FIELDING'S
VIETNAM
INCLUDING
CAMBODIA & LAOS

Fielding Titles

Fielding's Alaska Cruises and the Inside Passage
Fielding's America West
Fielding's Asia's Top Dive Sites
Fielding's Australia
Fielding's Bahamas
Fielding's Baja California
Fielding's Bermuda
Fielding's Best and Worst — The surprising results of the Plog Survey
Fielding's Birding Indonesia
Fielding's Borneo
Fielding's Budget Europe
Fielding's Caribbean
Fielding's Caribbean Cruises
Fielding's Caribbean on a Budget
Fielding's Diving Australia
Fielding's Diving Indonesia
Fielding's Eastern Caribbean
Fielding's England including Ireland, Scotland & Wales
Fielding's Europe
Fielding's Europe 50th Anniversary
Fielding's European Cruises
Fielding's Far East
Fielding's France
Fielding's France: Loire Valley, Burgundy & the Best of French Culture
Fielding's France: Normandy & Brittany
Fielding's France: Provence and the Mediterranean
Fielding's Freewheelin' USA
Fielding's Hawaii
Fielding's Hot Spots: Travel in Harm's Way
Fielding's Indiana Jones Adventure and Survival Guide™
Fielding's Italy
Fielding's Kenya
Fielding's Las Vegas Agenda
Fielding's London Agenda
Fielding's Los Angeles Agenda
Fielding's Mexico
Fielding's New Orleans Agenda
Fielding's New York Agenda
Fielding's New Zealand
Fielding's Paradors, Pousadas and Charming Villages of Spain and Portugal
Fielding's Paris Agenda
Fielding's Portugal
Fielding's Rome Agenda
Fielding's San Diego Agenda
Fielding's Southeast Asia
Fielding's Southern California Theme Parks
Fielding's Southern Vietnam on Two Wheels
Fielding's Spain
Fielding's Surfing Australia
Fielding's Surfing Indonesia
Fielding's Sydney Agenda
Fielding's Thailand, Cambodia, Laos and Myanmar
Fielding's Travel Tool™
Fielding's Vietnam including Cambodia and Laos
Fielding's Walt Disney World and Orlando Area Theme Parks
Fielding's Western Caribbean
Fielding's The World's Most Dangerous Places™
Fielding's Worldwide Cruises

FIELDING'S VIETNAM INCLUDING CAMBODIA & LAOS

by

Wink Dulles

Fielding Worldwide, Inc.
308 South Catalina Avenue
Redondo Beach, California 90277 U.S.A.

Fielding's Vietnam Including Cambodia and Laos

Published by Fielding Worldwide, Inc.

Text Copyright ©1997 Fielding Worldwide, Inc.

Icons & Illustrations Copyright ©1997 FWI

Photo Copyrights ©1997 to Individual Photographers

FIELDING WORLDWIDE INC.

PUBLISHER AND CEO	**Robert Young Pelton**
GENERAL MANAGER	**John Guillebeaux**
OPERATIONS DIRECTOR	**George Posanke**
ELECTRONIC PUBLISHING DIRECTOR	**Larry E. Hart**
PUBLIC RELATIONS DIRECTOR	**Beverly Riess**
ACCOUNT SERVICES MANAGER	**Cindy Henrichon**
PROJECT MANAGER	**Chris Snyder**
MANAGING EDITOR	**Amanda K. Knoles**

PRODUCTION

Martin Mancha   **Ramses Reynoso**

Craig South

COVER DESIGNED BY	**Digital Artists, Inc.**
COVER PHOTOGRAPHERS — Front Cover	**Glen Allison/Tony Stone Images**
Back Cover	**Mike Yamashita**
INSIDE PHOTOS	**Wink Dulles, Werner Funk, Praphqisri Jaiklom, Mike Yamashita, Destination: Vietnam—San Francisco, California**

Inquiries should be addressed to: Fielding Worldwide, Inc., 308 South Catalina Ave., Redondo Beach, California 90277 U.S.A., ☎ *(310) 372-4474*, Facsimile *(310) 376-8064*, 8:30 a.m.–5:30 p.m. Pacific Standard Time.

Website: http://www.fieldingtravel.com

e-mail: fielding@fieldingtravel.com

ISBN 1-56952-154-9

Printed in the United States of America

Letter from the Publisher

In 1946, Temple Fielding began the first of what would be a remarkable new series of well-written, highly personalized guidebooks for independent travelers. Temple's opinionated, witty, and oft-imitated books have assisted travelers ever since he guided tourists through postwar Europe. More important to some was Fielding's humorous and direct method of steering travelers away from the dull and the insipid. Today, Fielding Travel Guides are still written by experienced travelers for experienced travelers. Our authors carry on Fielding's reputation for creating travel experiences that deliver insight with a sense of discovery and style.

Wink Dulles personifies the Fielding attitude: seasoned, bright, obsessed with detail, and born to seek out new experiences for travelers. He has created the most enlightening travel guide available on modern Vietnam. Wink bought a beat-up 500cc motorcycle and drove down muddy roads and cow paths looking for the real Vietnam.

When you are in Vietnam don't be shy about looking Wink up and telling him about your experiences. Write us and tell us what you think should be in subsequent updates.

Welcome to the new Fielding.

RYP

Robert Young Pelton
Publisher and C.E.O.
Fielding Worldwide, Inc.

ABOUT THE AUTHOR

Wink Dulles

    Wink Dulles has spent the better part of five years in Southeast Asia, the last four as Southeast Asia correspondent for Fielding Worldwide. He's traversed Vietnam, Cambodia and Thailand by motorcycle, ducked artillery shells to get a better peek at Angkor Wat, exhumed the graves of Vietnamese villagers slaughtered by the Khmer Rouge deep in the Mekong Delta, talked with pangolins being smuggled from Vietnam into China, had his Saigon apartment raided by the cops at two in the morning, been mugged by a Vietnamese transvestite, chatted with Karen rebel leaders at Thai border refugee camps, got caught staking out a Muslim mosque by the Burmese army during religious unrest there, been mistaken as a Secret Service agent by President Gerald Ford (and Mel Gibson by 110 flight attendants) and witnessed the horror of one of Cambodia's 10 million land mines.

Dulles is the author of *Fielding's Vietnam Including Cambodia and Laos, Fielding's Thailand, Cambodia, Laos & Myanmar, Fielding's Bahamas* and *Fielding's Southern Vietnam on 2 Wheels,* as well as coauthor of *Fielding's Southeast Asia, Fielding's Far East* and *Fielding's The World's Most Dangerous Places. Fielding's Vietnam* was banned by the Vietnamese government in January 1995, presumably for reasons of candor. He was formerly senior editor and Bangkok bureau chief for *Escape* magazine, travel editor for *Vietnam Today* and Asia editor for *UFM* magazine.

The author's articles on Southeast Asian destinations and affairs have appeared in *National Geographic Traveler, New York Newsday, Salt Lake Tribune, Santa Barbara News-Press* and other national publications.

Ironically, Dulles, now a welcome part-time inhabitant of Vietnam, is the cousin of the late CIA Director Allen Dulles and former Secretary of State John Foster Dulles, who sent the first American military advisors into Vietnam in the 1950s after the French defeat in the First Indochina War. John Foster Dulles was considered "an enemy of the state," by Hanoi during his eight-year tenure as Secretary of State under President Dwight D. Eisenhower.

Wink Dulles also co-led the first American motorcycle tour of Vietnam in February 1996. When not traveling elsewhere, he divides his time between Thailand, Los Angeles and Ho Chi Minh City.

Jason Roberts

Jason was of particular help with the Cambodia section. After graduating from California State University Long Beach, Roberts blew off his glamorous and highly paid position at *Limousine and Chauffeur* magazine and moved to Bangkok to teach English. Tiring of Bangkok's hell, he moved on to Vientiane, Laos, in 1991, before finally settling in Phnom Penh, Cambodia, where he currently resides with his Cambodian wife, Thida, and their young son, Ernie. He was employed by the United Nations Transitional Authority in Cambodia (UNTAC) in 1992 as a media monitor in the Information and Education Division. Today, Roberts, fluent in Khmer, monitors prison conditions in Cambodia for the International Red Cross.

Fielding Rating Icons

The Fielding Rating Icons are highly personal and awarded to help the besieged traveler choose from among the dizzying array of activities, attractions, hotels, restaurants and sights. The awarding of an icon denotes unusual or exceptional qualities in the relevant category.

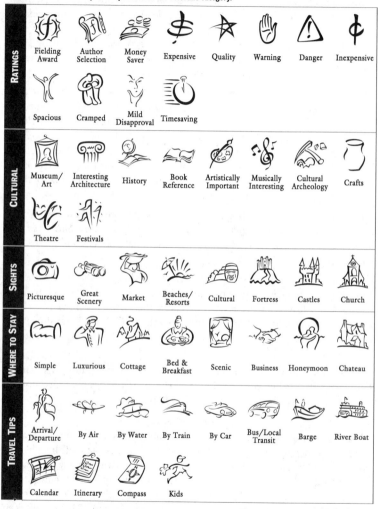

RATINGS

Fielding Award · Author Selection · Money Saver · Expensive · Quality · Warning · Danger · Inexpensive

Spacious · Cramped · Mild Disapproval · Timesaving

CULTURAL

Museum/Art · Interesting Architecture · History · Book Reference · Artistically Important · Musically Interesting · Cultural Archeology · Crafts

Theatre · Festivals

SIGHTS

Picturesque · Great Scenery · Market · Beaches/Resorts · Cultural · Fortress · Castles · Church

WHERE TO STAY

Simple · Luxurious · Cottage · Bed & Breakfast · Scenic · Business · Honeymoon · Chateau

TRAVEL TIPS

Arrival/Departure · By Air · By Water · By Train · By Car · Bus/Local Transit · Barge · River Boat

Calendar · Itinerary · Compass · Kids

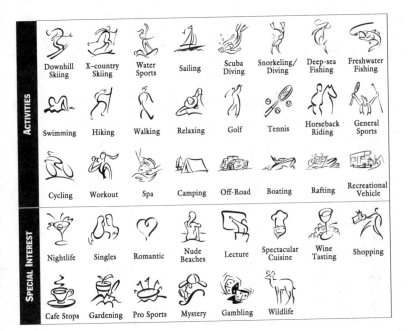

ACTIVITIES

Downhill Skiing	X–country Skiing	Water Sports	Sailing	Scuba Diving	Snorkeling/ Diving	Deep-sea Fishing	Freshwater Fishing
Swimming	Hiking	Walking	Relaxing	Golf	Tennis	Horseback Riding	General Sports
Cycling	Workout	Spa	Camping	Off-Road	Boating	Rafting	Recreational Vehicle

SPECIAL INTEREST

Nightlife	Singles	Romantic	Nude Beaches	Lecture	Spectacular Cuisine	Wine Tasting	Shopping
Cafe Stops	Gardening	Pro Sports	Mystery	Gambling	Wildlife		

Map Legend

Essentials

- 🏨 Hotel
- 🛏 Youth Hostel
- 🍴 Restaurant
- 🅂 Bank
- ☎ Telephone
- ℹ Tourist Info.
- ✚ Hospital
- 🍺 Pub/Bar
- ✉ Post Office
- 🅿 Parking
- 🚕 Taxi
- 🅂 Subway
- Ⓜ Metro
- Ⓜ Market
- 🅂 Shopping
- Ⓒ Cinema
- 🎭 Theatre
- ✈ Int'l Airport
- ✈ Regional Airport
- ★ Police Station
- ⚖ Courthouse
- 🏛 Gov't. Building

Attraction

- ■ Attraction
- ✈ Military Airbase
- 🧍 Army Base
- ⚓ Naval base
- 🏰 Fort
- 🏛 University
- 🏫 School

Historical

- ∴ Archeological Site
- ⚔ Battleground
- 🏰 Castle
- 🗼 Monument
- 🏛 Museum
- ⛪ Ruin
- 🚢 Shipwreck

Religious

- ✝ Church
- 🛕 Buddhist Temple
- 🛕 Hindu Temple
- 🕌 Mosque
- ⛩ Pagoda
- ✡ Synagogue

Activities

- 🏖 Beach
- ⛺ Campground
- 🍱 Picnic Area
- ⛳ Golf Course
- 🚤 Boat Launch
- 🤿 Diving
- 🐟 Fishing
- 🏄 Water Skiing
- ⛷ Snow Skiing
- 🦅 Bird Sanctuary
- 🦌 Wildlife Sanctuary
- 🌲 Park
- 🏕 Park Headquarters
- ⛏ Mine
- 🗼 Lighthouse
- 🗼 Windmill
- ⚓ Cruise Port
- 🏴 View
- 🏟 Stadium
- 🏢 Building
- 🐘 Zoo
- 🌳 Garden

Physical

— — — · International Boundary	🚶🚶 Hiking Trail
— · — · County/Regional Boundary	▬▬▬ Dirt Road
PARIS ⊙ National Capital	┼┼┼┼┼ Railroad
Montego Bay • State/Parish Capital	**RR** Railroad Station
Los Angeles ● Major City	— — ⛴ — Ferry Route
Quy Nhon ○ Town/Village	▲ Mountain Peak
— — ⑤ — — Motorway/Freeway	🝙 Lake
— — ⑯ — — Highway	— River
═══ Primary Road	◖ Cave
═══ Secondary Road	🪸 Coral Reef
— — — — Subway	⑅ Waterfall
— — 🚲 — — Biking Routed	♨ Hot Spring

©FWI 1995

ACKNOWLEDGEMENTS

The number of people I wish to thank for the preparation of *Fielding's Vietnam including Cambodia and Laos* in the countries of Indochina is vast, but as many as I can remember all deserve to be included in these pages. First and foremost I wish to thank Do Trong Tu. Known by his American-given name "Johnny" during the Vietnam War, Tu provided an invaluable amount of time and expertise in the preparation of this publication. By motorcycle, we explored the deepest regions of the Mekong Delta and traversed the coastal route National Highway 1 from Saigon to Hue. It seemed that every kilometer he wanted to stop and explain the cultural customs, topography and history of the area. We crossed rivers on tiny, dilapidated ferries unknown to tourists during monsoons. This is a guy who knows personally two out of every three persons living south of Saigon. The other one-third are members of his extended family. Traveling without such a man in Vietnam is like crawling through the old Viet Cong tunnels without light. Tu was my guide and is now my trusted friend. Thank you *(cam on)* Johnny, Mr. Tu. Tu can be reached at *FAX: 84-8-231071*. Or write him at his home: *322 Pham Van Hai Street, Ward 3, Tan Binh District, Ho Chi Minh City, Vietnam*. He'd love to hear from you if you're planning a visit to Vietnam, and he will enable you to get the most out of your visit.

For this new edition of *Fielding's Vietnam including Cambodia and Laos*, I am indebted to Mai Kim Hoanh. To Saigon resident and buddy-for-life Ron Van Wambeke: Thanks for the focus. For helping to update regions my steed couldn't get to this go-around, my thanks goes out to that crazy Swiss and "my older twin brother" Peter (where the hell are you?); Jim and Dan Tracy of Oakland, CA; Marty Wilson of Boulder, CO; and Timm Carstens and Mark Behrendt of Hamburg, Germany. Special kudos to Miss Chin of Saigon. Also to Kim Lynn Tran of Houston, TX, for looking so good although I hardly know yee; Tran Phan Ngoc Hue and his lovely wife, Hue; Phan Than; Nguyen Binh and the gang at B&B Motors; Tran Quoc Dai;

Michelle and Candace; the taxi driver who saved my ass in Bangkok; Misses Chung, Ha and Luong; Walter Ralphs of the Philippines; and, as always, Praphaisri Jaiklom. A big thumbs down to Dee Dee Dang of Huntington Beach, CA. You need help, sister.

In Laos, Doduangdy Diraphon of the Lao National Tourism Company made my job a lot easier. In Cambodia, thanks are in order to Fielding contributor Jason Roberts and his wife, Thida, as well as Martin Flitman, Pip Woods, Ker Munhit and "Tall Man."

In the U.S., I'd particularly like to thank Robert Young Pelton, an adventurer and the publisher of the Fielding guidebooks. Also at Fielding (in Redondo Beach, California), kudos to Amanda Knoles, Beverly Riess, Larry Hart, Chris Snyder and particularly John Guillebeaux.

And special thanks to my parents, Win and Patsy—who were there without being there.

—Wink Dulles

TABLE OF CONTENTS

LIST OF MAPS

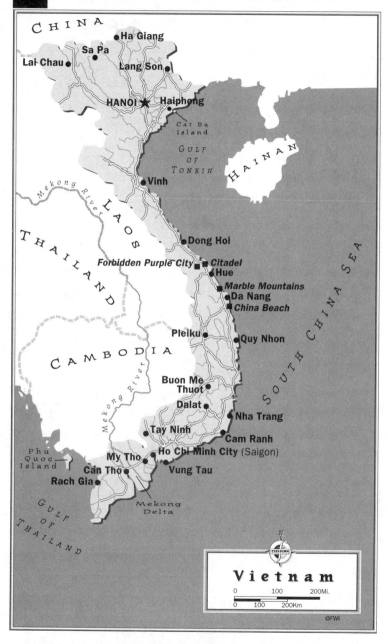

Vietnam

INTRODUCTION

Pulling Hairs in Vietnam

When I moved to Saigon four years ago to write the first edition of *Fielding's Vietnam*, it was still something of an oddity for the locals to see a Western face. I attracted curious crowds wherever I ventured. Children and some of the bolder adults pulled at the hair on my arms in fascination.

Today this only happens in the countryside.

Upon my arrival, skyscrapers were only on the joint-venturers' drawing boards. These days, they have transformed the city's skyline, turning Saigon from a crumbling Third-World socialist backwater into a modern capitalist metropolis.

I moved to Saigon on the threshold of the country's tourist boom. First to arrive were the French. Of course, that would be expected. Vietnam was a French colony from 1887 (some might say much earlier) until 1945 (some might say until much later). As Vietnam opened up to the outside world in the late 1980s, the French were among the first to discover the myriad changes the country had undergone. The French loss at Dien Bien Phu in 1954 to Ho Chi Minh resulted in their permanent exit from Vietnam, and, the fall of Saigon to the Communists in April 1975 marked America's exit.

In the early 1990s tourism was booming, growing at a clip of 50% a year. Vietnam, along with Laos and Cambodia, had become the new frontier for backpackers, adventure tourists, eco-travelers and bored old-timers who had already been everywhere else on the globe (save for North Korea, of course).

The French essentially fueled this boom and—although followed by the usual healthy portions of German and Australian backpackers—Hanoi poised itself for a tsunami of hard French francs by approving hundreds of hotel joint venture contracts, lodgings capable of handling the expected nine million annual visitors the government predicted would be arriving in Vietnam by the year 2010.

Americans were still reticent to tour Vietnam in 1994. After all, it was a "tour" in Vietnam that killed nearly 60,000 U.S. soldiers during the 1960s and 1970s. Vietnam was still a dark, evil place harboring millions of communists and even more malarial mosquitoes. Americans—from Jesse Helms to Jesse Jackson, from veterans to veterinarians—still had visions of screaming children running naked in the road, of body counts on the nightly news, and of heartland college students wailing in grief beside the corpses of their classmates. These are not the images in the storefront windows of your local travel agent. In 1994, Vietnam remained a war, not a country.

Even Americans with a deep sense of adventure, plus cultural and historical curiosity, feared how they would be treated if they traveled in Vietnam. But something happened; now they are coming, some for the first time, others for the first time in a very long time.

In February 1994, President Bill Clinton lifted the trade embargo on Vietnam. He then normalized relations with Hanoi on July 11, 1995. In May 1997, the first-ever U.S. ambassador—former Congressman and Vietnam War POW Pete Peterson—arrived in Hanoi. Americans considering traveling here breathed a little easier. These events also coincided with an ebbing of the tourism boom honeymoon in Vietnam. By the mid-1990s, Vietnam was no longer the final frontier. As more affluent visitors arrived for package tours, Hanoi decided to shed its shaggy backpacker scourge (which had been the country's tourism bread-and-butter since the late 1980s) by ending the extension of its 30-day tourist visas.

This was only part of the backfire. The French, who had rediscovered Vietnam, left again, yet this time of their own volition, bitching about an inadequate infrastructure, unqualified guides and lousy service at ho-hum hotels and restaurants. The affluent travelers of other nations followed suit, telling their friends at home harrowing tales of giant bugs, moped traffic jams and eight-hour layovers at Noi Bai after their non-English-speaking guides failed to show up to fetch them.

In 1997, some foreign investors—weary of bureaucratic red tape, endemic corruption and ambiguous, constantly changing legislation—began pulling out of their ventures in Vietnam. Bank of America recalled its staff in Hanoi in early 1997 and Chrysler Corp. pulled the plug on a US$160 million auto assembly venture at about the same time, the largest such project in Vietnam. Return foreign arrivals to Vietnam—including business arrivals—dropped to 10% by the end of 1996.

Put simply, Vietnam remains a source of contrasting expectations. It still has the Third-World lure of its early tourism years but has put up a facade of competence in handling its visitors—both vacationers and business travelers—after a decade-long dash to "international standards." Whereas in 1988, visitors expected—and received—little more than a bus ticket, a bucket of water and a stained mattress, these days the gleaming hotels and posh restaurants up and down the coast between Saigon and Hanoi suggest that Vietnam is at a stage of development where it has not yet arrived.

But do not let this turn you off. If the lure of Vietnam for you is where it should be—far away from chain mega-resorts, far away from French-trained chefs, far away from Windsor knots and Waterman pens—places where groups of curious children still pull the hairs on your arm to see if they're real, you'll still find a frontier.

Jumping Rope in Cambodia

With awe and some jealous envy, Cambodia has watched the changes taking place in Vietnam over the last 10 years.

Cambodia has had this pesky little civil war problem for the last 30 years, and has seemed capable of focusing on little else. Now that the Khmer Rouge threat has been mostly removed, folks here seem to need somewhere else to point their AKs. This means playing jump-rope to get a peek at the world's most magnificent ancient structures, the temples at Angkor. Jump-rope because the level of security changes with the wind, as political opponents lob grenades at each other in public places. The more public, the better. But jump at the right time and all the bad stuff will pass underneath. Heck, an estimated 100 of Interpol's most wanted international fugitives have found a home here, so it must be safe.

With a little planning, common sense and some loose change, it's quite possible to see and do a lot in this off again-on again war zone. In fact, the obstacles here to a sensible vacation are half the fun. I'll never get a key to the city from the Ministry of Tourism, but I've traveled Cambodia a dozen times and I'll keep going back. Whether it's motorcycling down Highway 4 to the beaches at Sihanoukville, off-roading it in Rattanakiri, rediscovering fabulous Angkor Wat, slow-ferrying it up to Siem Reap or hoisting sunset cocktails at the Foreign Correspondents Club along the Tonle Sap, the complete adventure Cambodia offers the hardy will always endure.

Laid-Back Laos

Laos offers today what Vietnam did 10 years ago—lazy cities and provincial towns, undisturbed hill tribes and magnificent religious monuments, all accessible only to the adventurous due to an all but nonexistent infrastructure.

Laos is a landlocked country with no railroads, a rudimental road system (only about 10% of the population lives anywhere near a road) that can be called a "road system" on maps only. And the maps themselves are like primitive cave etchings. External and internal telecommunications are only embryonic. Electricity is available in only a few urban areas—and even in many of these places, only for a few hours a day.

Vientiane, the capital, is as bustling as a South Pole bivouac. Nightlife translates into "being awake when it's dark out." If a break from the madness of Southeast Asian cities sounds like your kind of getaway, you've bought the right book and chosen the right place.

The technically Communist government here purposely hasn't rushed into tourism as Vietnam has, but also doesn't have spies following tourists around, as the authorities in Burma (Myanmar) feel comfortable doing with visitors to their fine land.

An increasing number of travelers are reporting to me that their most gratifying experiences in Indochina (if not all of Southeast Asia) were in Laos, along the 2030 kilometers of the Mekong River that run through the country, or high in the hills straddling the Chinese border, where one can totally discard civilization—where there is no other transportation than that provided by the generosity of the region's few inhabitants.

Laos isn't marred by civil war and internal strife, and you won't see hundreds of mini-buses screaming down the road shuttling tourists to different attractions. This gives the adventurous the unique opportunity to explore Laos' ancient culture in relative solitude.

Although the chunkiest part of this book is devoted to Vietnam, you'll miss a lot by not stopping next door at the neighbors. Both Laos and Cambodia are accessible by land from Vietnam—we tell you how—and by air are puddle-jumps from Saigon.

Enjoy your flight.

Destination: Indochina

If any books in the Fielding series of world travel guides require constant updating they are the ones that are written about Southeast Asia.

The Far East, particularly Southeast Asia, is the world's fastest changing region. From Myanmar to Mindanao, from Telukbetung to Nha Trang, Southeast Asia is exploding. Economic prosperity is rapidly transforming the face of countries such as Vietnam, as it makes the transition from an agrarian-based, Soviet-aided litany of economic failure to a major manufacturing and export player.

It took nearly a year for us to prepare this new update, which now includes Cambodia and Laos. It might have taken less had we stayed on the beaten path.

But we didn't. We took motorcycles from the Mekong Delta to the Chinese border—from Phnom Penh down notorious Highway 4 to Kompong Som, an occasionally bombed-out road and the stage for past Khmer Rouge abductions of foreigners. We elephant-trekked in Vietnam's Central Highlands, bounced on buses from Vientiane to Luang Prabang and scuba-dived the waters off Nha Trang. We joined musicians in Vietnam and Cambodia for impromptu jam sessions, both under the bright lights of Saigon and beneath a full moon in the jungle at Angkor Wat. We interviewed Cambodian army intelligence officers in Siem Reap province and visited active battlefields at Phnom Bok. We were summoned by the Cambodian Ministry of Tourism and chastised for our candor.

But it is still with some trepidation that we prepare this intro to *Fielding's Vietnam Including Cambodia & Laos*, because as these words are committed to paper, they become out of date. Asia has a maddening habit of doing exactly what you expect the least. Gentle people stage bloody uprisings, nations hurl themselves from capitalism to religious fanaticism overnight—and vice versa. If one thing is the same in Asia it is change.

Who Is This Guide For?

Fielding's Vietnam Including Cambodia & Laos is designed to be more fun than the penurious tones and dull squeaking of the backpacking guides, with less air-conditioned sterility of the business guides. It's more exciting than the white bread guides, and more opinionated than all of them combined. *Fielding's Vietnam Including Cambodia & Laos* is for the person with a lust for the foreign but with a healthy fear of the unknown. You're well read, have traveled before and really want to get into Indochina, not just surf. This is the guide to lean on when you get confused, tired or hurried—and the one to ignore when you're on a roll.

A Word About Guidebooks

Guidebooks, even this one, aren't the end-all for managing your Indochina adventure. Indochina is a highly dynamic and constantly changing environment. Although *Fielding's Vietnam Including Cambodia & Laos* listings are up-to-date right up to press time, businesses, eateries, hotels and tour companies both in and pertaining to Vietnam, Cambodia and Laos are in a constant state of flux. Phone numbers change; faxes are installed; businesses boom and bust. Tour companies come and go on the scene as fast as lip-synching pop stars.

Where the Heck Is Indochina?

Indochina is the region of Southeast Asia which comprises Vietnam, Cambodia and Laos. Indochina derives from the French *Indochine*, or the Indochinese Union, which was the colonial union of these three countries formed by the French in 1887.

For most Westerners it's on the other side of the world. Twenty-four hours aboard a plane or two or three and you're there. Sure it's a haul. But while Aunt Tess and Uncle Bill are getting toured to death on a bus in Belgium, you're checking out shrines built before there *was* a Europe—cultures and monuments so old they predate written history.

What's It Like?

Indochina offers some of the world's most mysterious and exotic attractions. It features beautiful topography—rainforests not unlike those found in the deepest jungles of Central and South America, vast deltas, and even boulder strewn mesas of the variety found in Mexico's Baja peninsula. If the region has had its fill of Western colonialism and domination, it is still very much the virgin for economic exploitation.

Vietnam's new riches have made more evident an astoundingly impoverished societal undercarriage, which really can only be called such because there are now other hugely-rich stratas for comparison. The average Vietnamese makes little over $200 a year. Any trip to this strange land will open your eyes to extremes you have never encountered before, from economic to religious.

The Indo-Chinese region is also home to the most spectacular ancient temples in the world, Cambodia's Angkor Wat in particular. Magnificent glimpses into ancient civilizations abound in Vietnam and Laos as well.

Some places are a little less staid than others. Cambodia is trying to shake off a 30-year-old civil war that's killed millions. Consequently, a dozen million or so land mines are buried in the ground and a lot of guys still carry big guns. Travel in much of the country is still quite unsafe. Whereas Laos, which may be even more primitive than Cambodia, today offers virtually unrestricted travel throughout the country—as does Vietnam.

Getting Wired

Hey, this is the '90s, and guidebooks aren't the only sources of travel information for vagabonds and wanderlusters. Web sites are popping up seemingly weekly with all kinds of Indochina offerings: some quite informative and useful, others quite awful and useless. We're not in the habit of pitching the products of potential competitors, but we also figure you won't be lugging along your PC or laptop into the jungle for hotel listings and restaurant prices. You'll need something a little less cumbersome, like this guide.

We haven't checked out all of the following sites for review purposes, so we're not recommending any (save for ours), but some of them might be useful as you prepare for your adventures. Here's a sampling.

Vietnam

http://www.fieldingtravel.com

    Fielding Worldwide

http://www.vietvet.org/visit.htm

    A Visit to Vietnam

http://grunt.space.swri.edu/visit.htm

    A Visit to Vietnam

http://www.well.com/user/gdisf

    Destination Vietnam

http://coombs.anu.edu.au/WWWVLPages/ VietPages/WWWVL-Vietnam.html

    Vietnam WWW VL

http://www.city.net/countries/vietnam

    City.Net Vietnam

http://marlowe.wimsey.com/rshand/ reflections/vietnam/vietnam.html

    Vietnam Memoirs

http://members.aol.com/jimm844224/ vietart1.html

    Vietnam Combat Art

http://users.aol.com/chaudoc

    Chau Doc

http://www.vietnamadventure.com

    Vietnam Adventure

http://www.branch.com/silkroute

    TravelASIA

http://www.vietvet.or/maps.htm

    Maps of Vietnam

http://www.erols.com/dreese

    Vietnam Tourism

http://www.webshingles.com/halong/ default.htm

    Halong Travel Company

http://www.fcaglp.unlp.edu.ar/~spaoli/ asiacountries.html

    Countries of Asia

http://www.well.com/user/gdisf/ portrait.htm

    Lou De Matteis' A Portrait of Vietnam

http://www.aduki.com.au

    Vietnam Economic Commentary

http://www.viam.com

    Vietnam Business Journal

http://www.ldc.lu.se/~eastasia

    Center for East and Southeast Asian Studies

http://www.lib.uci.edu/sea/seahome.html

    UCI Southeast Asian Archive

mkt03.htm#quinlan

    Vietnam Business Opportunities and Risks, by Joseph P. Quinlan

http://www.odci.gov/cia/publications/nsolo/ factbook/vm.htm

    1996 World Fact Book: Vietnam

http://www.sil.org/ethnologue/countries/ Viet.html

    Languages of Vietnam (Ethnologue Database)

http://www.hotelstravel.com/vietnam.html

    Hotels and Travel on the Net—Vietnam

http://www.interknowledge.com/vietnam/ index.html

    An Introduction to Vietnam (inter-Knowledge Corp.)

http://www.mindspring.com/~jrolls/cv.html

    Cycle Vietnam—From Hanoi to Saigon

http://www-students.unisg.ch/~pgeiser/ vietnam/vietnam.htm

    Internet Travel Guide—Vietnam

http://www.cdc.gov/travel/seasia.htm

    Southeast Asia Travelers' Health Information

http://travel.state.gov/vietnam.html

> *Travel Advisory: Vietnam (U.S. State Dept.)*

http://sunsite.unc.edu/vietnam/vnpic.html

> *Vietnam Pictures Archive*

http://www.usyd.edu.au/~bdrewnia/tales/tales.htm

> *Vietnam Travel Guide*

http://www.sunsite.nus.sg/SEAlinks/vietnam-info.html

> *Vietnam Information*

Cambodia

http://www.none.coolware.com/entmt/cambodia/cambodia.html

> *Holiday in Cambodia*

http://www.sunsite.nus.sg/SEAlinks/cambodia-info.html

> *Cambodia Information*

http://www-students.unisg.ch/~pgeiser/cambodia/cambodia.htm

> *Internet Travel Guide—Cambodia*

http://www.cdc.gov/travel/seasia.htm

> *Southeast Asia Travelers' Health Information*

http://www.ldc.lu.se/~eastasia

> *Center for East and Southeast Asian Studies*

http://www.lib.uci.edu/sea/seahome.html

> *UCI Southeast Asian Archive*

http://travel.state.gov/cambodia.html

> *Travel Advisory: Cambodia (U.S. State Dept.)*

http://www.fcaglp.unlp.edu.ar/~spaoli/asiacountries.html

> *Countries of Asia*

Laos

http://www.sunsite.nus.sg/SEAlinks/laos-info.html

> *Laos Information*

http://travel.state.gov/laos.html

> *Travel Advisory: Laos (U.S. State Dept.)*

http://www.fcaglp.unlp.edu.ar/~spaoli/asiacountries.html

> *Countries of Asia*

http://lox2.loxinfo.co.th/~seatimes

> *Laos Travel Information*

http://www.ldc.lu.se/~eastasia

> *Center for East and Southeast Asian Studies*

http://www-students.unisg.ch/~pgeiser/laos/laos.htm

> *Internet Travel Guide—Laos*

http://www.cdc.gov/travel/seasia.htm

> *Southeast Asia Travelers' Health Information*

http://www.lib.uci.edu/sea/seahome.html

> *UCI Southeast Asian Archive*

VIETNAM

Traditional Vietnamese dance and theater depicts Vietnam's history.

Vietnam has become the destination for the 1990s. In a word, Vietnam is hot. Tourism has become one of Vietnam's single biggest earners of foreign exchange. During the late '80s, these revenues multiplied many times over. Americans and others are descending upon this paradisiacal nation in droves—some to reflect on and make amends with past tragedy, others to see what Hawaii might have been like a couple of hundred years ago or so.

Although initial government predictions in the early '90s turned out to be slightly lofty as the end of the decade approaches, and the tourism boom has leveled off somewhat, Vietnam continues to enjoy about two million visitors per year.

THE FOREIGN TOURIST FORECAST		
YEAR	**TO VIETNAM (MILLIONS)**	**TO HCMC (MILLIONS)**
1995	1.40	1.0
1996	1.80	1.26
1997	2.30	1.56
1998	2.80	1.80
1999	3.33	1.90
2000	3.80	2.00
2005	6.20	3.10
2010	8.70	4.35

Source: Ho Chi Minh City Tourism Department

Whereas Europe has served as the traditional target of foreign jaunts by North Americans, travelers these days are tossing around names such as Danang, Ha Long Bay, Hue and Dalat like they once spoke of Amsterdam and Paris.

PURPOSES FOR ARRIVALS (%)				
YEAR	**HOLIDAY**	**BUSINESS**	**VISIT RELATIVES**	**OTHER PURPOSES**
1992	65.1	20.4	8.0	6.5
1993	56.0	21.3	23.0	11.7
1994	44.0	22.0	29.0	5.0

Source: Ho Chi Minh City Tourism Department

The annual growth rate of arrivals in Vietnam was between 40 percent and 50 percent for three years running in the early 1990s. The number of foreign tourists entering the country surged from 92,500 in 1988 to 1,018,000 in 1994—a tenfold increase in a mere six years. In 1995, 1.2 million foreign tourists came to Vietnam. This was a 15-percent jump over the figure for 1994. Fifty-two percent of the new arrivals in 1994 were from China, Hong Kong, Japan, Taiwan, France, the U.K., Canada and the United States.

The number of hotel rooms in the country has also shot up. At press time, there were 674 state-run hotels and 312 private hotels in Vietnam, with a total of 36,000 rooms—compared with 18,000 rooms in 1988. Today, there are at least 18,000 rooms up to international standards. Seven thousand rooms were added in 1994 alone. Foreign hotel investment is now nearly US$2 billion—one-fifth of all the foreign investment in Vietnam. Today, there are at least 231 foreign joint venture projects for tourism capitalized at nearly US$5 billion. There are at least 125 new hotel projects in the works, including 10 five-star, 24 four-star and 46 three-star caravansaries, projects that will add 13,500 international-standard rooms. It's projected that there will be 31,500 international-standard rooms in Vietnam by 1998.

And they're not just going up in Ho Chi Minh City and Hanoi. The provinces are getting their share. Resorts are springing up in Quang Nam, Ha Long Bay, Van Phong Bay and Ba Ria. Golf courses have been built in Ho Chi Minh City (two, actually), Dalat and Ha Tay Province. Vietnam's first casino has opened.

On the down side, only 10 percent of all tourists to Vietnam return to the country. Reasons for the low figure include a shortage of tourism representative offices in other countries, a poor infrastructure, insufficient investment in tourist sites and underqualified staff at tour companies, restaurants, hotels and tourist attractions. Ha Long Bay—one of the seven splendors of the world—and Hue, both certified as world heritage sites, fail to attract tourists for a return visit. Although the beautiful coastal city of Nha Trang is only 450 km north of Ho Chi Minh City, the grueling journey takes more than eight hours—and that's without stopping. And according to the tourism ministry, the hotel room occupancy rate in 1995 decreased by 10 percent compared with 1994. Compound these problems with substandard civil air schedules linking Ho Chi Minh City and Hanoi with other Vietnamese destinations such as Hue, Danang, Haiphong and Nha Trang, and it's easier to understand why the turnover from tourism amounts to only about US$60 per tourist. Let's face it—for many, beggars and touts are a turnoff. This is bound to change in the future. But in the meantime, keep in mind that if you're coming from Beverly Hills to see Beverly Hills, stay in Beverly Hills.

And, of course the real Vietnam lies beyond the cities. It's found on the rice terraces of the Central Highlands and the coffee plantations of Dac Lac province, around the spectacular stretches of sand such as China Beach, and in the incense-laced temples of Hue. It's found along the banks of the bountiful mouths of the Mekong. It's found in longhouses in the deepest jungles of northern Vietnam and aboard junks anchored in the Gulf of Tonkin. It's chronicled in the works of Somerset Maugham and Graham Greene.

Vietnam, for all its part proud, part shameful—and certainly lengthy—heritage, is just being born in many ways, and is most assuredly an embryonic host to the seasoned traveler.

Some say Vietnam has lost its lure as a frontier destination and to some extent, they're right. You see foreigners all around Saigon, Hanoi, Hue, Ha Long Bay and Danang these days. Many of the more affluent are looking to be catered to the same way they would be at the Hyatt in Orlando. But there is still so much of Vietnam left to be explored, so many places the tour buses and vans don't reach—places where foreigners have rarely or never been. Besides, if you've never been somewhere, it's a frontier.

VIETNAM AT A GLANCE				
The place	*Square miles*	*Population*	*Languages*	*Religions*
Vietnam	**127,330**	**73.9 million**	**Vietnamese, French, Chinese, Khmer**	**Buddhism. Hoa Hao, Cao Dai, Christianity, Islam**
Adult literacy rate	*Life expectancy*	*Number of Doctors*	*Pop. growth rate*	*Per capita income*
88%	**63 years**	**1 per 2882**	**2.5%**	**US$1140**
% labor force in agriculture	*Arable land as % of total*	*Rural pop.*	*Annual rate of deforestation*	*Growth of urban pop.*
67%	**17.5%**	**78%**	**0.6%**	**3.6% per annum**

Before You Leave

Travel Documents and Visas

Before you even schedule your trip, you'll need to get a passport. Check to find the closest passport agency in your area. Passport agencies are located in most large cities and selected post offices across the country. Passports cost $65 ($55 to renew). You'll need two passport photos (most photo shops can shoot them for you) and an original birth certificate. No copies. Allow about 30 days for processing, or pay an added fee for a rush turnaround. You'll need visas to visit some countries in Asia (Vietnam is one of them), although many nations will stamp U.S. and Canadian passports with stays from two weeks up to 90 days free of charge (such as Thailand and Malaysia, respectively). Visas are necessary for Vietnam and are good for 30 days. Extensions (I've seen up to 30 days) can be applied for and are usually granted when you're in-country though a travel agent. (Creative travel agents in Vietnam have the means to extend your visa even longer; check around.)

At the time of this writing, the U.S. has recently established normalized relations with Vietnam. Visas to Vietnam can now be arranged through the Vietnamese embassy in Washington, D.C. Previously, U.S. visitors to Vietnam had to procure visas through a third party which then obtained the visas through the Vietnamese embassies in Mexico or Canada. This is no longer the case, although it's still best to use a travel agent in the States rather than go directly through the embassy. You can contact one of the Asian tour companies listed in this chapter. They can generally provide visas for about US$70-90. A more prudent and cheaper way is to get to a place such as Bangkok first. There, most of the travel agencies that line Khao San and Sukhumvit Roads like a muster of slot machines at Las Vegas McCarran Airport might get away with taking about $50 from you. Or, you can go right to the Vietnam Embassy at *83/1 Wireless Road, Bangkok* (☎ *251-5835* or *251-5838*, FAX: *(662) 251-7201* or *251-7203*), fill out an application and give them about US$48, a couple of passport-sized photos and 24 hours and, presto, you're in.

I also recommend heading just a half-block down Wireless to **M.K. Ways** *(57/11 Wireless Road, Patumwan, Bangkok 1033*; ☎ *254-7770, 255-3390, 254-4765,* or *255-2892; FAX: (662) 254-5583).* If you're nice, they won't charge you much more than the 1200 baht you stood in the long line at the Vietnamese embassy to pay. They'll get you as cheap a fare into either Saigon or Hanoi as you'll find anywhere along Khao San Road. (My first visa only took a couple of days to get back to me from Hanoi, but it seems the capital is being besieged with visa applications and really doesn't appear as capable of handling the surging popularity of its country as quickly as it was only a year ago.) M.K. Ways has been known to pull some hemp-taut strings in Hanoi. Something to consider.

Tourist Visas

Individuals and tour operators can obtain visas for travelers, and the processing period doesn't take as long as a month as a lot of other guides claim. Visas are currently procured from the Vietnam Embassy in Washington, D.C. Usually it's just a matter of a week or 10 days before it's in your hands.

The best way to get a visa, as it is with all of the restricted countries in the region, is to get to Bangkok first. There you can pick up a visa in just a few days for around US$60–90 at the travel agencies or for US$48 at the Vietnamese Embassy at *83/1 Wireless Road*, directly across from the U.S. Embassy's ambassador's residence. They're usually open from 9–11 or 11:30 in the morning and 1–4 or so in the afternoon. Show up with a couple of passport photos. If you do use a travel agency, SHOP AROUND! In fact, rather than stand on line at the embassy for my visa, I just walked half a block down Wireless Road to the travel agency, M.K. Ways. They won't charge you much more than the embassy for the visa. They also specialize in Indochina tours and bookings and, frankly, will probably save you a lot of time prowling around Khao San Road for an airline bargain.

INSIDER TIP

Tour companies and travel agencies are extremely competitive and part of any particular company's lure is its ability to get you a visa quickly. With some companies, it might just take a couple of days, others as long as 10. But remember that in order for a tour company to get your visa quickly it has to press Vietnamese immigration officials to push the paper like a used-car salesman, some of whom don't like to be shoved around, even when tourist dollars are involved. A travel or tour agency known for its expediency in delivering your visa may ironically not be in such good favor with the Vietnamese authorities because they're such a pain in the rear to the Vietnamese. If you've got the time, settle for the longer visa processing time if your tour operator can compensate in other areas—and believe me, they can. Even so, never wait until the last minute to book.

One of the increasingly popular ways of getting to Vietnam is through Cambodia. Again, arrange for your Vietnamese visa in Bangkok, not Phnom Penh. If you do it this way, you can expect to pay as little as US$40 for the single-entry tourist visa. Making Vietnamese visa arrangements in Cambodia is both expensive and time consuming, as it is in Vientiane. In Bangkok, you'll need to get three passport-type photos.

From the U.S., you will need two photos and a copy of your passport. The cost is $65 per person. The application, photos and copy of your passport should be mailed to: **Vietnam Embassy**, *1233 20th Street N.W., Washington, D.C. 20036,* ☎ *(202) 861-0737 or FAX: (202) 861-0917.*

Selected Vietnamese Embassies Abroad

Canada
695 Davidson Drive, Gloucester, Ottawa, Ontario K1J 6L7
☎ *(416) 744-0698*   *FAX: (416) 744-1709*

United Kingdom
12-14 Victoria Road, London W8 5RD
☎ *071-937-1912*   *FAX: 071-937-6108*

Australia
6 Timbarra Crescent, O'Malley, Canberra ACT 2603
☎ *(062) 286-6059*   *FAX: (062) 286-4534*

France
62 Rue de Boileau, Paris 16
☎ *45-24-50-63*   *FAX: 45-24-39-48*

Germany
Konstantinstrasse 37, Bonn
☎ *(0228) 357-0201*

Keep in mind that a 30-day tourist visa is valid only from the dates stamped on the visa. This differs from places such as Thailand, where the clock on tourist visas begins ticking once you enter the country. For example, if your Vietnamese visa is stamped with a start date of January 1 and expiry date of February 1, you can stay only until February 1, even if you entered the country only a day before. This all means you should have already made your flight reservations before applying for the visa.

Additionally, you'll need to determine your point of entry into Vietnam before applying for the visa. If you come in by air, you'll need to specifically state whether you'll arrive at Ho Chi Minh City's Tan Son Nhat Airport or Hanoi's Noi Bai Airport, as this destination will appear on your visa as the only authorized point of entry. However, the visa will be stamped with both airports as departure points, giving you some flexibility in determining where you want to leave from should you change your mind once in Vietnam. Should you change your plans and want to leave by land, though, you'll need to have your visa changed to reflect the new departure point. This can be handled either through immigration or, better yet, a travel agent.

INSIDER TIP

On arrival in Vietnam, two copies of a customs declaration form must be completed, as well as a single arrival/departure card. You will be given one copy of the customs form and a portion of your arrival/departure card. Hold on to these documents as you would your passport. Do not lose them. You'll need to present them both when leaving the country. You'll most likely be fined if you've lost one form or both. And, for godsakes, don't lose your visa. Make a number of photocopies of it, as well as your departure card and customs declaration form.

Business Visas

Business visas are available for up to six months and extendable twice (for a total stay of 18 months) on a multi-entry basis. Also available are multiple entry three-month business visas. The policy has had a habit of changing over recent years; the best thing to do is to check with your sponsor, as you'll need one in Vietnam to procure a business visa.

Ask your Vietnamese sponsor to submit an application to the Ministry of the Interior. You'll need to give your full name, date and place of birth, profession, passport number (as well the date of issue and expiration), address, nationality, and time and place of entry into Vietnam.

The ministry will fax or telex the Vietnamese embassy or consulate in your country with an approval number usually between seven and 10 days. Remain in contact with your sponsor to determine when the ministry has approved your application. Ask the Vietnamese sponsor to give you the visa approval number and the date it was issued in order to track it down in the event that it is delayed.

The Vietnamese embassy or consulate will inform you when your application has been processed and the visa is ready. Show up with four passport photos and a copy of the approval stamp, which you can get faxed to you from your sponsor. You'll need to fill out an application form and pay the requested fee. From the U.S., the normal cost of obtaining a six-month business visa is about US$220. About US$110 of this will need to be paid to your sponsor for processing fees, and an almost equal amount to the Vietnamese embassy should you be picking up your visa in a place such as Bangkok. You can state specifically to your Vietnamese sponsor where you wish to pick up your visa, and it's highly advisable that you do so either in your home country or a third country en route to Vietnam. This will minimize hassles with immigration cops at the airport in Vietnam, who don't look kindly on empty passports. Similar to the tourist visa, the clock on a business visa begins ticking on the date stamped on the visa, not when you enter the country. And, also like tourist visas, your entry point into Vietnam must be determined before you apply for the visa. Exiting Vietnam is somewhat more flexible.

Who Should Travel to Vietnam?

Although Vietnam is becoming a travel destination at almost a fanatical rate, it's important to realize the country's infrastructure isn't close to having the ability of accommodating mass travel. Le Thieu Hung, Saigontourist's general manager, recently said that the country has yet to "meet the needs of mass tourism for pleasure and entertainment. Vietnam is still primarily a destination of business people and culturally minded travelers." At this time, Le Xuan Hien, manager of the operation department of Vietnamtourism, said, "We're rather interested in intellectuals, educated people who come here to see the specific cultural heritage and way of life in our country. We have to be very cautious with mass tourism so that we don't spoil our beautiful country."

Solo and Group Travel

Solo wandering is probably the purest form of adventure travel, while group or paired travel offers its own rewards. Wandering alone in faraway places takes on a romantic and nomadic aura. Getting from point A to B can become like a pilgrimage. This type of travel courts disaster but is also the most rewarding. It's exploration at its purest, with little to curb adventure except physical stamina and funds. In only a month or two, you will meet more people, do more things and experience more of life's ups and downs than in a year's worth of group or paired travel. If you travel in remote regions of Vietnam, prepare to be arrested, detained, celebrated, attacked, seduced and tricked. It's all part of the experience. But, remember, if you are a woman traveling alone, you're setting yourself up for thieves, thugs and worse. Men certainly aren't immune but are less likely targets.

The next best scenario is traveling with a single friend. The big drawback is the unintended barrier you'll create between yourselves and the locals. You will use the language less, be invited into fewer homes. But this is a better way for women from a security standpoint. Additionally, you won't get as lonely traveling in a pair—and you *will* get lonely traveling solo. A good way is to split up for portions of the trip, arranging to meet at a preset time and place.

AUTHOR'S WARNING

Although major, or organized crime in Vietnam rarely involves or has any consequences on foreign tourists, occasionally the errant tourist may become inadvertently involved in an illegal smuggling operation. The illegal export of timber is on the rise, particularly in the Bach Binh, Tanh Linh and Ham Tan districts, Binh Dinh province. This area has witnessed an alarmingly large scale of hardwood smuggling via freighters on the Mekong River. The Anti-Deforestation Task Force recently seized 100 cubic meters of timber in 14 cases of illegal transport. Independent travelers have been known to try to gain passage from Vietnam to Cambodia via waterway, sometimes hitching rides on freighters and other riverboats.

Group travel has its rewards if you've only got a week. But that's about it. Essentially, group travel is like relying on the weakest link in a chain. You can never travel faster than the slowest person; accommodations are always full; tables are too small; the prices are always higher—you name it. Group travel turns a simple pleasure into a military exercise.

What to Pack

Vietnam lies in tropical latitudes. This doesn't mean a prescription of Bain de Soleil and thongs. In the highlands of south and central Vietnam, and throughout the north, temperatures can get quite cold, especially in winter. Jungle areas can be so hot your brain turns to jerky. You'll want as much skin area covered as possible to ward off leeches, malarial mosquitoes and the fatal bites of scared, hungry, pissed-off or playful cobras, vipers, hanumans and kraits. (Lions and tigers and bears, oh my!) Ladies, remember where you're going. The Vietnamese on the whole are a tolerant lot and Western fashion has permeated urban areas, but a show of too much skin is taboo. Female lib hasn't gotten to Danang yet. And neither has Madonna's book. Longer dresses, pants and bras are *de rigueur* in most places other than the beach and other heavily touristed areas, especially in religious temples. Pretty Vietnamese girls who may wear the shortest, sexiest dresses and high heels on the street wear very modest swimwear at the beach.

Both sexes should bring along light cotton clothing and not a lot of it. You'll probably—and should—get a lot of what you need where you're going. For starters, a few pairs of trousers and a couple of pairs of shorts will do. Take two or three short-sleeved shirts max, and a single dress shirt. You determine the underwear. Sandals are a good way of getting around; the Asians seem to think so. Walking or hiking boots are a must for the jungle and the mountains. Sneakers are the best all-around bet. Slip-ons will be good if you'll be seeing a lot of temples; laced shoes are not a good idea if you've got a lot of pagodas on your itinerary. A small towel will also come in handy. Other good ideas are a day pack and a fanny pack. Don't bring things you probably won't need: sleeping bag, heavy outerwear, air mattress and such. Unless, of course, the nature of your journey requires this kind of bulk.

Take along a sewing kit, electrical current adapters, and a good Swiss Army knife. Bring contraceptives and condoms. Yeah, condoms. You can get them there, but Asian condoms break like soap bubbles in a pine forest. A *great* insect repellent is essential—like Deet. Some folks swear by preparations such as Avon's Skin So Soft to keep the little buggers away. Keep a marginal supply of duty-free liquor and American cigarettes handy to pay off officials and impress your friends. Johnnie Walker Black Label whiskey is generally the East Asian poison of choice, as are 555 or Marlboro cigarettes. In-country, carry a roll or two of toilet paper. In a lot of places, you won't find it; just a bucket of water. It's why there's not a lot of social grace in the left hand.

Medical/Health Certificates

You should receive inoculations against **yellow fever**, **hepatitis B**, **tetanus**, **typhoid**, **cholera** and **tuberculosis**. An **influenza** shot couldn't hurt either.

Some countries will require that you have, under International Health Regulations adopted by the World Health Organization, an International Certificate of Vaccination against yellow fever. Travelers arriving from infected areas will be required to show proof of vaccination against yellow fever. The certificate will also be stamped with the other inoculations that you have received. Any general practice will be able to provide this service.

A Word About AIDS (SIDA)

A local guide recently, on a trip in the Mekong Delta, decided he needed a rest at a truck stop (read that as whore house), where Vietnamese women obligingly take in weary travelers for some tea and a little "sympathy." Apparently, the man was not in the habit of using condoms during these little sojourns. He explained to me that, to avoid contracting the HIV virus, he had sex only with Vietnamese girls. "These girls don't have sex with foreigners," he said, his reasoning that the disease could only be spread by foreigners.

A Word About AIDS (SIDA)

Although government estimates of the spread of HIV in Vietnam are seriously lacking a firm data gathering procedure, AIDS in Vietnam is very real. At least the Vietnamese are becoming more aware of its dangers. The general awareness of HIV/AIDS has risen from 2.9 percent of the population in 1991 to more than 40 percent of the population now being aware of the danger and the spread of the disease.

As of August 1995, the National Prevention Committee reported 2777 people in Vietnam had contracted the HIV virus, 230 had AIDS and 69 of those with AIDS had died. HCMC has the highest number of people infected with HIV (1356). That using condoms prevents the spread of AIDS was known by 31 percent of the respondents in 1991, that figure jumped to 44 percent by the end of 1993 and to 50 percent by 1995.

Inoculations and Medical Advice

Arrival within six days after leaving or transiting a yellow fever zone requires an inoculation. But you should have all the proper vaccinations before coming to Vietnam. Disease is rife here. One source told me that Vietnam is the only country in the world where you can still get bubonic plague. Even if it isn't true, just the rumor itself is an indication that you would no more walk around Vietnam without inoculations than you would the surface of the moon without a space suit.

There is pneumonia here of every variety, malaria, diarrheal diseases, tetanus, tuberculosis, cholera, hepatitis, polio, rabies, leprosy, diptheria, dysentery, typhoid and rickets. You should be vaccinated for meningitis, hepatitis A and B, tuberculosis, typhoid, tetenus and diphtheria. Remember to have these performed well in advance of your trip as some will require boosters before you begin your journey. Also note that the period of efficacy differs by vaccination. Some will give you protection longer than others. And all of your vaccinations should be recorded in an International Health Certificate that you should carry with your passport.

Malaria is another story. Of course, you should obtain a larium prescription that you should begin taking about seven days before entering malarial zones. But the problem with this little monster of a disease is that it has this nasty tendency to become immune to virtually every medicine developed to fight it. Malaria mutates like Wolfgang Puck restaurants.

Also essential is a good first-aid kit with all the trimmings. And add to your booty when you get to Asia. A lot of the drugs you need a prescription for in North America, you can get over the counter in East Asia. And if you're going remote, painkillers are a great idea. You'll be thankful if you take a fall. We don't know too many docs Stateside who will write a downer "scrip" simply because you've said you'll be running in a road rally in HCMC for a month. But bring with you anti-diarrheal drugs such as codeine, Imodium or Lomotil along with an antiseptic and a laxative.

Medical Problems in Vietnam

Food and waterborne diseases are the biggest causes of illness in Vietnam. Diarrhea is the most common problem. Diarrhea is caused by ingesting contaminated food or water, as are other diseases such as parasites, typhoid fever, hepatitis, polio and cholera.

Cholera is caused by bacteria and is an acute intestinal infection transmitted through feces-contaminated food or water. Symptoms include vomiting, dehydration, massive diarrhea attacks and muscle cramps. These days, the risk of cholera infection in Vietnam is low if you stick to the usual tourist itineraries. Should you wander off the beaten track, drink only bottled or boiled water and eat only thoroughly cooked food. Peel vegetables before consuming them. You should be vaccinated against cholera if you're going to be spending significant time in rural and unhygienic places, or if you have stomach ulcers (use anti-acid therapy) or if you will be visiting areas known to have cholera outbreaks—in short, anywhere unsanitary or where floods occur, causing sewage to mix with drinking water. The available vaccine is only about 50 percent effective, and really isn't recommended for most travelers. If you decide to be vaccinated, you'll first receive two injections, and boosters every six months if you live in a high-risk area.

Typhoid fever is caused by a bacteria either consumed or transmitted between people. The symptoms include headaches, fever, constipation, lack of appetite and sluggishness. Typhoid fever can be treated effectively with antibiotics. The risks associated with typhoid fever are travel to rural areas and unhygienic places. Current vaccines are about 70 percent to 90 percent effective. A single injection of Typhim provides three years' protection and doesn't conflict with other inoculations and treatments (such as anti-malarial drugs, antibiotics, etc.) You should get inoculated against typhoid fever if you plan travel in remote parts of Vietnam or will be in the country a month or longer. To avoid risks, drink only bottled water (it's preferable over boiled water) and consume only thoroughly cooked food.

Dysentery is the worst diarrhea you've ever had, and more. It's accompanied by a high fever; you believe you are going to die. Bacillary dysentery is relatively easy to treat. Antibiotics will do the trick in only a couple of days. Even without treatment, bacillary dysentery will disappear after a few days. Amoebic dysentery is far more dangerous. Medical attention is usually necessary, as the disease will not disappear like the bacillary variety. If amoebic dysentery isn't treated promptly, liver damage is more than likely.

Hepatitis has three primary strains: A, B, and non-A/non B. Hepatitis A can be contracted in areas where there is poor hygiene and a lack of sanitation. It is spread through contaminated food and water and attacks the liver. Symptoms include fever, vomiting, loss of energy and acute depression—not unlike the symptoms of bacillary dysentery—which appear within three to eight weeks after infection. The disease will run its course after a few weeks of hell—there is no cure. Bedrest and a high-calorie diet are the recommended treatment.

Hepatitis B is far more dangerous and is spread though sexual contact, blood transfusions, contaminated needles—the same channels through which AIDS is spread. In Vietnam, don't even consider getting a tattoo or an ear pierced. If you get hepatitis B, you'll have it for the rest of your life. Non A/non B strains are simply other variations of the original. To avoid contracting hepatitis B, take the same precautions as you would to avoid AIDS. If you must have sex, do so only with a condom. Stay away from intravenous drugs, and insist that necessary injections be done with a sterile (preferably new) needle. In many areas of Vietnam, needles are reused and not properly sterilized. The other strains of hepatitis can be avoided by taking the same precautions outlined earlier to prevent contracting food- and waterborne diseases.

Malaria is also caused by a parasite, but one that is spread through the Anopheles mosquito rather than through food or water. There are four types of malaria, although only two strains represent most cases. The deadlier of the two is the P faciparum strain, found widely in the southeastern Mekong Delta. Symptoms usually develop about two weeks after being bitten. They include an intense fever, severe headaches, vomiting, shivering and sweating. The risks are greatest at lower altitudes in the south of Vietnam. Medical attention is a necessity.

Unfortunately, malaria has a tendancy to mutate into other vaccine-resistant strains when confronted with anti-malarial preventatives such as chloroquine, the most prescribed antimalarial, which has become largely ineffective if you're bitten by bugs carrying the P falciparum strain. You can't be inoculated against malaria, but are usually instructed instead to ingest chloroquine (one 500 mg tablet a week), starting two weeks prior to a trip into risk areas. The dosage must then be continued for 4-6 weeks after the trip is finished. Other malaria preventatives include maloprim—which is most effective when taken with chloroquine, but shouldn't be used longterm—and doxycycline, which also has dangerous, long-term effects. It particularly shouldn't be used by pregnant women.

The best advice to prevent malaria is stay away from high-risk areas. Cover exposed skin with a deet mosquito repellant and expose as little shin as possible in malarial areas. At night, sleep under a mosquito net. It would help if you had a fan blowing in your direction.

Dengue fever is also a mosquito-borne disease, but not nearly as severe as malaria, although you couldn't imagine anything more severe when you've contracted it. (Symptoms are similar to malaria, but usually subside after a few days, before returning to torture you for a couple of weeks.) But then it's gone. There is no vaccine, and antimalarial treatments and preventatives are ineffective against dengue fever. Take the same precautions as you would with malaria.

Medical Insurance

Before you depart for Vietnam, make sure your medical insurance covers you for such a trip. A number of policies will not cover you overseas, and those that do may not cover you in what they define as a Third World country, or for certain activities you partake in within the country, such as relatively dangerous expeditions and tours. Traveler's insurance is widely available in the U.S. Wallach & Company in Virginia (☎ *(800) 237-6615)* is a good choice, with two-month policies running US$100. Inside Vietnam, travelers—as well as expats—have a few options:

Bao Minh (Ho Chi Minh City Insurance Co.)

26 Ton That Dam, District 1
Ho Chi Minh City
☎ *8294180, 8230181, 8298911. FAX: 8294185.*

Bao Minh is Vietnam's state insurance company. I've heard a number of horror stories involving these folks in the past, particularly concerning the settling of claims. However, I think the operation has been streamlined in the past couple of years. But keep in mind the ceiling insured amount is only US$10,000, which amounts to little more than an ambulance ride and small tip to the nurses should you seriously mess yourself up. Premiums run from US$1.50 a day to as low as 50 cents a day depending on how long you're going to be in the country.

Asia Emergency Assistance (AEA)

65 Nguyen Du, District 1
Ho Chi Minh City
☎ *8298520*

These folks offer both emergency evacuation insurance as well expat medical insurance programs; the latter runs about US$385.

SOS Assistance

151 Vo Thi Sau Street
Ho Chi Minh City
☎ *8242866*
In Hanoi, ☎ *8226228*

Evacuation and repatriation insurance and assistance. Medical teams on call 24 hours, ready to airlift your butt out of a tight spot for transport to world-class health facilities in Hong Kong, Singapore and Bangkok. This costs about US$180 per year.

International Driver's License

These can be obtained at your state's department of motor vehicles offices or through AAA and other automobile associations. The fee is approximately US$7. If you're planning on driving in Asia, get one. Foreigners who have national or international driver's licenses are required to exchange them for Vietnam driver's licenses if they are planning on driving or riding a motorcycle in Vietnam. The cost of conversion is about US$150 and can be done at most police departments. Better yet, check out the expats at Kim Cafe in Saigon. They'll advise you how to do it cheaper and faster. Ask for "Eddie." In Vietnam, an international driver's license is required to rent a motorbike over 50 cc, although few rental firms will ask to see it. They're more interested in your passport. But don't allow that to make you lazy. The cops may ask to see it from time to time. And if you get into an accident over here, and don't have an international driver's permit, you're in trouble.

International Student Identity Card

The ISIC card can help with discounts on air tickets and lodging. There's been a surge in bogus cards, which have been readily available in Thailand

and Malaysia. To get a real one, contact the Council on International Educational Exchange (CIEE) at *205 E. 42nd Street, New York, NY 10017-5706;* ☎ *(212) 661-1414.*

International Youth Hostel Card

This will help you in the expensive places such as Japan, but may be totally unrecognized in Indochina. You can get this card through any youth hostel office. Or write *733 15th Street N.W., Suite 840, Washington, DC 20005;* ☎ *(202) 783-6161.*

Air Travel

There are now myriad airlines that call on the Pacific Rim from the U.S. and a growing number that serve both Ho Chi Minh City and Hanoi. With the lifting of the embargo in February 1994, United Airlines was the first American airline to announce that it would link the U.S. and Vietnam directly. Service to both Ho Chi Minh City and Hanoi may have started on United and Delta by the time you read this.

Take heed that some of the airlines offer better service than the others. It's a long way around to the other side of the globe, so you might want to pay the extra bucks for more comfort and better service—not in terms of upgrading your class, but in choosing an airline. For overall service, comfort, friendliness of the flight crew, food and all the amenities, our hats are tipped to Singapore Airlines. For the feeling of entering Asia the moment you step aboard, these are the folks to fly. Not far behind is Thai Airways, Cathay Pacific and British Airways are in the next league, followed by also-rans Northwest, Korean, Air New Zealand, MAS, Garuda Indonesia, JAL, and Philippines.

When choosing an airline, comfort may be as high a priority as price. Some Asian airlines, such as Singapore, Thai and Cathay Pacific, realize this and take extra pains to make the 15–25 hour flights enjoyable. Others, such as MAS and Garuda Indonesia, employ seat configurations and meal strategies designed for a maximum number of Asian travelers.

Flying to Vietnam

Flights to Vietnam from the United States in economy class with advance purchase cost between $1000 and $1500 round trip, although you may be able to get a cheaper fare through a ticket broker.

For many travelers to the region, Vietnam is not the only stop and is part of an itinerary that may include a number of other Southeast Asian destinations. Few travelers (especially those on extended journeys) book directly to Vietnam from their original points of departure. That's why it'll help to know approximately what the fares are to Vietnam from other cities/countries in the region.

THE STORY OF VIETNAM AIRLINES

Vietnam Airlines was formed in 1989, but its history dates back to 1954 with the takeover of Hanoi's Gia Lam Airport—now its headquarters—from the French. Then called the Civil Aviation Department, the airline went into service with a limited network of communications, meteorological information, fuel, cargo and only five aircraft. It launched its first international service—to Beijing—in April 1956. Over the next two years, the domestic service from Hanoi was extended to Vinh, Dong Hoi and Dien Bien Phu.

Unification of the country in 1975 brought about a boom in air services due to the dramatic increase in economic, political, cultural and social activities. As a result, the airline expanded its operations under a new organization formed in February 1976—the General Department of Civil Aviation. At the time, it had a modest fleet, many say a damned dangerous modest fleet of ailing IL-14s, Antonov-24s, LI-2s, Yak-40s, dilapidated DC-3s, DC-4s and then later a couple of Boeing 707s. The aircraft were poorly maintained, and safety procedures and equipment were all but nonexistent. The airline was considered, along with China's flagship carrier, perhaps the scariest airline on the planet. Many foreigners simply refused to fly VN altogether.

The GDCA also ran a network of aviation departments and airports throughout the country. In 1977, as Vietnam Civil Aviation, the airline carried 21,000 frightened passengers, of whom 7000 were even more frightened foreigners—3000 tons of cargo was also flown during this period. How frightened the freight was flying VN isn't known.

By the time it became Vietnam Airlines in 1989, the airline and its blue and white livery, lettering and precariously fluttering stork logo had become widely known to Vietnamese, foreign passengers and morticians alike.

On April 20, 1993, VN became a company under the Civil Aviation Administration of Vietnam. CAAV is a state-run organization controlling the entire aviation industry of Vietnam. The establishment of the Vietnam Airlines Company is part of the reorganization of Vietnam's aviation industry to meet the growth in air services to and from the country. It marks a significant stage in the development of the airline, namely because it's been forced to purchase newer and safer aircraft as well as seriously update its safety standards.

The new VN fleet now stands at 28 aircraft, including the likes of more modern and comfortable Boeing 737-300s and 767s, the Airbus 310 and 320, and ATR-72s. The old Soviet aircraft are being phased out of their remaining domestic flights—but they're still being flown. The airline began utilizing the Gabriel II reservation system in 1991 and is now planning to join Abacus and other global distribution systems to improve its sales system worldwide. Its computer system is also being upgraded to facilitate document management (which had previously been performed by surly, disgruntled bureaucrats), ticketing and check-in services. Phone bookings are now accepted. The number of passengers has been steadily increasing since 1976 at an average of 36 percent. In 1992, VN achieved 150 percent of its passenger and cargo targets—800,000 foreign and domestic passengers and 10,000 tons of cargo. In 1993, VN began scheduled services to Taipei, Moscow and Seoul using aircraft like the 737, A-310 and 320. In October of 1994, daily service was initiated to Singapore. In 1995, the airline carried 2.31 million passengers, a figure which was expected to rise to nearly 3 million for 1996.

THE STORY OF VIETNAM AIRLINES

VN now flies to 17 destinations overseas and operates 12 domestic routes. Not surprisingly, the domestic flights are still occasionally (very occasionally) aboard the aging and paint-flaked Soviet-era aircraft –most gratefully mothballed–that dot the tarmacs of Hanoi and Ho Chi Minh airports like exhibits at a Charles Lindberg museum.

VN's market share of passenger aircraft to and from Vietnam in 1992 was 35 percent–a significant growth from 1990's 12 percent and 1991's 27 percent. Its international passenger load grew by more than 70 percent.

VN now operates joint services with Cathay Pacific, Malaysian Airlines, Korean Air, Singapore Airlines and China Airlines–to name a few–on some international routes.

With the support of the International Civil Aviation Organization and the United Nations Development program, VN has invested tens of millions of U.S. dollars in upgrading its services as well as ground facilities. To meet new traffic demand to and from the country, VN inaugurated scheduled services to Japan, France and Germany in 1994. Could the U.S. be far behind? With the normalization of relations, it's a distinct possibility.

Not surprisingly, the place to get the cheapest airfares into Vietnam is Bangkok. The cheapest carrier to fly in and out of Vietnam is Vietnam Airlines (VN). At presstime, VN's one-way fare into Ho Chi Minh City was US$150, and US$160 into Hanoi. Advance purchase isn't required, and there isn't a discount for booking round-trip. To avoid the delays and hassles of running all around Khao San (or the equivalent in other Asian cities) looking for the cheapest airfares, simply contact and book through VN's representative offices charted later in this section.

The cheapest places to get to are Tokyo, Seoul, Taipei and Hong Kong (because these are typically nonstop). The more isolated the destination, the more expensive. But tickets to the Far East can be bought less expensively through the proliferation of ticket brokers in major cities. Flights that typically cost in the $900 to $1000 range at airline ticket counters and through travel agents can be had for as low as $725 through some brokers. But beware of these guys. Some of them are as fly-by-night as a red-eye to Seoul flanked by Soviet fighters. Don't give them your credit card number over the phone. Instead, try to pick up your ticket and render payment simultaneously at their offices. Many a traveler has made telephone arrangements only to watch his or her departure date come and go without having received the ticket in the mail. Look in the Sunday travel sections of big papers, such as the *Los Angeles Times* or *The New York Times*.

AUTHOR'S NOTE:
VN PRICE HIKES AND EXPANSION PLANS

Passengers departing on domestic flights from Hanoi, Hai Phong, Da nang, and HCMC are now required to pay an airport service charge of 15,000 dong (about US$1.50). The fees are said to be used to improve the airports' facilities. Vietnam Airlines has plans to more than double its fleet within the next six years. The airline said it needs an additional 30 to 40 of all types of aircraft by the end of the century. Boeing and McDonnell-Douglas are considered the primary contenders for supplying the new fleet. Currently VN utilizes aging Soviet-built Tupolev and Yak-40 aircraft on domestic routes, although Boeing 767s and A320s have been making the Hanoi-Saigon runs recently. Additionally, the airline flies nine other aircraft on international routes—five Airbus A-320s leased from Air France, two Boeing 767s leased from Ansett Airlines, and the two ATR-72s which the airline owns. Taking advantage of the growing number of travelers to Vietnam, VN hiked its fares in 1995 on domestic routes. Currently, foreigners pay about US$320 return fare between HCMC and Hanoi, an excessive amount that presumably subsidizes the current Vietnamese national fare of about US$64 each way. Pacific Airlines, a recent upstart that marginally competes with VN, has announced it will match the fares. Pacific Airlines currently has two aircraft that started a daily shuttle route between HCMC and Hanoi in April 1994 and also flies from HCMC to Panang. Pacific also flies from HCMC to Taipei and Kaohsiung. For reservations and flight information ☎ 84.8.8200978.

You can also obtain discounted multidestination airline tickets for about twice the usual return fare to a single destination. These tickets may permit three or four additional destinations but, of course, restrict you to the cities where the carrier flies. Advance Purchase Excursion tickets are also discounted, but you'll be as equally limited in your choice of destinations. Cancellation penalties can also be enormous.

Another cheap source of airline tickets into Vietnam is Asia itself. One-way fares, for instance, from Bangkok–Hanoi or Kuala Lumpur–Ho Chi Minh City are much cheaper when the tickets are purchased in Bangkok or Kuala Lumpur rather than in the U.S.—even aboard the same carrier. There are hundreds of travel agencies in most East Asian cities and, if you're looking for the cheapest fares, shop around. Once in Kuala Lumpur, I was comparing one-way fares from Singapore to Bangkok and, after having called at least a dozen KL travel agents, I couldn't find anything better than Korean's US$225 offering. Finally a last call I almost didn't make gave me an agent who put me on an almost empty Air New Zealand flight for a hundred bucks. It pays to shop around.

DISCOUNT TICKET BROKERS

American Travel Ventures	☎ *(310) 274-7061*
Angels International Travel	☎ *(800) 400-4150*

DISCOUNT TICKET BROKERS

Bi-Coastal Travel	☎ *(800) 9-COASTAL*
Discover Wholesale Travel	☎ *(800) 576-7770*
Eros Travel	☎ *(213) 955-9695*
Falcon Wings Travel	☎ *(310) 417-3590*
Moon Travel & Tours	☎ *(800) 352-2899*
Sky Service Travel	☎ *(800) 700-1222*
Silver Wings Travel	☎ *(800) 488-9002*
South Sea Tour & Travel	☎ *(800) 546-7890*
Supertrip Travel	☎ *(800) 338-1898*
Travel Mate	☎ *(818) 507-6283*

Tours

Taking a tour isn't the cop-out you might think it is. Tours can actually be a better alternative to independent travel if you have only a week or two. You won't experience the delays, language problems or other time-consuming idiosyncracies inherent in the culture you're visiting. Of course you won't be truly experiencing the culture with a few of the tours. Others, though, give you a surprising amount of freedom. Many of the "new breed" of tour operators are themselves formerly—and even currently—independent travelers. Young, and perhaps only entrepreneurial by default, their tours represent not only the spirit of independent travel, but the nuances as well. These days, you can spend a couple of weeks pedaling a bicycle up the coast of Vietnam from Ho Chi Minh City to Hue (courtesy of Velo Asia), while immersing yourself in the hospitality of rural Vietnamese, Khmer and Cham villagers. It's a tour only in the sense that you're sharing your experiences with a handful of other foreigners.

Experienced travelers will tell you that bigger things come in small packages. If you have only a couple of weeks it doesn't make sense to bounce around East Asia like a good pinball shot. Limit your destinations so you can get more out of them.

Hanoi has a slew of plans for both improving and expanding tourist areas throughout the country to attract more foreign visitors. In the Mekong River Delta region, the floating markets Phong Dien and An Binh are targeted for greater accessibility. The remarkable "Great Supermarket" of Phung Hiep (the markets distinctly dissimilar to the floating markets found in and around Bangkok), where seven of the Mekong's waterways converge, is an absolutely impressive sight; during the fruit season, hundreds of boats carrying rambutan, mango and other assorted fruit move in and out of the market areas. Visitors to the area can take an early morning coach from HCMC, eat breakfast at Tan An, and then cross the two ferries (at My Thuan and Hau Giang) to arrive at Can Tho, about 170 km from Saigon. There visitors can take a bus to Soc Trang in the afternoon, visit a Khmer museum and bat pagoda, and then return to Can Tho to view performances of "reformation" music.

The next morning, it's off to the Ninh Kieu wharf for a steamboat ride of about 25 km to reach the Phung Hiep market. There you can take a steamboat ride through the canals flanked by curious villagers, most of whom will insist that you stay at their homes for a meal of freshly slaughtered poultry and Vietnamese whiskey the villagers distill under the earth in their backyards. If you're part of the tour, the steamboat ride will probably prevent you from fraternizing with the villagers, as you'll have to go back to Saigon that evening, a ride that won't be a lot of fun if you've imbibed on too much rice whiskey.

Vietnam War vets and their families can take advantage of a visit to the former battlefield at Tay Nguyen on the Central High Plateau. Currently, there are very few tourists enjoying this ecological paradise, which has environmentally recovered completely since the end of the hostilities in 1975. In addition to Khe Sanh, Dien Bien Phu and the Ho Chi Minh Trail, there are a number of barely visited areas of the Central High Plateau. Interesting locales that see few, if any, tourists in the area include An Khe, Pleime and Dakto, as well as the mountain path to Lak Lake. A number of tourist agencies have combined their resources to make tours to the area viable.

The Central High Plateau has a number of attractions that tourists are infrequently aware of. There's the village of Bien Ho, and in the Lak district you can rent a canoe or ride on the back of an elephant. Hunting is also available for the outdoorsman.

Tourist agencies in HCMC may be able to cut out some of the more expensive portions of the tour, i.e. the airfares. You may be able to get from Da Lat to Buon Ma Thuot or from Buon Ma Thuot to Nha Trang through the Phoenix Pass (Phuong Hoang)—or take Highway 19 from Quy Nhon to Pleiku via the An Khe Pass. Ask around at the travel agencies spread across HCMC. Some of the better ones are listed in the "Directory" section of the "Ho Chi Minh City" chapter.

There are a lot of operators out there, and a lot of new ones trying to cash in on Vietnam's growing popularity. Get to know as much as possible about a firm before selecting it. Ideally, talk to some other people who've employed the company before. Remember, there are as many different types of tour companies as there are genres of travel.

Tours for Vietnam War Veterans

With improving Vietnam/U.S. relations, a few agencies now offer tours of Vietnam through areas where American soldiers fought, were based, and sent on R&R. As Saigontourist phrases it, "As understood by its appellation, war veteran tours have been set up by Vietnamese veterans for their foreign counterparts of the two Indochina Wars." These are special programs for those who served in Vietnam and would like to revisit former locations and areas of combat activities of their military units, of the Viet Cong war zones, and especially former battlefields. There are also more extensive programs for veterans from all countries (U.S., Australia, South Korea, Thailand, France and the Philippines) to visit the sites of former bases and areas of firefights. Vietnamtourism says these programs are designed to "promote understanding and friendship, thus helping to heal war wounds." Although the tours will have special appeal to returning American soldiers, all visitors to Vietnam are welcome who share an interest in visiting former battlefields as well as experiencing "the new Vietnam." Highlights of the tours consist of visits to the DMZ, Ben Hai River, Dong Ha, Quang Tri, the former U.S. base at Khe Sanh, Ashau-Aluoi valleys, "Hamburger Hill" (south of Ashau Valley) and the Ho Chi Minh Trail.

Some of the areas visited include:

BEN HAI RIVER, THE DMZ

From 1954 to 1975, The Ben Hai River served as the demarcation between the Republic of Vietnam (South Vietnam) and the Democratic Republic of North Vietnam. The Demilitarized Zone consisted of an area 5 km on each side of the river, or demarcation line.

HO CHI MINH TRAIL

Initially, this was only a small trail in the mountainous range of Truong Son only for foot soldiers. But it later developed into an intricate, intertwined road network along the majestic Truong Son range—consisting of a trail for foot messengers and guides, and a larger road for big trucks. For more than a decade, the Ho Chi Minh Trail was a special supply and communication line from North Vietnam to battle sites in South Vietnam.

Traveling by Road in Vietnam: National Highway 1

Totaling a distance of more than 1700 km, Vietnam's National Highway 1 (in its various stretches of smooth pavement and barely negotiable, dilapidated cattle trails) is the longest and most important roadway in the country. Including Highway 1A, it links Ca Mau in the far south all the way to Hanoi. For most of the route north of HCMC it is flanked by the gorgeous Truong Son mountains on the left and by the clear waters of the South China Sea on the right.

Ornate Vietnamese pagodas flank National Highway 1 in virtually uninhabited areas.

Between villages and cities, the route deteriorates from paved scenic pavement to pothole-ridden trenches meaning that bus drivers, and others who frequent the highway, need backsides of lead to endure. Rarely can you reach speeds of more than 50 mph (78 kph), except on a fast motorcycle, where far greater speeds are possible but dangerous due to the vast amount of pedestrian, bicycle and oxcart traffic. At times the shoulder of the highway will be in better shape than the roadway itself, and you'll constantly see motorbikers using the well-worn, but relatively smooth shoulders of the road rather than the highway itself. Roadworkers can be occasionally seen throwing large rocks into the deepest trenches, but there is, amazingly enough, little work that is done to improve NH1. Some of the bridges that were destroyed during the Vietnam War have yet to be repaired, many only crossable by planks and/or railway ties that have been placed over the crumbling grid foundations.

Women line the route toting astoundingly heavy baskets supported by bamboo poles with produce going to market, perhaps many kilometers. They seem to totally ignore the speeding motorbikes and dust- and exhaust-spewing buses and freight trucks that proceed along the highway as if they were its only users. Oxen and horse carts plod the highway, pulling their loads of sugarcane and rice. Bicycles may have as many as three passengers; I've seen as many as six individuals, entire families and maybe some of their friends, astride small Honda 50 cc motorbikes. You'll come across Lambrettas, motorcycles attached with a covered cart with benches running along the sides. They're slow moving and usually packed with at least two dozen people and as many chickens or ducks. It's an unbelievably unsafe way to travel, but is the most popular form for short-distance trips.

The most useful device on your own mode of transportation is the horn. If it isn't working, it may as well be the steering that isn't functioning. You'll see hundreds of the brightly colored Ford and Desoto buses packed with passengers like sardines in oil plowing their way to places such as Danang, Hue, Quy Nhon, Vinh, Phan Thiet, Saigon and the likes. Water spews from small pipes in front of the vehicles near the undercarriages. The water is from the large drums attached to the roofs of the vehicles—and they must stop every 100 km or so to have these refilled, as they serve as the vehicles' cooling systems. The occupants don't seem to mind the cramped conditions aboard the buses—perhaps because most are entirely accustomed to such travel. For the average Westerner, a long bus ride is intolerable and doesn't give the traveler the opportunity to really "be on the road," as the driver will stop every couple or so hours at a roadside cafe of his own choosing so the weary passengers can refill their own cooling systems. On the buses, you'll see two young men straddling straps on the stairs of the open doors, yelling at pedestrians and motorists in the bus path to move the hell out of the way.

The few cars you'll see along Highway 1 are usually hired by tourists or are government vehicles. You'll also see a number of microbuses of the various Vietnamese tourist agencies bouncing along the roadway usually carrying Viet Kieu (Overseas Vietnamese) tourists up and down the coast. The big trucks are usually relatively recently built Soviet heavy-duty trucks, although you'll also see a number of American- and French-made trucks left over from both Indochina wars that are still quite operational, the result of primitive, but ingenious maintenance.

INSIDER TIP

Because tourism is expanding so rapidly in Vietnam, some of the sites where locals rarely laid eyes on foreigners are becoming inundated with white-skinned Anglos with funny green eyes, cameras and Deet. Battle sites from the Vietnam War are becoming increasingly popular with foreign tourists. The village of My Lai and Son My village, where American soldiers massacred hundreds of Vietnamese civilians, have become hot spots to visit. Since the 25th anniversary of the massacre a couple of years ago, more than 7000 people have visited Son My. More than half the visitors were foreigners, whose number visiting the site increased fourfold from 1993 to 1994. The number of Vietnamese visitors has doubled. So if My Lai is on your itinerary, expect some company.

Frequently, you'll come across unhusked rice drying in the sun that may spread halfway across the highway. The larger vehicles will roll right over the grain—curiously, the farmers say it helps speed the drying process. The rice is left untended except for the occasional spreading of the path to even the terrain of the grain. Sugarcane and rice paper are also spread across the road at various points, although vehicles aren't meant to drive over the chips (markers in the form of stones or carts are placed in front of the piles to keep drivers off them). Think of the carbon monoxide and Michelin tire ingredients in your cuisine the next time you're dining.

At various points in the villages along NH1 the road narrows to a mere fly strip as motorcycles, bicycles and heavy trucks barge through the local markets that bulge out into the road like nonticket holders at a Grateful Dead concert. Additionally spilling out onto the highway are large groups of schoolchildren and people playing card games, again, totally oblivious to the traffic. NH1 is as much a social center as it is a thoroughfare.

Of course there are accidents—many of them. The sites where motorists or pedestrians have died are usually marked with a Buddhist-like shrine, and many drivers stop at these points to pay their respects. It is supposed to be good luck to do so. Near Ca Na, there's even a memorial where a busload of passengers died some years ago.

All along Highway 1 food stalls and cafes abound, their owners dangerously sprinting into the middle of the roadway as if there was an emergency to flag down motorists into their eateries. Usually the cafes are in clumps, so the competition for business, although friendly, is ruthless. In a way, customers at these stalls are a remedy to an emergency, as the stall owners are all quite poor. Wherever you stop, you will be swarmed by children, beggars and such, selling everything from lighter fluid to chewing gum.

Perhaps the great advantage of Highway 1, as well as other routes spread across Vietnam, is the number of Honda repair shops. Every few hundred meters you are bound to see a sign saying "Honda (spelled in various configurations such as 'Hun Da, Honza, Hon Daa', etc.) Xe Dap," the latter meaning the shop also works on bicycles. At virtually any point along Highway 1 if you break down, there will be a Honda repair hootch within rolling distance. Vietnamese, mechanics or not, will instantly try to determine and remedy your bike's malady. Most are quite adept, although they tend to smoke cigarettes so close to gasoline, it's amazing the country hasn't completely defoliated itself without the aid of hostile aggressors.

You'll find that after passing several kilometers through a village or town, a team of policemen will have set up roadblocks. Their purpose is usually to stop buses and trucks for bribes. Tourists are rarely stopped by the police (unless you're traveling independently by motorcycle—then expect to be stopped frequently), although you may find yourself on a microbus whose driver doesn't have the proper credentials to be transporting tourists. Some of these drivers employ imaginative ways of bypassing the roadblocks. One driver I met near Phan Thiet, before reaching a roadblock, unloaded his tourists and placed them on buses a kilometer before the checkpoint. He picked them back up again on the other side. Police, when they see a large motorcycle approaching, may step out into the road to flag you down with their batons—but upon realizing you're a foreigner will usually allow you to pass (Vietnamese are not allowed to operate motorcycles over 175 cc unless they're in "high positions," usually in the government—or they're police officers themselves).

NH1 is continually surrounded by rice fields, the workers under their conical hats stooped tending to the crop. You'll see statues of the Virgin Mary and ancient Cham towers perched on hilltops or right beside the roadway.

Near Cam Ranh, salt factories flank the roadside, and salt paddies extend out into the deep blue mountain-ringed bay.

Going north, after passing through Danang, you make a journey over one of the most spectacular passes in Vietnam, Hai Van Pass, which reaches an altitude of nearly 500 meters in the Truong Son Mountain Range. The views of both ocean and lush green mountains are unsurpassed anywhere in the world. This pass, many times shrouded in dense fog, is so dangerous and steep that ascending turn-off ramps on downgrades have been constructed for trucks and buses which lose their brakes, which happens constantly on this stretch of roadway. This is the ribbon of NH1 that drivers fear the most, and is perhaps the most dangerous stretch of NH1 in Vietnam. Hai Van Pass, during the 15th century, marked the border between the Kingdom of Champa and Vietnam. On top of the pass there is an old fort that was built by the French and then later used by the Americans and the South Vietnamese Army.

Between Danang and Lang Co Beach the Vietnamese climate changes dramatically—from sunny, hot and humid to damp, gray and cloud covered—and cold. From this point to Ha Long Bay and Hanoi, you'll think you're in a different country. The fog straddling the mountainsides of Hai Van Pass creates some of the best photo opportunities in Vietnam, but you'll soon become depressed by the lack of sunlight and heat which you despised only hours earlier. Villagers and farmers are dressed in winter clothing.

The one thing to watch out for on NH1 is that it forks frequently, the most confusing fingers of the road being in Quy Nhon and Phan Rang. You may travel several kilometers before you realize you screwed up.

Now that the Friendship Bridge has been completed linking Thailand and Laos, there's a lot of talk about linking Thailand and Vietnam through Laos at other points. Some of the projects seriously being considered are Highway 8, which would link Thailand's northeastern Nakhon Phanom Province with Vietnam's Cua Lo Port, near Vinh, via Khammouan Province in central Laos. Also being considered is Highway 12, which would link Thailand's Nakhon Phanom Province with the Vietnamese port of Hon La. This route is farther south than Highway 8. Highway 9 already links Danang and Hue with Laos and Thailand.

The government is interested in all three roads, but particular attention is paid to upgrading Route 9. This is to the benefit of Thailand's Mukdahan Province. There would be less investment involved, and the road traverses relatively flat terrain. Additionally, a port would not have to be built. But Nakhon Phanom has the edge in that Highway 12 through Khammouan to the Vietnamese coast is only 270 km, as opposed to the 570 km stretch along Highway 9 linking Vietnam with Laos and Thailand. One of the carrots being held out on the part of the Thais is that construction of Highway 12 would help reduce the pressure of population growth in Bangkok, and would more evenly distribute Thai manufacturing facilities. Laos favors construction of Highway 8, because it would be the shortest way of reaching its capital, Vientiane. Whichever route is chosen, the three countries will still have a modern roadway of international standards that will eventually become a major international transportation link.

AUTHOR'S NOTE

A little advice for travelers in Vietnam: There are 10,000 km of roads, 40 percent of which are rated "poor" or "very poor." There are 8280 road bridges, 50 percent of which are considered dilapidated. There are 2600 km of railways, seven major seaports, three international airports and 10 domestic airports.

Books

The following are some of the best historical and contemporary works on Vietnam:

Browne, Malcombe, *Red Socks and Muddy Boots* (New York Times Press, 1993); this is an excellent, fast-paced accounting of the famous journalist's observations of the Vietnam War based on his 11 years in-country during the 1960s and '70s. It's a humorous and depressing, no-punches-pulled analysis of the political and military blunders both sides struggled with in justifying both their moral, political and military ambitions in Indochina. Browne, journalists Peter Arnett and Neil Sheehan were primarily blackballed by U.S. and ARVN forces as traitors, so this makes for fascinating reading of life in a Huey and a suitcase.

Along the same lines is Sheehan's definitive work, *A Bright Shining Lie* (Jonathan Cape, London, 1989). This is a huge account of the war based around the life of John Paul Vann. Well-researched and as eye-opening as they come. This was a Pulitzer Prize winner. Sheehan also wrote *Two Cities: Hanoi and Saigon* (Jonathan Cape, London, 1992).

Another colleague of Sheehan's and Browne's was David Halberstram, whose *The Making of A Quagmire* (Ballantine Books, New York) is considered a gem in outlining U.S. participation in the war.

Also check out *The Real War* by Jonathan Shell (Pantheon Books, New York, 1987.

The Bamboo Cage by Leo Cooper (Cawthorne, Nigel, 1992). A tear-jerking account of POWs and MIAs in Vietnam during the war.

Francis Fitzgerald's *Fire in the Lake* (Vintage Books, New York, 1972) was also a Pulitzer Prize winner about U.S. involvement during the war.

Why Vietnam?, Archimedes Patti (University of California Press, Berkeley, 1980) is a compelling history of OSS (pre CIA) attempts to funnel weapons to Ho Chi Minh at the end of WWII. Patti was with the OSS during this time and was close to Ho when he claimed North Vietnamese independence in 1945.

A Death in November by Ellen Hammer (EP Dutton & Sons, New York, 1987) is the story of Diem's overthrow and execution in 1963.

One Crowded Hour, Tim Bowden (Angus and Robertson, 1988) chonicles the work of Australian film journalist Neil Davis, who shot footage of the NVA tank crashing through the gates of the presidential palace in April 1975.

The Tunnels of Cu Chi, Tom Mangold and John Pennycate (1985). A look at the hardships the Viet Cong faced in building and living in the famed tunnels west of Saigon.

The Fall of Saigon, David Butler (Simon & Schuster, 1985) is a look at the events and the chaos surrounding takeover of the South's capital in 1975, as is *55 Days; The Fall of Saigon*, by Alan Dawson (Prentice Hall, Englewood Cliffs, NJ, 1977).

Michael Herr's *Dispatches* (Knopf, New York, 1987) is a journalist's firsthand look at the bloody conflict.

Stanley Karnow's highly respected *Vietnam: A History* (Viking Press, New York, 1983) is one of the most respected works on Vietnam in the past two decades.

Chickenhawk, by Robert Mason (Penguin, 1984) is the recollections of a chopper pilot. Fast-paced, edge-of-the-seat reading.

The Pentagon Papers (Bantam Books, Toronto, 1971) were published by the *New York Times* and had the same effect, if not more, on America's sentiments toward the war as did the 1968 Tet Offensive.

Born on the Fourth of July, Ron Kovic (Pocket Books, New York, 1976). This grisly, heart-wrenching account of a soldier maimed during the war was made into a blockbuster movie starring Tom Cruise in an unforgettable role as the author.

The 13th Valley. It was written years before the motion picture *Platoon* hit the big screen and is easily the more horrific of the two in describing the terror of being a grunt in the jungle.

Brothers in Arms (Avon Books, New York, 1986), by William Broyles Jr. is a mildly interesting account of a former GI-turned-journalist returning to Vietnam some years after the war.

Portrait of the Vietnamese Soldier (Red River Press, Hanoi) is a provocative account of the North Vietnamese struggle against the Americans.

William Turley's *The Second Indochina War: A Short Political and Military History, 1954–1975* (Westview, Boulder, 1976), can be hard reading, but it's comprehensive and highly detailed.

Bungled military strategy is examined in *On Strategy*, by Colonel Harry Summers (Presidio Press, Navato, Calif., 1982).

Bloods: An Oral History of the Vietnam War by Black Veterans, by Wallace Terry (Ballentine Books, 1984).

Chained Eagle is a gripping account of the lives of American POWs by Everett Alverez (Dell, New York, 1989).

Viet Cong Memoir, by Truong Nhu Tang, is about the life of a former Viet Cong soldier who later rejected post-1975 Vietnamese politics. (Harcourt Brace Jovanovich, San Diego, 1985).

Ecological Consequences of the Vietnam War, SIPRI (Almqvist & Wiksell, Stockholm, 1976). An account of the environmental devastation of the war.

Other Books of Interest

The Quiet American, Graham Greene (Heinemann, London, 1954). In college most of us read this highly accurate fictionalized account of the impending American involvement in the Indochinese conflict. As relevant today as it was then. Some say it's a masterpiece.

A Dragon Apparent: Travels in Cambodia, Laos and Vietnam, by Norman Lewis (Eland Books, 1951). A superb travelogue.

Charles Fenn's *Ho Chi Minh: A Biographical Introduction* (Charles Tutteland Rutland Vermont, 1973).

Saigon, Anthony Grey (Pan, London, 1983).

The Birth of Vietnam, Keith Taylor (University of California Press, Berkeley, 1983).

J. Helzar, *The Art of Vietnam* (Hanlyn, London, 1973).

Elizabeth Kemp, *Month of Pure Light; The Regreening of Vietnam* (The Women's Press, London, 1990).

Gerald Hickey, *Village in Vietnam* (Yale University Press, New Haven, 1964).

Vietnamese Anticolonialism: 1885–1925, by David G. Marr (University of Berkeley, Los Angeles, 1971).

The Rise of Nationalism in Vietnam: 1900–1941 (Cornell University Press, Ithica, New York, 1976).

Australia's War in Vietnam by Frank Frost (Allen and Unwin, Sydney, Boston, and London, 1987).

All the Way: Australia's Road to Vietnam by Gregory Pemberton (Allen and Unwin, Sydney, Boston, and London, 1987).

Robert F. Turner, *Vietnamese Communism: Its Origins and Development* (Hoover Institution Press, Stanford, 1975).

When You Arrive

Vietnam is a surprisingly easy country to enter these days. The formalities are no more arduous than, say, entering Thailand. Frankly, it's more of a hassle entering Singapore than either Saigon or Hanoi. The infamous scams pulled by Vietnamese customs officials and policemen that were prevalent only a short time ago are all but nonexistent now. Foreigners, who are legitimate tourists of course, have little fear of being harassed or detained while an "illegal entry" fine is negotiated. Be warned, however, that a lot less English is spoken in Hanoi than in Saigon and, that if there is a problem, it probably will be both more expensive and time-consuming to solve it. It appears, however, that customs officials in both cities are under instructions in no uncertain terms that each and every stamp on a foreigner's passport is synonymous with much-needed hard currency; the likelihood of your being afforded the opportunity to tell your friends and other potential visitors of the hardships you encountered entering or leaving Vietnam are these days, fortunately, minimal. Even though Vietnam is a communist country, you will be surprised at how much freedom you're afforded.

On the plane you will have filled out a customs declaration form. Those items you have declared will be inspected in all likelihood. And even though the idea of having your belongings displayed is unappealing (and downright frightening if you've got on your person anything marginally to highly suspicious, such as gems, figurines, poached animal parts, Chinese elixirs or heroin paste), remember that what you don't declare doesn't exist. Say you're traveling with a laptop computer and don't declare it upon entry. If you're searched upon leaving and it's discovered, you may end up paying a duty on it, if not worse.

SOME ADVICE FOR RETURNING VIET KIEU

If you're an overseas Vietnamese, or "Viet Kieu," returning to Vietnam, here's a tip: don't show your bucks. Vietnamese can instantly spot an overseas Vietnamese, usually by behavior and attire. Many Vietnamese are wary of returning "Viet Kieu," and suspicious of their intentions. You may be only a tourist, but many Vietnamese will suspect you've returned to your home country to make a fast buck, especially if you dress flashy and exhibit the behavior and social customs you've acquired in your new home country.

Curiously, although they fanatically vie for it, the Vietnamese do not trust wealth, especially the display of it. Additionally, you may face criticism from your anti-communist friends at home, who may accuse you of supporting Marxism. Don't be surprised if many at home call you a VC (Viet Cong). Although relations between Vietnam and the U.S. have normalized, it is still very difficult for overseas Vietnamese to reintegrate with their people. You may feel like a stranger in your own country. The Vietnamese government will welcome your money, of course. Overseas Vietnamese send or bring into the country perhaps US$1 billion each year.

If you're an overseas Vietnamese wishing to return permanently to your homeland (as a growing number are), it may not be so easy.

Decision No. 59/TTg (implemented the day after U.S. President Clinton lifted the embargo in Feb. 1994) is somewhat complicated but essentially limits applicants to three categories of consideration: 1) elderly persons age 60 or more and children under the age of 16 if they are sponsored by close relatives living in Vietnam; 2) applicants with a post-graduate degree or professional skills needed by the government; 3) management directors of companies associated with investment projects in Vietnam as prioritized by the Law on Foreign Investment.

SOME ADVICE FOR RETURNING VIET KIEU

If you hold a foreign passport, forget it. If you hold no passport, forget it. If you left Vietnam illegally in the first place, forget it. In other words, the Vietnamese Vietnam will take back shouldn't have been tainted by counter-revolutionary lifestyles, or should be too old to do anything about it.

Language and Culture

There are a lot of nuances that differ among the peoples of the Far East. But for every contrast, there are 10 commonalities. Asians, as tolerant as most are, will behave in ways and speak with a body language that will fluster you at first. You'll be tempted to be amused by gestures and customs that seem everything from banal to compulsive. But don't be.

Just use good judgment. Knowing how to dress, present and compose yourself will dispel a ton of potential problems. Remember, it's better to blend in in Asia than to stand out. Dress coolly but conservatively. Shorts, but not short ones, are okay in informal environments. Ladies should cover as much of their bodies as reasonably possible. You don't have to look like a nun, but it wouldn't hurt. No short dresses; anything you consider sexy will be taken as offensive by your Asian hosts. And try not to look like a hippie. That sarong and the beads you bought in Ko Samui are fine on Ko Samui, but now you're in a land of pith helmets, business suits and olive drab uniforms. Take heed.

Displays of emotion—from affection to anger—are considered crass and rude. Never show anger, regardless of the situation. Most Southeast Asians abhor conflict. Smile even to the man you'd rather kick than converse with. Equally as offensive, in most places, are public displays of sexual affection. Kissing and even holding hands are discouraged in most Asian communities. Save it for the hotel.

When entering an individual's home, in some cases, you'll need to remove your shoes. However, unlike other predominantly Buddhist countries in the region, the Vietnamese are generally not inclined to follow this practice, even inside temples. If you're not sure, your host will not be offended if you politely inquire. Never will you be expected to remove your shoes at hotels and public structures other than some religious temples.

Don't pat anyone on the head, including children. It's a sign of disrespect. And what you do with your hands, do with both hands or your right hand only. The left hand is considered unclean. This includes for eating and passing objects to other people. It's a pain in the rear if you're left-handed, but try and follow the rule at least when it's most appropriate, as in ceremonial occasions, toasts in your honor, etc.

The feet are considered unclean as well. When seated, don't point them in anyone's direction. (A lot of people do it, anyway—it's no big deal unless you appear to be doing it on purpose.)

If eating with chopsticks, place them horizontally across your bowl or on the table when finished.

Finally, be especially careful of the gestures you make. Symbols that are considered innocent or even complimentary in the U.S. are construed differently abroad. However, it's only truthful to say that, as a foreigner, you won't be expected to understand proper gestures and behavior of the Vietnamese. Rather, you'll be expected not to understand. And, in most cases, violations will be dismissed with a smile, if they are even noticed. One reason the Vietnamese are more tolerant of Western idiosyncracies than other East Asian societies is the fact that 5 million Americans and a few hundred thousand other Westerners essentially occupied the southern half of the country for more than 10 years in the 1960s and '70s. Things are changing very rapidly here.

And a word about language. We'll admit it; the tongues of the Far East make the languages of Europe seem like dialects of English. Learning Mandarin Chinese, Japanese, Thai, Cambodian, Malay and Vietnamese virtually requires surgery for some people. But a little effort on your part to pick up some rudimentary Vietnamese phrases will go a long way. Unlike many huffy Parisians, Vietnamese people are honored when you make an attempt to speak their language, as futile and unintelligible as the resulting utterance may be. (See Vietnam's Language in "Vietnam Today.")

It's an old phrase, but not without relevance. When overseas, you are an ambassador of your country. How you treat your Vietnamese hosts will reflect on those who follow in your footsteps.

BEHAVING WITH THE VIETNAMESE SOCIALLY AND IN BUSINESS

A few notes on how to deal with Vietnamese customs, whether you're in the country on business or pleasure. Simply reading about the "customs" in Asian nations won't be enough to learn the idiosyncrasies of Vietnamese customs and behavior. In terms of business or official meetings, get a good interpreter. That person should teach you correct pronunciation for the individuals you'll be meeting with. Learn Vietnamese greetings (the "Crash Course in Speaking Vietnamese" in this book will help).

Learn now to recognize the individual you'll be meeting before the meeting, either through an interpreter's description or by seeing a photograph. That way, you'll immediately know who to address when entering the room. And do not greet an assistant first! When you shake hands, do so at arm's length rather than up close. Most Westerners are quite a bit taller than their Vietnamese hosts.

BEHAVING WITH THE VIETNAMESE SOCIALLY AND IN BUSINESS

Sitting at a table during a business meeting, do not cross your legs or show the soles of your feet (this is really not even acceptable in social situations, although the increasing influx of naive Westerners into Vietnam has made the Vietnamese more accustomed to this—but only in social environs). Although the custom of giving and receiving with both hands is common in Southeast Asia, it is not necessary in Vietnam.

When handing out business cards, start with the most important person you are with. But give cards to everyone! You never know where the mailroom clerk will be in a few years. If you're short on business cards and have to make photocopies, never mix the two when you're handing out cards. Either hand out a photocopy or the original.

One of the life-threatening habits I've acquired since being in Vietnam is that I've started smoking cigarettes. This was mainly due to the fact that I was incessantly offered them as gifts. Most Vietnamese men smoke, though few women do. Simply, if you're offered a cigarette, take it. Not doing so is somewhat of an insult (although this is changing rapidly as the Vietnamese become more accustomed to nonsmoking foreigners), even if you don't smoke. Either smoke it or place it on the table in front of you (in which case you will not be offered another).

One of the traditional tips offered to business people doing business with the Vietnamese has been this: If you're employing a translator, address the person you're speaking with, not the translator. When the Vietnamese is speaking with you, look at him and acknowledge him occasionally with a nod of the head. Again, don't look at the interpreter. He is only the conduit of your conversation with the person you are meeting with.

In reality, it usually doesn't work this way, and you'll find that many Vietnamese look and speak directly toward the interpreter, rather than at you. It's best when both talking and listening to divide your attention between the interpreter and your audience. It's more interactive and less a charade—as is the nature of all conversations between two people who can't understand a word each other says.

Vietnamese love to drink. If you do, too, you've come to the right place. There are different forms of toasting in Vietnam. One of them, which is used frequently, is called "Tram Phan Tram." It means you are required to empty the entire contents of your glass. If you don't drink alcohol, a soft drink or tea will do. But if you do enjoy an occasional whiskey or beer, be prepared to enjoy your imbibement excessively. In Vietnam, you should never refuse hospitality when it's offered.

Behaving in Temples

The rule of always removing your shoes before entering an Asian temple of worship is not always observed in Vietnam. It depends entirely upon the temple, the lifestyle of its hosts and local custom. As mentioned above, inquire first. At many temples, especially those frequented by tourists, a sign in English will be posted regarding the rule.

If seated before a Buddha, sit on your knees, thigh and hip, with your feet extending behind you. Do not sit in the lotus position (cross-legged). No shorts in temples, although some guides will tell you that it's okay. (They just don't want to offend you.) Cameras may or may not be permitted. Usually they're not in other East Asian temples, but in many Vietnamese temples, they are permitted—especially in those with connections to the state. They charge an additional camera admission fee! And remember, customs and behavior in the south are a lot more relaxed than in the north. It's like the difference between Venice, California, and Newport, Rhode Island.

A Word About Illegal Drugs

Leave them at home. Drug users and traffickers beware. A special squad formed by the Police Department's Economic Crimes Division will step up its efforts against both drug addiction and trafficking. It will become the most powerful anti-drugs force in Vietnam. In 1993, Vietnamese authorities siezed 1.4 kilos of opium and 10 kilos of heroin. During the past year, three drug smugglers have been sentenced to death, while two others were jailed for life.

In June 1995, a British national born in Hong Kong became the first foreigner executed in Vietnam for drug trafficking. In July, an American was sentenced to 20 years' imprisonment and fined US$200,000 for his role in attempting to bring 1600 kg of heroin into the country.

He got off light. Very light.

In May 1997, 12 important Vietnamese government officials went on trial for smuggling heroin into Vietnam, in what became the most heavily publicized trial in Vietnam's history. At press time, it was expected 10 of the 12 would be sentenced to death.

The government isn't screwing around.

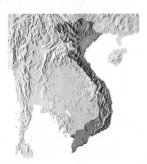

VIETNAM TODAY

Barbie, Barbwire and billiards. As Vietnam's economy becomes influenced by the West, so do its artists.

More than two decades after U.S. troops pulled out of Vietnam, Americans are returning to this still-battle-scarred country, only this time, they're coming as tourists and businesspeople.

Thanks to the U.S. government's removal of restrictions against travel to Vietnam in 1992, followed by President Clinton's lifting of the trade embargo in February 1994 and subsequent normalizing of relations in July 1995, a growing slew of tour operators now offer group and individual tour packages to Vietnam. Their numbers—and travelers' options—are expanding at a jackrabbit's pace.

Tours from the U.S. usually fly into Bangkok, Singapore or Hong Kong, convenient gateways for air connections into Vietnam. Although operators say most of their inquiries are for tours that combine Vietnam with Cambodia and Laos, you probably won't see many all-Indochina tours advertised until Cambodia's on-again/off-again political problems are resolved. You will, however, be able to choose from a fairly good selection of tour packages that combine Vietnam with other Asian destinations, including China. (There are good flight connections from Nanning, China, into Vietnam.) And soon, maybe by the time you read this, you may be able to fly directly to Vietnam from the U.S. (Look for Delta Airlines and United to be the companies to first offer these routes.)

VIETNAM IN A NUTSHELL

One of the most overwhelmingly beautiful countries in the world...with a people to match...73.9 million of them...of the 5 million Americans who fought here during the Vietnam War, 58,000 died and more than 2200 are still MIA in Indochina—more than 1600 in Vietnam alone...the subsequent international economic embargo of Vietnam crippled the country...it has one of the lowest standards of living in the world...certainly in SE Asia...however, the thawing of relations between the U.S. and Vietnam has spawned a surge in tourism...lifting of the embargo and the normalization of relations is now allowing American businesses to operate aggressively in Vietnam...there are more than 3200 km of coastline...more than the state of California...and most of it pristine...the U.S. dollar is accepted throughout most of the country...Hanoi is moving markedly toward a market economy...it's best to visit now, before the inevitable commercialism suffocates this country's innocence.

Ho Chi Minh City (Saigon)   *Although at one time on par with Bangkok, but now eclipsed by the Thai capital, Saigon is still one of the most thriving cities in all of Southeast Asia, certainly the most bustling in Indochina. It is vibrant, entrepreneurial, and with the exception of the revolutionary posters and hammer and sickle flags swirling about, you'd never know you were in a communist country. Population about 5 million. Natural attractions include the nearby Mekong Delta. Man-made wonders include the nearby Cu Chi tunnel network.*

Nha Trang   *This coastal area features beautiful beaches that are popular with both locals and tourists. There's great snorkeling and scuba diving as well as fishing and great seafood.*

Danang   *This is a historic city and one of Vietnam's major seaports. And although it bustles with shipping activity, the water is remarkably clean and the area boasts some good beaches. Some of the attractions include the local Cham architecture.*

VIETNAM IN A NUTSHELL

The Central Highlands	*Generally known for the great scenery, cooler climate and the Montegnard tribespeople. The verdant mountain scenery is unmatched in Vietnam save perhaps for some areas in the northern part of the country. There are waterfalls and many beautiful, clear lakes.*
Hue	*This city, although devastated during the war, retains a great deal of its historical charm. Hue is really the traditional cultural, art, educational and religious capital of Vietnam. There are all kinds of pagodas, palaces and museums to visit here. The royal tombs are just south of the city.*
Ha Long Bay	*Beautiful beach area with thousands of islands and spectacular grottoes rising from the Gulf of Tonkin southeast of Hanoi. The area is targeted by the government to become a major tourist area it says will rival those of Thailand and the Eastern peninsula of Malaysia. Visit this area now, while it is still absolutely pristine.*
Hanoi	*The charming capital of Vietnam but not nearly as colorful as its onetime rival in the south—Saigon. The people here are more reserved than their neighbors to the south. But it is a charming colonial city if charm is your thing. The Old Quarter is rapidly becoming transformed by weird-looking add-on building additions and satellite dishes, but the "gingerbread" style architecture and tree-lined boulevards make the capital worth a visit of moderate length.*

Americans who have already gone to Vietnam say they're amazed by the friendliness the people show toward U.S. visitors, given the recent history of the two countries. They're also surprised to find that just about everything is priced in U.S. dollars, rather than in Vietnamese currency, the dong (about 10,900 dong equals US$1), especially in the larger population centers. Even the departure tax of US$8 is paid in U.S. currency. Hotels and other businesses now accept U.S.-issued credit cards, and Vietcom Bank has also started issuing cash advances on U.S.-issued credit cards.

Despite poverty and a Third-World infrastructure, Vietnam—and particularly Ho Chi Minh City (which most people here still refer to as Saigon; in fact, the central part of the city is still officially called Saigon)—still retains its haughty, aggressive air. Rickshaws (called cyclos in Vietnam) buzz around town; street vendors hawk everything from lacquerware to old tires and city boulevards are graced by beautiful, newly restored colonial-era mansions built by the French.

The average hotel leaves something to be desired, although those frequented by monied tourists and businesspeople are overall surprisingly comfortable, if not downright luxurious. The townlike squares around the Rex and the Continental have the feel of Boston or New Orleans. There are currently about 10 or 12 hotels under construction in Ho Chi Minh City (which will be located in Saigon, Cu Chi—which saw heavy action during the Vietnam War—and Cholon, the city's Chinatown). Among the newer hotels are the 260-room Omni Saigon Hotel and the 600-room New World Hotel, in downtown Saigon. (Hong Kong-based New World is also building a hotel in Phnom Penh, Cambodia). Also, Club Med plans to build a vacation village sometime soon in Vietnam, but is first testing the waters by including the country in the schedules of its cruise vessel, *Club Med 2.*

Of the hotels already in operation in Ho Chi Minh City, the most luxurious (after the New World)—and the most intriguing—was the Saigon Floating Hotel. Operated by Australia's Southern Pacific Hotel Corporation, the boat-hotel was once a fixture on the Great Barrier Reef. It has about 200 air-conditioned rooms with all the modern amenities, including hair dryers in the bathrooms and a swimming pool on the mainland. However, as a testament to the current hotel glut in the city, the Floating Hotel battened its hatches in August of 1996 and was towed to the Philippines, where it began life anew off of Palawan.

Lots of Rooms—So Bring On the Tourists

At the end of 1996, there were 1800 hotels and guesthouses of all sizes in Ho Chi Minh City with 15,309 rooms, ranging in price from VND80,000-800,000 per night. About 13,000 rooms are considered to be of international standards.

Other good hotels in Ho Chi Minh City where tourists are accommodated include the century-old, but newly refurbished Continental Hotel, a favorite of W. Somerset Maugham, and the Century Saigon, which is operated by a Hong Kong firm and occupies the site of the former Oscar Hotel.

In Hanoi, the capital, the lovely former Metropole Hotel has gotten a new lease on life, thanks to Pullman/Sofitel, which restored this *grande dame* of the French colonial era. The Hotel Pullman Metropole has a superb French restaurant and a swimming pool.

Flora and Fauna

Vietnam's flora and fauna are something to behold, although the forests have been extensively denuded in the past century—particularly by warfare. But compared to other regions of Southeast Asia, Vietnam is Eden. The forests contain as many as 12,000 species of plants. Just more than half of them have been identified.

AUTHOR'S OBSERVATION

Peoples' Committees throughout Vietnam have recently received documents from the Vietnamese Ministry of Forestry banning the sale of wild animals, the products of wild animals (including food), skins, stuffed birds and animals, horns, antlers, bones, claws, elephant tusks and gazelle horns, tortoise shells and the skin of leopards and tigers. Additionally, interestingly enough, the husbandry of wild animals was approved in the Forestry Ministry decree for domestic use and export.

More than 250 species of mammals trod or trapeze the topography; 770 bird species traverse its skies. Nearly 200 species of reptiles slither about, hundreds of species of fish swim in its lakes and coastal waters, and 80 species of amphibians do both. The discoveries of new species continue. But, in sad contrast, hundreds more are expected to soon become extinct. Among those threatened are the tapir (which some believe is already extinct), the Javan rhino and the kouprey. The Sumatran rhino is already extinct in Vietnam.

Vietnam, like virtually all Southeast Asian countries, has been mired by an abysmal record of protecting threatened wildlife species. Although there's been growing pressure by international wildlife organizations on Vietnam to get its act together—and there have been many strides made in the past few years to eradicate the poaching and/or sale for private use of endangered species—it's still a major problem here.

A little side trip I took to Saigon's Cho Cau Mong animal market on Chuong Duong Street was evidence enough. The sign was marked "Exhibition and Sales of Birds and Animals." And we're not talking about canaries, angelfish and cute little poodles. This dilapidated "pet shop" is nothing short of a concentration camp for animals. Here, nearly extinct concolor gibbons and a myriad of other exotic species live packed in cages the size of toothpaste boxes; they're stacked upon each other like pallets in a warehouse with no platforms between them to prevent the excrement of the animals lucky enough to be imprisoned on the top level from dropping their waste onto the animals interred below.

Infant rhesus monkeys, separated from their parents at birth, huddle in fear or insanely leap back and forth in their cages like screaming balls in a short racquetball court—if there is enough room. Many of the species here are protected under the Convention of International Trade of Endangered Species, Flora, and Fauna (CITES)—but obviously not at this market. There are 113 signatories to the CITES measure. Vietnam isn't one of them. The animals here all suffered from scabies, mange and a host of other maladies. Prosemian slow lores groveled in feces, their tiny heads buried into their remaining fur, in cages beside workers pounding the concrete with iron rods and hammers. A pair of CITES-protected pangolins had been killed and stuffed, and were on display in glass counters. A magnificent 20-foot Indian python was coiled like a mammoth black firehose inside a cage the size of a suitcase, and a douc langur (a monkey indigenous to Vietnam), was for sale even though it is officially protected in Vietnam.

This "pet shop" and others like it have been substantially cleaned up by the government in the past few years. Previously, the conditions at the market were even more primitive and inhumane, nothing short of a landfill. And the market offered a greater array of threatened species than it does now. But the trade in exotic animals in Vietnam is still highly lucrative. Additionally, at the market, you can purchase ivory, snake and tiger skins, and the remains of other nearly extinct creatures but don't expect to get them through customs. If you choose to take pictures here (and can get away with it), be careful.

ELEPHANTS ON THE WANE

Although the number of elephants in Vietnam stands at between 5000 and 7000, according to the World Wildlife Fund—mainly living in the Central Highlands—the beasts have been rapidly disappearing in the past decade. The decrease in the past 10 years has been termed only as "substantial." Their demise has been mainly attributed to poaching tusks and the rapid loss of the elephants' natural habitat, due to farming extension and deforestation.

As the demise of millennia-old species proceeds unabated, on a brighter note, the discovery of new species of animals and plants continues. Apparently Dr. John MacKinnon, British-born ecologist, has discovered a fascinating new mammal species that resembles a goat, but is more closely related to the cow. DNA samples taken from the horns of the beast, believed inhabiting an area near Vietnam's 350-square-mile Vu Quang Nature Reserve, about 175 miles southwest of Hanoi near the border with Laos, have shown that the animal is nothing like scientists have ever seen. This is indeed the discovery of a large mammal previously unknown to science. The last time something happened of this magnitude was the 1937 discovery of the kouprey, a now nearly extinct species of wild cattle, in the forests of Cambodia.

The new creature is called *Pseudoryx nghetinhensis*—meaning the false oryx of Nghe Tinh (the former name of the province where it was found)—or the Vu Quang Ox. The villagers call the animal a spindlehorn. It's believed that until people began populating the region around 1950, the *Pseudoryx* had no natural enemies. The animal is horned and can weigh in excess of 200 lbs. It sports a brown coat with black-and-white markings and a scent gland used to stake its territory. MacKinnon argues that its existence suggests that cows may have come from the forests, and not from grassy plains and savannahs, as is most commonly believed. Two specimens have been captured alive, but have died in captivity. Scientists say that perhaps 300 of the creatures exist at most.

UPDATE ON THE RARE VU QUANG OX

During an expedition in June 1995, scientists discovered the remains of a rare Vu Quang Ox in an area of central Vietnam that was previously thought to be outside of the species' range. Consequently, researchers believe the nearly extinct ox may inhabit areas of the country where it wasn't previously thought to exist. The animal may have crossed north of the Song Ca River into other regions of Nghe An province. Return expeditions will focus on the forests of Bu Huong, Quy Cha district, Nghe An province. Since its discovery, the Vu Quang Ox has been thought to live in the highland forests of Vu Quang in Ha Tinh province and Pu Mat in Nghe An. The dead specimen was found about 60 km outside of the forest area which was previously thought to be the perimeter of the animal's habitat. Scientists from a British-based environmental NGO—Frontier—and the Xuan Mai Forestry College first witnessed the capture of a live animal by local Bu Huong hunters before coming across the carcass. Remains of the Vu Quang Ox were first discovered by Vietnamese scientists and MacKinnon during a survey of the Vu Quang forest in May 1992. But it wasn't until May 1993, that an ox was captured alive. Another was captured a short time later and both were sent to Hanoi, where they later died in captivity. The Vu Quang Ox is only one of seven new species of mammal to have been discovered this century.

Although the first-time visitor would hardly know it, huge parcels of Vietnamese topography were ruined during the Vietnam War. It's estimated that more than 70 million liters of defoliant were used on this country's forests during the war, resulting in a loss most experts put at close to 2.5 million hectares. Whereas nearly half the country was heavily forested during World War II, the figure has dropped to under 20 percent today. It is estimated that by the end of the decade, Vietnam will be virtually entirely denuded of its forests.

Traveling up National Highway 1, these estimates seem slightly exaggerated. The mountains as far as the eye can see appear immensely forested, save for areas where banana groves form columns on the hillsides. However, in the Central Highlands, one can see for miles deforested mountains and hillsides. But in defense of the Vietnamese naturalists' doomsday prediction, I think it's accurate to say that Vietnam's banning of the exporting of raw hardwood had more impetus than simply protecting the nation's forests. The move, many environmentalists believe, was a ploy to lure foreign investment in Vietnam's ability to produce its own wood-processing facilities. Quite simply, the amount of trees felled every year hasn't declined. Instead they're now processed inside Vietnam rather than Taiwan or Singapore; the exporting of processed wood from Vietnam (i.e., paper, cabinetry, furniture, etc.) is still quite legal.

National Parks

Some are more spectacular than others, and certainly some are more accessible than others, however, each of Vietnam's five "major" national parks is well worth a visit. And if the government follows through with its pledges, there will eventually be a total of 87 national parks and nature reserves, up from the current seven.

In the south, the principal park is **Nam Cat Tien National Park**, located on the fringes of four provinces: Song Be, Dac Lac, Dong Nai and Lam Dom. Located west of Bao Loc and Highway 20 and about 250 km from Ho Chi Minh City is this scenic new national park, which is home to rare and exotic wildlife, including elephants, leopards the gaur ox and the Javan rhino.

Few visitors get here and there are no organized excursions of the park through Dalat Tourist, at least at the time of this writing. Additionally, there are no accommodations in the park, making excursions out here at your own risk—which is 100 percent of the fun.

The best access to the park is from Highway 20. About 40 km south of Bao Loc a dirt road runs west from just below Da Huoai to Da Te. A bridge along this route collapsed but is in the process of being repaired. The road is accessible by car, but I'd suggest having some fun and doing it by motorcycle, especially if you can somehow arrange for a rare dual sport in Saigon (I've seen perhaps two in my life there). You'll be pretty much on your own, and can expect zero in the way of roadside services during the 20-km trip to the eastern edge of the park. At Da Te, a small village, it's unlikely you'll find an English-speaking guide, which would be nice to have out here.

In the center of Vietnam, near Hue, is **Bach Ma National Park**. There has been virtually zero development here and it's not geared up to handle tourists, but it's a gorgeous, mountainous chunk of real estate if you can get access to it. This is a former French hill station (and a national park since 1991) about 55 km southwest of Hue and rises majestically 1200 meters from the coast at Canh Duong Beach. The problem is getting in. The 16-km "road" to the hill station is a rutted mudslide, and presently, officials are less than cooperative about letting you use it. One reason may be the numbers of alleged poachers, who are reputed to be armed with AK-47s and quite willing to use them—as there's little chance they'll get caught. These days, the hill station is little more than a few crumbling walls, although the views are magnificent. There are no places to stay nor places to eat. You'll be on your own, save for, of course, the guide who will be assigned to you.

In the north is **Cat Ba National Park**, 30 km to the east of Haiphong and 135 km from Hanoi. Cat Ba Island is the largest island in the Ha Long Bay region. The park represents a small section of the island of Cat Ba that covers a forested area of 120 square km. The total area of Cat Ba is close to 355 square km. The area was declared a national park in 1986 to preserve the island's diverse flora and fauna. The mainly forested park is covered with tropical evergreens, coastal mangrove forests, freshwater swamps and lakes (the biggest being Ech Lake), and surrounded by fine beaches with coral reefs offshore. The principal beaches in the park include Hong Xoai Be, Cai Vieng and Hong Xoai Long beaches. There are reportedly three hotels on the island, although I could only locate one, the Cat Ba Hotel. It's said the other two go by the same name. Don't make plans to meet anyone at the Cat Ba Hotel. There are also two camping villages near the island's fishing village (Cat Ba Town) that attract a horde of both Vietnamese tourists and foreigners alike.

Cat Ba Island also features small waterfalls and grottoes in limestone rock formations (as many as 350 limestone outcroppings). There are high winds at the top of the grottoes and, frankly, sitting on the beach can get a little nippy at any time of the year, although on the rare summer sunny day, nothing beats kicking back on Cat Ba. In fact, there's no real "season" to visit the island, as the winters are cold, drizzly and gray and the summers rattled by typhoons.

Of particular interest have been the discoveries of stone tools and human bones on the island that indicate Cat Ba was inhabited 7000 years ago. Nearly 20 such sites have been found. Today, the island has at least a dozen species of mammals, including the rare Francois monkey. There are also deer and wild boar in addition to birds such as hornbills, hawks and cuckoos. Other species stop here on their migration paths. Most of the island's population of 10,000–12,000 people is located in Cat Ba Town. They eke out a living mainly through fishing and rice farming and by growing apples, oranges and cassava. Electricity on the island is limited to only a brief few hours in the evening. Some of the best beaches in Vietnam can be found here, or that's what Hanoi officials would have you believe. Cat Ba Island has largely been declared a protected region and, as mentioned, features tropical forests, mangrove swamps, towering dolomite hills, waterfalls, lakes, caves and, of course, gorgeous beaches. Daily ferries leave for Cat Ba from Haiphong's Ben Bach Dang Street Ferry Terminal, usually early in the morning (however, er, the schedules are subject to change).

Ba Be Lake National Park is one of the better kept secrets of the north. Located about 240 km from Hanoi, the park is in Cao Bang province and features magnificent waterfalls, caves, sheer rock walls and lakes carved into spectacular jagged mountains which reach heights of 1800 meters. The largest lake in the park is Ba Be (Three Bays) Lake, one of three in the area (hence the name). The park is inhabited namely by ethnic Dai, whose dwellings are built atop stilts. They'll be as curious about your presence as you about theirs, although they've seen enough tourists these days to start up their own clothing lines.

Puong Cave worms its way 300 meters entirely through one mountain; a navigable river sluices its way magnificently through the entire tunnel. Boats are available for the journey. The Dau Dang waterfall is also a draw here, as is the Nam Nang River, on which craft can be piloted from the falls to about 4 km above Cho Ra.

Cuc Phuong National Park is about 150 km south of Hanoi and west of Ninh Binh. Set amid deeply cut limestone mountains, this national park covers more than 25,000 hectares. It is an important archeological site discovered in 1974 in the Hang Dang (Bat) and Con Mong (Animal) grottoes. There have been numerous discoveries here of prehistoric tools and artifacts. This park is home to thousands of species of endangered and exotic tropical wildlife. A nature preserve was established here in 1962.

Vietnam's Geography and Climate

The terrain in Vietnam varies quite dramatically, from verdant mountainous edifices and dense jungle to coastal plains and delta. The climate is generally considered tropical monsoon, although it can actually get quite cool in the north, especially in the mountainous regions in northwestern Vietnam near Laos. Its 127,000,330 square miles (329,707 square kilometers) is roughly equal to that of South Carolina, Virginia and North Carolina together. Vietnam stretches some 2600 kilometers from tip to tip, but very little of the country is any more than 200 km at any given point, except in the far north. At its narrowest, Vietnam is barely 60 km wide. But Vietnam's remarkable coastline is nearly 3000 km long, offering miles and miles of virtually deserted white sand beaches.

The largest population centers are Hanoi (pop. 4 million), Haiphong (pop. 1.5 million), and bustling and relatively cosmopolitan Ho Chi Minh City (pop. 5 million).

The estuary of the Mekong Delta, extremely marshy, dominates the lower quarter of the country. The area is low and flat and perfect for the cultivation of rice in this rich soil. The area around Saigon to the north and the east changes—there is low-lying tropical rainforest and the rugged yet verdant chain of the Annamite Mountains.

The climate around Saigon and in the south of the country is year-round tropical, with sometimes intense heat and unbearable humidity, although it never seems to get quite as bad as Bangkok.

TEMPERATURE AND RAINFALL			
The place	Annual rainfall (mm)	Mean annual temperature (°C)	Mean annual variation (°C)
Hanoi	1680	23.5	12.4
Hue	3250	25.1	—
Danang	2130	25.4	7.8
Nha Trang	1562	26.4	4.2
Dalat	1600	19.1	3.4
Saigon	1960	26.9	3.1

Although never cold, the central highlands and the mountainous regions of the central part of Vietnam can become quite cool, with temperatures dipping as low as 50° F at night. During its northern hemispheric summer, the rainfall in the region can be quite heavy around the delta region—whereas the central highlands experiences the crux of its precipitation during the winter.

MONTHLY AVERAGE TEMPERATURES AND RAINFALL IN SAIGON AND HANOI													
CITY		Jan.	Feb.	Mar.	Apr.	May	Jun.	Jul.	Aug.	Sep.	Oct.	Nov.	Dec.
SAIGON													
Avg High	°C	32	33	34	35	33	32	31	31	31	31	31	31
	°F	89	91	93	95	92	89	88	88	88	88	87	87
Avg Low	°C	21	22	23	24	24	24	24	24	23	23	23	22
	°F	70	71	74	76	76	75	75	75	74	74	74	71
Rainfall	mm	15	3	13	43	221	330	315	269	335	269	114	56
	in.	0.6	0.1	0.5	1.7	8.1	13.0	12.4	10.6	13.2	10.6	4.5	2.2
HANOI													
Avg High	°C	20	21	23	28	32	33	33	32	31	29	26	22
	°F	68	69	74	82	90	92	91	90	88	84	78	72
Avg Low	°C	13	14	17	20	23	26	26	26	24	22	18	15
	°F	56	58	63	69	74	78	78	78	76	71	64	59
Rainfall	mm	18	28	38	81	196	239	323	343	254	99	43	20
	in.	0.7	1.1	1.5	3.2	7.7	9.4	12.7	13.5	10.0	3.9	1.7	0.8

With the exception of the Red River delta, northern Vietnam is heavily mountainous and not flat at all. The southwest monsoon climate means a hot, muggy period from mid-May to mid-September, while a cooler northeast monsoon from the middle of October to mid-March brings a seemingly perpetual drizzle the locals call *crachin* (rain dust). The jungle in the north is immensely thick in some areas and the canopy acts as a dome over much of the northern half of the country. There are, of course, lowlands in the north—referred to commonly as the Red River Delta Plain. This is a coastal plain that extends both south and north from the delta and is seasonally flooded. There is a complex dyke and levee system that prevents serious damage to the rich dark soil.

Waves gently roll onto the rocky beaches south of Nha Trang.

Rice fields cover much of the area and the region is densely populated with rice farmers and others who have something to do with its production and distribution.

Vietnam's People

The Vietnamese, with a 3-percent population growth rate, are composed primarily of ethnic Vietnamese with a smattering of Chinese, Khmer, Thai, Cham, Muong, Hmong and Meo—among other ethnic minorities. The major religions include Buddhism, Cao Daism, Christianity (brought in by the French and the subsequent arrival of American troops in the early 1960s), two forms of Islam (a variant of Middle Eastern Islam practiced by the Chams and the more traditional practices of ethnic Malays), and Animism.

The Vietnamese originally began their centuries-long migration southward around the year AD 940 from what is now southern China. The migration was part politically forced and part economically forced. They would eventually preside over the entire area known today as the eastern seacoast of the Indochinese peninsula. Pushed on by the promises of independence, a strong national identity of the Vietnamese people formed quickly, although their associations with Chinese culture weren't entirely discarded. Even today, Chinese culture plays a vast role in the identity of the typical Vietnamese. Although the 96-year French rule of the region (1858–1954) had a significant impact on Vietnamese life and culture, the Vietnamese still retain millennia-old family and societal values that have remained unblemished by colonialism and other forays by both the East and the West.

Today, more than a million Chinese make up the total Vietnamese population, and these people are mostly concentrated in the southern half of the country, and in particular the region of Ho Chi Minh City called Cholon. The Chinese make up the largest minority in the country. Although scorned by many ethnic Vietnamese, the Chinese population is largely to be credited with Vietnam's financial success, and particularly with the economic strides made since the end of the 1980s, when the Hanoi government recognized that opening up its economy was an absolute necessity in participating and harvesting gains in world markets.

VIETNAM TODAY

WHAT THE VIETNAMESE OWN (%)

HOUSEHOLD WITH	HANOI	SAIGON
At Least 1 Car	1	3
At Least 1 Motorbike	54	73
Air Conditioner	2	3
Refrigerator	6	40
Washing Machine	-	7
Stereo	3	64
Video Recorder	3	65
Video Camera	-	2
Computer	-	1
Telephone	4	5
Television	90	80
Radio	69	82

Source: SGR Vietnam

The Chinese are most involved with real estate, banking and rice trading in the south, and milling, shopkeeping and mining in the north. After the re-unification of the country, the Chinese community was ostracized by the Communist Party, leaving many Chinese with little choice but to flee the country, as they did in droves as boat people—perhaps as many as half a million in the middle and late '70s.

Today, though, the Chinese community in Vietnam thrives on Hanoi's reforms. Many thousands have returned to land they once fled and, officially at least, are welcomed with the open arms (and no doubt profit-twinkling eyes) of their one-time adversaries.

The next largest minority in Vietnam are the two main ethnolinguistic groups of Montagnards, mountain people of the Malayo-Polynesian and Mon-Khmer groups. These people generally occupy the highlands areas and speak so many tongues, no two of which seem to be mutually intelligible, that it's a small miracle that babies grow to speak the same languages as their parents. Perhaps 30 such groups of mountain tribes occupy these highland territories.

And last but not least are the Khmers of Cambodian descent of whom perhaps half a million reside in Vietnam. As expected, most are rice farmers and they're primarily to be found in the southern half of Vietnam near its border with Cambodia as well as along the mouths of the Mekong.

One other small minority in Vietnam of note are the Chams, who once were part of the powerful Champa Kingdom, which was annihilated by the Vietnamese in the 16th century.

Most Vietnamese are usually busier than this produce cart driver.

There are also the Tai who live in the extreme north of the country near the border with China. They speak a language called Tai-Kadai.

Other groups are the Nung, Muong and Hmong, who reside generally to the south, north and west of Hanoi and have been largely assimilated into mainstream Vietnamese culture, save for the hill people of the extreme north of the country. There is also a small group of people called the Meo, who live high in the mountains and cultivate livestock, grain and profitable opium. Not surprisingly, this group of people can also be found in the opium poppy growing areas of Laos, Thailand and Myanmar—the infamous Golden Triangle area.

Amerasians—those of Vietnamese mothers and American GI fathers—are perhaps the least-regarded of all the peoples of Vietnam. Generally, they're treated as scum and are often found in the streets—mostly in Saigon—looking for handouts. Many of the fortunate ones have emigrated to the United States.

HCMC police eye the author during a festival celebrating the Tet New Year.

Vietnamese of all ethnicities speak a surprising array of languages, helped in part by their remaining unscathed by the purges of Pol Pot in Cambodia, who effectively eliminated foreign-language speaking Khmers and ethnic Vietnamese in Cambodia during the late 1970s. Although Vietnamese remains the official language in Vietnam, don't be surprised to hear a fair amount of French being spoken, as well as Chinese and Khmer. English, however, seems to be making the biggest strides in Vietnam, as the language is universally considered the language of international business, and Vietnam is desperately seeking to align itself with the international business community. And don't be surprised to hear a 12-year-old girl speak better English than her 18-year-old brother. It's happening that quickly.

Literacy in the country stands at a remarkable 85 percent according to the latest estimates, and is at its highest among groups save for the Montagnards. Education is provided entirely free by the government, but is difficult to administer due to the continued high birth rate of Vietnamese children and a still largely undeveloped infrastructure. Vocational training is still most rigorously pursued by Vietnamese students, although with the demise of the Soviet educational style structure in Vietnam, liberal arts studies as found in the West are quickly making their way into Vietnam's educational system. No longer are Vietnamese students being sent by the thousands to school systems in the former Soviet Union and other Eastern European countries that have witnessed their own educational systems collapse. Additionally, Vietnam sends skilled laborers to parts of the world that include the Middle East and North Africa.

The average male in Vietnam can expect to live to 62 years, while a woman's average life expectancy hovers around 66 years. However, despite vast improvements in medicine in Vietnam, the infant mortality rate is just a little over 50/1000.

Vietnam's Religions

Vietnam has more diverse religions than any other country in Asia if not all the world, including a number of forms of Buddhism, Catholicism, Protestantism, Confucianism, numerous hilltribe hybrids of the above, Islam, Tam Giaoism, Hoa Hao, Hinduism, Taoism and the indigenous Cao Daism.

After the fall of Saigon in April 1975, the government made meticulous efforts to eliminate—or at least severely limit—the practice of most religions in the reunified country. Many outspoken clergy and their followers were sent to "reeducation camps" or simply thrown in jail. Religion had no place in the Marxist-Leninist scheme of the collective society. Those religions, Mahayana Buddhism in particular, that were permitted to function to some degree or less were strictly controlled by the state, as were those individuals permitted to become clergy.

Over the years, and especially since the latter 1980s, most doctrines have started to again become integrated into mainstream Vietnamese life, and the government has actually started to play a public relations role, albeit limited in scope, in appearing to associate itself with the importance of spirituality in Vietnam. Descriptions of the major religions practiced in Vietnam are as follows.

Mahayana and Theravada Buddhism

Mahayana Buddhism is the most extensively practiced religion in Vietnam. Theravada Buddhism is practiced mainly in the south in the Mekong Delta area by the country's inhabitants of Khmer descent. There are some fundamental differences in the two strains of Buddhism.

Mahayana Buddhism means "From the North," and the largest Mahayana sect in Vietnam is Zen. Dao Trang is the second-largest school.

The Chinese monk Mau Tu is usually attributed with introducing Mahayana Buddhism in the second century AD. While Indian Buddhists came in from the sea with their teachings of Theravada Buddhism, Mahayana Buddhism went to the north by way of Nepal, China, Tibet, Mongolia, Korea, Japan and Vietnam (thus it's called the Northern School). It wasn't until nearly 1000 years after Buddhism was introduced into Vietnam that it became the state religion (with the 1138–1175 reign of Emperor Ly Anh Ton). But even Buddhist teachings had become intertwined with the teachings of Confucianism, Taoism and Animism. By the 15th century, it had become so convoluted that Confucianism emerged as the dominant religion of the state. It wasn't until the first two decades of this century that Buddhism once again found a strong foothold in Vietnam; it came in the form of Mahayana Buddhism, which was spread from the north.

There are critical differences between Mahayana Buddhism and Theravada Buddhism, although all Buddhists believe in rebirth, which is common with Hinduism. Buddhists believe their action in this life will determine their manifestations in the next life. Acts in this life will govern those in the next. It's what's commonly called Karma, and it's not a concept looked lightly upon even by Christians, Muslims and others the world over.

Nirvana, or the ultimate enlightenment, is the goal of all Buddhists, and a life of chastity, fasting and minimal possessions is one of the keys to obtaining this state. Most monks own no more than three sets of clothing, a razor, a food bowl and a needle. Food cannot be consumed after noon and can only be procured by begging.

Mahayana Buddhists, centered mainly in the north and the central part of Vietnam believe only Gautama Buddha to be the one manifestation of Buddha. The Mahayana Buddhist believes in striving to achieve perfect ideals in the form of generosity, wisdom and patience. Perhaps the fundamental difference between Mahayana and Theravada Buddhists is that the former don't simply believe in enlightenment for themselves. The goal is to reach Bodhissatvahood, the state that allows the monk to stay on earth and help others attain nirvana.

Mahayana Buddhism rose primarily for the reason of making the religion more accessible and attractive to lay people. It was a response to the vast number of followers Hinduism was attracting. Monks began becoming more accessible solely for the purpose of helping others in the quest for enlightenment. As the number of Mahayana Buddhists began to swell, so were expanded the principles of the Mahayana doctrine. However, today, most Mahayana Buddhists also consolidate the teachings of Confucius and other Chinese religions, such as Taoism.

Theravada Buddhism, which came directly from India, more closely conforms to the original doctrines as they were developed in India, and is frequently called by Mahayana Buddhists as the "Lesser Vehicle," a mainly derogatory name that is indicative of the Vietnamese presdisposal to think of the Khmer people as a lower form of humanity. Theravada Buddhism is the most prevalent religion in Cambodia, Thailand and Laos.

The historic Buddha (Sakyumuni) is the Buddha most worshipped by Theravadans. For Theravadans, in theory Buddha images represent not supernatural gods, but shrines to aid in meditation. However, recently these images have been worshipped themselves, which is indicative of the influence Mahayanas are having on Theravada practices.

However, for their part, Theravada Buddhists consider their religion to be a less corrupt form of Buddhism.

Hoa Hao Buddhism (Dao Hoa Hao)

Huynh Phu So, an occultist who was miraculously cured of a serious disease, founded Hoa Hao sect of Buddhism in 1939. The religion is a type of reformed Buddhism which contends that elaborate rituals are not needed to honor Buddha, but merely a private, simple and unelaborate faith. He did not believe that intermediaries were needed between human beings and God, or the Supreme Being. There are perhaps more than a million followers of the religion today in Vietnam.

The French weren't fond of Huynh—they called him the "Mad Monk"—and suppressed his activities. He was thrown into an insane asylum after jailing him did little to affect his influence (he even converted the psychiatrist who was treating him to the Hoa Hao sect). The sect continued to grow, despite the monk's internment. During World War II, the sect formed its own army with the help of the Japanese. After the war, the sect fought the Viet Minh, and Huynh was assassinated by the Viet Minh. By this time, his army had grown rather strong in the Mekong Delta, particularly in the Chau Doc area. The Hoa Hao army disintegrated after one of its leading commanders was publicly executed by the South Vietnamese Diem regime. Much of the Hoa Hao then joined the Viet Cong.

Confucianism (Dao Khong)

Confucianism isn't really a religion in the traditional sense. The teachings of Confucius (551–479 BC) are more patterns of social behavior that have become entwined in the daily lives of most Vietnamese, more than an organized religion.

Confucius (Khong Tu in Vietnamese), born in China, saw human beings as both shaped by their society as well as having the ability to shape it themselves. It was social interaction that formed the basis of society. He devised a code of social interaction that specified an individual's obligation to his or her family, government and community. Hierarchy and sense of duty are principle ingredients of Confucianism.

Confucianism arrived in Vietnam via the Chinese 1000-year rule of the country, between 111 BC and 938 AD. Its philosophy stated that only the emperor could be the intermediary between Earth and Heaven. Virtue through education gave one the right to political power. In this form, there was some degree of equality among individuals, as education rather than birth, determined hierarchy. Virtue could only be acquired through education. As a consequence, education was widespread among the "religion's" followers. Young people were taught about duty, hierarchy and their responsibilities to both the family and the community at an early age. Each person would know his place in the community hierarchy.

A government-administered test was then given to the students to ascertain those with the greatest amount of education and virtue and it was these individuals who were selected as mandarins, members of the ruling class. Education was seen not only as a tool to acquire education but political status as well.

But only the emperor could establish this mandate between the secular and the spiritual. If virtue was lost, it was believed that rebellion was just, and that until virtue was restored natural calamities in the form of floods, earthquakes and typhoons would devastate the land.

Confucianism slowly met its demise in Vietnam during the 1400s as it became more regimented, and as kings became more arrogant and recognized themselves as divine rulers rather than intermediaries between the people and the gods. The Divine Mandate crumbled.

Cao Daism (Dao Cao Dai)

This is the one indigenous religion to Vietnam, and a strange one at that. It involves the worship of human beings as well as the worship of deities. It was founded to create the perfect religion—a blend of both secular and spiritual devotion. It was founded by Ngo Minh Chieu in the early 1920s and became so popular—gaining millions of followers—areas of southern Vietnam became a virtual political state, particularly in the Mekong Delta region and Tay Ninh, the religion's headquarters nearly 100 km from Saigon. This infuriated the South Vietnamese government to such an extent that it broke up the religion and conscripted many of its followers into the South Vietnamese Army. But after reunification of the country and relaxed religious mandates on the part of the Vietnamese government, Cao Daism flourishes again, but this time as a religion only. Cao Dai temples dot the southern Vietnamese landscape from the Mekong Delta to Hue. Above Cao Dai altars is an inscription that translates into "All Religions Have the Same Reason." Today, it's believed that as many as 2 million Vietnamese are Cao Dai followers.

Taoism (Dao Lao)

Taoism is another religion whose origins are in China. It's based on the philosophy of Laotse, or Thai Thuong Lao Quan, who lived during the sixth century, although the formal religion of Taoism was actually started by Chang Ling around 143 BC. Although there is some question as to whether or not Laotse actually ever existed (the debate continues today), legend has it that he was consulted by Confucius and was the custodian of the Chinese government's Imperial Archives. Sometime after 143 BC, the religion split into two branches: "The Way of the Heavenly Teacher" and the "Cult of the Immortals."

Taoists believe in the simplicity of life and eventually returning to what is called "The Way," the source of all things. Taoism is so complicated, few Vietnamese understand the religion—even Taoists themselves. But the essence of Taoism, namely its emphasis on contemplation and simplicity, has found its way into the various forms of Buddhism in Indochina. Taoism is a blend of superstitions, sorcery, magic and other mystical beliefs that are reflected in the architecture of Buddhist temples, which are adorned with dragons, snakes and other mythical beasts.

Christianity and Catholicism

Missionaries from France, Spain and Portugal brought Catholicism to Vietnam in the 16th century—mainly Portuguese Dominicans and French Jesuit priests. The first bishops to be sent to Vietnam were assigned by Pope Alexander VII in 1659, and the first Vietnamese priests were ordained in 1668. There were as many as a million Catholics in Vietnam by the end of the 17th century—and today, behind the Philippines, Vietnam has the greatest number of Catholics in Asia. Nearly a million Catholic Vietnamese were part of the hordes of boat people who fled Vietnam after the reunification of the country in 1975. (South Vietnamese President Ngo Dinh Diem was a Catholic.)

Over the centuries, Catholics suffered a tremendous amount of persecution in Vietnam. At many times during the 17th and 18th centuries, the religion was outlawed. After 1975, the practice of Catholicism was virtually untolerated by the new government.

INSIDER TIP

Although the government has become a lot more tolerant of religious practice in Vietnam, it once in a while lets religious hierarchies know in no uncertain terms that it is the state who's boss in Vietnam—that, yes, there's a degree of religious tolerance, but any clergy who had any previous association with the varying regimes of preunification Vietnam will not be tolerated, nor will they be allowed congregations. A case in point is Hanoi's recent falling out with the Vatican over a compromise that would have permitted the appointments of priests with ties to previous South Vietnamese regimes. Hanoi insists that the government must be consulted in the selection of clergy. Vietnamese Prime Minister Vo Van Kiet has said that the issue is one of "national sovereignty," as Vietnam has not signed any agreements with the Vatican allowing the Vatican to make "unfettered" decisions in its appointments. "Each country has the right to ensure stability and order through its own rules," Vo said. Things have heated up between the Vatican and Hanoi since September 1993 when authorities in Ho Chi Minh City said "no way" to the appointment of Bishop Huynh Van Nghi as a "supervisor" of the church instead of deputy archbishop. Saigon officials charged that the appointment was part of a "Vatican plot" to place an exiled nephew of former South Vietnamese President Ngo Dinh Diem as successor to the current archbishop. Hanoi, it appears, is taking very cautious steps in permitting a potential element of dissent, the church—which the government has always viewed as a hot bed for antistate activities—to return to its previous, prewar levels of influence.

But Catholicism flourished during French rule of Vietnam—as it did with the American presence in South Vietnam during the Vietnam War. Under French rule, Catholics were given high positions in the government and preferential treatment in general. From 1954 to 1989 in the north, and from 1975 to 1989 in the south, Catholic religious activities were heavily curtailed and monitored by the government. There were restrictions placed on the number of priests and the type of education Catholics could receive. Even today, the Catholic churches you see in both Hanoi and HCMC have become somewhat dilapidated, as the government still looks upon the religion as a capitalist poison.

Protestantism has flourished mainly among about a quarter of a million Montagnards in the Central Highlands. The religion first came to Vietnam in 1910 or 1911. The Montagnards have been harassed by the government for a number of years, and the introduction of Christianity into the populace didn't help matters any. After 1975, Protestant ministers, especially those trained by the Americans, were imprisoned for a number of years. Although you are free to practice the religion in Vietnam today, the state keeps a close watch on Christian activities.

Hinduism

Originally, Hinduism had its roots in Vietnam with the Cham people, and its influence can be seen in many of the early Cham towers in the southern half of Vietnam, which contain the phallic symbols of Shiva. When the Champa Empire fell in Vietnam in the 15th century, so did much of Hinduism's influence on the Cham people, who then absorbed Muslim ideas into their religious practices. But evidence of Hinduism is still evident even in today's Cham Muslim religious practices.

Islam

If you want to be a Muslim, but still want to partake in some of life's more secular vices, become a Cham in Vietnam. Although there are small communities of Muslims (such as ethnic Malays, Indonesians and Indians) that practice Islam, the Chams aren't so strict. They're permitted to drink alcohol and they don't make pilgrimages to Mecca. Rather than praying five times a day as do their traditional counterparts, Cham Muslims pray only on Friday and celebrate Ramadan for only three days. Traditional Muslims celebrate Ramadan (which requires dawn-to-dusk fasting) for an entire month.

In fact, Cham Muslims aren't entirely clear about the Islam concept. There are very few copies of the Koran in Cham villages and most of the villagers can't read it. Even the Cham Muslim religious leaders, who wear a white robe and an elaborate turban with colored tassels, can't read the Arabic script, or at least much of it. They've taken common expressions from the Koran and turned them into deities. Their religious services include only a few minutes of reading passages from the Koran, much of them decisively altered in meaning through a lack of understanding of the passages. They're also into animism and Hinduism, as they worship Hindu deities in addition to Mohammed.

The more traditional Muslims in Vietnam essentially fled the country after 1975, but there are still small pockets of Malay and Indian Muslim communities centered mainly in Saigon.

Worship of Ancestors

Introduced even before Confucianism in Vietnam, ancestor worship is the belief many Vietnamese have that their ancestors watch over and protect them. A person without descendants is doomed to have no home when they die. Ancestors play a role in all important events, including everything from tragedies to success in school to childbirth—and there are ancestor worship holidays on the dates of the ancestors' deaths. Sacrifices are offered to the ancestor. Families have altars in their homes devoted to their ancestors. Some pagodas feature pictures and other items ancestors once possessed on the altars. Usually the pictures depict the ancestors as young people. Ancestor worshippers usually also have plots of land that derive income for the ancestors. The cult also designates a male as the central figure to worship when he dies.

Vietnam's Government

The Vietnamese government is a socialist peoples' republic, a somewhat cantankerous hybrid of Marxism and Leninism. What this really means, however, depends upon who you talk to. An official in Hanoi may tell you something entirely different than a prosperous Chinese merchant in Saigon's Cholon district, whose perception of "socialism" may be afternoon tea with some neighbors. However, officially, there is one political party, called the Vietnam Communist Party, which was previously referred to as the Vietnamese Workers Party, a title that remained in effect from 1951–1976. This in itself was the offshoot of the Indochinese Workers Party, which was formed in the early 1930s by Ho Chi Minh. Vietnam's current constitution was ratified December 18, 1980.

In Vietnam, there are 50 provinces that are centrally controlled under the auspices of three municipalities (Hanoi, Ho Chi Minh City and Haiphong)—all under central government control.

In the north are Ha Bac, Cao Bang, Hoa Binh, Tuyen Quang, Lao Cai, Yen Bai, Bac Thai, Son La, Quang Ninh, Vinh Phu, Lang Son, Ha Giang and Lai Chau.

The Red River Delta Area has Ninh Binh, Ha Tay, Nam Ha, Thai Binh and Hai Hung.

North Central Vietnam includes Nghe An, Thanh Hoa, Quang Tri, Thua Thien-Hue, Ha Tinh and Quang Binh.

The Central Highlands is composed of Gia Lai, Dac Lac, Kontum and Lam Dong.

On the South Central Coast lies Quang Nam-Danang, Binh Dinh, Phu Yen, Quang Ngai, Khanh Hoa, Binh Thuan and Ninh Thuan.

In the South are Song Be, Tay Ninh, Dong Nai, Ba Ria-Vung Tau, Long An, Dong Thap, An Giang, Ben Tre, Kien Giang, Soc Trang, Can Tho, Minh Hai, Tien Giang, Tra Vinh and Vinh Long.

Vietnamese independence from the French occurred in September 1945, and the reunification of the north and the south officially took place in July of 1976. Some say the real unification took place with the temporary occupation of the United States embassy building during the Tet Offensive of 1968. Some venture to go back even further in time to 1963 when then-AP correspondent Malcolm Brown shot his historic photos of a Buddhist monk from Hue self immolating himself on a Saigon street in protest of the policies of the Ngo Dinh Diem government, a series of pictures that ultimately found their way to Washington's Oval Office and JFK's desk. The president, after gazing in horror at the human pyre in the street, orchestrated the roots of Diem's ouster.

Today's facets of the Vietnamese government consist of the executive branch, which is composed of the Council of Ministers; the State Council (or the Collective Chief of State), people's committees that have jurisdiction over local affairs; and the Legislative branch, which is also called the National Assembly (locally there are Peoples' Councils, and the Judicial branch, which is composed of the Supreme People's Court).

As far as defense goes, it's said that anywhere from 40–50 percent of the central government budget goes into the procurement and maintenance of defense-related technology and manpower—which explains why the Vietnamese are some of the poorest souls on the planet. But this is changing rapidly since the government's integration into the world community.

Vietnam's Language

As you might expect, the Vietnamese language is difficult both to speak and understand. It can be traced to Sino-Tibetan as well as to Austro-Asiatic and Mon-Khmer origins. Under ninth-century Chinese domination, the ideograms the Chinese used were adopted for use with Vietnamese (although gratefully, a Latin-style based script was adopted during the early portion of this century, making the reading of maps and signs possible for hapless Westerners). The original *chu nho* ideograms were utilized as the only form of communication up until the 20th century.

Vietnamese seeking to sever ties with the Chinese in the 13th century further complicated matters by taking the Chinese ideograms and adapting them for their own purposes. This was called *chu nom*, considered a "vulgar" or gutter form of *chu nho*.

In the 17th century, European missionary Alexandre-de-Rhodes mastered the Vietnamese language and actually created the first Romanized Vietnamese dictionary.

The biggest problem in understanding the Vietnamese language is the fundamental barrier that prevents Westerners from becoming proficient with other East Asian tongues—tonal usage. The same "word" can be used with a number of different tones and possess an equally different number of meanings.

The Vietnamese alphabet has 17 consonants, 12 vowels and nearly 20 double consonants. There are no prefixes and no suffixes. There is no use of plurals with nouns and there are double negatives that must be used to accomplish what Westerners can simply do with a simple positive. In other words, if you ask someone in Vietnamese, "Will you have dinner at my house tonight?" the actual translation is something like this: "You'll have dinner at my house tonight, will you not?" Instead of simply replying, "Yes, I will," an affirmative response goes something like this: "No, I will not." If you say the former, you're telling your host that "Yes, I will not be having dinner at your house tonight."

Ay!

Pronunciation

The Romanized letters of the Vietnamese language are pronounced as they are in French, and the pronunciation of consonants used in words is similar to how the sounds are pronounced in English. However, the Vietnamese do not use the letters 'F', 'J', 'W' and 'Z'. The following are the less obvious pronunciations.

CONSONANTS

c	*Pronounced as a hard 'c' in English, but without the aspiration.*
d	*Without a crossbar; pronounced as 'y' in the south and as a 'z' in the north. For instance, "ao dai" is pronounced as "ao zai" in the north and "ao yai" in the south.*
d	*With a crossbar; pronounced like a hard 'd'.*
gi-	*Pronounced like a 'z' in the north and like a 'y' in the south.*
kh-	*Pronounced like a 'k', but with aspiration.*
ng-	*Pronounced as the '-ng a-' in "sing along."*
nh-	*Pronounced as 'nya', or as the 'ñ' in Spanish.*
ph-	*Pronounced like an 'f'.*

Pronunciation

r	*Pronounced like an 'r' in the south and a 'z' in the north.*
s	*Pronounced as 'sh-' in the south and as an 's' in the north.*
tr-	*Pronounced as 'tr-' in the south and 'ch-' in the north.*
th-	*Pronounced as 't' but strongly aspirated.*
x	*Pronounced as an 's'.*
-ch	*Pronounced like a 'k'.*
-ng	*Pronounced like '-ng' in "song," but with the mouth closed.*
-nh	*Pronounced like '-ng' in "ring."*

VOWELS

i	*Pronounced as 'i' as in "this."*
e	*Pronounced 'e' as in "elf."*
ê	*Pronounced 'a' as in "hate."*
u'	*Pronounced 'ai' as in "mountain."*
o'	*Pronounced 'a' as in "alone."*
â	*Pronounced 'a' as in "ago" but shorter.*
a	*Pronounced 'a' as in "chance."*
a'	*Pronounced 'u' as in "cut."*
u	*Pronounced 'oo' as in "fool."*
ô	*Pronounced 'a' as in "call."*
o	*Pronounced 'o' as in "on."*

As anywhere you travel where the locals speak a different tongue, it can never hurt to pick up on a bit of the language. Simple greetings, phrases and requests in the local language can open a lot of doors. The Vietnamese, like the Thais, the Cambodians and most peoples of Asia, are impressed and even honored when even the slightest attempt by a foreigner is made to speak the host country's language, no matter how bad the result is (within parameters, of course. You don't want to tell a man that his wife looks like a swollen sow with udders for fingers when you've simply requested a glass of milk).

Proper Names

In Vietnam, as in other countries in Asia, the family name always appears first, followed by the middle name and then the given name. For instance someone named Nguyen Than Binh is called "Binh" by those who know him and perhaps "Mr. Binh" by those who know him only slightly or under formal circumstances. Nguyen is the family name and is rarely used when addressing someone. You'll notice quickly that everyone you meet in Vietnam will address you by your first name, even upon the initial meeting, preceded with "Mr." or "Miss." So get used to being called "Mr. Bob," "Mr. David," "Miss Sarah," etc. Even after knowing a Vietnamese for a long period of time, that person may still refer to you as "Mr." or "Miss."

For more extensive compilations of Vietnamese phrases, words, pronunciation, tone markers and usage, the following should be helpful:

Vietnamese for Tourists

> *Nha Xuat Ban The Gioi, 1996. 295 pages. US$6.95.*
> Available in bookstores in the tourist centers, particularly Ho Chi Minh City and Hanoi. Extensive and strong with phrases and conversations.

Tu Dien Viet-Anh (Vietnamese-English Dictionary)

> *Hanoi University Press (Truong Dai Hoc Tong Hop Ha Noi Xuat Ban), 1986. 992 pages.*
> Superb dictionary, easy to use, but unwieldy. Though not as massive as its 1960-page cousin, which goes by the same name.

Vietnamese Phrasebook

> *Lonely Planet Guidebooks. Hawthorn, Victoria, Australia.*
> Words, phrases, pronunciation, grammar. Very useful.

Essential English-Vietnamese Dictionary

> *Charles E. Tuttle Co. Rutland, VT and Tokyo. 1983.*
> Another good cross dictionary available in the U.S.

A CRASH COURSE IN VIETNAMESE
GREETINGS AND FORMALITIES

Hello	*Chao*
Good morning	
Good afternoon	
Good night	*Chao* **or** *Chuc ngu ngon*
Good bye	*Tam biet*
the above formal to older men	*Chao ong*
the above formal to older women	*Chao ba*
the above informal to men	*Chao anh*
the above informal to women	*Chao chi*
How are you?	*Có khoe khong?*
I am doing well, thank you	*Khoe, cam on*
Thank you	*Cam on*
Yes	*Vang (in the north)*
	Co, phai (in the south)
	Da
No	*Khong*

A CRASH COURSE IN VIETNAMESE

Excuse me			*Xin loi*
I am tired			*Toi met*

PRONOUNS

You	*On*	I	*Toi*
to an older man	*Ong*	He	*Cau ay, anh ay*
to an older woman	*Ba*	She	*Co ay*
to a man of own age	*Anh*	We	*Chung toi*
to a woman of own age	*Co*		

NUMBERS

1	*Mot*	6	*Sau*
2	*Hai*	7	*Bay*
3	*Ba*	8	*Tam*
4	*Bon*	9	*Chin*
5	*Nam*	10	*Muoi*
11	*Muoi mot*	16	*Muoi sau*
12	*Muoi hai*	17	*Muoi bay*
13	*Muoi ba*	18	*Muoi tam*
14	*Muoi bon*	19	*Muoi chin*
15	*Muoi nam*	20	*Hai muoi*
21	*Hai muoi mot*	1000	*Mot nghin*
30	*Ba muoi*	10,000	*Muoi ngan*
90	*Chin muoi*	100,000	*Mot tram nghin*
100	*Mot tram*	1 million	*Mot trieu*
110	*Mot tram muoi*	First	*Thu nhat*
200	*Hai tram*	Second	*Thu hai*

DAYS OF THE WEEK

Sunday	*Chu nhat*	Today	*Hom nay*
Monday	*Thu hai*	Yesterday	*Hom qua*
Tuesday	*Thu ba*	Tomorrow	*Ngay mai*
Wednesday	*Thu tu*	Morning	*Buoi toi*
Thursday	*Thu nam*	Afternoon	*Buoi sang*
Friday	*Thu sau*	Evening	*Buoi chieu*
Saturday	*Thu bay*	Right now	*Bay gio*

VIETNAM TODAY

A CRASH COURSE IN VIETNAMESE

MONTHS OF THE YEAR

January	*Thang gieng*	July	*Thang bay*
February	*Thang hai*	August	*Thang tam*
March	*Thang ba*	September	*Thang chin*
April	*Thang tu*	October	*Thang muoi*
May	*Thang nam*	November	*Thang muoi mot*
June	*Thang sau*	December	*Thang chap*
Year	*Nam*	Month	*Thang*
This year	*Nam nay*	Next year	*Nam sau*
Last year	*Nam ngoai*		

USEFUL WORDS AND PHRASES

My name is...	*Ten toi la...*	What is your name?	*Ten (your) la gi?* (see "you")
I would like...	*Toi muon...*	I would not like...	*Toi khong muon...*
I like...	*Toi thich...*	I would not like...	*Toi khong muon...*
I want...	*Toi can...*	I do not want...	*Toi khong can...*
I understand	*Toi hieu*	I do not understand	*Toi khong hieu*
I need...	*Toi can*	I am hungry	*Toi doi*
To eat	*An*	To drink	*Uong*
Thank you	*Cam on*	Please	*Xin*
Yes	*Da*	No	*Khong*
Come	*Toi*	Go	*Di*
Cheap	*Re*	Expensive	*Dat*
Man	*Nam*	Woman	*Nu*
Give	*Cho*		
Fast	*Nhanh* (in the north) *Mau (in the south)*	Slow	*Cham*
Old	*Cu*	New	*Moi*
Clean	*Sach*	Dirty	*Ban*
Hot	*Nong*	Cold	*Lanh*
Far away	*Xa*	Close by	*Gan*
Market	*Cho*	Office	*Van phong*
Post office	*Nha buu dien*	Museum	*Bao Tang Vien*

A CRASH COURSE IN VIETNAMESE

Pagoda	*Chua*	Church	*Nha tho*
Bank	*Ngan hang*	Tourism office	*Van phong du lich*
Telephone	*Dien thoai*	Mosquito net	*Man (in the north)* *Mung (in the south)*
East	*Dong*	West	*Tay*
North	*Bac*	South	*Nam*

ACCOMMODATIONS

Hotel	*Khach san* *Nha khach* *(guest house)*	Restaurant	*Tiem an*
Room	*Phong*	Room key	*Chia khoa phong*
Bathroom	*Nha tam* *Phong tam*		
Toilet	*Cau tieu* *Nha ve sinh*	Toilet paper	*Giay ve sinh*
I would like an inexpensive room.	*Toi thich mot phong loai re.*	How much does the room cost?	*Gia mot phong bao nhieu?*
Where is there a hotel?	*O dau co khach san?*	Air conditioning	*May lanh*
Fan	*Quat*	Hot water	*Nuoc nong*
Blanket	*Chan (in the north)* *Men (in the south)*	Laundry	*Tiem giat quan do*
Sheet	*Ra trai guiong*	Towel	*Khan tam*

FOOD AND DRINK

Water	*Nuoc*	Beer	*Bia*
Coffee	*Ca phe*	Tea	*Nuoc che*
Sugar	*Duong*	Beef	*Thit bo*
Chicken	*Thit ga*	Pork	*Thit heo*
Bat	*Con doi*	Snake	*Ran ho mang* *(Cobra)* *Con tran (Python)*
Goat	*Con de*	Venison	*Thit Nai*
Turtle	*Con rua*	Wild pig	*Heo rung*
Noodle soup	*Pho*	Rice	*Com*
Bread	*Banh mi*	Vegetables	*Rau*
Fish	*Ca*	Shrimp	*Tom*

A CRASH COURSE IN VIETNAMESE

Crab	*Cua*	Eel	*Luon*
Frog	*Ech*	Oyster	*So*
Fish and vegetable soup	*Lau*	Vegetable soup	*Xup rau*
White rice noodles	*Banh Pho*	Eel and vermicelli soup	*Mien Luon*
Yellow wheat noodles	*Mi*	Broth	*Nuoc Leo*
Dry noodles	*Kho*	Sweet rolls	*Nem Cha gio*
Apple	*Bom Tao*	Apricot	*Le*
Avocado	*Trai bo*	Banana	*Trai chuoi*
Cherry	*Trai se ri*	Chinese date	*Trai tao ta*
Coconut	*Trai dua*	Durian	*Trai sau rieng*
Grapes	*Nho*	Grapefruit	*Trai buoi*
Green dragon fruit	*Trai thanh long*	Guava	*Trai oi*
Jackfruit	*Trai Mit*	Khaki	*Hong xiem*
Lemon	*Chanh*	Longan	*Trai nhan*
Lychee	*Trai vai*	Mandarin Orange	*Trai quit*
Mango	*Trai mang cut*	Orange	*Trai cam*
Papaya	*Trai du du Qua du du*	Peach	*Trai dao*
Pineapple	*Trai khom Trai dua*	Plum	*Man Mo*
Pomelo	*Trai buoi Trai doi*	Rambutan	*Chom chom*
Starfruit	*Trai khe*	Strawberry	*Trai dau*
Tangerine	*Trai quit*	Tomato	*Ca chua*
Water apple	*Roi duong (Man)*	Watermelon	*Dua hau*

TRAVEL

Bus	*Xe buyt*
Bus station	*Ben xe buyt*
Train	*Xe lua*
Train station	*Ga xe lua*

A CRASH COURSE IN VIETNAMESE

Airport	*San bay*
Cyclo (Trishaw)	*Xe xich lo*
Map	*Ban do*
Schedule	*Bang gio giac*
	Thoi bieu
I want to hire a car.	*Toi muon xe hoi.*
I want to go to…	*Toi muon di…*
Highway	*Xa lo*
How long does the trip take?	*Chuyen di se mat bao lau?*
How far is it to…? (kilometers)	*Cach xa day bao nhieu kilomet?*
What time does the bus leave?	*Xe buyt se chay luc may gio?*
What time does the train leave?	*Xe lua se chay luc may gio?*
What time does it arrive?	*Xe se den luc may gio?*
What time does the first bus leave?	*Chuyen xe buyt som nhat se chay luc may gio?*
What times does the last bus leave?	*Chuyen xe buyt cuoi cung se chay luc may gio?*
What time does the first train leave?	*Chuyen xe lua som nhat se chay luc may gio?*
What time does the last train leave?	*Chuyen xe lua cuoi cung ce chay luc may goi?*
I would like a receipt.	*Toi muon bien lai.*
I would like a sleeping berth.	*Toi muon giuong ngu.*

GEOGRAPHY

Mountain	*Nui*	Island	*Hon dao*
River	*Song*	Boulevard	*Dai lo*
National Highway	*Quoc lo*	City square	*Cong truong*
Street	*Duong*	Bridge	*Cau*
	Pho		

AT THE MARKET

Expensive	*Dat tien*	Cheap	*Re tien*
Buy	*Mua*	Sell	*Ban*
Market	*Cho*	How much does this cost?	*Cai nay gia bao nhieu?*

A CRASH COURSE IN VIETNAMESE

EMERGENCIES

Help	*Cuu toi voi*	Police	*Cong an*
Thief	*Cuop*	Pickpocket	*Moc tui*
	Cap		

MEDICAL

Doctor	*Bac si*	Dentist	*Nha si*
Hospital	*Benh vien*	Pharmacy	*Nha thuoc tay.*
I am sick.	*Toi bi benh. (in the north)*		
	Toi bi om. (in he south)		
Please call me a doctor.	*Lam on goi bac si.*	Please get me to a hospital.	*Lam on dua toi den benh vien.*
Diarrhea	*Ia chay*	Stomachache	*Dau bung*
Malaria	*Sot ret*	Feverish	*Cam*
			Cum
Vomiting	*Oi*	Toothache	*Nhuc rang*
	Mua		
Headache	*Nhuc dau*	Backache	*Dau lung*

SOME OTHER USEFUL PHRASES IN VIETNAMESE

Where do I collect my visa?	*Toi nhan visa o dau?*
One of my bags is missing. Where do I make a report?	*Toi bi mat moy tui. Toi phai bao o dau?*
I bought this camera/video camera in ...	*Toi mua may anh/may quay phim nay o...*
I have had this camera/video camera for ...years.	*Toi mua may anh/may quay phim nay...nam roi.*
My flight number is...	*So chuyen bay cua toi la...*
What is your flight number?	*Chuyen bay cua ong/ba so bao nhieu?*
Have they called my flight?	*Ho da thong bao chuyen bay cua toi chua?*
Can I carry this as hand luggage?	*Toi co the xach tay tui nay duroc khong?*
Where do I pay the airport tax?	*Toi phai dong le phi san bay o dau?*
Over there, to the right/left.	*O dang kia, ben Phai/trai.*
How much is the airport tax?	*Le phi san bay la bao nhieu?*
Where is the transit lounge?	*Phong cho di noi chuyen o dau?*
Where can I get a taxi?	*Toi co the don taxi o dau?*

Cham brick columns at the Po Nagar Cham Towers in Nha Trang.

Vietnam's Food

Vietnamese food isn't cuisine that you either love or hate. There are as many as 500 traditional Vietnamese dishes. There's bound to be something you'll sink your teeth into.

The staple food in Vietnam is, of course, rice. Few meals are served without it. Seafood, beef, chicken, pork and other more exotic delicacies such as cobra, rat, dog, deer, bat, gecko, python, turtle, porcupine and the endangered pangolin round out the typical (and not so typical) Vietnamese meal.

Vietnamese food served in roadside stalls and restaurants is remarkably cheap. It's quite easy to consume three full meals a day for under US$3. On the other hand, it's equally as effortless to spend US$20 on a Vietnamese meal at an elegant restaurant.

Rice is served in a large bowl. You'll be given another small bowl for your portion and the meat, vegetables and condiments to mix with it. Rice is dished out with a large spoon, but you'll consume your meal with chopsticks. After adding rice and other ingredients, you hold the small bowl close to your mouth as you consume the contents.

Almost all Vietnamese meals consist of the staple *nuoc mam* (fish sauce), a fermented, odiferous concoction that takes some getting accustomed to. But it tastes a lot better than it smells. A more potent preparation is shrimp sauce *(mam tom)*, a fiery liquid that fewer foreigners find palatable.

Pho is the Vietnamese staple. It consists of soup (a broth brewed from bones, ginger, *nuoc mam* and prawns), noodles and shredded beef, chicken or pork. Vietnamese rarely consume the leftover broth after finishing the meat and noodles. You can add lemon, chiles or chile sauce to the concoction—I've seen some even add sugar, in the Thai style of garnishing dishes. The noodles served with *pho* and other noodle dishes are of three varieties: yellow wheat noodles *(mi)*, white rice noodles *(banh pho)* and rice noodles made with manioc powder *(mien)* that appear more like slimy strands of jelly.

Other popular dishes include *xup rau*, a vegetable soup; *lau*, a fish and vegetable soup; *cha ca*, filleted fish broiled over charcoal; *com tay cam*, gingered chicken or pork served with rice and mushrooms; and *bun thang*, rice noodles with shredded chicken and a fried egg—as well as some other "special" toppings.

Spring rolls *(cha gio)* are a popular appetizer. A sheet of rice paper is filled with sausage, shredded pork or other meat, as well as vermicelli, mushrooms and other ingredients, and then deep fried. Additionally, you can create your own spring rolls using the above ingredients and different vegetables and eat them without first frying them.

Vietnamese meals are typically served with complimentary iced tea—but not the type you're accustomed to back home. The Vietnamese variety is much weaker and is more akin to ice water than tea.

Western Food

Western food can be found in the cities these days, and even hotels in the boonies will offer an American-style breakfast. In Ho Chi Minh City and Hanoi, there has been a proliferation in recent years of upscale eateries offering all kinds of American and European offerings, using imported steaks from the U.S. and Australia, pasta and oils from Italy, cheeses from France, sausage from Germany, and so on. At some of the finer establishments, you'd never guess you're away from home. However, the Western food served at many of the cheaper Vietnamese restaurants is simply awful.

Additionally, dishes from the non-Western world can be found in the tourists centers. Some of the best Malaysian and Thai food I've tasted I've had in Vietnam. There are restaurants for Indian food, Russian food—even Algerian cuisine. But if you're going strictly native, be prepared to lose some weight. When you think you're full, you may not be, as noodles weigh you down with their liquid content. No one has ever gotten fat on a diet of rice.

GODS OF THE KITCHEN

Most Vietnamese houses are quite small and don't have a separate kitchen. Kitchens are typically located in an area of the house close to an opening to the outdoors. Today, the Vietnamese cook on a brazier over an open hearth. The brazier has three grills, or supports, above it to place pans and pots.

Before the introduction of braziers, Vietnamese cooks used to rely on three clay blocks as the hearth. These blocks, or stones, became known as the Kitchen Gods. In the mythology of Vietnam, the three blocks represent family fidelity and are based on an old fable that tells of a sailor and his wife.

The sailor spent a number of years at sea and the wife assumed that he had died, so she remarried. Then, of, course, the sailor came home. She was overcome with joy and bewilderment and hid her former husband beneath a layer of twigs so that her new mate wouldn't find out. The new husband came home with a freshly killed deer and decided to cook it on the stack of twigs. He set fire to the twigs, killing the sailor. The wife felt such guilt she threw herself into the flames. At a loss for seeing why his wife would kill herself, the new husband realized he couldn't live without her and immolated himself as well. All three were killed by the fire and martyred as the three stones. What some folks will do for a Whopper and fries.

VIETNAM TODAY

Overcharging

The Vietnamese overcharge Western tourists frequently at restaurants. Even in the boonies, most places are clip-joints and may charge you as much as twice what a Vietnamese would pay for the same dish. Many restaurants charge for some of the condiments they set out before you, although you didn't ask for them. There is even typically a charge for cold cloth that serves as your napkin. If you don't want something, ask the waiter/waitress to take it away. He or she will do so without a fuss.

Examine your bill very carefully. The writing will be in Vietnamese at most places, and it pays to have a Vietnamese with you. If not, go over the bill with the waiter. Ask what each item is and the cost.

Finally, when requesting your check, simply say *"Tinh tien."*

Restaurant Prices	
The "Where to Eat" listings in this book use a quick reference rating for the price category of the establishment. They are categorized as follows:	
$$$	$6 and up
$$	$3–$6
$	Less than $3

History of Vietnam

As Americans, we're all too aware of the recent history of Vietnam. For the last 35 years, its past has been entwined with our own. As Vietnam crippled the U.S. spiritually, we ravaged Vietnam economically. As Vietnam reshaped our own awareness of the world by repelling and finally bursting the bubble of the infallibility of American intervention abroad, we regrouped as a nation, only to witness the crumbling of an impotent strain of Southeast Asian Marxism. Nearly 60,000 young Americans paid for this social rebirth—both America's and Vietnam's—with their lives, along with perhaps 3 million Vietnamese.

Of course, Vietnamese history predates this conflict by centuries, if not millennia . Not surprisingly, much of the country's culturally rich history has been marred by conflicts.

If archeologists can be believed, human existence in what is present-day Vietnam stretches back some 500,000 years. The Vietnamese are thought to have practiced agriculture as far back as 9000 years ago. However, very little is known of the societies of Vietnam until the first few centuries AD, when

Oc Eo, near the present-day port city of Rach Gia in the Mekong Delta, became the capital of Funan.

The early Ly Dynasty seemed to be at war with everyone, and at the same time. There were the Chinese. And there were the Chams. And the Khmers. The list goes on. However, the ancient Vietnamese were a resilient lot. They pushed south toward the Gulf of Thailand and virtually annihilated the retreating Chams.

The Tran Dynasty ruled Vietnam in 1225 and faced its most potent threat from the north. The 300,000-plus Mongol soldiers of Kublai Khan attacked the nation and were repelled. But the dynasty would eventually crumble by 1400, when the Chinese again attempted to gain control. After a largely successful 20-year effort to eradicate Vietnamese culture, Le Loi emerged as the new leader of a free Vietnam. He was phenomenally wealthy and used his riches to help the poor, which made him extraordinarily popular. His family rule included the annexing of Laos and basically ended in 1524, but not until after a significant amount of reforms had been initiated, including civil rights for women. But it was also a time when China culturally dominated Vietnam.

The Split Between North and South

Soon after Le's demise, conflict again interceded. Vietnam was split between north and south, under the rule of two factions, the Nguyen and the Trinh. Fortified by Portuguese arms, the Nguyen lords prevailed and eventually conquered all of what is present-day Cambodia.

Various factions continued to battle each other and they intermittently ruled Vietnam. Finally, a rebellion in 1771 spread to the south and Nguyen Lu became king of the south, while Nguyen Nhac became king of the central part of the country and Nguyen Hue became king in the north. The Chinese, again seeking to take advantage of the internal turmoil in Vietnam, attacked in the north, but were defeated in 1789.

Nguyen Anh, an exiled prince, managed to gain the support of French traders in India and, with the help of French mercenaries, captured Vietnam in 1802. The Nguyen Dynasty lasted until 1945, at least on paper. But the Vietnamese, on the whole, began rejecting Western influences in the 19th century, in particular those transplanted via religious missionaries. Many of these missionaries' converts were executed by the Vietnamese, prompting the French to capture and control three southern provinces in 1862.

After a French merchant was killed in 1872 by pirates, French retaliation sent the north into anarchy. The emperor, Tu Duc, sought Chinese, English, as well as American assistance in repelling the French, to no avail. Soon, the French were in control of all of what is known today as Indochina. The Indochinese Union was formed in 1887.

The French are generally thought to have controlled the region poorly. There were heavy taxes. Bandits prospered. The opium trade flourished. A growing sense of Vietnamese nationalism then helped fuel the emergence of the Communist Party, led by Ho Chi Minh. After World War II had severely exhausted France's colonial resources and influence, the communists began emerging as the strongest political party in Vietnam. Incidentally, this group, which became known as the Viet Minh during WWII, were supported by both the Chinese and the Americans when they fought the Japanese.

DYNASTIES IN VIETNAM

DYNASTY	DATES	CAPITAL
Hong Bang Dynasty	2876–258 BC	Phong Chau
Thuc Dynasty	257–208 BC	Loa Thanh
Trieu Dynasty	207–111 BC	Phien Ngung
Trung Sisters	AD 40–43	Me Linh
Early Ly Dynasty	544–602	Around Hanoi
Ngo Dynasty	939–965	Co Loa
Dinh Dynasty	968–990	Hoa Lu
Early Le Dynasty	980–1009	Hoa Lu
Ly Dynasty	1010–1225	Thang Long
Tran Dynasty	1225–1400	Thang Long
Ho Dynasty	1400–1407	Dong Do
Post Tran Dynasty	1407–1413	
Le Dynasty	1427–1788	Thang Long
Mac Dynasty	1527–1592	
Northern Trinh	1539–1787	Hanoi
Southern Nguyen	1558–1778	Hue
Quang Trung	1787–1797	
Nguyen of Tay Son	1788–1802	Saigon
Nguyen Dynasty	1802–1945	Hue

The Japanese overthrew the French Vichy-appointed government in Vietnam in 1945. During their short reign, an estimated 10 million people starved to death due to Japanese requisitions of rice that year.

After the atomic bombs had been dropped on Japan by the Americans later that year, the Viet Minh assumed full control of the north. Other noncom-

munist groups wrestled for power in the south. The Democratic Republic of
Vietnam was formed in Hanoi on September 2, 1945.

Return of the French

Because of further Chinese incursions in the North and a volatile situation
in the South (which, incidentally, the British sought to control with both
French and Japanese support), the North was forced to bargain with the
French to purge Vietnam of the pesky Chinese. French rule of Vietnam was
the price Ho Chi Minh had to pay.

But less than a year later, Vietnamese opposition to the French had risen
again. With France foundering in Indochina on American aid, Vietnam again
became independent, but still divided north and south. The government in
South Vietnam, bolstered by Western support, lost support among the Buddhists as it sought to implement pro-Catholic policies. Protesters hit the
streets and a U.S.-backed coup in 1963 installed the first of a number of
puppet military regimes.

The Ultimate Backpacker: Uncle Ho's Early Years

*Few know that Ho Chi Minh (the name means "he who enlightens") left Vietnam in 1911 at
the age of 21 on an odyssey that wouldn't see him return to his native land for 30 years.
Ho was the ultimate backpacker, a world hitchhiker, brimming with passion and wan-
derlust.*

*Shortly before leaving Saigon for France in June 1911, Ho was a schoolteacher in the boon-
ies. He was born and grew up in the central Vietnamese province of Nghe An, in the village of Hoang Tru. His father, a low-level Mandarin who had studied the Confucian
classics and did a short stint behind the walls of Hue's Imperial City, left his wife and
three children shortly after dropping out of his imperial posting. Ho, who had changed
his name to Nguyen Tat Thanh (Ho was born Nguyen Sinh Cung in May 1890), followed
suit and left home at the age of 19. He moved to bustling Saigon and changed his name
yet again to Nguyen Van Ba. Sort of like changing your name to John Smith or Bob Jones.
Inconspicuous. The perfect name for someone signing on as a coolie aboard a French
freighter, which he did—the steamship Admiral Latouche Treville.*

*When the Treville arrived in Marseilles, Ho applied to get into the School of Colonies in
Paris and was turned down. He became a gardener for awhile before hopping aboard
another freighter and spending the next two years (1912 and 1913) traversing the seas and
outposts of Europe and North Africa. He spent time in the Belgian Congo, Algeria, Spain
and Portugal before arriving in the promised land of America.*

*Ho was enamored with New York and its mishmash of ethnicities. He remained in the U.S.
for a year, intermittently employed in menial labor.*

The Ultimate Backpacker: Uncle Ho's Early Years

Ho got his first taste of underground socialist thinking after he left for London in 1914. There he ran into a number of Irish nationalists and Fabian socialists. He became an apprentice under master pastry chef Georges Aguste Escoffier.

Ho rode out World War I in London and then took off again for Paris in 1917 where he came into contact with more leftist intellectuals and expat political dissidents from Africa and Asia. He also came into contact with Vietnamese socialists Phan Van Truong and Phan Tru Trinh, political refugees from the 1908 Hue uprisings and the defacto leaders of Paris' more than 100,000 politically restless Vietnamese expats. Ho ended up joining the Phan's secret nationalist group. He changed his name once again, this time to Nguyen Ai Quoc, meaning "the patriot."

It was in Paris where Ho began to create pamphlets and authored letters denouncing the French rule of Vietnam. He joined the French Socialist Party.

Disgruntled with the impotence of his efforts in Paris, Ho set out for Moscow in 1924. There he joined the Comintern, the Soviet agency tasked with spreading communism around the globe. Again Ho changed his name, to Ly Thuy, and as an assistant to Comintern's agent in Canton, China, formed the Revolutionary Youth League (RYL) for Vietnamese nationalists and revolutionaries in 1925.

Swept up in the communist tide that was surging through China, Ho was convinced Vietnam would follow suit and spent his time consolidating Vietnamese opposition to the French. Ho's movement gathered steam quickly until a trusted ally, Chiang Kai-shek, broke from the Moscow-backed communists, forcing Ho to flee back to the Soviet capital.

Realizing that his efforts to muster Vietnamese nationalists in Europe was pointless, Ho again returned to East Asia—this time to Thailand disguised as a Buddhist monk. He reignited the RYL in the northern Thai city of Udon, but left for Hong Kong shortly after to unite bickering elements of dissident Vietnamese.

In 1930, his efforts were successful and the Indochinese Communist Party was formed. But misfortune struck soon after as a French Comintern agent was arrested in Singapore, the authorities discovering his "black book" of Vietnamese and other dissidents. Ho was busted and ended up in a Hong Kong jail cell for the next two years.

In 1933 Ho was to leave Hong Kong for London after coming down with tuberculosis. But he never made it to the British capital, instead ending up back in Moscow, where he'd spend the next five years.

Comintern sent him back to China in 1939 at the brink of WWII after the Japanese conquered Manchuria. In the spring of 1941, Ho, now frail at 51, led a group of Vietnamese activists on a week-long trek into Vietnam from China—the first time he had been back to Vietnam in 30 years.

The Ultimate Backpacker: Uncle Ho's Early Years

He met up with some of his former buddies in Cao Bang province and formed the Viet Minh (officially called the Vietnam Independence League–or Viet Nam Doc Lap Dong Minh). It was at this time Ho finally assumed the moniker Ho Chi Minh.

Ho returned to China disguised as a blind beggar to consolidate other revolutionaries, but was caught by a warlord in China's Guangxi province and imprisoned for a year.

By the time he got out, the Japanese had taken Vietnam. Realizing the Japanese would have little sympathy for his efforts to create an independent Vietnam, Ho instead made the bold move of contacting the U.S. intelligence organization OSS. He offered the services of the Viet Minh to assist in locating and rescuing downed American flyers in Southeast Asian jungles. Ho's motive was clear: in return for their assistance Ho was gambling that the U.S. government would assist the Viet Minh in preventing the return of the French to recolonize Vietnam after the Japanese defeat–support that would never come. In fact, the U.S. provided massive aid to the French to retake Indochina.

So when the Americans defeated the Japanese in August 1945, Ho and his supporters moved toward Hanoi and took the capital on August 16.

In front of thousands of supporters in a speech given in Hanoi on September 2, 1945, Ho declared in the empyreal paradox of U.S.-Vietnamese relations: "We hold the truth that all men are created equal, and that they are endowed by their Creator with certain unalienable rights. Among them life, liberty and the pursuit of happiness," words very familiar to the Americans, who would 20 years later use their own interpretation of them to wage war against the ultimate backpacker for 10 years.

The War in Vietnam

Meanwhile, minds in the north were thinking unification. The Viet Cong was formed in 1960 to force the withdrawal of all foreign troops on Vietnamese soil. In 1964, North Vietnamese troops were making forays into the south. The rickety regime in Saigon was becoming weaker through mass desertions and disillusioned peasants.

The Americans, who had actually had troops inside Vietnam as early as 1955, made a full-scale military commitment to the preservation of the South Vietnamese government.

The turning point in the war came with the Tet (Chinese New Year) Offensive of 1968. Saigon was attacked by the Viet Cong. Mass devastation took place in the countryside. In one three-week period, more than 165,000 civilians were killed in the fighting.

Growing resistance to the war by Americans helped form the American policy of "Vietnamization," which marked the first efforts toward sending American troops home. But shortly afterwards, the U.S. began its massive carpet bombing of Cambodia. The public outcry in the U.S., combined with the phenomenal and unexpected perseverance and resiliency of the communist troops, ultimately forced the U.S. to negotiate with Hanoi. The withdrawal of all U.S. troops from Vietnam was ceded for Hanoi's recognition of the South's independence. But on April 30, 1975, North Vietnamese troops rolled into Saigon after a massive offensive and South Vietnam fell.

On April 30, 1975, a North Vietnamese Army tank smashed through this gate to Saigon's Presidential Palace, symbolizing the fall of South Vietnam.

Post-War Vietnam

The country then began the painful process of reunification and "reeducation." Hundreds of thousands of Vietnamese fled their country for the U.S. and Europe. Cut off from the West economically, Vietnam suffered greatly.

In 1977, Vietnam entered the United Nations. At the end of the following year, the army invaded Cambodia and deposed Pol Pot's murderous Khmer Rouge regime in January of 1979, installing a pro-Hanoi government. But not without tremendous consequences.

The Plight and Flight of the Forgotten Amerasians

While "glibertarians" like Jesse Helms pontificate on the Vietnamese, his last recourse is to ensure that Hanoi do something that is quite physically impossible: account for each and every American serviceman that was listed as missing in action during the Vietnam war. (No single foe in an American war has been so thorough as Hanoi in accounting for missing U.S. servicemen.) His banal, insipid efforts do little more than rip the sutures from a nation trying quite tearfully to put a 30-year-old conflict where it belongs–in the history books.

The Plight and Flight of the Forgotten Amerasians

Jesse James Helms realizes he's got an ace in the hole, of course—one that will remain there, obviously—and that is a number of these so-called MIAs aren't actually MIAs at all, but American guys shrimp farming in Soc Trang and Ca Mau with their Vietnamese wives. Guys who were sergeants and platoon leaders who've opened chick bars on Sukhumvit Road in Bangkok, or who are drowning themselves in Mekong whiskey in the sleazier joints of Pattaya. Guys who simply said "The hell with it; this isn't Kansas anymore, Toto—and you were an ugly poodle, anyway."

Mr. Helms, of course, has little concern for the only real MIAs that exist from the Vietnam War: the 86,000 Amerasian kids forgotten and abandoned by U.S. soldiers. These Amerasians aren't kids anymore. But they may as well be. Like children, they are unable to find employment in Ho Chi Minh City. (Few would dare to venture north!) Most have been unable or unwilling to find jobs. They grew up in orphanages. Many gravitate toward crime and drugs. They suffer from alcohol problems. They have intermarried, producing offspring equally ostrasized by mainstream Vietnamese society. They cannot even go to Vietnamese schools.

Few of the lucky ones find their way to the United States legally. After receiving hard-fought and laborious approval by the U.S. Orderly Departure program, for some, their problems are only beginning. First, they must endure months in Amerasian Transit Center (ATC) camps. Then comes a mandatory reimbursement to the U.S. government for their transportation and medical exam expenses.

The ATC was started in 1989. Since then, due in no part to Mr. Helms and Newt Gingrich, 52,000 of Vietnam's 86,000 Amerasians have been interviewed and processed by the ATC. There are perhaps 2000 Amerasians still left behind in Vietnam, a number nearly equal to the U.S. claim of soldiers missing in action in Indochina. A good number of these outcasts have been interviewed for immigration to the U.S., being done so by ODP personnel from the International Catholic Migration Commission (ICMC), a U.S. NGO. Many of the Amerasians fail their interviews—for a number of reasons. The criteria for passing? Among other more mundane concerns are the applicants' age and personal appearance, criteria that certainly haven't prevented so many Americans from receiving gainful employment with the U.S. Postal Service or in Ogilvy & Mather's creative department.

Although rejected for emigration to the United States, Amerasians are permitted to reapply to ICMC after several months, presumably to provide these folks ample time to find a barber and clothes that don't resemble pajamas. Others, though, face more formidable obstacles: they have lost their original identification papers, perhaps taken from them by officials at refugee camps in Thailand or swallowed by sharks while the rafters were bobbing in Desoto tires in the South China Sea off the coast of Vung Tau.

The Plight and Flight of the Forgotten Amerasians

*The ATC, located in a suburb of Ho Chi Minh City, has been funded by the U.S. govern-
ment. The money was used to house and feed 200 Amerasians on a mere US$5000 a
month. But in February 1996, the cash well dried up. Many fear the center will simply
close, and those remaining Amerasians will have little or no chance of reaching the
United States.*

*Understandable, of course, because folks like the honorable Mr. Helms say these people
don't even exist. But somewhere, goddamnit, there are 2000 dead Americans in the rice
paddies.*

By invading Cambodia, Hanoi had overextended itself, and the Cambodian conflict became what many call "Vietnam's Vietnam." While other
Southeast Asian countries were tasting a degree of prosperity for the first
time, Vietnam was sinking the vast crux of its economic resources into its war
machine, impoverishing its people to the lowest levels on the globe. Even
though Hanoi's forces had taken Phnom Penh, it spent the next 10 years
failing to crush the Khmer Rouge's perpetual insurgency. The war drained
Vietnam's already shaky centralized economy.

The Vietnamese government began withdrawing its troops from Cambodia in 1989 and agreed in October 1991 to the Paris Peace Agreement that
paved the way to the first free elections in Cambodia.

The Bill Clinton administration in the U.S. dropped the trade embargo on
February 4, 1994, and liaison offices were established in Hanoi and Washington by the end of the year.

On July 11, 1995, President Clinton announced normalized relations between Washington and Hanoi, a bold and controversial move welcomed by
the Vietnamese. Clinton has insisted that normalization will speed up the
process of resolving the POW/MIA issue. (See the "U.S. & Vietnam: Normalization" chapter.)

INSIDER TIP

*At presstime, the U.S. and Vietnamese governments had established full dip-
lomatic ties. When liaison offices were exchanged between the two countries
in the beginning of 1995, the agreement marked the first major talks between
the two countries since the Paris Peace Agreement in 1973 that technically
ended U.S. involvement in the Vietnam War. The U.S. office in Hanoi has primarily functioned to assess and aid trade improvements between the two
countries and also to continue to monitor human rights issues and American
MIA cases. America already maintains an office in Hanoi solely for the purpose of locating MIAs.*

INSIDER TIP

Vietnam's only official presence in the U.S. up to the liaison/normalization announcements consisted of its delegation to the United Nations in New York. The liaison offices have also been dealing with financial claims made by the two countries following the seizure of American assets by the Communists after the fall of South Vietnam in 1975, and Hanoi's claims of some US$290 million in frozen assets in the United States. American claims are approximately US$230 million, the crux of that being U.S. investments in the south, including seized properties and buildings and enormous assets in South Vietnam once held by Occidental Petroleum Corp (see below). On August 6, 1995, the U.S. Embassy opened at 7 A Lang Ha street, Dong Da District, Hanoi. The opening of the embassy will provide travelers with access to embassy/consular support and services should they get into trouble, lose their passport, etc. in Vietnam.

The Peace Process Is Complete

Settling financial and MIA claims have been the keys to achieving normalization, but there are still a number of issues to be resolved between Vietnamese and American negotiators. Part of the disagreement that remains between the two nations revolves around U.S. and Vietnamese assets left behind in Vietnam after the war. Some estimates put the number of U.S. assets lost after the fall of Saigon in 1975 at $230 million. U.S. government claims include the former U.S. Embassy in Saigon, which is currently being used by a Vietnamese oil company. The Vietnamese, in their behalf, claim that the U.S. maintains frozen Vietnamese assets totalling more than $290 million. U.S. oil companies were big losers with the U.S. withdrawl from Vietnam in 1973. Simply, American companies would prefer to have their old real estate back once they move back into Vietnam rather than having to be forced to procure new land and offices.

Vietnam has opened up its borders and military bases to the Americans to expedite the determination of the fate of the 1647 Americans still unaccounted for in Vietnam. Additionally, 505 Americans are still missing in Laos, 78 in Cambodia, and eight in China. The largest joint search with Vietnamese since the end of the war in 1975 was completed in January 1994. Five more operations occurred before the end of 1995. U.S. guidelines for a "full accounting" of all U.S. war dead include bringing back those who are still alive, which is unilaterally agreed as highly unlikely, as well as all remains. If the remains cannot be brought home, it must be demonstrated by the Vietnamese why this isn't possible. Groups, including families of missing veterans charge that Hanoi "calculatedly withholds" MIA information.

With the establishment of full ties between Washington and Hanoi, the investigation into these claims has accelerated.

In May 1997, Pete Peterson, who was a POW in North Vietnam for six years, became the first U.S. ambassador to Vietnam.

U.S.-VIETNAM RELATIONS

March 8, 1965	*The first U.S. combat troops reach Vietnam*
January 27, 1973	*The United States and North Vietnam sign the Paris cease-fire agreements, essentially ending the American combat role in the war.*
March 29, 1973	*The last U.S. combat troops leave Vietnam.*
April 1, 1973	*Hanoi releases the last 591 acknowledged U.S. POWs.*
April 30, 1975	*Saigon falls to communist troops. Vietnam is reunified. The American trade embargo is extended to all of Vietnam.*
February 1982	*The Vietnamese government agrees to talks with Washington on Americans still missing from the war.*
September-October 1988	*The United States and Vietnam conduct the first joint field investigations for American soldiers missing in action.*
April 21, 1991	*The U.S. and Vietnam agree to open an office in Hanoi to investigate the fate of American MIAs.*
April 29, 1992	*U.S. President George Bush eases the trade embargo by permitting American sales to Vietnam for humanitarian projects.*
December 14, 1992	*President Bush permits U.S. companies to open offices to do business feasibility studies and sign contracts in Vietnam.*
July 2, 1993	*President Bill Clinton ends opposition to settlement of Vietnam's US$140 million arrears to the International Monetary Fund, opening the way for Vietnam to acquire new loans.*
September 13, 1993	*Clinton permits American businesses to bid on projects financed by international banks.*
January 27, 1994	*The U.S. Senate approves a nonbinding resolution urging Clinton to lift the embargo.*
February 3, 1994 (Feb. 4 in VN)	*Clinton announces the lifting of the trade embargo against Vietnam.*

U.S.-VIETNAM RELATIONS

October 5, 1994	*The House passes a bill saying MIA accounting should remain central to U.S. policy in Vietnam and the principle function of a U.S. liaison office in Hanoi.*
January 27, 1995	*The United States and Vietnam sign an agreement to open liaison offices in Washington and Hanoi.*
May 23, 1995	*U.S. Senators John Kerry and John McCain, both Vietnam war veterans, urge Clinton to normalize relations with Vietnam.*
May 31, 1995	*Vietnam turns over 100 pages of maps and reports about U.S. servicemen killed or captured during the war. An American veteran's map helps locate a mass grave of communist soldiers killed during the war.*
June 1995	*U.S. Secretary of State Warren Christopher reccommends to Clinton that the U.S. establish formal diplomatic relations with Vietnam.*
July 1995	*Clinton's national security advisers draft a decision memo for him to approve full relations.*
July 10, 1995	*White House officials say Clinton will move to establish relations in a Rose Garden announcement.*
July 11, 1995	*Clinton establishes normalized relations with Vietnam.*
August 6, 1995	*U.S. Embassy in Hanoi opens.*

Planning Ahead

Vietnamtourism and Saigontourist

VT, Vietnam's official tourist information office, doesn't yet maintain an office in the U.S. (although this is bound to change shortly with the normalization of relations), but you can obtain informative brochures from the U.S. representative, (Ms.) Hont Nguyen, *200 Waterside Plaza, New York, NY 10010* (☎ *(212) 685-8001*). In Saigon, check out SAIGONTOURIST Travel Service at *49 Le Thanh Ton Street,* ☎ *84-8-8298914* or *8295834.* Or fax them at *84-8-8224987.* In all frankness, though, I didn't find these people particularly helpful save for all but the usual tourist package trips like three-hour expensive (US$15) city tours aboard buses that have to fight off thousands of bicycles and cyclos that swarm Saigon streets like bees in search of tulips to pollinate.

A NOTE ON TOURIST OFFICES, MAPS AND ROADS

Although tourist offices exist in most major Vietnamese destinations (and even some minor ones–although I couldn't locate one in Tay Ninh), they are often of little use to the independent traveler–this includes especially the major offices of Saigontourist and Vietnamtourism in HCMC.

Rather they cater more toward organized tours, providing guides (usually individuals with limited English capabilities at exorbitant prices), renting vehicles (also often at ridiculous rates) and providing little if any information on sites that aren't regularly visited by tourists–sights, regardless of their lack of scenic or cultural appeal, that independent travelers intuitively seek out. Their primary function is to procure dollars, and tour packages represent the best means of doing so. Even obtaining local maps at the tourist offices can be difficult if not impossible.

Saigon is the best place to obtain reasonably detailed maps of areas in southern Vietnam. And the best map stalls line Le Loi Boulevard, generally across from the Rex Hotel. Maps cost usually between US$1–$2, depending on the area. Hanoi is the best place to find maps to areas in the north.

Curiously enough, the least detailed maps seem to fetch the higher prices, and some of them seem virtually useless for ground travel. Many maps depict road routes but do not number them. If you're traveling by surface, before you depart, find someone who knows the numerical identifications of major Vietnamese roads and mark the maps at intervals, as route numbers have a tendency to change at times. In many cities, towns and villages where major routes pass through, the route numbers will become names, such as Le Loi Street, Nguyen Hue Boulevard, etc.

If you're not bringing a guide with you on independent travel along Vietnamese roadways, have someone mark on the map(s) where road conditions are particularly dismal. This is particularly important if you are drafting an itinerary and expect to reach specific locations at the end of the day.

A 150-km trek between Nha Trang and Danang is going to take a considerably shorter period of time than the same distance between Ben Tre and Soc Trang in the south. And the roads in the north, traditionally known for their resemblance to cratered cattle paths rather than vehicle highways, are improving.

Tourists traveling north in Vietnam from HCMC to Hanoi have traditionally gone only as far as Hue, at which point they opt to take the train or fly to points north. This still seems to be the case, even though the roads in the north are now in acceptable enough shape to be negotiated by means more sophisticated than a sow.

Entry By Air

Entry by air is by regularly scheduled flights into Hanoi and Ho Chi Minh City. Both cities are served by a variety of airlines, including Thai, Cathay Pacific, JAL, Korean Air, Garuda Indonesia, Philippine Airlines, MAS, Air

France and others depending on your departure point. There's also, of course, the infamous Vietnam Airlines, which has been likened by more than a few travelers to a fleet of coffins with wings. But I'll be honest, I've survived a number of smooth trips aboard a Vietnam Airlines Boeing 767 and Airbus 320, as well as the Aerospatiale ATR-72, and I figure any British pilot working for a Vietnamese airline had to have done something to get canned at British Airways, such as planting a 747 on a German autobahn. But we made it each time, and he sounded as if he was having a jolly good time of it. I had to admit it, though, it was a little unnerving to board a plane with absolutely no markings. The international fleet up until 1995 was painted white. A couple of numbers on the fantails, that was it. No logo or anything. I can think of a bunch of airspace in areas of the world where that would go over real well. But that's all changed now; the fleet is painted, save for its recent aquisitions from other airlines. One recent trip I took to Hanoi on Vietnam Airlines was aboard a Boeing 767, still wearing the colors and lettering of Royal Brunei Airlines. For a brief moment as we boarded, I did indeed think I was being deported. But the service was great.

There have been reports by Westerners of having to bribe Vietnamese immigration officials both in Hanoi and Ho Chi Minh City after arrival, even with all documentation in order. And it can be expensive—upwards of US$100. But these instances have become virtually extinct, especially since the lifting of America's trade embargo and Vietnam's joining of ASEAN in July 1995.

READ THIS: PREPARE FOR WHAT TO DECLARE

When entering Vietnam, be prepared to declare everything of value you're bringing along with you. Whereas you may be accustomed to flying into Bangkok, Manila or KL and taking a leisurely stroll through the Green Line with pounds of photographic equipment and the portable atom splitter your daughter bought you out of a Sharper Image catalog, don't expect such a smooth ride through Saigon's Tan Son Nhat Airport or Hanoi's Noi Bai Airport.

To keep the delay at customs to a minimum, write down the serial number and model name of all your electronic and photographic devices, etc. This includes the serial number of each of your lenses. The same goes for laptop computers and peripherals, even electronic datebooks.

You'll be required to do so on the customs declaration form—so it makes sense to have the numbers already handy in your wallet, rather than having to fumble through all your gear at the customs officer's desk.

READ THIS: PREPARE FOR WHAT TO DECLARE

On another note, foreigners have traditionally had to declare any amount of foreign currency more than US$5000 when entering Vietnam. By the time you read this, the amount will have risen to US$7000. The State Bank of Vietnam is planning to further increase that amount to US$10,000 in the near future.

According to the bank's Foreign Currency Control Department, the illegal transfer of foreign currency is principally executed through the banking system, while illegal transfer through entry and exit ports is rare.

Entry By Land

From Cambodia, the border crossing at Moc Bai is currently open to Westerners, who usually are on a bus from Phnom Penh to Ho Chi Minh City. There have been reports of Westerners being detained by Vietnamese border guards trying to solicit bribes. Be cool. The best bet is to pick up your visa (a 15-day transit visa has recently been lowered from US$20 to US$10) at the Cambodian consulate in Saigon (see Ho Chi Minh City "Directory" for the address and phone number).

The border between Vietnam and Laos has recently been opened to foreign tourists at Lao Ebbao. There's a little confusion about the costs of these visas. There is a free 3–5 day transit visa that can be issued at the border at Lao Ebbao, I was told. Another official at the Lao consulate in HCMC said that transit visas lasting a week cost US$25 and can be picked up at the Laos embassy in Hanoi and at both the Laos consulates in Ho Chi Minh City and Danang (Danang, I was told by the Lao consulate in HCMC, is your best bet). From north of Danang, National Highway 9 crosses Vietnam into Laos and finally into Thailand. This route can be traversed by foreign tourists by land. But the road in Laos is in dismal condition, and officials at the consulate said that foreigners should attempt a crossing into and through Laos from Vietnam in the dry season only—which runs from November through April. The roads in Laos west of Vietnam are not navigable during the rainy season between May and October. If you really want to get stuck somewhere for an extended period of time, say six months, in an area where there is virtually nothing that allows human beings to survive, I'd strongly suggest traveling into Laos from Vietnam by road during the rainy season.

The Chinese border to the north is becoming increasingly easier to cross for both Vietnamese and Westerners alike. Most travelers now say it's a piece of cake. Areas that were previously closed to foreigners, such as the border posts at Mong Cai and Dong Dang (20 km northwest of Lang Son), are now open for foreigners with the proper visa documentation. But if you are leaving Vietnam into China via these routes, your Vietnamese visa must specify these border gates as points of departure. You can easily change the departure point stamped on your current Vietnamese visa by paying a visit to the immigration offices in Hanoi or Ho Chi Minh City. Some travel agents in both these cities will also be in a position to do it for you.

Entry By Sea

Entering Vietnam by sea is legal only by freighter or cruise ship. It would 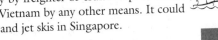 be dangerous to attempt a landing in Vietnam by any other means. It could mean months in jail. Keep your yacht and jet skis in Singapore.

Currency

The official currency in Vietnam is the dong, although U.S. dollars are accepted, even preferred, in the population centers. Bank notes come in the denominations of 200d, 500d, 1000d, 2000d, 5000d, 10,000d, 20,000d and 50,000d. Most travelers today are using the dollars over the dong for transactions worth more than US$20, and many upscale hotels require payment in dollars, even though an October 1994 law mandated that all major transactions in Vietnam must be made in dong. Carry a good amount of U.S. money in small denominations. Up until 1995, many travelers would use dong for all of their purchases. However, the dollar has gotten marginally stronger against the dong in the past year and, today, most travelers convert large U.S. bills into dong for the best exchange rate (11,000 to the dollar). You could get away using dollars entirely while you're in Vietnam, but it doesn't make a lot of sense these days. But if you must know, 10,900 dong is equal to a buck.

Tipping

Tipping is becoming increasingly expected in Vietnam, although it certainly isn't required. Some establishments add a 10 percent surcharge. Keeping some duty-free booze and foreign cigarettes on you is always a good idea. Marlboros and 555s are the best bets for the butts, Johnnie Walker Black Label whiskey for the booze. And remember, most waitresses in Vietnam make a salary of US$20 per month. Nearly all help support their families on this amount.

Official Language

The official language is Vietnamese, which is a combination of Chinese, Tai, Cham and Mon-Khmer. English is spoken by the many Vietnamese who worked with Americans during the Vietnam War as well as a number of schoolchildren and students. There's been an escalating interest in English since the country began opening itself to tourism in 1989. Many in the older set can speak French, and there are a lot of French tourists to practice with.

Business Hours

Most businesses open between 7 and 8 in the morning, shut down around 11–noon, and open again until 4 or 5 p.m. Government offices are generally open a half-day on Saturday. Museums are generally closed Mondays.

Telephone, Telex and Fax

Insider Tip: Collect Calls For Foreigners

Vietnamese law prohibited foreigners from making collect overseas telephone calls, but we've just gotten wind of AT&T's new Direct Service, which permits AT&T customers to use their calling cards when making international calls from Vietnam, and also allows others to phone collect to the U.S. from the GPOs in Hanoi and Ho Chi Minh City by dialing the following number: ☎ 120-10288. From GPOs in the provinces, the link-ups have yet to be established. So see the "Reach Out and Touch Someone" sidebar below.

These services are actually quite good, especially in Ho Chi Minh City, Hanoi and other tourist and business destinations. They used to be outrageously expensive, but prices are coming down. Faxing is your best bet. In fact, faxing from many places in Vietnam is cheaper than doing so from Thailand, Malaysia and Singapore, even from hotels. Most institutions with faxes in Vietnam charge by the page rather than by a three-minute minimum. It's a better deal if you're only faxing a single page. Expect to pay anywhere from US$6.75 to US$8.50 per page (compared to the thgree-minute minimum prices of around US$8-9 in Thailand). And beware. If you're faxing overseas from a hotel, ask to see the hotel's rate chart in print. Opportunistic clerks frequently pad the costs by a dollar or two per page. I've caught a few of them at it. International faxing and phoning is generally cheaper at post offices than at hotels.

AUTHOR'S NOTE: TELECOMMUNICATIONS

The official line is this: Calls to Singapore cost US$3.80 for the first minute and $2.95 for each subsequent minute. Calls to France cost US$4.60/ $3.82 for each subsequent minute. To Indonesia, the rates are US$4.55/$3.50, and to the U.S., US$5.50/US$3.82. In practice, I found these rates to be higher, not significantly, but high enough so that a business call that might take a certain amount of time adds up. Hotels are generally more expensive than going though a GPO, but don't count on it. Ironically, I've found it cheaper to fax the U.S. from small hotels in the middle of the boonies than to make the "less expensive" calls though the general post offices in the major urban centers. Who knows, you may be getting ripped off. But what the hell are you going to do about it? Interestingly enough, it's a lot cheaper to call into Vietnam than from Vietnam.

A phone call to the U.S. usually runs around US$5.50 for the first minute and a few pennies less than that for each minute thereafter. It's not cheap. Faxing is a better deal. The influx of foreign business into both Hanoi and

Ho Chi Minh City should soon bring these costs down as the country's communications infrastructure develops. Telexes aren't of much use any longer as the West has mostly discarded them in favor of the fax.

INSIDER TIP

Vietnam is a communist country. When faxing, avoid including information and/or opinions of a political nature. In some hotels, especially in the provinces, you can fax internationally direct—from hotel fax to destination fax—so there's little to be concerned about. This might be a little paranoid, but beware. In places such as Saigon, your fax is first transmitted to the general post office or other fax center before it is refaxed onto your destination. Usually, there's no hassle with this—and I have yet to experience a problem—i.e., state police battering down my hotel door at three in the morning. But just know that other eyes will see your communication before it's sent out of the country. Before you fax overseas, ask the fax operator (i.e. hotel clerk) if your message will be transmitted directly rather than through a middle source. As a rule of thumb, avoid sending anything even remotely controversial that could potentially raise a red flag. Literally. Foreign businesses in Vietnam generally can fax directly out of the country.

REACH OUT AND TOUCH SOMEONE

It's becoming a lot easier to make a phone call in Vietnam. The number of telephone lines in the country has increased by 200,000 to a total of more than 750,000 lines as of the end of 1995.

Most major cities provide relatively easy access to IDD (International Direct Dial) lines, most of them in the better hotels. Most budget travelers make overseas calls from GPOs in Vietnam's cities, and virtually all clerks at these post offices will tell you (seeing that you're a foreigner) that making collect calls overseas cannot be done. However, there is a way to make a collect call overseas. Get to know a Vietnamese local and have him do it for you. In some areas it's more difficult than in others, but generally it can be done.

Have an English-speaking Vietnamese friend explain to the clerk that he wants to make an overseas call, say to the U.S. (Vietnamese are given vast preferences over foreigners whenever trying to conduct any type of communications, accommodations, restaurant or utility-related business.) The Vietnamese person will have to give the operator his or her name, of course. Tell the Vietnamese friend to add your name to his when giving his own name to the operator.

For instance, if you're calling your parents in Georgia and the Vietnamese's name is Nguyen Tu, tell him to add your name to his. You can use your first name or surname depending upon whom you're calling (and the name the party will recognize you by).

REACH OUT AND TOUCH SOMEONE

If your name is Franklin Beethoven, have the Vietnamese say to the operator that his name is Nguyen Beethoven Tu. Your party in the States will probably recognize the situation and accept the charges. The operator may ask the Vietnamese how the hell he got the name Beethoven, but he simply needs to say it's a nickname. (In this case he might say his music teacher gave it to him, that it's a stupid one, but one that stuck.)

There is no guarantee that this will work, but it has worked for me on a number of occasions. A tip should be in order for the Vietnamese helping you. (It'll be a hell of a lot cheaper than paying for the call yourself.)

What to Wear

Vietnam has a sticky, tropical climate. Light cotton clothing is a must, particularly in the south. In the north (especially the mountainous north), it can become quite cool on winter evenings. A sweater or wrap would be appropriate. And places such as Ha Long Bay can get darn cold in January. Bring a coat. Jackets and ties for doing business only. (See the "Packing" section in the "Introduction.")

Local Time

Vietnam is seven hours ahead of Greenwich mean time. It's in the same time zone as Bangkok and Phnom Penh.

Newspapers and Magazines

Vietnamese English-language periodicals in Vietnam include *Vietnam Weekly, Vietnam Economic Times, Saigon Times*, the highly regarded *Vietnam Investment Review, Vietnam Today* and *New Vietnam*—all geared toward foreign business travelers, but most contain useful travel information on interesting destinations, some off the trodden path. Best bets in Ho Chi Minh City and Hanoi are the *Bangkok Post, The Nation, The Asian Wall Street Journal, USA Today* and the *International Herald Tribune* for newspapers and *Time* or *Newsweek* for magazines. There are a host of other foreign language publications. In addition, since the lifting of the American embargo, you can even pick up current issues of *People* magazine. Things are *really* changing here. Both the newspapers and the magazines are current. Expect foreign newspapers such as the *Bangkok Post* to be a day late. Although, sometimes if you're lucky, you can get the same day's edition in the late afternoon.

INSIDER TIP

Obtaining periodicals and newspapers dealing with the outside world used to be a hassle in Saigon—and an expensive one at that. This seems to be changing. American publications such as the Wall Street Journal, USA Today, Time, People and Newsweek are readily available, especially around the Rex and Continental Hotels.

INSIDER TIP

Swarms of children scour the streets hawking English-language rags to foreigners, but still, unfortunately, at inflated prices. Be aware that you may be able to bargain for many of the magazines and newspapers the kids are touting, namely because they've been pilfered from the hotels after the guests have finished with them. The bookstore across the square from the Rex has an especially well-endowed newsstand, selling current newspapers and magazines from all over the world.

The biggest disappointment is that the best locally produced periodicals, including the Saigon Times, the Vietnam Investment Review (highly recommended for business travelers) and Vietnam Today—all extremely useful and remarkably well-done publications—still fetch exorbitantly high prices. US$4–$5 is the norm. (The Saigon Times is only 5000 dong—and only worth 5000 dong.) For many travelers, though, the publications are an investment rather than a way to pass time in the toilet.

Electrical Current

Since Vietnam's infrastructure is still rudimentary, and power outages occur without warning, be sure to bring a flashlight. The electric current is 220V/50 cycles in most places. Take along adapter plugs and a converter.

AUTHOR'S NOTE

Vietnam's 500 kilovolt north-south power transmission line has started operation from Hoa Binh, about 75 km west of Hanoi, to Ho Chi Minh City. The line will supply 2.5 billion kwh for the southern cities and is currently the country's biggest infrastructure project. The goal is to provide power to southern cities that chronically suffer from seasonal shortages of power.

Local Transportation

Buses are one of the best ways to get around the country because they're so cheap and they get to so many places in Vietnam. And they're even better if you've got a lot of time—because they take a lot of time. Oh, yeah—they break down a lot, too. There are more runs during the night now that curfew restrictions have been relaxed. Keep in mind, though, that travel aboard Vietnamese buses (rather, reconfigured ancient Desotos) was designed for invertebrates and schools of very small fish. Anything or anyone with a backbone longer than a toothpick should be accompanied by powerful sedatives rather than a backpack.

Cars are a better way to get around than buses but are usually quite expensive, at least 25 cents a km on top of a day charge. And you can't rent them yourself yet, at least to drive. Alas, yours will have to come with a driver. It's better that way anyhow. There's right-side-drive in Vietnam and, although the cops are tough, one of the most common infractions is driving on the left (and driver's are rarely cited for doing so). There are a lot of companies that hire out cars and drivers in Ho Chi Minh City.

You can rent a **moped** (50 cc) without a special license in Vietnam for about US$6 per day, or hire a moped driver. You can even now rent a **motorcycle** in Ho Chi Minh City for about US$8-$25 per day. You will need an international driver's license with a motorcycle certificate, although few rental firms will ask to see it. But the police might. If you're staying for less than 30 days, have the license translated into Vietnamese and notarized (if you're planning on renting anything larger than 70 cc). For bikes larger than 150 cc, you'll need to convert your international license into a Vietnamese license for the ungodly cost of about US$100. At least that's the law. See the section on motorcycling in the Ho Chi Minh City chapter.

Trains are also a great way of getting around along the coast. They're slower than the buses, but are a helluva lot more comfy if you shell out enough dollars (you'll be required to pay in dollars) for anything more than a hard seat. The only problem is that the government slaps a surcharge on rail travel that makes it virtually as expensive as flying the same route (at least between Ho Chi Minh City and Hanoi).

Hitchhiking can be a piece of cake in Vietnam and not nearly as risky as in Cambodia, but expect to pay for your ride. A Westerner standing by the road with his thumb out in Vietnam is akin to holding out a billfold to beggars. The first thought of every driver going in your direction is "Ching! Ching!" And the thought of every driver going in the opposite direction, as well. A Western hitchhiker is a slot machine you don't have to feed quarters into. And it pays off on the first pull. The hell with Vegas. You may end up with a bigger queue of motorists than a police checkpoint.

Cyclos are also a cheap way to get around, especially in the cities. And they're everywhere tourists hang out. Bargain shrewdly. But keep in mind that the government has it in for cyclos. Like the *tuk tuk* in Thailand, the cyclo will soon become a dinosaur. The government doesn't particularly care for the image of old, tattered ARVN vets (which most of the drivers are) sharing war stories with curled-coiffured, camcorder-toting, notchless-belted Walter Cronkite groupies who would vote for Agnew if he wasn't dead. Besides, these awkward three-wheeled velocipedes—a cross between a coffin and an ice cream cart—maneuver in the dense Vietnamese urban traffic like a Goodyear blimp in a final approach pattern at Dallas-Ft. Worth Airport the day before Thanksgiving. They're great for tourists, but a pain in the backside to everyone else.

Bicycles are perhaps the best and cheapest way to get around in the towns and cities. They cost no more than a dollar per day and they can be rented at many places, including hotels, restaurants and sidewalk stalls. Some operators will ask for a deposit sometimes as high as US$20. Outside Saigon and Hanoi, most don't require any. I mean, what the hell are you going to do with a rented Chinese-made bicycle 11,000 miles from home? Break it down into parts and fence it off to the mafia in Laos?

INSIDER TIP:
TAXIS AND CAR HIRE IN VIETNAM

A service is available from Tan Son Nhat airport to Saigon. The 20 or so minute ride costs about US$7–$10 depending on your negotiating abilities. (When they run on the meter, as they should, from town to the airport, the cost is usually only about US$4.50!) Taxis are also available from Noi Bai Airport in Hanoi, costing anywhere from US$20–$25. The trip is a long one, sometimes taking up to an hour. Within the cities, with a proliferation of taxi companies and intense competition, taxis can be found cruising the streets looking for a fare. As well, they can be found at taxi stalls, or they can be arranged through hotels or by simply calling them. Some officials say that you can arrange for a car and a driver for about US$35 a day in both major cities, but I haven't found this to be true. Usually the rate, especially if you're considering excursions to the Mekong Delta and Cu Chi Tunnels in Saigon, or Ha Long Bay in Hanoi, can be considerably more expensive. In Saigon, for instance, expect to pay upwards of US$40–$70 a day (for a car and a driver in Saigon) and even more in Hanoi. Travel agents will do their best to make you think you're getting the deal of the century. But remember, the only deal of the century that can be found in Vietnam is drinking fresh beer (Bia Hoi). However, metered taxis in Saigon and Hanoi have become a bargain as well, costing usually only about VND5000-8000 (US$.55–$.88) for the first kilometer and a bit under that for subsequent kilometers. But don't use a taxi to go into the countryside. The private cars are a lot cheaper.

Tour Operators

The following is a partial listing of the ever-growing number of tour operators jumping on the Vietnam tour package wagon. Call around. Check out the prices and the itineraries that suit your budget and level of intrepidity. Some will merely bus your buns around the beaten track. Others will put you on a bicycle odyssey where you've got a decent chance of doing some pretty outrageous things or getting slammed head-on by a Russian-built freight truck.

(Note: Local numbers are for information; toll-free numbers are for reservations). In the U.S., you can contact:

Abercrombie & Kent International
   1520 Kensington Road
   Oak Brook, IL 60521-2106
   ☎ (708) 954-2944; (800) 323-7308

Absolute Asia
   155 W. 68 Street, Suite 525
   New York, NY 10023
   ☎ (212) 595-5782; (800) 736-8187

Adventure Center

1311 63rd Street, Suite 200
Emeryville, CA 94608
☎ *(510) 654-1879; (800) 227-8747*
FAX: (510) 654-4200

Apex World Travel

4620 West Commercial Way, Suite 3
Pamarac, FL 33319
☎ *(305) 733-4144; (800) 666-0025*
FAX: (305) 733-4456

Asian Pacific Adventures

826 South Sierra Bonita Avenue
Los Angeles, CA 90036
☎ *(213) 935-3156*
FAX: (213) 935-2691

Chinasmith

330 West 42nd Street
New York, NY 10036
☎ *(212) 239-2410; (800) US-CHINA*
FAX: (212) 643-1598

Cycle Vietnam

P.O. Box 4481
Portland, OR 97208
☎ *(503) 282-8499; (800) 661-1458*
FAX: (503) 331-1458

EastQuest

1 Beekman Street, #607
New York, NY 10038
☎ *(212) 406-2224; (800) 638-3449*

Far East Destinations

1001 4th Avenue Plaza, Suite 2401
Seattle, WA 98154
☎ *(206) 224-0117; (800) 879-2976*
FAX: (206) 467-9186

Himalayan Travel

112 Prospect Street
Stamford, CT 06901
☎ *(203) 359-3711; (800) 225-2380*
FAX: (203) 359-3669

IPI/InterPacific Tours International

111 E. 15th Street
New York, NY 10003
☎ *(212) 953-6010; (800) 221-3594*

All Adventure Travel

5589 Rapahoe, Suite 208
Boulder, CO 80303
☎ *(800) 537-4025*
FAX: (303) 4404160

Archaeological Tours

271 Madison Avenue, Suite 904
New York, NY 10016
☎ *(212) 986-3054*

Bolder Adventures

P.O. Box 1279
Boulder, CO 80306-9889
☎ *(303) 443-6789; (800) 642-2742*
FAX: (303) 443-7078

Creative Adventures Club

3007 Royce Lane
Costa Mesa, CA 92626
☎ *(714) 545-5888; (800) 544-5088*
FAX: (714) 545-5898

Diva Worldwide

☎ *415-777-5351*
FAX: (415) 334-6365

Express Travel

1050 S. Jackson Street
Seattle, WA 98104
☎ *(206) 324-6530*
FAX: (206) 328-6334

Gannon Tours

11495 Sunset Hills Road
Reston, VA 22090
☎ *(703) 471-9700; (800) GAN-TRVL*
FAX: (703) 742-0063

InterNation

620 Kearny Street
San Francisco, CA 94108
☎ *(415) 392-0244; (800) 553-3533*
FAX: (415) 392-3369

Here Today, There Tomorrow

1901 Pennsylvania Avenue, N.W., #204
Washington, D.C. 20006
☎ *(202) 296-6373; (800) 368-5965*

Intrepid Tours

315 Post Road West
Westport, CT 06880
☎ (203) 221-0332; (800) 558-2522
FAX: (203) 221-0816

Mountain Travel Sobek

6420 Fairmount Avenue
El Cerrito, CA 94530
☎ (510) 527-8100; (800) 227-2384
FAX: (510) 525-7710

Natrabu Indo-American Travel

433 California Street
San Francisco, CA 94104
☎ (800) 628-7228
FAX: (415) 362-0531

Pacific Holidays

2 West 45th Street, Ste. 1102
New York, NY 10036
☎ (212) 764-1977; (800) 355-8025
FAX: (212) 764-2396

South Sea Tour & Travel

210 Post Street Suite 910,
San Francisco, CA 94108
☎ (415) 397-4644; (800) 546-7890

The Global Spectrum

1901 Pennsylvania Avenue NW
Washington, DC 20006
☎ (202) 293-2065; (800) 419-4446
FAX: (202) 296-0815

Trade Services Co.

565 5th Avenue
New York, NY 10017
☎ (212) 697-1558; (800) 872-3386
FAX: (212) 697-2609

Velo Asia

1412 MLK Jr. Way
Berkeley, CA 94709
☎ (800) 884-ASIA

Viva USA

1840 W. 17th Street
Santa Ana, CA 92706
☎ (714) 972-2248
FAX: (714) 972-2034

Lotus Tours

2 Mott Street
New York, NY 10013
☎ (212) 267-5414
FAX: (212) 608-6007

Myths and Mountains

976 Tee Court
Incline Village, NV 89451
☎ (800) 670-6984
FAX: (702) 832-4454

Overseas Adventure Travel

349 Broadway
Cambridge, MA 02139
☎ (800) 221-0814
FAX: (617) 876-0455

Sino-American Tours

37 Bowery
New York, N.Y. 10002
☎ (212) 966-5866; (800) 221-7982

TBI Tours

787 Seventh Avenue, Suite 1101
New York, NY 10019
☎ (212) 489-1919; (800) 223-0266
FAX: (212) 307-0612

Top Guides

1825 San Lorenzo Avenue
Berkeley, CA 94707
☎ (510) 527-9884; (800) 867-6777
FAX: (510) 527-9885

Travcoa

2350 SE Bristol Street
Newport Beach, CA 92660
☎ (714) 476-2800; (800) 992-2003
FAX: (714) 476-2538

Vietnam Tours

1121 East Missouri, Ste. 115
Phoenix, AZ 85014
☎ (602) 230-1122
FAX: (602) 230-1029

VIETNAM TODAY

Or in Bangkok, Thailand, you can contact (country code, 66—city code, 2):

MK Ways
>57/11 Wireless Road
>Patumwan, Bangkok 10330
>☎ 254-4765, 254-7770, 255-2892, 255-3390
>FAX: 254-5583

Exotissimo Travel
>21/17 Sukhumvit Soi 4
>Bangkok 10110
>☎ 253-5240/1, 255-2747
>FAX: 254-7683.

Lam Son International Ltd.
>23/1 Sukhumvit Soi 4,
>Bangkok 10110
>☎ 255-6692/3/4/5
>FAX: 255-8859

Red Carpet Service & Tour
>459 New Rama 6 Road
>Phayathai, Bangkok 10400
>☎ 215-9951, 215-3331
>FAX: 662-215-3331

Viet Tour Holidays
>1717 Lard Prao Road
>Samsennok, Huay- Kwang,
>Bangkok 10310
>☎ 511-3272
>FAX: 511-3357

Vikamla Tours
>Room 401 Nana Condo, 23/11
>Sukhumvit Soi 4
>Bangkok 10110
>☎ 252-2340, 255-8859

FESTIVALS AND HOLIDAYS

January 1	New Year's Day	*Public Holiday*
February (moveable)	Tet (Traditional New Year)	*This is the big celebration of the year. It's the time that people forget their grievances; they pay off debts, kiss and make up—that sort of thing. Interestingly enough, Tet also marks everyone's birthday. The Vietnamese don't celebrate individual birthdays. On Tet, everyone's a full year older! The celebration is marked with a tremendous amount of eating. It's believed that the first full week of the year determines how the rest of it will go.*
February 3	Founding of the Communist Party Day	*Public holiday.*
March (moveable)	Hai Ba Trung Day	*Marks the revolt the Trung sisters led against the Chinese in A.D. 41.*
April 30	Liberation Day of South Vietnam	*Public Holiday. Marks the toppling of the Saigon government in 1975.*

FESTIVALS AND HOLIDAYS

April (moveable)	Thanh Minh, Holiday of the Dead	*Feast of the Pure Light. Vietnamese walk outdoors to contact spirits of the dead. Shrines and tombs are cleaned.*
May 1	May Day	*Public holiday.*
May 19	Birthday of Ho Chi Minh	*Public holiday.*
May 28	Celebration of the birth, death and enlightenment of Buddha	*Public holiday.*
August (moveable)	Wandering Souls Day	*After Tet, this is the second most important festival. By praying for the dead, their sins can be absolved. They can leave hell hungry and naked to their loved ones. Celebrations in temples and homes. Money is burned.*
September 2	National Day	*Public holiday.*
September 3	President Ho's Anniversary	*Public holiday.*
September (moveable)	Mid-Autumn Festival	*A children's holiday that features parades.*
November (moveable)	Confucious' Birthday	

VIETNAM TODAY

Vietnam: Potpourri

If you've never been to Southeast Asia before and are beginning your wanderings in Vietnam, get ready to be stunned. Although Vietnam is becoming more "modern" by the day, you will see and experience things completely the antithesis of your perceptions of reality. Your sensory network may transform you to emotional highs you never knew existed, as well as to deeper depths of despair than you've ever experienced—that's if you allow yourself to truly experience the country. Experiences and sights that will truly shock you will simply be a yawner for the Vietnamese. What seems cataclysmic to the Vietnamese, you may not even notice.

After getting off the plane at Noi Bai or Tan Son Nhat airport and riding a taxi into town, you'll come across your first I'm-not-in-Kansas-anymore-Toto experience: a decently dressed, grown man pissing on a wall or along the side of a car in full view of hundreds of pedestrians and motorists. Brace yourself, Butch; the trip's just starting.

The Cost of Traveling in Vietnam

Vietnam was one of the dirt-cheapest destinations to travel around in the world. And most folks have the impression it still is, particularly backpackers and other budget travelers. Not that it's become like Tokyo or Geneva, but I had a friend from Thailand recently come to visit me. She cut her trip short after a couple of weeks and returned to her home in Thailand's northeast, complaining about the "unbelievable" cost of living in Vietnam. The unbelievable cost of living—in Vietnam?! I had to admit it after thinking about it. A bowl of pho has gone up from VND4000 two years ago to VND8000 today. The cheapest food on the street in Vietnam is still more expensive than in some of Thailand's sit-down restaurants. Cyclo drivers are also charging about 50 percent more than they did a few years ago. A two-tiered pricing system—whereby foreigners are charged typically four or five times the amount locals are charged for the same goods and services—has made Vietnam the biggest clip-joint in the world. Still, Vietnam remains a bargain destination for those accustomed to $7 dollar hamburgers, $40 cab rides and $50 roadside motels. In Vietnam, decent hotel rooms can be found for US$15, delicious meals for US$1 and long cab rides for only a few bucks. In short, you can make your Vietnam stay as expensive or as cheap as you want. Backpackers who are on the last leg of a year-long hop on the Asia overland trail, and who ran out of travelers checks in Mandalay, can live as cheaply as US$10 a day in Vietnam (but they won't be doing a lot of partying). For US$25, you can live rather comfortably. And, of course, your standard of living rises from here. On US$1000 per month, you can live quite regally in Vietnam. Low-end travelers should stick to the backpacker caravansaries (US$5–$10 per night), eat at street stalls and travel by public transportation (buses are next to free). You get the idea. Vietnam started shunning backpackers in 1995 as more monied travelers came in tour groups. Backpackers, the bread-and-butter of Vietnam tourism until that point, became viewed as hippie cultural pollutants who were trickling only pennies into the economy. (The government even outlawed tourist visa extensions for a time to shed itself of the "freeloaders.") Then, about a year later, the boys in Hanoi started to panic as the tales of upscale visitors' woes of bad service, dirty hotels and lousy roads started to keep others like them away. The French, in particular, have stopped coming to Vietnam. Their early romance with Vietnam lasted from 1990-1994. Consequently, Vietnam has made a half-hearted effort to kiss and make up with the shaggy vagabonds. State tourism companies are now offering bargain-basement package tours (day trips for as little as US$8 and overnight trips for US$18, including accommodations). The business for budget travelers has become cut-throat, which is good news for hippies. Although faced with extinction in Vietnam, the backpack is making a comeback.

Beggars

Beggars have been a problem in Vietnam ever since there's been a discernable visual distiction between those with no money and those with anything more—which is probably since the Hong Bang dynasty. Beggars swarmed the streets (particularly

Ho Chi Minh City's) after the tourism boom started in Vietnam in 1990, but they've become a little less evident during the past couple of years, more likely due to police sweep-up campaigns than newly-found prosperity. Beggars in Vietnam are typically very old women; very young children; the infirmed, maimed or deformed of any generation; disabled Vietnamese war veterans (from both sides), and disheveled young women toting around grungy, sleeping infants covered with flies. (Unlike in America, able-bodied Vietnamese men—no matter what their appearance—stand little chance of collecting handouts from both tourists and Vietnamese alike.) Most of these people are truly destitute and have no other means of support; others are quite comfortable in life and ride new Honda Dream II motorbikes when no one is looking. These folks will pose a nuisance and some are quite aggressive. If surrounded by a group of beggars, it's best not to give anything—either food or money—to any one person unless you're prepared to give to the group at large. Food is better than money for the truly needy. Child beggars often surrender their day's booty to their parents (if they have any), who then use the proceeds to support alcohol or drug habits. Unmarried or childless women often carry another person's child for visual effect, and then split the take with the rented kid's mom. Do what your conscience—or reason—tells you. But if you do give, give in only very small amounts. (But I've seen more than one destitute old granny hop into the back of her son's late-model Toyota after a day of working the tourists on Dong Khoi Street.)

The Police

If you're not fond of cops in Houston, Portland or even King of Prussia, the constabulary of the Socialist Republic of Vietnam will do little to endear you to your local PBA. At their kindest, Vietnamese cops are aloof, stonefaced, noncommittal and suspicious. At their worst, well, it can't be printed here. Traditionally, Vietnamese police forces have been mired by corruption at all levels. It is especially prevelant when dealing with their own countrymen. Fortunately, foreign tourists have little contact with the police and, for the most part, the cops will leave foreigners alone in Vietnam, particularly tourists. The police are wary of foreigners, and many seem internally torn between the fear of reprisals from superiors if they apply the same systematic exploitation of the locals on foreigners, and the smell of money if they can get away with it. And many do. Taking bribes is engrained in the Vietnamese judicial system, at least on the street level, and basically all dealings with the police should be settled on the spot rather than "downtown." Fortunately, again, the government is coming down hard on police corruption, and incidences of impropriety on the part of police when dealing with foreigners are on a marked decline. But they still occur. Most police in Vietnam do not speak English, but they know the English words for numbers, which translate into dollars—your dollars. In most instances where a policeman requests a "fine" for an "infraction" the amount is low, and it can be bargained down to an even lower payoff. In most instances, it is wise to pay the officer the amount agreed upon, particularly if you are aware you broke a law, even a minor one. The rule of thumb here, and the locals will tell you this, is to never allow the situation to be removed from the scene of the "crime" to a police station, where all kinds of paperwork will have to be filled out and an official fine (usually higher than the street variety) levied. The trick is to resolve the problem—if it's minor—before it gets inked onto paper. If you are quite certain you did not break a Vietnamese law and an officer requests a large payment for a bogus offense, ask to write down his name and badge number. This will sometimes incite the policeman to merely shoo you away. If the amount of the fine is small, your best recourse is to pay it, regardless of your innocence or guilt. Vietnam is not a place to do anything on principle. It's very important to keep that in mind.

In Vietnam the police are always right. Do not think that carrying a foreign passport is a ticket to greater rights than the Vietnamese enjoy themselves. When dealing with the police do your best to behave as if you've been humbled, even if you're consumed with rage at their behavior. Act as if you were ignorant of the infraction and are now at their mercy (they know whether you're guilty or not). I was once arrested with another American for not having the "proper paperwork" to be riding a large motorcycle. It was my companion's first brush with the Vietnamese law and he behaved as if he had a diplomatic passport, angrily, arrogantly and recklessly accusing the interrogating officers of extortion and other infractions of Vietnamese law. Wrong approach. Some guy with green eyes, Earth Shoes and pressed underwear is going to know Vietnamese law? Right. We got off light with the confiscation of our motorcycles, owners' papers and a US$200 fine. In this case, the cops were at least partially right. However, stuffing a little pride back in the proverbial exhaust pipe would have reduced the "gravity" of our offense significantly.

As I mentioned, Hanoi has clamped down hard on hassling foreigners. Officers caught doing so are now routinely fired from their jobs and many imprisoned, where they're tossed into the same jail cells as some of the folks they busted. You can imagine the kinetics of this circumstance and why most law enforcement officers are mortally afraid of it. Before coming to Vietnam, swallow a large dose of respect for authority. A smile and a few bucks will make the bitter pill a lot easier to take. Again, most tourists experience no encounters with the law in Vietnam. And doing anything even marginally criminal in Vietnam is just simply stupid.

Insider Tip

Another piece of advice: carry on you at all times the address and phone number of your embassy, just in the event you really find yourself in the wrong place at the wrong time.

In Vietnam, the vast majority of police you will see or encounter are traffic police. They can be recognized by their light, pea-green trousers and caps and light, gray-blue shirts. They are a routine sight in the cities and towns as well as on the provincial roadways. In few instances will they help you should you become the victim of a crime. Though they won't be nasty, they are simply without jurisdiction or authority to intervene unless, of course, the crime involves a traffic accident. Criminal and investigative police wear a single-colored uniform and hat of drab green. These folks don't generally patrol the streets, but make themselves available for orchestrated busts and raids on bad guys' houses in the middle of the night. These are also the guys and gals you'll have to do business with if you're robbed or are the victim of another crime. Regrettably, horror stories continue to surface about the red tape and inefficiency travelers encounter with this group after being the victim of a crime. Expect to file lengthy reports and an even lengthier time for the cops to find their man—if they ever pop the perp at all.

Insider Tip: Squeaky Clean

If you talk to locals in the know in the south, they'll tell you the only place totally free of police corruption in the south is Kien Giang province in the Mekong Delta, home to the port city of Rach Gia. Do not, I mean do not, offer money to a policeman in this province. It'll get you in more trouble than you're already in.

Motorbike Safety: Rules of the Vietnamese Road

Anything can happen at any time, and it will.

The first Vietnamese cop who tickets a jaywalker should get a Nobel prize. Third World dogs will cross the road suddenly because Third World dogs have an apparent need to rapidly get somewhere they haven't been for 30 seconds. Spiritually, Third World dogs are bred to be under the generally correct impression they were inoculated against traffic at birth. If a dog appears interested in something across the road (particularly in another dog with mammaries that hang like fishing boots in a squall) and seems to be contemplating further investigation, ride with the appropriate foot extended and be ready to brake at a moment's notice.

Some Vietnamese people will cross the road suddenly because some Vietnamese people have an apparent need to rapidly get somewhere they haven't been for 30 seconds. Other Vietnamese people fail to sense the urgency of crossing a busy road with the necessary haste. Like their pets, these folks are under the impression—though generally incorrect in this instance—they were inoculated against traffic at birth. Many folks cross the entire road without looking once in either direction. Now as one cannot get any more skilled at this with experience, it's not safe to assume that older, more mature people are less likely to get hit than the rookies. Rather it's more likely that their card is closer to being dealt—and that your front end has some old guy's name on it.

Chickens aren't as predictable, and they're quicker off the line than dogs, making them the stealth bombers of highway hazards. Fortunately, if you play it right, upon impact, more of the chicken will splatter on the pavement than on you.

Cows and oxen can also exhibit traits of independent thinking, although they tend to arrive at decisions and implement them slowly enough to allow you ample time to brake and stop. We suggest doing so, based on simple physics and the negative correlation between the cow law and the chicken law.

And remember, nighttime doesn't stop a habitual jaywalker, which means it's more likely to stop you. Rather instantly, too.

Vehicles with four or more wheels do not recognize vehicles with any fewer as legitimate highway users. When confronting an oncoming vehicle that has moved into your lane to pass another vehicle, it is a certainty that the driver will move back into his own lane *only* when he has completed passing the vehicle and not in an attempt to avoid a head-on collision with you. Be prepared to move entirely off the road in such an instance, into the dirt, even a few dozen meters into a rice field.

Stay in the middle of your lane. Let the slower motorbikes have the far right. If being passed by a car, truck or bus, there's no reason to move to the far right if you're moving at a reasonable speed and there is no oncoming traffic. Would they move if you were passing them?

At speed, pass larger vehicles on the left. When congestion has slowed traffic, it's okay to pass on the right.

Vehicles with two wheels do not recognize other vehicles with two wheels as legitimate highway users. The vast majority of motorbike drivers use their mirrors only for looking at themselves, at least those who have mirrors.

When following another motorbike and not intending to pass, stay to the right of that bike. Motorbike drivers in Vietnam tend to make sudden U-turns without warning and without looking.

Deadly Toys

Tons of unexploded ordnance are still a lethal, daily reminder of three decades of war. Remaining on or just beneath Vietnamese soil, most of it is located in the central province of Quang Tri in and around the former DMZ area. Thousands of Vietnamese have been killed and maimed since the end of the Vietnam War while they were tilling fields or scavenging for scrap metal, accidentally detonating war materiel—such as white phosperous shells (Willy Peters), Bouncing Betty bombs and landmines. Many such devices, such as plastic landmines, cannot be located by metal detectors. Bouncing Bettys and other plastic-based landmines are particularly dangerous, as their bright yellow color and round shapes make them appealing as toys to kids who happen upon them in the countryside. Some estimates say—even today—an average of a kid a day in cental Vietnam gets blown up playing with these old toys of war. A landmine costs only about US$3–$8 to manufacture and plant in the ground, but between US$1000–$8000 to remove. Worse, they have a shelf life of many decades. A further slap in the face is that those most qualified to remove the little suckers are the same folks who manufacture them. Talk about having your cake and eating it, too. Needless to say, never pick up anything that might remotely resemble even a firecracker in the countryside, and never stray off well-trodden paths in the former DMZ area. Former—but still active—minefields may be known to the locals, but seldom, if ever, are they marked with warning signs.

Women Travelers

Vietnam, like most of Southeast Asia, is a relatively safe place for women travelers, even those going solo. Vietnamese men may stare a lot, but more out of fascination and curiosity than with an intent to do anything carnal or criminal. However, women are advised to dress modestly in all environments, including at the beach.

Toplessness, except in all but the most remote and deserted stretches of sand, is simply insulting to the locals and culturally sensitive visitors alike. It never ceases to make me cringe with shame and embarrassment when observing a nearly naked Western lady doing on a Buddhist beach—in full view of the locals, who mostly wear a full set of street clothes when sea bathing—what she would do in her backyard in Nice. Save it for Rio. Short shorts and miniskirts should be avoided in all social situations, as well. It's okay to dress in Western styles—even fashionably—but as much body should be covered as the Vietnamese women cover. Use common sense. In the cities, particularly Ho Chi Minh City, it's best to travel with a companion after 10 p.m.

Women should avoid traveling during the first three months of pregnancy—as this is the most likely time for a miscarriage—and during the last three months, when quick access to top-shelf medical facilities is a must. Third-World environments are typically not pregnancy-friendly—health care is less modern, accessible and reliable, and a proper diet—critical to pregnant women—is harder to come by. Yeast and other vaginal infections are also more likely to occur when traveling in the tropical boonies. Though it is not always necessary to see a doctor if you've come down with a yeast infection—a lemon juice or vinegar douche will sometimes do the trick—serious infections will require suppositories or cream from a reliable pharmacy. Yeast infections are more prevelant in the Third-World tropics due to the humidity, heat and lowered immunity levels caused by antibiotics taken for other ailments. Women travelers should dress in loose-fitting cotton clothing when possible.

Toilets

With the increasing number of tourist facilities in Vietnam have come the requisite number of Western-style, sit-down toilets. The Asian variety, squat toilets—which are little more than a hole in the floor—are still found at a number of downscale hotels, at many backpacker caravansaries and at numerous restaurants. And all but new, upscale Vietnamese homes are also fitted with squatters. The problem with most squatters, beside the awkward stance they require to heed the call of nature, is that they're indicative of primitive plumbing which can't deal with toilet paper. That's what the bucket of water beside them and the left hand were created for. Somewhat crude, but a fact of life in this part of the world. Many squatters will have a basket beside them, which means if you use toilet paper, it is to be disposed of in the basket, not the squatter. But you'll encounter a lot of toilets—of both varieties—in all kinds of establishments where toilet paper hasn't been budgeted for. When on the road, it'll always pay to carry an extra roll or two. Another problem with Vietnam is that public toilet facilities are all but nonexistent. This poses a greater problem for women than for Vietnamese men, who can be seen unabashedly urinating on all kinds of public terrain, natural or man-made. Women travelers in the countryside off the beaten path may want to consider wearing a sarong, which functions as a convenient tent when things get a little inconvenient. Oh, and a little advice: asking a Vietnamese waiter or hotel clerk where the rest room, or bathroom, or powder room, or lavatory, or men's room or ladies' room is will be met with nothing but confusion.

All of these quaint little euphemisms simply aren't known to the Vietnamese, who tend to call a spade a spade, anyhow. In this case, it's simply "toilet."

Bargaining

In most purchasing situations in Vietnam—other than at hotels, restaurants, fine shops, in metered taxi cabs and at sundry shops where items are tagged—the listed price isn't the real price. Most souvenirs, apparel, consumer goods and transportaion requirements are bargained for, from a cyclo ride to the monthly rent on an apartment. And, in Vietnam, it's a buyer's market. Inquire the asking price of a good or service before countering with an offer. It's silly to offer 10 dollars for a pair of three-dollar sunglasses. I usually counter with an offer of about 50 percent of the asking price, invariably settling for something in between and much closer to my side of the table. You'll find it emotionally more difficult to bargain for a good or service you find extremely desirable or absolutely need. Sellers are shrewd and quite perceptive of your body language and the level of urgency/desire in your voice. Acting as though you don't really give a damn about making a purchase will certainly get you a better price for it. On many occasions I have had my initial offer on a good or service accepted by the vendor simply by walking away or pretending to be distracted or preoccupied by something else, which is interpreted as a clue I simply might abandon the negotiations. Remember, it only takes one idiot to pay full price to alert the vendor he could probably get twice the amount for it. Consequently, many vendors of fashion accessories, basic handicrafts and other tourist items set an initial price tag as much as 10 times the fair price of the item offered. And that makes all of us fools who think we're getting a deal after paying half price—even me.

Bulls & Bears: What and What Not to Bargain For in Vietnam

Bulls: Don't Even Try	Bears: Go For It
Gasoline, anything in a department store, nearly full hotels, cigarettes, alcohol, restaurant or food stall meals, airport tax, airline flights, metered cabs running the meter, bar bills, train fares, bus fares, shoe or clothing repair, laundry, convenience store items, most club memberships, anything in a duty free shop, exchange rates at an official moneychanger, postal services, admission fees, bar or disco cover charges, parking fees, books, newspapers, magazines.	*Metered cabs when the driver won't run the meter, unmetered cabs, cab rides into town from the airport, traffic tickets, cyclo rides, anything found in a central market, hotel rooms at empty hotels, motorbike rides from private individuals, motorbike rentals, private tour guides, finished jewelry, cosmetic jewelry, cheap sunglasses, baseball caps, used motorbikes, used cars, unofficial moneychangers, souvenirs, artwork, handicrafts, roadside repair bills.*

Tipping

Tipping is rarely required in Vietnam (but becoming increasingly expected at establishments catering to foreigners), and many hotels and upscale restaurants add a 10 percent or 15 percent service charge onto their price tags. Tipping, as you'll hear the locals often say, "is up to you." Remember that you'll be charged in many places sometimes twice the price the Vietnamese pay for food, lodging and services. Why get ripped off for even more? Of course, you may be particularly enchanted with a certain waitress or hostess, in which case you should discreetly hand her a tip under the table. Discreetly because tips are often put in a communal kitty and divided among the establishment's staff at the more refined eateries. Tipping should never be done at food stalls, where prices are often so low there isn't a suitable bank note to justify a gratuity. Often, when tipping at a food stall, you'll find the proprietor giving you the money back in the belief you mistakenly paid too much. It disturbs me to see Westerners leaving a 5000 dong tip for a 10,000 dong meal. It simply suggests to the owner that he's not charging enough—and it's especially outrageous considering that foreigners' tips often exceed what the Vietnamese were charged for the same meal or service in the first place. If you've had to negotiate a price for a cab or cyclo ride, there's no need to tip, as the tip was already figured into the driver's poker hand. But it's not a bad idea to tip the driver of a metered cab. Tipping chambermaids and other hotel staff falls into more of a gray area. Many foreigners who tip hotel staff tend to leave a small gratuity on their hotel bed each morning. This may cause a problem if the room is being serviced by two chambermaids, who, when they become aware of your generosity, vie each other for getting into your room first. The other alternative is to leave a larger tip at the end of your stay, and give the gratuity in person to those you wish to tip. How much? Well, it's up to you.

The Moto Mafia and Rolling Graffiti

If you're riding a motorbike in Vietnam, you'll quickly discover that at virtually all public places you wish to park your bike, a man or woman will give you a small voucher and chalk a number onto the seat or fuel tank of your bike. Keep the voucher, as you'll need to give it back to that person when you wish to collect your bike. Invariably, the parking fee will be VND2000. You'll find these moto mafiosos in parking lots and on virtually all the sidewalks of the larger cities. In Vietnam you do not park on the street (virtually assuring the complete destruction of your machine) but up on the sidewak (virtually assuring a pain in the ass for pedestrians). If you lose your parking voucher, you will be in for quite a struggle to get your moto back. The ensuing arguing will also attract a lot of attention. Take this seriously: the moto mafia treats parking vouchers like wet-leased aircraft. They want them back. No voucher, no moto—period. The best-case scenario is having to cough up another 10,000 dong or so. But in many instances, even an offer of more money won't secure the release of your bike. Intervention by the police is sometimes necessary. But in the end, as it always is here, a handsome payoff will ultimately get you back in the saddle again. Be warned of sidewalk scam guys who will try to extort a parking fee from you without having given you a voucher. If someone hasn't given you a voucher, there's no need to pay for parking. The biggest hassle with Vietnam's parking system, besides losing your voucher, is the frequency of which you'll need to wash your moto. In just a couple of days of parking and getting your bike "tagged" by the moto mafia, your motorbike will end up looking like the side of a liquor store in the South Bronx.

Insider Tip

Whenever possible, park your motorbike indoors during the day and absolutely always indoors at night. Leaving a bike outside anywhere overnight is a guarantee of having to go to the police station in the morning and filing a vehicle theft report. Any probability of getting the moto back doesn't exist. Ironically, a larger-displacement, more-expensive motorcycle has a better chance of surviving the night on the street than does a beat-up old Honda Cub moped—for two reasons: 1) the bigger bikes are more conspicuous and more easily spotted by the police, and 2) most would-be thieves have no idea how to ride them.

Sidewalks

In Vietnam, sidewalks are an oxymoron. Rather than for walking, they make for better use as workplaces. Shops and stores spill out onto the sidewalks. Mechanics use them as a garage. For others, they are home. Entrepreneurs use them as soda pop bottle gas stations, jewelry shops, restaurants, nickle & dime shops, tobacco stores, auto parts warehouses, tire shops, hardware stores, parking lots, bakeries, discount sunglasses outlets, lottery centers and anything else you'd normally picture inside with a sign out front. And motorbike traffic will take advantage of any space remaining. Sidewalks are certainly not convenient for walking on, but still make for safer going than the street.

Crossing the Street

This would seem a silly subject in a book on any other country in the world—but not in this one. In the cities, motorbike, cyclo, automobile, bus, truck, food cart, bicycle and wheelbarrel traffic make for a never-ending sluice of humanity and rolling sheet metal in the streets—undisturbed by stop signs and traffic signals. Quite simply, you'll never find a break in traffic where it is safe to cross the street. Forget about intersections and the marked "pedestrian" crossings (a great vision, but whose implementation only kept a few dozen neo-impressionist street painters employed for a day). No one follows any rules here. You'll have no choice but to traverse the two-stroke spate unarmed. Venture into the street a step at a time, stopping after each step. This way you'll establish "presence," not unlike the presence, say, a concrete lamp post has. Motorbikes and other vehicles will adjust and whizz by you (hopefully) on both sides, like the current of a river when it snags up on an embedded log. The keys are keeping your eyes open, moving slowly and prayer. There won't be any Boy Scouts around.

Cockroaches

If you're coming to Southeast Asia, you had better get used to cockroaches, and not the cute silverfish variety found behind Maytag refrigerators in a Pittsburgh suburb. The suckers here are big, many the size of the roll you had for lunch on the THAI Airways flight over here. Cheap hotels also make an affordable place to stay for cockroaches. You can zap them one at a time with a can of Raid, but you'll be doing little thinning of the population by taking out an in-law or two. But for those whose pleasure is the thrill of the hunt rather than the satisfaction of the kill, the stuff will work, but not with the haste of a head shot. More than likely the sucker will scramble to a dark spot and ponder its brain damage for awhile before leaping into a shower drain in despair. Most people, though, want their proximity to a can of Raid about as close as they'd like to be under the fuselage of a crop duster. If you're totally unprepared, a good dose of hot water from the shower (if you've got hot water) will send these guys a message, usually immobilizing them. (You can decide what to do after that.) Boric acid, usually available in Vietnamese drug stores, will also do the trick. Sprinkle the powder around the corners of your room and in the toilet. Boric acid is extremely fatal to cockroaches, even in very small quantities. It's also quite harmful to humans if taken internally, but that shouldn't be on your menu.

Noise Pollution

I seriously suggest bringing a pair of earplugs or two with you to Vietnam. Unless you're in the remote countryside, this country, especially the cities, is damned noisy. The reasons are obvious. There are no emissions and noise laws in Vietnam and, consequently, many motor vehicles—especially trucks and buses—are entirely unmuffled, making for many potential sleepless nights. Also, Vietnamese kids are getting their hands on those beer-can screamer "Thai boy" motorbikes these days. You can't miss them, those skinny 125cc cafe racer-type motos that sound like a chain saw with diarrhea leveling a sapling. Also instrumental in the discordant cacophony are motorbike horns—which the locals punch like a Nintendo game boy—and bus, car and truck horns—which in Vietnam are custom-programmed by vehicle owners to sound like a bugle on acid doing the theme tune to "The Twilight Zone." Hotels along main thoroughfares should be avoided in most cases. Additionally, the Vietnamese have a propensity for beginning their day very early in the morning. By 5:30 a.m. the streets are teeming with traffic. Televisions (which the indiginous set at 11 on the volume dial) and tinny stereos are blaring. Funeral processions start boogying about 6 a.m., complete with live brass emsembles that sound like a defeated high school football team's marching band doing Herb Albert covers.

Air Pollution

Though not at nearly the levels of toxins aerating the lungs of Bankokians, air pollution is becoming a real problem in Hanoi and, in particular, Ho Chi Minh City. Like Bangkok, most of the pollutants in Vietnam's two largest cities are spewed from the tailpipes of motor vehicles, which are operated under no emission mandates. Billows of black clouds emit from ancient Desoto buses and old Russian trucks. Hundreds of thousands of motorbikes pack the streets of Saigon and Hanoi. Pollution in Ho Chi Minh City is becoming a problem. Respiratory diseases due to pollution are on a marked increase. Asthma cases have risen more than 62 percent since 1988; bronchitis has jumped more than 45 percent; sinusitis more than 40%. Pollution in HCMC is primarily caused by industrial waste and motor vehicle exhaust. Thu Duc district is considered the most polluted part of the city. Pollution levels in HCMC are almost twice as high in the dry season than during the rainy season. If you are really sensitive to pollutants, avoid visiting Saigon during the Tet New Year (late January-early February), when the ceaseless detonation of firecrackers (they've been outlawed in recent years, but may return) causes even the perfectly healthy to want to seek an oxygen tent. On New Year's Eve in February 1994, lead density in the air was 3.5 times higher than the minimum safety limits. It's also worthy to note that sewage and rotting garbage in the city pose a semi-serious hazard. Of the 16,000 cubic meters of garbage and the 2500 tons of manure that are disposed of daily, only about 27 percent of the garbage and less than 10 percent of the latter are properly treated. A lot of the trash ends up in the rivers, canals and lakes.

Power Outages

Up until 1995, power failures plagued Hanoi and Ho Chi Minh City, particularly the latter, where lengthy blackouts were a daily occurance (particularly in the dry season, when the hydroelectric generating plants lost their source of energy). I'm happy to report these days that outages in both cities have been drastically reduced through the development of new, modern power generating facilities. However, all of Vietnam's cities still experience outages—sometimes for as long as four or five (even 10!) hours—on roughly a weekly basis. Most of the mini-hotels and downscale caravansaries in the big cities do not have portable generators—so you'll be left to fester in darkness. All of the modern hotels have alternative power sources. In the provinces, power failures occur more frequently—and remote settlements and villages may only be supplied power for a few hours a day (usually from 6–10 p.m.), if at all. For budget travelers, a flashlight should be put on the packing list, and it wouldn't hurt to ask for a candle or two when checking into budget hotels in the provinces.

Telephone Numbers

Virtually every other guidebook to Vietnam—if not all—list the old system of dialing telephone numbers in Vietnam. In the beginning of 1996, the exchange system was modified to include the number 8 at the beginning of every phone number in the country. This was done to accommodate the rapidly increasing number of phone lines and users in Vietnam. The phone numbers themselves didn't change (so don't sweat it if you've got some old business cards) but are now preceded by the number 8. For instance, the phone number 84-8-444222 in Ho Chi Minh City is now dialed as 84-8-8444222. Calling locally, 444222 would become 8444222.

Collect Calls

As we've noted elsewhere in this edition, the making of collect telephone calls is generally prohibited for foreigners in Vietnam. However, at press time, AT&T announced that its Direct Service had been implemented in Vietnam—permitting AT&T customers to charge their calls on their AT&T cards or customers and non-customers alike to call collect overseas, from hotels and even from the general post offices of Hanoi and Ho Chi Minh City. To reach this service from the GPOs and the participating hotels, ☎ *120-10288.*

Telephone Call-Back Services

A booming US$500 million industry worldwide, call-back service—where the customer makes an overseas call from Vietnam using a U.S. third-party base as the billing source of the call—is only vaguely within the law in Vietnam and almost certainly will be completely illegal by the time you read this. Although that certainly won't eliminate the services. Call-back works like this: Clients subscribe to a U.S.-based telephone service and are given a toll-free access number in the U.S. to call when they need to make an overseas call from Vietnam. After listening to a ring, the caller hangs up the phone. A moment later, the caller receives a computer generated call producing a dial tone/calling instructions from the United States. The caller then dials the number overseas he or she wishes to call. The phone call is actually sourced in the U.S.—rather than Vietnam—so the customer is billed the U.S. rate for a call to that particular country, at a substantial savings over a Vietnam-based call to that same location. This irritates the Vietnamese government to no end, of course, because their monopoly on the phone system (Directorate General of Posts & Telecommunications) loses the revenue for that phone call. (IBM in Hanoi recently succumbed to government pressure and severed its relationship with a call-back firm.) Most Southeast Asian nations have cracked down hard on these call-back companies and have deported those involved in the business in-country. Frankly, call-back is a great deal for expats and foreign businesses in Vietnam needing to phone the home base on a frequent basis. But most of the call-back companies are sleazy, fly-by-night operations that typically go by unrevealing alphabet-soup names like ANA Network or ITD Systems, so as to remain as inconspicuous as possible. These companies, despite being chased by the cops, know they're in Vietnam for the short haul, to make as fast a buck as possible before scramming the hell out when the heat starts. However, because modern telecommunications are so problematic to monitor, I expect some of these folks will be cloak-and-daggering it around here for some time to come—and changing their names as often as did Ho Chi Minh.

Television Stations

Vietnamese television will bore most Westerners to tears, but has improved greatly over the past three years with expanded programming and coverage of world events from a surprisingly secular perspective. Many of the dramatic programs are bad copies of American soaps and corny movies about war heroes in love. There are also a lot of Chinese movies dubbed in Vietnamese. The dubbing of Western movies and serials is so bad, they really don't make any attempt at substituting Vietnamese words in the actors' lip movements. Rather, a single narrator speaks over the program's original score and soundtrack, speaking for the entire cast. The current rave throughout the country is the old American series "Little House on the Prairie." Don't expect to get caught up on a lot of international trends. Ho Chi Minh City has two TV stations, Channel 7 and Channel 9. Each broadcasts movies, soap operas, sporting events, variety shows, musical entertainment, children's shows and news programs. There is regular news and, at night, news programs are rebroadcast in English and French. As well, there are instructional programs which teach viewers English and French. VT3 is the national station and broadcasts from Hanoi. To the untrained eye, it differs little from the other stations, offering the same formats. But it does offer language instruction programs in English, French, Russian and Chinese. Satellite TV is offered in the good hotels, providing the Hong Kong-based Star TV network, which is a little hipper. All kinds of programs can be found on this network, including CNN and the MTV copycat, VTV.

Radio Stations

Vietnamese radio will also be of little interest to most foreign visitors. English-language broadcasts are provided by Voice of America, Radio Australia, Christian Science Monitor Radio and the BBC World Service.

English–Language Broadcasts	
Voice of America	17,730 kHz and 15,215 kHz in the a.m.; 11,755 kHz at night; 6110 kHz, 9760 kHz and 15,760 kHz (at night).
Radio Australia	21,725 kHz, 21,525 kHz, 17,880 kHz, 17,750 kHz, 17,670 kHz, 17,630 kHz, 15,575 kHz, 15,170 kHz, 13,755 kHz, 11,910 kHz, 11,880 kHz, 9560 kHz, 9510 kHz. The clearest broadcasts are 21,725 kHz and 17,750 kHz in the afternoon and 13,755 kHz in the evening.
Christian Science Monitor Radio	17,780 kHz (12 noon).
BBC World Service	15,360 kHz in the early morning; 15,280 kHz during the daytime hours; 15,310 kHz, 11,750 kHz, 9740 kHz, 6195 kHz at night. Also try 3915 kHz, 5975 kHz, 7145 kHz and 11,955 kHz.

Guns

Unlike in neighboring Cambodia, where an AK-47 is to the Khmers what baseball caps are to the Vietnamese, guns are largely absent in Vietnamese society. The Vietnamese love their shoot-em-up Hong Kong mob movies, but behavior on the screen has largely not personified itself in the actions of the Vietnamese. Most Vietnamese cops don't even carry weapons, other than a nightstick and the occasional sidearm. And they seem to get about as much practice with them as citizens of the Vatican. Simply, guns are a no-no in Vietnam. Even hardened criminals employ knives or sticks as their tools of the trade. Most Vietnamese criminals are frightened of guns, and are much more secure with pickpocketing, purse-snatching and knock-out drugs rather than armed robbery. In four years, I've yet to hear about even a single bank robbery in Vietnam. And it's equally rare for a foreigner to be the victim of a shooting. Of course, you do hear tales of peasants offing each other in the countryside occasionally. There is also the story of an American who packed up all he had, including a hunting rifle, and moved to Haiphong in 1996. He was arrested and sentenced to five years in jail.

Soldiers

Most Westerners, when they envision day-to-day life in a Communist country, picture rifle-toting soldiers staring down the populace on every street corner. This is certainly not the case in Vietnam. Armed soldiers are rarely seen by tourists and others alike. There is zero threat of a popular uprising in Vietnam, and the only order that needs to be restored in this country is the traffic. Occasionally one will see groups of soldiers strolling on roads in the provinces. But they're invariably unarmed and quite friendly. Also, armed soldiers occasionally man some intersections in Ho Chi Minh City during the wee hours to let the cops get some sleep. The threat of being detained is nil unless you're drunk and plow into something on the way home from the bar.

Secret Police

The secret police—plainclothed party cadres, informers and spies—is a fraction of the apparatus it once constituted. After 1975, the citizens could scarcely look up from the sidewalk while walking on city streets without being stared down by the party's Ray-Banned robots (sort of like the situation in Rangoon today). The secret cops were not only snooping on potential agitators, but shrouding coastal areas such as Vung Tau in search of doctors and lawyers armed with compasses and building rafts out of truck tires for the voyage to California. These days, the state has little worry over home-grown Che's and guys floating away on driftwood to Luzon. Unless you've come to Vietnam to stir up trouble or cop opium paste, you've got little to be concerned about in terms of attracting the attention of Amnesty International (who've probably got more informers in-country than the police). But remember, any cop not wearing a uniform is secret police.

Drug Stores (nhà thuôc tây)

Like some other countries in Southeast Asia, the Vietnamese are a self-medicated society—meaning that drugs that would normally require a prescription in the U.S. and much of the West are easily acquired over-the-counter at Vietnamese pharmacies. Everything from codeine cough syrup, tranquilizers and psychotropics such as Valium to anabolic steroids is yours for the asking. The drugs are also usually quite cheap. This is a good system if you're absolutely sure what ails you and what you need to cure it, and not such a good system if you're not. When buying any medication always check the expiry date. In the cities, most medications and other treatments are well within their expiry limits. This isn't always the case out in the provinces. Pharmacies are distinguished by their light pea-green signage with darker green lettering preceded or followed by a green cross. Many pharmacists in the major cities will speak some English, fewer in the countryside. Keep in mind that many Vietnamese see a pharmacist in lieu of going to a doctor. While pharmacists can be quite helpful in diagnosing and treating minor illnesses and injuries, they should not be substituted for a physician when you suspect your symptoms may be indicative of something more serious than a cold.

Girls & English Lessons

Unlike in Thailand—where no self-respecting female denizen of the community will be seen with a foreigner-sans-a-business-suit-on in the fear of being mistaken as a hooker—young and not-so-young Vietnamese girls of respectable status often make social overtures to Westerners. Many of the initiatives, as innocent as some may be, will stun Western men at first. Girls actually ask men for their phone numbers here, often only a moment after having gotten his name. And then, even more astounding, they call! Men, take note. When a female asks to see you again so she can improve her English, it usually means one of four things: 1) she actually wants to improve her English, 2) she wants to meet Westerners to broaden her perspective of the world, 3) she wants a new friend and, 4) she's looking for a marriage out of poverty or into relative riches. (Of course, there are more devious motives.) These, in my book, are all good reasons to comply with her request—save marginally for the last one. But keep in mind the cultural distinctions. Such invitations in the West immediately suggest a romantic liason. Do not apply this model to the foundation of Vietnamese romances. You'll be getting the wrong message in most instances. Vietnamese women are ignorant of the pick-up lines, and the necessity of them, of the West. Generally, their intentions are far more noble, and their naiveté of Western ways has caused many a strain on Western male/female relationships, as Vietnamese ladies consider unmarried men single. Never mind the guy has had a live-in girlfriend for a decade. Also unlike Thailand and other Asian societies, romantic liasons and marriages between Vietnamese women and Westerners are generally encouraged by the woman's family (probably for the ensuing financial strides it expects to take). Curiously, men particularly approve of these inter-racial unions. (They also speak excitedly of the possibility of netting a blond-haired California beach goddess for themselves, which might help explain their indifference at seeing their own most eligible bachelorettes jump ship.) If you're married, and make it known to inquisitors up front, you'll probably be left alone (if that's what you want). If you're single, and make it known to inquisitors up front, you probably won't be. Innocent or not, who's to know?

Postal Concerns

Through rain, sleet or snow, Vietnamese mail service doesn't go. And even without the meteorological concerns of sleet and slow, mail can take a painfully long time to get somewhere—if it gets there at all. But to give the Vietnamese postal service its fair shake, delivery service has improved tremendously in the past five years. Mail to the U.S. can take as little as a week from Saigon—although it can also take a couple of weeks or more. Mail is opened randomly, and all suspicious mail and parcels are opened, which may help explain some of the delay (see sidebar "A Postcard to Big Brother" below). Occasionally, suspicious parcels are held onto by customs and you will be summoned to the post office, where the package is opened with you present. Reportedly, this process is a hassle and can take as long as a day. Additionally, and without any apparent reason, you may be summoned to the post office to collect an innocuous airmail letter clearly addressed to you from abroad. For reasons unknown, the postal folks simply decided not to deliver it to your address. If you are summoned to the post office for either reason, be sure to bring along your passport.

I found that mail posted abroad from Ho Chi Minh City used to run through a meter, presumably because stamps didn't exist for the high denominations needed to post a letter overseas. However, this seems to have changed, and you're more likely to be given stamps which you will have to affix yourself. Keep in mind that most of the envelopes and stamps that you buy in Vietnamese post offices are not treated with glue. Don't lick a stamp nor seal your envelope in such a way. Instead, bowls of glue will be set up on the credenza. Give a few moments for the stamp to dry before depositing the envelope into a mail slot.

International postal rates in Vietnam are higher than they are in the U.S. One-page letters cost VND10,000 to the U.S., while post cards cost VND5000. To Europe, post cards cost VND6000. To Australia and most Asian destinations, postcards cost about VND4400.

Post offices in Vietnam normally keep long hours. The GPO in Saigon is open 7 days a week, including holidays, from 6 a.m.-10 p.m. Post offices out in the provinces also remain open 7 days, but usually close by 8 p.m.

A Postcard to Big Brother

"The weather's here; wish you were beautiful." That might get through the state mail readers, but don't pen a rocket formula on the back of a postcard and expect anything less than a midnight visit from guys in uniforms.

Mail into and out of Vietnam is randomly read by the Directorate General of Posts & Telecommunications, specifically by the Pre-Opening Office (POO), ostensibly for politically sensitive material–but it seems to be done more at random than with any design.

In the U.S., I've received simple form greeting cards from large hotels in Vietnam wishing me nothing more than a Merry Christmas that have been opened by the Pre-Opening Office. The POO is actually quite polite about their sanctioned voyeurism. Letters and parcels are not methodically resealed, masking evidence they've been tampered with. Nor are they sloppily taped back together like used giftwrapping paper. Rather, the office reseals the letters it's opened with a pleasant little decal on which is printed "Pre-Opening Office" along with its address and phone number.

Less and less mail appears to be being screened by Big Brother these days, and virtually all letters seem to make it through the net, unless you're sending a piece of mail to someone who has been red-flagged by the government or you have been red-flagged yourself and are stupid enough to list a return address. (However, some letters are opened because they don't list a return address!). Packages are a little trickier. The smaller they are, the less likely they will be opened. And the mail is a better way of getting something to someone unopened than the courier services.

Expect all packages sent to and from Vietnam via overnight services such as DHL or Federal Express to be opened and their contents examined. Some material the authorities will not allow to arrive at all. The material is simply confiscated and impounded (cultural items such as books, magazines, videos, etc. are most likely to get popped). You are not refunded the cost nor is the material sent back to you.

In fact, you're informed neither by the government nor the courier that the seizure has taken place. You don't become aware of it until you get a call from a guy who's had an empty box dropped off at his office that morning and is wondering what the hell you were thinking. Packages invariably arrive at their destinations resealed quite conspicuously by the Ministry of Culture or other cargo cops. One time I sent a package via FedEx from Ho Chi Minh City to Fielding's office in California containing some toy Coke can helicopters and a copy of a manuscript I was preparing on Thailand. The Coke cans arrived, delighting the publisher's kids; the manuscript didn't, marring what would have been a festive family dinner.

Air Couriers

Air couriers are hardly a bargain in Vietnam, but when something absolutely, positively has to be there, you now have a choice of five international air couriers servicing Vietnam.

Federal Express

1 Nguyen Hau Street, District 1, Ho Chi Minh City. ☎ *290747. FAX: 290477.*

DHL Worldwide Express

253 Hoang Van Thu Street, Tan Binh District, Ho Chi Minh City. ☎ *8446203, 8444268. FAX: 8445387.*
General Post Office, 2 Cong Xa Paris, District 1, Ho Chi Minh City. ☎ *8231525.*
49 Nguyen Thai Hoc Street, Ba Dinh District, Hanoi. ☎ *8267020, 8236061.*
Can Tho: ☎ *825305*
Dalat: ☎ *825586*
Danang: ☎ *821327*
Dong Nai: ☎ *822046*
Haiphong: ☎ *842596*
Nam Dinh: ☎ *849382*
Nha Trang: ☎ *823989*
Quang Ninh: ☎ *825135*
Vung Tau: ☎ *852343*

Airborne Express

General Post Office, 2 Cong Xa Paris Street, District 1, Ho Chi Minh City. ☎ *8294315, 8294310. FAX: 8292961.*
80C Nguyen Du Street, District 1, Ho Chi Minh City. ☎ *8292976.*

United Parcel Service

General Post Office, 2 Cong Xa Paris Street, District 1, Ho Chi Minh City. ☎ *8243597. FAX: 8243596.*

TNT Express Worldwide

56 Truong Son Street, Ward 2, Tan Binh District, Ho Chi Minh City. ☎ *8446476, 8446460, 8446478. FAX: 8446592.*

Photography Hassles

Vietnamese officials have gotten a lot less uptight about folks taking pictures and shooting videos of their country. But still be prepared to face some minor inconveniences. Although I'd stay away from shooting anything at airports, I'm told that it is now legal to take pictures from aircraft at Vietnam's airports. And I'm sure that if you want that shot of your wife descending the stairs from a Vietnam Airlines Boeing onto the tarmac at Tan Son Nhat airport, no one will stop you. Of course, you shouldn't take pictures of military facilities and seaports (not shooting policemen is wise, as well). More of an inconvenience are the ridiculous "camera charges" that tourist attractions impose on camera-toting visitors. Bringing a camera or video camera into many tourist attractions, such as the Forbidden City at Hue, will set you back up to US$5 above the cost of gaining admission—in fact, in the case at Hue, a whopping 100 percent increase over the US$5 admission price.

Banks

There are a number of foreign banks now in Vietnam in addition to the State-owned Vietcom Bank. Foreigners are welcome to start up accounts at most of them. However, checking accounts have yet to make their debut here. But remember, if you've got an account with a bank like Citibank or Bank of America in the U.S., it doesn't mean that you can walk into one of their offices here and simply withdraw cash from your account. Instead, you'll have to have cash wired just as you would if you stepped into a Vietnamese bank. Believe me, these folks will not treat you like the valued customer you are back home. Also, don't assume your American-issued credit card will be accepted in Vinh, even though you were able to take a cash advance out on it in Saigon. One American idiot, whom I won't name, started a bank account in Thailand and, knowing there were branches of the bank in Vietnam, brought along just enough traveler's checks to get by for "about a week or two." He just figured that if the cash ran out (it always does), he'd simply drop into the local branch of his bank for a withdrawal from a kindly Vietnamese teller. She told him he was bookoo American and was bookoo dumb for not bookooing enough bookoo to the Saigon branch from the Bangkok bank in the first place. "No biggy," my buddy said, "I'll just take an advance out on my VISA card." She said, "Yes, biggy. No can do." After only five days into a 30-day Vietnam tour, my buddy had to bookoo back to Bangkok for more buckeroos. However, it is worth starting a Thai bank account if you're going to be spending time in the region. You can even start an account and earn interest on it in Vietnam (if you do, we recommend it be with Vietcom Bank). And if you select a Thai bank (and start the account in Thailand) choose the bank carefully. For instance, an account with Bangkok Bank in Thailand won't give you access to your account at a Bangkok Bank branch of the bank in Saigon, unless you've made prior wire arrangements in Thailand. However, an account with Thai Military Bank, I'm informed, will allow you access to your money at a company branch in Vietnam. And also keep in mind that you will be charged on all withdrawals from a bank account in Vietnam, at least at last check. Usually the amount is US$1 for each withdrawal, no matter how small or large it may be.

Renting an Apartment

Some "experts" say Americans are permitted to rent an apartment during the first 30-day visa—others say you're not. Nonetheless, if the authorities discover that you're renting a flat rather than staying at a hotel when you apply for a visa extension, you're in trouble, pal. Tourists are expected to be lodging in Vietnam's hotels (of course because of the additional money it costs to stay in a hotel). When applying for an extension (or when leaving the country), your exit card must be stamped by a hotel showing the hotel as your lodgings in the country. If you are living in an apartment, make arrangements to stay in a hotel a few days prior to applying for your extension. The hotel will stamp your exit card and the authorities will be happy. If you don't, expect your apartment to be raided during the middle of the night by the immigration police. Not only will you have to pay an extensive fine yourself, but so will your landlord. You may even be asked (ordered, actually) to leave the country. When applying for an extension, you'll need to go through a sponsor (i.e. travel agent). Their prices for the extension will vary from between US$20–$40. Shop around. And it pays to have friends. Business travelers/expats these days report little hassles renting a flat in Hanoi or Saigon. But be prepared to bargain for your lodgings. A monthly rent which is quoted at US$500 can easily be haggled down to US$200–$300 (in most instances), especially if the place and surrounding or adjoining units don't seem to be terribly in demand. A lot of new apartment buildings designed to house expatriates have sprung up in recent years in Hanoi and Ho Chi Minh City. Lavish villas and suburb-type houses (complete with lawns and swimming pools) are part of new expat communities being built on the far side of the Saigon River off Highway 1 and Thanh Da. (The Thu Duc area is also being developed for residences.) These places can run anywhere between US$4000-$8000 per month. In town, luxury villas are also commanding outrageous rents, up to US$4000. These are usually rented by foreign businesses to domicile employees. Keep in mind that Vietnamese landlords have generally been successful in ripping off faceless foreign companies, and figure they can insist on the same terms with less well-to-do individuals looking for their own digs. It is typical for landlords of the newer, more desirable properties to require a one-year lease to be signed and a six-month deposit! Just walk away. You can generally find a large, comfortable apartment with a bedroom or two, living area, refrigerator, air conditioning and private bath and kitchen in the US$300-$400 range. The farther you get from central Saigon and downtown Hanoi, the cheaper the rooms.

"Extravagances"

The liberalization of the Vietnamese economy has spawned the influx of other Western influences or "extravagances" that would have been unheard of, or in this case, unseen, 10 years ago. A case in point is the rise in cosmetic sales. Just a short time ago, even lipstick was seen as a luxury for the very wealthy, models and actresses. Now Vietnamese are looking to the West for beauty aids, and companies such as Max Factor, Chanel, and Christian Dior couldn't be more ecstatic. Whereas once only Thai-made cosmetic products made poor girls even poorer, now beauty products from firms such as Chanel, Lancome and Revlon can be found in shops lining the boulevards of Hanoi and Saigon. A recent look at some of the shops found that a Suntory gift purse can be had for about US$25, while a bottle of Poison perfume fetches US$80.

Although there has existed a counterfeit market for such "brands" from Singapore, Thailand and China for years, it is dwindling quickly, as Vietnamese women are now insisting on the real McCoy. The cosmetic market though, according to most observers is still wide open, and will become increasingly lucrative as more Vietnamese women have the means to look "beautiful"—or use their meager means for beauty at the expense of food. Hopefully, we won't see the "Pepsi Generation" also become the Karen Carpenter generation.

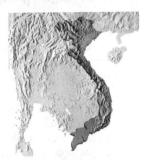

VIETNAM'S ECONOMY AND DOING BUSINESS IN VIETNAM

Vietnam's markets are crammed with vendors and buyers alike during the early morning hours.

Back in the 1980s, the real growth rate in the Vietnamese economy was estimated to be in the 6-percent range, but that would hardly be accurate today, as the country is courting foreign investment like a queen bee in heat. The drones of Japan, South Korea, Taiwan, Singapore, Malaysia, Indonesia, Canada, France and Australia have been more than happy to pollinate Vietnam's fertile embryo. Since the lifting of the American trade embargo in February 1994, U.S. companies have shoveled more than US$520 million into the Vietnamese economy, according to the U.S.-Vietnam Trade Council. Other estimates put the figure closer to US$550 million, making the United States Vietnam's fifth-largest foreign investor, up from 33rd a mere three years ago.

Vietnam enjoys an abundance of natural resources, including coal, phosphates, hardwoods, gems, manganese, chromate, bauxite, rubber, palm oil, marine products and—of particular interest to American oil interests—vast deposits of offshore oil reserves just waiting to heat every home from Anchorage to Albany—and perhaps even more important, from Quito to Asunscion.

Spices, coffee and tea account for 85 percent of all exports from Vietnam into the U.S. Vietnam is the fifth largest supplier of coffee to the U.S., ranked behind Mexico, Columbia, Brazil and Guatemala. Food processing, chemical fertilizers, cement, textiles, steel and electric power make up the crux of the country's exports, as does a US$900 million trade involving primarily agriculture, seafood, rubber, wood flooring and coal.

The owner of this hut is considered prosperous by his peers.

Exports of seafood, oil and apparel to Japan are substantial and exceed US$300 million.

Nevertheless, Vietnam is poor, one of the most impoverished nations on Earth—certainly one of the 10 poorest. We've already mentioned the typical American can spend on a pair of mediocre shoes what the average Vietnamese makes in a year. And Vietnam owes the International Monetary Fund some $1.5 billion in debts that its creditors are not likely to recoup. Perhaps the only plus in the whole scenario is that a lot of the cash is owed to the former Soviet Union, whose own crumbling monetary system makes the Vietnamese dong seem as solid as a Michael Milken junk bond investment of the mid-1980s. And this perhaps reveals one of the most ironic economic paradoxes of the nation—Vietnam as a single unique country sharing the same economic woes and monetary cemetery plots. This simply is without foundation. The two halves of the nation have evolved independently of each other, for all intents and purposes, for more than 50 years—and even the fall of Saigon to the north has done little to imperil the entrepreneurialism of the residents of the southern half of the country. Although the party virtually retains a subtle but Stalin-like grip on its people, it also covertly encourages perhaps the most liberal of all economic principles in Asia to function unabated. Some call the ideology schizophrenic, others believe it's just plain economic sense in dealing with a communist world that is collapsing around the last bastions of Marxist-Leninism like a ficus in an ice storm. Despite the loss of more than 58,000 American soldiers during the Vietnam War—and more than 3 million Vietnamese—Vietnam clearly remains two distinct countries.

The south is aggressive, outspoken, even pompous. The north, although tolerant—apparently for the gains it stands to realize—is more suspicious of the wave of Westerners (although first-time American tourists may be stunned on how warmly they're received). Hanoi, although charming enough, is void of the filigree of dissent, of muted protest—of diversity, in other words. It lacks an "edge," where youth and the free-spirited are thwarted from pushing the envelope of thought and art. Ho Chi Minh City makes no such pretense of Marxist piety. A curb may be built for keeping pedestrians from traffic, but they're also a lot of fun for bounding with skateboards and strolling on while donning headsets pounding with the likes of Metallica and Guns 'N Roses.

AUTHOR'S OBSERVATION: FYI FOR 'VIET KIEU'

Overseas Vietnamese, or "Viet Kieu," may or may not become a major component of foreign investment in Vietnam. Many analysts think their impact on the economy will be relatively marginal. Others are far more optimistic. The government is implementing incentive programs for overseas Vietnamese investors. A corporate income tax reduction of 20 percent may be the carrot overseas Vietnamese are looking for but, to date, only a few overseas companies have made any formal contact or inquiries with Vietnam's SCCI (State Committee for Cooperation and Investment).

Both the north and the south can be considered hard working, and it's one of the reasons Cambodians are so resentful of the ethnic Vietnamese that reside in their country, simply for their work ethic. The Vietnamese are educated, as mentioned earlier, but are beset with the problems of centralized government that continually results in grave shortages of staples and spare parts for machinery. Unemployment is rampant. Some put the estimates as high as 50 percent.

Why? Well, for once, it seems there are some easy answers. In fact, it's only one answer and it's twofold: the former U.S. trade embargo and Hanoi's insistence that so much of its budget go into military spending. There is China to the north, of course, relatively bitter foes. Cambodia to the west, hardly a cohesive and formidable foe, even against its own internal insurgents—and there is Thailand, whose real threat to the stability of Vietnam in the '90s is nonexistent.

But, despite the hardships created by war and international isolation, Vietnam has been a strongly resilient country. Despite the loss of massive economic aid from the former Soviet Union, Vietnam has stayed on its feet. It's dealing with new trading partners, and the relationships have been mutually profitable. Taiwan has emerged as Vietnam's largest trading partner—a far cry from Moscow in every sense of the word. Foreign investment has been growing at rates unparalleled outside Asia. By the first quarter of 1993, total foreign investments in the Vietnamese economy totaled more than US$3 billion, more than double the figure of only two years previously. Mid-1995 estimates put the figure at US$6 billion. By mid-1996, foreign direct investment in Vietnam totaled a whopping US$22 billion spread over 1700 projects throughout the country. Although, frankly, it's difficult to ascertain the precise figure, it's fair to say that the average capital growth rate here is 60 percent a year. Since 1991, Vietnam has seen an average 8.2 percent per annum growth rate, above the averages for all other Southeast Asian countries. Additionally, the ratio of total investment to gross domestic product (GDP) has doubled during the same time period to 30 percent, a rate similar to Thailand's and Malaysia's and above the rates of the Philippines, Indonesia and Myanmar. The country has established 16 industrial parks and export processing zones.

Money is pouring into Vietnam from Japan, Taiwan, Australia (even though it still steadfastly refuses to "Asianize" itself), Hong Kong, France, Great Britain and Germany—and now from the U.S. The rewards for Vietnam's trading partners can be astronomical. For instance, Vietnam's Foreign Investment Code, at the time of this writing, permits 100 percent foreign business ownership—astounding for a "communist" country. Foreign businesses are allowed up to 99 percent equity participation in joint ventures.

The joining of the Association of Southeast Asian Nations in 1995 (ASEAN) has also benefitted Vietnam tremendously. Between 1993 and 1994, trade between Vietnam and ASEAN nations increased from US$1.8 billion to US$2.5 billion. And in 1995, trade with ASEAN nations accounted for 32.4 percent of Vietnam's trade with the world, or about a third of all its foreign business. ASEAN investments in Vietnam have risen to a fifth of all foreign investment in the country. The creation of the ASEAN Free Trade Area (AFTA) and the propsed ASEAN Investment Area (AIA) will certainly further enhance Vietnam's relations and business ties with its neighbors, as well as attract capital from non-ASEAN economies. Bye-bye Moscow.

Vietnam's Top Investors

Although the investments of U.S. companies have soared in recent years, and Europe continues to retain a strong presence in Vietnam, the country's top investors remain giant Asian conglomerates, headed by those from Taiwan, South Korea, Hong Kong and Singapore. In April 1996, of the 33 licensed projects valued over US$100 million, more than 20 were committed by Southeast Asian companies. The majority of the investments are in hotel construction, infrastructure development, motorbike production and telecommunications.

South Korea's Daewoo, as of April 1996, topped the list of foreign investors with US$565 million tied up in 33 projects, including auto and electronics assembly, oil and gas exploration, hotel construction, a golf course and a US$177 million business center in Hanoi. The company intends to invest another US$2 billion in Vietnam by the end of the decade. The company is also involved in a US$136 million project to revamp Vietnam's public transportation network with 4000 new vehicles, including buses, taxis and trucks.

The Taiwan company Vedan has nearly US$500 million invested in an integrated food processing complex in Dong Nai province, and Fei-Yuen Investing and Development Company has US$468 million wrapped up into a commercial complex in Ho Chi Minh City.

The Chinfon Group, also out of Taiwan, has poured more than US$420 million into Vietnam, namely into the cement, banking and motorbike production sectors. One of the firm's ventures, Vietnam Manufacturing & Export Processing Company (VMEP), produces motorbikes in Vietnam (Bonus and Husky) and operates a cement plant in Haiphong and a bank in Hanoi.

In total in Vietnam, heavy and manufacturing industries account for US$9.5 billion of all foreign investment in Vietnam, US$6.6 billion has gone into infrastructure development and US$1.2 billion has been pumped into the oil and gas industries.

But if it all seems too good to be true, maybe it is. Foreign businesses are confronted in Vietnam with an essentially nonexistent infrastructure and excessive bureaucracy, in addition to the absence of a land title system and a consistent or uniform judicial system. Many charge that corruption runs rampant in the government, and accountings of how the pies of foreign investment are sliced and where the crumbs fall can be ambiguous if not down-right purposefully deceptive. And if Vietnam aspires to become a member of the World Trade Association (WTO)—as it indeed does intend to do—these problems will have to be tackled diligently.

Beer trucks have yet to make their debut in Vietnam.

But the money into Vietnam continues to flow like an aqueduct sourced at a deep snowpack. Tourism, of course, has skyrocketed. In 1989, about 60,000 tourists visited Vietnam, most of whom were overseas Vietnamese living in foreign countries taking advantage of Hanoi's increasingly liberal policies dealing with repatriation and the visiting of relatives inside Vietnam by political and "economic" refugees. Another significant chunk of that figure was the flow of tourists from communist countries, who have more access to communist-controlled tourist destinations than to places such as Miami or Rio.

But the figure jumped to nearly 190,000 tourists just one year later, in 1990. Optimistic government officials then predicted that by 1995, the 1991 figure would double. It turned out to be a pessimistic forecast at best. The figure authorities in Hanoi now openly speak of is over 1.4 million. No wonder it's easier to declare a camcorder at customs.

The problem is a lack of facilities to accommodate all these people. Maybe "facilities" isn't the word. Change that to quality hotel rooms. The number of hotel rooms in Bangkok alone today stands around 30,000. Compare that with fewer than 16,000 international-standard rooms in the entire country of Vietnam, whose population exceeds that of Thailand's by nearly 20 million.

AUTHOR'S NOTE

By the year 2000, Vietnam will need between 12,800 and 17,300 tourist cars and between 47,000 and 63,000 commercial vehicles. If the country decides not to build its own plants, it will have to spend nearly US$1.5 billion to import them. If Vietnam decides to build its own plants, government officials will be looking primarily at the United States, Western Europe and Japan for the necessary technology.

But these rooms, and thousands more, will come—if for no other reason than there is so much money to be made here. It's believed that northern Vietnam has some of Asia's greatest coal deposits. Offshore oil reserves make your head spin. A recent survey estimated that Vietnam's oil reserves are somewhere between 2 and 3 billion barrels—more than half a million barrels could be output in a single day in about 10 years from now. With the lifting of the U.S. trade embargo and the recent normalization of relations between Washington and Hanoi, Vietnam is poised to become a huge exporter of oil in the near future.

The New Wave of American Investment in Vietnam and Some Tips for Entrepreneurs

The lifting of the trade embargo and the subsequent normalization of ties between the U.S. and Vietnam has spawned a wave of American business people seeking opportunities in the country. Whereas in 1994, the U.S. ranked 33rd among foreign investors in Vietnam, it leapt to between the 13th and 7th largest investor in the country by the middle of 1995, depending on who you talk to.

The Asia Pacific Chamber of Commerce (APCC) based in Seattle, Washington, sent a commission to Vietnam in April 1994 called the "Business Opportunity Mission to Vietnam." Its purpose was to help American entrepreneurs learn Vietnamese business and social customs and how to do business in perhaps the world's fastest growing economy. According to APCC execs, American companies attending the mission included Caterpillar, Clark, Microsoft, Sun Micro Systems, US West and McCaw Cellular (both telecommunications companies), Crate & Barrel, Advanced Technology Labs and Space Labs (a hospital monitor company).

Official members of the delegation included Senator Patty Murray of Washington, Adlai Stevenson and Paul Cleveland (The U.S. trade ambassador).

There were also participants from the American Grocer's Association, the Washington Apple Commission, and officials from Washington State's Department of Agriculture.

Among the many American companies rushing into Vietnam to sign deals are the Texas-based WG Ripley Group (assembly lines for cotton production, a US$2.5 million deal) and DuPont (which has opened an office in Ho Chi Minh City and said that Vietnam is now a focal point for its efforts to quadruple sales—to move global sales from 7 percent to 20 percent—in the region by the turn of the century). (Incidentally, DuPont was one of the first U.S. businesses to open shop in Vietnam after the lifting of the embargo.) DuPont's energy subsidiary, Conoco, has been seeking to obtain offshore oil exploration rights. The company, like a slew of others, is forecasting increasingly sophisticated consumer and industrial markets for electronics, automotive products, electrical goods, construction materials, clothing and crop protection.

Mobil now has a big contract to drill in the South China Sea off southern Vietnam. Chrysler recently opened its first offices and showrooms in Hanoi and Ho Chi Minh City (although the carmaker recently pulled the plug on what would have been Vietnam's largest auto factory). RJ Reynolds is building a US$21 million factory in Dalat and is starting a 6000-hectare tobacco planting project in nearby Quang Nam-Danang province. Citicorp is here. Delta Airlines will be starting air service soon. Even Baskin Robbins is vending its 31 flavors in HCMC.

Vietnam may become a major importer of U.S. farm products, perhaps procuring as much as US$300 million annually. Vietnam purchased US$213 million worth of food in 1992, the last year statistics are available. About a quarter of the products were purchased from the European Union, Singapore, Japan and Hong Kong.

Because Vietnam is looking at moving toward an economic strategy that would increase its growth rate between 8 percent and 10 percent annually, agricultural imports are likely to skyrocket in coming years, according to a U.S. State Department report. Total agricultural purchases in Vietnam could reach U.S.$1.7 billion annually. Vietnam's interest in American agricultural products include wheat, wheat flour, feed grains, poultry, pork and processed meats, vegetable oils and oil seeds, cotton and processed fresh fruits.

Business people considering doing business in Vietnam may want to consider that there may be only limited demand for branded consumer products. But assistance with the country's agricultural industry should provide self-starters with boundless opportunities. But remember, you've got some catching up to do. The U.S. currently ranks 13th (at press time) in foreign investment in Vietnam. Investment opportunities flourish. Nearly all of the country's 50 provinces and cities are openly vying for overseas investment.

AUTHOR'S NOTE

Hollywood, not one to miss scouting a good location, is also jumping in on the post-embargo feeding fray in Vietnam. The American film Fields of Fire *will be the first post-embargo American film shot in Vietnam. The film, of course, will be a Vietnam War film, and more than likely feature the rising Vietnamese-American actress Kieu Chinh in the lead role. Production began in May 1994. The film was adapted from the novel of the same name written by the film's director James Webb, who was a lieutenant in the U.S. Army during the war stationed at Quang Nam-Da Nang. Webb also served as secretary of the Navy under the George Bush administration. Fields of Fire chronicles the fates of soldiers on both sides of the conflict. The film's primary locations are set in the districts of Duy Xuyen and Dai Loc. Up until now, most movies depicting the war, including Francis Ford Coppola's epic* Apocalypse Now *and* Platoon *used the Philippines, Thailand, Malaysia, and other Southeast Asia locations for shooting.*

In addition, aviation will undoubtedly provide a slew of opportunities for American firms. American aviation companies jumping on the Vietnam bandwagon include United, Continental, Northwest and Delta Airlines. Boeing and McDonnell-Douglas are lobbying hard to replace Vietnam Airlines' aging fleet of 20 Soviet-built airlines. Delta, as well, is working with Vietnam Airlines to establish direct links between the United States and Vietnam. Up until this point, travelers have had to endure long layovers in places such as Bangkok, Singapore, Hong Kong or Seoul before boarding flights on different carriers to Vietnam.

U.S. INVESTMENT IN VIETNAM (IN US$ MILLIONS)

SECTORS	1994–1995	1998
Energy & Transportation	1062.0	2493.0
Road Construction	100.0	210.0
Telecommunications	223.5	457,5
Oil & Gas Equipment	113.3	11375.5
Aviation Control Equipment	87.0	195.0
Oil Exploration	25.7	41.3
Refrigeration	4.5	24.0
Computers	24.5	118.8

U.S. INVESTMENT IN VIETNAM (IN US$ MILLIONS)

SECTORS	1994–1995	1998
Airplane Engines	200.7	750.0
Hotel Construction & Management	36.1	54.8
Automatic Products	33.3	65.8
Pharmaceuticals	13.3	54.0
Air Services	44.8	68.2
Medical Equipment	3.0	9.8
Chemicals	25.5	110.1
Construction Materials	20.0	73.0
Petro-chemical Products	45.0	10.0
Other Industrial Products	60.3	138.2
Consumer Goods	390.6	1303.3
Automobiles	30.6	57.4
Banks & Stocks	21.9	68.8
Shipping	100.0	438.0

Source: U.S.-ASEAN Council

In the areas of construction, major U.S. companies either seeking to establish contracts in Vietnam or those whose ink has already dried include Fluor Daniel (66th among the largest diversified service companies in the world, according to *Forbes* magazine), and Indochina Partners.

In the north, conditions for conducting and initiating business transactions are far more problematic than in the south. American businesspeople are now jamming airliners headed to Hanoi, and officials in Vietnam are having a difficult time accommodating all the interest American companies are developing in the country's economy. As one observer noted, "The Vietnamese economy still lacks the fundamental preconditions for high, sustainable growth."

In a way, Vietnam is going through a potentially dangerous phase. Central planning has been all but eliminated entirely. But the country has yet to establish a free market system that works within any predictable or regulatory network. The budget deficit continues to widen, currently about 7 percent (See "Author's Note" below).

But some of the other numbers sure look good: The gross domestic product expanded by 8 percent in 1993, without any measurable degree of inflation. (Prices rose slightly more than 5 percent.) Nearly 1 million jobs were created in the country in 1994 (although countless millions of Vietnamese still remain under- or unemployed). These new workers are helping to construct houses and produce durable goods, efforts that have yielded more progress in the country in the past five years than in the previous half century.

Recent projects that have been capitalized comprise more than US$300 million, and experts say that foreign investment in Vietnam soared to US$20 billion in 1996.

Taxation law in Vietnam remains a problem and is generally considered to still be administered mainly by corrupt party officials. The "savings rate," a prime indicator that gleans the mobilization of capital by commercial banks, has risen slightly (to 11 percent of the gross national product) but needs to double, according to the experts, in order for Vietnam to move up to par with the economies of Thailand and Singapore. Additionally, Vietnam's economic growth must be more concurrent with progress in social change, according to government officials. Economic management must match social efforts to reduce or eliminate entirely corruption, drug abuse, prostitution and especially smuggling, officials say. This disparity could possibly dissuade foreign investors in utilizing the country's vast work force. One has to remember that Vietnam is starting from Ground Zero.

SOME OF THE U.S. FIRMS DOING BUSINESS IN VIETNAM

American International Group	*Insurance*
Ashta International, Inc.	*Consultancy*
Baker Hughes	*Oil and Gas*
Coca Cola	*Soft Drinks*
Pepsico	*Soft Drinks*
Baker McKenzie	*Lawyers*
Carrier	*Air Conditioning Equipment*
Caterpillar	*Heavy Equipment Supplies*
DeMatteis Development Corp.	*Construction*
Connell Bros.	*Commodities*
General Electric	*Electrical Equipment*
Gemrusa	*Gems/Mining*
L.A. Land Resources	*Property*
Manolis Co. Asia	*Development and Architecture*
Esso/Exxon	*Petroleum*
Otis Elevator	*Lifts*
Philip Morris	*Tobacco and Food*
Spivey International	*Medical Supplies*
Vatico	*Consultancy*

SOME OF THE U.S. FIRMS DOING BUSINESS IN VIETNAM

VIIC	*Consultancy*
VINA-USA	*Financial Services for Overseas Vietnamese*
South Sea Tours	*Tourism*
Vietours Holidays	*Tourism*
Bank of America	*Banking*
Citibank	*Banking*
Russin Vecchi	*Lawyers*
American Trading Co.	*Trading*
Deloitte Touche Tohmatsu	*Accountants*
Digital Equipment Co.	*Computer Technology*
Apple Computer	*Computer Technology*
American President Lines	*Shipping*
Du Pont Far East Inc.	*Chemicals*
International Direct Marketing, Inc.	*Marketing*
Technomic Consultants	*Consultancy*
American Service Co.	*Consultancy*
Eastman Kodak	*Photographic Materials & Equipment*
IBM	*Computer Technology*
Motorola	*Telecommunications*
Leo Burnett Co.	*Advertising*
White & Case	*Lawyers*

The Post Normalization Outlook: A Level Playing Field

What will the normalization of relations between Washington and Hanoi mean for American companies doing—or planning to do—business in Vietnam?

Formal diplomatic ties will put American businesses on the same playing field with companies that have been reaping the fruits of Vietnamese investment for years, according to businesspeople I spoke to in both Saigon and Hanoi. The normalization of political relations between the two countries will boost commercial relations as well. The U.S. government will now be in a position to support its private sector, such as granting import-export credits. The aircraft and oil industries are to be the top beneficiaries of this, as they can now get official support from the U.S. Export-Import Bank and from the Overseas Private Investment Corporation. Vietnam's banking sector will become more strongly developed, as the Vietnamese acquire the advanced technology of U.S. banking.

U.S. exports to Vietnam have surged since the lifting of the embargo. American exports to Vietnam in 1994 topped US$172 million—.03 percent of U.S. total exports that year—up from a scant US$7 million in 1993, according to Vietnam's Trade Ministry. In 1994, Vietnamese exports to the U.S. climbed to US$52 million. Although that figure was only .01 percent of all U.S. imports in 1994, consider that in 1993, not even a mere ton of Vietnamese exports reached U.S. shores.

Vietnam is desperately seeking American technology, and as it now has access to the huge U.S. market for its goods, Vietnam will be in a position to purchase the computer equipment and technology it so direly needs.

Although most American businesspeople in Hanoi and Ho Chi Minh City are welcoming Clinton's decision, some of the smaller American firms that made big gambles by starting operations in Vietnam before even the embargo was lifted are a little worried—but just a little—of the normalization move being premature.

"The next move is most-favored trading nation status," said Ronald Van Wambeke, an American businessman whose construction and infrastructure company Asia Pacific International, Inc. opened a Ho Chi Minh City office eight months prior to the lifting of the embargo. "It's happening a little too quickly. We've been in place a long time and we're poised to make a killing here. And timing is everything. If the most-favored status happens too quickly, there are going to be a lot of cherry (American) bozos coming in here and throwing wrenches into the spokes we've taken years to connect to the wheels of this country."

At press time, there were 115 U.S. representative offices in Vietnam. Fifty-five were involved in trade and investment, while 28 others were doing business in the consultancy, legal and technical arenas.

What the Businessperson Should Know

Investors in Vietnam should be prepared to expect a lot more red tape than they're used to at home, but also considerably more concessions. The economy is hovering around a double-digit growth rate. Labor is phenomenally cheap, especially compared to labor costs in the U.S. The taxes are low. And there are options for 100 percent foreign ownership of your business.

But remember, Vietnam is a socialist state. Private enterprise in Vietnam is hardly fully developed. The move toward a free-market economy is still embryonic and is, at best, an experiment. Private businesses are operating under a Socialist political umbrella, deflecting all types of influences that may compromise its integrity. You'll want to grab for the country's economic opportunities, but be prepared for long delays.

You cannot, at the time of this writing, own land in Vietnam. You can lease but can't own. And the land you lease from the government may be claimed at some point in the future by its former owner(s). It could become a sticky litigation problem lasting years. You need to acquire licenses from the Vietnamese State Committee for Cooperation and Investment (SCCI) as well as local and other authorities, a process that can take months, even years, depending on the nature of your business. The structuring of joint ventures can be difficult and time-consuming as well.

But there are routes through the yarn ball, many of them.

The most important element is to establish trust with the Vietnamese you contact. The only way you'll get business transacted relatively smoothly is by networking with as many people as possible in Vietnam, both Vietnamese and foreigners who have already established businesses and/or contacts in Vietnam. The better you treat your hosts, the better you will be treated in return. It also pays to know what does and doesn't offend the Vietnamese during formal discussions. Here are some tips.

1) If you've made an appointment with a Vietnamese official—government or otherwise—know as much about the person as possible before your first meeting. If possible, get a snapshot of the principal individual before the meeting through a local guide, or other source, so you'll immediately recognize the person you're meeting with.

2) If the meeting involves more than one person, go directly to the principal participant upon being introduced and offer your business card. Presenting yourself to an assistant first is considered an insult. Present your cards based upon the chain of command.

3) Vietnamese men smoke like a train climbing Pike's Peak. Virtually all men in Vietnam smoke. You will undoubtedly be offered a cigarette. It is important to accept the cigarette, even if you don't smoke. (Many a self-righteous anti-smoker has taken up the habit after spending significant time in Vietnam.) If you don't smoke, simply place the cigarette on the table in front of you. You won't be offered another—not in contempt, but in respect.

4) Try not to cross your legs during the meeting, as, in Buddhism, pointing the sole of your foot at someone is a sign of disrespect. However, I've seen an increasing number of men cross their legs in both casual and business environments.

The key to getting things done rapidly in Vietnam is by developing trust and friendship with your Vietnamese contacts. Favors and gifts are also highly appreciated by Vietnamese businesspeople, and will more than likely be reciprocated by means of a smoother and swifter transaction of business.

The Dong vs. Dollar Debate

Vietnam's official currency—the dong, or VND, and sitting at 11,000 dong to the U.S. dollar—has been in a supremacy battle with the dollar for years, with various Vietnamese government decrees aimed at eliminating the use of the dollar—and all foreign currencies—making little impact into the widespread use of the American currency. About US$2 billion in notes are circulating throughout Vietnam.

In theory, foreign currencies can be legally used in only 30 government-authorized stores and duty- free shops in Vietnam. In reality, the story is far different. The dollar remains the preferred tender for all major transactions in Vietnam, such as for hotels and higher-priced consumer goods, and is accepted—and even preferred—by everyone from restaurateurs to cyclo drivers and shoe-shiners. In many transactions, the customer uses dollars and is given dong in return. Although it may seem confusing to tourists at first, you'll find that many street-level transactions involve a VND10,000 to US$1 exchange, simply because few will take out a calculator to struggle with such an insignificant difference in the exchange rates, particularly regarding small purchases.

Large purchases are regularly made in U.S. dollars, even by the Vietnamese themselves. High-ticket items such as motorbikes and home appliances are priced by the Vietnamese in "notes." The notes, of course, are US$100 bills. For instance, a new Honda Dream motorbike costs 23 notes, or US$2300. And most Vietnamese believe that the sellers of these items will only accept U.S. cash.

The dong has generally devalued against the dollar over the past 10 years, and though it has stabilized to a degree, the face value of dong notes remains ridiculously low. Regardless, many analysts here believe eventually the dong will replace the dollar as the principle—and perhaps the sole—currency of Vietnam. However, for the time being, the dollar is likely to be around for awhile. For the purchasers of motorbikes, automobiles, computers and houses, it's simply a pain in the ass to have to cart around barrels of cash.

The Dong or the Dollar?

In a dramatic and somewhat confusing shift in Vietnam's tourist and business travel economy, as of October 1, 1994, hotels in Vietnam have been required by law to accept only Vietnamese dong in payment for rooms. And a new decree in July 1996 required that all transactions in Vietnam be made in Vietnamese dong–on every level of monetary transactions. Whereas the American dollar had previously not only been the preferred currency for hoteliers, many establishments across the country–especially the finer ones–required payment in U.S. currency. The highest Vietnamese monetary note in wide circulation is the 50,000 dong bill, which, until recently, was about as readily available as a personal meeting with the pope. Sounds like a lot, but it's worth only US$4.54. That's it, folks. (The highest bank note in Vietnam is actually VND5 million–or US$454.50–but I've yet to see one of these bills and know of no one else who has either.) Lines at hotel cashiers' counters were feared to rival the queues at Ticketmaster for U2 tickets as clerks would be forced to count barrel-loads of dong notes, especially at the higher-ticket hotels.

The Dong or the Dollar?

The move is part of the Vietnamese government's effort to replace the U.S. dollar with the dong for most currency transactions. It's scaring some foreign businesses and may send some shivers up the spines of tourists planning to visit Vietnam, as the dollar has remained stable with the dong since the government began opening up the economy in the late 1980s. Foreigners generally have paid for higher-priced goods and services with the dollar during the past seven years. Many experts believe that as much as US$2 billion is floating around the country in U.S. dollar notes. Authorized businesses that have previously accepted or required U.S. dollars in payment are now required to reapply for their licenses. Banks and hotels will be required to set up more currency exchange booths. Airlines are continuing to accept U.S. dollars. Credit cards are still accepted at the time of this writing, but may become more difficult to use. The question is how vigorously the law will eventually be enforced.

Consider this: US$150 in "large" 5000 Vietnamese dong notes is about as thick as this book. That's just for one night in an upscale hotel. Well-heeled tourists planning on visiting Vietnam better pay a visit to a camping shop and get some advice on backpacks.

Vietnam's Copyright Laws

Up until September 1996 they were nonexistent. Simply anything creative that exists was fair game in Vietnam, from bootleg music CDs to photocopied ripoffs of Lonely Planet books being hawked by kids in the street. Although this is likely to remain the case for some time to come—regardless of the anticipated government decrees and a pending bilateral copyright agreement with the United States—the government has initiated moves to create legal tools for protecting the intellectual property rights of artists, musicians and film producers.

Decrees announced in September 1996 raised the maximum US$182 fine for copyright infringement to US$9100 (VND100 million). Computer software pirates also face these fines, as well as imprisonment under Vietnam's penalty code. Of course, the problem will be implementing these statutes. Hanoi admits that "the government cannot do everything. Artists, writers, singers and software developers should form their associations to protect their own rights." The Copyright Office of Vietnam is considering joining the Berne Convention on Protection of Literary and Artistic Work, which was adopted in Paris in 1896. The Berne Convention is the most important international convention protecting the rights of writers and artists. However, at press time, Vietnam has signed no copyright agreements with any foreign country.

The Copyright Office has claimed in defense of shunning these types of agreements the need for refining Vietnam's own copyright law, implementing it and enforcing it before joining any international conventions or signing agreements with other countries.

Vietnam is on the brink of approving a bilateral copyright agreement with the U.S., which would be the former country's first international agreement. Most analysts, both Vietnamese and foreign, agree that stricter copyright laws in Vietnam and vigorous enforcement of them would create more commercial opportunities for Vietnam—that protecting the rights of foreign works in Vietnam would increase the credibility of the business climate here and attract more foreign investment, as well as reveal the maturity of the Vietnamese market. In reality, it should be slow going.

AUTHOR'S OBSERVATION

Besides the high-profile measures the government of Vietnam has made in recent years to lure foreign investors, many of its fledgling and more subtle, recent decrees to placate potential investors tend not to make the headlines. But they're being noticed by companies that stand to make a lot of money in the consumer products sector. For instance, the government has begun a serious crackdown on counterfeit consumer products, including locally-produced and bottled fake Coca-Cola, fake Johnnie Walker Black and Red Label whiskey, Marlboro cigarettes, and counterfeit Lacoste shirts. Around Hanoi, and especially Saigon, it's been commonplace to find electronics outlets peddling cassette players with names suggestive of the real McCoys, brands called "Pensonic," "Sonv," and "Toshida." It's called intellectual property rights and, for years, they've been virtually entirely unprotected in major metropolitan areas throughout Southeast Asia. At least in Hanoi, it seems to be changing. The government has promised to be in a position to effectively enforce these rights within the next four years. Granted they have a tough task before them. Hanoi has even established an economics police unit to deal with the problem.

Vietnam's Patent and Trademark Bureau of the Chamber of Commerce and Industry, along with other state-owned enterprises, act as the patent attorney for foreign businesses that have registered their invention rights and industrial property in Vietnam. Much of the counterfeit products are available in Vietnam for a fraction of the cost of the originals. Because the Vietnamese have enjoyed greater buying powers over the last few years, there's been a tremendous surge in patent and trademark applications by foreign firms doing or planning to do business in Vietnam. More than 50,000 trademarks have been registered in Vietnam—80 of them by foreign companies. It's turned out to be an overwhelming amount for the government to process. In 1994, the Ministry of Science, Technology and Environment received nearly 8500 applications to register service trademarks, patents and industrial designs. This was up from 6617 from the previous year. The system has become bottlenecked, a system which has always been marred in red tape.

AUTHOR'S OBSERVATION

Much of the counterfeit merchandise comes from abroad. "Pensonic" products come from China. And other counterfeits, such as bogus Hennessey cognac smack so much of the original, right down to the seal, it would be impossible to make this product in Vietnam, whose own domestically produced liquor caps virtually disintegrate after the seal is broken. (If you purchase Vietnamese spirits, be prepared to consume them in one sitting). Additionally, imitation and substandard medications are rampant in Vietnam.

To its credit, Vietnam became a member of the Geneva-based World Intellectual Property Organization, an arm of the U.N. The country became affiliated with the International Patent Corporation Treaty. Vietnam was also a participant at the Paris Convention on patents, trademarks and other forms of industrial property protection. After the U.S. embargo was dropped, another 200 U.S. companies applied for patent protection, bringing the number of American applications to nearly 1500. So far, there is no copyright protection for film or literary works in Vietnam. These are areas that will have to be addressed in attracting hundreds of foreign cultural imports.

Top 10 Tips for U.S. Investors

1) The first step U.S. companies should take is to get a grasp on the legal environment and the market for their products in Vietnam. Companies need to study the legal framework of each specific field they want to invest in.

2) Companies must prepare feasibility studies and prepare a list of potential local partners. Feasibility studies should be jointly composed by the company and its local partner.

3) The laws in Vietnam are continuously changing and evolving. This presents one of the greatest risks for U.S. investors. U.S. investors should always have contingency plans for changes in laws, especially those pertaining to taxes.

4) The gap between the time for obtaining an investment license and the time for projects becoming operational in Vietnam could be a wide one.

5) Carefully choose the form of investment. Business in Vietnam can be done as a wholly owned foreign company, as a joint venture with one or more local partners, or through business cooperation contracts with local companies. The Vietnamese government might prohibit foreign companies from certain types of investments.

6) Consider foreign exchange issues. If a company establishes a manufacturing or production facility in Vietnam to produce goods that will be purchased locally, it should consider exporting a percentage of its production to obtain hard currency for the purpose of profit remittance.

7) FYI: Most of the foreign loans procured by joint ventures in Vietnam have offshore security.

8) In Vietnam, it is extremely difficult to use land use rights as collateral security for a project. Land regulations in Vietnam have yet to be clearly clarified.

9) State-owned companies generally have more experience, resources and bigger pools of labor than do the relatively newer private firms.

10) Vietnam, at the time of this writing, is most interested in investment in infrastructure projects.

List of Goods Prohibited to Export and Import

The import of used electronics, electrical equipment, motorcycles and automobiles is prohibited by the government.

1) Prohibited Exports: Weapons, ammunition, explosive materials, military equipment, antiques, certain drugs, toxic chemicals, round timber, sawed-up timber, kinds of semiprocessed wood products, rattan material, wild and rare animals and plants.

AUTHOR'S NOTE

In special cases, the import of goods belonging to the above list can be permitted by the prime minister with a written statement. The prohibition of export of wild animals to protect the environment is guided by a written statement from both the Ministry of Forestry and the Ministry of Science, Technology and Environment. The government also says that to avoid being "backward" about industry, complete equipment as well as separate machines being used and valued from US$100,000 or more must be checked by the leading offices (Provincial People Committees or Ministries) of the business and the Quality Standard Measurement Office; a license to import will be issued by the Ministry of Commerce. The Ministry of Commerce, the Ministry of Home Affairs and the Customs Office will together approve a concrete list of special vehicles and automobiles addressed under Article 11.8. After making an agreement with the Ministry of Commerce and the Ministry of Foreign Affairs, the Customs Office will apply guidelines for the article "Property." It all sounds pretty complicated.

2) Prohibited Imports: Weapons, ammunition, explosive materials, military equipment, kinds of drugs, toxic chemicals, reactionary and debauched cultural products, firecrackers, "toys harmful to children's personalities or social order" (I wonder if this includes Barbie dolls and squirt guns), cigarettes (except quantity fixed in personal luggage), used consumer goods (including sewn or weaved goods), under 12-seat automobiles, motorcycles and motor and non-motor tricycles, family-used electronics and electric equipment (except quantity fixed in personal luggage), material that may cause environmental harm or "other inconvenience" (such as used accessories, used tires, abolished products—abolished materials are also classified as prohibited imports—automobiles and vehicles with steering wheels on the right side (including accessories and dismantlements)—except some special vehicles and automobiles having narrow circulation.

Employment Opportunities in Vietnam

Okay, so you don't have the big bucks to get a business going in Vietnam—and perhaps you punch a cash register for Merle's Auto Parts and Custom Aluminum Siding in Waco, Texas, where the opportunities of being assigned to the firm's new rep office in Ho Chi Minh City are about as realistic as an ATF agent being elected mayor. How to get a job in Vietnam?

A rapidly expanding number of Westerners are living and working in Vietnam—at last count more than 10,000 in Ho Chi Minh City alone. But most of these folks represent corporations of their native countries, both large and small, some fly-by-night in-country for a quick kill (like call-back companies), others huge international oil and consumer products concerns in town for the long haul. Most of the lads and lasses under their employ are young, green and were sent to Vietnam with about as much knowledge of Vietnamese culture and language as the chairman of your local Young Republican's Club. Frankly, many of these pubescent expats are in their positions for one of two reasons: to impress their friends, or no one else would go. More on that in a bit.

Vietnam didn't open up for foreign (noncommunist) job-seekers until after the demise of the Soviet Union in 1990. Until then, foreign workers in Vietnam were mainly composed of Soviet and other East Bloc engineers and technicians working in Vietnam's infrastructure, oil and defense sectors. Even today, years after the Russians packed it in and bundled up for the Aeroflot jaunt back up north to the ice pack, Westerners may still be greeted (usually taunted) in the provinces with less than affectionate calls of "Xien Lo" ("Soviet") from the children, sometimes to the accompaniment of rocks and sticks. East Bloc workers weren't known as appreciative guests, and regarded their positions as lateral moves from the tundra to the frying pan.

These days it's a different story. Finnish hippies are opening gyms. Viet Kieu are returning from Dallas and starting up barbecued ribs joints. Lost souls of all ages are teaching English, both in Vietnam's schools and privately. Fledgling journalists are taking stabs at contributing to Vietnam's expanding number of English-language publications. Bad art directors from in-house ad agencies in Des Moines are finding new life as creative directors at Saigon's ad houses. Burned-out vets are working as tourist guides in the Mekong Delta. Doctors are finding work with NGOs and private evacuation and medical assistance firms. Airline pilots who've ditched an Airbus or two at Air France are flying the friendly skies of Vietnam Airlines. And, of course, foreign lawyers are trickling in to represent them all.

The two principal things to keep in mind if you intend to come to Vietnam to work are these: the experience won't make you rich and it probably won't help your CV, or resume, much. In fact, if you're already on a career path that would normally and decidedly miss Vietnam as a pit stop, you may be doing yourself more harm than good by venturing out from the fold. If you're a young management wannabe and you get posted to run a company's small branch or rep office in Vietnam, the people-management (or money-management) experience will indeed be helpful—especially in money-management, as Vietnam's financial environment is still quite primitive, providing raw, roll-your-sleeves-up commercial experience. But if you're in high-tech or any other cutting-edge field, you may as well go back to coloring books.

As far as your resume is concerned, if it's got Vietnam on it, the fact is that most employers back home will simply say, "So what?" And if your working experience in Vietnam does appeal to a prospective employer back home, the chances are you'll be sent back to Vietnam, and only Vietnam, to utilize it for your new company.

In many fields, time spent in Vietnam is simply time spent away from the latest trends and developments in that particular occupation, as well as time spent away from those who might be useful in propelling your career back at home—if that's what you ultimately intend to pursue. Vietnam, for instance, is an instant black mark to corporate headhunters. "Two years is the maximum time someone in journalism, marketing or advertising should spend in Vietnam," said one Sydney, Australia-based job broker. "After that you're no longer relevant. Any job that you seek after having worked in Vietnam would have to have some relevance to Vietnam, where your knowledge of Vietnam would be a distict commodity to that company. Otherwise, why would anyone care?" Additionally, your Vietnam experience may simply be a red flag to a prospective employer with no business interests there, who may simply think that you're an unfocused flake, someone who'll take off to teach English or take yoga lessons in Kashmir two months into a management training course.

That being said, if I haven't thoroughly demoralized you, there are work opportunities in Vietnam. Besides, you may have no intention of returning home to future corporate stardom. But if you come to Vietnam not having been sent here by someone to work, you'll have to start in the mail room—teaching English.

English teaching positions abound in Hanoi and Ho Chi Minh City (privately, at universities and at the burgeoning number of private language centers)—particularly for native English speakers, and even more so for American English speakers. There has been a marked trend in the evolution of English-as-a-second-language in Vietnam toward American English, and many Vietnamese versed in English are boastfully proud of their "American accents." American and Canadian teachers are prized by the universities, as well as by upscale Vietnamese families seeking tutors for their children. Why these children should say "schedule" rather than "shedule," or "can't" rather than "cawn't" is a mystery, but a reality nonetheless. And the only qualification would-be English teachers seem to need these days is the ability to speak English. Although some schools and others require teaching certificates of teaching candidates, many more don't—although it would certainly help to have a bachelor's degree.

The pay isn't good, usually US$2–$3 an hour at the government universities and up to US$5 an hour teaching privately. These jobs are typically not advertised, so the longer you stay in town and the more you poke around, the better your chances of landing a job. Presently, these jobs are only semilegal for those with a tourist visa, as you'll need a business visa to officially be permitted to teach in Vietnam. Although this seems to be only intermittently enforced, business visas are available through sponsoring universities and private language centers. Also, it has been relatively easy in the last few years to get a business visa through travel agents, even without any business purpose in the country. However, at press time, the government was coming down on this, and applicants are being required to more thoroughly disclose their "business" activities/intentions before a business visa will be issued.

Barnstormers Wanted

The one occupation in Vietnam for foreigners that seems to be immune from potential resume blemishes is that of an airline pilot. A Boeing 767 is flown the same way over Danang as it is over Denver or Amsterdam.

With the replacement of Vietnam Airlines' (VN) fleet of ancient Soviet Tupalov bolt-buckets with modern, digitized Boeings and Airbuses has come the need for folks who know how to fly them. While there are many Vietnamese first officers in the cockpits of these new aircraft, virtually all scheduled commercial flights are flown by foreigners. Vietnam Airlines has only about a half-dozen Vietnamese chief pilots for the six new Boeing 767s and 10 A320s the airline flies. Each plane requires three or four teams of pilots (one pilot and one first officer) to keep it in the air. The A320s alone require a roster of at least 40 chief pilots.

VN's fleet in all requires 90 chief pilots—one reason why the airline has hired 70 foreign pilots. Although we will eventually see the "Vietnamization" of VN's flight crews, it won't be any time soon. To apply, fax your resume (sans cropdusting experience), salary history and requirements, a brief essay (no more than 10 words) about what Vietnam looks like from 40,000 feet, and notarized autobiography to 84-4-8273003—and see what flies.

Ho Chi Minh City

HO CHI MINH CITY

Rush hour in central Saigon makes traffic in Los Angeles seem like a Utah interstate highway.

HO CHI MINH CITY IN A CAPSULE

Formerly known as Saigon...Still called Saigon by most...Renamed after reunification in 1975...but central district is still called Saigon...population of about 5 million...Once called Paris of the East because of its French colonial architecture and sidewalk cafes...Much more open than conservative Hanoi to the north...Free enterprise abounds on the streets...City is about 70 km from the South China Sea...Vietnam's economic reforms are most evident in Ho Chi Minh City...Tourism here is booming...Compared with other SE Asian cities, there is little crime–but it's rising rapidly.

145

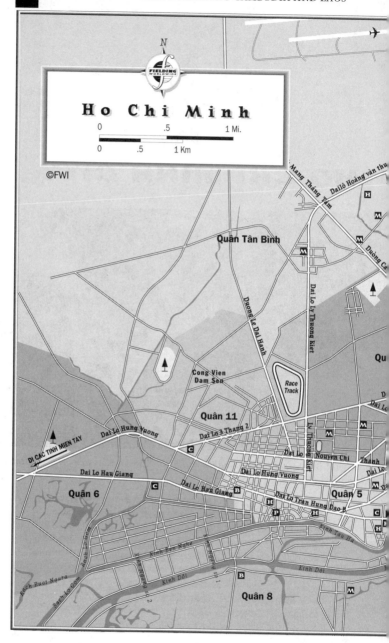

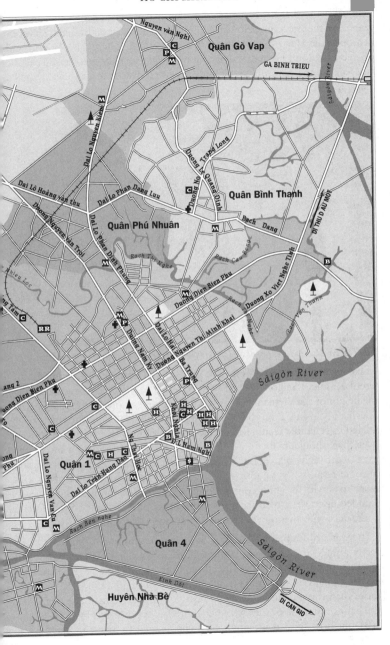

This is a city that has been called no fewer than seven names through the years, and the latest one, Ho Chi Minh City, is about as embraced by its population as the Marxism that tagged it. People who live here call it Saigon, and people who don't live here call it Saigon. In fact, so many people still call the city Saigon, the government allows the central district to be officially called Saigon.

The Opera House in central Saigon is the district's social hub on Sunday.

Like its neighbor to the west, Phnom Penh in Cambodia (although for different reasons), Saigon swelled with refugees from the countryside during the height of the Vietnam War as North Vietnamese forces were toppling the South and closing in on the capital. After the fall of Saigon, the city actually started to resemble Hanoi for a while—with its glum-faced citizenry looking over their shoulders for someone to tout, but instead catching the narrow gaze of the secret police. But all that's changed and it's "Happy Days Again" in some respects for Saigonese, who are starting to come out of the woodwork to service the burgeoning number of Western tourists who have descended upon the city in relative swarms in recent years, and to join foreign companies with their newly acquired language and technical skills.

There is no doubt that bustling Saigon is the industrial, business and—many argue—the emerging cultural heart of Vietnam. There are thriving markets, discos and eateries. The ethnic Chinese of Cholon (Hoa) are again exerting their economic might. Before the fall of Saigon, the Hoa controlled more than three-quarters of the industry of South Vietnam and nearly half the banks. After 1975, they were persecuted as opportunists by the Vietnamese—but now they're accepted, even encouraged to invest by the government. In fact, Hanoi sees Hoa prosperity as integral in its efforts at moving toward a free-market system. Of course, the move toward free enterprise has its inevitable victims. It's estimated that hundreds of thousands of Vietnamese in Saigon alone are unemployed.

In terms of lifestyle, Saigon is like the Southern California of Vietnam. If you're real lucky (or unlucky, depending upon your viewpoint) you might catch a glimpse of a young Saigonese skateboarding along a rutted sidewalk boogying to an old American rock anthem blasting in his headset.

The people of Saigon are remarkably friendly to Americans, considering the horrific experiences most had to endure just a generation ago. In fact, once it's gleaned you're not a Russian, you're still likely to be followed down the street by a posse of curious children.

Even during the short period I was away from the metropolis between November 1994 and June 1995, Saigon's changes were vast. New sidewalks now line Tran Hung Dao Street and other major arteries. No more of that Bangkok fear of falling into a 10-foot pit. You can actually get around in high-heels these days.

Elegant new hotels and apartment buildings have sprung up on Le Loi and Nguyen Hue Streets. Two golf courses opened in the suburbs of Song Be and Thu Duc. Trendy eateries and nightclubs have opened along Thi Sach Street. There are more cars on the roads—and more new motorbikes.

This place is changing daily. If you get into town and are a little confused and want to get pointed in the right direction, drop Do Trong Tu, one of the best local guides, a line at *FAX: 84-8-8231071.*

Backpacking in Saigon

Tay ba lo. That's the local Vietnamese name for the increasing number of Western backpackers plodding HCMC streets. The Vietnamese know the backpackers have few dong and are mainly interested in Vietnamese culture and sights on a tight budget. *Tay ba lo* range from students to teachers to unemployed sheet metal workers. But the one thing in common they all have in HCMC is where they eat and sleep. Most eat at small food stalls for around 5000 dong and stay in guesthouses in District 1 on Le Lai, Calmette, Pham Ngu Lao, De Tham and Bui Vien Streets. Guesthouses on these avenues cost in the US$5–$15 range. If you're lucky, you may be able to get by for as little as US$2–$3 a day for accommodations in HCMC.

Getting around by cyclo is cheap, although you must be a shrewd negotiator. Agree on the price beforehand, and make sure that both you and the cyclo driver understand the amount. There is an increasing problem in cities such as HCMC, Hanoi, Danang, Hue, etc., with drivers demanding additional payment after they've dropped you at your destination, saying it was the agreed price. They will not accept the money you give them, nor will

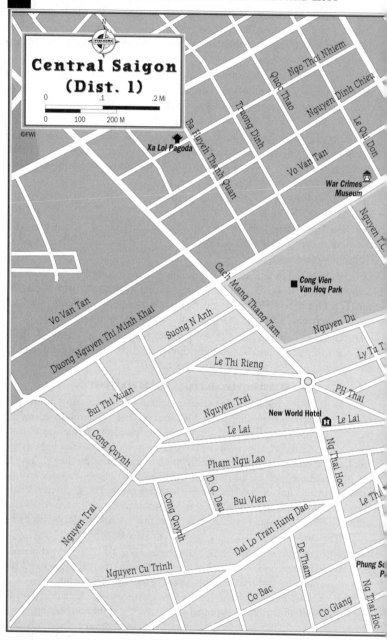

Central Saigon (Dist. 1)

0   .1   .2 Mi

0   100   200 M

©FWI

Ngo Thoi Nhiem

Quoc Thao

Truong Dinh

Nguyen Dinh Chieu

Le Qui Don

Ba Huyeh Thanh Quan

Xa Loi Pagoda

Vo Van Tan

War Crimes Museum

Nguyen T.C.

Cach Mang Thang Tam

Cong Vien Van Hoq Park

Vo Van Tan

Duong Nguyen Thi Minh Khai

Suong N Anh

Nguyen Du

Ly Tu T

Le Thi Rieng

Bui Thi Xuan

Nguyen Trai

PH Thai

Cong Quynh

Le Lai

New World Hotel   Le Lai

Pham Ngu Lao

Ng Thai Hoc

D. Q. Dau

Cong Quynh

Bui Vien

Le Thi

Nguyen Trai

Dai Lo Tran Hung Dao

De Tham

Nguyen Cu Trinh

Phung S Pa

Co Bac

Co Giang

Ng Thai Hoc

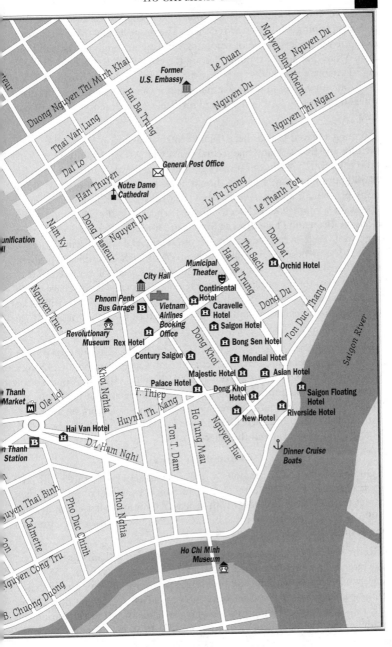

they leave, but will instead stand around like a cheated card player, sulking and complaining while a crowd gathers. The point here is to gain sympathy from the bystanders, some of whom may insist you cough up the additional cash. More than likely, though, among the crowd will be an English-speaking Vietnamese who knows precisely the scam the cyclo driver is up to. In all probability, you will find the Vietnamese on your side, and the cyclo driver will end up "losing face." The loss of his face is preferable to the loss of your cash.

Renting a bicycle is also cheap. Many rental shops are on or near the above-mentioned streets. Many bike rental firms will ask for 10,000 dong a day (about US$1), but you can usually get this price down, sometimes to as low as 5000 dong per day. But you should never have to pay more than 10,000 dong per day for a bicycle. Make sure the tires are full before you depart. If you want a motorbike (150cc or under), check out the shops and hotels along **De Tham** and **Pham Ngu Lao Streets** in District 1. Remember that renting a motorbike over 50cc requires an international driver's license, and over 70cc a Vietnamese license (although proof of such a certificate probably won't be asked for by rental shops). In most cases, you will be asked to leave your passport for the duration of your rental. No sweat, GI. Just have a photocopy made to keep on yourself as well as your original visa. This will be appropriate documentation should you be stopped by the police or get into an accident.

Many foreigners can get by in Vietnam for as little as US$500 per month. In HCMC, most backpackers frequent the Sinh Cafe, Pham Ngu Lao Street, where meals can be had for as little as 5000 dong (US$0.45). A bottled soft drink will cost you another 2000 dong. Around the area of De Tham and Pham Ngu Lao Streets there are maybe a dozen restaurants or food stalls with similar prices. Included here are the Lotus Cafe, Kim Cafe, Long Phi, Thang Com Binh Dan and the Saigon Cafe.

Rooms for Rent

On Pham Ngu Lao Street alone, there are at least 14 guesthouses with 110 rooms for rent. De Tham Street has six guesthouses and 30 rooms. Bui Vien Street features 13 guesthouses with at least 41 rooms at last check in mid-1996. The vast majority of these businesses are unlicensed—some estimates say as high as 85 percent.

In the sanctioned hostels and hotels in the De Tham/Pham Ngu Lao area, the price for a double room with fan and private bath runs about US$10 per day, while a room with air conditioning, some furniture and a refrigerator runs at US$15 a day. These are steep rates for a backpacker, but they generally only last during the high season between January and April. During the rainy season, the rates drop, usually from US$10 to eight dollars and from

US$15 to $12 a day. Evening arrivals to the area may find comfortable rooms for as little as US$5 a day. Private guesthouses have the luxury of being able to slash their prices when the demand calls for it, but the hotels aren't permitted to do so.

But the high season also brings some great bargains if you really want to get down-and-dirty. The number of backpackers in this small section of HCMC rises to nearly 400 new arrivals a day during the high-season months, and some enterprising homeowners have gotten creative with their use of space. Additional beds and "sedge mats" are laid out in many private homes on the side streets off Pham Ngu Lao and De Tham. Families utilize every square inch of their homes to accommodate the overflow, and travelers will find bargains at these homes for as little as US$1 per night on laid-out sedge mats. Backpackers can share small rooms in these homes for about US$2 per person a day. Floor space is rented out—even closets and furniture.

It's a snap to find these places. Just hang out at Kim Cafe for a BGI or two and the touts will spring from the woodwork. They range from cyclo drivers to chewing gum sellers, who make a 10 percent commission on first-time arrivals and 5 percent on repeat business.

The guesthouses will do your laundry and usually have bicycles and small motorbikes for rent: motorbikes can be had for US$5–$6 per day, and bicycles for US$1 a day.

As the De Tahm/Bui Ven area began evolving as a backpackers' haven, the number of coffee shops and cafes proliferated. Formerly, there were only two "in" spots—Kim Cafe and Sinh Cafe. Now, there are no fewer than 15 cafes and coffee shops in the area. Meals typically range in the 10,000 dong (US$1) range and are generally rather tasty, representing the best food bargains found in the city. The service is invariably friendly (with the competition, it has to be) and employees can at least speak restaurant English.

Guesthouse Tour Services

Many of the guesthouses along De Tham/Bui Ven/Pham Ngu Lao Streets offer tour services in addition to accommodations—or they work in association with operators working in their lobbies. Tours from two to 15 days can be booked—at amazingly low prices. Nearly 10 itineraries are offered. For instance, a 15-day tour of Saigon/Dalat/Nha Trang/Quy Nhon/Hoi An/Danang/Hue/Vinh/Hanoi/Halong Bay ranges from US$220–$330, depending on your mode of transportation. Car tours are the most costly, while going via a 24-seat bus can cost as little as US$100 per person. Day trips to such places as the Cu Chi Tunnels and My Tho runs for as little as US$8, and overnight packages to the Mekong Delta and the Vung Tau peninsula run a scant US$18. But, beware of these "packages." Like the old saying—you get what you pay for. Travelers have reported being abandoned during the middle of the night. They wake up at some Quy Nhon flea bag only to discover that the guide and driver have split.

Other Services

Laundries, photo shops, souvenir stores and book "rental" shops have sprung up along the backpacker streets—all of which are not nearly as expensive as similar kiosks and shops found on the more fashionable streets of Nguyen Hue and Dong Khoi. You can get your laundry done on the side streets for as little as 1500 dong an article, depending on the material. T-shirts, film, Chinese-pirated CDs and souvenirs can be had at heavily discounted prices. And, yes, you can even rent books here—for about 4000 dong per day.

Insider Tip: Saigontourist's 'Backpackages'

After years of ignoring the only consistent contributor to Vietnam's tourist industry—the backpacker's dollar—Saigontourist has finally gotten around to a tour booking desk at 187 Pham Ngu Lao Street in the heart of Ho Chi Minh City's backpackers' mecca. Saigontourist says it's an attempt to lure the increasing numbers of budget travelers stopping in Saigon.

The tour desk is offering one-day tours of Cu Chi Tunnels-Tay Ninh for US$4 per person and My Tho for US$8 per person. Two-day tours of My Tho-Soc Trang-Can Tho cost US$18 per person, and two-day tours of Binh Chau-Tan Phu run US$22 per person. Accommodations are included. Also offered is a five-day, four-night tour of My Tho-Vinh Long-Can Tho-Chau Doc-Ha Tien. As you might imagine in this newly capitalist cutthroat market, other tour desks in the backpacker zone, such as Sinh Cafe and Ben Thanh Tourist, put out identical packages before lunchtime.

A Word About Shopping in HCMC

Souvenir stores and kiosks abound in Saigon. If you're looking for simple souvenirs for your friends and relatives back home, it's best to find them on the street rather than in the fancy, ornamental and expensive shops that line Le Loi Boulevard and Dong Khoi streets in District 1. (See the "Shopping in Ho Chi Minh City" section in this chapter.) Although the souvenirs aren't as finely crafted as those found in the shops, they are incredibly cheap. Printed T-shirts go for as little as US$1. Small, handcrafted wooden boats run from between US$5–$50 dollars. These are incredible bargains. Not to mention the Coke cans that have been crafted into the uncannily realistic shapes of warplanes and helicopters. (These can be had for the remarkable price of about 10,000 apiece!) A lot of it, of course depends upon your ability to bargain. You can also purchase collections of ancient stamps, coins and silk paintings at astoundingly low prices. But remember something: Never pay anything more than 50 percent of the asking price.

JUNK SHOPPING: 'THE MENEST SOB IN THE VALLEY'

Take a stroll down Dong Khoi Street and not only will you find the good stuff, but the bad stuff, as well. Numerous vendors offer for sale trinkets they say are spoils from the war—such as Zippo engraved lighters and GI dogtags with shibboleths such as "Yea though I walk through the valley of death I will fear no evil, because I'm the menest SOB in the valley." The bad English invariably gives the items away as fake. But the fake stuff may be what you're looking for. Rolexes from the Vietnam War era may be real or fake. Some are obvious, others dangerously less so, as the asking prices usually start at about US$100 or more. Mont Blanc and Parker fountain pens can be had. Are they fake or real? Or, check out the old Russian box cameras like Praktica, Rolleiflex and Rollei. Interested? Before you buy, shoot a roll of film and have it developed. And mark the camera.

But remember the bargains are becoming fewer in HCMC, as the number of tourists continues to escalate. Prices for local art and sculpture in both HCMC and Saigon are spiraling. One artist in Hanoi, Nguyen Quan, who only just two short years ago was peddling his art to diplomats and business people looking for cheap souvenirs to bring home, has witnessed his art double and even triple in price—and it continues to ascend at a remarkable rate. "The artists in Vietnam now have the freedom to paint subjects other than peasants, workers and soldiers," he said.

Art in Saigon and Hanoi has taken on distinct Western influences, mostly in the European abstract style. The ban on painting nudes has also been lifted. Paintings that sold for as little as US$300 a year ago are now fetching US$1000 or more. And this is in a country where the per capita annual income hovers around US$200. Private galleries in both HCMC and Hanoi are proliferating to capitalize on the demands of foreign tourists and businesspeople.

Lacquerware is a better bargain in HCMC than in Hanoi, namely because most of it is produced in the Saigon area. You can pick up some of the smaller vases and pots for under a dollar if you bargain hard. More expensive items include four-panel wall hangings that start at about US$40.

Vietnamese silk is generally thinner than Chinese and Thai silk, but the quality can be good. Most prices start at US$14 per two meters.

Crime in Ho Chi Minh City

During the past few years, petty theft has surged dramatically in Saigon, particularly in the most touristed areas. One night on Dong Khoi street, I was mugged by a transvestite who relieved me of my US$20 Bangkok Rolex. It was totally professional. She/he posed as a drunken hooker on a dark street and grabbed my arm and crotch. I pushed the lady-boy on her ass and continued my evening stroll, noticing my watch was gone 15 minutes later. A professional hit. Like the Vietnamese who are victims of such crime–and know better– I didn't bother reporting the crime to the police.

On another occasion, in broad daylight in the heart of the city's financial district on Nguyen Hue Street, I watched as a gang of youths–both male and female–accosted a shocked Western businessman, stealing his watch and briefcase to the amusement of dozens of onlookers.

The Vietnamese themselves will not get involved. Pleas to nearby traffic policemen–who may have witnessed an incident–will invariably fall on deaf ears. "I'm a traffic policeman," is the typical response. "I deal with traffic offenders; I don't chase thieves."

Until a few years ago, HCMC police periodically made sweeps of petty street criminals and hookers and hoarded them off to "reeducation camps" in the suburbs. Soon, though, the thugs and prostitutes were back on the streets. The crackdowns are far less frequent these days. And victims who report street crime must supply a photo of themselves and pay US$2 for a crime report, often standing in line with other victims. The thieves are rarely caught.

Most street punks operate on motorbikes, where they snatch satchels, purses and briefcases from unsuspecting foreigners as they walk on the streets, ride a cyclo, or ride pillion on other motorbikes. Pickpockets favor hanging around major hotels, such as the Floating Hotel, the Rex and the New World.

Dung, the owner of Saigon's best foreign-language newsstand across from the Rex, witnesses daylight street crime frequently. "It's gotten really bad in the last year," he told me. "Robbers don't care about being seen robbing tourists. In fact, they want to be seen. All these kids have been watching Hong Kong and American movies for the last couple of years, and they want to be like the criminals they see on the screen. It's a macho thing to make a broad daylight hit."

Crime in Ho Chi Minh City

The rule of thumb is to stay off the streets after 9 p.m. in Saigon. The police, whose presence on the streets is highly visible during daylight hours, seem to go into hibernation after dark. At any time, if you're wearing a money belt or fanny pack, keep at least one hand on it. And clutch it rather tightly. The same goes for anything else you're carrying. Thugs and ruffians have no scruples, particularly concerning women, the largest victim category of street theft. It pays to be big, or at least act big. The more intimidating you appear, the least likely you are to become a victim. Army boots, a few visits to the gym, and a tight black Megadeath T-shirt can't hurt. If you're strolling, do it with friends. If you're a photographer with a monopod, carry the case with you on the streets. Sure, it's for encasing your monopod—but it looks (and feels) like a billy club. Scares the hell out of the locals.

The police do make arrests, but they offer better advice. (Vietnamese crime victims know they have a better chance of recovering their stolen items by waiting at home for a call from the thieves, and offering cash for the return of their papers, valuables and identity cards.) To one Japanese businessman who had his cellular phone swiped, the police simply suggested that he phone his own number and ask how much money the crooks wanted for its return.

What to See and Do in Ho Chi Minh City

Places that are must-see in the city generally include the Reunification Palace, formerly the Presidential Palace; the War Museum, which is filled with photographs and memorabilia, including exhibits that depict the horrors of the Vietnam War; the Historical Museum, containing some noteworthy archaeological artifacts and a beautiful bronze Buddha that dates from about the fifth century A.D.; the former U.S. embassies, and the Cu Chi tunnels, which were originally built during Vietnam's battle for independence from the French. The tunnels were greatly enlarged during the war with the U.S. to accommodate the Viet Cong, and contain living quarters, kitchens and surgical areas for the wounded.

War Remnants Museum (formerly American War Crimes Museum) ★★

28 Vo Van Tan, Dist. 3. Located on Vo Van Tan Street near the intersection of Le Qui Don Street.

Open daily from 7:30–11:45 a.m. and 1:30–4:45 p.m.

This may be the most popular attraction in Saigon. Built on the site of the former Information Service Office of Saigon University, the museum exhibits a slew of photos depicting events of the Vietnam War in general, and alleged and real American atrocities in particular. Many of the shots are absolutely gruesome. Some of the events covered here are the My Lai massacre and the effects of Napalm, Agent Orange, and phosphorous bombs on the Vietnamese people. The museum has been remodeled since my last visit—it seems they've done away with the deformed human fetuses that were once displayed. Outside the museum is a collection of war materiel, U.S. choppers and tanks. Here you can see a bunch of downed trainer fighters, light aerial and slow bombers that would hit their targets accurately, but weren't very fast. There's an array of machine guns from both sides of the war—

weapons in poor condition. It's all just a testament to a war that, if one didn't know any better, looks like it may have taken place during the last century.

Americans are depicted as murderers, without any real perspective that war itself is hell. You won't see photos here of U.S. GIs giving candy bars to VC children while they sit in Bob Hope's lap. There are a lot of photos depicting carnage all over the place and weapons mounted on pods. Some of the stuff looks pretty bizarre, like microwaves at one of the first Burger Kings. In another room there are many aerial photos depicting bombardment from B-52s—also some evidence here that looks like animal experiments being performed by U.S. scientists—DNA stuff that was conducted by Americans, genetically altering animals to be Robocops trained to destroy the VC.

The worst sight are the photos of babies hideously deformed, the alleged consequences of exposure to Agent Orange. Most of the material here is pure propaganda, but there's a lot to be said for the proportion of it that is correct. Also here are prison and torture cells where VC prisoners were held—cement torture chambers. Scrawled words cover the walls. Above the cells are gridlike floors where the captors could observe the torture below. The Huey helicopter in the courtyard is in good shape. All in all, despite the fetuses, this is not an unnerving sight. Worth the visit.

AUTHOR'S NOTE

The state curators have conspicuously toned down the anti-American rhetoric at this museum in the past couple of years, from photo captions to the actual name of the place. On my arrival in Vietnam at the start of 1994, the place was called the American War Crimes Museum, and it left little doubt that Iran wasn't alone in its condemnation of the U.S. as the Great Satan. Phrases and captions such as "M-16 typical of that issued to the imperialist American aggressor troops" have been changed to simply "M-16." The new name of the exhibition grounds, the War Remnants Museum, sounds like a family run carpet warehouse outlet in Queens rather than a propagandized testament to the horror of war. The times, they are a changin'.

Botanical Gardens

At the end of Le Duan Boulevard, where it meets Nguyen Binh Khiem.

There were once thousands of species of beautiful orchids and other flowers here, although the war did a lot to dilapidate the place. It's still worth a visit though, if for nothing other than the small zoo on the grounds. The gardens are 130 years old, while the zoo features rare and endangered Vietnamese indigenous animals, as well as some exotic animals from overseas. A couple of big cats, lots of birds and a pair of Komodo dragons donated by the Indonesian government. Admission: 10,000 dong.

Central Market   ★★

Ben Than Market, at Le Loi and Pham Hong Thai streets.

Here's where you'll feel the economic pulse of the "new" Vietnam. This is Saigon's Ben Thanh, and it's definitely a must-see if you're going to hit the market scene—there are maybe 40 or so sprinkled about Saigon. Here you'll find an incredible array of imported goods, including the usual assault of Japanese electronic goods. VCRs are becoming popular—as are the peripherals that come along with them, namely Hong Kong skin flicks.

Cholon ★★

District 5.

Talk about the economic pulse of the new Vietnam. This is Saigon's Chinatown, where nearly 400,000 ethnic Chinese are helping to breathe new fire into the Vietnamese economy. There are also pagodas here. The beautiful **Thien Hau Temple** was built in 1825 and is dedicated to the cult of Thien Hau, the goddess of the sea and protector of fishermen. The **Quan Am Pagoda**, built in 1816, has some incredible ceramic illustrations of traditional legends. The **Phuoc An Hoi Quan Pagoda** may be the most elaborately decorated in the city. There's also **Cha Tam Church**, where South Vietnamese President Ngo Dinh Diem fled during his escape in 1963, and the Taoist shrine **Khanh Van Nam Vien Pagoda**. Also check out the produce market of **Binh Tay**.

Historical Museum ★

Open 8–11:30 a.m. and 1–4 p.m. Tues.–Fri. Small admission fee.

This was formerly called the National Museum and is the best place to step back into Vietnam's 4000-year-old history. In addition to the art of the early Chinese and Indonesians, the museum houses artifacts from the Bronze Age and the Dongson period (3500 B.C.–A.D.100). The building was built in 1928 and now also contains items related to the early communist presence in Vietnam. There's a bronze standing Buddha from the fifth century and artifacts from the country's various hilltribes. Also look for Khmer and pre-Angkorean statuary of the Funan period. See if you can get a guide. At last check, none of the labeling was in English.

Notre Dame Cathedral

Opposite the GPO, facing Dong Khoi Street.

Built in 1883 and designed by the French architect Bouvard, this Catholic church (near Tu Do Street) is constructed of granite and red brick. It's quite a magnificent sight in contrast with its surroundings. Tu Do Street was the old red-light district in Saigon.

Cha Tam Church

25 Hoc Lac, on the western end of Tran Hung Dao.

This is the famous church where South Vietnamese President Ngo Dinh Diem and his brother Ngo Dinh Nhu sought refuge after the 1963 coup attempt at the Presidential Palace. Both Ngos later gave up after realizing they hadn't any political support left and were assassinated a short time after coup leaders picked them up at the church with an armored personnel carrier. The church is worth visiting more for its history than for its architecture. But it's an attractive cathedral, having been built in the early 1900s. Today, its parishioners number in the thousands.

Reunification Hall (Presidential Palace)

Open 7:30–10:30 a.m. and 1–4:30 p.m. Mon.–Sun. There is a US$4 admission charge.
This is the modern administrative center, located to the southeast of Nguyen Thi Minh Khai Street, where, in a famous photograph, an NVA tank slammed through the gates on April 30, 1975, which symbolically marked the South Vietnamese defeat in the war. The president and the entire South Vietnam cabinet were in the palace at the time and were arrested shortly afterwards. You can tour the former palace in a group.

Ho Chi Minh City's Reunification Hall was formerly called the Presidential Palace before Saigon fell to the North Vietnamese in 1975.

The Rex Hotel

141 Nguyen Hue, Dist. 1. Located at the intersection of Nguyen Hue and Le Loi boulevards.
This was the famous hangout of American officers during the war. It has regained some of its previous glory and now features a number of almost luxurious amenities (at least by Vietnam standards). There's a beauty parlor and an on-site tailor. There are also some respectable business services, such as photocopiers and a fax machine. The place is always packed, so if you're planning a stay, reserve early. Europeans cover the place like bees in a jar of jelly. Rex Regal splendor. If Vietnam is communist you'd never know it. Mahogany and marble all over the place. The breezy rooftop bar's a good place for expensive drinks.

Ho Chi Minh Museum

1 Nguyen Tat Thanh Street. ☎ *8291060.*
The museum is open on Tues.–Sun. (Fri. afternoons only) from 7:30–11:30 a.m. and 1:30–4:30 p.m.
Chronicles the life and adventures of Uncle Ho, who reportedly made this building his last stop before leaving for France on a freighter in 1911. He wouldn't see Viet-

nam again for another 30 years. Lots of Ho's personal items are on display here, including clothes and an old American radio he used to listen to. (See "The Ultimate Backpacker: Uncle Ho's Early Years" in the Vietnam Today chapter.) Its seven rooms contain more than 1000 exhibits—there were a mere 400 in 1982. Photos of the young Ho in London and the brick that he used as a heater when he lived in Paris during the early 1920s. The building was constructed between 1862 and 1864 and is characterized by the two dragons on the roof—giving the structure the nickname "Dragon House." The building originally served as the office of the French Royal Shipping Co. It was later converted into a fueling supply base for U.S. ships during the Vietnam War. After reunification in 1975, the building became part of Vietnam's Maritime Transportation Department. The Dragon House didn't become a museum until 1979—although it wasn't opened until January 1, 1982. Admission fee: 8000d.

Saigon City Hall

Le Thanh Ton Street at Nguyen Hue, Dist.1.

This is probably the most photographed building in Saigon. It was formerly the Hotel de Ville and built between 1901 and 1908 by the French. This is a magnificent pastel-yellow building that is now the HCMC People's Committee Building. Getting inside, though—to see its magnificent interior—is a little tricky, as it's not opened to tourists. You may be able to get in with a special appointment through a local travel agent who's connected.

Military Museum

Across Nguyen Binh Khiem Street at the corner of Le Duan Boulevard.

Here's an array of Vietnam War-era Soviet and Chinese weapons such as a 57 anti-aircraft gun which supported the Army Corp 4 in the Xuan Loc battle; it was laboriously moved along with the unit to Bien Hoa to liberate that city. There's also an 85 mm gun that was one of the guns of Division 5, Engineering Unit 232, that was used to support the unit as it crossed the Vam Co River to attack Phulam Radar station, a strategic outpost near the capital. Next to that is a 105 mm gun that was one of the guns that was used to stun the ARVN military position northeast of Saigon to support the unit that was attacking the Dong Hu base. Right next to this is a 130 mm gun that was one of the guns of the Nhon Trach battle used to attack Tan Son Nhat on April 29, 1975, which marked the beginning of the victory of the Ho Chi Minh campaign. There's also a 37 mm anti-aircraft gun that belonged to the 7th Anti-Aircraft Regiment of the 7th military zone, which took part in the liberation of Loc Ninh, and later in the liberation of Bien Hoa. There's also an American aircraft, a Cessna A-37, used by the South Vietnamese Air Force. Under Nguyen Thanh Trung's command, five planes left Thanh Son to bomb Tan Son Nhat airport on April 28, 1975. There's also an engineering vehicle and vehicles belonging to various information/propaganda regiments, which don't really bring back a lot of memories other than the truck used by the Beverly Hillbillies. These information units were primarily propaganda units that supported the army units as they moved south. There's also an ARVN armored personnel carrier here, which was captured at Phuoc Long in January 1975. There are also some bulldozers that are only worthy of note because they were supplied by the Cubans, as was engineering aid by Castro advisors. There's an area of destroyed U.S. and South Vietnamese aircraft that clutters some of the grounds of the compound, and it seems nobody has been able to identify the wrecks. Perhaps the most interesting attraction of the museum is the F-5 fighter plane that was flown by the renegade pilot Nguyen Thanh Trung. According to the description, this was the aircraft that bombed the "Puppet President's Palace" and then landed in a liberated area. It took off with South Vietnamese markings. The plane bombed the palace and then fled the capital. There is also the interesting T-54 tank, Number 848, which was the tank that attacked the Independence Palace at 10:30 a.m., April 30, 1975. Inside, the museum chronicles the history of Vietnamese campaigns ranging from the first Indochina War through the American war. There's an assortment of photos as well as a number of small arms that were used during the wars. The guides here speak relatively decent English, and the photos and maps have English descriptions, although the English is a bit shoddy and not nearly as descriptive as the Vietnamese captions to the museum's artifacts. There's also a large VC and tactical map showing troop movements and firefight sites at American military positions.

The Former U.S. Embassies

39 Ham Nghi Boulevard; Le Duan Boulevard and Mac Dinh Chi Street.

The older U.S. embassy is located at *39 Ham Nghi Boulevard.* The Americans abandoned it after it was bombed in 1967. They moved to a much more attractive compound at the corner of *Le Duan Boulevard and Mac Dinh Chi Street.* This is the famous structure that Viet Cong guerrillas nearly seized during the Tet Offensive of 1968 and the same building where millions around the world saw on television the rushed rooftop evacuation of hundreds of Americans and Vietnamese as communist forces sped like a torpedo toward central Saigon. Thousands of South Vietnamese, who had been promised evacuation by the U.S., massed outside the embassy gates, repelled by the U.S. Marine guards. U.S. choppers shuttled the lucky passengers between the rooftop and waiting U.S. warships off the coast of Vung Tau. At each corner of the embassy compound, there are concrete pillboxes with explosive shields. The main building is covered with a concrete shield that was to protect it from bombs, grenades and rocket attacks.

Vinh Nghiem Pagoda

339 Nam Ky Khoi Nghia, Dist. 3.

This is one of the largest pagodas in Saigon. It was built in 1967 in the modern Japanese style. It's an impressive sight, with a stupa reaching up to seven stories, and one of the largest pagodas in Vietnam. The pagoda is 35 meters long, 22 meters wide and 15 meters high. There are a number of wooden carvings, depicting the four sacred animals—unicorn, dragon, tortoise and phoenix, as well as carvings of other famous pagodas. Fantastic bell tower.

Xa Loi Pagoda

Bay Huyen Thanh Quan Street. Located near the War Crimes Museum.

This temple was built in 1956 and features a multistory tower that houses a sacred relic of the Lord Buddha. There's a huge bronze-gilded Buddha in the main sanctuary. The pagoda was the site where monks self-immolated themselves in opposition to President Ngo Dinh Diem in the mid–1960s.

Artex Saigon Orchid Farm
5/81 Xa Lo Vong Dai, Thu Duc district, on the Korean Highway.
Started in 1970, the orchid farm now boasts more than 1000 types of orchids and around 60,000 plants. A beautiful and relaxing place to kill a Sunday afternoon. This is the largest orchid farm in Vietnam, with orchids indigenous to Vietnam and from abroad. The best time to visit is during the dry season. The only problem is that you need reservations to visit here. You should do it a couple of days in advance. ☎ *8240124.*

Where to Stay in Ho Chi Minh City

> ### AUTHOR'S NOTE: TELEPHONE PREFIXES
>
> *When dialing telephone numbers in Ho Chi Minh City, the country code is 84. The city code is 8, followed by the local exchange. Numbers listed are local exchanges.*

Asian Hotel   US$75
146/150 Dong Khoi Street. ☎ *8296979. FAX: 8297433.*
One restaurant; no charge for children under 12. Service charge and breakfast are included in the tariff.

Bat Dat Hotel   US$10
238-244 Tran Hung Dao B Boulevard. ☎ *8555817.*
117 rooms.
Recommended by the backpack set. Cheap rooms with air conditioning; cheaper still with fan; Chinese restaurant.

Caravelle Hotel   US$50–$180
17-23 Lam Son Square, Dist. 1. ☎ *8293704/8. FAX: 8299746, 8296767.*
115 rooms.
Not as well kept up on the outside and more run down than its French neighbor the Continental across the square. Very, very French. Once the hangout for journalists during the war and also once owned by the Catholic Church. Recently renovated; 9th floor continental restaurant; conference facilities; foreign exchange counter; Japanese restaurant; disco; coffee shop; air conditioning; IDD; gift shop; gym; sauna; tailor in-house; massage; excellent location. Friendly.

Chains First Hotel (First Hotel)   US$65–$125   ★★★
18 Hoang Viet, Tan Binh Dist. ☎ *8441199. FAX: 8444282.*
90 rooms.
Near the airport; tennis courts; business services; airport shuttle; gift shop; coffee shop; three restaurants; sauna; air-conditioned; refrigerator. Has separate area with rooms with fans.

Cholon Hotel
Su Van Hanh Street. ☎ *8357058.*

HO CHI MINH CITY

Popular with visiting Taiwanese; clean rooms; restaurant.

Century Saigon Hotel   US$115–$200   ★★★★
68a Nguyen Hue Boulevard. ☎ *8293168, 8231818. FAX: 8292732, 8222958.*
Sort of nouveau colonial; big bucks in the first district. Mainly for business travelers. Business center, health club, visa extension assistance service, in-room movies, restaurants and lounges plural. With what the Big Bens people shell out here, this is the definition of "Marksism."

Continental Hotel   US$85–$170   ★★★★

132-134 Dong Khoi Street. ☎ *8299201, 8299255. FAX: 8290936.*
87 rooms.
This was the setting of Graham Greene's novel *The Quiet American*. Built in 1880, this French colonial building is kept in exquisite shape. It was renovated in 1989. Large, open courtyard. Large rooms with air conditioning; Bamboo Bar; Azur Bar; La Dolce Vita Bar; expensive Italian restaurant; Continental Palace Restaurant serves great Vietnamese fare. Good service. Business services.

Duc Huy Hotel   US$15–$25

422 Hai Ba Trung Street, District 1. ☎ *8442937. FAX: 8230132.*
This is one of the best bargains in town, for businesspeople as well as for backpackers and other tourists. Opened in April 1994. The upper-end rooms are immense and comfortably appointed. Attached bath with hot water. Refrigerator, karaoke and video facilities, meeting rooms, air-conditioned, color TV. Car, motorbike and bicycle rentals. Organized sightseeing tours throughout the country. There are even backpacker tours at "backpacker rates." Hotel, airline and rail bookings. The staff, all English speaking, are extremely friendly.

Dong Khoi Hotel   US$50
12 Ngo Duc Ke Street. ☎ *8294046.*
34 rooms.
Old French colonial building. Air-conditioned suites with high ceilings. Friendly proprietors; good security. Was being totally renovated at press time, so we'll see what the new rate card looks like.

Ecumenical Guest House   US$10–$12
15 Tu Xuong, Dist 3. ☎ *8222642, 8251701. FAX: 8231071.*
Perhaps the best bargain I've found in HCMC. They could easily get away charging two times the amount. Modern, clean rooms with air conditioning and private bath. Quiet setting. Breakfast. A deal and a half. Highly recommended.

Embassy Hotel   US$60–$100   ★★★
35 Nguyen Trung Truc, Dist. 1. ☎ *8231981. FAX: 8231978.*
New hotel in the center of town. Nice rooms with air conditioning, TV, minibar, refrigerator. Business center and restaurant.

Emperor Hotel   US$30–$66   ★
117 Nguyen Dinh Chieu, Dist. 1. ☎ *8290811. FAX: 8230515.*
Moderate in every respect. Rooms with air conditioning, TV, refrigerator and minibar. Restaurant, conference facilities. But this place doesn't take credit cards at last check.

Evergreen Hotel   **US$35–$45**   ★

261B Hai Ba Trung, Dist. 1. *8291237. FAX: 8291835.*
Close to central location. Brand new hotel that's clean and comfortable, and definitely worth the price. One of the increasing bargains in HCMC as the city is experiencing a hotel glut, and there's something of a price war going on. Spacious rooms
with air conditioning, TV, refrigerator, minibar. Friendly service.

Equatorial   **US$100–$400**   ★ ★ ★ ★

242 Tran Binh Trang, Dist. 5. *8390000. FAX: 8390011.*
334 rooms.
District 5 is a little out of the way, but maybe these people thought a lot of rich people would enjoy being a little out of the way. At press time, this was indicative of the
race to establish the "best" in Saigon.

Festival Hotel   **US$28–$44**   ★

31 Cao Thang, Dist. 3. ☎ *8390704. FAX: 8390553.*
Clean and comfortable. Worth the price. Rooms with air conditioning, TV, minibar
and refrigerator. Restaurant.

Hai Van Hotel   **US$14–$25**

69 Huynh Thuc Khang-Quan 1. ☎ *8291274, 8230400. FAX: 8291275.*
For under US$25, this was one of the best places in town, but no one seemed to
know about it. It has since fallen into a state of disrepair—or I should say a perpetual
state of constant repair. The construction of the adjacent South Hai Van didn't help
with the racket around this place. A new locally popular disco in the hotel makes the
lobby busier than a beehive—and it doesn't help with the noise problem. But the
staff couldn't be friendlier, perhaps more so than in hotels twice as expensive.
Ground-floor restaurant serves decent Vietnamese fare. Karaoke club on the second
floor. Hot water. No TVs in the rooms. It's been a shame to watch the demise of
this place, and I hope they'll bring it back up to speed.

South Hai Van Hotel   **US$50–$99**   ★ ★

132 Ham Nghi Street. District 1. *8211679, 8211680; FAX: 8224174.*
This place is far nicer than its sister next door. Far nicer. Brand new, the US$50 rate
is a true bargain. Clean and comfortable with a friendly staff, this place is up to international standards, in stark contrast to the adjacent Hai Van. All rooms with air conditioning, color TV, minibar, private bath with hot water. There's a decent
restaurant and bar, as well as karaoke. Secured parking for both autos and motorbikes. Souvenir shop and travel center for booking air and train tickets. IDD phone.
Take advantage of this place while its new. Recommended.

Hotel Bongsen   **US$55–$210**   ★ ★ ★

117-119-121-123 Dong Khoi Street, Dist. 1. *8291516. FAX: 8298076.*
130 rooms.
This is actually two hotels: Bongsen I and II, the first being the pricier of the two.
Breakfast included and children under six stay free at both. Air conditioning, minibar; private baths with hot water; VCRs; IDD and other business services; sauna;
shopping arcade; laundry and valet; photo lab on site; medical staff; travel reservations. Bongsen I is moderate to expensive, Bongsen II inexpensive to moderate.

Huong Sen   US$38–$100   ★★

70 Dong Khoi, Dist. 1. ☎ 8291415, 8290259. FAX: 8290916, 8298076.
50 rooms.
Air-conditioned; IDD telephone; TV; hot water; refrigerator; minibar; sauna; coffee shops and restaurants; laundry and valet; cars for hire; express photo services; travel reservations and services. Great location for business and shopping. Cozy and modern. Rooms with the standard amenities. Restaurant, bar, small business center.

International Hotel   US$85–$165   ★★★

19 Vo Van Tan, Dist. 3. ☎ 8290009. FAX: 8290066.
New and luxurious rooms for businesspeople, but I gave it only three stars, because, at press time, there were no computers in the business center. Restaurants, shopping area.

Kim Do Hotel   US$119–$479   ★★★★

133 Nguyen Hue Blvd., Dist. 1. ☎ 8225914. FAX: 8225913.
133 rooms.
Newly opened by Saigontourist. Mucho dinero. Great location; handsome, utilitarian appearance. Business center, in-house movies, health club, orchid and rose garden deck on the sixth floor, satellite TV, restaurant, two bars, health club, IDD phone, ballrooms and conference center.

Ky Hoa Hotel   US$40–$90   ★★

12 February 3 Street, Dist. 10. ☎ 8655037. FAX: 8655333.
Way out of the way, but clean and friendly if you need to be out here. Rooms with air conditioning, minibar & refrigerator, TV, telephone, restaurant.

Mekong Travel Hotel   US$66–$95   ★★★

243A Hoang Van Thu, Tan Binh Dist. ☎ 8442986. FAX: 8442981.
Near the airport if that's where you want to be. Most businesspeople and travelers are settling into the newer hotels closer to downtown. But this place is nice enough. Standard amenities.

Mercure   US$95–$230   ★★★★

79 Tran Hung Dao, Dist. 1. ☎ 8242525/555/537. FAX: 8242533.
Good location near Ben Thanh market. Shopping arcade, business facilities, great restaurant, conference facilities. Friendly staff.

Metropole (Binh Minh Hotel)   US$85–$150   ★★★

148 Tran Hung Dao, Dist. 1. ☎ 8322021/2. FAX: 8322019.
Nice place but the rooms generally have a lousy view, if any. Business and conference facilities, superb restaurant. Rooms with minibar, refrigerator, air conditioning, IDD, TV.

Majestic Hotel   US$50   ★★

1 Dong Khoi Street, Dist 1. ☎ 8295515. FAX: 8291470.
100 plus rooms.
Once the city's best hotel, a fire ravaged it. Now passable. Some of the rooms have a river view; two restaurants; postal and some business services.

Mondial Hotel   US$62–$112   ★★★

109 Dong Khoi Street, Dist. 1. ☎ 8296291 or 8296296. FAX: 8296324.

40 rooms.
Some rooms with balconies; most have private baths, bar and lounge. Elegant and expensively decorated. Great location in Saigon's 1st District. French restaurant with Continental cuisine. Orchid Lounge; quiet, comfortable. Ornate lobby. Exotic place. There are traditional Vietnamese cultural shows here three times a week.

New Hotel — US$25–$65

14 Ho Huan Nghiep St., Dist. 1. *8230656, 8231343. FAX: 8241812.*
Located just off Me Linh Square, this really is a new hotel. The best way to describe it is to say quaint. It's tight and tall, five stories, but it has one of Saigon's only B&B atmospheres. The suites facing the street are impressive and run only about US$65 a night. Cheaper singles run around $25. Friendly staff; fax; laundry, cafe. This is one of the quietest hostelries in the 1st district, yet you're right next to all the action.

New World Hotel — US$140–$500 ★★★★

76 Le Dai, Dist. 1. *8228888. FAX: 8230710.*
To date, this is the largest hotel in Saigon and it dominates the downtown skyline. They rushed to get this thing up, and I would've given it 5 stars if it weren't for the reports I've heard about shoddy craftsmanship. But an inspection in 1996 didn't glean anything that should discredit the place. It is a little anonymous—or I should say you'll feel a little that way here. Great dining and business facilities. Huge conference center. All the amenities.

Norfolk Hotel — US$85–$220 ★★★

117 Le Thanh Ton, Dist. 1. *8295368. FAX: 8293415.*
45 rooms.
Located in central Saigon. Usually booked solid. Australian owners/managers. Attached bathroom; air-conditioned; well-furnished; elegant lobby; hot water; color TV with Star satellite network; wet bar; business center with secretarial services; fax; meeting facilities; restaurant; bar; rooftop BBQ.

Omni Saigon Hotel — US$150–$800 ★★★★

215 Nguyen Van Troi Street; Phu Nhuan District. *8449222. FAX: 8449200.*
250 rooms.
This is an extravagant facility, opened in Feb.'94 near the airport with rooms, suites and longer-term apartments. The business services here are outstanding, including fully-serviced satellite offices. Also a ballroom, health club, outdoor swimming pool, IDD, color TV, air-conditioned rooms, minibar, etc., and the full array of capitalist running-dog amenities that would have V.I. Lenin spinning in his formaldehyde.

Orchid Hotel — US$50 ★

29A Don Dat Street. 🕿 *8231809. FAX: 8231811.*
30 rooms.
Air-conditioned rooms; bathroom; telephones; refrigerators; bar; restaurant; coffee shop.

Palace Hotel — US$40–$145 ★★★

56-64 Nguyen Hue Blvd., Dist. 1. 🕿 *8297284, 8292860. FAX: 8299872, 8290457.*

Rooms have bathrooms and hot water; swimming pool; bar; restaurant; great location.

Rang Dong Hotel   US$25–$47

81 Cach Mang Thang 8, Dist. 1. ☎ *8322106.*
Decent location and a clean hotel with great prices. Rooms with air conditioning, hot water, minibar and refrigerator.

Regent Hotel

700 Tran Hung Dao Blvd., Dist 1. ☎ *8353548. FAX: 8357094.*
Also called the Hotel 700. Located in Cholon. Joint Vietnam/Thai venture.

Rex Hotel   US$80–$800   ★ ★ ★ ★

14 Nguyen Hue Blvd., Dist. 1. ☎ *8296042/3. FAX: 8291269, 8296536.*
120-plus rooms.
A favorite of American officers during the war. Enjoying a new life with the opening of tourist and business frontiers in the city. Air-conditioned; color TV; refrigerators with wet bars; three restaurants; IDD telephones; hot water; cassette players; large statuary and topiary; art gallery; dance area; business center; cinema; tailor in-house; large gift shop; tennis court; swimming pool. Expensive as hell. Get there for a drink if nothing else. See description under "What to See and Do in Ho Chi Minh City."

Riverside Hotel   US$25–$50

19 Ton Duc Thang Street. ☎ *8224038. FAX: 8298070.*
34 rooms.
Rooms have TV; telephone; refrigerator; self-contained bathrooms; business center; bar; restaurant.

Saigon Hotel   US$50   ★ ★

41-47 Dông Du Street, Dist. 1. ☎ *8230231/2, 8241078, or 8299734. FAX: 84-8-8291466.*
105 rooms. 16 deluxe suites.
Room rates include breakfast, and fruit baskets and newspapers come with the deluxe suites. Children under 6 stay free. Satellite color TV in the deluxe rooms and suites; IDD; 24-hour service. Minibar; hot water; air conditioning; conference center; bar on the 9th floor and restaurant in the lobby. Also will do air ticket booking. Moderate.

Saigon Lodge Hotel   US$78–$305   ★ ★ ★

215 Nam Ky Khoi Nghia, Dist. 3. ☎ *8230112. FAX: 8251070.*
Suggested for businesspeople. Close to the business center of District 1. A little expensive. Big rooms with air conditioning, minibar & refrigerator, TV, IDD. Restaurant, bar.

Saigon Star Hotel   US$90–$180   ★ ★ ★

204 Nguyen Thi Minh Khai, Dist. 3. ☎ *8230260. FAX: 8230255.*
Another hotel catering primarily to businesspeople. Business center, conference facilities.

Sol Chancery Saigon   US$107–$180   ★ ★ ★ ★

196 Nguyen Thi Minh Khai, Dist. 3. ☎ *8299152. FAX: 8251464.*

A businessperson's delight. All the rooms are suites, and this is one of the most comfortable and friendly business hotels in town. Recommended restaurant. Gym, sauna, business center. Nice site overlooking the main city park.

Sunny Hotel US$30–$57 ★

54 Dang Dung Street, District1. ☎ *8442192, 8442056. FAX: 8440543.*
34 rooms

Comfortable although a bit overpriced just off Hai Ba Trung Street in a quiet residential area that's one of the best-kept secrets in HCMC for expats. The suites are little more than partitioned rooms, but the effect is certainly achieved. But a super-friendly staff. My only gripe (at least for the price) is about the tacky furnishings. The interior design appears to have been done by a drunk, 13-year-old Japanese samurai apprentice—right down to the linen. But there's a certain Bohemian ambience that appealed to me, whether it was by design or not (it wasn't). Rooms with air conditioning, stereo-cassette player, color satellite TV with in-room videos, minibar, IDD telephone, private bath, refrigerator, bathtub, hair dryer. Vietnamese restaurant, fax and photocopy services, secured parking. The adjacent Forget-Me-Not Hotel offers the same fare but is a little cheaper and sans suites. I actually like these places, especially this neighborhood north of Tan Dinh Church.

Tan Loc Hotel US$50–$110 ★★★

177 Le Thanh Ton, Dist. 1. ☎ *8230028. FAX: 8298360.*
Rooms with air conditioning, satellite TV, IDD, minibar, refrigerator. Nice restaurant.

Thanh Binh 1 Hotel US$30

315 Hoang Van Thu, Tan Binh Dist. ☎ *8440984. FAX: 8640262.*
A bargain in the boonies. Comfortable rooms with air conditioning, minibar & refrigerator, telephone.

Victory Hotel US$30–$80 ★★

14 Vo Van Tan, Dist. 3. ☎ *8231755. FAX: 8299604.*
This place has been recently renovated and is one of the best bargains in HCMC. Three-and four-star amenities at budget prices. Recommended. Located just north of District 1's central business district.

Vien Dong US$25–$50 ★

275A Pham Ngu Lao, Dist. 1. ☎ *8393001.*
Great budget hotel. Rooms with air conditioning, hot water, telephone. Cheers disco is located here.

Where to Eat in Ho Chi Minh City

Probably the heartiest places to eat in Saigon are at the hundreds of street stalls and *pho* shops. For the most part they're safe, excellent and extremely inexpensive—with prices usually less than a dollar. But if you want more ambiance or are simply not one to take chances with your body, there are a number of decent establishments in town.

Insider Tip: Amerip-offs

Be warned: if you're tiring of the local cuisine and searching for a juicy steak or something else you're more accustomed to, there is an increasing number of Western-style restaurants opening in town. It's a pity most don't put the same effort into the food as they do into the interior designs of these places. Yeah, you might think you're in an American grill or bistro until the food arrives—usually poor attempts at such things as hamburgers, spaghetti, pizza and sandwiches served in microscopic portions at outrageous prices. Unless an American-style eatery is located where there are a lot of tourists, stay away. One tip-off to these places is that most tout their Italian ice cream, coffee and their establishment as a café. They usually go by pompous, silly and pseudo-chic names.

The best, and also the most expensive, were formerly found at the better hotels. But that's not the case anymore. The proliferation of international-class eateries here in Ho Chi Minh is perhaps unmatched anywhere in the world. Here's a look at some of the hundreds of restaurants around HCMC.

INSIDER TIP

As might be expected, Saigon is experiencing a degree of the "Bangkok Syndrome," an Asian City homogenizing Eastern and Western influences with the pâte of the Chao Phraya River and 30-weight motor oil. Western food is invading the palates of Saigonites like a mozzarella revolution. Four pizza joints have opened in HCMC in just the past few months, a couple of them not half bad. Swiss-born Danny Koeppel, sort of the Wolfgang Puck of Indochina, whose credits include more than a year at the internationally famous Chez Guido at the Continental Hotel, has become something of a consultant to the increasingly popular pizzerias springing up around the city. His new "consultancy" venture is with the new Pizzeria Cappuccino, 11 Ho Huan Nghiep (off Dong Khoi Street, ☎ 8291051). Because the competition is getting stiffer in Saigon, Koeppel has decided to broaden the offerings. The specialty of the house is pasta, of course. Mozzarella, as well as the anchovies, are shipped from Italy. Koeppel claims to be the first to create "spaghettata," an "island" of pasta surrounded by sauces prepared in minutes for businesspeople on the run. The homemade bread with a dish of chopped chilies in sauce is delicious. Ho Huan Nghiep Street is known for its bars, and a lot of people come into the eatery without the intention of investing the time in a full sit-down dinner. So try the cheeseburgers if you've got the dong (they run nearly US$4), or even a hot dog; the sausage is imported from Germany. There's also ice cream and, of course, coffee.

180 Restaurant   **$$$**   ★

180 Nguyen Van Thu, Dist. 1. ☎ 8251673.

Usually, restaurants named for their addresses in Vietnam are simply glamourized food stalls. Not the case here. Imported American and Australian beef. Try the smoked salmon. Wide drink menu; garden villa setting.

13 Restaurant $$

13 Mac Thi Buoi, Dist. 1.
Not as fancy as the 180, but highly popular with expats, tourists and locals alike. Cafe-style. Great Vietnamese food, great prices.

Ashoka $$$ ★

17A-10 Le Thanh Ton, Dist. 1. ☎ *8231372.*
North Indian fare in this Vietnamese yuppie hangout. Try the chicken marinated in yogurt or tandoori. The cooking is done in traditional Indian clay ovens. Recommended, but pricey.

A Nhat $$

86 Ngo Duc Ke, Dist. 1. ☎ *8210494.*
Excellent Vietnamese fare in a French setting. Cafe-style seating.

Annie's Pizza $$

57 Nguyen Du, Dist 1. ☎ *8392577 (home deliveries) or* ☎ *8223661 (reservations).*
Popular family-style place for expat and Vietnamese folks. The pizzas and burgers are quite passable. Also pies and sausages. Typical of the new wave of Western fast-food/boutique settings. Also—naturally—with home delivery. Popular.

Augustin's $$ ★★★

10 Nguyen Thiep. ☎ *8292941.*
Popular French eatery favored by Saigon's French expats.

Cafe Brodard $$

131 Dong Khoi Street. ☎ *8225837.*
A hangout for expats, backpackers and hipsters.

Buffalo Blues $$$ ★

72A Nguyen Du, Dist. 1. ☎ *8222874.*
Great place for barbeque and jazz, but expensive. Elegant setting.

Bavaria $$

20 Le Anh Xuan, Dist. 1. ☎ *8222673.*
Opposite the New World, this is a haunt of German expats and tourists. Don't expect a lot of English spoken willingly, but the schnitzels and wursts are fabulous.

Cafe Latin $$ ★★★

25 Dong Du Street, District 1. ☎ *8226363.*
Great Spanish fare, especially the stuffed peppers, stuffed squid. All can be washed down with the tastiest margaritas in HCMC. Four floors in this Soho-type venue. Personable Aussie owner Joe Cilia makes sure that every visitor is satiated. Next to the Saigon Hotel, but not well signed. Recommended.

Cafe Mogambo $$ ★

20 Thi Sach, Dist. 1. ☎ *8251331. FAX: 8226031.*

"American" bar and grill, but looks more like a Polynesian theme joint in Cancun. Dark, bamboo interior. Western food at Western prices. Friendly management. Filled every night for dinner, entirely by expat suits.

Chez Guido   **$$$**   ★★

Continental Hotel, 132 Dong Khoi, Dist. 1. ☎ 8299252.
Expensive Italian cuisine; good portions. All imported ingredients.

Fook Yuen   **$$**   ★★★

International Hotel. 19 Vo Van Tan Street. ☎ 8290009; ext. 812.
Cantonese fare prepared by Hong Kong Chefs. You'll need to make reservations here, so make you sure you dial the number correctly—otherwise it'll sound like you're insulting someone.

Givral Cafe   **$$**

169 Dong Khoi Street, Dist. 1.
Like the Brodard, mostly expats and journalists, but better food.

Harbor View Restaurant   **$$$**

At the curve where Ton Duc Thang and Ben Chuong Duong Streets meet.
Lavish eatery right on the riverfront overlooking the harbor. The food (Asian, Vietnamese, and Western) is superb but expensive. This place is frequently rented out for wedding receptions.

Kim's Cafe   **$**

De Tham St., Dist. 1.
The place to be seen for the backpacker set. Reasonable food at rock-bottom prices.

Krua Thai   **$$**

2 Thi Sach, Dist. 1.
The best Thai in Saigon. Excellent green and red curry dishes.

La Bibliotheque (Madame Dai)   **$$**

84 Nguyen Du.
Very good Vietnamese fare and excellent beef.

Le Bordeaux   **$$$**   ★★★

7-8 Duong 2, Van Thanh Bac, Binh Thanh District. ☎ 8999831.
One of the newest eateries in town. The word is out on this place and it's become quite popular with the expats in Binh Thanh district. But others make the trip from downtown.

La Camargue   **$$$**   ★★

16 Cao Ba Quat, Dist. 1. ☎ 8243148. FAX: 8290603.
Goat's cheese and ratatouille tartelette, roasted whole poussin stuffed with spinach and cheese with garlic and thyme sauce. If this sounds like your kind of evening, this is your place. Bring a wad of cash to this beautiful villa-turned-upscale-restaurant. There's a small, open-air bar with a television set downstairs if the scene upstairs gets a little stuffy.

La Couscoussiere   **$$$**   ★

24 Nguyen Thi Manh Khai, Dist. 1. ☎ 8299148.

Persian, Indian and Arabian fare. Absolutely delicious. Great sausage, lamb, chicken and mixed- grill dishes.

Le Mekong $$ ★

32 Vo Van Tan St., Dist 3. ☎ *8291277.*
French fare at great prices.

Lemon Grass $$ ★★★

4 Nguyen Thiep Street. District 1. ☎ *8220496.*
Vietnamese and Western cuisine in a cafe-style setting. Still one of the best restaurants in Saigon for Vietnamese.

Le Pierrot Gourmand $$

19 Le Thanh Ton, Dist. 1. ☎ *8908156.*
French cafe specializing in cakes, pastry and ice cream.

Liberty $$ ★

Dong Khoi Street. District 1.
Excellent Chinese in a cheesy-elegant setting. I don't know what it is that bothers me about this place. The chessboard tile floor? The white tablecloths and red napkins? Can't put my finger on it, but I always feel like a guest at a cheap wedding reception. Live music, sometimes Vietnamese traditional.

Lotus Court $$$ ★

Omni Hotel, 251 Nguyen Van Troi, Phu Nhuan Dist. ☎ *8449222.*
Beijing Duck prepared by Hong Kong chefs. Get ready to spend a bundle.

L'Etoile $$$ ★

180 Hai Ba Trung. ☎ *8297939.*
Elegant and expensive French and Vietnamese as you're serenaded by guitar music.

Lu'o'ng So'n $$ ★

31 Ly Tu Trong. District 1. ☎ *8251330.*
Large, semi-outdoor cafe setting that is one of the most popular gathering spots for Saigon yuppies in town. The Vietnamese fare is absolutely delicious. Try the curried eel. Crowded and festive.

Mae Krua Thai $$

2 Thi Sach Street. District 1. ☎ *8298919.*
Just up the street from the Apocalypse Now. The Thai fare is passable, but the service is a little snooty. The Vietnamese waitresses are clearly uncomfortable in their northern Thailand *chud thai* dresses and seem like off-duty hookers. And the owner appears to be their role model. Home of the most expensive fried rice this side of Guam.

Manhattan $$

Nguyen Thi Minh Khai Street (just west of Hai Ba Trung Street). District 1.
American-style fast food joint complete with bolted-to-the-floor tables and chairs. You'll swear you're in Orange County, California. The main fare here is hamburgers and pizza, both of which are reasonable facsimiles of the real things. But, as is the case with most Vietnamese versions of pizza, the tomato sauce is either still being

held up at customs or it is simply a concept. Still worth a weekly visit for expats. This is perhaps Saigon's best candidate for the country's first drive-through.

Marine Club $$

17A/4 Le Thanh Ton, Dist. 1. ☎ *8292249.*
Brittany crabs in a setting that's a cross between Long John Silver's and Gilligan's Island.

Max Amerique $$

144 Hai Ba Trung Street. District 1. ☎ *8296616.*
Amerip-off bar and restaurant more popular with young locals than foreigners. Cozy, dark interior with an American motif. But overpriced for the small, forgettable portions of your favorite American dishes, which may taint your opinion of such things as ham-and-cheese sandwiches and spaghetti permanently. The sandwiches, particularly, are about as thick as a Communion host. Be warned. But the staff is friendly and they get your order right. Something to be said for that in this town. A little out of the way from the downtown scene unless you're motorized.

Maxim's $$$ ★★★

13 Dong Khoi Street, Dist. 1. ☎ *8299820.*
Live music, decent food, high prices. But this remains a HCMC icon and shouldn't be missed if you're going to be in town for awhile. The staff is especially friendly, and I've been able to get these guys some rare techno tapes. Superior sound system. Downstairs dinner theater, upstairs disco.

Monte Rosa Cafe $$

125A Hai Ba Trung Street, Dist. 1. ☎ *8244425.*
Typical of the Amerip-offs with a dark interior and a facade of elegance, but the inadequate, expensive portions of Western-style Denny's fare leave a lot to be desired. If you're hungry, you'll need two entrées. Only for the desperate.

Napoli $$

79 Nguyen Hue, Dist. 1. ☎ *8225616.*
Small, clean Italian pizzeria in the center of the business district.

Nha Hang 5 Me Linh $$ ★

Near the statue of Tran Hung Dao.
Great Vietnamese fare. Even Cobra!

Nha Hang 51 Nguyen Hue $$

51 Nguyen Hue Blvd.
Ditto.

Nhon Bashi Japanese Restaurant $$$ ★

On the ground floor of the Rex Hotel.
Excellent Japanese fare but expensive.

Noodles Restaurant $$

72 Ngo Duc Ke, Dist. 1. ☎ *8290894.*
As the name suggests, that's what you'll get here, Japanese style. Good tempura.

Ohan Restaurant $$ ★★

67 Pasteur Street. ☎ *8292063.*

The beach at Quy Nhon

Chinese temples line Tran Phu Street, Hoi An.

A ferry on Ha Long Bay

Fish is the main source of protein in Vietnam.

Saigon's Ho Chi Minh Museum chronicles the life of Ho Chi Minh in 1000 exhibits.

Some of Vietnam's best meals can be found on the street.

Superior Japanese dining, but you may feel a little awkward if you're not Japanese, as the place is almost exclusively patronized by visiting Japanese businessmen and expats. But the staff certainly won't make you feel uncomfortable, and neither will the generous helpings of Japanese food.

Papaya Verte $$

33A Ben Van Don, Dist. 4. ☎ *8253652.*
French cafe style, a bit out of the way, but worth it for the prices.

Palace Hotel $$$ ★

15th floor restaurant.
The best view of Saigon in town.

Pho Dien Bien $ ★

165 Dien Bien Phu, Dist. 1. ☎ *8290286.*
One of the best-kept secrets in Saigon. Not any longer. Local eatery. Great food. Cheap prices.

Red Rhino $$ ★

8A/1/D2 Don Dat, Dist 1. ☎ *8292216.*
One of the newer and trendier eateries/bars in town. Excellent seafood. Western and Vietnamese dishes. Reasonably priced. Recommended.

Restaurant A (The Russian Restaurant) $$ ★

361/8 Nguyen Dinh Chieu, Dist. 3. ☎ *8359190.*
Azerbaijan-style dishes along with blintzes, borscht, caviar and black bread. For Russian, this is Saigon's best (if not only).

Restaurant Ami $$$ ★

170 Pasteur, Dist. 1. ☎ *8242198.*
Extensive and expensive wine list. Mostly expat clientele. French. Expensive.

Restaurant Huong Rung $$ ★★

462 Pham The Hien Street, District 8. ☎ *855323.*
This is one of the most bizarre dining experiences in HCMC. Eccentric owner Tran Van Kien has created a setting where live pythons, cobras, iguanas, lizards and all sorts of other reptiles and birds freely roam the environs of this posh and expensive restaurant. While eating such exotic delicacies as cream of goat testicles soup, you may suddenly find a snake slithering into your pants pocket or a turtle traversing your beef satay. This seems to be a popular place with noisy expats drinking vats of Tiger beer.

Restaurant Vietnam Indochine $$$ ★

173 Nguyen Van Troi, Phu Nhuan Dist. ☎ *8444236.*
Vietnamese with a French twist. Superb and expensive. Opened only recently.

Rex Garden Restaurant $$

86 Le Thanh, Dist 1. ☎ *8292186.*
The only place in town with both a tennis court and a tank as backdrops for dining. In back of the Rex. A little pricey and curiously nearly always close to empty.

Sawaddee $$ ★

252 De Tham Street, District 1. ☎ *8322494.*

Superb Thai atmosphere—albeit with a backpacker flavor—and food here in the heart of Backpacker Barrio.

Sawaddee   **$$**   ★

29B Thai Van Lung (Don Dat) St, Dist. 1. ☎ *8221402.*

Excellent new sister restaurant to the De Tham location. This one's a bit classier, but equally as cozy. Superb Thai; try the curried chicken *(khaeng kai)*, the omelette-like *kaiyatsai*, stuffed with minced pork, fried tomatoes and green beans—and the fried fish and vegetables *(plachon patkuenchai).*

Saigon Cafe   **$**

De Tham Street, Dist 1.

Backpacker hangout on De Tham.

Saigon Times Club   **$$$**   ★

37 Nam Ky Khoi Nghia, Dist. 1. ☎ *8298676.*

Great Vietnamese. Dark atmosphere. Vietnamese yuppies and live music.

Saigon Lodge Hotel   **$$**   ★

215 Nam Ky Khoi Nghia, Dist. 3. ☎ *8230112.*

For Malaysian, this may be the best in town. Malay Muslim, Chinese and Western dishes.

Sa Pa   **$$**   ★★

8A/8 Don Dat, Dist 1. ☎ *8295783.*

Swiss, Indonesian and Vietnamese fare. Semi-outdoor setting. Relaxed ambience in a cozy setting. The upstairs dining room is where to head for the superb dishes; downstairs is found the popular bar—with limited seating for food. Recommended.

Sinh Cafe   **$**

6 Pham Ngu Lao Street. District 1.

A good mingling place for hipsters, vagabonds and other L.P. types. Passable travelers' food. The cafe arranges for minibus tours to Cu Chi, Tay Ninh, the Mekong Delta, Phan Thiet, etc. HCMC's mecca for the backpacker set.

Spices   **$$**   ★★★

132 Ham Ngi Street. ☎ *8211687.*

Indian style curries are what makes this place hot—no pun intended. The cuisine, featuring nasi goreng and gado gado make this eatery more Indonesian and Malay than southern Indian. A great change of pace.

Tex-Mex   **$$**

24 Le Thanh Ton, Dist. 1. ☎ *8295950.*

The bar's the best thing going here. A French attempt at Mexican. Taco Bell authenticity.

Thuan Tuan   **$$**

3/6 Nguyen Van Thu, Dist 1. ☎ *8244051.*

Specializes in lamb dishes. Small, family-style place.

Vietnam House   **$$$**   ★

93-95 Dong Khoi Street. ☎ *8291623.*

Posh. Expensive Vietnamese cuisine. Live, traditional Vietnamese music performances accompany dinner. Attentive and friendly service. But I've heard that they've re-served food that wasn't eaten by other customers. Maybe a disgruntled former employee.

Wild Horse Saloon   **$$**   ★★

8A1/D1 Thai Van Lung (Don Dat) Street, District 1. ☎ *8251901.*
The food, continental, American and Asian, is passable and worth the price in this American Old West theme bar and restaurant. I regularly jam with the house bands here on Thursdays and Saturdays—regrettably usually clearing the joint.

Yeebo   **$$**

97B Ham Nghi, Dist. 1.
Cantonese and seafood.

Pho Stalls

Pho is a staple of the northern Vietnamese diet. And it's developed a strong foothold in the south, particularly in Saigon. Essentially, *pho* is a beef-based broth smothered with noodles and beef *(bo)* or chicken *(ga)*, to which the customer then adds chiles, lemon juice, hot sauces and sweet basil and fennel leaves to the liking of his or her palate. It's eaten with chop sticks and a spoon. A bowl of the spicy concoction usually runs no more than VND6000, although many places will try to charge foreigners more—around VND10,000. Regardless, it's tasty and worth both prices. But don't make *pho* the heart of your diet, unless you want to lose weight. It works for the Vietnamese—and they're not even trying to.

Ice Cream Parlors

Ice cream, like pet dogs and golf courses, was once considered a bourgeois indulgence in Vietnam. Now it's simply a tasty way to cool off. Ben & Jerry's has to yet to open up shop here, but there are a number of American-style stores with ripped-off names, such as American 31 Flavor and Nestly. In the marketing boardrooms of Hanoi and Saigon these must've come out sounding better than Vladmir and Ho's or 1975 Flavors.

District 1

Hoang Gia

32 Le Van Huu Street. ☎ *8296538.*
VND7000 per cup.

Linh Phuong

128A Pasteur Street. ☎ *8295775.*
One scoop cup: VND18,000; two-scoop cup: VND30,000; three-scoop cup: VND45,000.

American 31 Flavor

257 Tran Hung Dao Street. ☎ *8357573.*
One scoop cup: VND18,000; two-scoop cup: VND30,000; three-scoop cup: VND40,000.

Vinamilk

36-38 Ngo Duk Ke Street. ☎ *8244227.*

Ice cream bars: VND1000–1700; VND2100 per cup; one-liter box: VND11,500; half-liter box: VND6800.

District 3

Thien Ly

225 Nam Ky Khoi Nghia Street. ☎ *8439162.*
VND3000–4000 per cup; VND15,000 per box.

Penguin American Ice Cream

91 Vo Thi Sau Street. ☎ *8231199.*

Pinky (Italian Ice Cream)

2B Su Thien Chieu Street. ☎ *8296631.*
VND8000 for two scoops; 750 grams for VND50,000; home delivery.

District 5

Pinky (Italian Ice Cream)

251 An Duong Vuong Street. ☎ *8353987.*

American 31 Flavor Ice Cream

148 Tran Hung Dao B Street. ☎ *8553517.*
VND18,000 for a one-scoop cup; VND30,000 for two scoops; VND45,000 for three scoops.

District 6

Igloo

127 Hung Vuong Street. ☎ *8550289.*

Binh Thanh District

Tan Hiep

252 No Trang Long Street. ☎ *8940601.*

Sierra

217/10 No Trang Long Street. ☎ *8434290.*

Kem My

16 Dinh Tien Hoang Street. ☎ *8434432.*
VND4000–18,000 per cup.

Phu Nhuan District

Anh Hung

211 Le Van Sy Street. ☎ *8442938.*

Nightlife in Ho Chi Minh City

Over the past few years dozens of trendy nightspots have sprung up all over the city. Many of the hipper spots are opening up along District 1's Thi Sach Street. Thi Sach means "beer street" to the Saigonese. It's appropriate. If you're into nightlife, it'll be tough to get bored in Saigon. Imagine saying that 10 years ago. This town is starting to rock.

Bars

Apocalypse Now

2c Thi Sach, District 1.

This was the former hangout for grungers in Saigon, but the clientele has evolved into a mish-mash of ponytailed guys (who are actually clean), upscale backpackers and too-cool expats whose shirts don't stink. If you miss the college bar back in Wisconsin, you'll feel quite at home here. Expect about as much Vietnamese flavor as a pizza. Blaring old rock music din in a cavelike setting. This place has been around for a few years but just recently moved to the new location in the expat ghetto around Thi Sach, the East Village of Saigon. Loud tunes, pool table, relatively cheap beer and the recent arrival of "hostesses" who mostly hang out at the pool table and are inclined to bend over it for more time than it normally takes to line up a pool shot. Works for me, though. Does a booming T-shirt business.

Baby Blue

63 Ly To Trong Street. District 1. ☎ *8226818.*
Too hip on some nights, no hips on others. Good restaurant, though. Imported beers and spirits.

Buffalo Blues ★

72A Nguyen Du, Dist. 1. ☎ *8222874.*
A spotlessly clean and elegant New Orleans-type jazz club. Once in awhile, it gets some out-of-town acts to complement the house band, the Jazz Brothers Band. Frequented by expat businesspeople. Serves Bass Ale and Tennent's Lager. Worth a stop, but it's rather expensive.

Cafe Boong, Hammock Bar

1A Ton Duc Thang Street (next to the Floating Hotel). District 1. ☎ *8291468.*
This converted cargo boat on the banks of the Saigon River makes for an excellent change of pace in watering holes. The upstairs bar is cozy and overlooks the nighttime river traffic. A little expensive, but as I said, a great change of pace. Good place to bring a date. Downstairs restaurant. Closed at press time, but hopefully only for a face lift.

Cay Thung

20 Mac Thi Buoi, Dist. 1.
A good, cheap bar but lacking the "action" of some of HCMC's other venues. Some outdoor tables. Quiet, but a good stop with a date or a few friends.

Chi-Chi's

4A Le Thanh Ton Street. District 1. ☎ *8226585.*
Boasts the longest bar in Saigon. Pool table and dart board.

Cheers!

Vien Dong Hotel, 275A Pham Ngu Lao Street. District 1. ☎ *8392052.*
Bar and disco with karaoke rooms in a casual setting. More popular with visiting Taiwan and Hong Kong businessmen than with Westerners, probably for the hostesses. Boring.

Doors Pub ★

10 Pham Ngu Lao, Dist 1.
Not a bar to let your hair down in, but the atmosphere's cozy and they show American movies in the early evening. Cheap prices for beer and other beverages. Serves snacks and light meals.

Gecko Bar ★

74/1A Hai Ba Trung, Dist. 1. ☎ 8242754.

Small bar with a good crowd of regulars. This is the place to go if you miss your Boddington's.

Hard Rock Cafe

24 Mac Thi Buoi Street. District 1.

This venerable institution has come to Saigon, and if it's your style, well...But if you think the Hard Rocks of London, Bangkok, Everywhere Else in the World, etc., are staid, you're in for a real yawner here.

Ice Blue ★

54 Dong Khoi Street. District 1.

Popular with both expats and Saigon yuppies. Female bartenders tend a long bar packed with mainly a male clientele. But this is a fun place; the staff is gregarious and everyone seems to be having a great time.

I Don't Know the Name of This Place ★★

Off Cach Mang Thang Tam, about 200 meters from the circle next to the New World Hotel, Dist. 1.

I really don't know the name of this bustling, loud and get-loose outdoor bar. But it's great. Waiters serve mussels and milk-baskets full of Saigon beer to your table as you're serenaded by beautiful Vietnamese girls in Johnnie Walker T-shirts cooing you into buying a sample drink or three from the bottles they carry around. Almost an all-Vietnamese crowd. The action's loud until only about 9, then the place gets dead quick. Definitely make a stop here and then tell me what the bloody name of the place is!

Press Club ★

Corner of Hai Ba Trung and Le Duan, Dist. 1.

Semi-outdoor cafe/bar that's a great place to bring a date. Mostly a Vietnamese clientele, mixed with foreigners. Especially cozy when it rains. My only complaint is that the Vietnamese pseudo-techno rock is played way too loud for the ambience. This is a place for conversation, and the two don't mix. Recommended, though. Run by the Ho Chi Minh Journalist's Assn. Art exhibits are occasionally presented here.

Q Bar ★★

Saigon Opera House (Theater) opposite the Caravelle Hotel, Dong Khoi, Dist. 1.

This is where the movers and shakers retire to martinis and business news in Saigon. Run by an expat New Yorker, the Q Bar is becoming what the Rex and the Caravelle were to expats during the war. Elegant and expensive. Better to be in suit than thongs here.

Rex Hotel Terrace Bar ★

141 Nguyen Hue, Dist. 1. ☎ 8292185.

This is the famous rooftop bar of the Rex Hotel where so many American officers nursed cognacs while bitching about Neil Sheehan and Jane Fonda. Sculpted shrubbery and totally outrageous cocktail prices. A single small-pour Johnnie Walker will

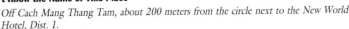

HO CHI MINH CITY

set you back seven bucks U.S. Worth it only to say you've been there, although it's a good place to gaze down on the phenomena of Saigon Sunday night cruising.

River Bar ★

5-7 Ho Huan Nghiep, Dist. 1. ☎ *8293734.*

A great place for burgers and beer. The music's only okay, but there's a pool table and satellite TV for sports and news freaks.

Rootz ★

44 Dong Du Street. District 1.

Lively and relaxed at the same time at this two-level bar near the river. An odd blend of West and East, both in decor and clientele, that seems to work, especially between dinner and the real late-night partying elsewhere. The miniskirt-clad hostesses seem a bit out of place, but who's complaining? Definitely worth a stop.

Saigon Headlines ★

Saigon Opera House (Theater), opposite the Continental Hotel, Dist. 1.

This was the "Q Bar" of Saigon before the Q Bar came around. Low, Moorish ceiling arches (watch your head) separate areas of the bar like caverns in a cave. Now that the full-wallet expat crowd has moved over to the Q Bar, SH has been taken over by Saigonese yuppies. Live music by musical-chairs Vietnamese pop performers. The biggest problem with this place is that they haven't changed the house band in three years, which hasn't changed its sets in three years. Worth a stop if only to see inside.

Sa Pa

8A/8 Don Dat Street. District 1. ☎ *8295783.*

The downstairs bar here gets a colorful collection of expats most nights of the week. Amiable Swiss owner who doesn't mind treating his customers to the odd drink. When was the last time you saw that—especially in Asia? A good conversational watering hole.

Stephanie's

14 Don Dat Street, Dist. 1. ☎ *8258471.*

Australian steaks and cold beer. Pool tables upstairs. A good place if you live here, but it can be skipped by tourists in for a night-on-the-town. The upstairs bar is usually deserted. Charming Viet Kieu owner who enjoys mingling with her customers. Recommended for a quiet evening out.

Tex-Mex

24 Le Thanh Ton Street, Dist. 1. ☎ *8295950.*

After hearing that a genuine south-of-the-border kind of place with real quesadillas, chile verde burritos and Dos Equis beer had opened in town, I—hailing from close to the border myself—was thrilled. But I was in for a small letdown. The place is more French than salsa. More mocking than authentic. I'll just have to wait for the next "hog" run with the boys down to San Felipe.

Wild Horse Saloon ★

8A1/D1 Thai Van Lung (Don Dat) Street, District 1. ☎ *8251901.*

I regularly jam with the house bands here in this American Old West theme bar and restaurant on Thursdays and Saturdays—regrettably usually clearing the joint. But the American West theme seems to work here, and there's a steady stable of hard-core regulars. The action heats up after dinner, usually about 10 p.m.

Wild West

Hai Ba Trung Street (between Mac Thi Buoi and Dong Du Streets), District 1.

Old West setting and run by a couple of Viet Kieus from the States. This place used to be better when there was live music. These days it's relatively dead, but occasionally gets lively on the weekends. Super-friendly staff and, despite the fact that the place may no longer be operating by the time you read this, it's possible to have a real good time here. Come alone and you may find another lonely soul to help brighten the evening.

Bia Om Joints/Hostess Bars

Bia om literally translates into something like drinking beer with someone's arms wrapped around your waist. In reality, it's not much different. *Bia om* venues in HCMC are no more than bars where men are served by pretty hostesses who will make themselves available for other extracurricular services should you have a bigger budget for the evening than a few bottles of Tiger. If you wanna get laid and don't much mind that half the city will know about it the following morning, these are the places for you.

Most of Saigon's *bia om* joints catering to Western tourists and expats are centered in the downtown area on and off Hai Ba Trung Street near the opera house. Others, for Vietnamese and other Asian (particularly Chinese) adulterers can be found scattered throughout the city, namely in and around Cholon—many simply whorehouses masquerading as karaoke and hostess joints. Unlike the charade found at most American (and Bangkok, for that matter) girlie clubs, where the hookers are seasoned and do about as good a job of faking an orgasm as passing for a nun, the girls found at the Hai Ba Trung venues are generally friendly and more concerned with finding a husband than wearing stupid Nguyen Dynasty ball gowns and seducing every 300-lb. tourist with a camcorder and an American Express gold card. These lasses are simply trying to make ends meet, and most of the money they make goes to their folks. I'd suggest not butterflying around if you're going to be in town for more than a few days. Finding a good girl in these places is almost ridiculously easy—making the whole bloody scene so damn melancholic. Take a good girl home (i.e., back to your hotel) and you may have just found a concubine for life. Perhaps even a loving and devoted lifelong wife. Leave for another, and you'll crush her heart.

Bia oms are typically small and dimly lit. I'll remain shy of actually stating them as intimate, as the subtle bouquets of urine, stale beer and cheap perfume have a way of flickering the candles, if you get my point. But think with the big head and you'll actually make some friends here and experience some quite enjoyable evenings at many of the places.

Oh, yeah—I forgot. Girls typically cost between US$50–$100 for an overnight. Somewhat less expensive for a short time, if that's what you're into.

Pub Sông Ngân

74/6 Hai Ba Trung Street. District 1. ☎ *090803641*

Small and dark, about the size and appearance of the cabin of a rich hooker's Lear jet. Owner Thuy is one of the most interesting women in Saigon.

(Tuyet Trang) Snow Bar

74/5 Hai Ba Trung Street. District 1. No telephone.

The Gecko

74/1A Hai Ba Trung Street. District 1. ☎ *8242754.*

The management of this establishment might blast me for calling this a *bia om*, so I won't—but it does indeed precariously straddle the fence between a mainstream, tastefully appointed watering hole and a place to meet ladies. It's just not as apparent.

Ngôi Sao (Star)

74 Hai Ba Trung Street. District 1. ☎ *090909195.*
Virtually a carbon copy of the Pub Sông Ngân.

Paradise

Hai Ba Trung Street (opposite the corner of Le Loi).
This is perhaps the coziest of the hostess bar settings, with its bamboo, Polynesian motif. A couple of pool tables here—the ladies are friendly and quite profficient at the game. Not a *bia om* in the sense of being able to smooch with a girl in a dark booth between guzzles on a BGI—so don't expect it. But the place is pleasant enough and quite popular.

Bia Hoi

In addition to the tourists and expat hangouts, no visit to Saigon is complete without a stop at one or more of the hundreds of *bia hoi* (fresh beer) joints in the city. Although more abundant and popular in the north of Vietnam—where the Vietnamese swill some 100,000 liters of the stuff every day—there are plenty of food-stallish *bia hoi* venues in the heart of HCMC.

Bia hoi is so fresh and perishable that it has to be consumed within 24 hours of being produced. With less chemical content than bottled beer (*bia hoi* has a similar alcohol content—but it's the chemicals that usually cause a hangover) *bia hoi* has become the life-blood of Vietnamese men. *Bia hoi* was only introduced to Vietnam about 30 years ago from Czechoslovakia with the arrival of the Czech *houblom* yeast. You can get drunk on the stuff, but it's not as easy as imbibing bottled or canned beer. Small *bia hoi* stalls can be found throughout the city (and are even more numerous in Hanoi). They're typically sidewalk perches where the owner has thrown out a few stools. They're dirty looking, and the brew attracts flies the way—well, you know. The conditions under which the beverage is consumed naturally keep all the tourists away—grungy-looking stalls and sticky floors strewn with cigarette butts, dried squid, peanut shells, goat meat, snake meat, fish sauce and stray, mangy Third World dogs.

WHAT TO EAT WITH BIA HOI

No bia hoi experience is complete without sampling the gourmet cuisine that is served with it. May your taste buds tingle in delight.

Chan Ga   *Boiled chicken feet (mmm!)*

WHAT TO EAT WITH BIA HOI

Dau Phu	*Soya cake*
Khoai tay ran	*Chips*
Lac	*Peanuts*
Muc	*Dried squid*
Nem chua	*Spring rolls*
Nhong	*Silkworm (plenty of protein!)*
Nom	*Salad*
Nuoc mam	*Fish sauce*
Oc	*Snail (gimmee more!)*
Thit bo xao	*Fried beef*
Thit cho	*Dog (Lassie—mmmm!)*
Thit de	*Goat meat in fish sauce*
Thit ran	*Snake (chase it quickly)*

In the south, *bia hoi* is produced by the Saigon and Dong Nai breweries—in the north by the Halida and Hanoi breweries. Vietnamese from all levels of society congregate together when the *bia hoi* barrels are tapped. And they can afford it. *Bia hoi* sells at 2000-3000 dong a glass—a large glass.

Bia hoi has been so popular since the mid-'60s, the Vietnamese once had to be rationed the brew. With coupons in hand, they queued at state-run stores waiting for their meager two glasses a day. However, now *bia hoi* is everywhere. But not all the time. The brew is so popular that many stalls run out of their daily supply by mid-day. Most of the stuff is gone by the early evening.

Want to hoist a few?

Thanh Nha

> 6 Hai Ba Trung, Dist. 1.
> This is my favorite *bia hoi* stall in Saigon. It's one of the cleaner venues in town (or at least it looks something akin to a bar—i.e., there's a roof over your head). But the flies abound and your hands just may get stuck to the table. It's one of the bigger *bia hoi* stalls around. If you're timid, but have been lured by the above words, this place will make a great introduction.

Bia Hoi

> 20-26 Thi Sach, Dist. 1.
> This is my second choice. More foreigners here, who have already gotten their feet wet, literally.

Bia Hoi Dong Nai

> 1 Nguyen Sieu, Dist. 1.
> Another popular stall that sees some foreigners from time to time.

Bia Hoi ★

79 Nguyen Dinh Chieu, Dist. 3.
This place is packed throughout the day. Few foreigners.

The Garage ★

90G Tran Quoc Toan, Dist. 3.
As authentic as they come. You'll be greeted with smiles and back-patting, and the
stories of toothless old war vets.

Nightclubs/Discos

Cheers

Vien Dong Hotel, 275 Pham Ngu Lao, Dist.1. ☎ *8392116.*
Hostess disco that attracts a large Chinese clientele at times. Cross between a pub
and a disco. The karaoke seems more popular than anything else. Private karaoke
rooms with English- and Chinese-speaking hostesses.

Cinta ★

Saigon Lodge Hotel, 215 Nam Ky Khoi Nghia, Dist. 3. ☎ *8230112.*
Depending on the night, you'll find expats, locals or tourists. European, Asian and
American DJs at the helm play contemporary Western and Asian pop hits. Popular.

Gossip ★★

Mercure Hotel. 79 Tran Hung Dao Street. District 1. ☎ *8242525/555.*
For Westerners and hip locals, this is the most happenin' throb joint in town. Excellent sound and light systems, blaring techno and patrons groomed straight out of a
16-month-old copy of *Vogue*. Large and airy, and very, very popular with Saigon's
foreign expats, in addition to the city's most beautiful and endowed (monetarily and
otherwise) women. Groovy, man.

Hai Van Disco

Hai Van Hotel, 69 Huynh Thuc Khang, Dist. 1. ☎ *8291274.*
This place, on the third floor of the hotel, gets packed—entirely with Vietnamese.
But the odd thing about it is its hours. The most popular time to be boogying away
to the live music here is 10 a.m. Sunday mornings! Or even more bizarre, at 2 p.m.
Monday afternoons! And yet it's closed 11 p.m. Saturday nights. You figure it out.

Orient Club

104 Hai Ba Trung, Dist. 1. ☎ *8222547.*
More popular with locals than with foreigners. This place is dark, the way young
Vietnamese couples like it. Mostly Vietnamese "white" pop.

Planet Europa

A43 Truong Son Street, Tan Binh District (next to the Saigon Superbowl).
One local rag described this Starship Enterprise of Saigon's discos as "cheezy," and
the guy who penned it wasn't far off. Part of a Singapore chain of upscale rave joints,
the Planet's all decked out in a loony interstellar motif—all the waiters dress up like
a cross between Dorothy's Tin Man and Star Trek's Worf. The music is pretty tame
and lame, definitely intent on bulging the Bee Gees' royalties coffer. The biggest
problem, though, is the location in the boonies out by the airport. Expats needn't
bother, as they can get the same action back in town.

Saxophone Bar

New World Hotel, 76 Le Lai, Dist. 1. ☎ 8228888.

What you'd expect at a five-star hotel. On Saturday nights, it becomes pretty busy. Mainly Asian clientele dancing to spun music and the occasional international live act. But I've never been comfortable at a bar most folks head for because there's no other choice—as in hotel bars and airport bars. And this place is no exception. I prefer tanking amongst friends.

Saxo Club

91 Hai Ba Trung Street. District 1. ☎ 8228305.

Really more a bar than a nightclub, but the nightly live music gives it a bowery jazz club feel. Pool table and darts—even putt-putt golf.

Starlight Nightclub & Disco

Century Saigon Hotel, 68A Nguyen Hue, Dist. 1. ☎ 8231818.

Way up on the 11th floor for some great views of Saigon when the action's slow. The disco recently introduced an expat night on Thursdays to attract those who have been staying away.

Venus Club

Saigon Star Hotel, 204 Nguyen Thi Minh Khai, Dist. 3. ☎ 8230260.

Better for the karaoke than for the disco, which is too small.

Wine Delivery

International Fine Foods

☎ 8420212. Mobile ☎ 090909012. FAX: 8420288.

When pizza delivery came to Saigon, some folks were outraged, others curious, and the balance simply hungry. Now HCMC wine connoisseurs can let their fingers do the walking. IFF, which formerly served only the restaurant and hotel sectors, has gone retail. There are more than 50 wines from six countries in the IFF cellars. French, Chilean and Australian wines can be found here and prices range from US$6.50 to US$30 a bottle. These folks will deliver a case or merely a single bottle to your doorstep, at no extra charge.

Shopping in Ho Chi Minh City

Cosmetics & Perfumes

Angela

132 Dong Khoi, Dist. 1.

Very expensive and specializing in Maybelline and Christian Dior products. Behind the Continental Hotel.

Fuji Cosmetics

96 Nam Ky Khoi Nghia. Dist 1. ☎ 8223100.

Small little shop in the downtown area with Fuji, Revlon, Max Factor and Chifune products available.

Paris Beaute

127 Le Thanh Ton, Dist. 1.

Cosmetics shop that specializes in Joseph, Eclat d'Ete, Masculin and Galenie products.

Sporting Goods, Clothing & Fashion

Ben Thanh Market

At the intersection of Le Loi and Pham Hong Thai, Dist 1.
Some of the best bargains in Saigon are found here. But be warned that much of the clothing is counterfeit.

Dung Cu

82B Nguyen Thi Minh Khai, Dist. 3.
All types of sports equipment, from tennis rackets to golf clubs. Sportswear, as well.

Eskmo

82B Nguyen Thi Minh Khai, Dist 3.
A small, elegant shop for women. European designs.

Haia

68 Ly Tu Trong, Dist. 1. ☎ *8295085.*
A wide selection of sports shoes from Reebok, Nike, etc. And some of them are real!

Khanh Dang Silk & Fashion

112 Nguyen Hue, Dist. 1. ☎ *8296708.*
One of the best places for silk in HCMC. Everything from suits to T-shirts. Tailored men's silk shirts and trousers, as well as ties, dresses for women and fabric. Recommended.

Kim Phuong

39B Ngo Duc Ke, Dist. 1. ☎ *8225665.*
Silk products and tapestries. Beautiful tablecloths.

Ly Ly

229 Ly Tu Trong, Dist. 1.
Sportswear and swimming attire.

Minh Doan

120 Le Thanh Ton, Dist. 1. ☎ *8231687.*
Custom-tailored European styles for men and women.

Moiselle Collection

128C Hai Ba Trung, Dist. 1. ☎ *8295579.*
Women's dresses and business suits, all custom-tailored.

Tropic

73A Le Thanh Ton, Dist. 1. ☎ *8297542.*
New silk shop that offers lingerie, embroidery and linen for the home.

Jewelry

Most jewelry in Saigon is sold along Le Loi and Dong Khoi Streets. Numerous shops offer gold as well as stones. Be warned that items aren't particularly a bargain. Better bargains on gold can be had in Cambodia.

Alpha

163 Dong Khoi, Dist. 1. ☎ *8258356.*
Gold and silver items in the heart of the shopping district.

Saigon Girl

176 Ly Tu Trong, Dist. 1.

Popular with European tourists for clothing as well as jewelry and cosmetics.

Art

Hoang Hac

73 Ly Tu Trong, Dist. 3. ☎ *8223198.*
Large collection of abstract and contemporary oil paintings.

Tu Do Art Gallery ★

142 Dong Khoi, Dist. 1. ☎ *8298540.*
This gallery offers the finest selection of oil and lacquer artwork in town, as well as silk prints. Vietnam's most prominent artists are represented here, including Thu Ha, Bui Ngoc Tu and Nguyen Pham. Recommended.

Food/Supermarkets
District 1

Donamart ★

63 Ly Tu Trong, Dist. 1. ☎ *8244808.*
Big supermarket in central Saigon where most expats do their shopping. Good selection of imported foods as well as other household items. Expensive. Restaurant upstairs.

Mademoiselle de Paris

249 Le Thanh Ton, Dist 1. ☎ *8222890.*
French food and wines. Next to Ben Thanh Market.

Nhu Lan ★

66 Ham Nghi, Dist. 1.
Some say this is the best bakery in town, but it's getting tough to tell these days, with a proliferation of boutique food shops opening in HCMC. Cheeses, meats, breads, cakes, sandwiches.

Saigon Food Center

393b Tran Hung Dao, Dist. 1.
Brand-new connoisseurs' market that's splashy and expensive. Best bet for pastries, cakes and cheeses. More a series of deserted restaurants and banquet rooms than a market. It doesn't seem to do a roaring business.

Sana Epicerie ★

35 Dong Du, Dist 1.
A good place to stock up on meats, sausages, wines, champagne, chocolates—and Bass Ale.

Shop 125 ★

125 Le Thanh Ton, Dist 1.
Fancy new establishment offering an array of liquors and soft drinks, as well as food.

7-Eleven Gesevina

16 Nguyen Hue, Dist. 1. ☎ *8290046.*
Nice selection of fine foods. Specializes in ice cream.

Co-opmart

189C Cong Quynh Street. ☎ *8325239, 8394973. Open 9 a.m.-9 p.m.*

Packaged food, cosmetics, clothes, children's toys, fresh food department. Free home delivery services by phone.

Minimart

101 Nam Ky Khoi Nghia Street. ☎ *8292035. Open 8 a.m.-6 p.m.*
Packaged food, cosmetics, clothes, children's toys, household items, footwear, children's accessories. Free home delivery services by phone.

Komart

41 Hai Ba Trung Street. ☎ *8222284.*
Food, household items.

Megamart

71 Pasteur Street. ☎ *8222578.*
Food, household items, childrens' accessories.

Phong Lan

85 Dong Khoi Street. ☎ *8297846.*
Packaged food, household items, cosmetics, hair & body care products.

Saigon Mart

196 Hai Ba Trung Street. ☎ *8228913.*
Packaged food, household items, cosmetics, health care products.

Student Mart

138 Tran Quang Khai Street. ☎ *8444068.*
Heath care products, stationery, school supplies, packaged food products.

U-Save Mart

57 Nguyen Du Street. ☎ *8258359.*
Food, heath care products, beauty products, cosmetics, stationery & supplies.

District 3

Unimart

228A Pasteur Street. ☎ *8201166.*
Food, heath care products, beauty products, cosmetics, stationery & supplies.

Bill's Minimart

142 Vo Thi Sau Street. ☎ *8200326*
Food, heath care products, beauty products, cosmetics, stationery & supplies.

Liquormart

241 Hai Ba Trung Street. ☎ *8223883.*
Name brand liquors from around the world; no counterfeits.

Rose Food Super

145 Nam Ky Khoi Nghia Street. ☎ *8281760.*
Packaged foods, cosmetics, household items, health care products.

SB Center

272B Pasteur Street. ☎ *8223230.*
Packaged foods and snacks, some household items, beauty aids, heath care products.

Van Khach Den

419 Hai Ba Trung Street. ☎ *8295629.*

Packaged foods and snacks, some household goods, beauty & health care products.

Yvonne

418 Nguyen Thi Minh Khai Street. ☎ *8334967.*
Household items, health care & beauty products.

District 5

Citimart   ★

235 Nguyen Van Cu, Dist. 5. ☎ *8358692. Open 9 a.m.–noon and 2:20–9:20 p.m.*
The largest and best supermarket in HCMC. Name it and it's here: imported foods,
wines, clothing, jewelry, toys, household items.

Citimart Lakai

121 Nguyen Tri Phuong Street. ☎ *8578552.*
Smaller but with a good selection of household items and packaged food.

District 6

Binh Tay Shop

258 Thap Muoi. ☎ *8554394.*
Packaged foods, household items, beauty & health care products.

District 10

Maximart

3C Ba Thang Hai Street. ☎ *8356617. Open 9:30 a.m.-9:30 p.m. (Sat. & Sun. until 10
p.m.)*
Packaged food, cosmetics, fresh food, fashion apparel (Vietnam-style).

Phu Nhuan District

Vinamart

157 Phan Dang Luu Street. ☎ *8441962. Open 9 a.m.-9 p.m.*
Packaged food, electronic goods, cosmetics, textiles, apparel, household items, children's toys and accessories.

PNJ Mart

52 Nguyen Van Troi Street. ☎ *8444547.*
Household goods, packaged food.

Binh Thanh District

Tonamart

37 Xo Viet Nghe Tinh Street. ☎ *8400017.*
Packaged foods, household items, heath care & beauty products.

Sports in Ho Chi Minh City

What would have been unheard of 10 years ago is a reality today, as HCMC is beginning to resemble Los Angeles more than Moscow. All types of sporting activities are available today, including golf and even betting on horses.

Golf Courses

Golf Vietnam Thu Duc

An Phu Village, Thu Duc. ☎ *8960756, 8252951.*
I don't know how they keep the fairways in shape here, but they do. Not a particularly challenging course for the seasoned golfer, it's still a helluvalot of fun to be
playing golf in Vietnam. Full, 18-hole course with driving range (US$3 for a bucket

of balls), clubhouse, 19th hole. You'll need to hire a caddie here. And, yes, you—Joe Public—can call ahead and get a starting time. But—fore!—be prepared to shell out some cash. Greens fees are US$73–$92. Club rentals are US$13. A caddie runs US$15. Expats take note: membership fees range from US$15,000 for an individual membership to US$100,000 for a top-end corporate membership, which results not in more privilages, but in the higher cost of consumer goods—or whatever your company makes.

Song Be Club

Thuan Giao Commune, Thuan An Dist., Song Be Province. ☎ *(65) 55800.*
This is perhaps the area's better course, but it's open to members only at press time. 18 holes, par 72, 6647-meter course. Song Be is about 20 km north of HCMC. Get a member to invite you.

Horse Racing

Phu Tho Club

2 Le Dai Hanh, Dist. 11. ☎ *8551205.*
Nice track with a VIP club overlooking the venue. Racing on Saturday and Sunday afternoons, and on two Tuesdays per month. You can place bets here between 1000-50,000 dong on the first two places *(quinellas)*. Long-distance cycling events are also held here.

Gyms and Fitness Centers

Cu Ta The Hinh Club

Phan Dinh Phung Stadium Annex, 132 Pasteur, Dist. 3.
Gym with a less than modern weight training system. But it's still a good place for a heavy workout. Be warned: there's no air conditioning here. You'll fry.

World Gym

26 Le Thanh Ton, Dist. 1. ☎ *8221416.*
This is where most of the expats go. Imported, relatively modern weight equipment. Sauna, fitness instruction, custom training programs.

Bowling

Superbowl

A43 Truong Son Street, Tan Binh District (1 km from the airport).
That ubiquitous cornfield icon has arrived in Saigon. Can Chris Schenkel be far behind? Ultra-modern lanes with Saigon's only escalator (beside a couple at the airport). Any kid who's anybody in Saigon does the scene here. The only drag is having to change shoes into those nerdy clown slippers. Glancing around, you'd think Saigon was the hippest place between Hong Kong and Sydney. The fact that the city still has some catching up to do is evidenced by the many folks who journey all the way out here just to look at the escalator. Expensive at three bucks a game during peak hours—a bit less at other times (when anyone sane is sleeping).

Motorcycling

Motorcycling, quite simply, is damned dangerous in Vietnam and particularly in Saigon. But if you're going to be here on a long-term basis, you'll eventually have no other choice but to rent a motorbike or larger motorcycle. The motorcycle has been my means of transportation in Vietnam for years, and the joys of biking out in the Vietnamese countryside are nothing less than enthralling. I've led organized tours of Vietnam by mototcycle, both long and short—and if you're into bikes, there's no true Vietnamese experience like letting 'er rip in the provinces. Those who have done it, whether solo or in a "pack," have no comparable memories—of anything, including sex.

Whether it be a short jaunt to the Mekong Delta or the Central Highlands, or a longer trip up the coast, biking is a total rush here. If you're planning or would consider motorcycling in Vietnam—whether it just be around town or on a longer road trip—I strongly suggest you pick up a copy of my book *Fielding's Southern Vietnam on 2 Wheels*, available at most bookstores. The book contains the essentials for motorcycling in Vietnam, and outlines both day and extended trips, complete with maps, route descriptions and distances. If you can't find it in your local bookstore, call ☎ *(800) FW-2-GUIDE* to order a copy for US$15.95.

Motorbike (175cc and below) rentals are available at the backpacker guesthouses along De Tham Street in District 1, as well as other selected hotels. At these venues you'll also find some of the Russian- and East Bloc-built Minsks and Jawas. Note that the Vietnamese are not permitted to ride anything larger than 150cc, so the availability of anything larger in Saigon is extremely limited. The police definitely stare down the larger bikes, and there's a good chance you may be stopped and asked to present your paperwork if you're riding anything larger than 150cc. So be warned. However, foreigners are permitted to rent the larger bikes, as scarce as they are. Smaller Honda Dreams and 50cc–70cc Honda Cubs, and similar models, run only about US$6–$8 a day. A 125cc Bonus will set you back US$8–$10 a day. While the larger 250cc–750cc rent for US$20–$25 per day. Insurance is not available. You make the bed you sleep in.

Technically, you'll need an international drivers license with a motorcycle endorsement, your home state drivers or motorcycle license and, of course, your passport. However, in reality, few if any of the rental firms require the documents (although the police probably will if you're stopped). And if you're staying in Vietnam any longer than 30 days, you'll need to trade your international license in to the local police for a Vietnamese operators permit, at a cost of about US$100. (The international license will be returned to you upon request—which should be made just prior to leaving Vietnam.). When renting a motorbike or motorcycle make sure you obtain a copy of the bike's registration. This is essential, namely to keep bribes to a minimum.

You might also be disappointed to learn that no dual sport bikes are available in HCMC. They simply can't be found. The larger-cc configurations are limited to Japanese street bikes and "choppers," such as the Honda Magna, Yamaha Virago and Honda Rebel—as well as the occasional and very expensive Honda Steed (called the Shadow in the U.S. market). I've seen only one Harley Fat Boy in Saigon and it ain't for rent.

For renting machines, contact Mr. Binh at:

B & B Motor Service
   258/112 Tran Hung Dao Street
   District 1
   Ho Chi Minh City
   ☎ *8393125, phonelink 281-15001*

Binh is a man who knows his stuff and is the regular Vietnamese tour leader for organized motorcycle tours that are conducted in Vietnam. He's also a nice guy, but his English is limited—so bring a friend and tell him I sent you.

Directory

INSIDER TIP: VIETNAM'S BURGEONING MOTORBIKE PROBLEM

Saigon is one of the most dangerous cities in the world to travel through via car, bicycle, motorbike and motorcycle. To the uninitiated, two-wheeled traffic here is so overwhelmingly intimidating that few Westerners venture into traffic through their own means. And the motorcycle problem in HCMC is only going to get worse. In 1995, there were 2.7 million registered motorbikes on the streets of Vietnam, compared with 600,000 in 1990. Honda accounts for about 70 percent of these machines. And more than 400,000 motorbikes and motorcycles are imported into the country each year. Most come from Japan, Taiwan, Korea, Indonesia, Singapore, Thailand, Russia and Germany. But an increasing number of the machines are being smuggled into Vietnam through the Cambodian border. In 1993, 200,000 motorcycles were registered in HCMC alone, bringing the total number of motorbikes in the city to 1,060,000. Motorbike imports reached 350,000 a year in 1995, and will rise to 500,000 annually until the year 2000. This is making congestion virtually unbearable. The number of motorbikes—many dangerously traversing Vietnamese streets—has seriously hampered HCMC's mass transit capabilities. Quite simply, the Vietnamese's increasing ability to purchase motorbikes has far outpaced the government's ability to improve the traffic network. And the death toll on the nation's roads is mounting. In 1996, more than 5000 people were killed in traffic accidents in Vietnam—and this is in a country where the majority of people still get around by bicycle. Fully 70 percent of all road accidents in Vietnam involve motorbikes. If you have the insane inclination to rent a motorbike in Saigon, remember this important regulation: For any bike you rent over 50cc, you must have an international driver's license. Vietnamese themselves are not permitted to own or operate a motorcycle more than 175cc, although foreigners are permitted to rent bikes with far greater power (which you'll greatly appreciate on good roads out in the provinces on long journeys). A Vietnamese spotted by the police on a big motorcycle will invariably be pulled over, although foreigners rarely are. (I have been pulled over by the police on a number of occasions, however, sometimes through inadvertently violating a Vietnamese law, and sometimes for having done nothing wrong at all.)

Transportation

Ho Chi Minh City is 1710 km from Hanoi, 1071 km from Hue, 965 km from Danang, 445 km from Nha Trang, 340 km from Ha Tien, 300 km from Dalat, 250 from Rach Gia, 165 km from Can Tho, 115 from Vung Tau, 147 from Vinh Long and 72 km from My Tho.

By air:

Downtown Ho Chi Minh City is about a 20-minute ride (8 km) from the airport (Tan Son Nhat Airport). It's a relatively modern airport by Southeast Asian standards, but still is far from the likes of Bangkok's Don Muang or Singapore's Changi

Airports. But the facilities here are quite a bit better than at Hanoi's Noi Bai Airport. If you do a lot of international traveling, do not let your film, computerized camera, laptop computers, etc., go through the airport's primitive X-Ray machines— although they display signs in English saying they are "film safe," which simply means that your equipment won't actually melt or come out the other side as an Egg McMuffin.

There is a branch of the Vietcom Bank here for changing money, as well as Vietnamtourism, Saigontourist and Cuu Long Tourist offices. There is also a post office. Don't rely on any of the tourist organizations for hotel suggestions if you're on a budget. Instead, just outside the airport, you will find at the taxi stand an acceptable list of accommodations in Saigon with their prices posted. Many backpackers arrive at the airport without any idea as to where they'll be staying, but instead rely on travel guides that often list accommodations that simply don't exist anymore. Remember, hotels in Saigon are generally quite expensive, and if you're only planning on spending US$3–$5 a night here, be prepared to share your "room" with various other manifestations of Southeast Asian life forms.

Use the list at the taxi stand to determine where you'll spend at least your first night in HCMC. You should choose a hotel in the US$10–$20 range, and one preferably close to District 1 (Downtown Saigon).Get a feel for the city and where other travelers are staying, but don't do this at the bar atop the Rex Hotel. Be sure that all your paperwork is in order, and carry additional passport photos than the required three. Any lapse in presenting the correct documents will send you back to the end of the customs lines, which have become massive waits in recent months with the armies of tourists arriving in Vietnam. If you're an American, at the time of this writing, your visa will not be stamped into your passport, but instead will be a separate document with your picture attached. You'll also need additional photos for your declaration forms. If you don't have the necessary photos, there is a desk behind the customs area where you can have the photos taken. But this can take as long as customs processing itself.

Upon arrival at HCMC airport, assuming everything is kosher, it'll take more than an hour before you're on the street. Outside the airport are numerous touts with license badges attached to their shirts signifying they are official taxi drivers. They will swarm upon you like bees on new lotus blossoms. By taxi, you shouldn't pay any more than US$8 to get to your destination. There are regular international connections to Jakarta, Bangkok, Manila, Kuala Lumpur, Singapore, Vientiane, Moscow, Paris, Frankfurt and Amsterdam (to list a few) on airlines including Vietnam Airlines, Air France, Philippine Airlines, Garuda Indonesia, Thai, Lao Aviation, SK Air, MAS, Singapore Airlines—and soon on Delta and United.

By bus:

The **Mien Tay** terminal (in An Lac, about 10 km west of HCMC) serves the Mekong Delta. To get there, take Hau Giang or Hung Vuong boulevards west from Cholon. ☎ *8255955*). It is quite a distance southwest of town on Hung Vuong Boulevard, and serves the Mekong Delta area, including My Tho, Vinh Long, Can Tho, Chau

Doc, Rach Gia, Long Xuyen, Long An, Ca Mau and other delta locations. Buses to points north, including Phan Thiet (6 hours), Vung Tau 3 hours), Dalat (8 hours), Nha Trang (11 hours), Qui Nhon (17 hours), Danang (25 hours) and Hue (29 hours)—as well as other locations—depart from HCMC's **Mien Dong** terminal, which is on the north side of the city on Xo Viet Nghe Tinh Street off National Highway 13 near the Saigon River. Wake up early, as the express buses leave between 5 and 5:30 a.m. To be safe, purchase your tickets a day in advance for both terminals, although this is often not necessary.

(Note: Express buses receive priority treatment at ferry crossings and, although I've heard horror stories of tourists waiting an hour or more to cross the two rivers by ferry from HCMC to Can Tho, I've never had to wait more than just a few moments. Automobiles and motorcycles also receive priority treatment at the ferry crossings.) Book your tickets in advance—although, in many instances, you won't need to, as they depart when they are full (first come, first serve). You can also take a bus to Cambodia's Phnom Penh, which leaves from the Phnom Penh Bus Garage at *155 Nguyen Hue Boulevard*. You'll need a Cambodian visa; tickets are cheap (about US$5 one way) and the trip takes from 10–12 hours, although I've heard of some taking as few as 8 hours due to a lack of delays at the border.

Local buses are a hassle. There is indeed a route system, but it is followed irregularly and buses sometimes stop where they want to. Routes are extremely limited. Bus stops are generally unmarked and, frankly, very few foreigners are seen aboard local buses due to these reasons. To the uninitiated, local buses in Saigon are a crapshoot. Experiment if you want to, but bring a map, a Vietnamese-English dictionary and a change of underwear. And don't make any plans to meet anybody. (It might help to register with your embassy in the event you get really lost.) Fares range from VND1000 to VND3000.

By microbus:

You can also travel by microbus (or minibus), which has become an increasingly popular form of travel for overseas Vietnamese, Vietnamese and foreign tourists. However, there never seem to be any permanent departure points for these vehicles. Hotels are the best places to ask about microbus service. There is a microbus office at *39 Nguyen Hue Boulevard*. Buses here leave for Dalat, Vung Tau, Nha Trang, Hue, Danang and Quy Nhon. Another office, I was told, is at *89-91 Nguyen Du Street*.

By train:

The Saigon railway station (Ga Hoa Hung) is about 2 km from District 1 and has regular daily connections with all points north of Saigon. If you're going anywhere by train for more than eight hours, get a sleeping berth. The trip to Hanoi can take from 40–50 hours. Ouch! Foreigners are charged extraordinarily more for tickets than are Vietnamese. To get to the dilapidated station, take Cach Mang Thang Tam Street to the turn-off at *132/9*. Or take the roundabout at *Cach Mang Tam Street* and *3 Thang 2 Boulevard*. A cyclo ride from the city center should cost between US$.50–$1. Train schedules change often, so it's pointless to list them here.

By ferry:

To get down to the Mekong Delta, go to the ferry landing on Ton Duc Thang Street at the end of Ham Ngi Blvd. To get to Can Tho takes about a day and costs US$1. To Chau Doc, count on another 12 hours and an additional 2000 dong. There are also high speed river **hydrofoils** that make the trip to Vung Tau down the Saigon River from near the Harbor restaurant on Ton Duc Thang and Ham Nghi Streets. It's an exhilarating and fast ride (about 1.5 hours) but expensive (US$10).

By car:

Cars with drivers (the only way you can rent a car) rent for anywhere between US$40–$70 a day from HCMC travel agents. However, there are many private operators who hang out in the square next to Reunification Hall and will undercut the tourist and travel agents. To the Cu Chi tunnels, a car can be had for about US$50; although this is only a half-day trip, most of the tourist companies will insist that the minimum car rental period is a full day. Also, some of the larger hotels can provide autos, but filled with five passengers, for as low as US$30 a day. Check around.

By Taxi

Taxis swarm Saigon like bees on honey. All you need to do in most parts of the city is simply stand on the sidewalk and flag one down. It'll take no more than a moment or two. This is particularly true in the downtown area. (Regrettably, you'll also attract a swarm of cyclos.) If you're concerned about price, Festival is the cheapest. But be prepared to wait a few minutes after you've called them. Fares (in dong) range from 5000–6500 for the first km, and 5000–7500 for the following km. The price gets lower on some after the ninth kilometer, and fares are always negotiable if you have the patience to haggle over the price and the distance you're going.

If you have called a taxi, wait for that taxi company's car to show up. While you're waiting, you'll no doubt be swarmed by other cabs looking for your business. But you telephoned ahead, so wait for the right one. The driver should turn on the meter as soon as you begin rolling. Make sure the driver does this or get out of the car. He's looking to bilk some bucks from you.

HO CHI MINH CITY

Taxi Services

Airport Taxi (white)
☎ *8446666*

Saigon Taxi (white)
☎ *8448888*

Ben Thanh Taxi (red)
☎ *8422422*

Saigon Taxi (dark blue)
☎ *8424242*

Cholon Taxi (white)
☎ *8226666*

Saigontourist Taxi (red)
☎ *8222206*

Davi Taxi (white)
☎ *8290290*

Star Taxi (white)
☎ *8651111*

Festival Taxi (gray)
☎ *8454545*

Tanaco Taxi (red)
☎ *8226226*

Gia Dinh Taxi (white)	**Taxico (white)**
☎ *8226699*	☎ *8350350*
Phnom Penh Bus	**V Taxi (red)**
☎ *8230754*	☎ *8202020*
Saigon Airport Service Co.	**Vinataxi (yellow)**
☎ *8295925*	☎ *8422888*

Getting around Saigon is easy and cheap. **Cyclos** are the slowest but cheapest form of transportation (the drivers who hang out at the more expensive hotels usually charge more), but you can also rent **bicycles** from numerous hotels and bike rental shops throughout the city for 8000–10,000 dong per day. Negotiate. You can also rent small **motorbikes** such as Honda Cubs and Dreams for as little as US$6 per day. I recommend **Kolo Rentals** at *7 Lam Son Square* (across from the Continental Hotel). ☎ *8296499*. They'll rent even larger bikes if you've got the proper international driver's license (see "Motorcycling" for a more complete description). If you break down within a 100 km radius, they will provide the necessary repairs free of charge.

Banks and Moneychangers

Vietcom Bank is located across the city, at Nguyen Hue Boulevard across from the Rex, at *123 Dong Khoi Street*, and a large main branch on Ben Chuong Duong and Nam Ky Khoi Nghia Streets. **The Foreign Exchange** bank is located at *101 Nam Ky Khoi Nghia Street* (Vietcom as mentioned above). There is also a Vietcom bank at the airport's international terminal.

Many foreign banks have now opened offices in Saigon. **Bangkok Bank Ltd.** has a branch on Nguyen Hue Blvd about halfway from the Rex to the River. The **Thai Military Bank** is also in Saigon, and banking with them you have the advantage of withdrawing funds directly from the office in Saigon even though your account may be in Thailand. Bangkok Bank offers no such service. Remember, at many banks, you will not be permitted to convert dong into dollars.

You can also change money at hotels, although the rate you may receive is 10,000 for every dollar (if you change small amounts), whereas the official exchange rate is 10,900-11,000 dong to the dollar. Some hotels will offer rates as high as 10,900 dong to the dollar—not bad considering the hotels aren't banks. You can also change money in jewelry and gold shops at favorable rates, but don't change money on the street. At the various markets around HCMC you will be approached by black marketeers offering to exchange money. Keep in mind that 50 or so foreign banks have recently opened offices in HCMC, and the number rises daily.

General Post Office

2 Cong Xa Paris, next to the Notre Dame cathedral, open from 7:30 a.m.–10 p.m. every day. There are international telephone and fax connections here, although you won't be able to make a collect call overseas without getting a Vietnamese to do it for you. Faxes aren't much cheaper to send from here compared with from your hotel, perhaps 30 cents a page internationally. Besides, all faxes sent from here must go through the Fax Center on Hai Ba Trung Street before they're sent to their final destination. So, even if there isn't a line at the GPO fax window, you'll still have to wait up to 15 minutes before you'll get a confirmation report—much longer if there is a line at the window. Frankly, I don't think the savings are worth it. Of course, you can send faxes directly from the Fax Center itself. It's located on Hai Ba Trung Street in District 1, directly across from the large Catholic church. At the GPO, there's also a window for making international and domestic phone calls. You'll need to fill out a form listing your name and address in Saigon and the name, phone number and address (you can usually skip the latter) of the party you're calling. You'll be required to pay first—so choose the number of minutes you think you'll need to be on the line. (If your call lasts a shorter duration than the time you paid for, you'll be refunded after you've finished the call.) You'll then be directed to a numbered booth. Pick up the receiver and wait for the operator's instructions. English is spoken quite well, and few people have hassles making calls from the GPO.

A portait of Ho Chi Minh dominates Saigon's General Post Office.

TNT International Express

406 Nguyen Tat Thanh Street. ☎ *8222886 or 8225520.*

DHL Worldwide Express

DHL

253 Hoang Van Thu Street, Tan Binh District, Ho Chi Minh City. ☎ *8446203, 8444268. FAX: 8445387. General Post Office, 2 Cong Xa Paris, District 1, Ho Chi Minh City.* ☎ *8231525.*

Located at the GPO. The major hotels such as the Rex and the Saigon Floating Hotel offer all types of international business services. See "Air Couriers" in the Vietnam Today chapter for more information.

Federal Express

Federal Express (FedEx)

1 Nguyen Hau Street, District 1, Ho Chi Minh City. ☎ *8290747. FAX: 8290477.*

You'll find FedEx in the GPO building, but through a separate entrance on the left hand side of the building near the corner of Hai Ba Trung. International courier services. See "Air Couriers" in the Vietnam Today chapter for more information.

Foreign Affairs Office

6 Thai Van Lung Street. ☎ *8223032 or 8224124.*

Immigration Office

161 Nguyen Du Street. ☎ *8299398.*

Hospitals

Cho Ray Hospital. *Nguyen Chi Thanh Boulevard.*

Airlines

Vietnam Airlines

(International Office) *116-118 Nguyen Hue Blvd.* ☎ *8292118.* Across from the Rex next to City Hall. (Domestic Office) *15 Dinh Tien Hoang Street.* ☎ *8299980.*

Air France
130 Dong Khoi Street. ☎ *8230746.*

Cathay Pacific
49 Le Thanh Ton Street. ☎ *8223272.*

China Airlines
132-134 Dong Khoi Street.
☎ *8251387/9: FAX: 8251390*

EVA Air
129 Dong Khoi Street. ☎ *822488. FAX: 8223567*

KLM Royal Dutch Airlines
244 Pasteur Street, Quan 3.
☎ *8231990, 8231991. FAX: 8231989*

MAS
116 Nguyen Hue Boulevard, just above the VN office. ☎ *8292118.*

Pacific Airlines
27B Nguyen Dinh Chieu Street.
☎ *8200978*

Philippine Airlines
☎ *8292200*

Quantas
311 Dien Bien Phu Street. ☎ *8396194. FAX: 8396199*

Singapore Airlines
6 Le Loi Street. ☎ *8231583*

Thai Airways
116 Nguyen Hue Boulevard.
☎ *8223365.*

Tourist Offices

Saigontourist
49 Le Thanh Ton Street. ☎ *8295834. FAX: 8224987.*

Vietnamtourism
69-71 Nguyen Hue Boulevard. ☎ *8290772. FAX: 8290775.*

Private Tour Operators

Diethelm Travel

International Business Center, 1A Me Linh Square, Dist. 1. ☎ *8294932. FAX: 8294747.* Diethelm is a giant in Southeast Asia, with offices in all major Asian cities.

HO CHI MINH CITY

Fiditourist

71-75 Dong Khoi, Dist. 1. ☎ *8296264. FAX: 8223571.*
Package tours and air ticket booking.

Hung Vai Travel

110A Nguyen Hue, Dist. 1. ☎ *8225111.*
Specializes in business, research and investment tours for businesspeople. Visa services, car rentals, ticket booking.

Mai Linh Tours

32 Nguyen Hue, Dist. 1. ☎ *8224491.*
Specializes in tours to the northern part of the country, as well as to Cambodia and Laos.

Media Service

4C Le Thanh Ton, Dist. 1. ☎ *8294600. FAX: 8295126.*
French company specializing in housing, warehouse rentals.

Minh Chau

39/3 Tran Nhat Duat, Dist. 1. ☎ *8442807. FAX: 8439471.*
Specialists in Laos and Cambodia. Veterans' tours and Central Highlands trekking. Business introductions.

Saigon Shipchanco

2 Nguyen Hue, Dist 1. ☎ *8292424.*
Boat cruises up and down the Saigon river in less than luxurious vessels.

Superbco

110A Nguyen Hue, Dist. 1. ☎ *8225111. FAX: 8242405.*
One of the best in HCMC. In-country tour specialists and veterans' tours. Comprehensive services.

T&P Reisen

Saigon Business Center, 57 Dong Du, Dist. 1. ☎ *8904340. FAX: 8298155.*
Caters to German tourists and specializes in Indochina.

Voiles Vietnam

17 Pham Ngoc Thach, Dist. 3. ☎ *8296750, 8231589. FAX: 8231591.*
Specializes in custom junk tours along the Mekong River and Nha Trang. Also offers land services.

Vyta Tours

52 Hai Ba Trung Street, Dist. 1. ☎ *8230767. FAX: 8243524.*
Friendly service and comprehensive tour packages, including motorcycle and four-wheel-drive tours. Country-wide packages as well as day tours. Some of the best prices in town. Recommended.

Consulates in Ho Chi Minh City

Australia

The Landmark Bldg., 5B Ton Duc Thang Street, District 1. ☎ *8296035.*

Cambodia

41 Phung Khac Hoan Street, District 1. ☎ *8294498.*

France

27 Nguyen Thi Minh Khai Street, District 3. ☎ 8297231.

Germany

126 Nguyen Dinh Chieu Street, District 3. ☎ 8291967.

Indonesia

18 Phung Khac Hoan, District 1. ☎ 8223799.

Japan

13-17 Nguyen Hue, District 1. ☎ 8291341.

Korea (South)

107 Nguyen Du, District 1. ☎ 8225836.

Laos

181 Hai Ba Trung Street, District 1. ☎ 8299262, 8297667.

Malaysia

53 Nguyen Dinh Chieu Street, District 3. ☎ 8299023.

New Zealand

455 Nguyen Dinh Chieu, District 3. ☎ 8396227.

Singapore

5 Phung Khac Hoan Street, District 1. ☎ 8225173.

Thailand

77 Tran Quoc Thao, District 3. ☎ 8222637.

United Kingdom

261 Dien Bien Phu, District 3. ☎ 8298433.

United States (liason office)

8 Doc Ngu Street, Hanoi. ☎ 8236050.

Important Phone Numbers

Ambulance. ☎ 15

Emergencies. ☎ 8296485

Police. ☎ 13

Traffic Police. ☎ 8296449

Fire. ☎ 14

Maps

The best and perhaps the only places to get maps of areas and cities of Vietnam are sidewalk stalls on Le Loi Boulevard opposite the Rex Hotel. Do not rely on obtaining maps on the road, as you will be severely disappointed—even in the major cities. Saigon is the only place in the south where you can obtain maps of various destinations. Don't say we didn't tell you.

Books, Magazines & Newspapers

There are only a few places in HCMC where foreigners can purchase English-language books and recent magazines and newspapers. The stand with the widest selection is the Lao Dong Shop.

Lao Dong Shop ★

104 Nguyen Hue, Dist. 1. ☎ 8251951.

The best in town. Owner Dung's been doing this for years and has met anyone who's anyone who has ever made it to HCMC. *Time, Newsweek, People,* you name it. English-language newspapers from Bangkok, Hong Kong and Singapore arrive at the stand the same day at 7 p.m. Dung also carries the *Asian Wall Street Journal* and the *International Herald Tribune*. Can't find something you'd like? Ask Dung and he'll get it for you. I've requested daily copies of Thai language newspapers and off-the-wall periodicals, and have gotten them all. If you can't get to the stand, Dung has an army of touts all over District 1 with the latest newspapers. You won't be far from one. In fact, they'll find you first.

Khai Minh Bookshop

154 Dong Khoi, Dist. 1. ☎ *8291439.*

French newspapers and hard-to-find rags about computers, medicine, science, fashion, etc.

Rex Hotel

141 Nguyen Hue, Dist. 1. ☎ *8292185.*

There is a stall at the rooftop Terrace Bar with offerings such as the *Financial Times, Le Monde, Weekly Express, Le Figaro*—and a garnishing of pop culture rags, such as *Teen* and *Hot Rod.*

Photography

There are dozens of film shops along Nguyen Hue Boulevard between the Rex and the Saigon River and on Le Loi. However, the kiosks that formerly lined Nguyen Hue have been torn down. I have no idea what happened to them. Kodak recently opened its first lab on the northeastern side of Nguyen Hue Boulevard about halfway between the Rex and the river. A year ago, the majority of shops developed and sold Fuji film only. Kodak had a long way to go to catch up, and it has.

Laundry

Hey, man, what other travel guide to Vietnam will tell you where to get suds to your duds? Most hotels in HCMC offer laundry service, but it's usually expensive—at least VND7000 per shirt. And these folks use soap that's more like crushed coral than Tide. And they tend to forget the rinse cycle altogether. The result is clothes that look and feel like a burlap sack. After three or four washes, your shirts are ready to be donated to a car wash. Saigon's big laundries are fitted with modern equipment and your clothes will receive the loving care of imported chemicals and equipment. The cost is between VND5000-6000 for shirts and pants, including ironing. Dry cleaning a shirt, a pair of jeans and a brocade ao dai costs VND10,000, 15,000 and 20,000 respectively. And delivery to your home or hotel is typically free of charge. For businesspeople, the best laundries are located near the New World Hotel. They generally charge VND30,000 to have a shirt washed and ironed and about VND35,000 to have a shirt dry cleaned. Expensive, but worth it when you have to look your best.

Ho Chi Minh City Environs

Cu Chi Tunnels ★

This is a vast network of more than 200 km of underground tunnels in Tay Ninh, a little under 70 km northwest of Saigon. These tunnels were constructed and used by the Viet Cong to conduct operations, sometimes within the perimeters of U.S. military bases, and hide from the enemy. These are thoroughly fascinating subterranean vestibules, where the VC lived, slept and ate. There are underground hospitals, kitchens and communications centers, living areas, sleeping quarters and munitions storage centers. There are even "street" signs under the earth to help guide errant guerrillas and newcomers. When operational, these tunnels amazingly stretched all the way from Saigon to the Cambodian border. What you'll crawl through today are actually widened versions of the originals. Getting access to tunnel areas other than the touristed ones is problematic. You may even get a chance to fire an AK-47 or an M-16 for a U.S. buck a bullet. Fully automatic can be pricey. Admission: 45,000 dong. Buses to Cu Chi leave from the Tay Ninh Bus Station in Tan Binh district. Take Cach Mang Thang all the way out to about 1 km past where Cach Mang Thang merges with Le Dai Hanh Street. Cars and drivers for hire can be found at the **Phnom Penh Bus Garage** *(155 Nguyen Hue—next to the Rex)*. A lot of private owners hang out in the square in front of Reunification Hall. Expect to pay between US$20–$30 for a half-day trip out to the tunnels.

Cu Chi Tunnels were remarkably well hidden during the Vietnam War.

The Iron Triangle (Tam Giac Sat)

This is an area, not far from the Cu Chi Tunnels, that was named by American troops during the war because of their inability to penetrate this Viet Cong stronghold. Although the area isn't far from Saigon, in the forests between Ben Cat, Cu Chi and Dau Tieng, the region was impenetrable. The "Triangle" served as the base for attacks by the VC on Saigon, in particular the battles during the 1968 Tet lunar New Year as well as bloody battles at Binh Long and Dong Xoai. Now that a greater number of visitors are coming out to the tunnels at Cu Chi, there has developed an interest on the part of tourists to see the Iron Triangle area. To get there, take Highway 13 about 17 km, crossing the Binh Trieu Bridge. You'll arrive at Lai Thieu, a small village known for its handicrafts and lacquerware. You'll also pass Binh Nham and Suoi Don before reaching the town of Thu Dau Mot. From there, on the road to Dau Tieng, you'll see a trail on the left, which is the path to the Iron Triangle. Although devoid of any cultural, natural or topographical attractions, the region is bound to become popular with returning American veterans of the war. Tours of the area can be arranged through Vietnamtourism and other local operators (see the "Directory" portion of this chapter). You'll visit former battlefields, military bases and villages heavily damaged in the war.

My Tho ★

In the Mekong Delta, about 70 km southwest of Saigon, this is the former capital of Dinh Tuong province and now the capital of Tien Giang province. This fertile area is home to several interesting temples—including **Vinh Trang Pagoda** and **My Tho Church**. There's also a bustling central market. This area is often included on tours outside of Saigon. (See a more complete description of the area under the My Tho section.)

Vung Tau Beach

This is a popular beach resort a couple of hours or more (130 km) southeast of Saigon at the mouth of the Saigon River. The front and back beaches are the choice of Vietnamese surf frolickers, while secluded Pineapple Beach features villas and a large statue of Christ overlooking the South China Sea. There are several decent temples here, including the largest one in Vietnam Niet Ban Tinh Xa. Long Hai is a better beach about 30 km closer to Saigon (See a more complete description of the area under Vung Tau.)

Tay Ninh ★

Usually combined with a visit to the Cu Chi tunnels, Tay Ninh is a town about 100 km northwest of Saigon. This is the capital of the Tay Ninh Province, which borders the Cambodian border. Back in the 1970s, Cambodian Khmer Rouge guerrillas, in their campaign of terror against anyone Vietnamese, attacked villages in the province frequently and relentlessly. These attacks were part of the reason the Vietnamese Army invaded Cambodia in late 1978. A few weeks later, in January 1979, Pol Pot's Phnom Penh government collapsed and the Khmer Rouge fled into western Cambodia. Tay Ninh is primarily known for the indigenous religion of Cao Daism and the **Cao Dai Great Temple.** Set inside a complex of schools and other buildings and built between 1933 and 1955, the temple is distinctive for the European influences in its Oriental architecture. It's one of the most intriguing temples in Vietnam, if not all of Southeast Asia. Tay Ninh Province was also the strategic end of the Ho Chi Minh trail during the Vietnam War. (See a more complete description under the Tay Ninh section.)

Can Gio

Believe it or not, there's actually an ocean beach in Ho Chi Minh City—at least technically. At the mouth of the Saigon River, 60 km from Saigon, rests a mucky island called Can Gio, which is actually nothing more than a giant mangrove swamp. Home to some shrimp harvesters, salt farmers, clam diggers and a smattering of folks who vend produce from Saigon, Can Gio—again, technically—lies facing the South China Sea but may as well be a landfill in the Passaic River. No tourists get out here as no decent thoroughfares link the village with HCMC (nor with close-by Vung Tau, for that matter), and the shabby one that does requires two ferry crossings. There's not even any fresh water out here. As a foreigner, you will be treated as an oddity—or perhaps as just simply odd for having made the trip.

But if you do decide to make the journey, there are a few must-sees. There's a Cao Dai temple in town (next to the bustling market), a war cemetery and the massive Cofidec shrimp ponds that compose most of the area's beaches.

You'll be hard pressed to find both good food and a clean place to stay. The island's only hotel, the **Duyen Hai Hotel** (☎ *8740246*; US$5–$10) is a dump and only has a few rooms. The only place you might consider eating anywhere in a 50-km radius is the **Duyen Hai Restaurant** (next to the hotel). If you're new to Vietnam, stay away from both the food stalls and the ice in Can Gio.

The first ferry crossing is at Cat Lai, about 17 km from Saigon. With a motorbike, you can make the crossing relatively easy by employing any one of the numerous small boats which make the crossing, rather than waiting for the car ferry, which lumbers along every half-hour or so. With a motorcycle, you can probably get away with only VND2000 for the crossing. The second boat ride is at Dan Xay and connects the mainland with the "island" of Can Gio. Again, motorcycles can cross via a small ferry—this time for about

VND4000. With a car, you'll have to wait a lot longer. It takes a surprisingly long 2-3 hours to get out here. Don't say I didn't warn you.

Da Chong-Dinh Quan

These rock formations in Dong Nai Province, alongside Highway 20 about 112 km from Ho Chi Minh City and 82 km from Bien Hoa, are themselves certainly not worth the visit from Saigon, but make a decent pit-stop on the way to Dalat. This eight-hectare area features an unusual array of rock formations that link the plains of southern Vietnam with the Central Highlands. The most intriguing formation is the 100-meter-tall Ba Chong Mountain, and two equal-size boulders that straddle each other so precariously it's a wonder the top one doesn't simply roll off and crush a minibus on the highway below.

Geologists place the rocks' formation to the Kreta era; meaning the penetrated magma stone pile is about a million years old. Its main composition is granodiopt. The factors of climate and time have subsequently carved the rocks into the peculiar formation in which they sit today.

Here can also be found the Thien Chon Pagoda at the Elephant Mound and there's a statue of Sakyamuni at the top of the formation. Southwest of Ba Chong there are a couple of elephant-shaped boulders quite appropriately tagged the White Elephants. The "male elephant" stands at 40 meters high, while a Sakyamuni statue is found alongside the smaller "female elephant."

To the northwest of the Ba Chong are found other interesting rock formations, namely plate-shaped configurations that reach 50 meters high. Da Chong-Dinh Quan has been designated by the Ministry of Culture and Information as a natural wonder, as well as a cultural and historic relic. You'll find it a good place to stop for a Coke. You'll see the formations at kilometer marker 112 on Highway 20. You won't miss them as they flank the road.

Con Dao Islands ★★

It's now possible to reach the relatively unexplored and serene Con Dao Islands, beautiful peaks that rise from the sea much like the islands of Hawaii, about 100 miles off the coast of Vung Tau. Air service had connected the islands with Ho Chi Minh City, but was temporarily discontinued at press time. However, ferries make the 14-hour journey from Vung Tau.

When planes are operating it takes about 40 minutes from Ho Chi Minh City and you're there. Con Dao Island has only been accessible for the past couple of years, and a visit to these nearly deserted islands is well worth it, even considering the exorbitant US$200 round-trip airfare from HCMC (that's when the planes are flying).

There are miles of deserted beaches, jungle roads and paths to explore. The water is calm and clear here, not like the silty surf of Vung Tau and Long Hai.

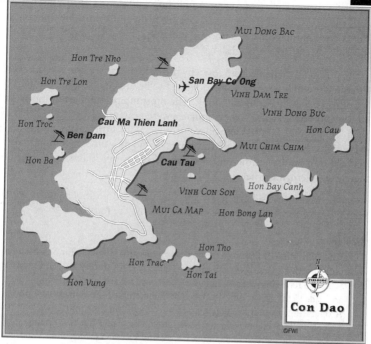

The group of islands that make up the Con Daos numbers 14. The largest is Con Dao (also called Con Son) itself, with a small airstrip that's only manned every couple of days or so when a turboprop plane drops from the sky from HCMC. Con Dao Island is only about 20 square kilometers and its inhabitants number perhaps 2000 or so fishermen and their families. It is a heavily forested island with a number of steep mountains that drop right into the sea, the highest of which reaches 600 meters. Climbing the peaks affords fantastic vistas of the surrounding coral reefs and pristine, white sand beaches.

The island was formerly home to a French prison (built in 1861 and still standing about a kilometer outside the island's main town) for political dissidents and Vietnamese nationalists under French colonial rule of Vietnam. The former South Vietnamese government also used the island as a prison for anti-regime elements. It could house 12,000 inmates.

After touching down at the island's airport, you'll take a minivan or jeep about 13 km into town (where the only accommodations are), most likely without seeing another soul along the way, for 15,000 dong. In town, the only attraction—other than the slow way of life itself—is a house that served as the prison camp warden's home. It's now called **Bao Tang Tong Ho Tinh** and has been turned into a museum. Admission: 5000 dong. The museum depicts the island's prison years and species of plant and animal life found here. Tours are conducted when someone shows up. The assistant director of the museum speaks decent English.

The prison is reachable from town by the Vietnamese version of a *tuk tuk*, a three-wheeled Honda that looks designed to be driven by a circus bear,. The roundtrip fee is about 20,000 dong. The most interesting part of the prison are the old "tiger cages," where inmates were beaten, tortured and killed by their French and South Vietnamese captors. With little imagination, it's a grisly sight. Near the prison are the graves of and monuments to hundreds—perhaps thousands—of the prisoners who died on this island, including the legendary Vietnamese heroine Vo Thi Sau.

On the southwest side of town are a couple of Buddhist pagodas worth seeing simply for the panoramic vistas where they're located.

Doing It:

Vasco Co. formerly flew from the domestic terminal at HCMC's Tan Son Nhat Airport directly to Con Dao on Tuesday, Thursday and Saturday at 8:30 a.m. using Jetstream turboprop aircraft, and may well resume the schedule after improvements are made to the airport on Con Dao. The flight returned the same day at 9:30 a.m. If operating, the flight takes only about 30–40 minutes, but costs US$200 roundtrip. If the flight is running, book through Vietnam Airlines. Or call ☎ *84-8-8445999*. The more intrepid can take a colorful Vietnamese ferry from Vung Tau. The one-way journey costs only VND150,000 for a berth depending on your bargaining skills and takes about 12–14 hours. Bring plenty of provisions (water and food). A taxi ride from Vung Tau to the ferry terminal to Con Dao costs about US$12. The ferry ticket office on Con Dao is not at the dock but rather at *430 Truong Cong Dinh Street*. English is only barely spoken or understood.

Where to Stay:

There are a couple of guesthouses on Con Dau, but you'll first be taken to the island's only hotel, the **Phi Yen** (☎ *0164-30168*). There are 10 rooms here, the cheapest being US$20 a night. A double runs US$30. The hotel also rents boats and jeeps for island excursions, but access around the island seems to have become more limited. The staff speaks limited English. Very limited. Cozy place—you'll like it. There is a police guesthouse on Le Duan Street that will sometimes handle the rare overflow at the Phi Yen. As only about 100 foreigners a year make it out here, according to local sources, the overflow is rare.

Where to Eat:

There are a number of stalls with excellent seafood. The best "restaurant" in town is the **Cong Quan Restaurant** (☎ *830106*), which is on the ocean next to the pier. Great seafood and cheap.

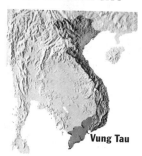

Vung Tau

Vung Tau

Beach umbrellas shroud Vung Tau's Paradise Beach.

Vung Tau

VUNG TAU IN A CAPSULE

Saigon's closest beach resort, about a three-hour drive from Saigon...Mostly frequented by weekending Saigonese...The beach sees few, but a growing number of foreign tourists...Back and Front Beaches are the least attractive of the resort's beaches...Paradise Beach is the best...For fewer crowds, nearby Long Hai is a better bet...Kiosks and restaurants line Vung Tau's beach-fronts...The drive out from Saigon is over flat terrain and not particularly scenic...But there are a number of decent hotels in town.

This (along with Long Hai) is the closest beach of any note to Saigon, about 130 km from the city, and where most Saigonese head on out to when the heat becomes too much and they don't mind the two- to three-hour ride along generally good roads. Frankly, I find the beaches here a disappointment. They're more silty than sandy, and the sea is gray-colored, typical of beaches found at river mouths the world around. (This area is where the Saigon River dumps out into the South China Sea.) The surf is choppy rather than rolling, and not particularly suited for effortless sea bathing—although the body surfer will find the occasional swell to ride in on. Even the drive out to Vung Tau is mainly lacking in any natural beauty. Perhaps Vung Tau is best recommended for Saigon locals and expats with desk jobs who can only get out of town for a day or two.

Vung Tau has changed so radically in the past three years, you wouldn't believe your eyes if it has been that long since your last visit, and such return visitors will be stunned at its increasing similarities to Thailand's Pattaya, Bangkok's sleazy beach getaway. In fact, save for the blatant sex venues (they're here, believe me) Vung Tau seems to be in the process of out Pattayaing Pattaya. The growth is phenomenal and equally as unchecked and mismanaged as that of the Thai seaside resort. Hotels have sprung up like mushrooms from cow dung after a summer rain. A full time job for any cartographer would be to keep track of them. In fact, as this edition goes to print, there will be another half-dozen hotels built before you even read this.

Hookers prowl the beach areas but are restricted from banging on the doors of guests' rooms at some of the more upscale hotels. But on and near the beaches—with the exception of Paradise Beach—don't be surprised to be openly propositioned. And feel free to openly reply "Get lost." They especially seem fond of the bungalows and tattered cafes of Back Beach. Massage parlors abound, and Westerners are considered a real catch, as they've got the real bucks. Regretably, Vung Tau is becoming a sex mecca—although families staying at some of the better hotels may fortunately remain oblivious to this.

But if there's a bright side to all this, it' the sanctuary of the new, modern caravansaries. Whereas a few years ago Vung Tau was nothing more than a dirty beach, today it's a dirty beach with some nice places to stay. And when the sun goes down, there are actually some decent places to party. (Vung Tau looks better when you can't see it.) I'll even go as far to say that it's worth coming out here for the weekend if you're stuck in Saigon with—eeks—a job. Though not as flashy as Pattaya, it's not far behind.

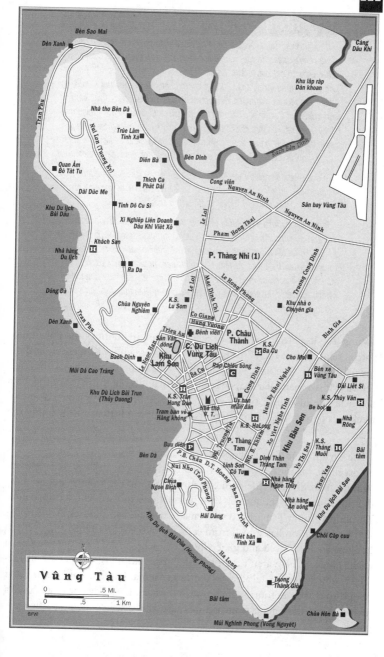

Bến Sao Mai
Đèn Xanh
Cảng Dầu Khí
Trần Phú
Khu lắp ráp Dàn khoan
Nhà thờ Bên Đà
Núi Lớn (Tương Kỳ)
Trúc Lâm Tịnh Xá
Diên Bà
Bến Đình
Quan Âm Bồ Tát Tu
Rạch Bến Đình
Thích Ca Phật Đài
Công viên
Nguyễn An Ninh
Dài Đức Mẹ
Tịnh Độ Cư Sĩ
Sân bay Vũng Tàu
Khu Du lịch Bãi Dâu
Xí Nghiệp Liên Doanh Dầu Khí Việt Xô
Phạm Hồng Thái
Nguyễn An Ninh
Khách Sạn
Lê Lợi
Nhà hàng Du lịch
Ra Da
P. Thắng Nhì (1)
Lê Hồng Phong
Mạc Đĩnh Chi
Trương Công Định
Đông Đà
Khu nhà ở Chuyên gia
Chùa Nguyên Nghiêm
K.S. Lư Sơn
Lê Lợi
Cô Giang
Đèn Xanh
Bình Giã
Trần Phú
Triệu An
Hưng Vương
Bệnh viện
P. Châu Thành
K.S. Bà Cù
Cho Mới
Sân Vận động
Lê Ngọc Hân
C. Du Lịch Vũng Tàu
Bạch Dinh
Khu Lam Sơn
Bà Cù
Bến xe Vũng Tàu
Mũi Đá Cao Trắng
Rạp Chiếu bóng
Đại Liệt Sĩ
Nam Kỳ Khởi Nghĩa
Công Định
Khu Du Lịch Bãi Trun (Thủy Dương)
K.S. Trần Hưng Đạo
Trương Văn
Uỷ ban nhân dân
Xô Viết Nghệ Tĩnh
K.S. Thùy Vân
Bẻ bởi
Nhà Rồng
Trạm bán vé Hàng không
Nhà thờ V. T.
K.S. HaLong
N.C.B. Nhiều
Khu Bầu Sen
Bưu điện
P. Thắng Tam
K.S. Thắng Mười
Bến Đà
P.B. Châu
D.T. Hoàng
Võ Thị Sáu
Bãi tắm
Linh Sơn Cổ Tự
Đình Thần Thắng Tam
Núi Nhỏ (Tao Phùng)
Phan Chu Trinh
Nhà hàng Ngọc Thủy
Chùa Ngọc Bích
Thùy Vân
Nhà hàng Ăn uống
Khu Du Lịch Bãi Sau
Hải Đàng
Chồi Cấp cứu
Khu Du lịch Bãi Dứa (Hương Phong)
Niết bàn Tịnh Xá
Hạ Long
Tượng Thánh Giớa
Bãi tắm
Chùa Hòn Bà
Mũi Nghinh Phong (Vọng Nguyệt)

Vũng Tàu

0   .5 Mi.
0   .5   1 Km

©FWI

Vung Tau

Insider Tip: Vung Tau's Cops

Although Vung Tau is beginning to take on the trappings of tourist-friendly Thia resort cities, the cops here don't seem to get it. One of the most enjoyable ways to get out to and explore Vung Tau is by motorcycle. If you're riding anything larger than 70cc, prepare to be pulled over and hassled by Vung Tau's finest. Without a Vietnamese driver's license (even if you have an international license) be even further prepared to be brought "downtown" for a less-than-polite debriefing. The fine for such an infraction is supposedly US$100. But expect these guys to change their minds as fast as a kid in a toy shop. Especially if you insist on a written citation. And they're not nice.

On one recent occasion I was threatened with arrest, the confiscation of my motorcycle, lulled with promises that I'd be released with my motorcycle, and then threatened with arrest again—all in about 15 seconds.

Despite such efforts at building tourism, Vietnam has yet to develop methods of dealing with tourists. Consequently, even minor dealings with the police here can leave visitors with a taste so sour for the constabulary that even a lemon tastes like bread. As tourism booms here in places such as Vung Tau, there has become an even greater need for a "Tourist Police" division in Vietnam, similar to the marvelously developed one in Thailand. Until such a unit is formed, intimidation will mar most dealings with the police. Be warned.

Vung Tau used to be called Cap Saint Jacques, in honor of the Portuguese patron saint. Before the 17th century, the city was under Khmer rule and the town began to develop as a seaside resort near the beginning of the 20th century. It is a triangular shaped peninsula that juts out into the South China Sea near the mouth of the Saigon River. The beaches are jammed on the weekends despite the strong currents and high winds that usually buffet the area.

The Thanh Truc Cafe is at about km marker 62 from Vung Tau and makes an excellent roadside rest area for a cool drink about halfway from Saigon. Rubber trees dot the side of the roadway. You pass a former military base that looks just like the former U.S. installations you see all over the south. The strip at Vung Tau is lined with small cafes and bath houses. Not surprisingly, prostitution has spread from one side of the strip to the other, yet the hookers are low-keyed and generally, the beaches make for a suitable family environment. There aren't the roadside "truck stops" that generally characterize some other coastal areas of southern Vietnam beaches, although this is bound to change as tourism increases in the area. Presently one doesn't see a lot of Westerners here, primarily because the beaches aren't particularly good.

As I mentioned, to Vung Tau's credit, there is a growing number of very decent hotels appearing in the area. They are primarily frequented by Vietnamese and other Asian tourists, although Westerners are warmly welcomed everywhere.

The beachfront itself is fairly dilapidated, the structures weather-beaten. Strangely, most cafes and beachside eateries have seating areas that face the road rather than the beach, which makes for sort of a ridiculous view of nothing really—a couple of hills. The reason for this is that the onshore winds are extremely brisk much of the time, making ocean-facing seating in open-air cafes impossible. Even a full beer would get blown away. Consequently, those who want to swim and frolic in the sea pitch up tents on the beach. Those looking to relax prefer to sit in the cafes, facing roadside.

There are two "mountains" in the city (a giant statue of Jesus looks down upon the ocean from one) and they make for good bike riding. In fact, this may be the best activity here, both for the view and the fact that the beach is usually so windy that it feels like being pelted by small weapons fire due to the blowing sand. The big Jesus has a Rio de Janeiro look with its outstretched arms overlooking the sea. The statue was built in 1974. The best way to get up to it is by a rocky path.

Vung Tau was an area very popular with the Russians during the period when Russians had a great degree of influence here. Here was the headquarters of VIETSOVPETRO, and many Soviet expats used to live in villas around Front Beach, most of which have been razed for the building of hotels for tourists. Many villas also look over Back Beach; they're very attractive and almost Mediterranean in appearance.

Vung Tau is also famous as a departure point for the hundreds of thousands of Vietnamese who fled the country during the latter 1970s through the mid 80s. This may explain why Vung Tau possessed one of the most vast secret police networks after reunification in 1975.

Vung Tau, along with being targeted for tourism, may also become one of Southeast Asia's largest heavy container ports. Vietnam's largest single infrastructure project, at US$637 million, will have a total of eight container wharves. The total handling capacity will be about 60 million tons per year. How this will affect tourism to the area isn't clear.

What to See and Do in Vung Tau

Recently, there was not a lot to do here other than swim or look at the rapids-like surf and contemplate swimming—or take a bike ride around the area. But that's changing. The burgeoning number of hotels and attractions are luring more and more tourists here. There's even a golf course planned for Vung Tau.

Front Beach (Bai Truoc)
Western edge of town.

This is commonly referred to as Front Beach, and was probably the best beach in town, which isn't saying a lot, until the beach erosion brought the sea nearly to the road. This is Vietnam's version of Coney Island. Beggars and touts abound. But the shellfish being hawked is excellent. Unfortunately, the beach itself is dirty, rocky and only acceptable if you close your eyes and dream of being somewhere else. But, all in all, it does make for a nice break from the congestion and hustle & bustle of Saigon.

Back Beach (Bai Sau)

2 km south of town.

This beach is about 2 kilometers south of town and is the area that attracts the most tourists, most of them Saigonese getting out of the city for some fresh air and visiting Asian tourists. You can rent a beach chair and tent for a couple of thousand dong and gaze out at the dangerous surf, which is usually only frolicked in by locals lounging in inner tubes. What the beach has going for it is that it is the only beach in the area with actual sand. Vendors, kiosk proprietors and a lot of folks carrying strings of dried squid provide the culinary delights. Soda pop and beer are readily available. If you can, get a Vietnamese to do the buying for you; it'll be cheaper. Like other areas in the town, the water can be dangerous for swimming. Sometimes flags will be posted warning of the conditions. A white flag means the water is safe (from what I'm not sure). A red flag means the conditions are unsafe.

Paradise Beach ★

Northern stretch of Back Beach.

This is undoubtedly the best beach in Vung Tau and is the northern stretch of Back Beach. Bright red tents shroud the beach like a Christo exhibition. If you head north on the sand a few hundred meters from the bath house and restaurant, the crowds suddenly vanish and the beach is yours. But I expect a lot more development on the outer reaches of Back Beach in the future. There are a number of decent hotels near here, and good facilities at the beach for dining and souvenir shopping. The bar/restaurant is surprisingly comfortable. Take Le Hong Phong Street and make a left where it intersects with Vo Thi Sau.

Bai Dau Beach

4 km north of central Front Beach.

There's a pagoda on a hill near here and it's about the only attraction. The beach is nothing special and it's a hike, about 4 km north of town.

Bai Nghinh Phong

This is a relatively nice bathing area for Vung Tau. The surf seems more predictable but locals say the swimming can still be quite dangerous, with strong undertows. The few people you do see in the water are rarely swimming but just standing around in the surf getting their street clothes sopping wet.

Hon Ba

Right off Back Beach (Bai Sau)

This is an impressive looking small pagoda on a tiny island only a few hundred yards off the headland, accessible by foot at low tide.

The Lighthouse

Overlooking Bai Truoc Beach.

This offers the best view of the area. It was built just after the turn of the century and rises some 200 km above sea level and can be reached by bicycle, although by foot may be the more attractive alternative. You can also get up to the top from Back Beach, but the roads can be muddy, especially during the wet season.

Pagodas

There's the island pagoda of **Hon Ba**, of course, but there are others in Vung Tau worthy of a visit only if pagodas run like heroin through your veins. **Niet Ban Tinh Xa** is easily the most impressive pagoda in Han Ba. It features a giant bronze bell. There is the 1000-year-old **Linh Son Co Tu Pagoda** at *61 Huang Hoa Tham Street.* Also you might want to see the **Whale Dedication Temple**, again not spectacular, but if you've come this far, well...**Thich Ca Phat Dai Park** is where the locals hang out. There's a huge Buddha statue that sits on the side of a hill. There are also a lot of animal and people figurines. Lots of restaurants here as well as a number of souvenir kiosks. The park is on the eastern side of Large Mountain.

Boat Yards

About 500 meters south of the bus station on Nam Ky Khoi Nghia Street.

This is where to go to check out how the local fishing vessels are built. We didn't have any problem exploring the yards independently.

Vung Tau Market

North of town on Tran Phu Street.

The market is on Tran Phu Street north of town and was "built" in the beginning of the century. The gardens are a pleasant place to relax.

Where to Stay in Vung Tau

**AUTHOR'S NOTE:
TELEPHONE PREFIXES**

When dialing telephone numbers in Vung Tau, the country code is 84. The city code is 64, followed by the local exchange. Numbers listed are local exchanges.

Hai Au Hotel 9   US$45–$85   ★★

100 Halong Street. *852278. FAX: 859868.*
64 rooms.

This is a small, clean place that was opened about five years ago. Pool, air-conditioned.

Thang Muoi Hotel   US$15

4-6 Thuy Van Street. Back Beach. ☎ *852665.*
90 rooms.

This is an old place on Back Beach and one of the nicer places in the area despite its age. It's a quiet place with a pool, air conditioning, restaurant and an open courtyard-type area surrounded by the single-story guest units.

Beautiful Hotel   **US$40–$60**   ★★

100-102 Thuy Van Street. Back Beach. ☎ 852177, 853174. FAX: 853177.
100 rooms.
New hotel with comfortable rooms, air conditioning, telephone, minibar. Restaurant. Worth the price.

Ha Long Hotel   **US$25–$40**

45 Thong Nhat Street. Front Beach. ☎ 852175.
This place has been totally renovated to keep up with the new places opening in town, and the prices have gone up accordingly. But a nice place with improved amenities such as air conditioning. Restaurant.

Lu Son Hotel   **US$15–$20**

27 Le Loi Boulevard. ☎ 852576.
65 rooms.
Here is a bargain if you don't mind being some distance from the beach. The rooms are spacious and clean, with air conditioning, minibar, hot water, private bath, TV.

Grand Hotel   **US$20–$40**

26 Quang Trung Street. Front Beach. ☎ 852469. FAX: 859878.
60 rooms.
Nice location across the street from the beach. Non-air conditioned rooms have fans and private bath, but I'd splurge the extra five dollars or so for an airconditioned room. All rooms with private bath, hot water. Restaurant, disco, sauna, Thai massage, gift shop.

Saigon Hotel   **US$10–$35**

72 Thuy Van Street. Back Beach.
The lower-price rooms here are a bargain, although you can't go wrong anywhere here. Airy, spacious rooms with air conditioning, hot water, private bath.

The Seabreeze Hotel   **US$50–$80**   ★★

11 Nguyen Trai Street. Front Beach. ☎ 852392, 859856. FAX: 859856.
The hotel was opened in 1992 and is Australian-owned and managed. The rooms are expensive by Vietnamese standards but appear to be worth it. Air-conditioned, TV, refrigerator, telephone, fans and clean bathrooms. The more expensive rooms are three-room suites. Also a swimming pool and restaurant.

Canadian Hotel   **US$40–$80**   ★★★

48 Quang Trung Street. Front Beach. ☎ 859852. FAX: 859851.
This hotel, opened in 1991. It's well-managed and clean—you'd expect it for the prices. Rooms have views of the sea. Restaurant, tennis court, business center, air-conditioned, minibar, disco and a bar.

Rex Hotel   **US$35–$100**   ★★★

1 Duy Tan Street. Front Beach. ☎ 891766, 852135. FAX: 859862.
This is a huge structure by Vung Tau standards, nine stories. Restaurant, tennis courts, air-conditioned, disco.

Hoa Hong La Rose Mini Hotel   **US$20**   ★

39 Thuy Van Street. Back Beach. ☎ 859455.

A service oriented inn on the beach with a dining room. Comfortably and tastefully furnished with secure parking. Staff, although their English is limited to nonexistent, is extraordinarily friendly.

New Hotel
US$35–$60 ★★

Next door to the Rex at Duy Tan and Quang Trung Streets. Front Beach.
Just like the New Hotel in Saigon, this is also a new hotel, completed just a couple of years ago. On Front Beach. Good views of the sea.

International Hotel Hai Dau
About US$20

242 Ba Cu Street. *852178, 852571.*
Only five years old, this place looks like it could have been used as a fire base by American troops during the war. The amenities, though, belie the trashiness of the place. There's a swimming pool, business center and two restaurants.

Pacific Hotel
US$16–$30 ★★

4 Le Loi Boulevard. Front Beach. *852279.*
The more expensive rooms have a view of the sea. This is a large, drab complex with air-conditioned rooms, refrigerators, hot water, a disco/nightclub, and a decent massage.

Palace Hotel
About US$40

Nguyen Trai Street near Quang Trung Street. Front Beach. *852411, 852265. FAX: 859878.*
105 rooms.
This is also a sprawling but stale and plain place that at least offers all its rooms with air conditioning, TV and a refrigerator. It can be tough getting up in the morning in some of the rooms as they have no windows; they almost create a prisonlike feel. But there are a couple of restaurants, a "nightclub," a massage parlor and a tennis court.

Phuong Dong Hotel
US$35–$60 ★★★

2 Thuy Van Street-VT. Back Beach. ☎ *852158, 8525983.*
This is a new and impressive hotel in Vung Tau, perhaps the town's finest. It sits on the hillside overlooking Back Beach and just above a complex of some of the architecturally attractive Mediterranean style villas in Vung Tau. Service is extremely considerate and the grounds are immaculately kept. Karaoke, massage and a host of other amenities. It is frequented primarily by visiting businessmen apparently, but the manager, Dinh Van Ha, made it clear that tourist bookings are on the rise.

Diamond Hotel
US$15–$20

8 Tran Nguyen Han Street. ☎ *895930; FAX: 895930.*
Not much here but a restaurant and a room to watch videos. Rooms with air conditioning.

Backpackers generally head for the **Bai Dau** beach area, where a number of no-longer-cheap guesthouses can be found. Bai Dau is the quietest part of Vung Tau, which is part of its attraction—however, like the rest of the peninsula, the beach isn't particularly nice. But it is less crowded and a good place to meet other travelers. Most of the guesthouses (Nha Nghi) go by numbers and run between US$10–$20 a night. Most offer private rooms and a shared toilet. Hot water isn't always available. The best place along this strip

Vung Tau

is probably **Nha Nghi 29** *(Tran Phu Street, US$20)*. It's on the beach and relatively clean; rooms with air conditioning. See "Insider Tip" below.

INSIDER TIP

In Bai Dau, there are dozens of guest houses catering to budget tourists, but many of them only accept Vietnamese. These are sometimes nothing more than short-time hooker stops. (If you must, these "ladies" can be had for as little as 40,000 dong, or about US$4. Don't expect a wake-up call.) Although the area itself is not particularly unappealing, the beach along Bai Dau is. Some of the "cement-floor" types might want to try the Nha Nghi My Tho at 47 Tran Phu Street, the Nha Nghi 29 on the beach, the Nha Hang 96 (not on the beach), or the Nha Nghi DK 142, although it's a bit pricier. One thing to remember is that places come and go virtually overnight in this part of the country. Construction of new dwellings is rampant around here, albeit slow. A lot of the older hotels and kiosks appear to be changing their names, or at least recreating their marquees in a grandiose manner to attract customers. Sometimes the addresses of the establishments will be displayed with far more prominence than the actual hotel or restaurant name. So it pays to know where you are rather than where you want to be going.

Where to Eat in Vung Tau

There are dozens of eateries lining the beach along Ha Long, Quang Trung and Thuy Van Streets. Of note on Thuy Van Street along the Back Beach: Thuy Van Cafe, Quan An Binhean Cafe, Don Qui 59, Quai Quan Thuy Tien, Lam Thon Thung, Dai Dung, Nha Hang and Quang Hang. Also try: Thanh Nien, 55 Quang Trung Street.

Nightlife in Vung Tau

There has been a proliferation of nightclubs and karaoke clubs springing up in and around town. Most of the good hotels have some form of nightlife. Expats have yet to start up beachside reggae bars. But they'll be here soon on the heels of **Apocalypse Now**, a popular watering hole for Westerners at *438 Truong Cong Dinh Street*. Definitely do not confuse this place with the one in Saigon, although there seem to be as many white faces at times.

Directory

Transportation

The bus station in Vung Tau is at *52 Nam Ky Khoi Nghia Street*. There are minibuses that depart from Tran Hung Dao Blvd. and Ly Tu Trong Street. The minibuses depart for Saigon as soon as they're filled, usually around every 40 minutes or so and cost about 8000 dong (US$.80). They usually take about three hours, but frequently longer. The regular nonexpress buses take a lot longer (maybe four hours), but cost only about 2000 dong (US$.20). It may not be necessary, but it's probably a good idea to buy your tickets to Saigon in advance, even as much as a day. Buses from Saigon for Vung Tau from the Mien Dong Bus Station also leave when they're filled. You can also take a bus to Vung Tau from the station at Nguyen Hue Blvd. These are express buses that usually take about three hours and cost about US$5 return fare. If you want to go by car, ask around, but feel lucky if you can get a ride for less than US$70 round trip for a day excursion. Getting around Vung Tau is best by bicycle or motorbike, and there are plenty for rent, despite what people might say. Most of the hotels now rent bicycles, as do a number of beachside cafes.

Perhaps the most enjoyable—and certainly the fastest—way to get to Vung Tau from Ho Chi Minh City is by high-speed hydrofoil ferry. The trip takes only 75–90 minutes and costs VND110,000 (US$10) one-way. (Children under 12 cost US$5 one way.) Contact the following:

Vina Express Ferry Service

6A Nguyen Tat Thanh Street. District 4. ☎ *8253888, 8224621. FAX: 8253333.*
Ticketing Booth: Ho Chi Minh City Jetty (opposite main customs office, 200 meters from the site of the former Saigon Floating Hotel). ☎ *8297892.*

The firm has two high-speed hydrofoil boats that run back and forth between Saigon and Vung Tau twice a day (see below). It's a splendid trip down the Saigon River to the South China Sea, and a running time of 75 minutes makes the US$10 fare entirely worth it. Beverages and snacks aboard. Don't plan on bringing a motorbike or bicycle with you, though, nor any—as the company phrases it—"foul smelling items." Presumably durian and cyclo tires.

Vina Express Ferry Schedule

HO CHI MINH CITY	VUNG TAU		HO CHI MINH CITY
Departure	Arrival	Departure	Arrival
8 a.m.	9:15 a.m.	11 a.m.	12:15 p.m.
2 p.m.	3:15 p.m.	4:15 p.m.	5:30 p.m.

Banks and Money Changers

Vietcom Bank, *27 Tran Hung Dao Boulevard.* It will exchange travelers checks and, at last check, issue advances on American-issued credit cards.

Medical Clinics

Veterans' Clinic

Opposite 99 Le Loi Boulevard, 1.5 km north of downtown. ☎ *852573, 857348.*
This is a project run by veterans of the Vietnam War from both sides, including U.S.-based Veteran's Vietnam Restoration Project. These folks provide general medical care if you've got cash.

General Post Office

4 Ha Long Street, near the Hai Au Hotel.

Tourist Office

Vung Tau Tourism, *18 Thuy Van Street.* ☎ *852314.*

Vung Tau

Long Hai

Long Hai, about 120 km southeast of Ho Chi Minh City and 35 km northeast of Vung Tau, has become something of an alternative to Vung Tau for those seeking refuge not only from the stress of Saigon but from the commercialism of Vung Tau. Although the beaches here are hardly any better than those of Vung Tau, there are certainly fewer people here, and fewer accommodations to house them.

Long Hai is a gritty little town with a gritty beach that mostly attracts Vietnamese day-trippers and backpackers. Route 51 from Bien Hoa to Vung Tau splits after about 75 km at Ba Ria. (Although a large town, Ba Ria is little more than a truck stop.) The left fork heads to Ba Ria, a kilometer or so away, and then another 12 km to Long Hai. There is little reason to overnight here unless you plan on staying at the one diamond in the rough here, the surprisingly elegant, fun and relatively inexpensive Thuy Duong Hotel, about 3 km north of town on the beach. In fact, it is this area of Long Hai that makes the trip worth it. North of the town the beaches beome almost deserted and are set against a backdrop of rugged hills and outcroppings, giving the area a California-like appearance. The road meanders along the rocky coast and the water actually seems cleaner here. Microbuses from Saigon pick their own secluded inlets, and the souvenir and seafood hawkers that abound at Long Hai's town beach are refreshingly absent just a couple of klicks north of town.

In town itself are muddy roads and the usual collection of food stalls and Honda repair shops, as well as a couple of vastly overpriced hotels. In the center of town, the road forks. Most tourists and beachgoers take the right fork for another half-kilometer to the crowded beach. The left fork leaves town and meanders along the uncrowded coastline for a few kilometers before reaching the Thuy Duong. The area is surprisingly scenic. There are few tourists—other than those staying at the Thuy Duong—and the beach is actually quite decent. With rolling hills swooping down toward the palm-lined sands, you could actually picture this place in a brochure. It is a far cry from both Vung Tau and Long Hai town beach.

There's no way to get out here other than by private transportation. But most folks get out to Long Hai by minibus or car anyhow. My advice for day-trippers is to skip the town of Long Hai, other than for provisioning, and head up the left fork at the center of town to the beaches approaching the Thuy Duong. They're mostly clean and empty and make for a surprisingly supurb day outing. But just a note, if you've come out to the beaches looking for some nightlife, stick with Vung Tau. After dark, Long Hai gets about as hoppin' as a Franciscan monastery on Holy Saturday.

Where to Stay in Long Hai

AUTHOR'S NOTE: TELEPHONE PREFIXES

When dialing telephone numbers in Vung Tau, the country code is 84. The city code is 64, followed by the local exchange. Numbers listed are local exchanges.

There are perhaps four hotels in Long Hai that will accept foreigners. With the exception of the Thuy Duong Resort, they're overpriced and deserved to be skipped. Only a couple are worth mentioning—even if it's to not recommend them.

Long Hai Hotel   US$50

Long Hai Townlet, Ba Ria. *868010. FAX: 868010.*
25 rooms.

This is the first hotel on the main drag as you come into town. At first glance it seems to be a rather decent place—relatively new with tidy landscaping and set on the beach. But the beach is grotty (too many fishing boats) and the rooms are hugely overpriced. The staff is polite at best, with limited English abilities. Rooms have air conditioning (they'd better), private bath and hot water. Restaurant serves passable Vietnamese, Chinese and Western fare. Also dancing, karaoke, massage, steam bath. The weathered tennis court is about as popular as ice hockey. Despite the rakishness of the place, it's often fully booked, always on holidays. Reserve in advance.

The Palace Hotel   US$25

1 km up the left fork from the center of town.

What a disappointment this place is, as it's got every reason to be the best bargain in the region, especially for backpackers. Set on a secluded knoll overlooking Long Hai's north beach, this grand old stone building would make for the perfect getaway—but it's in total disrepair. The foresty grounds, once neatly manicured and spiked with bright flowers, have been consumed by weeds and underbrush. At 25 bucks, the drab, unaccented and prisonlike rooms are a ripoff—they come with neither air conditioning nor a fan. A sea breeze might make up for these deficiencies, but it's cut off by sand banks, knolls and trees. This place has a decision to make: opt for either a total facelift to justify the rates, or send the room prices in a nose dive to bring the backpackers in. Do it and they will come.

Thuy Duong Hotel   US$35–$90   ★★

Phuoc Hai Village, Long Bat District. *886215/7. FAX: 886180.*

A gem of a new "resort" set at the base of boulder-strewn, California-like mountains dipping to the sea three kilometers north of Long Hai. Out of the way and self-contained, it's a world away from the grit of Long Hai. There's both a sparkling-clean main building set up on a hill overlooking the beach as well as a number of equally tidy beachside bungalows (US$45). All rooms with air conditioning, hot water, private bath, telephone, color TV, minibar. Hotel and beachside restaurants. Myriad watersports activities, including jetskiing, rafting and boating. Two kilome-

Vung Tau

ters of mostly empty beach. The room prices for this kind of quality and friendly service in Vietnam are unmatched in my travels. At present, this place is secluded and void of the tackiness that seems inherent in Vietnamese-designed and executed tourist projects. The only bad news? The Thuy Duong Company has set aside an additional VND140 billion for tourist development in the vicinity. Can they keep the daffy duck boats and plopping ponies away, I wonder?

Directory

Transportation

Long Hai is about 120 km from Saigon and 35 km from Vung Tau. The best way to get out here is by minibus or motorcycle from Saigon. Many hotels offer minibus service to Long Hai, but don't expect to leave on a whim unless you want to pay for the ride by yourself. Also, check with Sinh Cafe on Pham Ngu Lao Street (District 1) in Saigon to see if it's presently running any minibuses out to Long Hai. Day trips usually run about US$8. Overnights, if available, will set you back about US$18, including accommodations.

Ba Ria to Xuan Loc

So close to Saigon and so little traveled by foreigners is a great 55-km stretch of pavement that begins in Ba Ria and ends up at National Highway 1 at Xuan Loc, about 15 km north of the intersection with National Highway 20. The drive—or ride—is both scenic and smooth. The road is flanked by rubber plantations that were former battlefields (Benh Gia and Nui Dat battles) of the Australians, New Zealanders and VC during the Vietnam War, as well as by verdant mountain ridges. The road is relatively sparsely traveled, making for a great motorcycle day-ride from Saigon, and offers three historical attractions. To find the road to Xuan Loc, take the Ba Ria fork left off Highway 51 to Vung Tau (about 20 km north of Vung Tau) and follow it into downtown Ba Ria. Go around the clock square and continue on the road one more block. At this next intersection (you'll see a large Catholic church on the left just before the intersection), hang a left. This is the road to Xuan Loc.

What to See and Do: Ba Ria to Xuan Loc

Tunnels of Long Phuoc

Long Phuoc

These former VC tunnels, bravely located along the perimeter of both former American and Australian military bases, are so infrequently visited by foreign tourists that the tunnels' sole guide doesn't speak a word of English. Although less significant in scope than the Cu Chi Tunnels—Long Phuoc has only 200 meters of the tunnels open to tourists—they are far easier to explore than Cu Chi, are visited by few tourists, and are refreshingly lacking the ideological diatribes spouted by uniformed cadres. There is no mandatory propaganda film to be tortured by here. The

Long Phuoc Tunnels' guide wears a silk tank top and high heels and was born during the Jimmy Carter administration. She's about as anti-American as the governor of Hawaii. In a few ways, a visit here beats one to Cu Chi. A big reason is that tunnels are high enough to walk through without crouching. That's right—upright. And, unlike Cu Chi, these tunnels were not adulterated to accommodate the expanded girths and wingspans of overfed Westerners. They are seen today as they were originally constructed. And they were probably constructed after the tunnels' engineers toured the micro-environs of Cu Chi and said "Screw that!" The soil in the vicinity is extremely sandy, and the Viet Cong used concrete to ballast the network. Like at Cu Chi, living and sleeping areas, medical stations and gun vents can be explored. And, also like Cu Chi, three levels of tunnels were built under the surface. Visitors can wander on each of the levels. There's a small museum with a few remnants of the war, including small arms and the casings of phosperous and anti-tunnel, ground-piercing corkscrew bombs—also some other odds-and-ends, such as an oil drum lid used to cover a tunnel entrance and digging tools. There is a large model/map depicting the tunnel network and the surrounding American and Australian bases. I was told by the guide the only foreigners that usually come here are Australian vets on an annual pilgrimage to the site each August 20. There is no admission fee, but a donation—or guide tip—is more than appropriate; it should be about VND10,000 per person. To get here, take the Ba Ria-Xuan Loc road from Ba Ria north about five kilometers to where it splits. The left fork heads to Xuan Loc while the right fork heads to Long Phuoc and Long Than, the site of a major Australian-Viet Cong battle in August 1966. After a few kilometers, you'll see a sign on the left (in English) announcing the tunnels' entrance.

Nui Dat Battlefield

Long Than Village

Continuing on the road five km past the Long Phuoc Tunnels, this little known but horrific battlefield was the site of brutal fighting between the VC and Australian and New Zealand troops in August 1966. Today the site is little more than a rubber tree plantation that can be reached only after getting permission from the local People's Committee. The People's Committee building can be found on the left side of the road in Long Than village. This place (or I should say the local People's Committee) is a total ripoff and should only be visited by those who actually fought here—although they won't recognize it. The custodian of the People's Committee demanded US$15 to visit the muddy, totally unremarkable site—a Christian cross placed in the center of a rubber tree orchard—and then threatened one in my group for opting not to go on the "tour," saying she would be heavily fined should she attempt to reach the site on her own. Of course, her only counter-revolutionary idea was to get as far away from the site—and the surly comrade—as possible. This kind of place is one reason Vietnam doesn't get a lot of return visitors. And the comrade should be sent to a boat-people refugee camp in Hong Kong for a couple of years to think things over amongst friends. Interestingly enough, you can learn the story about the cross without wasting the time to visit this site. After the war, the Australian government requested the Vietnamese government send the cross, inscribed with the names of the Australian dead, to Australia as a memorial to the war. Vietnam complied, but sent a fake cross, holding on to the original. Of course, the Aussies weren't duped. But the original was never sent, and can now be found in a Vietnamese museum. As for the fake? A fake now sits where the original did at the Nui Dat battlefield—er—rubber tree farm. A good view of the former battlefield and Australian post can be seen after getting back on the Ba Ria-Xuan Loc road. You can't help but notice the large, solitary rise on the east side of the road a few kilometers north of the Xuan Loc-Long Phuoc fork. The rise was the site of the Australian encampment. Keep the fifteen bucks for beggars.

Hang Gon Tomb

Just about halfway up the road from Ba Ria to Xuan Loc is an unusual tomb of a person or persons unknown that's thought to be around 4000 years old, making it the oldest tomb in Vietnam. No one's quite sure who's inside or where the massive stones that seal this person(s) came from. Some archeologists believe the mystery dead dude is actually the ashes of an entire Mnong family from the Central Highlands, as suggested by a large urn found here. In 1987 the government tried to remove the massive rock "lid" to solve the nagging mystery, but to no avail, as these were the days before foreign direct investment and machinery capable of the task. The tomb isn't marked, but is just 20 meters off the west side of the highway down a nondescript and unmarked path, next to a tractor yard and a white Catholic church about 30 km outside Ba Ria. It's worth stopping for, although the gate surrounding the meticulously upkept garden and tomb may be locked. Simply hop the fence, but be careful of the tourist-unfriendly spikes. Only for the fit.

Binh Chau

At the termination of a recently paved road, some 50 km northeast of Long Hai and six kilometers northwest of Binh Chau town (nothing but a stagecoach stop), is found Binh Chau Hot Springs. Not a lot of foreign tourists get over here (but the resort gets packed with domestic Saigon escapees), but those that do will find some decent hot springs which can be visited for VND2000. The trip is easily made by motorcycle (see "Getting There" below), and has to be done privately as no public transportation yet serves the area from Long Hai or Vung Tau. The springs themselves are too hot to bathe in for some, but others make the plunge in the steaming pool at Cumi Binh Chau Resort—which is fed from the springs—for the reputed medicinal and remedial properties of the mineral-rich water. For an overnight there are few options—in fact, only one. The Binh Chau Resort (Cumi) is hardly a resort, but has decent though overpriced rooms for about US$25. The dormitorylike main domicile overlooks a small outdoor restaurant and picnic area, which is packed with Vietnamese on Sundays. For the amusement of guests, monkeys and birds are trapped in cages next to the picnic tables.

You can wander away from the resort by foot or motorbike about 3000 meters along a series of sand paths to some hot springs and a lazy brook, a journey the resort insists can only be done with the expertise of a guide so as not to get lost in the brush. Skip the guide and do it yourself. The resort sends tourists out to the hot springs and brook via oxcarts. The walk takes about 45 minutes in each direction—15 minutes by moto.

Camping can also be done in the surrounding brush; the resort supplies camping equipment. **Vyta Tours** *(52 Hai Ba Trung Street, Ho Chi Minh City;* ☎ *8230767; FAX: 8243524)* runs overnight trips on Saturdays to the Binh Chau Resort, costing US$35 a head. The price includes transportation, meals and lodging. But the highlight of their trip to Binh Chau is the visit to Ho Coc Beach, a five-kilometer strip of deserted beach (save for the main restaurant and bathing area), set amid verdant jungle and rolling hills against the backdrop of the Truong Son Mountains—on a clear day (see below). The area is protected by the Vietnamese government, and the attempt at keeping the environment pristine has worked well up to press time.

Getting There

To get to Binh Chau from Saigon, take route 51 toward Vung Tau to the Ba Ria fork, about 25 km from Vung Tau. Take a left to Ba Ria and continue straight through town toward Long Hai. About a kilometer east of central Ba Ria the road forks—the right fork runs to Long Hai and the left fork 48 km to Binh Chau (Xuyen Moc). The fork is clearly marked. At Binh Chau, the road forks again. A sign clearly marks the hot springs and resort as being 6 km up the left fork. When the weather's nice, the ride up here provides some great visitas of rubber tree plantations set against the backdrop of the South China Sea. Tour buses make the 3.5-hour trip from the offices of Saigon travel agents. Another way is to follow the above directions, but instead go directly to Long Hai. In Long Hai, take the left fork (away from Long Hai town beach) and head for the resort of Thuy Duong for lunch. Continue on that road up the coast about 15 km to the only major intersection you'll come across. Turn right here, as this is the aforementioned road to Binh Chau.

Ho Coc Beach

Ho Coc Beach is a bit far as a day trip from Saigon at about three hours, but makes for a decent stop when combined with an overnight trip to Binh Chau. This far north from the mouth of the Saigon River (about 40 km north of Long Hai) means that Ho Coc is considerably cleaner and less silty than the waters of Vung Tau and Long Hai. But domestic tourists have discovered Ho Coc, and on Sundays the beach is packed with tour buses of all sizes. Ho Coc's attractiveness is its isolation from the tourist spots of Vung Tau and Long Hai. But don't expect to be alone unless you wander away from the main restaurant and picnic area. Pitiably, like at most Vietnamese beaches accessible to tourism, you'll be expected to pay for something here, such as one of the beach's two dozen or so lean-tos. There are also bungalows here now for spending the night.

Getting There

To get to Ho Coc Beach from Saigon, take route 51 toward Vung Tau to the Ba Ria fork, about 25 km from Vung Tau. Take a left to Ba Ria and continue straight through town toward Long Hai. About a kilometer east of central Ba Ria the road forks—the right fork runs to Long Hai and the left fork 48 km to Binh Chau (Xuyen Moc). The fork is clearly marked. Follow this road about 35 km. A sign on the left side of the road will designate the turnoff to Ho Coc. Turn right here and follow the flat dirt road 7 km to its termination at Ho Coc Beach. Tour buses make the 3-hour trip from the offices of Saigon travel agents. Another way is to follow the above directions, but instead go directly to Long Hai. In Long Hai, take the left fork (away from Long Hai town beach) and head for the resort of Thuy Duong, 3 km away, for lunch. Continue on that road up the coast about 15 km to the only major intersection you'll come across. Turn right here, as this is the aforementioned road to Ho Coc Beach and Binh Chau.

Vung Tau

Tay Ninh

Tay Ninh

TAY NINH IN A CAPSULE

Headquarters to the Cao Dai Sect, one of the most intriguing religions in Asia, if not the world...features some of the most ornate and intricate religious symbolism in the world...there are elements to the temple that are unique in the world...Cao Daism is an odd blend of both Eastern and Western faiths that were somehow coagulated to form the "perfect religion"...There are elements of Christianity, Buddhism, Confucianism, Hinduism, Taoism, Islam and God knows what else...There was a major conflict between Cao Daism and the South Vietnamese government back in the mid-1950s that ultimately led to the reannexation of Cao Dai territory to the Vietnamese...Tay Ninh itself is nothing special and not worthy of a journey simply for the town itself...It's a typical Vietnamese village with avenues flanked by food stalls, electronics shops, etc....There seems to be an increasing number of petrol stations, though...Before the 17th century, this province, close to the Cambodian border, was under Khmer rule.

Tay Ninh, the capital of Tay Ninh Province and about 100 km from the capital, is home to the famous and magnificent, if not bizarre, Cao Dai headquarters, a complex of temples and fields including the Cao Dai Great Temple. The excursion is an easy day trip from Saigon and can be done by rented car, bus, or motorcycle. By motorcycle (you can rent one in Saigon with the proper international driving permit for about US$10 per day), the ride is an exhilarating experience, although the countryside isn't all that magnificent. Unless you plan on being at the temple for noon prayer (there are also prayer services at 6 a.m. and 6 p.m.), just getting there might be the highlight of the day, as the roads are well paved and suited for touring by motorcycle (be careful).

Once you get out of Saigon (from District 1, take Cach Mang Thang Tam to Huong Lo and follow the highway past Cu Chi to Go Dau, then take a right), which can take a very long time (the locals insist the entire trip to Tay Ninh takes two hours by car or fast motorbike). It can easily take as long as 3.5 hours from central Saigon even at speeds as high as 70 or 80 mph and drain your nervous system entirely. The highway becomes relatively free of heavy-vehicle traffic outside the sprawling metropolis and you soon become surrounded by rice fields and then, amazingly enough, a few more after that. There are a number of small, pastel yellow pagodas along the route, but few, if any are worth a detour, unless the road starts to become a little too much and you want to prime yourself for the sights of Tay Ninh.

Between 1975 and 1979, Tay Ninh Province was increasingly encroached upon by Cambodian Pol Pot's Khmer Rouge, who invaded villages and reportedly raped women and killed men and children indiscriminately. It was these deeds that gave the Vietnamese government the impetus (or at least a damn good excuse) to invade Cambodia in December 1978.

The best reasons to visit Tay Ninh, of course, are the Cao Dai temples, particularly the Great Temple, or Holy See. Cao Daism's roots stem from the 1920s in southern Vietnam after the religion's founder, a civil servant named Ngo Van Chieu, received a "visit" from "God," or Cao Dai. Similar to Moses, who descended Mount Sinai with God's gifts of the tablets of the 10 Commandments (not ironically, Cao Dai means "high tower"), Ngo received a message from Cao Dai that the religion was to be based on the "Giant Eye." (The Giant Eye is above each altar in a Cao Dai temple.) In fact, the religion subscribes to five commandments: don't kill anything living, don't practice excessive or extravagant living, do not slander, do not be tempted, and do not covet. This Giant Eye was apparently the manifestation of the vision of a number of lay people, from politicians to poets. Included as saints in the Cao Dai religion are such illustrious luminaries as Winston Churchill, Moses, Joan of Arc, the French writer Victor Hugo, Sun Yat Sen, and Brahma. This helps explains Cao Daism's attempt to merge secular and scientific principles with religious or spiritual devotion. Followers of Cao Daism interpret the "scriptures" through meditation and sort of a séance that contacts the saints utilizing a corbeille-a-bac, an odd wooden planchette.

Their religion became formalized in 1926 and soon developed an almost nationalistic fervor. Within a short time, Cao Daism had tens of thousands of followers.

A year later, Cao Dai convert Le Van Trung staged a religious coup and assumed leadership of the fledgling faith. He built a temple in the village of Long Hoa, near Tay Ninh. Ten years later, the following of Cao Daism had become massive; there were an estimated 4–5 million followers of the sect. It essentially became a political state that, of course, didn't amuse the government. In 1955, when as many as 15 percent of southern Vietnamese were Cao Dais, there was a major confrontation between the religion and the state that ultimately gave the government back control of territory that it had "lost" to the Cao Dais. The South Vietnamese government then conscripted tens of thousands of Cao Dai adherents as soldiers.

After the fall of the south in 1975, Cao Daism all but ceased to exist. Because they refused to support both the Viet Cong and the South Vietnamese forces during the protracted war, Cao Dais faced especially intense scrutiny and hardship after the Saigon leadership collapsed. Since the relaxation of tensions between the peoples of the north and the south, Cao Daism has re-emerged and nearly 1000 Cao Dai temples can be found throughout Vietnam, primarily in the south, receiving the worship of an estimated 2 million adherents to the religion. Cao Daism has the strongest influence in the province of Tay Ninh and in the Mekong Delta region.

Cao Dais aim to break the cycle of reincarnation by following the five commandments. The principle deities are the Mother Goddess and God. Men and women equally share positions of supreme authority; both men and women become clergy, except at the highest levels. If men and women clergy of the same status are based in the same temple area, the men are bestowed greater authority. Male priests are called "Thanh," while female clergy are referred to as "Huong." Cao Dai temples are built in a fashion where male clergy enter the structures from the right, while the women enter from the left. The same goes for worship; men worship on the right side of the temple while the women do their praying on the left side of the temple.

Prayer services—conducted four times daily (6 a.m., noon, 6 p.m. and midnight)—are the best times to visit the temples. Clergy and dignitaries wear ornate red, blue and yellow ceremonial robes and hats, and there are offerings of fruit, flowers, alcohol and tea. During the normal prayer sessions on weekdays, hundreds of clergy members may be present. But there are special Cao Dai holidays where you may actually find yourself among thousands of Cao Dai priests.

Cao Dai priests practice celibacy and vegetarianism. The Cao Dais separate history into three distinct periods or revelations: the first was when the existence of God was revealed to human beings through Laotze and the influences of Taoism, Buddhism and Confucianism. The second phase involved Sakyamuni Buddha, Jesus Christ, Mohammed, Moses and Confucius. During the second period, the Cao Dai came to believe that the conduits carrying the divine messages from these individuals had become convoluted and impure.

INSIDER TIP

Visitors to the temples should remove both hats and shoes. Similar to Cao Dai clergy, women enter the temple through an entrance on the left, while the men do so on the right—similar to how Cao Dai clergy enter and exit their temples. You'll usually be accompanied by a Cao Dai priest (man or woman), and you will be expected to provide a small donation—the amount entirely up to you. Curiously enough, my guide barely spoke a word of English, and I found that other clergy at the Cao Dai Great Temple weren't exactly fluent in anything but what they seemed to be muttering either. So be prepared. Read the section on Cao Daism in this book (or other more extensive selections, such as Cao Dai Spiritism: A Study of Religion in Vietnamese Society, *by Victor Oliver (EL Brill, Leiden, 1976) before visiting the temple. Without doing so, your visit may be virtually meaningless, save for a few snapshots. You will understand none of the artistic depiction of three periods of history that hang on the walls. In the main temple two rows of pink pillars line the aisle, inscribed with dragon figures. These aisles lead up to the main altar, above which is the Giant Eye. Visitors watch the service from a balcony overlooking the cathedral. Plan on staying for the entire service, which lasts about an hour. It would be a disruption as well as an insult to depart earlier. At no time should you walk down the center portion of the nave, although when I inadvertently did I was met with a kindly but "you stupid Hoa Ky" smile from my guide. You may be allowed to take pictures, taking photos of clergy members is forbidden unless they grant you permission, which may mean a small "donation."*

The new, or third phase, of Cao Daism has its followers believing that the convoluted previous messages have been eliminated through their communication with the spirits. These "spirits" include former Cao Dai leaders as well as an eclectic blend of both lay people and clergy. Many Westerners are spirits the Cao Dai contact frequently. Among them are Shakespeare, Louis Pasteur, and V.I. Lenin (who, curiously enough, didn't appear to inspire the Cao Dai to align themselves with Marxist Viet Cong forces during the war, even though Cao Dai members sided with the French against the Japanese, the Americans against the Viet Minh, and the Viet Minh against the South Vietnamese government). The spirits are communicated with in a number of languages, including French, Vietnamese and English. In one ceremony, the priest seals a blank piece of paper in an envelope and places it above the altar. When he takes it down, a message is contained in the envelope.

Although formal Cao Dai seances have been held in temples across the country since 1925, the only "legitimate" seances that reveal divine truth can be conducted at Tay Ninh.

What to See and Do in Tay Ninh

Cao Dai Great Temple (Holy See) ★★

Long Hoa village, 2 km east of Tay Ninh.

This is the principal temple of the Cao Dai religion and the focal point of the Cao Dai complex called Holy See. Its colorful pastel yellow architecture (which seems to get a new coat of paint hourly by the hordes of workers one sees on scaffolds all the time) is set among a large complex of schools, dormitories and a "hospital," which utilizes traditional Vietnamese herbal medicine. The main temple consists of an intriguing complex of architectural styles, ranging from Oriental to European. The large front facade features reliefs with depictions of Cao Dai saints. Some have called the building the most impressive structure in the Orient, while others have compared it with Disneyland. If you're impressed with Disneyland, though, you may be disappointed by the lack of roller-coasters at the temple.

The temple is constructed on nine levels, which represent the nine steps to heaven. On each level you will find a pair of columns. There are impressive columns in the nave decorated with dragons. Above the altar, of course, looms the Giant Eye with an eternal flame. The domed ceiling that the columns support represents the heavens.

There is a mural in the entry area displaying the three signatories of the "Third Alliance Between God and Man." There are seven large chairs at the far end of the temple in front of the globe, the largest of which is supposedly "reserved" for the Cao Dai pope, a position that hasn't been filled since the early 1930s. Three of the chairs are for the use of those Cao Dais responsible for the religion's law books. The remaining three chairs represent the seating areas for the leaders of the religion's three branches.

A must is to attend a prayer service at the temple. Although the place is swamped with tourists at noon prayer time (held each day at 6 a.m., noon, 6 p.m. and midnight), it is a highly impressive experience. Visitors remove their shoes at the left and right entrances of the temple (resulting in an enormous, odiferous mountain of footwear at the base of the church) and then climb stairs to the overhead viewing gallery which perches from along three sides of the temple. Hundreds of Cao Dai male and female clergy in bright yellow, blue or red robes then enter the temple for an hour of chanting and praying. Cameras and VCRs can be used by tourists from the upstairs viewing balcony to record the proceedings, but shouldn't be used for individual portraits or other photos of Cao Dai clergy outside the temple.

Long Hoa Market

Middle of town.

In the middle of Tay Ninh, about a kilometer or two from the Cao Dai complex. Nothing really worth writing home about here; just the basic staples bought by the basic crowds you see in marketplaces all over provincial Vietnam. Foodstuffs, fake designer clothes, etc.

Tay Ninh

Where to Stay and Eat in Tay Ninh

Near the bridge there are a few places to stay in the US$10–$20 range, but Tay Ninh is not an area worth more than just a few hours' visit, which can easily be arranged from Saigon by tour group or rented car. Most visitors combine day tours of Tay Ninh with a visit to the Cu Chi Tunnels, which lie along the route (National Highway 22) to Tay Ninh from Saigon.

For food, your best bets are the numerous food stalls that surround the Long Hoa market. Two restaurants of note are the **Nha Hang So 1**, which is on the western side of the river near the bridge, and **Nha Hang Diem Thuy**, located at 30/4 Street. Both restaurants, as are all in Tay Ninh, are extraordinarily cheap, with most meals costing as little as 5000 dong (about US$.50).

Directory

Transportation

The best way to get to Tay Ninh is by minibus or car, the latter of which can be rented for the US$70–$90 range a day, although some private entrepreneurs will offer cars and drivers for as little as $40 a day ($20 per day if you're going only as far as Cu Chi.) Buses leave for Tay Ninh regularly from Saigon via Cu Chi from the Tay Ninh bus station and the Mien Tay bus station in An Loc. They take about three hours, sometimes longer. The other alternative is to rent a motorcycle. Make sure you leave Tay Ninh (if you're not spending the night) by 3 p.m. to avoid the extremely dangerous nighttime traffic, both on treacherous Route 22 and in Saigon, where nighttime motoring is something akin to a circus bumper car ride without electricity. Unless you know what you're doing, it's better to get out to this area with a guide or in a group. Buses back to Saigon leave from the Tay Ninh bus station regularly to the same stations.

Tay Ninh Environs

Black Lady Mountain

This is also called Nui Ba Den, and it's located about 15 km from Tay Ninh. I've heard this is the highest peak in southern Vietnam. There are a number of temples on the mountain (the main temple can be reached in about 45 minutes via a relatively simple hike from the base of the hill), the result of centuries of Khmer, Cham, Vietnamese and Chinese domination of and influence in the area. The term Black Lady Mountain is based on the legend of a young woman named Ly Thi Huong who, despite being wooed by a rich Chinese Mandarin, ended up marrying the man of her dreams. (Another version of the tale has Huong leaping off the side of the mountain in protest of the wealthy Chinese's romantic pursuits.) While the husband was away fighting wars, Huong would make pilgrimages to the summit of Nui Ba Den to visit a magical Buddha statue. One day, as legend has it, there was an attempt by bandits to rape the woman, who, believing death was the more virtuous alternative, threw herself off the face of the edifice. The story became known through her communication with a local monk.

The mountain, which reaches about 900 meters or more above the rice fields was also the setting of intense firefights between the Viet Minh and the French during the first Indochina War, and between the Americans and the Viet Cong during the Vietnam War. Americans heavily defoliated the region during the war, though one can hardly tell today. (If your grandchildren are born resembling cauliflowers, you'll realize that the American defoliation of Vietnam is a lot like AIDS—you may look verdant on the outside, but something inside is ripping you apart.)

The principal temples of pilgrimage on the mountain are Lang Chang Pagoda and Chua Linh Son Pagoda. Some of the fortune tellers in and around the pagodas speak English.

Tay Ninh

Tay Ninh

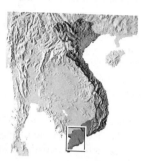

THE MEKONG DELTA

THE MEKONG DELTA IN A CAPSULE

Vi Thanh *(60 km south of Can Tho) was one of the first "strategic hamlets," a largely unsuccessful attempt by the South Vietnamese government to create artificial urban centers for farming that would be safe from Viet Cong infiltration...***My Tho** *is the closest delta destination to Saigon...***Can Tho** *is considered the capital of the Mekong Delta...***Thot Not** *(40 km upriver from Can Tho on the Bassac River) was where the Trotskyite revolutionary Ta Tu Thau was born...***Thap Muoi,** *or The Plain of Reeds, at the junction Long An and Dong Thap provinces, is a former Viet Minh and Viet Cong base that neither the French nor the Americans were able to occupy...***Ca Mau** *(348 km from Ho Chi Minh City, 210 from Vinh Long.) is the biggest city in the Ca Mau peninsula on the Gonh Hoa River. Ca Mau is famous for the U Minh forest, the second largest mangrove swamp in the world. There are many precious and endangered birds and animals...***Ha Tien** *(340 km from Saigon, 250 km from Vinh Long) is a small town of Kien Giang Province in the Gulf of Thailand, 8 km from the Cambodian border. It has many beautiful beaches, caves and romantic settings. Phu Tu Islet (Father-Son Isle), with its panoramic views, looks like Ha Long Bay in miniature...Stone Cavern...Dong Ho Lake...Cape Nai...Offshore island of* **Phu Quoc** *accessible by air and being developed for tourism.*

This is the richest and the most prolific agricultural region of Vietnam. In fact the majority of all Vietnamese are fed with agricultural products from the Mekong Delta. It's an extremely rural area covering some 67,000 sq. km but, surprisingly it is one of the most densely populated areas of Vietnam, and more than half of the entire region is under cultivation. The only regions of the delta that are to date sparsely cultivated or not cultivated at all are the areas around Minh Hai Province.

The Mekong Delta was formed primarily by mud from the Mekong River spreading in forklike directions out to the South China Sea. The area itself was sparsely populated until the 19th century, when Vietnamese settlers moved slowly down south to take advantage of the newly formed region's rich agricultural potential. They called the area "Mien-tay," or the "West." Most of the area's geographical, cultural and architectural attractions are, by Vietnamese standards, new. Temples that may appear to be hundreds of years old may in fact have been built as recently as the 1930s and '40s. The oldest area of the Delta is Ha Tien, on the southwestern coast at the border of present-day Cambodia. Ha Tien was settled and highly prosperous as early as the start of the 17th century.

Crops grown in the delta include mango, mangosteen, jackfruit, oranges (believe it or not), guava, pepper, durian and pineapple, among others. Also under cultivation are coconut, sugarcane and seafood—if you can call shrimp cultivated. In fact, although the rice yields are lower in the delta than in the north of Vietnam, there is nearly three times as much rice acreage per person as there is in the north. The region is entirely flat and contains a vast network of rivers and waterways that comprise the tributaries of the Mekong River—locally called Song Cuu Long (or the River of the Nine Dragons).

The Mekong's source is high on the Tibetan Plateau, making the river perhaps the mightiest and longest in Asia. It flows nearly 4500 km through China, Laos, Cambodia and Myanmar before finally splitting into both wide and thin branches of waterway in Vietnam's southern region.

In Vietnam, the Mekong splits into two major channels. The river itself moves through Hung Ngu and Vinh Long, where several fingers then branch out on their journeys to the South China Sea.

INSIDER TIP

The Vietnamese government plans to spend US$9.2 billion each year on improvement of the country's waterways. Investments are also expected to be made to develop modern passenger ships as well as domestic touring vessels.

The Bassac River, which runs through Long Xuyen and Can Tho, is the other main branch. The best time of the year to see the Mekong is in the fall, when the runoff from upriver all through Southeast Asia makes the waterways an incredible sight, as the flow of the river reaches nearly 40,000 cubic meters (compared with 2000 during other times of the year).

INSIDER TIP

There has been increasing interest among independent travelers to creatively find their own ways of exploring the Mekong River. Beware, though, that pirate attacks are not infrequent along this vast stretch of interior waterway. Pirates recently boarded a Cambodian freighter bound for Phnom Penh and beheaded 18 people, including children, and dumped their bodies into the river. Armed with AK-47 rifles and grenade launchers, the pirates escaped before being apprehended by Vietnamese authorities.

Not surprisingly, because the mighty river's force continues to extend the shoreline of southern Vietnam by as many as 15 meters a year and extend the shorelines at the mouths of the river by about as much as 80 meters a year, the Mekong Delta region is geologically relatively recent in origin. As mentioned, the land of the delta was formed by the silt being pushed down the river from the highlands of China, Myanmar and Laos, and the area—save for the Ha Tien region, which was settled in the 17th century—remained virtually unpopulated until the 19th century. Vietnamese settlers moved south into the "Mien-tay." Consequently there is very little of any deep historical significance in the delta. The temples are new, although some appear to be centuries old.

Perhaps the amazing oddity of the Mekong occurs not in Vietnam, but in Cambodia, where, when the river is at flood stage, it drains up the Tonle Sap River, which prevents flooding in the Mekong Delta region and brings Cambodia's Tonle Sap Lake to enormously high levels.

AUTHOR'S OBSERVATION

The Irrawaddy dolphins of the Mekong River are getting blown out of the water. Literally. The increasing use of explosives by Khmer fishermen to more easily harvest fish from the waters of the Mekong is including in its carnage the slaughter of the Irrawaddy, a rare dolphin that inhabits the waterways of the Mekong in Laos, Cambodia and Vietnam. This is the report from the Bangkok-based Project for Ecological Recovery. According to the report, and travelers visiting the region, the blasting of fish out of the river is on the rise, and has increased steadily in the past 10 years (and even to a greater extent since the signing of the Cambodian Peace Accords in October 1991) occasionally during the high-water rainy season but much more frequently during times of the year when the water levels go down. Many visitors to the region report hearing 10–20 explosions per day in the river.

Originally, the delta region belonged to the Cambodians and wasn't settled by the Vietnamese until centuries later (see the Ha Tien chapter). Although most of the region's population is composed of ethnic Vietnamese, you'll find a number of Khmer descendants living particularly in the lower end of the delta.

The Mekong Delta is a fascinating area to tour, but it is also a monotonous glut of real estate, the topography changing very little, if at all, for thousands of square kilometers. I toured the area by motorcycle and boat, and, frankly, would not have done it any other way simply for the reason that the numerous rest stops I took were the most enjoyable part of my adventure. The people of the delta are truly its attraction, not the topography nor the historical sights. Being invited into families' homes for meals, falling in love with the locals and trading love messages that have to be translated by relatives, these are the real attractions of the delta. At one cafe in the tiny southern delta village of Soc Xoai, I was grilled by a young lady's parents over Vietnamese whiskey and BGI beer about my background and profession in order to gain permission to marry the young woman (which was essentially granted) even though my only request was to exchange addresses with the young lady for correspondence purposes.

There are ferry trips across the Bassac and Hau Giang rivers to villages whose inhabitants have rarely—if ever—laid eyes on a Westerner. But keep in mind that traveling the delta below Can Tho isn't easy, and can be quite dangerous. The roads are in dismal shape. I've experienced numerous flat tires and broken clutch cables—many parts of my motorcycle have simply fallen off—due to the harshness of the terrain. At the end of the day, you will be covered in dust, vehicle exhaust and mud if you travel by any other means than by bus or with a tour group in a car or microbus. The water at many hotels in the region may turn out to be nothing more than motivation to remain as dirty as you'll get. Travel by regular bus in the delta below Can Tho is *excruciatingly* uncomfortable for taller Westerners. Nowhere else in the southern half of the country will you have to "rough it" like you will in the Mekong Delta.

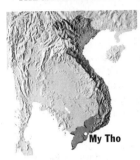

My Tho

MY THO IN A CAPULE

Just two hours from Saigon...Capital of Dinh Tuong Province...Under Khmer rule until the 17th century...The French colonized the area in the mid-1800s...A strategic American military base was here in the mid-1960s...Considered the site of the Viet Cong's first major military victory...Makes for an easy day trip from Saigon.

My Tho, one of the first stops in the Mekong Delta, is only about a two-hour drive from Saigon (about 76 km) and is the capital of Dinh Tuong province (also known as Tien Giang province), with a population of about 100,000. It sits on the banks of the My Tho River, one of the many Mekong River tributaries near the mouths of the Mekong. It was under Cambodian rule until the 17th century and was settled mainly by Chinese after the Nguyen Lords took control of the area later that century. Thai forces subsequently invaded the area but were forced out in 1784. The French took control of the region in the mid-19th century. In the mid-1960s, an important American military base was here.

My Tho is often considered the site of the first Viet Cong victory over ARVN forces, but the fight actually took place in nearby Ap Bac.

Today, My Tho is a relatively prosperous city known for its rice production and fruit orchards. The city itself isn't as drab as Vinh Long. My Tho can easily be seen in a day visit from HCMC, but if you take this kind of excursion, get the most out of it. I especially recommend visiting the nearby islands of Ben Tre and Phung Island, former home of the Coconut Monk—although don't expect a lot of truly magnificent scenery at either. It's the history of the area that makes it worth seeing.

My Tho

What to See and Do in My Tho and Environs

Trung Trac Central Market

Located on Trung Trac Street near the Bao Dinh channel on the eastern edge of town.
If you've seen one market, you've seen them all. At least the streets are closed to traffic here and you'll see a lot of produce and fruit—I mean a lot. Most of it, I'm sure, ends up in HCMC. You'll also see a lot more tobacco sold here than in other delta markets. However, this is the best place to get a sample of life in My Tho, as it is the city's most bustling area in an otherwise laid-back environment.

My Tho Church

32 Hung Vuong Street.
This is a big pastel yellow church with twin towers that was built about 100 years ago, making it ancient by Mekong Delta standards. The church serves the city's 8000 or so Catholics, but it's open only about six hours a day: very early in the morning (you'll still be in bed), and in the afternoon for about four hours. Masses are held twice every day and at least three times on Sunday. The plaques on the wall inside the church are dedicated to Fatima.

Vinh Trang Pagoda

60A Nguyen Trung Truc Street.
Open from 9 a.m.–noon and from 2 to 5 p.m. in the afternoon.
This is an unimpressive little pagoda that's a little tough to get to without asking for directions. Well, here they are: Cross the bridge at Nguyen Trai Street and then turn left down Nguyen An Ninh Street to the end. Then walk down a dirt path to Nguyen Trung Truc Street. You'll come across a painted bamboo gate on the right. This is the entrance. The actual entrance to the pagoda is through a porcelain gate. Architectural styles range from Chinese to Vietnamese to French colonial (the temple was built in the mid-1800s). I'd simply avoid this place altogether if only for the fact that the animals kept here in the "zoo" live in dismal conditions. It seems the pagoda's lure is not spiritual or architectural, but purely capitalistic. It's sad to watch the microbus loads of tourists gawk at the animals and behave as if they were at Disneyland. The only thing worth seeing here is the portrait of Ho Chi Minh, complete with real beard hairs from Uncle Ho's face.

Quan Thanh Pagoda

3-9 Nguyen Trung Truc Street.
This is a nice restored temple with plaster figures. Otherwise not a lot to see here.

Con Phung (Phung Island)

The island of the Coconut Monk is about 3 km from My Tho. After World War II, the Ong Dao Dua (the Coconut Monk) built a small village on Con Phung and started a new religion, which was a mishmash of Christianity and Buddhism. In its early years it might have reminded you of singer Michael Jackson's ranch in California, with parklike attractions in an attractive setting (although Disneyland's influence seems all too apparent in and around My Tho). The grounds used to contain ornate structures: dragon-wrapped columns and the like, but today, they're run down and musty. The Ong Dao Dua, who was born Nguyen Thanh Nam, was given his moniker because he reputedly ate nothing but coconuts for three years on a stone slab where he also meditated both day and night. Before his monastic life, he was educated in France, married and had a daughter. Later, during his coconut diet, he was persecuted and imprisoned by the various South Vietnamese governments as he sought to reunify Vietnam though a peaceful process. To get out to the island, you can hire a boat at the south end of Trung Trac Street. Prices vary depending on the size of the boat, ranging anywhere from US$3 an hour to US$20 for a round trip and "tour."

Tan Long Island

This is worth seeing only because it's a cheap five-minute boat trip from My Tho. Fishing boats cover the palm-lined shores. Take some pictures and then come back.

Snake Farm ★

8 km from My Tho toward Vinh Long.

Many varieties of snakes, all indigenous to Vietnam, are raised here, from pythons to deadly cobras. The military runs the place and raises the animals for their medicinal qualities. I assure you these snakes have not had the lethal venom removed and the ability of the soldier/snake handlers in dealing with these vicious creatures is a sight in itself. The belief is that the snakes have healing powers in their flesh and glands. These medicines are then bottled and sold to the hordes of tourists who've climbed off the microbuses.

Where to Stay in My Tho

> **AUTHOR'S NOTE: TELEPHONE PREFIXES**
>
> *The following telephone numbers are local exchanges. The country code is 84. The city code is 73.*

Hotel 43   US$6–$8

43 Ngo Quyen Street. ☎ 873126, 872126.
24 rooms.

The expensive rooms are the doubles with air conditioning, while the cheaper rooms can sleep three and have an attached bath. Service here is some of the friendliest in My Tho. Great value.

Song Tien Hotel (formerly the Grand Hotel)   About US$20

101 Trung Trac Street. ☎ 8712009.
35 rooms.

This is a relatively expensive place that used to have a better reputation as the eight-story Grand Hotel. The staff has been reported to be dishonest. And honestly, the place is overpriced. The upper-end rooms have refrigerators and air conditioning.

Thanh Binh Hotel   US$3

44 Nguyen Binh Khiem Street.
4 rooms.

Forget it. Like spending the night in a janitor's closet. I wouldn't let them pay me to stay here. In fact, I'm not even sure they still allow foreigners. No fans; no bath.

My Tho

Rach Gam   US$3–$6

33 Trung Trac Street.

This is one of the cheapest accommodations in town and it shows. Backpackers only.

Lao Dong Hotel   About US$6

Le Loi and 34 Thang 4 Streets.

This is a relatively new hotel that hasn't yet gotten the opportunity to descend into uncleanliness. And it's cheap. Again, for the backpacker set—but a definite bargain.

Where to Eat in My Tho

My Tho is known for a couple of specialty dishes, the best being *hu tieu my tho*, a spicy and garnished soup packed with herbs, shrimp, vermicelli, pork and chicken. Find it, or in its various forms, at:

Restaurant 43

43 Ngo Quyen Street.

Vietnamese, Asian. Inexpensive and good.

Nha Hang 54

54 Trung Trac Street.

Vietnamese, Asian fare. Ice Cream.

Nha Hang 52

52 Trung Trac Street.

Vietnamese, Asian. One of the best in town.

Directory

Transportation

By **bus** or **car**, My Tho is about 76 km from HCMC and another 70 km from Vinh Long. It's about 180 km to both Rach Gia and Chau Doc, and 275 km from Ha Tien. You can get to My Tho in only a couple of hours from Saigon's Mien Tay Bus Station. The bus station at My Tho is 4 km back on the road toward Saigon and Vinh Long. The station is open from about 4 a.m. to 5 p.m. Take Ap Bac Street to National Highway 1 to get there. There are also buses to Vinh Long, Can Tho, Rach Gia, Chau Doc and other destinations in the delta. Buses generally leave when they are full.

By **boat**, ferries leave to My Tho in the afternoon from Saigon and take about 6-7 hours, sometimes quite a bit longer. They leave from the wharf on Ton Duc Thang Street at the end of Ham Nghi Street. Price about US$1. Transportation around My Tho is by cyclo or by small motorized boats which can be rented from the ferry landing on Trung Trac Street. You can hire a car at Thuan Hung, *130-156 Le Loi*. Note: if you're traveling by car from Saigon to My Tho, remember the road (NH1) splits about 68 kilometers from HCMC. Proceed straight (which is a fork off NH1) to get to My Tho, or turn right to proceed on to Vinh Long. Signs are well marked.

Tourist Office

Tien Giang Tourism, *66 Hung Vuong Street.* ☎ *872154.*

Ben Tre

Just below My Tho is the province of Ben Tre, with its capital of Ben Tre. What really separates Ben Tre from My Tho is the number of tourists. Most tourists take a boat trip on the Cua Dai (Tien Giang) River and then head on their way to Vinh Long or back to Saigon. Few actually cross the river and continue their travels in Ben Tre province, namely because the road dead-ends at Ba Tri. There are few tourist facilities in the province, but certainly enough to accommodate the few who get here. The town of Ben Tre itself is small and uncluttered with tourist trappings. Boats can be hired for journeying on the Ben Tre River just off Hung Vuong Street near the Hung Vuong Hotel and the Floating Restaurant. Ben Tre Tourism has a speedboat for rent for about US$30 an hour. There's a small lake in town (Truc Giang Lake) where small paddleboats can be rented, but only if you really have nothing to do. The lake can be crossed in just a minute or two.

What to See and Do in and Around Ben Tre

Vien Minh Pagoda

Nguyen Dinh Chieu Street

This is a Chinese-style pagoda that was built in 1958, replacing the original structure which was thought to be more than a century old when it gave way to the current structure. The pagoda is easily identified by the large white statue of Quan The Am Bo Tat (the Goddess of Mercy) in the curtilage in front.

Nguyen Dinh Chieu Temple

This temple is about 30 km from the town of Ben Tre. Not worth the drive out unless you're headed in that direction for another reason.

Boat Rides on the Ben Tre River

Next to the bridge small boats can be hired to explore the tributaries of the Mekong for about US$5 an hour.

Where to Stay in Ben Tre

Dong Khoi Hotel   US$25–$35

16 Hai Ba Trung Street. ☎ *822240.*
35 rooms.

The best place in town, with comfortable singles and doubles with air conditioning, hot water and private bath. TV, restaurant and gift shop. Staff might arrange for boat rentals. Set by Truc Giang Lake.

Ben Tre Hotel   US$8–$15

226/3 Tran Quoc Tuan Street. ☎ *822223.*

Dumpy rooms with fan or air conditioning, but still not a bad value for the price. The doubles with air conditioning are the best bet.

Hung Vuong Hotel   US$7–$15

166 Hung Vuong Street. ☎ *822408.*

On the riverfront. Air-conditioned doubles and singles with fan.

Where to Eat in Ben Tre

The best place to eat in Ben Tre is the restaurant at the **Dong Khoi Hotel**. The other option is the **Floating Restaurant** on the Ben Tre River next to the bridge. Both places offer superb river delights.

Directory

Transportation

See the My Tho section for getting to My Tho. From My Tho, ferries depart for the other side of the Tien Giang at the Ben Tre ferry landing on Le Thi Hong Gam Street, 500 meters west of Nam Ky Khoi Nghia Street. You might also try the ferry landing on Trung Trac Street if you're traveling by bicycle or small motorbike.

Tourist Office

Ben Tre Tourism

West of Truc Giang Lake near the corner of Dong Khoi Street. ☎ *829618*.

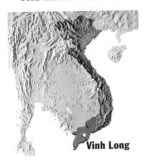

Vinh Long

Vinh Long

VINH LONG IN A CAPSULE

Vinh Long, *(about 135 km southwest of Saigon) is the site of a major temple dedicated to Tong Phuc Hiep, general of the Nguyen Dynasty... It was also the home of Petrus Ky (Truong Vinh Ky), the 19th-century spirit who sought to modernize Vietnam.*

About 145 kilometers from Ho Chi Minh City on the Hau River, Vinh Long province occupies a core area of the Mekong Delta. It may be regarded as a microcosm of the entire Mekong Delta due to its primordial prosperity. An Binh Island and Binh Hoa Phuoc Islands dot the huge networks of meandering rivers, bisected by countless arroyos under the dense tropical delta foliage. When you pay a visit to the orchards you can taste ripe fruits you pick from the trees yourself or have friendly conversations with the local people.

Vinh Long (the capital of Vinh Long province) is not the kind of place you'll really want to spend a lot of time in, however, save for taking boat trips along the Co Chien River to visit the orchid-covered islands. There are some decent hotels that have gone up in recent years that make the town a more attractive resting spot in your journey to areas farther south and to the west such as Can Tho, Long Xuyen, Rach Gia and Ha Tien. Vinh Long is also the nucleus of the spread of Catholicism in the Mekong Delta region, so you'll come across a couple of cathedrals and a seminary. There's also a Cao Dai church near the second bridge into town coming from both Saigon and My Tho. Vinh Long is about 140 km south of HCMC. The city was also the home of Truong Vinh Ky (Petrus Ky), a legendary figure of the 19th century who sought to bring Vietnam into the "modern" age.

If you visit the islands around Vinh Long, you'll have to hire a boat, the smallest of which can be had for around 10,000–20,000 dong per hour (about US$1–$2). The best islands to see are unquestionably An Binh Island

and Binh Hoa Phuoc. The town of Vinh Long itself is rather dreary, but is becoming an increasingly comfortable place to spend the night.

What to Do and See in Vinh Long and Environs

Tong Phuc Hiep Temple

This temple was dedicated to Tong, who was considered a great general during the Nguyen Dynasty. It's worth a few minutes' visit.

Binh Hoa Phuoc and An Binh Islands

Just a short ride across the Mekong (the finger here is called the Co Chien) are islands teeming with tropical fruit plantations, fruit that's eventually trucked or shipped up to HCMC. You could actually spend a few hours out on the river as there are other islands dotting the river, many having never been visited by tourists. Again, though, there are not a lot of sights out here, and the boat ride may be worth it just for the ride itself and the breeze to break up the intense delta heat. For boat info check with the Long Chau Hotel or the Vinh Tra Hotel (addresses below). The boat trip runs about US$30.

Where to Stay in Vinh Long

AUTHOR'S NOTE: TELEPHONE PREFIXES

The following telephone numbers are local exchanges. The country code is 84. The city code is 70.

An Binh Hotel   US$5–$15

3 Hoang Thai Hieu Street. ☎ *823190.*
40 rooms.
Although not on the riverfront, this is a decent value for the money. Rooms with air conditioning or a fan. Air-conditioned rooms have private bath. Massage, restaurant—even tennis!

Vinh Tra Hotel   US$12–$35

1 Thang 5 Street. ☎ *823656.*
20 rooms.
Cheapest rooms get you a fan, the more expensive hot water, air conditioning and refrigerator. Hotel offers Mekong River tours, car and microbus rentals, restaurant with Asian and European cuisine and dancing. Hotel overlooks the Mekong.

Cuu Long Hotel   US$15–$35

Next door to the Cuu Long Restaurant. 1 Thang 5. ☎ *822494.*
24 rooms.
One of the best places in town. Comfortable if not particularly attractive rooms with fan or air conditioning. But this is a good place to book river trips. Hotel also provides car rentals and arranges local tours.

Long Chau Hotel   US$6–$12

11 Thang 5 Street. ☎ *823611.*
$6 rooms with public toilet. $8 rooms have private bath. The more expensive rooms also have air conditioning. Hotel offers river tours, car and microbus rentals. Res-

taurant featuring Asian and European cuisine. Dancing hall, orchestra and entertainment nightly. This is a hell of a good deal and popular with backpackers.

Truong An Tourist Villas   **US$22–$30**
4 km from Vinh Long toward the ferry. ☎ *823161.*
Fantastic riverside location for these bungalows. Clean, comfortable and relaxing. Restaurant. Recommended.

Where to Eat in Vinh Long

Phuong Thuy Restaurant
Thang 5 Street, across the street from the Vinh Tra Hotel.
Excellent seafood at some of the cheapest prices in the delta. There are a number of restaurants serving river fish and seafood specialties along Thang 5 Street. However, the Phuong Thuy may well be the best.

Directory

Transportation

Hired motor car or motorcycle is the best way to move between Saigon and Vinh Long, and many tourists will combine a day trip with a visit to nearby My Tho or even Can Tho (about US$70 for the car and another $20 a day for the guide). (Frankly, I don't think a day trip to Vinh Long is worth it. The stop is only reasonable if you're planning an extended trip into the delta.) But if you must travel by bus, buses from HCMC's Mien Tay Station to Vinh Long take between 3.5 and 4 hours, as does the return trip from Vinh Long's bus station next to the post office and central market. Buses leave when they're full. There is also bus transport from Vinh Long to other areas in the delta, including My Tho, Can Tho, Rach Gia, Ha Tien and Long Xuyen.

Tourist Office

Cuu Long Tourism. *1 Thang 5 Street;* ☎ *823616.*

Post Office

Just behind the bus station on Doan Thi Diem Street.

Tra Vinh

Tra Vinh is an infrequently visited province to the southeast of Vinh Long, namely because once you get there you have to come back the same way. There are no roads nor towns of any significance on the southern banks of the province on the Bassac (or Hau) River which might provide a link with Soc Trang or Can Tho provinces (i.e., there are no ferries). But the heavily ethnic-Khmer province is accessible and Tra Vinh town can be reached by bus from Vinh Long or Can Tho. Those on motorbike can also explore surrounding areas such as Chua Co and Luu Cu. Tra On is also accessible, but the trip is better done during the dry season, as the "road" linking the town with Vinh Long is in awful shape.

Tra Vinh town sits on the banks of the Long Binh River and features a number of Khmer and Chinese pagodas. Although 300,000 ethnic Khmers

Vinh Long

call Tra Vinh province home, so does the Mekong Delta's largest concentration of ethnic Chinese.

What to See and Do in Tra Vinh

Khmer Pagodas

There are said to be nearly 150 Khmer pagodas in Tra Vinh Province, the majority of them buried in the boonies. **Ong Met Pagoda (Chua Ong Met)**, however, can be found in the center of Tra Vinh town. This is a large Khmer pagoda accessible to tourists. **Wat Angkor Icha Borei** is another superb example of Khmer-style Theravada temples and can be found at Ba Om Pond, on the road to Vinh Long 8 km from Tra Vinh town. The lake itself is something of a pilgrimage spot for the area's ethnic Khmers. **An Pagoda (Chua An)** is about 5 km southwest of Tra Vinh town and features a small museum. Forty-five kilometers from Tra Vinh town can be found **Co Pagoda (Chua Co)**, a nesting ground for huge numbers of storks.

Den Tho Bac (Uncle Ho Temple)

Long Duc, 5 km from Tra Vinh town.

This is a somewhat brash temple built ostensibly to honor Ho Chi Minh, but more realistically to attract tourists. Few locals use it as a place of worship.

Ong Pagoda

Corner of Tran Phu and Dien Bien Phu Streets, Tra Vinh town.

This is a beautiful Chinese temple in an extraordinary state of repair that is said to have been originally built in 1556. It has undergone a number of rebuilds and restorations since and is probably unrecognizable from its original state, but is worth a visit to admire the intricate work that has gone into its present form.

Oyster Island

Boats can be rented in Tra Vinh town for a journey down the Long Binh River to Oyster Island. Nothing really to be seen here on this mucky island other than oysters. However, the boat trip is a pleasant one.

Where to Stay in Tra Vinh

Thanh Tra Hotel   US$10–$35

1 Pham Thai Buong Street, Tra Vinh town. ☎ *863622. FAX: 863769.*

The best place in town at press time and popular with Vietnamese tour groups. The lower-end rooms have fan and private bath, while the better rooms come with air conditioning, TV, private bath, hot water. Restaurant.

Huong Tra Hotel   US$5–$7

67 Ly Thuong Kiet Street. ☎ *862433.*

Shabby rooms with a fan and shared bath. Pass on by.

Cuu Long Hotel   US$15–$25

999 Nguyen Thi Minh Khai Street. ☎ *862615.*

Rooms with air conditioning, private bath, hot water.

Transportation

Tra Vinh town is 210 km from HCMC and 67 km southeast of Vinh Long. Buses reach Tra Vinh town from both Vinh Long and Can Tho.

Tourist Office

Tra Vinh Tourist Company

Cuu Long Hotel, 999 Nguyen Thi Minh Khai Street, Tra Vinh town. ☎ *862491. FAX: 863769.*

Sa Dec

Sa Dec, halfway between Vinh Long and Long Xuyen, is about 135 km from Saigon and is probably most famous for the many flower nurseries that transport fresh flowers daily to Saigon. Ho Chi Minh's father used to spend time here and his grave is located in Sa Dec. Here is also the tomb of Nguyen Van Nhon, the mandarin who helped Emperor Gia Long defeat the Tay Son. Also, the commander of the French Forces in Cochin China, General Chanson, was assassinated here, as was Thai Lap Thanh, the governor of Cochin China, in July 1951. The killings were the work of a dissident Viet Minh Cao Dai follower.

Sa Dec is worth a visit for the beautiful nurseries in the area. As well, Ho Chi Minh's father settled and was buried here.

Where to Stay and Eat in Sa Dec

Sa Dec isn't worthy of an overnight stop. The few food stalls offer standard Vietnamese fare, but watch where the proprietors crack the ice. If they're doing it on a sidewalk or in the street, avoid it.

Directory

Tourist Office

The tourist office for Dong Thap Province is located at *108 5/A Hung Vuong Street* in Sa Dec. It's called Dong Thap Tourist. ☎ *861430* or *861432.*

Cao Lanh

Cao Lanh has only been visited by tourists for the past couple of years, as travelers seek to get off the Mekong Delta ant trail. Cao Lanh is accessible by Route 30, which runs northwest from Highway 1A from a point 12 km north of the ferry crossing to Vinh Long. Cao Lanh is reached 30 km later. The town sits about 10 km north of the main branch of the Mekong River, but is surrounded by waterways that can be traversed by small boats. There is even water-skiing here, as Dong Thap Tourist has gotten hold of a decent speedboat, which can be rented out for US$25 an hour with skiis. Contact

Vinh Long

Dong Thap Tourist *(2 Doc Binh Kieu Street.* ☎ *851547, 851343).* These folks also run boat tours on the area's arroyos.

Other things worth taking in here include the gravesite of Ho Chi Minh's dad, Nguyen Sinh Sac. The tomb can be found about 1000 meters southwest of town. Before reaching the center of Cao Lanh coming west on Highway 30, you'll come across the War Memorial, the gravesite of more than 3100 Vietnamese communist soldiers.

What to See and Do Around Cao Lanh

Rung Tram Forest

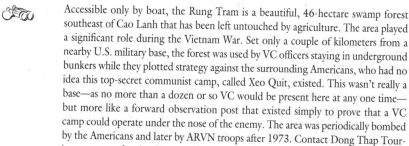

Accessible only by boat, the Rung Tram is a beautiful, 46-hectare swamp forest southeast of Cao Lanh that has been left untouched by agriculture. The area played a significant role during the Vietnam War. Set only a couple of kilometers from a nearby U.S. military base, the forest was used by VC officers staying in underground bunkers while they plotted strategy against the surrounding Americans, who had no idea this top-secret communist camp, called Xeo Quit, existed. This wasn't really a base—as no more than a dozen or so VC would be present here at any one time—but more like a forward observation post that existed simply to prove that a VC camp could operate under the nose of the enemy. The area was periodically bombed by the Americans and later by ARVN troops after 1973. Contact Dong Thap Tourist to arrange for their speedboat to get out here at US$25 an hour. Slower boats take about 40 minutes and cost about US$4 a person if the trip coincides with a visit to the White Stork Sanctuary.

White Stork Sanctuary

Also reached only by boat to the northeast of Cao Lanh is this preserve for white storks, which can be seen by the dozens poking around the marsh for food. This is actually a small area and it's a lengthy one-hour speedboat ride from Cao Lanh (90 minutes by slow boat).

Where to Stay in Cao Lanh

Song Tra Hotel   US$25–$45
Nguyen Hue Street, center of town.
New hotel and the best in town. Comfortable rooms with air conditioning, hot water, private bath, minibar, color TV. Restaurant, tourist services.

My Tra Hotel   US$15–$30
Highway 30 (Nguyen Hue Street), opposite the War Memorial. ☎ *851469.*
20 rooms.
Rooms with fan or air conditioning, hot water, private bath. Good restaurant.

Tam Nong Nature Reserve
(Tram Chim Tam Nong)

Forty-five km north of Cao Lanh is the village of Tam Nong and the Tam Nong Nature Reserve, home to hundreds of species of birds, including cranes and beautiful red herons, which make their nests here from December to June. If you are able to visit during these months, the herons can best be seen at sunrise and sometimes at dusk when they return to their nests.

The reserve is quite accessible, by either an uncomfortable 90-minute drive or via boat from Cao Lanh. The speedboat can be rented from Dong Thap Tourist; the journey takes an hour and the boat rents out for US$25 an hour. Slower boats also ply the canals up here and cost US$4 with a minimum of 20 people. At Tam Nong, another boat will have to be rented at US$15 an hour to reach the reserve (a one-hour trip).

If visiting the reserve it makes more sense to stay in the village of Tam Nong rather than Cao Lanh, especially if you're planning to be up early in the morning to get a glimpse of the red herons. There is one guesthouse in Tam Nong open for foreigners. It's about 2 km outside of town and costs US$6–$10. Some of the rooms have air conditioning.

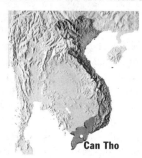

Can Tho

Can Tho

This skipper negotiates a narrow canal near Can Tho.

CAN THO IN A CAPSULE

Can Tho *(170 km southwest of Saigon) is the capital of Can Tho Province and the region's transport center. Since the colonial days, it has been the delta's major center of rice cultivation...There's an important rice research institute here, as well as a university.*

Can Tho (about 170 km south of Saigon), capital of Hau Giang (or Can Tho) Province on the Bassac—or Hau River—is considered to be the Mekong Delta's Capital of the West and is the largest population center in the delta, with more than 200,000 inhabitants. It's probably the cleanest

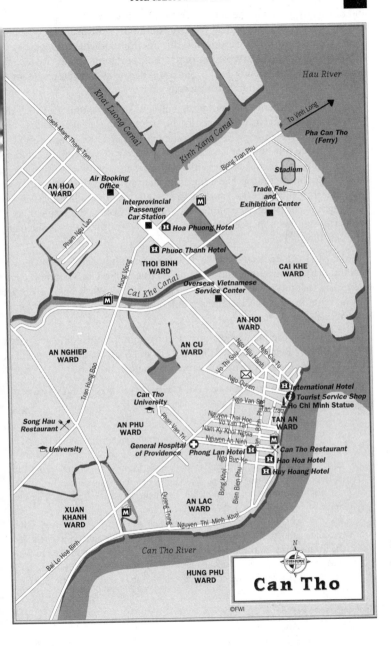

Hau River

To Vinh Long

Pha Can Tho
(Ferry)

Khai Luong Canal

Kinh Xang Canal

Cach Mang Thang Tam

Bjong Tran Phu

Stadium

AN HOA
WARD

Air Booking
Office

Trade Fair
and
Exihibition Center

Interprovincial
Passenger
Car Station

Pham Ngu Lao

Hoa Phuong Hotel

Phuoc Thanh Hotel

THOI BINH
WARD

CAI KHE
WARD

Hung Vuong

Cai Khe Canal

Overseas Vietnamese
Service Center

AN HOI
WARD

AN NGHIEP
WARD

AN CU
WARD

Tran Hung Bao

Vo Thi Sau

Ngo Hiu Hanh

Ngo Gia Tu

Ngo Quyen

Can Tho
University

International Hotel

Tourist Service Shop
Ho Chi Minh Statue

Ngo Van Sao

Phan Van Tri

Song Hau
Restaurant

AN PHU
WARD

Nguyen Thai Hoc
Vo Van Tan
Nam Ky Khoi Nghia
Nguyen An Ninh

Phan Dinh Phung

Han Trao

TAN AN
WARD

University

General Hospital
of Providence

Phong Lan Hotel

Ngo Duc Ke

Can Tho Restaurant

Hao Hoa Hotel

Huy Hoang Hotel

Bong Khoi

Bien Bien Phu

XUAN
KHANH
WARD

Quang Trung

AN LAC
WARD

Nguyen Thi Minh Khai

Bai Lo Hoa Binh

Can Tho River

N

Can Tho

HUNG PHU
WARD

©FWI

and nicest city to visit in the delta—certainly the city with the best accommodations. Can Tho makes a great base to explore the outlying villages and islands. Canals and rice fields surround this intermittently picturesque city. I also serves as the delta's most important transportation center. Roads and ribbon-thin river tributaries lead to surrounding towns and villages, many of whose inhabitants have rarely seen foreigners.

Can Tho is certainly the political, cultural and economic hub of the Mekong Delta, and many farmers in the surrounding villages possess vast parcels of land (recently given back to the farmers after the communist government seized most private land after 1975) used for agriculture, including tropical fruit, cotton and pepper. Along the canals (that rise to the rims of their banks and then drop like a flushing toilet with the tides) outside Can Tho, visitors will be surprised at the increasing number of tall, modern deco-like structures being erected along the waterways' banks, the result of local prosperity and the money sent back to families by wealthy overseas Vietnamese (Viet Kieu).

In the city's center, along Hai Ba Trung Street on the Can Tho River, is a bustling market and a huge, silver painted statue of Ho Chi Minh in the riverside park that looks like a carved brewery vat. City dwellers and tourists get around by motorcycle cyclos that are unique to the delta; they aren't found anywhere else in Vietnam.

Can Tho is also the site where Nguyen Khoa Nam, commanding general of the 4th Military Region, and his deputy Le Van Hung committed suicide in May 1975 after the fall of South Vietnam to the communists.

What to See and Do in Can Tho and Environs

Binh Thuy Temple   ★★

3 km west of Can Tho

Just a few kilometers west of Can Tho, this structure was built in 1852 by Binh Ton and features shrines to the king of longevity. There are some beautiful portraits—and others that are rather amateurish and less flattering—of Vietnamese and Chinese leaders such as Phan Boi Chau, Bui Huu Nghia and Nguyen Hue. Perhaps the most striking features of the temple are the numerous cranes that are built near dragon-wrapped columns. Other figures of cranes and dragons are built of brass that frankly, could use a bit of polishing. There is also a large 150-year-old stuffed tiger. The symbol of the giant cranes reflects the large white birds' visits to the area to be fed marijuana by the locals (as legend has it). Others from Can Tho to Long Xuyen will attest to the birds feeding on the illegal crop each day near sunset on the river's islands. The temple was designated a cultural and historical area by the Hanoi government in 1989.

Munirangsysram Pagoda   ★

36 Hoa Binh Blvd.

Here is a Khmer Hinayana Buddhist temple that features a 1.5-meter-tall figure of Siddhartha Gautama, the original Buddha, sitting beneath a bodhi tree. It was built in 1946, at which time more than 200 monks lived at the pagoda. An extremely elderly monk lives here as well as a few much younger monks, youths really. They are extremely friendly and will invite you into their quarters for tea before viewing the inside of the relatively small pagoda. The temple serves the several thousand Khmer Theravada Buddhists who live in the Can Tho area. I felt guilty neglecting to leave a donation, but if the monks were displeased, they didn't show it. Prayers are held early in the morning and in the evening.

Quan Thanh De Pagoda

Le Minh Ngu On Street.

Also known as Minh Huong Hoi Quan. Built by a Cantonese contingent nearly 75 years ago, this small Chinese pagoda was the house of worship for Can Tho's enormous ethnic Chinese population, who mainly evacuated the city—and Vietnam—in the late 1970s during the Vietnamese government's anti-Chinese persecution program. Quan Cong, as well as administrative mandarin Quan Binh and General Chau Xuong, are in the main dais, while Ong Bon, the Guardian Spirit of Happiness and Virtue are situated to the left of the dais. The Goddess of the Sea (Thien Hau) is on the other side.

Can Tho University

30 Thang 4 Blvd.

This small university was founded in 1966 and is worth only a brief stop for most visitors.

Central Market

Just down the river on Hai Ba Trung street from this statue of Ho, is a busy, cluttered market lined by numerous food stalls.

The Villages Surrounding Can Tho (Ba Se, O Mon District)　★★★

These are the real attractions of the city, and if you can get a guide with relatives in the area, the US$20 expense will be more than worth it. All along the main highway to Long Xuyen, are rutted paths that lead deep into the delta's heartland. Small villages line the canals and motorized and oar-propelled boats navigate the sometimes dangerously shallow canals, with amazing ingenuity. The best reason for the guide is the opportunity to be invited into his relatives' homes for meals and Vietnamese whiskey, whose distillers have no qualms of beginning their imbibing as early as 10 in the morning. In many of these areas, villagers have never set eyes on foreigners, and wherever you stop you'll be surrounded by dozens of children and women offering coconut milk. If you can go by boat it's better, especially one that can be arranged through a relative of your guide. In one day I had no fewer than five chickens slaughtered in my honor by families scattered along the banks of the canals. I was shown grave sites of family members killed during the war, as well as rich, vast parcels of deep black, rich soil covered with fruit and eucalyptus trees. There are boats for hire in Can Tho that usually rent for around US$2 an hour. They can be found along the riverfront. You won't have to look hard.

Can Tho

The other way to get out to the villages in O Mon district is to catch a minivan west to O Mon from Can Tho and ask the driver to stop after about 10 km—about halfway to O Mon. At that point, ask any of the numerous locals to bring you back along the arroyos on the back of his motorbike. Most won't hesitate to oblige for US$1–$2. Ask to go to Lo Te Ba Se—or show the rider the following: **Rach Xeo De**, **Ba Se**, **Xa Tan Thoi**, **O Mon**, **Tinh Can Tho**. This means you'd like to go to Xeo De canal, Tan Thoi village, O Mon district, Can Tho province. The rugged ride is a truly remarkable 15 km journey back in time. Few travelers get back here. Small villages line the slim path deep into the heart of the delta. Canals line the path, where women wash clothes and canoe skippers pole themselves out of the mud as they traverse the ribbon-thin arroyos beneath a canopy of tropical vegetation. When you reach Ba Se, you can dispatch the driver—as there will be many villagers eager to bring you back to the highway after you've finished exploring the region. Ask anyone in Ba Se for a man named Mr. Hai Ky (Ong Hai Ky). Not only will you be treated to a meal, this elderly gentleman will be your proud escort through one of the most colorful experiences you'll have in Vietnam. He'll get one of his sons or nephews to fetch a canoe and bring you along the Mekong's thinnest tributaries. I'm not saying any more. Trust me on this one.

Where to Stay in Can Tho

AUTHOR'S NOTE: TELEPHONE PREFIXES

The following telephone numbers are local exchanges. The country code is 84. The city code is 71.

Hotel Song Huong   US$10–$12
101 Nguyen Trai. ☎ *825074.*
12 rooms.
Rooms with double or multiple beds. US$6 for a small room with a fan. Restaurant, private toilet. Foreigners accepted and management is quite proficient in English.

Tay Ho Hotel   US$7
36 Hai Ba Trung Street. ☎ *823392.*
12 rooms.
Rooms have two beds with fan and private bath. Foreigners encouraged. Next door is the Mekong Restaurant. Great Vietnamese cuisine at shamefully low prices.

Tay Do Hotel   US$4–$5
61 Chau Van Liem Street. ☎ *821009.*
27 rooms (14 double, 13 single).
This place is quite popular with backpackers. Private bath with the doubles, public toilet for the singles. Fans in all rooms.

Ninh Kieu Hotel   US$25–$40
2 Hai Ba Trung Street. ☎ *825285, 824583.*
One of the best places in town with a great riverside location. Excellent restaurant. Comfy rooms with air conditioning, hot water and private bath.

Huy Hoang Hotel   US$7–$10

35 Ngo Duc Ke Street. ☎ *825833.*

Ten bucks gets you air conditioning and little else here, perhaps the most popular spot in Can Tho for backpackers.

Phong Nha Hotel   US$4–$5

75 Chau Van Liem (Nguyen An Ninh Old). ☎ *821615.*
24 rooms.

Singles and doubles both have private baths. Reception friendly. For the price, it's well furnished. Gets the overflow from the popular Huy Hoang.

Hotel Phuong Phu   US$4–$5

79 Chau Van Liem. ☎ *820149.*
14 rooms.

One of the best bargains in town for the price. Private rooms with bath. No hot water, of course, but hot water in southern Vietnam is for tea, not bathing in. Electric fan. Currently the hotel is adding more rooms and air conditioning.

Saigon Can Tho Hotel   US$58–$98   ★★★

55 Phan Dinh Phung Street. ☎ *825831/822318. Fax: 84-71-823288.*
46 rooms.

With the rebuilding of the former Viet Hong Hotel, this place has become the best place in Can Tho, hands down. In fact, it's the best in the Mekong Delta. These guys tout themselves as the first business hotel in Can Tho. Although the International makes a better claim to the stature, there was never any real reason for foreigners to be doing business in Can Tho to begin with. Perhaps now there is. And now there's an even better place than the International to do it. Air-conditioned rooms. Two-hundred seat restaurant offering Vietnamese, Chinese and Western dishes. Business and conference center, massage & sauna, karaoke, car rentals. The hotel provides tourist services from Can Tho Tourism. They'll also book flights to Phu Quoc Island, which leave on Mondays. For foreigners the cost is US$30 (the cost from Can Tho to Saigon to Can Tho is the same). Get a room on the upper floors (5th and 6th floors) for a great view of the surroundings.

Viet Huong Hotel   About US$10–$15

33 Chau Van Liem Street. ☎ *824832.*

Good central location close to the market and the river. A little cramped.

Khach San Khai Hoan   US$4

83 Chau Van Liem. ☎ *835261.*

On and off again in terms of accepting foreigners. The only thing going for it is the price.

Hotel Hoa Binh   US$6–$18

5 Hoa Binh Street. ☎ *820530, 820536.*
22 rooms.

The single rooms at six bucks aren't much, but there is a fan. Rooms with three beds can be had for US$11, and nonair-conditioned doubles for US$8. Check the different rooms. There are a lot of configurations. For instance, 13 of the rooms offer

Can Tho

only a public toilet. There is air conditioning offered in nine of the twin bed rooms, which run US$18. Foreigners are welcome and the price includes breakfast.

Hao Hoa Hotel   US$10–$15

8 Hai Thuong Lang Ong Street. ☎ *824836.*
Small, but it finally is open to foreigners.

International Hotel   US$25–$40   ★

12 Hai Ba Trung Street. ☎ *822079, 822080.*
40 rooms.
This was the classiest place in Can Tho until the redo of the Saigon Can Tho. You might even be tempted to say that it's up to international standards which, in my opinion, it is. Its well-maintained, modern exterior and interior stand out in distinct contrast with the surrounding environment. Right on the waterfront. Air conditioning, restaurant, friendly service.

Hau Giang Hotel   US$23–$36   ★

34 Nam Ky Khoi Nghia Street (Can Tho center city). ☎ *821851, 821189. FAX: 821806.*
35 rooms.
Nicely appointed and friendly staff who know English well. Rooms have private bath, air conditioning, refrigerator, telephone (IDD in the lobby), radio cassette and TV. Hot and cold water systems. Photocopy services, foreign exchange services, car rental service and river tours to orchid-covered islands. Air-conditioned restaurant with 200 seats; Vietnamese, Asian, seafood, Chinese and European dishes. Open from 6 a.m. to 11 p.m. 7 days. Price includes both breakfast and lunch. Dancing hall and karaoke room.

Nha Nghi Hotel   US$15–$20

1 Dien Bien Phu Street. ☎ *820049.*
New and clean, this hotel is a value indeed. Singles and doubles with air conditioning, private bath and hot water.

Where to Eat in Can Tho

Those on a budget or those who simply want to immerse themselves in the local color should definitely head for Nam Ky Khoi Nghia Street, between Dien Bien Phu and Phan Dinh Phung Streets, where can be found a number of good local joints serving the catch of the day from the nearby Bassac River. The following are also worthy.

International Hotel $$ ★

12 Hai Ba Trung Street. ☎ *822079, 822080.*
Perhaps the best place in town. The upstairs restaurant is the best, offering superb river fish, snake and prawns.

Restaurant Can Tho $

52 Nguyen Trai Street. ☎ *822186.*
Vietnamese, Asian, Chinese.

Restaurant Can Tho $

27 Chau Van Liem Street.
Vietnamese, Chinese, European. Romantic setting, nice ambience.

Can Tho

Restaurant Hoang Huy $

65 Phan Dinh Phung, 1st floor.
Vietnamese.

Restaurant Rain-Bow $

54 Nam Ky Khoi Nghia.
Vietnamese, Asian.

A Chau Restaurant $

91 Chau Van Liem Street. ☎ *822129, 822130.*
Vietnamese, Asian. Expect your meal to be served quickly.

Vinh Loi Restaurant $

42 Hai Ba Trung Street.
Soups are the tastiest here. The Vietnamese cuisine is both delicious and a total bargain.

Nighlife in Can Tho

International Hotel

12 Hai Ba Trung Street. ☎ *822079, 822080.*

The upstairs disco is the place to be most evenings, particularly on the weekends. The pretty hostesses may avail themselves to extracurricular activities. The outside balcony offers great nighttime vistas of the river activity and is a breezy place for quiet conversation and romantic liasons.

Saigon Can Tho Hotel

55 Phan Dinh Phung Street. ☎ *825831/822318. FAX: 84-71-823288.*

Requisite karaoke and becoming popular.

Directory

Transportation

Can Tho is 170 km from HCMC, 104 km from My Tho, 115 km from Rach Gia, 35 km from Vinh Long, 115 km from Chau Doc, 62 km from Long Xuyen and 50 km from Sa Dec. By **bus**, you'll leave from HCMC's Mien Tay bus station. Express buses take only about 4 hours to get here and leave HCMC when full. Non-express buses take about 5-6 hours. Can Tho's intercity bus station is located next to the ferry dock on Nguyen Trai and Tran Phu.

There are two ferry crossings—one at Vinh Long and the other at the north side of the Bassac River at Can Tho. Just a note: motorcycles and express buses have priority at the ferry crossings. With a motorcycle, you'll certainly catch the next ferry (two are typically run simultaneously) and probably won't have to wait much more than 15 minutes. Express buses may sometimes wait 30 minutes, but it's rare. Non-express buses frequently wait 30 minutes or more.

Getting around town is best by flagging down a *xe honda loi*, a **motorized cyclo** (a motorcycle pulling a pushcart) that is unique to the Mekong Delta. Nowhere else in Vietnam are these contraptions found. They make for a bumpy ride but are relatively cheap at VND5000–10,000 for jaunts around town.

Can Tho Police Dept.

☎ 8270281.

Fire Department

☎ 820170 (An Hoi Quarter, ☎ 821286).

Post Office

25 Hoa Binh Street.

Emergency Medical Services (EMS)

213 Hoa Binh; ☎ 6l: 824644, 824244.

Can Tho Tourist Co. (Headquarters)

27 Chau Van Liem Street; ☎ 821804, 821853; FAX: 822719.

Can Tho Service Center

18 Hai Ba Trung Street; ☎ 821852; FAX: 822719
(In Ho Chi Minh City) 01 Nguyen Tat Thanh Street-4th District; ☎ 8291053.

Phung Hiep

About 25 km southeast of Can Tho on the road to Soc Trang is the small town of Phung Hiep, which is noted for its morning floating market. National Highway 1 passes right over the market on a bridge. If you get up early enough (the market gets going about 6 a.m.; the cast strikes the set about 10:30 a.m.) you can stand up on the bridge and get some excellent photos of the activity taking place just a few meters below.

The town and market are best accessible by private transport from Can Tho. There is no reason to overnight here.

Thot Not (Can Tho Subdistrict)

On the northwest side of Can Tho is Thot Not. There's not much here, unless you're moving at night east to Can Tho (about 40 km away) and are extremely tired and want to spend the night at one of the cheapest hotels in Vietnam. The one attraction in this area is **Tan Lap Island**, another area *very rarely* seen by foreigners. You can hire a boat in Thot Not and cross the Hau River for a visit to the orchid-covered island.

Where to Stay in Thot Not

Thot Not Hotel   US$2.50–$3

No address, across the bustling main drag from Thanh Binh Restaurant; ☎ 851309. *10 rooms.*

This lies on a busy main street lined with cafes, food stalls and small restaurants. The hotel itself is a converted office building that's dirty and musty and sees few foreign travelers. The rooms are relatively clean, but if you've gotten a room with two single beds attached, don't move them apart. The floor will reveal a putrid display of dead cockroaches, rat excrement and used condoms. The public toilet is abhorrent. Don't use it unless you've got a good, high pair of trout fisherman's boots. The water in the showers is like grape vinegar. The manager, though, is eager for business, and is eager to please tourists.

Where to Eat in Thot Not

There are numerous food stalls up and down the "strip" in Thot Not with—perhaps not surprisingly—great sea and river food. Most of the proprietors are relatively old and speak both French and English—i.e. they fought or were associated with the South Vietnamese/American efforts to win the Vietnam War. They'll want to practice their English with you and will often trade conversation for libations, and even food. You can have a night on the town here without even having a town to have a night on.

Long Xuyen

Long Xuyen

Long Xuyen (about 182 km southwest from Saigon) is the capital of An Giang Province with a population of about 100,000 situated on the west bank of the Bassac River. It's a rather shabby city, as are many in the delta, and seems virtually indistinguishable from Can Tho save for the riverside parks and cafes, of which I couldn't find any in Long Xuyen. It was once a major area of the Hoa Hao sect, an interesting religion without temples or priests that act as the bond between man and God. But the Hoa Hao people were extremely influential in the area and even had their own surprisingly strong and disciplined military force. Today the city is the home of the Hoa Hao University, which was founded in 1970.

My impressions of the provincial capital were redundant with some of the other city centers of the delta: bustling markets, shabby hotels, a river transportation system that takes some asking around to get pointed in the right direction, and small temples and pagodas that are only really worth seeing if you haven't seen some finer examples in other areas of the delta.

There's not a lot to see and do here, and perhaps its greatest attractions are the locations on the other side of the river, many of which have not been seen by foreigners.

What to See and Do in Long Xuyen

Dinh Than My Phuoc Temple

Le Minh Nguy On Street, near the intersection of Huynh Thi Huong Street.
There's an impressive roof here and the walls near the altar are covered with murals. Worth a quick stop.

Quan Thanh Pagoda

8 Le Minh Nguy On Street.

This isn't far from Dinh Than My Phuoc Pagoda and is probably more worthy of a visit. The entrance wall is covered by beautiful murals, and the altar features a figure of Mandarin General Quan Cong as well as other Mandarin leaders including Quan Binh and General Chau Xuong.

Cao Dai Church

Tran Hung Dao St.

Near the end of Long Xuyen toward Chau Doc on Tran Hung Dao street is a small Cao Dai temple that, again, is really only worth a visit if you haven't already been to Tay Ninh.

Long Xuyen Catholic Church

Center of the triangle formed by Nguyen Hue A, Tran Hung Dao and Hung Vuong Streets.

This is a huge Catholic church that's an easy landmark in the city and can be seen from several km from outside Long Xuyen. It was finished just prior to reunification of the country in 1975. There's a 50-meter-high bell tower and two giant hands clasped together form the spire of the church. This church is reputedly one of the largest in the delta. Masses are conducted here quite early in the morning (around 4:30 a.m.) and in the evening from 6 to 7 daily. On Sunday, there are three masses.

Protestant Church of Long Xuyen

At 4 Hung Vuong Street.

This is much smaller than its Catholic cousin close by and is only really worth a visit if you feel compelled to attend service. Services are held every Sunday.

Cho Moi ★

North side of the Bassac River.

This is the verdant agricultural district on the other side of the Bassac River reached by ferry from the ferry terminal at the base of Nguyen Hue Street. It features bountiful tropical fruit groves of mango, banana, jackfruit, guava, durian and longan. It's worth a few hours' visit.

My Hoa Hung Memorial House ★★

My Hoa Hung village, north side of Bassac River.

Do you want to visit a fascinating island across the Basac River from Long Xuyen where giant, brilliant, white, flamingolike storks arrive by the thousands each evening to munch on marijuana? Do it. The island is also home to the My Hoa Hung Memorial House, which is where Ton Duc Thang, one of the best-known architects of Vietnamese communism and the Vietnamese labor movement lived from 1888-1906. The memorial house, across the road from Ton's magnificent tropical and eerie hardwood home, features photos of the Viet Minh's—and North Vietnam's—eventual leader at the usual state and formal functions. More interesting are the letters he wrote that are on display in glass cases, as well as his shoes, uniforms, suitcases, spectacles and other clothing items. The memorial house is visited seldomly, and the only Westerners to have seen the area (which have been very few indeed) have arrived via the fledgling Anziang Tourist Agency in Long Xuyen as part of small tour groups crossing the ferry at An Hoa. The place was deserted when I got there. There is no admission fee, but small donations (say 2000 dong) are appreciated. As far as getting out there, forget the tourist agency. (They'll tell you that the storks don't feed on marijuana because it's illegal to grow or possess marijuana in Vietnam. I guess someone's gotta tell that to the storks.) Nothing's marked, so read carefully. If you're coming west from Can Tho continue to Long Xuyen via Lien Tinh Street. Go around the first roundabout in Long Xuyen and continue straight on Lien Tinh. At this point stop and ask someone where Binh Duc Bridge is (it's located along the same route, but you'll need to know EXACTLY where it is!). Just before reaching Binh Duc Bridge, at the last possible meter, there will be a dirt turnoff to the right. Keep going on this path, which flanks the Dra On canal, for about 500 meters to an extremely small ferry landing. On the other side (only bicycles and motorcycles permitted on the ferry) of the river, you'll pass through My Hoa Hung village. You'll then see a bridge off to the right after about 3 km. Make a right over the bridge. The Memory House isn't much farther. Plan your visit to see the stoned storks between 5 and 6 p.m. The ferry to My Hoa Hung village is 700 dong; tack on another 600 dong for a bicycle, or 800 dong for a motorbike. Instead of returning the way you came, continue straight along the dirt road to the An Hoa ferry, which runs across the river into downtown Long Xuyen.

Where to Stay in Long Xuyen

AUTHOR'S NOTE: TELEPHONE PREFIXES

The following telephone numbers are local exchanges. The country code is 84. The city code is 76.

Long Xuyen Hotel   US$16–$26

17 Nguyen Van Cung Street. ☎ *852927.*
37 Rooms.
Newly renovated, at least to an extent, within the past two years. Hot water, air conditioning. Cheaper rooms have a fan, no air conditioning. It's run by An Giang Tourism.

Khach San Cuu Long (Mekong Hotel)   US$25–$30

21 Nguyen Van Cung Street. ☎ *852365.*
24 rooms.
Huge rooms here with private bath. Perhaps the best hotel in town. Hot water, air conditioning.

Tien Thanh Hotel   US$6–$10

240 Tran Hung Dao Street.
On the road east to Can Tho, several km out of town.

Thai Binh   US$6–$12

12 Nguyen Hue Street. ☎ *852184.*
24 rooms.

A good value for the price. The more expensive rooms have air conditioning. Restaurant. Public and private toilet.

Kim Thinh   US$6

39/41/43 Nguyen Trai Street. ☎ 853137.

Air conditioning for only six bucks, which makes this place a deal. Popular restaurant.

Xuan Phuong Hotel   US$15–$20

68 Nguyen Trai Street. ☎ 852041.

This is also not a bad deal. It's a clean hotel, and the more expensive rooms can accommodate four people. Air conditioning.

Song Hau   US$6–$10

10 Hai Ba Trung Street. ☎ 852308.
26 rooms.

The cheaper rooms come with fan, while there's air conditioning in the others. Private bath. This is the most popular spot in town for backpackers.

Where to Eat in Long Xuyen

As in other Mekong Delta destinations, food stalls abound in Long Xuyen, and they're understandably the cheapest places to eat. Most of the small restaurant/cafes can be found along Hai Ba Trung Street, as can the **Long Xuyen Restaurant**, perhaps the best eatery in town, on Hai Ba Trung and Nguyen Trai Streets. Cuisine is Vietnamese, Chinese, and European.

Directory

Transportation

Long Xuyen is about 65 km from Can Tho and 126 km from My Tho. The distance to HCMC is about 190 km. **Buses** leave from Saigon's Mien Tay Bus Station. The express bus to HCMC leaves Long Xuyen at 4 a.m. every day. The Long Xuyen bus station is about 1.5 km east of town on Tran Hung Dao Street, not far from the Catholic cathedral. The ride to Saigon takes about 7 hours along generally good roads. Bus connections from Long Xuyen can also be made to Can Tho, Vinh Long, Chau Doc and Rach Gia. It's important to note there are other bus stations around town that can provide more comfortable express bus service to HCMC. An express microbus leaves from near the GPO about 2 a.m. There's also a tourist express bus service (at *93 Nguyen Trai Street*) to HCMC at 4 a.m. each day. It can be confusing to figure out what the best situation is for your own needs, so ask the folks at **Angiang Tourist Office** (*6 Ngo Gia Tu Street*). There are a few private bus companies that offer faster and more comfortable solutions to your transportation needs. Transportation around town is generally via the type of **"cyclo"** which is unique to this part of Vietnam. They are in effect wagons that are pulled by either motorcycle or bicycle. They are the easiest way to get around town.

Post Office

101 Tran Hung Dao Street.

Banks and Moneychangers

Vietcom Bank is located, *1 Hung Vuong* near the intersection of Hung Vuong and Nguyen Thi Minh Khai Streets. Money can also be changed at reasonable rates at gold and jewelry shops about town, usually about 10,800 dong to the dollar. Many hotels, if they do change money, render 10,000 dong per dollar. But it's gone up at many places in recent months to close to the exchange rate of 10,900 dong per dollar.

Tourist Office

An Giang Tourist Office is at *6 Ngo Gia Tu Street.* ☎ *852036.*

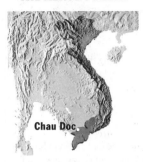

Chau Doc

Chau Doc

CHAU DOC IN A CAPSULE

300 km from Saigon, 150 km from Vinh Long...Chau Doc is part of An Giang Province near the Cambodian border...There are many ranges of spectacular mountains, beautiful landscapes and a lot of historical relics...Mount Sam...Ba Chua Xu Temple...Tay An Pagoda...Thoi Knock Hau Mausoleum...Breeding fish rafts on the rivers.

Like Can Tho, Chau Doc (population about 50,000), is a relatively attractive and clean city for the Mekong Delta and a major commercial center in the western delta—it attracts a lot of Vietnamese and particularly Chinese, Taiwanese and Hong Kong tourists. It sits on the west bank of the Bassac River near the Cambodian border and possesses perhaps both the largest Khmer and Cham populations in Vietnam. Until the middle of the 18th century, Chau Doc was under Cambodian rule but was ceded to Lord Nguyen Phuc Khoat after his help in suppressing an uprising in the area. You'll notice that many of the women here, rather than the traditional Vietnamese conical hats, don Khmer scarves on their heads. The area is also home to the Hoa Hao sect, which was founded by Huynh Phu So in 1939 and claims more than a million members, most of whom live in the Chau Doc region.

An interesting and curious feature of Chau Doc are the floating houses in the river. They're not built on stilts, but rather float directly on the river. Fish are raised in nets under the houses and are fed whatever the owners want to feed them. Of course, raising fish this way makes them easier to catch. Perhaps of greater benefit, fishermen don't have to drop explosives into the river to reap their bounty.

What to See and Do in Chau Doc and Environs

Chau Doc Church

459 Lien Tinh Lo 10.

Chau Doc

This is a tiny church that really isn't worth a stop unless, of course, you're Catholic and it's Sunday at 7 a.m.

Chau Doc Market

This large market stretches along the riverfront on Chi Lang, Le Cong Thanh Bach, Bang Dang and Doc Phu Thu Streets. In addition to an array of fresh produce, you can also find an abundance of goods smuggled into Chau Doc from Thailand via Cambodia.

Chau Phu Temple

Gia Long and Bao Ho Thoai Streets.
This temple was erected in the mid 1920s in honor of Thoai Ngoc Hau. There are both Vietnamese and Chinese influences here, and funeral markers commemorating deceased dignitaries.

Chau Giang Mosque

Take the ferry from the Chau Giang ferry terminal and proceed about 25 meters before taking a left and going another 50 meters.
This attractive mosque features a large dome and arches and is where Chau Doc's Cham Islamic population comes to worship.

Sam Mountain (Nui Sam)   ★

3 km southwest of town.
This is perhaps why the Chau Doc area attracts so many tourists. On Sam Mountain there are pagodas and temples that number in the dozens. The mountain was designated as the "Famed Beauty Spot" in 1980 by the Vietnamese Ministry of Culture. Many of the pagodas are set in deep caverns and caves within the mountain. The mountain itself is not a particularly impressive sight from a distance, but its religious and historical significance—as well as the labyrinth of caves makes a visit here well worth the trip. Most of the tourists here flock to the Tay An Pagoda, which is at the base of the mountain, the tomb of Thoai Ngoc Hau, Lady Chua Xu Temple, and the Cavern Pagoda. But that's no reason not to ascend to the top of the mountain, where vistas of the countryside give testimony to the area's agricultural bounty.

Tay An Pagoda   ★

Base of Sam Mountain.
Here there are hundreds of wooden carvings of religious figures. There are both Islamic and Hindu elements in the architecture of the pagoda, which was built in the mid 1800s. It was rebuilt in 1958. Tombs of various monks surround the temple, and close to the temple is the statue of Quan Am Thi Kinh (the Guardian Spirit of Mother and Child). Carvings of dragons and lions can be seen above the bilevel roof of Tay An Pagoda as they fight for possession of lotus blossoms, pearls and apricot trees. There are statues in front of the pagoda of a black elephant with two tusks, a white elephant with six tusks.

The Tomb of Thoai Ngoc Hau

Sam Mountain.
Thoai was once a powerful Nguyen lord who served the Nguyen Dynasty. He ordered that his own tomb be built at the base of Sam Mountain and it isn't far from Tay An Pagoda. The steps leading to the platform where the tomb is (and those of

his two wives) are made of red stone imported from the eastern and southern portions of Vietnam. There are other less impressive tombs in the area of some of the men who served under Thoai Ngoc Hau.

Temple of Lady Chua Xu

Sam Mountain.
This inauspicious temple faces Sam Mountain and is also not far from both the tomb of Thoai Ngoc Hau and Tay An Pagoda. It was built in the early 19th century from bamboo and shrubbery but was later reconstructed in the 1970s. Legend has it that the statue of Lady Chua Xu, which now stands at the base of Sam Mountain, was originally at the peak of the hill, but was brought on its way back to Thailand by Siamese warriors in the early part of the 19th century. But they never made it. It was so burdensome, they dumped it by the side of some path. Local villagers then brought the statue back to their town to build a temple for the statue. A young woman in the village, who pronounced herself Lady Chua Xu, instructed 40 virgins to bring the statue down to the base of the hill. After they reached the plain, the statue became too heavy for the women as well, and it was believed by the locals that because the women had stopped carrying the statue out of pure exhaustion, that this was the site where Lady Chua Xu had chosen for a temple to be constructed around it. And that's where it remains today. There's an important festival surrounding the temple from the 23rd to the 26th of each lunar month.

Cavern Pagoda ★

Sam Mountain.
The upper section of this pagoda, which lies about a third to halfway up the western slope of Sam Mountain, is composed of two areas: the main sanctuary, where there are statues of Thich Ca Buddha and A Di Da (Buddha of the past). In the back of the cave is a shrine dedicated to the Goddess of Mercy (Quan The Am Bo Tat). The lower area of the pagoda houses the pagoda's monks and also contains two tombs where Thich Hue Thien and a lady named Le Thi Tho are buried.

Where to Stay in Chau Doc

AUTHOR'S NOTE: TELEPHONE PREFIXES

The following telephone numbers are local exchanges. The country code is 84. The city code is 76.

Hang Chau Hotel   US$20–$30   ★

On the river on Le Loi Street near the ferry terminal. *866196.*
This is the best and most expensive hotel in Chau Doc. There's a swimming pool, restaurant and a busy nightclub. All the rooms come with air conditioning. The more expensive rooms have a great view of the river.

Thai Binh Hotel

37 Nguyen Van Thoai Street. *866221.*
15 rooms.

Foreigners have not been allowed to stay here, but this may change by the time you read this.

Hotel 777   US$6

47 Doc Phu Thu Street. ☎ *866409.*

A small hotel popular with backpackers. Very inexpensive.

My Loc Hotel   US$10–$15

51 Nguyen Van Thoai Street. ☎ *866455.*
20 rooms.

Double rooms with ceiling fans. Some of the rooms have air conditioning. The more expensive rooms sleep up to four guests. Popular with backpackers.

Chau Doc Hotel   About US$8–$10

17 Doc Phu Thu Street. ☎ *866484.*
42 rooms.

Relatively dismal but with enough life-support systems for backpackers, who seem to fill the place.

Nha Khach 44 (Guesthouse)   US$6–$10

44 Doc Phu Thu Street. ☎ *866540.*

Another popular backpackers' stop. There are doubles and triples here.

Where to Eat in Chau Doc

The best place undoubtedly is the restaurant at the **Hang Chau Hotel**. There's live entertainment offered here. There's also the **Tourist Restaurant** at the corner of Doc Phu Thu and Phan Ding Phung Streets. Also try **Lam Hung Ky** (*71 Chi Lang Street*).

The cheapest places to eat are at the food stalls that are in and surrounding the Chau Doc market. The river-caught fish is particularly tasty.

Directory

Transportation

Chau Doc is about 245 km from HCMC, 118 km from Can Tho, 180 from My Tho, and 96 from Ha Tien. The Chau Doc bus station is on the southeast side of the city on the south side of Le Loi Street, about 1.5 km out of town. **Buses** to Saigon take about 7 hours and arrive at HCMC's Mien Tay bus station. There is supposedly an express bus that leaves for HCMC from in front of Chau Doc Hotel. Buses to Long Xuyen take about 2 hours. There are also connections to other destinations in the delta area, but remember, there is no direct road from Chau Doc to Ha Tien. You'll have to go east nearly to Can Tho (Thot Not) before Highway 1A heads south to Rach Gia. **Ferries** to Saigon often take over 24 hours and leave daily from the wharf at Ton Duc Thang Street (about US$1.20). Ferries, I am told, also ply their way down a series of canals to Ha Tien. Buses to Chau Doc leave from HCMC's Mien Tay station. The principal form of transport around Chau Doc is by **motorized cyclo**.

Post Office

On the corner of Bao Ho Thoai Street opposite Chau Phu Pagoda. ☎ *894550.*

Rach Gia

Rach Gia

RACH GIA IN CAPSULE

Unattractive coastal city on the Gulf of Thailand...But the seafood is great...Considered to be the most prosperous province in Vietnam...One of the two gateways to Phu Quoc Island...Large numbers of ethnic Khmer and Chinese live here.

Rach Gia, the capital of Kien Giang Province with a population approaching 125,000 people, is a major port city on the Gulf of Thailand at the very bottom of Highway 1A. The flies here outnumber the residents by about five to one. Yet despite its appearance, it's considered to be the center of Vietnam's most prosperous province. Many of the hotels allow prostitutes into guests' rooms, and it is very likely one, or perhaps more, will knock on your door after you've checked into your hotel. Both the hotels and the hookers are the cheapest in all of Vietnam. You'll frequently see men about town with large red circles on their backs and chests. This usually means they've recently been in the company of a massage girl, who performed a flaming alcohol massage by placing the bases of hot glasses on their skin in addition to employing more traditional sexual duties.

The population contains a large number of ethnic Chinese and Khmers. This is one of the oldest population centers in the Mekong Delta, so a number of pagodas and temples in the area are relatively old (if you consider the 18th and 19th centuries old). The city center itself lies on an island between two branches of the Cai Lan River. This is where you'll find most of the hotels, restaurants and shops. Rach Gia is also one of two ports with ferries bound for Phu Quoc Island (Ha Tien being the other).

Rach Gia is a delta boom town—with many goods entering Vietnam here from Thailand and other points in Southeast Asia (many of them smuggled)—and is expected to become even more prosperous in the future as the Vietnamese government continues to open its economy.

Rach Gia

INSIDER TIP

The ferry from Rach Gia to Phu Quoc Island (about a 9-hour ride), is supposed to leave at about 9 a.m. and around 10 p.m., but usually leaves when it is filled with passengers. The round trip costs approximately US$8 (about 80,000 dong) and you can bring a bicycle or motorcycle aboard the ferry for an added surcharge (for a motorcycle, 80,000 dong roundtrip). Warning: If you are traveling in this part of the Mekong Delta by motorcycle and want to bring the machine with you out to Phu Quoc Island, only depart from Rach Gia, and not from Ha Tien (which is much closer to the island with lower fares to match). The boat trip to the island from Ha Tien is aboard a much smaller craft, and even the locals consider the ride a dangerous one. Do not bring a motorcycle from Ha Tien to Phu Quoc by ferry. If you plan on bringing your bike to Phu Quoc, you won't be able to go with it. It will leave on the night ferry. You yourself will then be required to leave by the ferry the next morning. The gamble's yours.

Despite being directly on the Gulf of Thailand coast, there are no beaches in Rach Gia. There's a dirt road (Tran Hung Dao Street) that leads from the harbor to a small waterside "park" called Hoa Bien Park, which is nothing more than a big dirt patch where you can rent a chair, watch the sea, drink beer (there are a couple of food stalls here) and swat away at the flies.

What to See and Do in Rach Gia and Environs

Phat Lon Pagoda

Just off Quang Trung Street.

The name means Big Buddha. It's a big Khmer Hinayana Buddhist temple that features figures of the historical Buddha Sakyamuni. Eight small altars are scattered around the exterior of the pagoda. You'll see two curious-looking towers that are used to cremate dead monks. Tombs of other monks surround the temple. The pagoda was constructed 200 years ago. Although the monks that live here at the pagoda are ethnic Khmer, you'll also see ethnic Chinese worshipers. Prayers are held in the wee hours of the morning and in the early evening.

Nguyen Trung Truc Temple

18 Nguyen Cong Tru Street.

Nguyen Trung Truc was the fellow who led the Vietnamese resistance forces against the French colonists in the mid 1800s. He was responsible, at least for the most part, in the destruction of the French warship Espérance, after which he fled to Phu Quoc Island and eluded French capture for a number of years. This infuriated the French so much that they kidnapped his family and took hostage a number of other civilians in 1868. Nguyen gave himself up to the French authorities and then was executed in the Rach Gia marketplace in October of the same year. Although the first temple bearing his name was primitive in structure, it has been rebuilt a number of times over the years. On the altar in the main hall is a portrait of Nguyen.

Pho Minh Pagoda

At the corner of Nguyen Van Cu and Co Bac Streets.

There's a Thai-style Sakyamuni Buddha here that was a gift to the Pagoda by Thai Buddhists in 1971. The small pagoda itself was built in 1967. Close by is the Thich Ca Buddha in the Vietnamese style. There are nuns here that live behind the pagoda. Prayers are held at the practical hour of 3:30 in the morning and also at 6:30 in the evening.

Ong Bac De Pagoda

14 Nguyen Du Street.

This pagoda has on its main altar a statue of Ong Bac De, a reincarnation of the Emperor of Jade. To the left of the statue is Ong Bon (the Guardian Spirit of Happiness and Vitue), and to the right is the likeness of Quan Cong. The pagoda was built about a hundred years ago by Chinese living in Rach Gia.

Tam Bao Pagoda

The corner of Thich Thien An and Tran Phu streets.

Although rebuilt in the early 20th century, the pagoda was originally constructed in the early 1800s. The garden of sculpted trees and bushes depicting dragons and other creatures is quite beautiful. The pagoda is open from 6 a.m. to 8 p.m.

Rach Gia Museum

21 Nguyen Van Troi Street.

Not a lot here.

Rach Gia Catholic Church

Vinh Thanh Van subdistrict, across the channel from the Vinh Than Van Market.

This is an unimpressive Catholic church built of red bricks in 1918. It's worth a visit if you're Catholic and don't want to miss Mass, which is conducted at 5 a.m. and 5 p.m. on weekdays. Sunday mass is at 5 a.m., 7 a.m., 4 p.m. and 5 p.m.

Vinh Thanh Van Market

Sprawled along at Bach Dang, Thu Khoa Nghia and Trinh Hoai streets.

There's an imported-products market close by between Pham Hong Thai and Hoang Hoa Tham Streets.

Oc Eo

10 km from Rach Gia toward Vong.

Oc Eo is an ancient city near Vong. The village, about 10 km from Rach Gia, was in its prime during the 1st through 6th centuries and was a major commerce center when the area was ruled by the Funan empire. Many archeological discoveries have been made here with relics found representing ancient Malay, Thai, Indonesian and even Roman Empire societies. Many of these artifacts can be seen in HCMC's History and Art Museum and the History Museum in Hanoi. There used to be travel restrictions to Oc Eo but, at the time of this writing, they have been lifted.

Soc Xoai

16 km from Rach Gia toward Ha Tien.

There is absolutely nothing to do in this small village about 16 km west of Rach Gia on the dilapidated, rutted and chokingly musty highway 9 to Ha Tien (about 90 km to the west) except make a pit stop at the Phuong Mai Cafe on the right side of the highway about halfway through town.

Where to Stay in Rach Gia

> **AUTHOR'S NOTE:**
> **TELEPHONE PREFIXES**
>
> *The following telephone numbers are local exchanges. The country code is 84. The city code is 77.*

Palace Hotel   US$9

41 Tran Phu Street. ☎ 863049.

Not only perhaps the best hotel in Rach Gia, but certainly the best bargain. Clean comfortable rooms and good restaurant. The staff is exceptionally friendly and goes out of its way to make you feel at home. Better yet, they'll even purchase your ferry tickets to Phu Quoc Island—and not mark them up.

Nha Tro Dormitory   US$3

No address nor phone, but it's located right at the wharf on the gulf where the ferries leave for Phu Quoc Island.

This may be the best deal in town at US$3 for a double room with fan. Popular with Westerners, I was told, although the only foreigner I saw was Clint Eastwood on a nearby video screen. Fan; no hot water. Public toilet and shower; the water seemed a little dirty and was another reason it's best to visit this part of the world with a crew cut. But if you're going to take the ferry, this is a good place to be, because there really isn't a schedule out to the island. Some ferries leave at 9 at night, others early in the morning. Stay at this hotel and you'll know at a moment's notice. And you can't beat the price. I stayed in only one hotel in the Mekong Delta that was cheaper. Also here is the Caphe Hung (it closes early) for libation and the Xuan Hai Restaurant next door.

Nha Khach 77.77   US$4–$10

77.77 Tran Phu Street. ☎ 863375.

Not much here. Dumpy rooms with public water closets. Inexpensive.

1-5 Hotel (Khach San 1-5)   US$5–$20

38 Nguyen Hung Son Street. ☎ 862103.

The biggest problem in what seems to be a nicely decorated hotel is that I couldn't find anyone who could speak English. Rooms have air conditioning, telephone. There's a large parking area if you've come by car. Restaurant with European and Asian dishes. The manager was able to somehow explain that both the receptionists and waitresses were "young." Whether this was for my benefit or yours, I couldn't tell. The business card says the waitresses are "warn careful." Okay. Sounds like a government SIDA (AIDS) brochure. Souvenir shop, tourist cars, barber and beauty shop. Massage available.

Rach Gia

Hoa Binh Hotel   **US$3.50**

5A Minh Mang Street. ☎ *863115.*

Another cheapie popular with the backpacker set. There are double rooms with a private bath and single rooms with no air conditioning or hot water. Bargain basement.

To Chau Hotel   **US$15–25**

4F Le Loi Street. ☎ *863718, 863746; FAX: 84-77-862111.*
29 rooms

The best thing about this place are the suites for US$25, a real bargain. The rooms are clean, pleasantly furnished and air-conditioned. Beware, though, these folks will not accept a photocopy of your passport when checking in.

Where to Eat in Rach Gia

Thien Nga   **$**

4A Le Loi Street.
Vietnamese, Asian, and some hybrid European food. Cheap.

Rach Gia Restaurant   **$**

Intersection of Ly Tu Trong and Tran Hung Dao Streets on the water.
Delicious seafood.

Hai Van Restaurant   **$**

Khu 16 ha. ☎ *86305.*
On the rutted dirt road leading to Hoa Bien Park near the harbor. Shrimp, lobster, squid, frog, chicken and fish. Overlooks the water

Palace Hotel & Restaurant   **$**

41 Tran Phu Street. ☎ *863049, 866146.*
The restaurant attached to this recommended hotel is also recommended for superb seafood at cheap-moderate prices.

Vinh Hong I   **$**   ★

So 39b Tran Hung Dao Street. ☎ *866183.*
This is a Fielding choice in Rach Gia for the seafood feast and pleasant and quick service.

In addition, there are numerous food stalls all across the city.

Directory

Transportation

Rach Gia is about 250 km from Saigon, 115 km from Can Tho, 180 km from My Tho and 90 km fro Ha Tien. The bus station is on Trung Truc Street south of town. Buses leave regularly for Saigon's Mien Tay station when full. The trip takes about 8 hours. Express buses leave for HCMC from *33/40 Thang 4 Street.* There are also buses to Can Tho, Long Xuyen, Ha Tien. Buses to other local areas including Soc Xoai, Tan Hiep, Vinh Thuan, Tri Ton, Duong Xuong, Hong Chong, Go Quao and Giong Rieng usually leave the station very early in the morning, between 4 and 5 a.m. Buses leave Saigon's Mien Tay station for Rach Gia regularly. By **air**, VN will get you to Rach Gia via Phu Quoc Island on Tuesdays, Thursdays, Saturdays and Sundays at 11:20 a.m. The connecting flight leaves Phu Quoc for Rach Gia at 1:30 p.m. The total journey time is 2.5 hours.

Flights to HCMC from Rach Gia also connect through Phu Quoc Island, and leave Rach Gia at 2:30 p.m. the same four days. From Phu Quoc, the connecting flight leaves at 3:40 p.m. Check with Vietnam Airlines for any schedule changes, which occur frequently. Cyclos are the best way to get around town.

Post Office

The general Post office is on Tu Duc Street, near the corner of 207 and Duy Tan Streets.

Tourist Office

Kien Giang Tourism is at *12 Ly Tu Trong Street.*

Banks and Moneychangers

Vietcom Bank is next to the post office at *2 Duy Tan Street.*

Phu Quoc Island

This is a verdant mountainous island with a population of 50,000 about 45 km in the Gulf of Thailand west of Ha Tien, although it is better reached by ferry from Rach Gia. Its exquisite beaches are becoming more popular by the year, but you'll still be only one of a handful of tourists that are here at any given time. The island is about 50 km long with an area of 576 sq. km. It provides fantastic fishing for the locals and the water is clear and calm. It's great for swimming and snorkeling and features some of the finest coconut tree-lined beaches in Vietnam, especially in the southern portion of the island. The island lies only about 15 km off the Cambodian coast and, although there's a lot of nasty, verbose talk about sovereignty of the island, it seems that it will remain in Vietnamese control for some time.

Phu Quoc is generally devoid of tourists, but its overall pristine environment and fabulous beaches are luring some takers. There's talk of a Club Med going up on the island, and a Sinaporean consortium is planning a resort here.

In addition to the superb beaches found throughout the island, the market at **Duong Dong** is worth seeing for the variety of fresh seafood being offered—and is also the place to change money if need be. There are a number of small shops in Duong Dong, as well, namely for mingling with and enjoying the locals.

Author's Note

On Phu Quoc, there are about as many people who speak English as there are glaciers and Chechen rebels combined, so be prepared to do a lot of pointing.

Where to Stay on Phu Quoc

Huong Bien Hotel   **US$10–$15**

Duong Dong Town. ☎ *84-77-846113, 846050, 846082.*

Slightly seedy but it's directly on the beach. There are only four rooms here, but it's probably still not necessary to make a reservation in advance. If you're lonely, you may find some equally lonely women. The grounds around the place appear to be in the process of being cleared. Word is they might throw up some bungalows on the beach.

"Guesthouse"   **US$10**

Duong Dong Town

This is a tiny place with three rooms on the first floor—only one comes with a private toilet/shower. But the place is quite clean, and the staff very pleasant. There's also an excellent, equally small restaurant.

Where to Eat on Phu Quoc

The **"Guesthouse"** has an excellent small restaurant serving the local catch. The food is superb and runs between US$2–$3. Don't expect anyone to speak any English. Just point and enjoy. There's another backwater eatery between the river delta and the beach. It's grungy looking and you'll have your doubts, but give it a shot. The seafood is excellent here, as well.

THE INDUSTRIALIZATION OF PHU QUOC

Phu Quoc has an area of 576 square km and is roughly the size of Singapore. There are more than 100 km of beach and thousands of square km of fishing areas. 500,000 tons of sea products are pulled from the Gulf of Thailand each year. The island's fish sauce is very popular in Vietnam. There are 80 such fish sauce processing plants on the island that have a capacity of producing 5 million liters of the sauce each year. Pepper is also grown here, but production is down in recent years. However, cashew nut growing areas are increasing rapidly. But to Phu Quoc's credit, the island is investing billions of dong into reforesting 300 hectares that have been denuded within the 370-square-km area of forests. There is also a boom in industrial products and handicrafts on Phu Quoc. The island now makes some 100 billion dong a year from food processing, building materials and forest products. The Vietnamese government has now permitted Phu Quoc (Kien Giang province) to directly work with foreign companies to build roads, a sea harbor, an export-processing zone, and to install electrical and water supply systems. A total investment of more than US$500 million is planned for such projects. This island is going to change very quickly.

Directory

Transportation

There are a few ways of getting there, flying in from HCMC being the easiest and the most expensive (about US$140 round trip). Or you can take a **ferry** from either Rach Gia (about 8–10 hours) or from Ha Tien (about 4 hours, but sometimes as many as 6). The trip from Rach Gia leaves daily at 10 a.m. and costs 44,000 dong one way per person, and another 60,000 if you bring a **motorcycle**. There is an additional VND50,000 unloading charge once you reach the island town of An Thoi. Make sure you bring plenty to eat and drink, as the onboard concessions seem to consistently be out of sustenance after about three hours into the trip.

One of the obstacles with the ferry arrival at An Thoi is that the island's main town of Duong Dong—and the only accommodations on the island—are 20 km away. The ferry gets in between 6 and 7 p.m., in near darkness. If you've got your own motorcycle, make a left after traveling 7 km to Duong Dong. Make a note of the mileage as the turnoff isn't marked.

The return trip from An Thoi to Rach Gia departs at 10 a.m., so you should check out of your Duong Dong hotel before nine. Curiously, the return to Rach Gia comes with a different price tag: VND35,000 one way for both you and your motorcycle. There's a VND30,000 charge for loading the motorbike.

Do not attempt to take the ferry from Ha Tien to Phu Quoc with a motorcycle. The police in Ha Tien, as well as some of the locals, say the trip on the small ferry is dangerous enough in itself. The ferries leaving Rach Gia are considerably larger. Also, do not plan on a day trip to the island from Ha Tien. Theoretically, you might board a 9 a.m. ferry (that supposedly only takes 4 hours) and return on the afternoon ferry. But don't try it. You'll have to spend at least one night on the island, and in relatively expensive accommodations.

By **air**, VN will get you to Phu Quoc Island on Tuesdays, Thursdays, Saturdays and Sundays at 11:20 a.m. There is a connecting flight to Rach Gia at 1:30 p.m. From Phu Quoc, flights leave for HCMC at 3:40 p.m. on the same days. Check with Vietnam Airlines for any schedule changes, which occur frequently. The flight's about 50 minutes.

Emergencies/Communications

There's a post office in town and a "hospital" just opposite it. The "tourist office" is located at the Huong Bien Hotel.

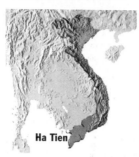

Ha Tien

Ha Tien

HA TIEN IN A CAPSULE

The southwesternmost town in Vietnam...Sits on the Cambodian border...The road leading to the city is in dismal shape, but it's being repaved rapidly...Used as a springboard to Phu Quoc Island...The sight of mass killings by Cambodia's Khmer Rouge in the late 1970s...Has perhaps the most intriguing history of any area in Vietnam...Was once the best link for sea traffic crossing the South China Sea for India.

Situated in the far southwestern corner of Vietnam on the Cambodian border, Ha Tien, with a population of about 90,000–100,000, is a seaside anomaly, a mishmash of Khmer, Chinese and Vietnamese (many from the north and other sections of the Mekong Delta) working to construct something reminiscent of roads along the dilapidated dirt paths that connect Ha Tien with the rest of the Mekong Delta.

Although most of the few tourists who venture to this remote corner of Vietnam use Ha Tien as a springboard to nearby Phu Quoc Island, the city of Ha Tien has perhaps the most interesting history of all the regions of southern Vietnam. In 1671, a young Cantonese named Mac Cuu left China's Fukien Province at the age of 17 for the capital of Cambodia, Oudong. There, he impressed the Cambodian monarch King Chey Chettha IV so much that he was indoctrinated into royal service. He was an aggressive individual capable of attracting vast commerce and exploiting the far away, completely undeveloped reaches of Cambodia. Most of his efforts were in the far southeastern edge of Cambodia in the Ha Tien area, the southern coast of the Cambodian state. Through his vast successes in developing agriculture in the region, the King granted him governorship (Oc Nha) of the region.

Soon, the area that is currently known as Ha Tien became a huge commercial success. Chinese settlers were offered free land. Agriculture flourished in the region, as did the trade in fishing and the distribution of agricultural tools.

Soon, Mac Cuu's "kingdom" without defined borders took on a more formal statelike structure. It became an essentially autonomous state maintaining a precarious existence between neighboring Cambodia, Thailand and Vietnam.

Because of Ha Tien's location as Cambodia's only important port of entry (and the best harbor on Indochina's western peninsula), it attracted the Siamese, who invaded the area in 1708 and essentially ruined the area's prosperity. (Ha Tien had become the strongest link for sea traffic traversing the South China Sea from India.)

Mac Cuu understood that the only way to maintain his "kingdom" was to enlist the aid of more powerful neighbors. So, in 1708, he sent a delegation to the then Vietnamese capital of Hue for a visit with Minh Vuong, southern Vietnam's leader at the time and one of the Nguyen Dynasty's most effective and dynamic Lords, chiefly responsible for expanding Vietnam's empire in the south. Minh liked the idea of essentially annexing territory from the Siamese and Cambodians at virtually no expense without concessions.

When the Siamese invaded the Ha Tien area a short time later, Vietnamese forces quickly drove the aggressors away. Ha Tien was then transformed from a colony of refugees to a full-fledged state, and it regained its prosperity, this time as a southern Vietnamese political state on the southern coast. It remarkably retained a separate identity, even as a province of the Nguyen empire.

Mac Cuu died at 80 in 1735 and is today considered the father of the southern peninsula. His grave, along with those of his family, is located outside the city center and is ornately looked after by the descendents of his family.

Prince Mac Tu Kham, the seventh generation of the family of Mac Cuu, was the last Vietnamese ruler of province—until 1857, when the French decided to annex Ha Tien with the rest of the Mekong Delta. Under French control, pepper plantations were established, but little was done to improve the lives of the region's people.

Much of the recent history of Ha Tien surrounds Khmer Rouge military raids of the city during the savage Cambodian leader Pol Pot's reign of terror, where hundreds of Vietnamese men, women and children were slaughtered by unspeakable means by Khmer Rouge guerrillas. The graves of the Vietnamese victims are scattered at different sites across the town and, by chance, I came across a remote site near the memorial tomb of Mac Cuu, where a sweat-soaked lone man surrounded by a score of children was digging into the claylike earth beside a dirt path. At first I thought he might be digging a latrine or well. I stopped and found out that he was exhuming the remains of his mother and three sisters who had been buried at the site in a single plastic bag 15 years earlier. It is customary for the inhabitants of Ha Tien who had relatives murdered by the Cambodians to exhume the remains of their relatives and have the remains burned and then sealed in a large lacquer pot. I watched in near horror as the man dug and picked his way through four feet of earth, finally reaching a tattered black plastic bag, which he then unceremoniously pulled from the ground as if he were simply removing the roots of a tree. Opening the bag, he sifted through the bones and the still-intact clothing his relatives had been wearing the day they were executed. The children, he told me, had been ripped apart alive limb by limb by the guerrillas' own hands. On a decayed, crumbling finger of his mother, he pulled off a gold ring, stained brown by the years of its clay earthen environment. The bones of the corpses had become part of the soil and he meticulously separated bone from the earth. The clothes of the woman and the children were then placed back into the grave and set on fire.

Author helps Ha Tien local exhume the remains of his family, slaughtered by the Khmer Rouge.

Ha Tien's topographical setting in the Mekong Delta is unlike the rest of the region, and might remind you to a degree of northern Vietnam's Ha Long Bay, with its huge rock formations and caves towering above the seascape.

You'll be disappointed to discover that Ha Tien is one of the more expensive areas to stay and eat in the Mekong Delta. Even Vietnamese nationals are overcharged in many places, and it isn't unusual to pay US$2.50 or so for a meal, about three or four times the rate you'll pay in most places in the delta. Hotels tend to be expensive because fresh water has to be hand-carried to each establishment from the city's water tower. Throughout the city, one sees sun-withered men stoically hauling giant drums of fresh water stacked on dilapidated carts. Even in the few hotels that are marginally habitable, the water is often brown and silty, water that you'll eventually be required to bathe in if you decide to spend a few days here. Although it's expensive, I recommend bathing and brushing your teeth with bottled water only.

What to See and Do in Ha Tien and Environs

Thach Dong ★

3.5 km from town on the Cambodian border.

This is a massive, cavernous subterranean temple just a stone's throw from the Cambodian border, where you can watch farmers and other merchants pedal their wares through the border gate from a few locations high in the cave. It's an odd sight, because just on the Vietnamese side of the frontier, formations of Vietnamese police officers can be seen lined up in the style of 18th-century British combat techniques, training in the use of mortars, automatic rifles and small arms—all the weapons pointed toward Cambodia and the flat Khmer countryside (although, admittedly, I didn't see any rounds fired).

It was at Thach Dong where the Khmer Rouge massacred at least 130 people (some of the locals say the number was higher, 162 exactly). Chambers in the grotto feature altars to the Emperor of Jade (Ngoc Hoang) and the Goddess of Mercy (Quan The Am Bo Tat). Some of the more adventurous types might be tempted to make an ascent to the summit of the cave/mountain, but the only route is up a slippery, vertical tunnel which serves as the home to hundreds of bats and, consequently, their droppings. Don't try it.

Dong Ho

Ben Tran Hau St.

Granite hills surround this lagoon formed by the Gulf of Thailand. It's just east of Ha Tien. The other side of the lagoon is flanked by the To Chau hills.

Ha Tien Market

Just southwest of floating bridge.

Located in the center of town to the left after you cross the floating bridge. It's a bustling place that's worth noting mainly for the smuggled goods you can purchase from Thailand and Cambodia. And it may be the only market south of HCMC where some of the goods (probably smuggled) can probably be bought cheaper than in Saigon.

Tam Bao Pagoda

328 Phuong Thanh Street.

Mac Cuu founded this temple in 1730. A statue of the Goddess of Mercy (Quan The Am Bo Tat) can be found in front of the pagoda standing in the middle of a pond surrounded by lotus blossoms. The area surrounding the temple contains the tombs of 16 monks. The bronze statue of the Buddha of the Past (A Di Da Buddha) is inside the temple. Prayers are held in the morning and the afternoon.

Phu Dung Pagoda

Off Phuong Thanh Street.

Founded just a short time after Tam Bao Pagoda by Mac Cuu's second wife, this temple features a statue of nine intricately carved dragons surrounding the newly born Siddhartha Gautama (Thich Ca Buddha). The bronze statue of the pagoda came from China and is encased in glass. Beside the pagoda the tombs of Nguyen Thi Xuan and other monks are carved into the hillside. (Supposedly Mac Cuu was killed in battle in Thailand and is buried there, although some locals who claim to be of the eighth generation of the family say that his tomb is not in Thailand but on the hillside, as well. The history books indicate there are no longer any living descendents of Mac Cuu.) From the hillside you can look across the bay at the mountain the locals call the "Sleeping Elephant."

Behind the temple is a smaller structure, Dien Ngoc Hoang based on the Taoist Emperor of Jade. Figures beside the emperor include Nam Tao on the right (Taoist God of Happiness and of the Southern Polar Star) and Bac Dao (God of the Northern Polar Star and Longevity) on the left. It is in this area where other unmarked graves contain the victims of Khmer Rouge massacres in the area.

The Beaches of Ha Tien

3 km west of town.

Don't expect the crystal clear waters of Ca Na, Nha Trang or those found farther down the Gulf of Thailand coast, but the water here is calm and extremely warm—hardly refreshing. **Bai No Beach**, one of the best, is about three km west of Ha Tien. It's clean, has some snorkeling opportunities and it usually isn't as crowded as **Mui Nai Beach**, which is about 3 km west of town. Mui Nai is usually where the tour microbuses stop for the afternoon after reaching Ha Tien from Saigon. The beach is small and the sand dark. Women are frequently seen here trying to peddle their recent crab catches. There are two restaurants here, the **Sea Star** and the **Sao Bien** (which also means Sea Star), which are in fact one and the same, but in two different structures. I was disappointed with this beach.

Hon Giang Island   ★

This is a small, beautiful island about 15 km off Ha Tien's coast. The island offers a great beach but absolutely no tourist facilities. It is reachable by boat from Ha Tien and makes for a great day trip. But provision yourself accordingly.

Mo So Grotto

17 km east of Ha Tien, 3 km off the road to Rach Gia.

This grotto and tunnel network makes for a good diversion from the road trip between Rach Gia and Ha Tien. The caves are accessible by foot during the dry months, but can only be reached by small boat during the rainy season. It would be best to utilize one of the locals as a guide here.

Hang Tien Grotto

25 km from Ha Tien off the road to Rach Gia.

This is another interesting grotto but only accessible by boat. This is where the Tay Son rebels chased future Emporer Gia Long into hiding in 1784.

Ha Tien

Phu Quoc Island ★★★

45 km west of Ha Tien.

This is a verdant mountainous island with a population of some 50,000 about 45 km in the Gulf of Thailand west of Ha Tien. Phu Quoc is reachable by ferry from Ha Tien, but it makes better sense to do it from Rach Gia, although the trip from Rach Gia takes twice the time. The boat ride from Ha Tien is scary at best and not for the timid. For a complete description of Phu Quoc, see the "Phu Quoc Island" subchapter in the Rach Gia chapter.

Where to Stay in Ha Tien

INSIDER TIP

Although Ha Tien has accommodations that are ridiculously inexpensive, most of the hotels (and the food they serve if they have a restaurant) come with price tags that are the highest in the Mekong Delta. The primary reason is the water, which through the city's water lines is more akin to used radiator antifreeze than anything potable. Fresh water has to be hand carted to the hotels, restaurants, homes, etc., from a storage tank on the edge of town. Most of the water you will find for bathing in Ha Tien hostelries is the color of Jamaican Rum. The point is to be careful in Ha Tien. This is not a clean city, and many Vietnamese were surprised that I didn't contract viruses related to the water. Be careful of both what you eat and drink. A good guide is your best source of where to eat and drink in Ha Tien. The following is a list of hotels and eateries I personally experienced, although it is no guarantee that you won't become sick in any of them.

AUTHOR'S NOTE: TELEPHONE PREFIXES

The following telephone numbers are local exchanges. The country code is 84. The city code is 77.

To Chau Hotel   US$5–$6

299 Ben Tran Hau. ☎ *852148.*
7 rooms.

There are singles and a couple of classes of doubles here. Fans and public water closet. Dirty, but acceptable for Ha Tien, where prices are traditionally higher than in all other areas of the delta.

Dong Ho Hotel   US$4–$6

Ben Tran Hau Street. ☎ *852141.*
19 rooms.

Run of the mill but cheap with a pleasant staff. Fan, public water closet.

Phuoc Thanh Guesthouse   US$.50–$2

This place costs only 5000 dong for Vietnamese for a room and 1500 dong for a dormitory setting. Conditions are dismal here, and the water is as black as Ha Long coal.

Public toilet and "shower" that guests also frequently use to urinate in. Don't brush your teeth here or wash yourself unless it's with bottled water. In fact, I'd avoid the place altogether, despite the fact that you can get a room for as little as US$.50.

Binh Minh Guesthouse   US$5

Duong Du Street. ☎ *852035.*
8 rooms.
Standard guest-house fare but better than the Phuoc Thanh, and more expensive. Public toilet, no hot water, no air conditioning. Accepts foreigners but staff English is limited.

Khach San Du Lich   US$10

Cong Ty pu Lich, Kien Giang. ☎ *852169.*
18 rooms.
Ceiling fan, no hot water, but has private Western-style toilets; cafe. Moderate, and probably worth the added cash because they spend more money purifying their water.

Where to Eat in Ha Tien

There are a number of places to eat in Ha Tien, and you'll find that they're relatively more expensive than elsewhere in the Mekong Delta. After crossing the floating bridge, immediately to your left and right will be a number of semi-outdoor cafes and restaurants. If possible eat at sidewalk stalls, as they tend to be about half as expensive as anything indoors, with or without air conditioning. It is not uncommon to spend US$2.50 a meal at an indoor restaurant, and about half that for food just as palatable as that served in the indoor eateries. Be careful what you ask for at an outdoor stall. They'll promise to serve it, but may have to run across the street to have the meal prepared at another restaurant. You'll end up paying more. Eat only what you know the stall or cafe can prepare itself.

Ha Tien reputedly grows coconuts not found elsewhere in the country. Many places serve the exotic coconut milk. If you must eat indoors, perhaps the only place I can recommend is **Xuan Thanh Restaurant** across from the market on Ben Tran Hau street. The food seemed to be prepared in soiled surroundings, but I found it quite good, although Johnny Tu, my guide, was appalled at both the prices and the food, and swore never to return. I guess that means I won't be going back either.

Directory

Transportation

Ha Tien is about 92 km from Rach Gia, 96 from Chau Doc, 205 km from Can Tho, and 340 from Saigon. The bus station at Ha Tien is on the southeast side of town, just across the floating bridge on the right hand side of the road. The trip to Saigon takes about 10 hours over some amazingly dismal but rapidly improving roadways. **Buses** arrive at HCMC's Mien Tay Station. They usually leave for Saigon in the wee hours of the morning, so don't plan on sleeping. Buses for Rach Gia leave at least four times daily, the trip taking about 4–5 hours or more depending on the roadwork being done. By fast motorcycle, the trip is much quicker, by at least an hour, than by car. But again, the roads in the southern Mekong Delta area are in such disrepair it is unlikely Lewis and Clark would have ventured across them. Currently there is no air service between HCMC and Ha

Ha Tien

Tien, although you can fly to the island of Phu Quoc from HCMC. Travel into Cambodia, which is terribly tempting, is not permitted. Border police at Ha Tien, although mostly friendly, will turn nasty if you ask too many questions. They say that Khmer Rouge units still operate regularly on the Cambodian side of the border. You can try to get authorization at Ha Tien's immigration police office, but they'll turn you down as well.

Hon Chong

Hon Chong lies at the tip of a round peninsula that juts out into the Gulf of Thailand about 35 km southeast of Ha Tien. This area features the finest beaches in the Mekong Delta, which isn't saying a lot. But nonetheless, the area is untouristed, remote and makes for a decent getaway off the ant trail. The only problem, and it's a big one, is the cement factory they've built down here, a huge backside boil on what were once pristine surroundings that had the potential of being lightly developed for tourism. The cement guys decided definitely not to consult with the tourism guys when they built this dust pit less than a kilometer from Duong Beach.

Duong Beach certainly isn't the prettiest in Vietnam, but its calm waters invite swimming. From the southern end of the beach you can see Hon Phu Tu (Father & Son Island), which is supposed to resemble a father holding onto his son but looks more like a kangaroo driving the kids to preschool. Anyhow, I suppose it depends on what you're taking when you see it.

Also on the southern end of the strip at the base of a hill is **Chua Hang Grotto** and the Buddhist temple **Hai Son Tu**, which must be entered to gain access to the grotto. The grotto itself is the geological version of Tubular Bells—the hollow stalactites produce musical tones when tapped.

Also worth it here is a boat trip out to **Nghe Island**, which takes about 90 minutes. The island is a scenic, relaxing place with a decent beach and another cave temple. A trip out here can be managed through **Hon Tren Guesthouse** at Duong Beach. The cost is steep at US$40 for the day, but it can be made a lot cheaper if you bring some buddies. The Hon Tren (☎ 854331) itself is a big bungalow with 10 or 12 rooms which can be had for US$6. The ammenities are primitive, but the "staff" is friendly and they'll cook up some fresh seafood for you. Another decent guesthouse at Duong Beach is the **Binh An** (☎ 854332; FAX: 854338), an enclosed structure with a pleasant garden and 16 passable rooms. The air-condtioned rooms run about US$12, while doubles with a fan cost only US$6.

Doing It

Hon Chong and Duong Beach can be reached by getting to Ba Hon, about 25 km east of Ha Tien on the road to Rach Gia. At Ba Hon, a dirt road cuts south another 15 km or so to Hon Chong. Motorbike drivers will be happy to bring you the distance from Ba Hon to Hon Chong if you don't have your own transportation.

Soc Trang

Soc Trang

SOC TRANG IN A CAPSULE

About 60 km east of Can Tho...The capital of Soc Trang province...Province population about 1,172,000...65 percent ethnic Vietnamese, 28 percent Khmer, 7 percent Chinese...About 90 Khmer pagodas and 47 Chinese pagodas can be found in the province...Colorful feasts and festivals take place here each year.

Rather than taking the highway southeast toward the South China Sea, most tourists in the Mekong Delta head northwest to Long Xuyen and Chau Doc or south to Rach Gia and Ha Tien. Soc Trang is an infrequently visited city by foreigners, mainly because it has few attractions—although they are growing.

The reason to come here is to see the bizarre Vietnamese Pagoda, which is covered with swastikas, Buddha figures (mainly heads) and the statues of animals that cover the grounds. There's also another pagoda here, a Khmer monastery called the Bat Pagoda, where fruit bats live in the trees. They make for good photo opportunities. There are a number of murals here.

With a little digging, you'll find there are other attractions to the area, as well. Nearly 140 pagodas dot the countryside in the province. There are numerous festivals and traditional feasts, exquisite gardens in the city and, of course, the large influence of Khmer culture in the area.

What to See and Do in Soc Trang

Stork Garden of Tan Long Thanh Tri (Vuon Co Tan Long)
About 40 km from the city.
Tens of thousands of white storks make this "garden" their home. The sight of so many of these birds frolicking in the treetops and in the marshes shouldn't be missed.

Fresh Water Lake (Ho Nuoc Ngot)
Center of town.

Soc Trang

This is an attractive, little, pine-surrounded lake in town that's a good place to kill a few hot afternoon hours.

My Phuoc Isle (Cu Lao My Phuoc)

In the middle of the Hau River.

This is an attractive island featuring gardens and fruit trees. The fifth day of the fifth month of the lunar calendar marks the annual Doan Ngo Tet festival—the start of the annual harvest—and the island becomes a focal point. Soc Trang natives return from all over Vietnam to partake in the festivities.

Tran De Fishing Port (Moo)

30 km out of town at the sea.

This area is being developed, albeit slowly, for tourism. The Tran De estuary flows into the South China Sea from here. There's a quaint fishing port here as well as Mo O Beach, at the mouth of the river. Don't expect an azure sea.

Museum of Khmer Culture

Right in the middle of town.

Depicts the lives of southern Khmers. A few nice displays here. Attractive and clean as a whistle.

Moon Worshipping Ceremony ★

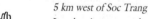

Celebrated on the 15th night of the 10th lunar month, this is a colorful festival dedicated to the moon's role in producing bountiful crops. There's a special offering of flattened rice *(com dep)* to the Man on the Moon. Earlier in the day is the Oc Om Bok Ceremony, when the spectacle of the Ngo Boat Race is held. This is one of the most colorful events in southern Vietnam. Dozens of brightly clad boat teams row 15-meter canoes in the river while hundreds of revelers on the banks delight to Vietnamese, Khmer and Chinese theater artists.

Ma Toc Pagoda (Chua Doi—The Bat Pagoda)

5 km west of Soc Trang

Local estimates say that more than 100,000 bats live in the trees around this four-century-old Khmer monastery. Thousands of bats can be seen sleeping upside down on the branches of trees during the daytime. They are most active just after sunrise and just before sunset. The creatures make some incredible noises. A word of caution. Bats don't drop the pretty white stuff that sparrows do. Be warned. It's like being hit by a skunk.

Clay Pagoda (Chua Dat Set)

Located 1 km from town.

This is a 200-year-old pagoda filled with animal sculptures and giant candles weighing in at between 100-200 kg. The candles have only been about one-third melted in 20 years of continuous use.

Where to Stay in Soc Trang

AUTHOR'S NOTE: TELEPHONE PREFIXES

The following telephone numbers are local exchanges. The country code is 84. The city code is 79.

Khanh Hung Hotel   **US$5–$22**

15 Tran Hung Dao Street. ☎ *821027.*
Big new hotel with a wide range of rooms. The best place and best bargain in town. The cheapies come with a fan and private bath, while the air-conditioned rooms run from 10 bucks up. Big restaurant with decent food.

Phong Lan Hotel   **US$15–$25**

124 Dong Khoi Street. ☎ *821619.*
Nice location by the river. The lower-priced rooms have a fan and private bath, while the air-conditioned rooms also offer hot water.

Tay Nam Hotel   **US$20**

133 Nguyen Chi Thanh. ☎ *821757.*
One of the three cleanest hotels in Soc Trang. This place even has a tennis court. Rooms with air conditioning, private bath. Restaurant.

Phong Lan (Orchid) Hotel   **US$20–$35**

124 Dong Khoi Street. ☎ *821619.*
Was the best in town until the Khanh Hung came around. Rooms with air conditioning, private bath. This is where the tour group set calls it a day. Has the best restaurant in town.

Where to Eat in Soc Trang

Undoubtedly the best place in town is the Orchid Hotel. These guys also do a number of weddings and banquets. Also recommended are:

Hung Restaurant   **$–$$**

74-76 Mau Tham 68 Street. ☎ *822268.*
Great eatery with local fare.

Nha Hang Huong Duong (Sunflower Restaurant) $

Fresh Water Lake. ☎ *821638.*
Great area for a picnic with food bought at the restaurant.

Bong Sen (Lotus) Restaurant   **$**

National Route 1. ☎ *821344.*
Nice eatery with Vietnamese specialties. Centrally located.

Directory

Tourism Office

Soc Trang Tourist Company

131 Nguyen Chi Thanh Street. ☎ *821498. FAX: 821993.*

Bac Lieu

Bac Lieu is a small town about halfway between Soc Trang and Ca Mau that serves little purpose other than breaking up the trip between the two towns. Unlike in most areas of the Mekong Delta, there is little grown or harvested here (other than oysters) due to high salt content of the soil. It's a ramshackle little town with a disproportionate number of hotels.

There are a few "attractions" in the area. About 12.5 km south of Bac Lieu on the road to Ca Mau is the Khmer pagoda **Moi Hua Binh**. This is a slightly unusual pagoda in design but not terribly old, having been built in the early 1950s. It's located on the east side of the road and visible from the highway.

Another Khmer pagoda, **Xiem Can**, can be found about seven kilometers from town on the road to **Bac Lieu Beach**, a grotty coastal strip that invites neither sunbathing on the mud nor swimming in the murky surf. The **Bird Sanctuary**, or San Chim, is located on the same road about five kilometers from Bac Lieu but is not a particularly impressive sight.

Although there is little reason to overnight in Bac Lieu unless you have business or relatives in the area, there are a couple of hotels in town. The **Bac Lieu Hotel** *(4 Hoang Van Thu Street.* ☎ *822621)* is in keeping with its name-sake: dingy and cheap. Closet-sized singles with a fan and shared bath run about US$7, while air-conditioned rooms cost about US$20. A step away is the similarly-priced-and-endowed **Rang Dong Hotel** *(6 Hoang Van Thu Street.* ☎ *822437)*.

Soc Trang

Ca Mau

Ca Mau

CA MAU IN A CAPSULE

On the southern edge of the U Minh Forest...Considered the largest mangrove swamps outside the Amazon Basin...Few Westerners visit here...American defoliation during the Vietnam War obliterated the area...Has a zoo that's more like a leper colony...Take medical precautions while visiting this vast swamp.

Ca Mau on the banks of the Ganh Hao River is 180 km from Can Tho and 350 km from Saigon. It is the largest settlement on the Ca Mau peninsula and is at the southern edge of the U Minh Forest, a giant cajeput swamp that covers approximately 1000 sq. km of Minh Hai and Kien Giang provinces.

Apart from the Amazon basin in South America, the U Minh forest is considered by most to be the largest cajeput (or mangrove) swamp in the world. Aerial defoliation by the Americans during the Vietnam war practically ruined the area. However, nature has incredible resilience and, today, much of the swamp has regained its beauty (although nearly a quarter of the swamp remains a dank wasteland). Much of the waterfowl have returned to the area, and bees pollinate the mangrove blossoms. However, the area is still being depleted of its natural resources today via shrimp breeding ponds. Locals also use the cajeput in a number of different ways: as charcoal, as a source of timber, and thatch for dwellings.

Ca Mau also features a "zoo," which is a dilapidated, inhumane environment designed for tourism that houses diseased, dismally treated animals that survive (barely) here for the benefit (or the nausea) of the few foreign tourists that visit this area. I'd stay away from it.

Bring your deet and malaria pills (although they might not be effective). Mosquitoes in the mangrove swamps and the town abound. They're espe-

Ca Mau

cially bothersome at night, and eating at outdoor food stalls can be a miserable experience for this reason alone.

Where to Stay and Eat in Ca Mau

The **Khach San Sao Mai** *(38-40 Phan Ngoc Hien Street.* ☎ *831035.* US$15-25) on the corner of Duong Ly Bon and Phan Ngoc Hien Streets appears to be nothing more than a whorehouse, as are most of the hotels in Ca Mau. Most of Ca Mau's hotels are on Phan Ngoc Hien Street, as is the best hotel in town, the **Phuong Nam Hotel** *(41 Phan Dinh Phong Street.* ☎ *832129.* US$20–$55). The upper-end rooms here are worth it purely for the escape value the satellite TVs provide. The **Ca Mau Hotel** *(20 Phan Ngoc Hien Street.* ☎ *831165)* also offers some decent but overpriced rooms for US$20–$50. However, the cheaper rooms are a rip-off. Everything else in town ranges from around US$7–$20, and most of the places are filthy, run-down, or just plain dumps. It's one of the many reasons so few Westerners make it down this far. There is little tourism infrastructure in Ca Mau, and even fewer reasons to stay here.

On Ly Bon Street can be found a number of roadside food stalls. You'll need nourishment, so eat at them, although the food is nothing to write home about. You should only travel to this area after having spent enough time in Vietnam to become accustomed to eating food stall fare, drinking boiled water, and bathing in rancid water. This is an easy place to get sick, and if your immune system hasn't yet adjusted to rural Vietnam, I'd avoid this area until it has. The one decent restaurant in town is the **Thanh Thanh Restaurant** *(9 Phan Ngoc Hien Street.* ☎ *831076).*

Directory

Transportation

Ca Mau is about 350 km from Saigon and 180 km from Can Tho. **Buses** leave for Ca Mau from HCMC's Mien Tay Bus Station and the trip usually takes between 10 and 11 hours by express bus and up to 13 by other buses. The road from Can Tho to Ca Mau is like other roads in the southern delta; they can only peripherally be classified as "roads." Potholes the size of B-52 bomb craters make the trip a roller-coaster ride. The long trip by bus from HCMC is unendurable. If you want to go by boat from Saigon, the trip takes well over a day; boats leave for Ca Mau about every other day. Local transport is by water taxi, motorbike or cyclo. You cannot reach Ca Mau by air.

Tourist Office

Minh Hai Tourist
17 Nguyen Van Hai Street. ☎ *831828.*

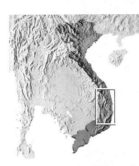

THE CENTRAL
HIGHLANDS

Vietnam's Central Highlands offer some of the best vistas in the south.

THE CENTRAL HIGHLANDS
IN A CAPSULE

*Some of the most spectacular mountainous scenery in Vietnam...The hillsides
are dotted with hilltribe villages...The southern region of the highlands has
Vietnam's best climate, warm days, cool nights...Many of the natural attractions have been somewhat spoiled by overcommercialism...Tourists are fewer
and the accommodations sparse in the northern areas such as Pleiku...There
was considerable military action in the highlands during the Vietnam War.*

The lush Central Highlands is home to many ethnic groups and famous for spectacular scenery. The area is part of the southern chain of the Truong Son Mountain Range, with a cool climate, beautiful lakes and waterfalls. Although not many people live in the Highlands, the area was considered strategically important during the Vietnam War, and travel restrictions to areas of the Central Highlands even exist today—although they are decreasing.

Independent travelers can reach (if they are physically able to) many areas that were once prohibited. Provinces in the Central Highlands consist of Dac Lac, Kon Tum, Lam Dong and Gia Lai. During the war, a lot of fighting took place around Pleiku, Kon Tum and Buon Ma Thuot. However, Dalat was remarkably spared from the fighting. Supposedly, top military brass on both sides of the conflict used Dalat as a summer retreat, and it's said that officers from opposing armies spent R&R time in villas only a few kilometers from each other.

Americans were recently prohibited from visiting the Central Highlands with the exception of touristy Dalat due to the continuing conflict between government forces and FULRO (the United Front for the Struggle of the Oppressed Races); there are even rumors of Reeducation Camps still existing in the area. These restrictions have been almost entirely removed. And at the few remaining restricted sites, you no longer need to be guided by Vietnamese Army soldiers. Instead tourism permits can be arranged at provincial tourist offices for a nominal fee of about US$5 (although you'll still have to hire one of their guides and perhaps a vehicle, even if you have your own).

The road leading from Saigon to Dalat is a generally good one (excellent by Vietnamese standards) and scenery is spectacular, particularly between Bao Loc and Dalat. You'll want to stop and take pictures in numerous places, across verdant mountainous vistas as well as the bridge spanning a small section of the Ho Tri An Lake between Bien Hoa and Bao Loc, where floating hootches dot the marshes and lake. The final 20 km to Dalat are almost straight up and, although it's a treacherous ride, the road winds deep through some of the greenest mountainsides you'll ever have a chance to see.

Good news for travelers wishing to take in the highlands are the vast improvements that have been made on Highways 27 and 14. Up until 1996, these roads were in dismal shape and foreigners weren't even permitted to make the trip between Dalat and Buon Ma Thuot using the mountain roads. Instead, travelers to Buon Ma Thuot were forced to divert to the coastal cities of Phan Rang and Nha Trang before heading back into the hills for Buon Ma Thuot. Today, the travel time has been cut from 10 hours to as little as four with the opening of Highway 27 and its subsequent improvements. Additionally, the former guerrilla trail turned cattle trail Highway 14 now smoothly connects Buon Ma Thuot with both Pleiku and Kon Tum, making travel between the Central Highlands' principal towns a snap.

Hill Tribes

The highland areas of Vietnam are considered by most as the most culturally and linguistically numerous and diverse in the entire world. In the southern Central Highlands, there are as many as 35 tribes, and as many as 50
throughout the country. Some of the ethnic groups have as few as 500 individuals; the largest may number in the millions. Here's a look at some of the
hill people, including those in the north:

Bahnar

Mostly concentrated in the central highland provinces of Gia Lai and Kon
Tum, the Bahnar are an ethnic minority group who speak Mon-Khmer.
Their population is estimated at about 100,000. After enjoying nearly four
centuries of power in the region (15th–18th centuries), the group was nearly
wiped out in the 19th century by the Harai and Dedang people. The Bahnar
became close with the French, and Christianity (particularly Catholicism)
became widespread. Men and women are considered equals. Wealth is evenly distributed among a Bahnar family, and marriages can be arranged by the
parents of either the man or the woman.

Koho

These matrilineal people, also called the Kohor, inhabit Lam Dong Province near Dalat on the Lam Dong Plateau. Today's population of around
100,000 live in longhouses in extended family groups. These houses can
each 30 meters in length. Men who marry often live with the family of the
wife. Settled agriculture provides the Kohos' subsistence.

Rhade

This is another matrilineal group that primarily inhabits the Central Highlands. They're also known as the Edeh, and their population is believed to be
approximately 170,000. They also befriended the French and Christianity is
prevalent in their communities. They are considered to be among the most
"modern" of the ethnic hill people. Extended families, such as the Koho,
also live in longhouses. Inheritance is usually given to the highest ranking female member of the family. Wet rice agriculture is the Rhades' primary form
of subsistence, although some communities still practice the more traditional
forms of shifting cultivation.

Gia Rai

Found primarily in the hills in and around Pleiku in the provinces of Gia
Lai and Kon Tum, these 260,000 matrilineal people represent the largest
ethnic minority in the Central Highlands. They are also known as the Zrai
people.

Sedang

Another Central Highlands tribe, the Sedang (or Xo-dang) number about 100,000 people who live in longhouses in the Gia Lai and Kon Tum province areas. Subsistence is by wet rice cultivation and shifting agriculture. These are a violent people; they have fought both the French and the Viets, and they were the group that nearly made the Bahnar extinct in the 19th century.

Muong

As we move north, we find the Muong who are, numbering at nearly 600,000, one of the largest ethnic minorities in Vietnam. They inhabit the central and northern provinces of Hoa Binh, Son La, Thanh Hoa, Ha Tay and Nghia Lo provinces. There are many similarities between the Muong and ethnic Vietnamese, both in culture and language. Wealth is inherited through the male line, and their subsistence is through the cultivation of both wet and dry rice. However, unlike the ethnic Vietnamese, the Muong were not confronted with the Chinese and Christian influences that permeated Vietnamese culture. Some Muong still apply a black lacquer to their teeth in their mid-teens to symbolize entry into adulthood.

Hmong

The Hmong, who can be found in highland areas throughout Vietnam, have a population of about 750,000 people, making them one of the largest groups of ethnic hill people in the country. Originally settling in Vietnam in the 19th century from China, most Hmong can be found near the Chinese border and south to about the 18th parallel. The Hmong are a very isolated people, choosing to live at altitudes far higher than those inhabited by other ethnic hill people. Usually they live some 1500 meters higher then their lower neighbors. Like the Sedang, they are warlike and fought both the French and the Vietnamese. They use slash-and-burn agricultural techniques. There are different groups of the Hmong: the White Hmong, the Flowered Hmong, the Red Hmong and the Black Hmong.

Nung

These mostly Buddhist people, centered primarily north of Hanoi in the provinces of Ha Bac and Bac Thai, number more than a million people. They subsist on settled agriculture and are known for their bravery in battle. They have been strongly influenced by both the Chinese and the Vietnamese.

Zao

There are perhaps 400,000 Zao (also called Yao, Dao or Man) people living in the highland areas of northern Vietnam. Most are Buddhists, although some Zao are into Taoism and Confucianism. They usually live in the mountains at between 700-1000 meters high.

Thai

This is the largest ethnic minority in Vietnam, inhabiting primarily north-west Vietnam, whose numbers exceed 1.4 million. They first came to Vietnam from China during the 4th century. The Thai consist of three groups; the Red Thai *(Thai Do)*, the Black Thai *(Thai Den)* and the White Thai *(Thai Trang)*. The names are based on the color of the tunics worn by the women of each group. They live in the provinces of Lai Chau, Son La, Thanh Hoa, Nghia Lo, Nghe An and Hoa Binh. They use Chinese ideograms for writing and subsist on the cultivation of wet rice.

Other ethnic minority hill people with significant populations include the **Hre**, who number about 80,000 in the provinces of Gia Lai and Kon Tum; the **Mnong**, who number about 65,000 in the provinces of Lam Dong and Dac Lac; and the **Stieng**, who number about 50,000 in the provinces of Dac Lac, Song Be and Lam Dong.

The Bigfeet of Vietnam

Legend has it that a group of Vietnamese living in Hue were cast under a spell by a "witch doctor," which forced them into the mountains of the Central Highlands in western Quang Binh Province. This "spell" made these people grow hair all over their bodies, similar to apes, and took away their ability to speak. After first establishing settlements in this rugged, mountainous region, they were forced farther into the highlands as Vietnamese and other ethnicities migrated into these areas. They made no contact with anyone, but at night would surround the new villages established by the migrating Vietnamese and howl from deep in the forest in remorseful memory of who they once were and the human capabilities they formerly possessed. Many believe these "monkey people" still exist and torment villages, without being seen, late at night with their baying.

In reality, the legend isn't far from the truth, although it's doubtful they metamorphosed as the result of magic. They're called the Ruc ethnic group and they do indeed inhabit the high jungles of western Quang Binh Province in north-central Vietnam, living by hunting and gathering. By the best estimate, there are only about 200 surviving members of this primitive animal-like tribe. They live in highly remote and mountainous stone caves that are entirely inaccessible. Earlier, the Ruc people had civilized knowledge as well as their own language. They also had a concept of the sun and earth and of different species of living animals. But due to scientifically unknown historical events, they were forced to retreat higher and higher into the western mountains near Laos, where they lived totally cut off from the rest of Vietnam's population. The untamed forests, wild animals and severe environment made their lives quite primitive. At night they creep into their caves or primitive huts. In the daytime, the men stalk through the forest and boulders in search of monkeys, deer and bees for food. The men wear only tree bark loin cloths, while the women wear loin cloths of the same material, covering the lower parts of their bodies only. The children do not wear clothes. Fire is created by rubbing black stones together. The fires are kept burning for months and even years. When women give birth, the woman will go deep into the forest and dig a hole where she will bear the child alone. The husband is not allowed to be with his wife, but passes food to her with a long stick. After the birth of the child it is the husband's duty to search the forests for seven white monkeys. Only after the wife has eaten all the monkeys can she return home. This is an important rite for the Ruc, as they believe the practice of giving birth in the forest prepares the newborn child immediately for the severe climate. God decides whether the child will live or die, and the Ruc pray to God by rubbing two bamboo pipes together. The Ruc people are a deeply attached community. For instance, when a water hole is discovered, the person making the find gathers the entire community together to drink at the site. If a man discovers a tree called *nhuc*, he will summon the women and the girls of the community to get the heart wood for food. When a group of men returns to the "village" after a hunt, they share their catch with everyone—and the man who killed the beast severs the head. The rest of the meat is shared by the tribe. There are Ruc festivals, where tribespeople gather around fires to listen to primitive *K Teng* and *T Lenh* songs. These people have been more exposed to the outside "world" in recent years and their customs are changing quickly. Regrettably, the "Bigfeet" of the remote Vietnamese forests will soon start donning Nikes.

A floating village on Ho Tri An Lake off National Highway 20 near Tan Phu

Bao Loc

Spectacular Dambri Waterfalls outside Bao Loc cascade some 50 meters.

BAO LOC IN A CAPSULE

Gateway to the Central Highlands...A good stopover from Saigon to Dalat...Site of some of the most spectacular waterfalls in southern Vietnam...110 km south of Dalat on Highway 20...Surrounded by lush, rolling hillsides supporting coffee and tea plantations...A major center of silk production...Dambri waterfalls often bypassed by tourists...Relatively new and upscale hotel called the Seri.

Bao Loc (or B'Lao) is 110 km south from Dalat (and about 200 km from Ho Chi Minh City) on Highway 20, or Tran Phu Street as the highway is called in town. It makes for a convenient stopover between Saigon and Dalat. The area consists of lush rolling green hills that support a number of coffee, mulberry leaf and tea plantations. Silk production is big in this area. There are also a number of small waterfalls, and one massive one that only a handful of foreigners bother getting out to, the falls at Dambri. These falls make the waterfalls in Dalat seem like bathroom showers, and they well may be the most spectacular falls in Vietnam. The vast majority of travelers bypass Bao Loc completely. This is bound to change.

What to See and Do in Bao Loc and Environs

Dambri Waterfalls   ★ ★ ★

Located about 17 km west of Bao Loc.

These are perhaps the most magnificent waterfalls in Vietnam, in southern Vietnam for sure, surpassing in magnificence even the Drai Sap falls near Buon Ma Thuot. Nearly 50 meters high, the rushing water cascades down a solid rock edifice creating a thunderous cloud of mist and multihued spray. Wonderful photos can be taken from both the summit and the base of the falls. But down below, you'll get wet, so keep your camera dry. The best times of the day to see the falls are in the early morning, where the spray creates spectacular rainbows, or late in the afternoon, when the low sun spills angles of light directly on the rushing water. The best thing about the falls is that few travelers know about them, although now there is a newly built restaurant at the falls, attracting the tour buses. On some visits here, I have not seen a single other tourist, yet on others, the place seems to be a theme park. Regrettably, the silly floating duck boats and plopping ponies of Dalat have found their way south to Dambri. Though Dambri is not yet as overcommercialized as the attractions of Dalat, how long can it be? From Bao Loc, you turn west at the post office and then have to make a number of turns on side streets before reaching the road toward the falls, a magnificent stretch of winding roadway, flanked by silk, tea and coffee farms and offering magnificent vistas of the surrounding mountains, including May Bay Mountain. Ask for specific directions at The Bao Loc Hotel or the Seri Hotel. There's the big, but usually empty Dambri Restaurant at the admission area. Admission: 12,000 dong for foreigners, up from VND10,000 a year ago—obviously to pay for the daffy duck boats and the restaurant. Frightful but worth it. Not to be missed.

Bay Tung Falls

23 km south of Bao Loc, off Hwy 20.

Take Highway 20 seven km south from the Bao Loc Hotel. Then take a trail, 3 km after crossing the Dai Binh River, to the hamlet of Ap Dai Lao in the village of Xa Loc Chau. The trail starts on the right side of the road. You'll walk about 400 meters through tea bushes and coffee trees as well as banana and pineapple groves to reach Suoi Mo, the Stream of Dreaming. There the path goes left through thickets of bamboo. Soon you'll see the Bay Tung Falls and the pools of the Stream of Dreaming. Worth a visit only if you're planning on spending a day or two in Bao Loc—few people do. The falls pale in comparison to the Dambri Waterfalls.

Bao Loc Church

In town, north of Bro Loc Hotel.

Nothing spectacular, but if you're Catholic, you may want to pay a visit. It's located about 300 meters on Highway 20 north of the Bao Loc Hotel.

Tea, Silk and Coffee Factories

Surrounding hillsides.

Get a local to show you around some of the factories that produce coffee, tea and silkworms. You can find the factories on Highway 20 south of Bao Loc and also on the well-paved road leading to the Dambri Waterfalls.

Where to Stay in Bao Loc

AUTHOR'S NOTE: TELPEHONE PREFIXES

The telephone numbers listed here are local exchanges. The country code is 84. The city codes for both Bao Loc and Dalat are 63.

Bao Loc Hotel & Restaurant   US$12–$20

So 11 A Tran Phu-Bao Loc (National Highway 20). ☎ 84107 or 84268; FAX: 84167. 12 rooms.

There are only three "hotels" in Bao Loc that foreigners might consider, this one, the Hong Hoang Mini-Hotel and the more upscale Seri. Once I suggested that budget travelers stay here, but now only with hesitation, even for a single night breaking up the trip to Dalat. It's a pretty big place considering the number of rooms, but the rooms are somewhat shoddy and don't expect your toilet to work. The staff is friendly but dizzy enough to collapse the building, which has been in disrepair since its construction in 1940. The deceivingly large structure has two large, empty restaurants. Everything here seems spacious and empty. Yet on my last visit toward the end of 1996, I was told there were not two rooms available for myself and a traveling companion, despite the place being devoid of travelers. Overpriced, but there is hot water. If you order a cocktail in the bar, you'll have to pay for the bottle—at an exorbitant price you'll have to negotiate down from an even higher price! Don't expect to be served what you ordered in the restaurant.

Seri Hotel   US$40–$80   ★

Bao Loc-Lamdoc Province, just off Highway 20 in the center part of town. ☎ 84150, 84430 or 84065. FAX: 82183.
57 rooms.
Reservations: Direct or through HCMC, 28 Mac Dinh Chi. ☎ 8298438 or 8231375. FAX: 84.8.8294086.

This place also once had a better recommendation in this book. It does its best of putting on a facade of luxury, but is actually pretty standard, somewhat pretentious and overpriced, unless your idea of value is singing karaoke to yourself. But the Seri, somewhat a cross between Saigon's Floating Hotel and the Pentagon, is the only upscale place in town. But why it would expect to fill its spacious, tastefully decorated rooms is well beyond my comprehension given the lack of reasons to put in an extended stay in the Bao Loc area. The higher priced rooms are decently furnished and comfortable suites. Singles and doubles, all with TV, hot water, telephone. Restaurant, snack bar, dance hall and karaoke. The staff is especially friendly, well-dressed and surprisingly fluent in English. A shop sells locally produced silk clothing, but at relatively exorbitant rates. Hotel also offers minibus transportation to tea and coffee plantations, as well as to the area's waterfalls, including the Dambri Waterfalls. The falls are what make this hotel worth the visit.

Hong Hoang Mini-Hotel   US$15

Tran Phu Street (National Highway 20), about a half-kilometer south of the Bao Loc Hotel.

New, comfortable, clean and reasonably priced. Hot water. Security for you motorbike if that's how you arrive.

Where to Eat in Bao Loc

There are a number of food stalls and cafes that line NH20 (Tran Phu Street) through Bao Loc.

Restaurant Dang Nguyen

02b Tran Phu Street.
Vietnamese, cheap.

Tram Anh Tra Cafe

5 Tran Phu.
Comfortable, shaded and popular.

Restaurant Hung Phat and the Hung Phat Cafe

Tran Phu Street, across from the Bao Loc Hotel, 20 meters south.

One of the best restaurants in town with friendly service. There's an outdoor dining area which consists of one-table gazebolike booths. If you happen to get a date in Bao Loc, bring your friend here.

Dream Cafe

Across Tran Phu Street from the Restaurant Hung Phat.
Nothing to write home about.

Bao Loc Hotel

So 11a Tran Phu Street.
Usually empty, but vegetable dishes are great. Also Western food.

Seri Hotel Restaurant

Seri Hotel.
Better then average Vietnamese and Western fare for the area.

Dambri Restaurant

Dambri Waterfalls.
New, big and modern establishment; average food.

A rainbow cuts through the mist at Bao Loc's 50-meter-high Dambri Waterfalls.

Cat Tien National Park

Located southwest of Bao Loc and Highway 20 and about 160 km from Ho Chi Minh City is this beautiful new national park that is home to rare and exotic wildlife, including elephants, leopards the gaur ox and the Javan rhino.

Few visitors get here and there are no organized excursions of the 380-square-kilometer park through the state-run tourist companies, at least at the time of this writing—but visits can be arranged privately or through private tour operators, and I imagine through the state companies, as well, if you ask. Additionally, there is a guest house on the eastern edge of the park (see "Doing It" below), but most excursions out here should be at your own risk—which is 100 percent of the fun.

Don't expect any marked nature trails or signs designating flora and fauna species nailed to tree trunks. There are no observation platforms and neither are there any touts, chewing gum hawkers, food stalls, cowboys with plastic six-shooters astride plopping ponies nor packs of aggressive child-guides fluent in a half-dozen languages. This place is so far totally pristine and without any of the tourist trappings that plague so many of Vietnam's natural attractions. A few thin dirt roads ribbon through this semimountainous, electrically-lush park, many of which are flooded out during the wet season, particularly in areas near the Dong Nai River, which flows in fast-forward during the southwest monsoon. There are no walking trails that branch from the road. Instead, you'll have to leave your vehicle or motorbike and hack

your way through the jungle, which I heartedly suggest you do. Besides my
iad species of birds, you'll probably be treated to sights of macaque monkey
wild boar and ox, and giant lizards, as I was. Butterflies in a kaleidoscope c
bright hues travel in clouds, massing where shafts of sunlight have found th
earth after poking through the rainforest canopy. Dazzling orchids can b
found roosting on the trunks of the many varieties of hardwood trees foun
in the park.

For a complete description of what can be found in the park and where t
find it, I suggest making contact with Mr. Duyen after you arrive at the Ca
Tien Guesthouse. He's the congenial park director and Cat Tien's residen
botanist/biologist/engineer/naturalist/guide—and a wealth of informa
tion. His English is passable though hardly fluent, but his vast knowledge c
Vietnamese flora and fauna more than makes up for it.

Perhaps the best part of a trip is getting out there. The two "roads" tha
cut west from Route 20 will transport you back to another time. Nowhere i
Vietnam have I encountered so many shouts of "Xien Lo!" (Soviet) from th
children of the villages, most of whom had never seen a foreigner. Villager
of all ages gawked at me in astonishment. On the flanks of the meandering
path are rolling hills checkered with coffee and banana plantations. The
roads themselves are nothing short of dangerous. Deep trenches and chunk
of laterite make the going quite hazardous by any means of transportation
They are best negotiated by small motorbike. (Even rugged 4x4s will have a
rough go of it.) The 750cc cruiser beast I was mounted on stalled and stum
bled at every turn, becoming swallowed by the thick, soupy clay. Teams o
delighted but purposeful villagers would push and stablize the rear end
along the trickier sections, and then follow me to the next obstacle simply to
see if I'd dump the bike.

Cat Tien Park is best attempted during the dry season from November
through April. Any other time and expect a very muddy visit—that's if you
can get here.

Doing It

Although only about 160 km from Saigon, this is no day trip. The park is accessible
from two points off National Highway 20. Coming north from Saigon, a dirt road
cuts west to the park from the village of Tan Phu. You can't miss it as it cuts west
from Route 20 in the center of town at the market. If you're on a motorbike, I'd
suggest refueling anywhere from Dinh Quan north. Your last chance will be at a
small "soda pop bottle" fuel hootch about 20 meters on the right side after you
make the turnoff (although in a pinch, a few hootches farther along the path may
offer a soda pop bottle of the dirty, low-octane stuff). You'll be pretty much on your
own, and expect zero in the way of roadside services during the 17-km trip to eastern edge of the park. The "road" is in dismal condition. At one long stretch after
turning in Dong Phu, every 50 meters or so, you'll be faced with a field of laterite

chunks to negotiate, flanked by deep mud trenches. There about 15-20 such sections currently on the 17-km length from Tan Phu to the ferry, the vast crux of them after the Dong Phu turnoff. After leaving Route 20, you'll travel about 7 km before reaching the small village of Dong Phu, where there's a distinct right side turnoff. You'll need to turn right here if you're looking to reach the Cat Tien Guesthouse. If you continue straight, the following three kilometers will lead you to the ferry crossing at the small village of Ta Lai on the Dong Nai River. There are no accommodations here. If you cross the ferry here into the park, you'll be SOL. The road into the park that leads to Tec Lon and Dong Phu from Ta Lai doesn't actually lead there—it is only negotiable for about 10-15 km west of the Dong Nai River before it simply disappears in the wedge of a mountain and a river—a dirt biker's nirvana. Instead, make the right at Dong Phu three kilometers before the river. This is a rocky and barely traversable road that runs another seven km or so before it Ts. Make a left here onto another dirt road, this one a lot smoother going. It also Ts after about 3-4 km at a small village. Make another left here (also on dirt) 300 meters to the ferry to the Cat Tien Guesthouse. **Note:** You'll need to stop at the park's entrance facility before reaching the ferry. It's on the right-hand side about 50 meters before reaching the ferry. Here you'll need to register with park officials. The ferry itself is a beat-up old platform hull that looks like a legally blind welder's attempt at recreating the landing craft MacArthur stepped off from in the Philippines. This ferry can accommodate both a car or two and motorcycles. The trip across the Dong Nai River is a precarious one, especially in the extremely strong currents caused by the southwest monsoon. The ferry uses more distance powering up and down the river than the actual width of the river. The Cat Tien Guesthouse is directly across the river at the landing. The ferry costs a ridiculous US$4 return if you bring a motorcycle, perhaps a couple of thousand dong if you don't.

Also, about 40 km south of Bao Loc another dirt road runs west from below Da Huoai (at the Dalat 158 km marker heading north and the HCMC 141 km marker heading south) to the same ferry. As I mentioned, both roads are accessible only by a rugged, high-clearance 4x4 vehicle and motorbikes, but I'd suggest having some fun and doing it by motorcycle, especially if you can somehow arrange for a rare dual-sport in Saigon (I've seen perhaps a dozen in my life there, but the number is growing daily). This road is also in dismal shape, but slightly less brutal on motorcycles. It carves its way 18 km through rugged terrain to the same ferry crossing at Cat Tien Guesthouse. At Da Te or Dong Phu, tiny villages, it's unlikely you'll find an English-speaking guide, which would be nice to have out here. Your best bet for a guide is at the Cat Tien Guesthouse, though it's not assured he will speak English. If going it solo directly into the park, go right after embarking from the ferry. The narrow track winds its way deep into a jungle full of exotic wildlife. You will see no people nor evidence anyone's been there before you, save for a pathmaker. During the rainy season the path becomes completely flooded by the surging Dong Nai and is impassable after about 14 km into the park. But you'll have an absolute blast just getting this far.

Where to Stay

You've only got one choice here. It's the **Cat Tien Guesthouse** (☎ 061-856449), compound of four or five ramshackle, spartan buildings on the west bank of th Dong Nai River. Almost no foreigners stay here (none were seen during both of m visits), and the "hotel" was primarily built to serve the park's workers and biolog students. But the staff and locals are very friendly. A comfortable gazebo overlook the river. Singles run US$5 in the wooden structure and rooms with four beds (usu ally only two with mattresses) run US$10 in the more modern but drab cemen structures. All rooms have a fan, mosquito nets (use 'em; see Insider Tip below) and nothing else. And there's no hot water. There are couple of shared toilets/shower outside the buildings and a dilapidated restaurant on the river serves absolutely deli cious river food and huge portions—which you can help drain into your stomach with Saigon beer. No one, save for the hotel's (and park's) director, Mr. Duyen speaks any English, so ordering anything is all but impossible. Eat what you are served.

Warning: Mozzie Scare

The one drawback to a trip to Cat Tien is the preponderance of mosquitos. They are big and they are everywhere. I was eaten alive at Cat Tien and covered with enormous welts each morning, despite using a mosquito net. The little buggers seemed to have found a hole in it, or simply dug one themselves. I've heard there's malaria in the park and am actually a lab rat for that hypothesis at this moment. Apply anything and everything you've got, and remember to gobble larium or other antimalarial as prescribed well before a trip here. Keep as much of your body covered as is reasonably possible. I'll let you know later whether the possibility of contracting the disease should deter you from coming.

Dalat

Dalat's railway station used to serve Saigon via Phan Rang until continuous Viet Cong attacks ruined the track and made the journey impossible.

DALAT IN A CAPSULE

Founded by French scientist Andre Yersin as a French hill resort in 1897...Offers the best climate in Vietnam...a primarily temperate zone with huge tea and coffee plantations as well as silk-production facilities...A favorite honeymooning spot for Vietnamese newlyweds...Much of the mountainsides have been heavily deforested in recent years...Very little fighting took place here during the Vietnam War...Montagnard, Da Hoa and Lat hill people live in the region...Waterfalls and lakes surround this mountainous area.

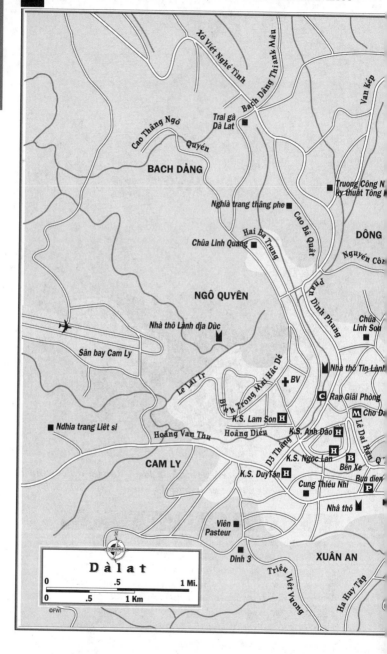

Dalat

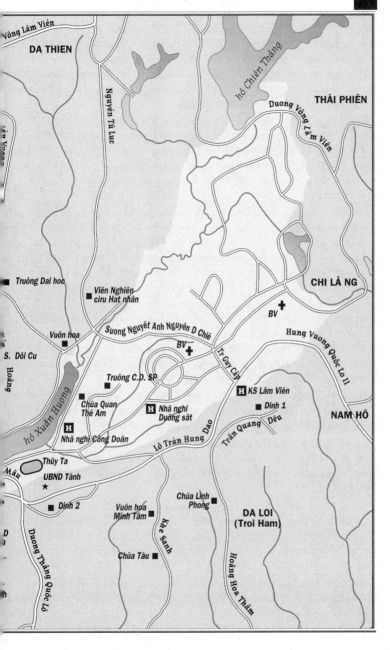

What can you say about Dalat (population about 130,000)? It's certainly one of the most beautiful cities in all of Vietnam and sits atop a mighty plateau at nearly 1500 meters. It features the best climate in Vietnam (warm days and cool nights all year round). Temperatures average here 24°C (78°F.) in the day and 15°C. (60°F.)at night. There is a rainy season from April through November, although even during these months it still rains infrequently and only for a short duration.

The Lang Biang Mountains to the north rise to nearly 2500 meters. They're inhabited by a number of ethnic minorities, including Montagnards Lat and Da Hoa tribespeople. In the center of the city is pristine Xuan Huong Lake. Around town there are waterfalls, beautiful gardens of temperate flora, deep pine forested valleys, a man-made reservoir, lakes and even a golf course.

Dalat was founded by Frenchman Andre Yersin, who convinced the French government to establish a hill station here in the late 1890s. There was a railway station here that linked Dalat with Phan Rang and Saigon (although it is defunct now). During colonial times, the Frenchmen of Saigon used Dalat as a summer resort to escape the intense heat of Saigon. Much of the architecture is French.

Dalat is still a popular resort destination with more than 2500 villas surrounding the region. Dalat is a more popular resort with the Vietnamese, rather than with Europeans and other Westerners, and the area is a favorite for newlyweds. Caravans of balloon- and streamer-covered cars and minivans traverse the hilly area, and honeymooning couples can be found at practically every attraction site dressed elegantly for photos.

Dalat was once well known as a big game hunting resort as late as the 1950s, but the wild animals—bears, rhinos, tigers, elephants and deer—that once roamed these once dense forests have disappeared.

I find Dalat mildly disappointing in a number of ways. Massive deforestation in the area has created bare mountainsides in every direction. This wasn't a result of the war, but instead the result of relentless commercial timber activities.

There was actually very little fighting in and around Dalat during the Vietnam War. In fact, high-ranking officers on both sides of the conflict used Dalat villas as retreats not more than a few kilometers apart. But comparatively little remains of the lush environment of the highlands surrounding Dalat.

Dalat has also become overcommercialized. At virtually every attraction in and surrounding the area are dilapidated paddle boats with duck heads that look like a cross between old Soviet submarines and floating bathtubs. "Cowboys" in attire out of the "Wild, Wild West" lead tourists around on ponies in these circuslike environments. There are "zoos" with poorly treated animals, and some unlucky enough to have been stuffed by omnipresent Vietnamese taxidermists and glued to trees and rocks. The sight of these rare and sometimes endangered species is sad. And these poor creatures are everywhere. In shops, at the parks, at the waterfalls, etc. If you care about animals, a visit to Dalat may be extremely depressing.

Thousands of Dalat dwellers were resettled by the new government after 1975 to areas down the plateau outside the city. One such Lat village is 20 km south out of town along Highway 20.

In previous years, you needed a police permit to visit many areas outside of Dalat—and the horror stories abound of corruption and bribery. But when I visited the immigration police station, I was politely told that a permit was only needed to visit Lat Village, about 12 km northwest of town. The permit costs US$5 and could be obtained through Lam Dong Tourism. You'll have to hire a guide through the tourism agency, however. At least it won't be a policeman or soldier.

There also used to be problems with foreigners checking into the few foreigner-permitted hotels. You'd have to file a phenomenal amount of information with the police. This is no longer the case. As in most of Vietnam, travel by foreigners is basically unrestricted in Lam Dong Province.

What to See and Do in Dalat and Environs

Xuan Huong Lake

Central Dalat.

This is an artificial lake that was created in central Dalat by a dam on the west end of the valley in 1919. The lake itself isn't particularly spectacular but it's surrounded by kiosks and cafes. Rent a bike and take the road that runs around the perimeter of the lake. Many locals swim here, but I'd avoid it, seeing what they toss into it. The lake was named after a controversial 17th-century Vietnamese poet. Unfortunately, this is one of the many water sites in Dalat where you can rent one of those Bozo bathtubs and paddle around for an hour or two.

Dalat Flower Garden

Set on the northeast end of the lake.

These beautiful gardens were established in 1966 by the South Vietnamese Agricultural Service. After becoming nothing more than a weed patch, the entire gardens were renovated in 1985. Here you can see both tropical and temperate flora, including hydrangeas, orchids, roses, fuchsias, lilies and camellias. How some of the flowers are grown is interesting—orchids are grown inside coconut palm trunks. Admission: 2000 dong.

Dalat's Cathedral, with its 48-meter-high spire, began construction in the early 1930s but wasn't completed until 1945.

Dalat Cathedral

Yersin and Tran Phu Streets, next to the Dalat Hotel.

Begun in the early '30s and not finished until 1945, the impressive 48-meter-high spire can be seen from all over town. The medieval-style stained glass windows were imported from France and were crafted by Louis Balmet. There are wood carvings of Jesus lining the nave. Masses are conducted every day at 5:15 a.m. and 5:15 p.m., and on Sundays at the ungodly hour of 4:00 a.m. as well as 5:15 a.m., 7 a.m., 8:30 a.m. and 4 p.m. This might be why the pastor seemed a little exhausted during our brief conversation.

Quan Am Tu Pagoda

2 Chien My Street.

Not a lot here, except for the Buddha with the electric halo around its head. The gardens are nice here, too. Worth a brief stop if you can tear yourself away from the nice monk, who'll want to keep you there for hours.

Linh Son Pagoda

120 Nguyen Van Troi Street.

There's a huge gold and bronze bell here. I did not see any women here and was told women weren't allowed by an old man trying to sell me incense. There are two dragons in front of the sanctuary with small ponds on each side of them.

Su Nu Pagoda

1 km south of Le Thai To at 72 Hoang Hoa Tham Street.

This pagoda is strictly for nuns, although men are allowed to visit. Don't visit here during the lunch hours, you'll offend the praying women, who are all bald-headed and wear gray or brown robes. It was built in 1952.

Domaine de Marie Convent

6 Ngo Quyen Street.

Built in the early 1940s, this convent once housed more than 300 nuns. The few nuns still around today make fruit and spice candies as well as the fruit they grow in an orchard out in back.

Minh Nguyet Cu Sy Lam Pagoda

At the end of Khe Sanh St.

Built in 1962, this is a Chinese Pagoda just across from the Thien Vuong Pagoda (see below). It is a round structure representing a lotus blossom. The sanctuary is to the right of the main gates after entering the path. Inside the pagoda is a statue of Quan The Am Bo Tat (the Goddess of Mercy). Lotus flowers can be seen all over the gates and the bars on the windows. The pagoda, as is Thien Vuong Pagoda, is very popular with Chinese and Hong Kong visitors. Take off your shoes before entering the pagoda after passing the few stalls that sell vegetable and fruit concoctions.

Thien Vuong Pagoda ★

At the end of Khe Sanh Street.

This is Chinese and one of the more interesting pagodas in Dalat. At the end of Khe Sanh Street a dirt path rises up a pine-covered hill leading up the pagoda. Souvenir stalls line the path up to the pagoda where there are two large yellow wood-built buildings. In the first building you will not be required to remove your shoes. In this structure is a statue of one of Buddha's protectors, Ho Phap and another statue of Pho Hien, an aide to the A Di Da Buddha (Buddha of the past). In the next building, where you'll be required to remove your shoes, are three huge Buddhas brought over from Hong Kong. These Buddhas are thought to be the largest sandalwood Buddhas in Vietnam. They represent Quan The Am Bo Tat on the right Sakyamuni (the historical Buddha) in the center, and Dai The Bo Tat on the right Behind the second building further up on the hill is a giant white Buddha overlooking the valley. The pagoda was built in 1958.

A large white Buddha at Dalat's Thien Vuong Pagoda overlooks the pine-covered Central Highlands.

The Tomb of Nguyen Huu Hao

The tomb is atop a 400-meter high hill northwest of Cam Ly Falls.
Nguyen Huu Hao was the father of Bao Dai's wife, Nam Phuong. Nguyen died in 1939.

Cam Ly Falls

57-59 Hong Ven Thu Street.
Busloads of tourists—that's what you'll find here along with cowboys, plastic guns and a lot of kids selling chewing gum and cigarettes. A guide here costs US$1 an hour and it ain't worth it, folks. You can adequately tour the small falls in under half an hour on your own quite well, thank you. Animal lovers will cringe at the stuffed jungle animals.

Valley of Love

Five km north of Dalat.
This place was given the name by students in the early 1970s who used to hang out here with their lovers. The original name was the Valley of Peace after Emperor Bao Dai decided *that's* what it should be called. Obviously, he was happy by himself. Now the place is a circus, with cowboys and others running around in bunny suits. You can rent those insufferable floating bathtubs here, as well as buy everything from lottery tickets to straw hats. The cowboys are the most annoying aspects of a visit here as well as the chewing gum hawkers. Refreshment stalls abound, as do tourists.

Dalat (or Crèmailllère) Railway Station ★

Five hundred meters east of Xuan Huong Lake and off Quang Trung Street.
This is a sight not to be missed. About a half-dozen ancient train cars and a black steam engine that has to be at least a century old lie on the track next to the pastel yellow railway station. Opened in 1938, the station used to serve Saigon through Phan Rang until continuous Viet Cong attacks on the track made the journey impossible, and the routes were shut down in 1964. However, tourists can now take the "train" about 7 km out of town to Trai Met Village for the ridiculous price of US$10 round trip. The journey's a novelty and pleasant—you pass well-tended, dense vegetable fields—but for 10 bucks?

Central Market

Located at the end of Nguyen Thi Minh Khai Street.
This is one of the most interesting markets in Vietnam and certainly the best for getting temperate produce and fruit such as strawberries, carrots, plums, avocados, cherries, potatoes, loganberries and apples. Friends in the south will be highly appreciative if you bring back a gift of some of these foods.

The French District

Hoa Binh Square area.
This is the area around Rap 3/4 cinema that's right off the Universal Studios lot. Move from Vietnam into France in only a few short footsteps.

Dalat University

1 Phu Dong Thien Vuong Street.
With the aid of New York's Cardinal Spelman, Dalat University opened its doors in 1957 as a Catholic learning institution by Hue Archbishop Ngo Dinh Thuc, who

Dalat

was the older brother of President Diem, assassinated in 1963. When Dalat was "liberated" in 1975, the university shut down but was reopened a couple of years later. Now more than a thousand students study here, from English to agriculture.

Dalat's Quang Trung Reservoir was created by a dam in 1980.

Quang Trung Reservoir (Lam Tuyen Lake)   ★

Head down Highway 20 toward Bao Loc. About 5 km from town, turn right down a rutted, dangerous rock and dirt path to the reservoir.

It was created by a dam in 1980 and, today, about 30 people live on floating houses in the reservoir. It was named after Quang Trung, one of the Tay Son rebellion's great leaders, who was responsible for repressing a vicious Chinese attack in 1789. The reservoir is situated in a deforested valley (there are some recently planted pine trees) beneath a spectacular new Vietnamese pagoda. There's not much to see here and there are only a few visitors, so the child gum and cigarette hawkers are at a minimum. There is one cafe and supposedly small power boats for rent, but I didn't see one on the entire reservoir.

Truc Lam Thien Vien Pagoda   ★

Overlooking Quang Trung Reservoir.

Also called the Bamboo Forest Meditation Center, this is a spectacular new Vietnamese pagoda of 24 hectares high on the bamboo forest hillside overlooking Quang Trung Reservoir. But it's a hike to get up there (222 steps). The new domiciles are now home to 52 monks and 45 nuns. The chief monk, Thong Triet (who will not leave the hillside pagoda for at least three years) will be more than happy to show you the giant sand and cement Buddha trucked up from Saigon at the altar, the four-layer curved roof of the Main Sanctuary as well as the 1100-kg bell that's rung twice a day (at 3 a.m. and 6 p.m.) cast and brought over from Hue. On the bell is carved a poem by Truc Lam Dau Da (Buddhist name of King Tran Nhan Ton, founder of the Vietnamese zen sect, 1258-1305). This is a magnificent new structure (built in 1994) with beautiful temperate flora landscaping. Inside the pagoda "giang huong" hardwood covers the ceiling and altar archways. Next to the main sanctuary is the Hall for Zen Consultations where, on the 14th and 19th days of each lunar month, the chief monk and his disciples gather to contemplate some of the mysteries of Zen. There's also a brand new guesthouse (Noi Vien) for visiting monks alongside the pagoda. If you're out of shape, a trek up to this pagoda is a day trip.

"Cowboys" toting plastic six-shooters are typical of Dalat's commercialism.

Lake of Sighs   ★

About 5 km on Phan Chu Trinh Street northeast of Dalat.
This lake, a natural one that was enlarged by a French-built dam, is supposedly named after girls who were brought here by students at Dalat's military academy. Another story says that it was named after the lovers Hoang Tung and Mai Nuong, who met and fell in love here during the 18th century. Hoang Tung then joined the army to help fight the Chinese, but left Mai Nuong unaware of his new duties and travels. When he left to fight the Chinese, Mai felt that she had been abandoned and drowned herself in the lake. The lake itself is nothing spectacular and largely denuded of its once-dense vegetation. There are a few souvenir stands here and the usual stuffed animals. Again, you'll find those cowboys with their little plastic six-shooters looking to bring you around the lake on horseback.

Datanla Falls

200 meters farther down Highway 20 from Quang Trung Reservoir.
The falls themselves aren't as impressive as some of Dalat's other waterfalls (and pale in comparison with Bao Loc's Dambri Falls), but the pleasant thing about them is that they lack the carnival-like environments of Dalat's other attractions. There is only a small viewing area, which is usually full of tourists picnicking. The down side

to these falls (again, forgive the pun) is that you've got to be a decathlete to reach them. The walk down the path is steep and long. If you're not in shape, forget it.

Prenn Falls

At the base of Dalat on Highway 20 at the Prenn Restaurant.

These are perhaps the nicest falls in Dalat, but they're packed with tourists, souvenir touts, mini-sailboats and Vietnamese on horseback dressed like Red Skelton on the set of Mel Brooks' *Blazing Saddles*. At an altitude of 1125 meters, water cascades off a 15-meter edifice into a brown-colored pool the size of a backyard swimming pool in Lubbock where you can rent these tiny toy ships for a "voyage" that's more like an ant crossing a cup of coffee. Kiosks and food stalls abound. The parking area is packed with minibuses. The park around the falls, sprinkled with palm-thatched gazebos was dedicated to Thailand's Queen in 1959. Admission: 5000 dong.

Prenn Pass ★★

This is the steep stretch of roadway on Highway 20 that leads down from Dalat past Quang Trung Reservoir, Datanla Falls toward Prenn Falls.

This is a beautiful, but sometimes narrow and dangerous road that's surrounded by tall palms and thick vegetation. Some of the scenery is magnificent. By motorcycle, you'll be tempted to do a Pike's Peak climb in record time. Don't try. The veering minibuses treat the road as if it was their own and use both sides of the road. A collision here and you're in for "dalat" of trouble.

Duc Trong Village (Quang Hiep)

20 km south of Dalat down Highway 20, flanking the roadway on the west side.

On one trip, a guide insisted that this small village was Lat Village. He was wrong. Instead this small agricultural community on the right side of the road is where displaced ethnic Da Hoa were forced to move into the valley by the government after 1975. There's not much here save for the kind villagers and a giant statue of a chicken. No one seems to have an answer for why it's there or what it means. Here, you'll want to visit Mrs. Nguyen Thi Kim Phung, an English teacher whose knowledge of the relocation of Dalat residents after 1975 is vast and interesting. She'll also want to guide you to the summit of Elephant Mountain, a four-hour, round-trip hike up the heavily deforested peak. In the past couple of years, perhaps because of this book, the gentle minority village has seen a surge of tourists, explaining all the new souvenir and crafts kiosks that have gone up along the path from the entrance. Regrettable, perhaps, but it's brought needed income to the area and hasn't seemed to have jaded the inhabitants' dispositions any. Worth a brief visit unless you want to do the hike, which offers spectacular scenery at the summit.

Lat Village

About 12 km north of Dalat.

Here is the only area around Dalat you'll need a permit to visit, which can be obtained through the Lam Dong Tourist Office for US$5. You'll have to use one of their guides and that'll cost you more. Why you need to obtain a permit to visit these nine small hamlets is a mystery to me. And by the time you read this, the conditions of visiting the village may have been lifted. The ethnic Lat, Koho, Ma and Chill tribes that inhabit the area really don't seem like the insurgent types, although many Lat and Montagnard people worked for the Americans during the war. Here, the houses are constructed of thatched roofs built on piles. There are about 300 hectares where the villagers grow rice and produce charcoal. Lat Village also has two Christian churches. It's worth a visit, but the US$30 or so you'll have to spend to make the trip may create some reservations about doing it. If you're able to visit the village independently, take Xo Viet Nghe Tinh Street north from Dalat. At the road fork in Tung Lam hamlet stay to the right. From Dalat's bus station there are a couple of buses a day to Lat Village

Lang Bian Mountain (Lam Vien)   ★ ★

30km north of Dalat.

These are five volcanic peaks, heavily deforested, and about a four-hour hike from Lat Village. The two highest peaks are called K'Biang and K'Lang, which reach up to about 2400 meters. Not so many years ago, tigers, bears, elephants, boars and rhinos roamed the peaks. But not anymore. The hike is worth it for the spectacular views.

Ankroët Lakes & Falls

About 20 km northwest of Dalat.

The lakes are actually part of a hydroelectric project. Many hill tribes in the area. The falls aren't spectacular, reaching a height of about 15 meters.

INSIDER TIP

There are a number of falls in the Dalat area that require a considerably long and steep hike to reach. Although most tourists in Third-World countries are in generally good shape, others aren't. If you have a heart condition or just plain can't blow out a candle from three feet, I recommend staying at the top, purchasing a souvenir or two and a postcard, and telling your friends at home how beautiful the falls were.

Where to Stay in Dalat

Even though tourism in Dalat is exploding it still seems that two of every three hotels in the city will not allow foreigners. If you find yourself in the center of Dalat and are not sure where to stay, it will be a waste of time to roam the streets—which are packed with hotels and mini-hotels (guest houses)—looking for a suitable hotel. You'll get frustrated. Even though the number of foreigners that visit Dalat is increasing rapidly, the overwhelming majority of visitors are Vietnamese on holiday. However, on the plus side, the cheaper hotels that once didn't provide hot water now usually do. And you'll want hot water in Dalat, even during the warmer months.

AUTHOR'S NOTE: TELEPHONE PRFIXES

The following telephone numbers are local exchanges. The country code is 84. The city code is 63.

Thanh The Hotel   **US$5–$12**   ★

118 Phan Dinh Phung Street. *822180.*

42 rooms.

Friendly English speaking staff; comfortable singles and doubles. Private bath, clean rooms. Hot water. Restaurant, cafe. Incredible value for the price, and one of the few hotels on Phan Dinh Phung Street that accepts (and welcomes) foreigners. A similar room in Saigon would go for twice as much money. This makes the Thanh The one of the best values in Dalat. Also, it is enhanced by its central location in the middle of town.

Thanh Van Hotel   US$20–$25

9/1 Phu Dong Thien Vuong Street. ☎ 822818; FAX: 822782.
21 rooms.

Clean, comfortable rooms, but a little pricey. Price includes breakfast. Restaurant. Private bath. Centrally located. Large, comfortable rooms. Car hire for local tours of the Dalat area.

Palace 2 Hotel   US$30–$50   ★

12 Tran Hung Dao Street. ☎ 822092.
28 rooms.

Hotel has been open for about six years. This place, an elegant structure and built in 1933, was formerly the Governor-General's Residence, and then was used as a guest house for dignitaries and for official receptions. Now anyone can stay if you're willing to pay the price, which includes breakfast. The pricier rooms are deluxe suites. There are 19 first-class rooms, seven second-class rooms. Rooms are large, almost palatial. Attached bathroom, restaurant, telephone and television in all the rooms as well as IDD services. Organizes area tours via vans, coaches and microbuses. I found the service here a little too stuffy, although friendly enough.

Hang Nga's Guest Home and Art Garden   US$15–$35

3 Huynh Thuc Khang. ☎ 822070.
12 rooms.

This is the most bizarre-looking hotel in the Milky Way, a treelike, dripping, sculpted building designed by Hang Nga (who may be the Southeast Asian reincarnation of Salvador Dali) that resembles an outcropping on Uranus. Something right out of a Steven Spielberg flick. Even if you don't stay here, if you're in Dalat, make sure you give this place a visit. They even charge 2000 dong just to go in and see the place. It's right out of Disneyland. However, the rooms are spacious and adorned in a cavelike motif with carved dragons and stuffed bears. Big baths. Sitting areas. The lighting is romantic and the place would make a good honeymooners' spot. A giant sculpted giraffe sits next to the complex—it's gotta be 20 meters high. Why it's there and what it has to do with the rest of the hotel's motif is a total mystery. The only hesitations about staying here are a couple of recent reports from travelers suggesting that the highly eccentric Ms. Nga has become a bit grumpy lately. I'd still stay, anyhow.

Sofitel Dalat Palace Hotel   US$120–$350   ★★★★

12 Tran Phu. ☎ 825444, 823496.
43 rooms.

Dalat's Hang Nga's Guest Home and Art Garden features some of the most bizarre architecture in the country.

This hotel has been thoroughly renovated, and it's taken four years. The building was originally erected in the early 1920s. It is a magnificent, big building with great views of the Xuan Huong Lake. The grounds themselves are beautifully landscaped. The hotel is seeking to get five stars. Whether or not it does, it's still the classiest in town.

Bao Dai's Summer Palace   US$30–$40   ★★
Biet Dien Quoc Truong.
This is a beautiful 25-room villa that was constructed for Emperor Bao Dai in 1933. This is now actually a hotel, but the place is a little ambiguous because it closes for "lunch" for a couple of hours during the day and you simply can't get into the place. Even the reception area is closed. I'm not sure what you'll want to do while you wait for the office to reopen about 1:30 p.m. You can also tour the palace/hotel when it is open whether you're staying there or not. Even if you're already a guest I'm still not sure you can get into the structure between 11:30 a.m. and 1:30 p.m. The attractions here are many. There's an engraved glass map of Vietnam that was given to the Emperor during the early '40s by Vietnamese studying in Paris before World War II began really taking its toll on the French people (and others studying there). The palace also features an ornate dining room and Bao Dai's office, which contains some of his books and other personal effects as well as his desk. The "palace" doesn't look really either like a palace or a hotel. Bao Dai spent his enormous amount of money on airplanes while stashing the rest in Swiss and U.S. bank accounts in anticipation of his political demise.

Savimex Guest House   US$25
11b 34 Street. ☎ 822640.
This is one of the first hotels you'll run into after cresting the mountain and heading down toward Dalat. Its hillside location offers good views of the mountains and the valleys. Relatively new building. English speaking staff. Hot water, restaurant.

Cam Do Hotel & Restaurant   US$10–$30   ★
81Phan Dinh Phung Street. ☎ 822732, 822482, 828010. Fax: 84-63-822661.
15 "standard" rooms.
Run by Dalat Tourist, this is one of the classier budget hotels—if not the best—in Dalat and quite a bargain. Price includes breakfast. Friendly, English speaking staff. Elegant lobby. Quite popular with foreigners in the fall. Clean, friendly and tastefully furnished. Rooms have private bath and hot water, as well as a refrigerator, color TV and telephone. Restaurant serving quite passable Asian and Western fare. There are also microbus tours of the Dalat area run by the hotel. Other tourist services, including airline booking. The hotel also provides one-way minibus service to Nha Trang, Phan Rang and HCMC.

Mimosa Hotel   US$7–$20
170 Phan Dinh Phung Street. ☎ 822656 or 822180.
31 rooms.
This is a friendly, centrally located hotel located in the heart of Dalat that looks more expensive than it is. Private bath, restaurant in the lobby. You can rent cars here for sight-seeing and the hotel will arrange bus and travel tickets. Mr. Long is

the man to talk to about Dalat, especially if you're planning an itinerary within a tight schedule. Popular with backpackers, but I also saw a couple of families here as well.

Nha Hang Huong Son   US$25

27 Duong 3 Thang 4. ☎ *822124.*
10 rooms.
Perhaps overpriced but comfortable. Hot water. Restaurant. Check to see whether they'll allow foreigners. For some reason, there's a disproportionate amount of hotels in Dalat that do not accept foreigners. One employee said yes, the other no.

Buu Tram Hotel   US$20–$30

138B Phan Dinh Phung Street. ☎ *822887.*
15 rooms.
A mostly non-English-speaking staff here that at present doesn't accept foreigners. However, the mamasan said this may change soon. Eight rooms with private bath, seven with public toilet. Room service.

Thang Long Mini Hotel and Restaurant   US$10–$20

154 Phan Dinh Phung Street. ☎ *822690.*
This is another one of those places that may or may not accept foreigners. Call in advance.

Ngoc Lan Hotel   US$32–$55

42 Nguyen Chi Thanh Street. ☎ *822136.*
25 rooms.
This is near the southern entrance to Dalat on a hill that overlooks the lake and the bus station. You can decide which is the better view. Totally renovated and enjoying a new life in the current tourist boom in Dalat.

Dalat Hotel   About US$25

7 Phan Tru Street. ☎ *822863.*
65 rooms.
A bit run down and the rooms are large, but I think it's too expensive, even though the views are nice. Hot water.

Anh Dao Hotel   US$29–$55   ★

50 Hoa Binh Square, up the hill from the Central Market. ☎ *822384.*
This is a renovated, spotless place with good service. Private bath. Hot water. Restaurant.

Minh Tam Hotel   About US$35–$50   ★

20A Khe Sanh Street (about 3 km out of town). ☎ *822447.*
17 rooms.
A bit out of the way but the views of the surrounding forests and valleys are nice. It was built in 1936 as the palace of South Vietnamese President Ngo Dinh Diem's infamous sister-in-law Madame Nhu. It was renovated in the mid 1980s and is especially popular with domestic tourists. All the amenities one would expect for 50 bucks.

Thuy Tien Hotel   US$20–$25

73 Thang 2 Street. ☎ *822444.*

This hotel is close to both the market and the bus station. A little run down for the price at last check, and this before they doubled the prices, as everyone in town seems to be doing. Hot water, restaurant.

Nha Khach Com   US$6

48 Phan Dinh Phung Street.
Out of the way, but cheap. Reasonable rooms.

Thanh Binh Hotel   US$7–$26

40 Nguyen Thi Minh Khai Street. ☎ 822394 or 822909.
42 rooms.
Near the Central Market and a decent value. Hot water. Attached bath. Restaurant.

Hai Son Hotel   US$15–$40

1 Nguyen Thi Minh Khai Street. ☎ 822379, FAX: 892889.
This is a musty, dirty and overpriced place, but the price includes breakfast. Hot water, attached bath. Not worth it.

VYC Hoa Hung Hotel   About US$15–$20

Lu Gia Street. ☎ 822653.
Reservations: Direct or VYC Tourism in HCMC, 180 Nguyen Cu Trinh. ☎ 84-8-8298707.
This is away from town but relatively new, clean and friendly. Attached bath, hot water; restaurant.

Duy Tan Hotel   US$20–$45

83-3 Thang 2 Street. ☎ 822216.
Too expensive. Dormitory setting as well as nondescript, private rooms with attached bath. Hot water.

Triaxco Hotel   US$35

7 Nguyen Thai Hoc Street. ☎ 822789.
8 rooms.
This overlooks Xuan Huong Lake and some of the rooms have a great view of the lake. But others don't. The rooms vary considerably, so look at a few before deciding (granted the place isn't full, of course). Hot water.

Phu Hoa Hotel   US$8–$15

6 Tang Bat Ho Street. ☎ 822194.
You could do worse in this price range. A little grotty but acceptable, if not comfortable. The higher-priced rooms get you hot water, necessary in the winter. The restaurant is passable, like the rest of the place.

Hoa Binh Hotel   US$6–$15

84 Truong Cong Dinh Street. ☎ 822787.
For foreigners, this is about as basic as you get in Dalat and, consequently, popular with backpackers. There's no hot water. The staff ranges from aloof to friendly, but the rooms need to be sandblasted; they wouldn't look any different if you threw a frag grenade inside.

Where to Eat in Dalat

Dalat has a reputation throughout Vietnam of offering only mediocre food. Of course these are Vietnamese comparing the Vietnamese food of Dalat with that available in other cations. However, most foreign travelers won't be disappointed by the food (particularly vegetarians), especially the Vietnamese food available in Dalat. Most of the hotels have their own restaurants and they are often empty, with a bevy of uniformed waitresses sitting around and not doing much. One reason for this is that food in restaurants is generally more expensive than dishes found in private restaurants or food stalls. One exception would be the Hoang Restaurant at the Thanh The Hotel listed above. The food is good and cheap. Because of Dalat's relatively temperate climate, it is an excellent source of vegetables and is a vegetarian's paradise. There are a number of small restaurants and cafes long Nguyen Thi Minh Khai Street that offer an excellent variety of Vietnamese dishes. Just pick the one that looks the cleanest. And something to remember about eating in Dalat: Restaurants where the prices are included in the menu are generally more expensive than eateries that don't list prices on menus. If the menu has been professionally printed, the same is true. If the menu is handwritten in Vietnamese only (with poor English translations, such as "Freid Eeg"), you'll know you're getting rock-bottom prices.

You may want to avoid the lakeside eateries, which are generally overpriced and serve average food. Backpackers mostly hang out at the Long Hoa and the Hoang Lang Restaurants. Some of the other places to eat:

Shanghai Restaurant   **$$**   ★

8 Khu Hoa Binh Square.
Vietnamese, Asian and European fare including "delicacies" such as goat testicles and beef penis. Interesting.

Thanh Thuy Restaurant   **$$**

4 Nguyen Thai Hoc Street. ☎ *822262.*
On the lake beneath the Triaxco Hotel. Vietnamese, Asian, European cuisine. Average but very popular.

Dang A   **$$**

82 Phan Dinh Phung Street.
Vietnamese and exotic Asian fare.

Cam Do   **$$**

81 Phan Dinh Phung Street.
This is typical of the cheap, good food that can be found outside of the hotels, but close by.

Xuan Huong   **$$**

Ho Xuan Huong Street. On the west side of the lake overlooking the water.
Vietnamese, Western dishes.

Pho Tung   **$$**

Near the Shanghai Restaurant.
Excellent bakery, average food.

My Canh   **$**

41 Nguyen Thi Minh Khai Street.
Excellent Chinese fare.

Thuy Ta   **$$**   ★

Just below the Palace Hotel.

If not for the food, which is decent, come here for the views of the lake. Breakfast is the best time.

Long Hoa $

6-3 Thang 2 Street.
Western-style breakfast, but open all day. Although the morning is the best time to hang out here.

La Tulipe Rouge $$

1 Nguyen Thi Minh Khai, between the market and the Hai Son Hotel.
Vietnamese, Chinese and Western dishes.

Nhu Hai $

In front of the Central Market.
Known for great vegetable dishes.

Cafe Tung $

6 Khu Hoa Binh Street.
Not really a restaurant, but a cafe with a rich history. Artists used to hang out here before 1975.

Directory

Transportation

Dalat is about 320 km from Ho Chi Minh City, 110 km from Phan Rang, 210 km Nha Trang, 1510 km from Hanoi, 320 km from Saigon, and 110 km from Bao Loc.

INSIDER TIP

Dalat's Lien Khuong Airport is slated for an upgrade, which will include lengthening the runway to 2600 meters, allowing direct flights from Singapore when Dalat's proposed US$500 million Dankia-Suoi Vang tourist complex opens. The airport lies about 4 km from downtown Dalat. Before 1975, it served as an air base.

By air:

There are four flights weekly from Saigon to Dalat (Tuesday, Wednesday, Friday and Sunday at 10:45 a.m.) and they cost about US$80 round trip aboard a YAK 40 or ATR-72. Flights from Dalat to HCMC are on the same days, departing at 12:30 p.m. You once could also fly to Hue on VN on Wednesdays and Saturdays at 10:40 a.m. But check the current schedule. Flights to Dalat from Hue leave Wednesdays and Saturdays at 1:20 p.m. when the Dalat-Hue route is being run by VN. Flight time is about 40-50 minutes to Saigon and 2 hours to Hue.

By bus:

Dalat has two bus stations (Dalat Bus Station—the long-distance station at the end of Nguyen Thi Minh Khai Street—and the local bus station which is a block north of Rap 3/4 Cinema). From the long-distance station, express buses leave for Saigon at about 5 a.m. (11,000 dong, 310 km) and take about 8-9 hours, Nha Trang (8400 dong and 5–6 hours, 205 km), Phan Rang (4,600 dong and 2–3 hours, 100 km), Hue (30,000 dong and a very long time), Danang (27,000 dong, 745 km),

Quang Ngai (22,500 dong), Quy Nhon (16,400 dong), and Buon Ma Thuot (17,000 dong, 395 km). Intra-Provincial buses connect Dalat with Bao Loc, Cau Dat, Da Thien, Di Linh, Ta Nun, Ta In and Lac Duong. The fastest way of getting away is by minibus from the local station, however.

Minibuses leave for Hanoi (69,000 dong), Hue (40,000 dong), Danang (35,000 dong), Vinh (55,000 dong), Quy Nhon (55,000 dong) and Nha Trang (11,500 dong).There is also hourly minibus service to Saigon for about 18,000 dong. Many hotels offer their own minibus services to Nha Trang, and some offer them even as far as Saigon.

By car:

Dalat is about a 6-7 hour trip by a late-model sedan. I did the trip in a little under 5.5 hours by large motorcycle, although I do not recommend you try to break that record. The road from Saigon to Dalat is usually quite wide and primarily in excellent shape (by Southeast Asia standards) but, nonetheless, there is a significant amount of pedestrian, ox cart, motorbike and bicycle traffic—so driving (or riding a motorcycle) is very dangerous. Fortunately, after the fork that splits off NH1 to Dalat, the traffic becomes quite light, except in the villages. There is far less traffic on Highway 20 than on NH1. Be especially careful on the road that ascends from Bao Loc to Dalat through the forested mountains. The road narrows significantly and becomes very steep and winding. Minibuses seem to take great pains to give their passengers the feeling they're on a roller coaster and frequently use the wrong side of the road when negotiating corners at extremely high speeds.

By train:

There is no train service presently to Dalat from anywhere but a couple of suburbs, rides that are usually taken on these ancient trains by tourists.

Around town, the best way to get around is on the back of a **motorbike**. You shouldn't have any problem finding someone willing to lend you their services for a day or two. Some will not even require payment. I paid one driver US$7 for two full days of journeying around the Dalat area. You can also travel by **horse cart** or ancient Peugot **taxis**. You can also rent a **bicycle** (if you're in good shape—the terrain is hilly). But you won't find a **cyclo**, because the drivers aren't in good shape.

Post Office
14 Tran Phu Street.

Banks and Moneychangers
Industrial and Commercial Bank of Vietnam. *46 Hoa Binh Square, above the market.* ☎ *822495.*

Tourist Offices
Lam Dong Provincial Tourist Office. *12A Tran Phu Street.* ☎ *822125.*
Dalat Tourist. *9 Le Dai Hanh.* ☎ *822479.*

Immigration Police
Lam Dong Provincial Public Security Immigration Office. *10 Thanh Binh Trong Street.* Hours are between 7:30–11:30 a.m. and 1:30–4:30 p.m.

Buon Ma Thuot

BUON MA THUOT IN A CAPSULE

500 meters above sea level...Principal cash crop is coffee...Fell to the North Vietnamese Army on March 11, 1975, 50 days before the war ended...Home to Rhade and M'nong hilltribe people...Population about 67,000...The M'nong are skilled at catching and taming elephants...Many new Chinese arrivals cashing in on the coffee trade.

Much of this area of the remote central highlands used to be off-limits t foreigners—especially Americans. But this is no longer the case.

Deep within the Central Highlands on the Dac Lac Plateau is the provir cial capital of Buon Ma Thuot (population about 67,000 and considered b many as the capital of the Central Highlands), not far from the Cambodia border. This is one of the least accessible areas in Vietnam, although you ca get there by car and bus. The bus journey from Saigon can take a grueling 4 hours in the rainy season.

The immigration police in Dalat told me that because of the lengthy and r diculous road routes to get there, very, very few Westerners make it out t Buon Ma Thuot. Although it is only perhaps 130 km or so as the crow flie northwest from Dalat (see below), to get there by road, you must first tak the highway east to the coastal city of Phan Rang (about 110 km), the NH1 north about another 160 km or so, well above Nha Trang (about 3 km), before heading on the road west to Buon Ma Thuot, a now decer roadway, for perhaps another 200 km or so. It means a trip from Dalat Buon Ma Thuot equals well over a whopping 400 km via public transporta tion!

But tourists can visit this city. This is an area that was designated a Nev Economic Zone after the fall of South Vietnam in 1975. Peoples of the Re River region near Hanoi and a significant number of Saigonese were dis laced to this area, where villages were created and the forests cleared. The leared land has yielded little in the form of crops, although the government alls Buon Ma Thuot a "major commercial center." Coffee is the principal rop grown here.

Buon Ma Thuot has the distinction of being the site of the last major battle etween NVA and South Vietnamese troops during March 1975 (guess who von?). Then South Vietnamese President Nguyen Van Thieu ordered a vithdrawal from the area (in fact the entire Central Highlands) and it was nly a short month later before NVA tanks rolled into Saigon.

Today, Buon Ma Thuot's population is ethnically divided, and there is ten-ion with the Rhade minority groups, who have been considered second-lass citizens for a number of years.

Buon Ma Thuot shares a similar rainy season with Dalat, but is usually varmer because of its lower elevation.

Along the 250 kilometers from Buon Ma Thuot to Kon Tum there are a umber of ethnic minorities, most noticeably the Austronesian tribes Jarai nd Raday. Buon Ma Thuot was also home to an American military base luring the Vietnam War.

In the center of town is the main square, which formerly featured the first NVA tank that entered the city poised on an angled monument. It has since een removed and will be placed in a museum, according to Dac Lac Tourist fficials.

Highway 27's Heart of Darkness

Our Dac Lac Tourist guide hunched down on a cluster of sharp porous rocks, the spray from Buon Ma Thuot's Drai Sap Waterfalls beading on his face and creating a miniature falls as it cascaded off the peak of his baseball cap and tumbled into his lap. His attention to my question was diverted a moment as he warned one of the Americans not to swim in the pool at the base of the thundering falls—he was sure to slice up his legs on the razor-sharp boulders, deceptively formed like a bed of nails only a meter below the surface. The guide issued the warning self-assuredly, as if he himself had the centipede scars of Drai Sap Falls' stitches as a testament to such foolhardiness. The American shrugged off the advice and stripped to his shorts. He dove head-first into the swirling waters. When oth-ers in the group saw his grinning face bobbing on the surface a few seconds later, they also stripped and entered the torrent. Dai, our guide for the morning, flicked his cigarette in the water and shrugged. "Nobody does that," he said. "Much too dangerous."

Dai had forgotten my question, seemingly more concerned about losing face should the Americans all emerge from the giant whirlpool unscathed. By the look of his mug—which reflected resignation rather than the concern for safety commonly seen etched into the faces of lifeguards—I uncomfortably discerned I was probably correct. He had no idea what lurked beneath the chop of the current.

Highway 27's Heart of Darkness

I repeated the question. Perhaps because he wanted to, Dai forgot the would-be drowning victims as quickly as he had sidestepped my first inquiry. Perhaps it was a cultural thing.

"Highway 27," he said finally. "It's very, very difficult. Very hard."

"Have you ever been to Dalat on 27?" I asked, stubbing my own butt and pocketing it, more concerned for the water than the Americans swimming in it. I'd hardly call myself an eco-traveler, barrelling unmuffled 750cc motorcycles through pristine mountain Mnong villages, but occasionally I make amends for my myriad environmental shortcomings.

"Of course I have," Dai said defensively.

"What's it like?"

"It goes through the mountains."

"I'll bet you can see some trees, too," I said.

Dai nodded and smiled, a little more confident that I was buying it. Of course, I wasn't. Now thoroughly relaxed, he went on almost arrogantly about the little-traveled route that connects Buon Ma Thuot and Dalat, claiming it was only 70 kilometers long and, that except for some 10 kilometers "somewhere in the middle" of it, it was a "fine road."

Later that day we were to find out how typical Dai's answer was with the responses of everyone else we asked. There was one thing all the briefings from the locals had in common—no two were alike. One guide said the road wasn't open to foreigners. Another said it didn't exist. A dentist who gets his supplies from Dalat said Highway 27 was in the hands of rebel Montagnards and that it was mined. An elephant trainer in Lak, about 50 kilometers south of Buon Ma Thuot, said that 27 was a four-lane divided highway, complete with street lamps, royal palms planted in the median, community service cleanup projects—complete with Port-O-Johns—and motorist aid call boxes. At least that was how our interpreter—whose entire family of nine ended up in Ocala, Florida in 1982 via a raft—described it.

Suffice it to say our group of 10 American motorcyclists and a crazy Spaniard were a little unsettled that night over BGIs and a bucket of ice at Buon Ma Thuot's Ban Me Hotel. We had come a long way over the past 15 days—from Ho Chi Minh City up the coast to Hue, back down Highway 1 to Binh Dinh, where we headed over to Pleiku on Highway 19 and then down to Buon Ma Thuot on Highway 14. Fortunately, only one in our "moto posse" had suffered an accident in the two-plus weeks on the road—an American rider went down in the sand at Nghia Lap, a beachside Cham village above Ca Na. He busted some ribs and retreated to the relative M*A*S*H unit the support van provided. He was taped up and forced to endure Bryan Adams and Whitney Houston tapes for the balance of the expedition.

Highway 27's Heart of Darkness

From Buon Ma Thuot we had to be back in Saigon in two days, namely because most of the guys had desks in San Francisco and Des Moines they had to get back to. So the soon-boozy discussion centered on whether to depart before dawn on Highway 26 for Nha Trang on the coast or cut our way through the remote Central Highlands along uncharted and perhaps even nonexistent Highway 27. In this case, the beer tipped the scales in favor of Lewis-and-Clarking it down 27 to Dalat. First, the suds inspired adventure. Secondly, we wouldn't have to get up as early—the suds also inspire unmitigated slumber.

We knew the first hop—the first 50 klicks to Lak—would be a snap. After all, tourists ride elephants down there. And tourists do little that's not a snap. The path, we assumed, had been carved for us by 18-seat Mitsubishis packed with accountants and schoolteachers swathed in safari shirts and SPF 32 sunscreen. We motored our way on the relatively paved first leg of 27 to Lak. Greeted by school kids roasting shellfish on the shores of Dac Lac Lake, we took a breather and an elephant ride through the rice fields in the valley that Dac Lac Lake encompasses—an olive drab, denuded bowl during the dry season that appears to have seen better times.

Riding an elephant isn't recommended for breaking up a long motorcycle trip. It's something akin to footballers doing windsprints at halftime. In fact, unless you have something really meaningful to be doing on the back of an elephant—say hauling hardwood or trotting around in a circle beneath a circus tent (and getting paid for it, of course)—the experience really isn't worth breaking up anything with. Our derrieres resembled the barnacle-studded hull of a shrimper, but we set out from Lak for Dalat at 11 a.m.—and the totally unknown. Quite simply, no foreigner had ever ventured down Highway 27—at least to the knowledge of anyone from Vientiane to Guam. I was told this beforehand by some folks who laughed when they said it. And then by some more folks, who also found it amusing. Again, it could have been a cultural thing.

We discovered quite suddenly that Highway 27 south of Lak became a winding, congealing mishmash of stones, dirt, mud and chunks of granite the size of basketballs. Motorcycle wheels churned into a deep-copper fog of dust so thick it created its own meteorological patterns. Clothes that had been recognizable as such at dawn had become bodysuits of sandstone armor. All of the riders appeared sculpted, and drying sweat threatened to immortalize us all as permanent roadside attractions.

What little of the road I could see resembled little more than a riverbed, as it carved its way high into the mountains. There were few other vehicles, mostly ancient motorbikes riding on their rims, piloted by tattered Mnong ethnic hillpeople ferrying goods and supplies to and from the few villages that flanked the full 80 kilometers of this sandstorm of the heavens. The area is so rugged and remote that occasional Montagnard villagers we came across dropped their jaws and chores in astonishment at the "long-noses," which, of course, they had never set eyes upon before.

Highway 27's Heart of Darkness

Tiny villages and settlements flanked the roadside every 10 km or so. Amazingly, ancient French buses plied the route, but none dared to make the entire journey from Dalat to Buon Ma Thuot, or vice versa. Instead, they ventured perhaps two-dozen kilometers from the cities into the mountains, where they deposited passengers and consumer goods and then gratefully returned. I saw that cigarettes, beer, gasoline and household items were moved by motorbike or by foot to other villages deeper in the rainforest along the roadway. Ancient, tiny Hondas and even bicycles were laden with hundreds of kilograms of wares. And only on a few sections of the roadway could the bicycle riders actually ride their bicycles. More often I saw cyclists walking their flimsy Chinese-made spoke buckets with these loads up seemingly insurmountable grades. Occasionally, a lone bulldozer or steamroller could be found deep in the heart of the jungle highway—idle, and with perhaps only one person around who knew what it was or how to use it. God knows how these machines got there, or what really anyone intended to do with them.

Without the benefit of anyone around I could speak the same tongue with having done this trip before, I was tricked into an chimera of relief by a mirage—the sight of pavement—about halfway through this highway from hell. I stopped and waited for the others along the first meter of asphalt. (We spaced ourselves about a hundred meters apart in order to attain enough visibility to see our front wheels.). Broiling in the midday sun, the group took refuge in the shade of a bamboo thicket. The Vietnamese tour organizer, Than, decided to recon the terrain which lay ahead. When he didn't come back with the big 750 cc Magna 10 minutes later, I became concerned and considered going out after him. But then I heard the report of the big machine laboring up the hillside. Than returned, but drenched in blood. The Honda was mangled, but with some forceful bending of its parts, it would ride again. Than wouldn't, having shred his arms and hands in a decidedly nasty spill.

"Good news and bad news," he said stoically, although in shock. "Good news is we're at the top. We start going down from here. Bad news is the road ends in 500 meters."

The trip from Buon Ma Thuot to Dalat took nine hours, covering a mere 165 kilometers. This was in March 1996. Today, the road has been paved, and the tiny Mnong villages that were only recently separated from the 17th century only by the two-stroke motor are bound soon to become "Dalatomized," as the Mitsubishis and camcorders move in. I've recently heard that the improvements on the road—stamping your feet would have improved it—have cut the trip from nine hours to a mere four, as progress claims yet another Vietnamese heart of darkness.

The desk clerk at the hotel in Dalat gazed upon this gritty assemblage of bikers in bewilderment as we checked in. When we walked through the lobby, we were followed by a young man in a white suit with a mop.

"We were told you came from Buon Ma Thuot today on Highway 27," the clerk said. "What is it like?"

"It goes through the mountains," I said, quite truthfully.

Highway 27's Heart of Darkness

Doing It:

Buon Ma Thuot is now quite accessible from Dalat, and "doing it" these days is far less problematic than my last pilgrimage to the region. By road, Buon Ma Thuot is about 460 kilometers from Ho Chi Minh City. Take Highway 1 north from Ho Chi Minh City to Trang Bo Ni, where Highway 20 begins meandering through the Central Highlands to Dalat. Highway 27 cuts north at Duc Trong (Lien Nghia) about 28 kilometers south of Dalat. I highly recommend breaking the trip up in Dalat, however.

For motorcycle rentals, there are few options. The best is **B&B Motor Service** *(258/75 Tran Hung Dao Street, District 1, Ho Chi Minh City;* ☎ *8393125)*. Ask for Mr. Binh, but bring a translator if you can't speak Vietnamese. You'll need an international motorcycle license which has been either translated into Vietnamese officially or exchanged for a Vietnamese license.

The less adventurous can go by minibus or car. See what kind of deal you can get from **Dalattourist** *(21 Nguyen An Ninh Street, District 1, Ho Chi Minh City;* ☎ *8230227; FAX: 8222347)* or **Vyta Tours** *(52 Hai Ba Trung Street, District 1, Ho Chi Minh City;* ☎ *8230767; FAX: 8243542)*.

What to See and Do in and Around Buon Ma Thuot

Museum ★

1 Me Mai Street.

This is a relatively interesting museum devoted to the ethnography of the Central Highlands. There are displays and artifacts representing Montagnard and Rhade traditions, among the traditions of other ethnic groups. There is earthenware here as well as agricultural tools. There are also displays of traditional Montagnard dress, musical instruments, ancient weapons and other artifacts from more than 30 ethnicities of the Central Highlands. There's also a traditional Rhade house here as well.

Draylon, Drai Sap, Drayling and Draynor Waterfalls

These are the several waterfalls that can be found outside town. None are terribly impressive but they rarely see tourists, which makes them that much more delightful to visit. Drai Sap Falls, about 12 km from Buon Ma Thuot, are the most dramatic; the falls are surrounded by massive hardwood trees. Regrettably, litter is becoming a problem. And be careful swimming here, as you'll be very tempted to do; ragged rocks ring the perimeter of the river and lie beneath the surface.

Lak and Dac Lac Lake

Lak is a small Mnong fishing and rice cultivating town about 50 km south of Buon Ma Thuot along the only decent stretch of Highway 27. Former Emperor Bao Dai used small amounts of money to build a small palace at Dac Lac Lake, also about 5 km south of Buon Ma Thuot and next to Lak. It's not much to see these days. But the lake itself makes for a relaxing way to meet the locals over grilled prawns. Students particularly like to relax here on Sundays. There's an elephant camp along the perimeter of the lake at Lak where visitors can take elephant rides lasting from one to three hours for up to US$50. However, the shorter rides have the beasts plod through nothing much more than rice fields and villagers' back yards. You'll notice the heavy deforestation of the surrounding hillsides. Many visitors erroneously attribute this to the defoliation of the region during the Vietnam War. Not the case, folks. That stuff all grew back; it was all simply cut down again.

Local Villages ★★

Foreigners are permitted to visit the local ethnic villages in the vicinity of Buon Ma Thuot and no longer need permission from the police to do so. You can visit the Rhade village Buon Tuo—13 km from Buon Ma Thuot. Here there are longhouses where matriarchal Rhade families dwell, although, in many instances, a male will preside over the community. There are also supposedly elephants in the Buon Don area that are captured and trained by the M'nong ethnic group. But there are elephants trained in Buon Don, a M'nong village about 56 km northwest of Buon Ma Thuot. Elephants can also be found at a camp in Lak, 50 km to the south of the city. They are captured through the use of domesticated elephants. The M'nong, like the Rhade, are a people whose surnames are passed down through the female rather than male lineage. The M'nong have a lot of animosity against all other ethnicities of the region, including ethnic Vietnamese, although the few Westerners that come to this remote pocket of Vietnam are greeted with great curiosity. There is also a 13th-century Cham tower in the area, about 35 km to the north in Ya Liao.

Yukdon National Park ★

The Don village is the gateway to this scenic 58,200-hectare national park, the largest in Vietnam. In addition to pristine tropical rainforest, rivers, waterfalls, mountains and lush jungle, this makes a great place to come for an elephant ride, whether it be for an hour or a week. Many of the elephants raised in the Don village have been bought by the park for transporting the few tourists who get here on guided tours of the park. The riders are either ethnic M'nong or Lao and have come from generations of elephant trainers in the Central Highlands. When not bringing the rare tourist through the jungle—or being put to work hauling lumber or having their tusks sawed off for the ivory market—the park's 45 trained elephants roam the park's hectares freely, although dragging along 15-meter-long chains so the trainer can track them and round the beasts up when they're needed to provide a few tourists (or an occasional busload of them) with a thrill. Although the dry season brings sparse vegetation to the jungle and an overall diminished lushness to the tropic flora, it is perhaps the best time to visit here, as the park's other exotic inhabitants—leopards, tigers, bears and deer—tend to congregate in the few isolated places where there is water, and are more easily spotted by park visitors. During the rainy season it can be quite difficult to catch a glimpse of anything that moves other than birds. The park offers what it stylishly calls "eco-tours" aboard the tuskless beasts ranging from a couple of hours to up to three days. A three-day tour aboard four elephants runs US$460 total, including guides, camping equipment (there are no accommodations in the park) and food. Those not wishing such a spartan existence can take day-long tours for US$60 per person, or simply an elephant ride at US$15 per hour per person. Contact **Dac Lac Tourist**, *3 Phan Chu Trinh Street.* ☎ *852108.*

Where to Stay in Buon Ma Thuot

AUTHOR'S NOTE: TELEPHONE PREFIXES

The following phone numbers are local exchanges. The country code is 84. The city code is 50.

Thang Loi Hotel   **US$25–$30**

1-3 Phan Chu Trinh Street. ☎ *852322.*
This is the largest hotel on Buon Ma Thuot. Dingy but comfortable.

Tay Nguyen Hotel   **US$20–$30**

106 Ly Thuong Kiet Street. ☎ *852250.*
The US$30 rooms have air conditioning. Comfortable. Restaurant.

Guest House   **US$7–$10**

42 Ly Thuong Kiet Street. ☎ *853921.*
Basic and popular with backpackers. Rooms with fan.

Hong Kong Hotel   **US$10–$15**

30 Hai Ba Trung Street. ☎ *852630.*
Basic accommodations. Public toilet.

Hoang Gia Hotel   **US$6–$10**

62 Le Hong Phong Street. ☎ *852161.*
Ditto. Inexpensive.

Where to Eat in Buon Ma Thuot

Stick to the hotels. Like a number of areas in the Mekong Delta, the folks here don't boil their water. I'd stay away from the food stalls unless you want to spend quite a bit of time in a stall of quite a different variety.

Directory

Transportation

Buon Ma Thuot is about 350 km from HCMC as the crow flies (and about 450 km by Highways 20 and 27 from Ho Chi Minh City), 1430 km from Hanoi, 160 km from Dalat, 225 km from Quy Nhon, 665 km from Danang and 190 km from Nha Trang.

By air:

From Saigon, VN flies to Buon Ma Thuot daily at 6:40 a.m. (Wednesdays at 10:30 a.m.), with a second flight added Mondays, Fridays and Saturdays at 10:30 a.m. VN flies from Buon Ma Thuot daily at 8:05 a.m. for HCMC (Wednesday at 4:30 p.m.). A second flight is added Mondays, Fridays and Saturdays at 4:30 p.m. Call VN for the latest schedule changes.

By bus:

There is regular bus service to Saigon, Hanoi, Dalat, Nha Trang and most other provincial capitals and major cities. Buses from Saigon leave from Mien Dong bus station. Although the trip formerly took an exhausting 20 hours (as the bus was forced to go up the coast to Nha Trang before cutting west to Buon Ma Thuot), by the time you read this, the time will have been cut nearly in half with the paving of Highway 27 linking Dalat with Buon Ma Thuot.

By train:

There is no rail service to or from Buon Ma Thuot.

By car:

See the above mileage information. Buon Ma Thuot is now accessible directly from Dalat along fledgling and treacherous Highway 27. The distance is only about 130 km, but it will be the roughest 130 klicks you've ever traversed. The route is not served in its entirety by public transportation (i.e., bus) but it is possible to negotiate the "road" by minibus, motorcycle or 4-wheel-drive vehicle. The key is finding someone willing to submit his vehicle to the punishment it will take. And if you break down, be prepared to settle in for awhile. There are absolutely no services in the heart of the roadway, save for a small store and "gas station" about 30 km from Route 20. You may receive food and shelter from the ethnic minority villagers, but don't expect a new alternator.

Tourist Offices

Dac Lac Tourist Office. *3 Phan Chu Trinh Street.* ☎ *852108.*

Hospital

6 Nguyen Du Street.

Post Office

4 Doc Lap Street.

Pleiku & Kon Tum

Pleiku (with a population of about 40,000 and an elevation of 780 meters) is a market town in the center of a massive and fertile plateau whose red soil is of volcanic origin. Most of the town's inhabitants are from a variety of ethnic origins. Pleiku was also the site of an American base that went through vicious shelling and mortar attacks by the VC during the war in February 1965. The attack was used as justification for the U.S. escalating its military presence in Vietnam (there were about 25,000 U.S. military "advisers" at the time in South Vietnam).

Kon Tum, about 50 km north of Pleiku, is also inhabited primarily by ethnic minority groups. Some of these peoples include the Sedeng, Jarai, Bahnar and Rengao. Kon Tum was the site of massive bombing by American B-52s during the Vietnam War and was essentially leveled by that and the fighting that took place between NVA and ARVN troops in the area in 1972. Kon Tum is extremely remote and should be seen by only the hardiest of travelers. Some government immigration officials told me that permits and fees were required to visit Kon Tum, while others said such documentation and fees were not necessary to see the region.

INSIDER TIP

Although virtually all of Vietnam is open to independent travel, always check with the local immigration police if you want to visit remote, inaccessible areas. The big problem here is that, in many instances, officers within the same province will tell you different stories, especially the farther away you are from the central tourist areas. And, believe me, Pleiku and Kon Tum are off the beaten track.

What to See and Do in Pleiku

There is not a tremendous amount to do here; but do see the magnificent **Gia Lai Forest** and **Yali Waterfall**. Also don't miss the elephant village of **Nhon Hoa**, where you may be able to ride an elephant (and that probably depends whether or not you're part of an organized excursion). There are also ethnic dance shows and cultural and folk shows in town.

INSIDER TIP

Unfortunately, one of the few ways to visit Pleiku is through one of Saigon-tourist's expensive tours of the area. If you take the tour to Pleiku, you'll have to surrender at least nine days of independent travel time, as the tour will also bring you to sights in Nha Trang, Buon Ma Thuot, Quy Nhon and Dalat, places you can easily reach on your own—and should. The following is the tourist agency's itinerary while stopping in Pleiku: After visiting the hill-tribe museum and Tua Village near Buon Ma Thuot, you'll travel overland and spend the night in Pleiku. Here you'll get an elephant ride in the village of Nhon Hoa and spend the evening seeing cultural and folk shows put on by ethnic minorities. That's it, folks. Even if you're on a tight budget, you might want to consider flying to Pleiku, as the cost is relatively cheap at about US$80 one way from Saigon. From Hanoi, it's about twice as much. The best bet is to fly to Pleiku from Danang for a day or two. The cost is US$80 round trip at last check.

Where to Stay in Pleiku

AUTHOR'S NOTE: TELEPHONE PREFIXES

The following phone numbers are local exchanges. The country code is 84. The city code is 59.

Pleiku Hotel   US$12

124 Le Loi Street. ☎ *824628.*
Considering you've got little choice in Pleiku, this isn't bad—and it's where most of the backpackers settle in. Clean upon last inspection.

Yaly Hotel   US$10–$40

89 Hung Vuong Street. ☎ *824858.*
The best place in town. Rooms with private bath, some with air conditioning. Restaurant. Clean and comfortable.

Directory

Transportation

Pleiku is about 550 km from Saigon, 425 from Nha Trang, 200 km from Buon Ma Thuot and 185 km from Quy Nhon.

By air:

VN flies to Pleiku from HCMC on Sundays, Mondays, Tuesdays, Wednesdays, Thursdays and Fridays at 11:50 a.m. From Pleiku, flights depart for HCMC on the same days at 4:30 p.m. Flights from Pleiku to Danang leave at 1:35 p.m. every day of the week except Saturday. Flights from Danang to Pleiku depart at 3:10 p.m. on the same days.

By bus:

There are non-express buses that leave from Pleiku to the coastal cities between Nha Trang and Danang. From Saigon, there is express bus service to Pleiku (about 22 hours).

Airlines

Vietnam Airlines Booking Office. *Yaly Hotel.* ☎ *823834.*

Post Office

69 Hung Vuong Street. ☎ *824006.*

Hospital

Tran Hung Dao Street. ☎ *824125, 24111.*

Tourist Office

Tran Phu Street. ☎ *824271.*

What to See and Do in Kon Tum

The spectacular 40-meter-high **Jrai Li Waterfalls** are perhaps the best reason to visit the region. They can be found about 20 km southwest of Kon Tum.

Directory

Transportation

Kon Tum is about 900 km from HCMC, 50 km from Pleiku, 248 from Buon Ma Thuot, 200 km from Quy Nhon, and 435 km from Nha Trang.

By air:

You'll have to fly into Pleiku (see the above VN air schedule) and I suggest combining a trip to Kon Tum and Pleiku by flying into Pleiku from Danang.

By bus:

Buses leave Kon Tum for Danang, Pleiku and Buon Ma Thuot.

By car:

You can rent a car (and driver) to get to Kon Tum. It's worth only a day trip from Pleiku, as Kon Tum has few accommodations for foreign travelers.

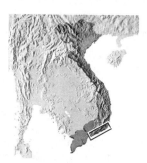

THE SOUTH COAST

Scenic Cam Ranh Bay has been used as a naval base by several countries, including the Russians, the Japanese, the Americans and the Soviets.

Bustling National Highway 1 runs north from Saigon nearly 200 kilometers before you get your first glimpse of the sparkling blue South China Sea near Phan Thiet.

Yeah, sparkling for a change. If Saigon's closest beach towns of Vung Tau and Long Hai were your introduction to the South China Sea and the Vietnamese coast, you're probably wondering what all the fuss about Vietnam's beaches is really about, and glad you didn't spend your three or four grand on a beach vacation. Not only are the two towns somewhat an eyesore themselves, the waves lapping onto their silty stretches of "sand" aren't all that appealing either. The problem, of course, is that Vung Tau and Long Hai lie close to the mouth of the Saigon River, and a number of other riverines that have carried mud and the refuse of every riverside dweller from the Cambodian border to Saigon to the open ocean.

Such isn't the case with Vietnam's southern coast. Far enough away from Saigon in a number of ways, the beaches of southern Vietnam are perhaps unmatched by the balance of the Asian mainland. And the beaches and topography of the southern Vietnam coastline vary more than in any other coastal region of the country. Just north of the historically rich and scenic coastal city of Phan Thiet, the Vietnamese landscape becomes dry and barren. Rock outcroppings and cacti poke the sky from the base of the Truong Son Mountains, whose magnificent peaks now begin to parallel the coast for nearly a thousand kilometers. The region here will remind you more of Mexico's Baja peninsula than anything you pictured Vietnam to be. Further north the coastline becomes verdant and lush, with sweeping mountains cascading to the sea's edge.

For the watersports enthusiast, the relentless slicing breezes of Phan Thiet create ideal windsurfing and jetskiing conditions, and the burgeoning number of watersports resorts here are answering the call. The azure, glass-smooth inlets at Ca Na present secluded, pristine marine environments for snorkelers, set against a backdrop of old gun turrets used during the Vietnam War.

Cam Ranh Bay, arguably the most scenic strip of Vietnamese coastline, is void of any development altogether—allowing for breathtaking Hawaii-like vistas of electric-green banana and palm forested hillsides and vast stretches of deserted white sand beaches.

The southern coast also introduces visitors to the relics of the once-great Champa kingdom, which stretched from Phan Thiet to Hue in the 15th century. Some of the best examples of Cham architecture can be found in and around the Ninh Thuan provincial capital of Phan Rang, including the 13th century Po Klong Garai towers and Po Re Me Cham tower. Small Cham villages still dot the roadside along Highway 1, and the more adventurous can journey off the beaten path to more remote inland and beachside villages offering an undisturbed, untouristed culture and mores unchanged for 400 years.

Enough with the tourist brochure fluff. Fortunately, Highway 1 straddles the sea for much of the journey up the coast. Unfortunately, it is also Vietnam's most congested artery. A combination of internal bickering among government deep pockets; shoddy, cut-corner engineering and severe wet seasons the last couple of years have left the highway in miserable repair for much of the year—good reasons to make the journey slowly if going by car, bus or motorbike.

Phan Thiet

Phan Thiet

Colorful fishing boats flank the Phan Thiet River.

PHAN THIET IN A CAPSULE

Largest city in Binh Thuan province...About 120 miles northeast of Saigon...Population of 75,000...Clean, casuarina-lined, breezy beaches... Famous in Vietnam for its fish sauce (nuoc mam)...A Cham-controlled area until the late 17th Century...Now targeted as major tourist destination.

Phan Thiet is usually the first stop travelers stay overnight when heading north from Saigon, and the last when heading south from Hue, Danang or Nha Trang to Saigon. There's not a lot to note here, but the beaches—both Phan Thiet and Mui Ne, 25 km to the east—are clean and expansive and offer a refreshing way to kick back after a hot ride from Saigon. Crossing over the Phan Thiet River on National Highway 1 near the river's mouth at the South China Sea, you'll see row after row of brightly colored fishing boats tied along both banks. The roads are wide and tree-lined in and outside of Phan Thiet and are usually uncrowded, making sidewalk dining at food stalls comfortable. The enormous width of National Highway 1 leading to Phan Thiet from Saigon was the work of the U.S. Army Corps of Engineers during the Vietnam War. In the effort to widen this central artery between Saigon and Phan Thiet, engineers razed countless buildings, but only partially. It's a bizarre sight to see houses and other structures that appear as if they had gone through a jigsaw. Their owners simply slapped on corrugated metal siding and continued their lives—in half a house. For miles these half-houses flank the highway south of the city.

The north bank of the Phan Thiet River was home to European settlers in the 18th and 19th centuries when Phan Thiet was a relatively bustling port. Prior to European colonization, the city was under Cham control. And this part of Vietnam is still heavily populated with Cham descendents. In fact, even today, the plains and mountains around Phan Thiet have a population consisting of only about 30 percent ethnic Vietnamese.

In Phan Thiet, swimmers don't bother donning bathing suits.

Phan Thiet is the southernmost city of the former principality of the Cham. Once known as Panduranga, it was once, until the 18th century, entirely left to itself by the Vietnamese because of its inhospitable climate. Slanting from the northeast to the southwest, the region remains relatively free of the monsoons, which, like Ca Na to the north, create an environment not unlike

Mexico's Baja peninsula. What was originally the coast of Panduranga extended nearly 250 kilometers. Panduranga once reached 100 kilometers west into the valley of the Ndau Nai, which is now referred to as the valley of the Dong Nai River which flowed down to Saigon (then called Raigauv). The Mnong Plateau to the east once served as a natural barrier between Panduranga and Cambodia. The region was comprised of a number of towns that still exist today: Tanh Linh, Di Linh, Dalat and Bao Loc.

Today, Phan Thiet is poised to become a hotbed of tourism. The Hai Duong Resort has just opened at Mui Ne Beach, and with it Western-style attractions, such as windsurfing and kayaking. Other resorts are planned for the area as well as an 18-hole golf course. More and more Saigonese are flocking out here on the weekends and bypassing the dirtier Vung Tau area.

The tourist office is located at *82 Trung Trac Street,* which is just on the south side of the Phan Thiet River near the bridge.

What to See and Do in Phan Thiet and Environs

Phan Thiet Beach

Phan Thiet Beach, covered with casuarina pines, isn't your typical palm-lined tropical beach, but it's clean and offers some pretty heavy surf, almost the kind of surf you can surf in. But don't get out the board. There are beach chairs for rent in this parklike atmosphere. You can sit and drink for free but you've got to rent a chair. It's a popular place with the locals and, as with the vast majority of Vietnam's beaches, the Vietnamese remain in the protective shade of the pines and coconut palms above the beach, leaving this wide aisle of buttery sand nearly deserted save for occasional bathers. Only foreigners are stupid enough to lie in the sand nearly naked under a burning sun. The best way to reach Phan Thiet Beach is to head east at the pointed Victory Monument. You can't miss it. You'll reach the dunes just a few hundred yards later. It's usually pretty windy here.

Harbor

South side of town, east of the bridge over the Phan Thiet River.
Phan Thiet's harbor, which is usually packed with bright, multicolored fishing boats, makes for great photos. Try photographing from the bridge that spans the Ca Ti (Phan Thiet) River.

Mui Ne Beach

About 12 miles east of Phan Thiet.
This is also a nice strip of sand at the end of the Mui Ne peninsula with rising sand dunes and gusty winds. You can get here either by car or bus. Previously, if you were just looking for a beach to relax on, the trip out probably wasn't worth it, as Phan Thiet Beach offers as much in scenery and more in amenities. But that's starting to change, as resorts are beginning to go up along this stretch. Mui Ne is no longer nearly as isolated as it was, which is good news and bad news.

Vinh Hoa

Off NH1 between Phan Thiet and Phan Rang.

Vinh Hoa is most famous for its mineral water, which is bottled and sold all over Vietnam. It's a small town just off the highway.

Where to Stay in Phan Thiet

AUTHOR'S NOTE: TELEPHONE PREFIXES

The following telephone numbers are local exchanges. The country code is 84. The city code is 62.

Mercure Ocean Dunes Resort & Golf Club   US$100–$300   ★ ★ ★ ★

Phan Thiet. ☎ *822393. FAX: 84-62-825682. For information on the golf course,* ☎ *84-8-8997443.*

123 rooms

The Mercure Phan Thiet Hotel is the first southern Thailand-style oceanside mega-resort to hit the shores of Vietnam and is shaping up to be one of the best resorts in Vietnam, in fact, the only real resort in the country. Nautical theme throughout. Perhaps the friendliest and most capable hotel staff in Vietnam. Rooms with all the amenities; the suites are fitted with Jacuzzis. Restaurant with international cuisine specializing in seafood. 24-hour room service, full business facilities and conference rooms, fitness center, steam bath, massage, shops, swimming pool, two tennis courts and watersports activities, including windsurfing and jetskiing. But the real kicker here is the Nick Faldo-designed, 18-hole, par-72, 6825-yard Ocean Dunes Golf Club, managed by International Management Group. This is actually a helluva course, casuarina-lined and set alongside the sea—meshing splendidly with the natural surroundings. The whole resort is quite mind boggling, surreal really—particularly when you're reminded where you are by the red flag flying out in front of this place.

Phan Thiet Hotel   US$15–$25

40 Trang Hung Dao Street. ☎ *82573.*

This is where you should stay if you're on a budget while staying in Phan Thiet. It's in the center of town, but it's only about a 10-minute walk to the beach. All the rooms have air conditioning, attached bath, and they're generally quite clean. There are doubles and triples in this hotel.

Khach San 19-4   About US$15

1 Tu Van Tu Street. ☎ *82460.*

This big hotel is just across the street from the bus station and formerly didn't permit foreigners to stay. But this has changed. Air conditioning, restaurant.

Vinh Thuy Hotel   US$45   ★

This expensive hotel is right on the beach on Ton Tuc Thang Street. ☎ *821294 or 22394.*

This is a new structure, built in 1989, although it looks older. And it's expensive. But it's the only choice in town if you want to stay on the beach. Air conditioning, restaurant. Rooms are clean. To get to the hotel follow the directions given above to Phan Thiet Beach. You'll see the multistoried hotel on the left.

Hai Duong Resort Coco Beach   US$32–$56   ★ ★

Mui Ne/Phan Thiet Beach. ☎ *823591. FAX: 823590.*

New resort at Phan Thiet/Mui Ne Beach that seems to be poised to become a harbinger of what's to become of this growing area. Comfortable bungalows. 15 villas. Restaurant, bar; private beach with bar. Watersports, including windsurfing, sailing and boat rentals. Mountain bike and moped rentals. Hurry, because these prices won't last long, I'm told.

Where to Eat in Phan Thiet

Extremely cheap sidewalk foodstalls offering great Vietnamese fare and seafood abound in this port city, but if you must:

Phan Thiet Hotel $$

3rd Floor, Phan Thiet Hotel; 40 Tran Hung Dao Street.
Vietnamese. Relatively expensive.

Vinh Thuy Hotel $$

Ton Tuc Thang Street, on the beach.
Great seafood at moderate-expensive prices.

Directory

Transportation

Phan Thiet is about 200 km from HCMC, 248 km from Dalat, and 250 km from Nha Trang.

By bus:

From HCMC, buses depart for Phan Thiet at Mien Dong Bus Station. The bus station in Phan Thiet is on Tu Van Tu Street on the northern edge of town. Non-express buses leave here for HCMC, Bien Hoa, Phan Rang, Long Khanh, Phu Cuong, Madagoui, Mui Ne Beach and other destinations. Best to purchase your tickets in advance.

By train:

The Reunification Express train runs in both directions up and down the coast from the town of Muong Man, which is about 10 km northwest of Phan Thiet.

By minivan:

Minivans leave the Sinh Cafe on Pham Ngu Lao Street, Dist. 1, daily at 7:30 a.m. The price of a one-way ticket is US$10. The journey takes about three hours. This is no day trip.

Around town:

Cyclos were the cheapest and only way to get around Phan Thiet. However, bicycles and small motorbikes can be had from some of the hotels these days. About US$1 for the bicycles and about US$6–$8 for the mopeds.

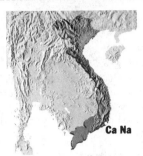

Ca Na

Ca Na

Former U.S. military turrets dot the beaches around Ca Na.

CA NA IN A CAPSULE

Isolated and arid...a great overnight stop on National Highway 1...Few people, lots of clean, clear ocean...Take panoramic photos from the tiny mountainside pagoda...Terrain is much like Mexico's lower Baja peninsula...Popular stop for tour buses making their way both north and south.

There's not a helluva lot here, and that's Ca Na's appeal. After a grueling ride over rutted National Highway 1 south from Nha Trang or north from Phan Thiet, Ca Na is what the doctor ordered, as long as you're not expecting a five-star hotel, or even a one-star hostelry for that matter. The accommodations are a little primitive and you'll think the tiny town is a winter destination for migrating flies. But get it out of your mind, snap the tab off a cold one, and enjoy the warm clear waters of this magnificent bay. The sea- food in the town's three restaurants is superb and the scenery is some of the most unique in Vietnam. If you didn't hear Vietnamese being spoken around you, you'd swear you were in Baja, Mexico. Cacti poke from the rug- ged, boulder-strewn mountains that lace this semicircular transparent bay. Casuarina pines tower from the bluffs overlooking the long, deserted beach. There's even a gun turret and bunker left over from the war facing the ocean, defiantly keeping the masses from developing this unique little spike in the South China Sea that will remind you as much of Vietnam as Mazatlan does.

Ca Na

Arid Ca Na offers Baja California peninsulalike vistas.

What to See and Do in Ca Na

There's basically nothing to do here but swim in the warm ocean and enjoy the views. Take a hike up into the mountains. (Be careful. Although the locals say the area has been pretty much depleted of its indigenous fauna, there may be snakes.) Take a brief visit up the stairs to the Chinese pagoda resting precariously on the hillside opposite the Hai Son Restaurant and take photos of the clear bay. At night, drunk new friends that you've made will invite you up into the hills to shoot wild animals. Best to decline the offer un- less he has the gun pointed at you.

Where to Stay and Eat in Ca Na

Hotels

Ca Na Hotel   **About US$15**

National Highway 1. You can't miss it.
10 rooms.

A backpacker's type of place, but the accommodations are sufficient for more upscale visitors. Breezy and desertlike. The Ca Na Hotel looks like a beat-up '50s American motel, but it's right on the beach. The ocean here is very calm and clear, turquoise in hue. The rooms are large and airy and have ocean views. Private toilet but no hot water. Electricity problems. You'll need the mosquito net more for the flies than for the mosquitoes. If you're traveling with a Vietnamese guide, you may get away with paying as little as US$8 a night.

Hai Son Hotel   US$15

Right next to the Hai Son Restaurant.
10 rooms, all facing the sea.
A small Chinese pagoda overlooks the town perched on the side of a mountain. You can climb a bunch of steps to get up there.

Restaurants

Ca Na Quan Restaurant $

National Highway 1.
Right on the beach, patio over the water. Excellent seafood, from lobster to urchin to squid. Cheap.

Nha Hang Hai Son $

National Highway 1.
You can rent cars out of this place; great seafood, right down the street from both hotels.

Phan Rang

The four brick Po Klong Garai Cham Towers date from the 13th century.

Phan Rang (population about 50,000) is sort of a dumpy little nondescript semi-seaside city along the coast a little more than halfway between Phan Thiet and Nha Trang. It also serves as the capital of Ninh Thuan Province. Its attractions have nothing to do with the city itself (there are even few hotels for foreigners) but the surrounding Cham towers that rise above the landscape, in particular Po Klong Garai towers, offer magnificent views of the surrounding mountains. And it is this tower complex that is really the only reason you should veer off NH1 through Phan Rang, unless you need to change money or buy table grapes (which are grown here and sent to Saigon).

The climate of Phan Rang itself is relatively dry and arid, although from the Po Klong Garai towers, you can view the arid landscape south toward Ca Na and the more lush mountainside bordering the sea toward Cam Ranh Bay in the north. As well, you can see the concrete remnants of the U.S. air base called Thanh Son to the north. It was used by Vietnamese Air Force as well as the Soviets until the collapse of that nation. Also you can view from the hill the water tower the Americans built during the war in 1965. Surrounding it are the gun turrets the French built during the First Indochina War. There's a bunch of prickly cacti in the area as well as poinciana trees.

The reason so many towers are in the area is that Phan Rang was once the capital of Champa when it was known as Panduranga. There is still a significant number of Chams that live in the area, and they all seem to be horribly poor, despite the city's trickling trek toward relative economic prosperity.

You'll be tempted to try to find a map of the surroundings identifying sites of Cham towers, but you'll be disappointed. In fact no maps at all (including of Vietnam) are available at any of the newsstands/bookstores in Phan Rang. As I mentioned earlier, buy all the maps you'll need in Saigon or Hanoi. You'll be hard pressed to find any anywhere else.

What to See and Do in Phan Rang and Environs

Po Klong Garai Towers ★★

About 7 km from Phan Rang off the road toward Dalat.

This is a spectacular set of four brick Cham towers, highly visible at Thap Cham. To get there take the road to Dalat and turn right onto a dirt road about 2 km past the village Thap Cham. A landmark will be a water tower. When you see it, turn right. The towers are atop a granite, rock-strewn hill called Cho'k Hala Hill just about 200 meters down the road. The biggest of the four towers *(kalan)*—all of which are in remarkably great shape—built as Hindu temples in the 13th century, was constructed in 1306. There's an image of Siva with six arms appearing to be dancing above the entrance. The image itself was reputedly carved in the 12th century, although recently renovated. The pillars surrounding the entrance have detailed inscriptions. Inside it's dark, and the thick incense constantly burning can be overwhelming and make the visit inside a short one, as you'll soon need fresh air. But inside on a raised dais is a lingam featuring a human face, which is said to be that of King Po Klong Garai. It is believed to have been carved in the 16th century. The face is covered with a white dough mask, which is changed during every ceremony. Inside the narrow vestibule is the carving of a bull which was called Nandin, a symbol of agricultural prosperity. There is a tower opposite the kalan's entrance that was originally the main entrance to the kalan. Here there are renovated inscriptions carved into the brick. This definitely is worth a visit if you're passing through Phan Rang. Don't be surprised to find a number of young Vietnamese girls dressed in *ao dais* eager to practice their English with foreign visitors. It was here that I met one such woman who had brought her teacher along to help. The man insisted that the

Vietnam War was lost by the Americans because of a mind-control machine a Vietnamese scientist developed in the early 1960s, giving him the power to redirect American opinion of American involvement in the war. He insisted that the device is still in use today, and that it's thought-control waves are delivered through television. Then he said he spent a year in a Saigon mental hospital. Even though he insisted I give him my address, I have yet to receive one of his ears in the mail.

Po Nagar Cham Towers were built between the 7th and 12th centuries.

Thap Cham Rail Yards

About 300 meters southeast of Po Klong Garai, next to the railroad station.

The main purpose of the yards, built by the French around 1915, is to repair the old railroad engines used by Vietnamese Railways. The Vietnamese are ingenious in their repair methods, as spare parts are made by hand through thoroughly antiquated machinery processes. There was an 85-km-long line between Thap Cham and Dalat, but it was closed in 1964 due to repeated VC sabotaging of the tracks. Chains used to pull the trains up the mountainsides. You can see the steepest mountain along the rail line from the road to Dalat from Phan Rang.

Po Re Me Cham Tower

It's on a rocky hill about 10 km southwest of Phan Rang and 5 km toward the mountains south of Phan Rang off NH1.

This is more recently constructed than the towers of Po Klong Garai. It can easily be seen from the summit of Cho'k Hala Hill. It was one of the many towers and sanctuaries that encircled the capital, as these towers do in all Cham capitals. It was named for the last Champa ruler King Po Re Mi (1629–1651). Many archeologists believe the structure was built much earlier than the king's reign, perhaps as early as the beginning of the 16th century. Paintings decorate the interior. There are also two statues of the bull Nandin here. There is an excellent life-size image of Siva carved into a relief on a stele. However, this image of Siva has eight arms rather than the six found at Po Klong Garai. There are five figures that are next to the statue— one is a wife of King Po Re Me (Bai Tan Chun). There's another wife of the king, Princess Po Biah Sucih. A third figure was another wife of the king, the Vietnamese princess Po Bia Ut. There are also chapels in the area with Hindu influences, but they lack the classic Cham style. They are located in the Huu Duc village of Hau Sanh.

Po Nagar

This pagoda is about 15 kilometers east of Phan Rang.

It's a 19th-century Vietnamese pagoda that celebrates the Goddess Po Nagar. Here there are statues of women and a stone which represents the Mother Goddess.

Tano Po Riya

50 kilometers from Phan Rang at the base of the mountains.
This is a small chapel in Malam. Ask for directions.

Po Rayak

This means God of the Sea and the Rains and rests on the mountain of Cape Padaran. There is a large festival that takes place, in the southern part of the province in March which draws virtually the entire province's population.

Ninh Chu Beach

This is a relatively nice stretch of unspoiled and deserted beach (for the most part) sand. About 4 km south of Phan Rang.

Tuan Tu

South on NH1.
This is a small Muslim Cham village 5 km south of Phan Rang. Go about 250 meters after you cross a large bridge. Here, you'll come across a smaller bridge, after

which crossing you'll turn left onto a dirt path. You'll come to a market which is just after a Buddhist pagoda. Turn right on the road at the market for 2 km. You'll then cross two small foot bridges. Depending on the mood of the Provincial Immigration office, you may need a permit to visit here, as well as dishing out fees for a guide, even if you already have one. There is a Cham Mosque. The elected officials of the village can easily be recognized by their ornate costumes, featuring white robes and a turban with long red tassels. The women wear traditional Cham headdress.

Where to Stay in Phan Rang

Huu Nghi Hotel   **About US$12–$25**

1 Hung Vuong Street (just off the road to Thap Cham). ☎ *822606.*
20 rooms.
Some rooms with air conditioning here, but the staff is friendly and they welcome foreigners. The lower priced rooms are a little dingy.

Phan Rang Hotel   **US$10–$20**

254 Thong Nhat Street.
20 rooms.
Didn't get a chance to visit here, but I'm told it's the most popular hotel in Phan Rang with foreigners.

Thong Nhat Hotel   **US$15–$20**

164 Thong Nhat Street. ☎ *822515.*
16 rooms.
This is a relatively new hotel. Restaurant, hot water, air conditioning in the high-end rooms.

Where to Eat in Phan Rang

Huu Nghi   **$**

1 Hung Vuong Street.
Great Vietnamese fare.

Nha Hang 426 (Restaurant)   **$**

Across the street from the bus station.
Vietnamese, Asian dishes. A good place to hang out while waiting for your bus.

Thu Thuy Restaurant   **$**

Thong Nhat Street.
Vietnamese, Asian. Delicious and cheap.

Nha Hang 404 (Restaurant)   **$**

404 Thang Nhat Street.
Vietnamese.

Directory

Transportation

Phan Rang is about 330 km from Saigon, 105 km from Nha Trang, 110 km from Dalat, and 147 km from Phan Thiet.

By bus:

The Intercity Bus Station is opposite *66 Thong Nhat Street*, about 500 meters north of the center of the city. There are regular connections with Saigon, Danang, Nha Trang, Dalat, Ca Na, Cam Ranh Bay, Don Duong, Long Huong, Phan Thiet, Noi Huyen, Song My, Nhi Ha and Phan Ri, to mention some. Buses leave Saigon from Mien Dong Bus Station. The local bus station is at *428 Thong Nhat Street*, south of town.

By train:

The station is located at Thap Cham, 5 km west of town and within sight of Po Klong Garai Cham towers. Trains serve all coastal destinations.

By car:

From Dalat, the trip takes about 2 hours. From Saigon on NH1, about 7–8 hours.

Banks and Moneychangers

Foreign Exchange Service. *334 Thong Nhat Street*. There are also a couple of jewelry and gold shops along Thong Nhat Street (which is what NH1 is called going through Phan Rang) that will exchange money, but be prepared to accept a sack of small 2000 dong notes.

Tourist Office

Ninh Thuan Tourist (in Vietnamese: *Cong Ty Du Lich Ninh Thuan*). Inside the Huu Nghi Hotel.

Phan Rang

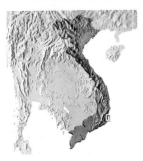

Cam Ranh Bay

Hootches hide behind coconut palms and banana trees south of Cam Ranh.

CAM RANH BAY IN A CAPSULE

Hawaii of the Orient...Laid-back and lush...This was the site of the largest U.S. naval base in Vietnam during the war...Has been utilized as a naval base for five nations since 1905...The Russians even managed to maintain a presence here after the Soviet Union collapsed...The area is a major salt-production site....A great place to build a summer home and start your own navy.

Traveling up NH1 from Phan Rang toward Nha Trang lies some of the most beautiful coastal topography in southern Vietnam, much of it in the Cam Ranh Bay area. Salt paddies and small, primitive processing plants dot the roadside—and on both sides of this beautiful natural harbor are towering, lush mountains supporting banana plantations and fringed by dense coconut palm groves. The water here is a crystal-clear, sky blue. Perhaps the most disappointing (or rewarding, depending on your viewpoint) aspect of the area is its distinct lack of tourist facilities. This is simply because Cam Ranh Bay has traditionally served as a major naval station for nations including the Russians in 1905, the Japanese during WWII, the Americans during the Vietnam War, and the Soviets again after the Americans left; the area is still a military zone. In fact, even after the fall of the Soviet Union, Russia still managed to maintain a small fleet in Cam Ranh Bay (it was once their largest base outside the Soviet Union)—as a symbolic gesture of defiance if nothing else. Now, in the strangest turn of events, there's talk about the U.S. Navy returning to lease the base—but this time from Hanoi!

In the 1960s, U.S. forces made this area a massive naval institution, and the area has not yet shed it's militarylike milieu. Touring the area today is still difficult—even though the Russians have mainly left. It is still considered militarily sensitive, which is a shame, because there's really nowhere to stay and it's the kind of environment you could see yourself spending a few days in, if not longer. The beaches all along the bay are terrific—unspoiled, empty white sand stretches for kilometers.

Where to Eat in Cam Ranh Bay

The number of food stalls along NH1 approaching Cam Ranh is staggering. Proprietors dart out into the middle of the highway with each approaching vehicle to entice the driver to stop at their eatery. Choose among the dozens that are here. The seafood, including eel, squid and fresh fish crab, is excellent. But be warned. If you're traveling independently without a Vietnamese, you will be charged as much as three times higher than a Vietnamese would, or foreigners traveling with a Vietnamese.

INSIDER TIP

When traveling with a Vietnamese, let this person do all the work for you, in both restaurants and in hotels. Never order or ask for anything yourself. Don't even point at what you want. Tell the Vietnamese guide or friend what your wishes are. If the proprietor has even the slightest indication that you are requesting something yourself, you will be charged more, even if your Vietnamese companion is present. You don't believe me? Go ahead and order that 333 beer, and later see on your bill that it cost 10,000 dong, while it would have cost 5 or 6 thousand dong had your Vietnamese companion ordered it for you.

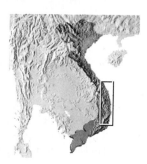

THE CENTRAL COAST

This might not be an example of Vietnam's sandy white beaches, but the rugged coastline makes for a nice change of pace between Nha Trang and Danang.

As it is along the southern coastline of the country, the lifeline of the central coast of Vietnam is National Highway 1, which straddles the coast in this part of Vietnam from Nha Trang to Danang to Hue, offering both spectacular coastal vistas and superb mountain scenery as well as glimpses into Vietnam's both distant and recent past.

The most magnificent coastal pass I've ever had the opportunity to ride is found a few kilometers north of Danang. Hai Van Pass winds and cuts its way through cloud-shrouded jungle and finally reaches an altitude of 500 meters before snaking back down to the gin-clear flats at Lang Co. For the most impressive scenery make the crossing early in the day, because after about 11 a.m. this place lives up to its name, Pass of the Ocean Clouds, and you'll get lost in the stratosphere.

359

Vietnam's central coast begins at Nha Trang, a popular tourist stop with an absolutely gorgeous seaside location at the base of the Truong Son Mountains. Nha Trang is to Vietnam's coastline what Dalat is to the Central Highlands. Heavily touristed, the city offers both cultural attractions, such as pagodas, the Po Nagar Cham towers and the Pasteur Institute, and superb topographical features offering the outdoors enthusiast a bounty. The waters of Nha Trang's numerous offshore islands make for some great (or lousy!) scuba diving, windsurfing and jetskiing. Resorts have recently sprung up here solely for these purposes. For the adventurous, many of the islands off Nha Trang, such as Bamboo Island and Salangane Island, can be reached by small boat.

About 85 kilometers up the coast from Nha Trang is found secluded and scenic Dai Lanh Beach, a resort that never came to be (fortunately), which offers a little-touristed, relaxing place for lunching on local seafood delicacies, washed down with ice cold beer. Yummy.

Quy Nhon was the site of some bitter fighting during the Vietnam War and was the venue where most of the South Korean contingent in-country saw action. There are a couple of Cham towers in the vicinity, but most use the town as an overnight stop between Nha Trang and Danang. The beaches here are unimpressive. About 175 kilometers north of Quy Nhon is Quang Ngai, an undistinguished spec on the map inland from the beach that is known by most for its proximity to the site of the 1968 My Lai massacre, where more than 500 Vietnamese civilians were gunned down or killed otherwise by American soldiers sniffing out alleged VC enclaves. A small memorial park and museum mark the site today.

The "ancient village" of Hoi An, about 30 kilometers south of Danang, is perhaps the most unusual of all Vietnamese towns, at least in appearance. The town, with its iconoclastic mix of 17th-19th century European, Japanese and Chinese architecture, was once a major international seaport. It was left unscathed during the Vietnam War. The only drawback is that the town has been "discovered" by tourists, and has started resembling a theme park.

Close by is China Beach of Vietnam War fame, or at least the beach the tourist officials have designated as China Beach. The real China Beach, which was used as an R&R spot for war-weary GIs, is reputedly about five kilometers north of this spot, which features a popular restaurant and usually booked hotel. There's some decent surfing here when the typhoons kick up the waves in the deep South China Sea. The Marble Mountains are also another popular attraction of the Danang area, as is the Cham Museum down-town.

Then head over to Hai Van Pass to Lang Co Beach for some shell collecting before heading up to Hue, the ancient capital of Vietnam, and the venue for some of the fiercest fighting of the Vietnam War. Although Hue is heavily touted by tourism cadres, it can be a disappointment unless you're a true scholar of ancient Vietnamese history. Many of the area's attractions, such as the Imperial City, were pulverized into rubble during the 25-day siege of Hue during the Tet Offensive of 1968. Most of the other royal sites aren't in any better condition. Oh, well.

Cham clergymen rarely see foreigners, and are even less likely to give you permission to photograph them.

Nha Trang

Nha Trang

Nha Trang

Nha Trang's huge white Buddha was built in 1963.

NHA TRANG IN A CAPSULE

Lazy and beautiful fledgling beach resort city of 200,000 that may one day unfortunately acquire the commercialism and gaudy trappings of Thailand's Pattaya or Bali's Nusa Dua Beach...Offers some of Vietnam's best year-round weather...The beach here is nearly four miles long...Port was established in 1924 and was a popular recreational spot for American sailors during the Vietnam War...The site of some of Vietnam's most magnificent Cham towers...The Po Nagar Cham towers offer spectacular views of the city and harbor, the ocean and islands, and the surrounding verdant mountains.

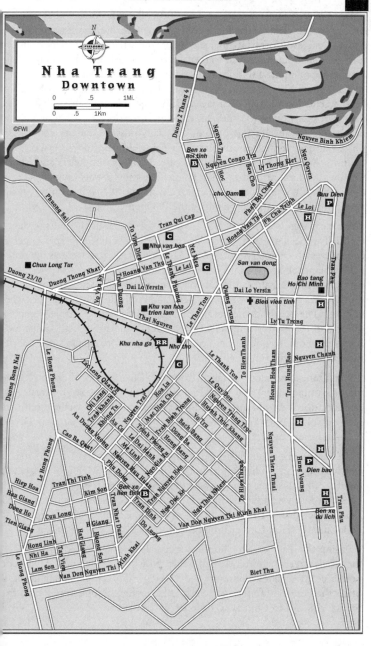

Nha Trang

Nha Trang
Downtown

©FWI

Nha Trang (population about 210,000) offers the best combination of clean beaches, clear water and traveler's amenities for the least amount of people than any coastal city in Vietnam. Asked what city travelers would return to after doing a coastal tour of Vietnam, most say Nha Trang. Other than its topographical setting, architecturally it's not a particularly beautiful city. It's not a historical and cultural icon like Hue. It lacks the colorful and heart-wrenching Vietnam War sagas of Danang. It is, though, probably Vietnam's closest answer to a developed tropical resort city. Its four miles of beaches are clean and uncrowded, especially outside the city center. The water is usually quite clear, making Nha Trang a diving and watersports destination. And, yes, jet skis—the bane of ecotourists, snorkelers and jellyfish worldwide—have arrived in Nha Trang. We knew it was only a matter of time. Only a couple of short years ago, watersports in Vietnam was taking your family on an inner-tube raft to the Philippines.

The clear waters of Nha Trang are great for scuba diving and snorkeling, especially off Mieu Island, which can easily be reached by ferry, passenger excursion vessels or small private boats. Unfortunately, this area has the potential of being developed into a major seaside tourist mecca of the likes of Pattaya or Phuket, although this will take some years. The small pockets of tourist areas are packed with foreigners, and rarely do you see any elsewhere in town. The beachside boulevard of Tran Phu is usually virtually empty of traffic and there are a number of hotels lining the street, although they're across the boulevard from the beach, which is coconut palm-lined and features a number of comfortable cafes.

Nha Trang (the name is taken from the Cham word "Yakram," which means bamboo river) also has perhaps Vietnam's best coastal climate, as it can cool down significantly here in the evening. Unlike farther south, the rainy season in Nha Trang runs only from October through early December—and even then, rain usually falls only at night.

There are some magnificent Cham towers (the Cham Po Nagar Complex) which sit high atop a hill on the north bank of the Nha Trang River, near its mouth, offering spectacular views of the city, beaches, the harbor and mountains that reach west far off into the distance. Few tourists visit areas of Nha Trang other than the seaside, except to see the Cham towers, Long Son Pagoda, and the Hon Chong Promontory.

During the Tay Son rebellion in the late 18th century, Nha Trang fell to the rebels after nine bitter days of battle. Now it is a two-tiered city offering both a sleepy seaside community and a bustling city center, which, ironically offers the best food found in the city. Nha Trang's architecture ranges from French colonial to Chinese to post-1975 Vietnamese.

What to See and Do in Nha Trang

The Beaches ★

Nha Trang offers some of the best beaches in all of Vietnam. There is Nha Trang Beach, which runs parallel with Tran Phu Blvd. The coconut-palm lined white sands are dotted with cafes and food stalls. This is where most visitors to Nha Trang come to sun themselves and bathe in the warm, clear waters. As you move down the beach south toward the Bao Dai Villas, strollers, sun worshipers, bathers and souvenir hawkers become fewer and farther between. This is a beautiful, clean stretch of sand surrounded by calm waters that is nearly 6 km long. Hon Chong Beach is actually a few beaches which surround the Hon Chong Promontory. The palm-lined sands are on a beautiful sky-blue bay surrounded by tall, lush, banana and mango tree-covered mountains. Many of the area's fishermen live here.

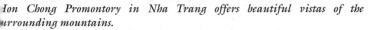

Hon Chong Promontory in Nha Trang offers beautiful vistas of the surrounding mountains.

Hon Chong Promontory ★★

Just north of Nha Trang (about 3.5 km from the city center).

A tall granite hillside overlooks the small crystal-clear bay where Hon Chong Beach is. You can get here by following *2 Thang 4 Street* past the Po Nagar Cham Towers and turning right on Nguyen Dinh Chieu Street, which leads up the hill to the promontory. There's a decent restaurant and souvenir kiosks at the promontory and a small run-down hotel nearby (Nha Nghi Hon Chong) that's currently closed. From the bluffs of the promontory, you can view the Fairy Mountains, three peaks that are supposed to look like a sleeping fairy (I'll tell you, these Vietnamese!) but look like nothing more than three verdant peaks. Toward Nha Trang, down Hon Chong beach, you can see the small island of Hon Do and its Buddhist temple on top. To the northeast is Tortoise Island. You can also see the two islands of Hon

Nha Trang

Yen in the distance. The giant rocks of the promontory here are reputed in legend to have been carved by the hands of a giant. A large "handprint" is on one boulder on top of the promontory. Local lore has it that the print was made by a drunk male fairy after he was caught peeking at a female fairy swimming in the buff and then fell down. (Unfortunately, today the only carving in the rocks is being done by drunk vandals with spray paint cans. Graffiti covers some of the stones.) Although the two fairies eventually married, the male was caught by the gods and sent off to "prison" for his previous voyeurism. After the female could wait no longer for her lover to return, she lay down and turned into Fairy Mountain. I think that Disney could use some of these guys as writers. Admission is 6000 dong per car.

Gallery

20 Tran Phu.

Vietnamese artists' and sculptors' works on display and for sale. Oil paintings, lacquer paintings, wood engravings, silk paper paintings, etc. Universal Sciences of Library of Khanh Hoa Province.

Phong Trung Bay My Thuat Gallery

16 Tran Phu. ☎ *822277.*

The various works of several Vietnamese artists and sculptors. Works for display and sale.

Pasteur Institute ★

Tran Phu Street, across from the beach.

Andre Yersin, who came to Vietnam from Paris after working for Louis Pasteur and lived for four years in the Central Highlands documenting his experiences, was perhaps the most beloved of all the Frenchmen by the Vietnamese in the late 19th and early 20th centuries. Yersin was the man who "discovered" Dalat and recommended that the French government establish a hill station there. He also was the first to introduce quinine and rubber-producing trees to Vietnam. But perhaps he is best known as being the man who discovered the cause of bubonic plague. Yersin founded the Nha Trang institute in 1895 to help research ways of improving Vietnamese hygiene and immune systems. Today, the institute performs the same functions. It develops vaccines and conducts research in microbiology, epidemiology, and virology, and develops disease vaccines using primitive equipment. Yersin's library has now been made into a museum. On display here are antiquated research equipment, personal items and the doctor's books. Open every day from 7:30–11 a.m. except Sunday and holidays.

Po Nagar Cham Towers ★★★

On 2 Thang 4 Street (just on the north side of the Xom Bong bridge).

There were once eight magnificent towers on this granite hilltop overlooking the picturesque Nha Trang region, but only four remain today. Po Nagar (locally called Thap Ba) means "Lady of the City," and the towers were built between the 7th and 12th centuries. Well before then, during the 2nd century AD, the area was an important Hindu worshipping hilltop. The largest tower is the 23-meter-high Thap Chinh, built in AD 817 by a minister of King Harivarman I named Pangro, which houses the statue of Lady Thien Y-ana (the wife of Prince Bac Hai). Lady Thien

Y-ana taught agriculture to the people as well as weaving. The remaining towers were constructed in honor of the gods, the central tower (or Fertility Temple) in honor of Cri Cambhu. The northwest tower was built for Sandhaka (the foster father of Lady Thien Y-ana) and the south tower for Lady Thien Y-ana's daughter, Ganeca.

Some 40 years before the north tower was built, it was raided by Malay corsairs from Sumatra who burned and ransacked the area. A gold mukha-linga was put in the north tower by King Indravarman III in AD 918, although it was later hauled off by raiding Khmer bandits. The mukha-linga was replaced with the stone figure of a shakti of Shiva by King Jaya Indravarman I in AD 965.

The central tower was erected in the 12th century, and is considered the least well-built tower in the complex. Its pyramidal roof possesses no terracing or pilasters.

There's a museum next to the north tower that contains examples of Cham stone-work, but relics that hardly rival the magnificent examples of Cham stonework found at the Cham Museum in Danang. The towers are worth a visit if only for the views from the top of the hill. Don't do Nha Trang without seeing them. Admission: 5000 dong.

ong Son Pagoda ★

23 Thang 10 Street.

The Buddha in this temple, founded in the late 19th century, is lit by natural light from behind it. The pagoda itself has been rebuilt a number of times and is now dedicated to the monks and nuns who perished through self-immolation protesting the South Vietnamese Diem regime during the Vietnam War. There are ceramic tile and glass images of dragons on the roof and the entrance to the structure. There are also murals telling of jataka legends covering the upper walls of the pagoda. The principal sanctuary is decorated with dragons wrapped around the columns on both sides of the main altar. Stairs on the right side of the complex head up the hill toward an approximately 10-meter-high white Buddha seated on a lotus blossom. The big Buddha can be seen from many parts of the city.

au Da

About 5 km south of Nha Trang.

This is a tiny, nondescript fishing village best noted for being a good way to get out to Mieu Island, for the Bao Dai Villas and also for the Aquarium. But there are some superb views of Nha Trang from the promontory which is the site of the villas. There's an abundance of souvenir kiosks in Cau Da for tourists while they haggle over private boat fees to the island. Many of the "souvenirs" are stuffed sealife, but you can purchase some fine, polished seashells and seashell jewelry.

ceanographic Institute and Aquarium

From Nha Trang, go down (south) Tran Phu Boulevard toward the Bao Dai Villas, which becomes To Do Street south of the airport.

Built in the early 1920s, this is a disappointing display of ocean creatures and plant life in Cau Da. The aquarium's more than 20 tanks contain seahorses, lobsters, turtles and the like. There's a museum of preserved sea creatures behind the aquarium featuring perhaps 60,000 preserved specimens of local sealife. As well, there are stuffed fish and sea birds.

Where to Stay in Nha Trang

> ### AUTHOR'S NOTE:
> ### TELEPHONE PREFIXES
>
> *The following telephone numbers are listed as local exchanges. The country code is 84. The city code is 58.*

Ana Mandara Resort   US$80–$150   ★★★

Nha Trang Beach. ☎ [66] (2) 354-4775/6 in Bangkok for reservations. FAX: [66] (2) 354-4566. Internet: http://www.sonevapavilion.com.
16 villas with 68 rooms and suites.

This is the new standard in Nha Trang. Right on the beach and set in 20,000 square meters of tropical gardens overlooking the ocean. Traditional Vietnamese-styled rooms with all the amenities and private terraces. Restaurant, lounge. Watersports center offers scuba diving, snorkeling, windsurfing, jetskiing, parasailing. The noisy sports are done on an island offshore. Tennis court, swimming pool, fitness center, sauna and massage. Business and conference facilities..

Cau Da Villas (Bao Dai Villas)   US$40-plus   ★

Tran Phu Street at Cau Da. ☎ 822449, 822249 or 821124.

These villas, about 3.5 miles south of town off Tran Phu Street, were once the classiest accommodations in town and used to be the estate of the former Emperor Bao Dai. The villas were renovated recently and offer incredible views of the sea, the harbor, and Bamboo and Mieu Islands, although it's a little disappointing when freighters are anchored offshore, as they often are down here. But the villas are an outstanding bargain for the price. The rooms are large, open and airy—with bathrooms to match. All the amenities you'd expect at twice the cost.

Thuy Duong Hotel & Restaurant   US$7–$15

36 Tran Phu.
10 rooms.

Air conditioning in the cheap rooms. Restaurant. Sort of a lazy place frequented by beer-swilling, but polite, locals. Pool tables in front. Not much going on. I saw no tourists here, but they are accepted.

Hotel Hoa Hong (Mini Hotel)   US$15

26 Nguyen Thien Thuat. ☎ 822778; FAX: 823842.

A bit off the beaten track. Not particularly close to the beach, nor the hustle and bustle of the city center. But clean enough. Few tourists.

Thong Nhat Hotel   US$12–$27   ★

18 Tran Phu Street. ☎ 822966 or 822511.
86 rooms.

On the beach strip. Tall, attractive building—the upper floors offer a great view of the islands if you can get a room facing the water. The cheaper price gets you a reasonably comfortable room with two beds, a ceiling fan and hot water. The splurge price gets you the above plus air conditioning, a refrigerator, telephone and TV. Overall, this is a very nice place for the price.

ıst Hotel
US\$20–\$25

2 Tran Phu Street. ☎ *821181.*
24 rooms (2 suites).
Located on the far north end of the Tran Phu strip across the street from the beach. Brand new building and hotel. Opened only a year ago. Friendly, helpful and eager staff—perhaps because they're new. Glamourous white deco building. Clean as a whistle. Get a room on one of the higher floors for a view of the sea. Although it's quiet enough, I'd stay away from the rooms off the lobby if you can. Telephone, refrigerator, TV, air conditioning.

uy Tan Hotel (Khach San 24)
US\$11–\$30 ★

24 Tran Phu Street. ☎ *822671.*
83 rooms.
This building, across Tran Phu from the beach, looks like a toppled ice-cube tray, but it's a popular place. A word of caution. It seems each room has a different price. I counted at least eight different prices, so know what you're getting into. A number of rooms offer separate meeting areas. Restaurant, car rentals, tours, catering, laundry, barber/beauty salon. Photo developing.

ien Dong Hotel
US\$7–\$50 ★★

1 Tran Hung Dao Street. ☎ *821606 or 821608; FAX: 821912.*
84 rooms (6 suites).
This is the most happenin' place in town. Just up Tran Hung Dao from the beach, this place is truly a bargain if you take one of the cheaper rooms on the top floor. You'll be able to take advantage of the hotel's amenities which, on a Vietnam scale, make the Vien Dong a full-blown resort. There's a large swimming pool, pool tables, a tennis court, badminton court, and a huge outdoor cafe where traditional Vietnamese dance shows are performed a few times a week. There's a top-shelf gift shop, restaurant and bicycle rentals. The service is friendly, albeit a little slow. The cheap rooms offer fan, hot water, public WC. The pricier digs come with air conditioning, color TV, telephone (IDD) and refrigerator. This is my choice when in Nha Trang, although it's somewhat sterile, packed with foreigners, and you have to pay to use the pool.

ai Au 1 Hotel
US\$15–\$20

3 Nguyen Chanh. ☎ *822862.*
21 rooms.
Tucked away off the beachside drag of Tran Phu, this is a small, unassuming, quiet, and basic hotel that might be just a little overpriced. But the service is friendly and laid-back. Popular with both overseas Vietnamese and Westerners. Air conditioning, hot water.

Hau Au 2 Hotel
US\$15–\$25

4 Nguyen Chanh. ☎ *823644.*
15 rooms.
This is a more attractive and newer building than its sister up the street. Hot water, air conditioning, restaurant, rest area.

Khatoco Hotel
US\$30–\$60 ★★

9 Biet Thu Street. ☎ *823724, 823725, or 823723; FAX: 821925.*

Nha Trang

Nha Trang's Khatoco Hotel leaves no guessing who it's owned by—a giant tobacco monopoly.

26 rooms.

This is the classic example of the invasion of capitalism in Vietnam. In the middle of relative squalor with no particular strategic or marketing reason to be there, rises this modern, elegant, dazzling white monolith founded in marble, smoked glass and chrome that looks right off the set of *Miami Vice*. Atop the roof are suspended giant packs of cigarettes produced by the hotel's owners (the Khanh Hoa Tobacco Company). This is truly a bizarre sight, and worth the short walk from the beach just for the chuckle and a snapshot. Opened in April 1993, it has most of the conveniences: guide services, tours, restaurant, air conditioning, refrigerator, international TV, telephone. Very friendly staff. But for the price, make sure you get a view of the water.

Nha Trang Hotel   US$8–$20

129 Thong Nhat Street. ☎ *822347 or 822224.*
74 rooms.

This towering (by Vietnamese standards) seven- or eight-story hotel is clean and priced right but out of the way unless you have business in the vicinity. Air conditioning.

Hai Yen Hotel   US$7–$80   ★

40 Tran Phu Street. ☎ *822828 or 822974; FAX: 821902.*
107 rooms.

This is a popular place across Tran Phu from the beach, and despite its amenities of conference rooms, car rentals, a dancing hall, restaurant, currency exchange, gift shop and traditional Vietnamese dance performances, the reception—when I visited—ranged from aloof to rude. I don't see what all the fuss is about.

Hotel La Fregate (Khach San Thang Loi)   US$20–$38

4 Pasteur Street. ☎ *822241 or 822523; FAX: 821905.*
55 rooms.

This hotel has undergone a recent renovation and the staff seem as cheerful as the new masonry. Conference hall, large restaurant, cafe, two bars, two banquet rooms, beauty salon/barber, massage and sauna, and gift shop. Also car and bike rentals, boat tours. The upper-end rooms come with refrigerator, hot water, air conditioning and bathtub. Luxurious for the price.

The Grand Hotel (Nha Khach 44)   US$10–$40

44 Tran Phu Street; ☎ *822445.*

This yellow French colonial mansion sits right across Tran Phu from the beach and has some breezy, large and elegant rooms. But the cheaper prices put you in a barracks-like annex next to the main building with a fan and a hard, thin mattress. The grounds look more like a boarding school campus than a hotel, but the price—at all levels—includes a full breakfast on the patio. It's relaxing in the early morning sunlight. Beauty salon/barber services.

Lehoang   US$8–$16

86 Tran Phu; ☎ *824070, 824076.*
9 rooms.

On the road just south of town. The $8 rooms are a bargain that would run as high as $12 or more closer to town. Across the road from the beach. Air conditioning, big beds, hot water, individual baths. Nhat Thong is the manager; a real friendly guy. Tell him Fielding sent you and you may get a Vietnamese's rate. Restaurant right next door. Inexpensive.

Hung Dao Hotel   US$8–$10   ★

3 Tran Hung Dao Street; ☎ *822246.*

This is where everyone heads when the cheaper rooms at next door's Vien Dong are full. Consequently, this place is full a lot of the time, too. Call in advance. Or better yet, call the Vien Dong in advance. I've heard a rumor about "nasty" elements frequenting this place. Hookers perhaps? Nonetheless, it's an attractive place with a decent location (although not on the beach) and a good restaurant. Bike rentals, too.

Hai Duong Bungalows

Tran Phu Street, about two miles south of town on the beach.

This place appears to be nothing more than a beachside whore village for Vietnamese soldiers on R&R. As a foreigner, I wasn't allowed to take a "hut." And my inspection of the grounds turned up nothing more accommodating than some drunken Army officers fondling hookers in the bar next to reception. I only mention this place so you'll avoid the temptation to inquire here, because Hai Duong is on the beach and the setting's not bad amid the casuarina trees. If you can get in, I'd like to hear from you.

Where to Eat in Nha Trang

Nam Phi Restaurant $

12 Tran Phu Street.
Local fare.

Coco Bar $

Tran Phu Street, across from the Pasteur museum on the beach.
Cafe.

Dich Vu Du Lich $

Thuy Trang, 9a Le Loi.
Vietnamese, Asian.

Ninh Hoa $

So9 Le Loi.
Specialty is hash.

Hoang Yen Guide and Tourist
Services Center $$

26-28 Tran Phu; ☎ *822961.*
Yes, this is a restaurant. Great seafood.

Quan An $

11 Le Loi.
Seafood.

Ninh Hoa $

13 Le Loi.
Vietnamese, Asian.

Vi Huong $

> *19 Le Loi;* ☎ *822872.*
> Cuisine of Vietnam.

Quan Nem $

> *1 Hoang Van Thu.*
> Vietnamese.

Com Phan Dia $

> *33 Le Loi.*
> Vietnamese, Asian.

Khanh Phong $

> *6b Yersin.*
> Vietnamese, Asian.

Cafe Tho $

> *1 Quang Trung.*
> Vietnamese, Asian.

**Banana Splits (formerly The Second Best
Ice Creamery in Vietnam)** $$ ★

> *58 Quang Trung.*
> Yogurt, fruit salad, fruit juice, banana splits galore, soft drinks, sour soft drinks, fruit shakes, coffees, teas, a hodgepodge of stuff. Frequented by Westerners. Very friendly. The owner says the original name was a takeoff on an ice cream parlor in Saigon called The Best Ice Creamery in Vietnam. But her scheming neighbor, hoping to cash in on some of the success she was seeing next door, suspiciously and less than fluently renamed her own food stall as the "First Best Offering" store and posted an identical menu alongside the one hanging in The Second Best Ice Creamery. If you're not careful, you'll think the two shops are one and the same and end up getting served by the imposter. But on my visit, First Best Offering was empty and SBICV nearly packed, mostly with dollar-toting foreigners. The owner of SBICV changed the name to Banana Splits and tacked a poster-sized photo of yours truly to the wall of the place just so Fielding readers won't mistake the two restaurants and inadvertantly wander into her competitor's shop. And should you still manage to stray toward the enemy, she'll run out into the street with yet another photo. The power of the printed word. Now you've got the scoop (tee hee).

Cafe Vy $

2 Ly Tu Trong, just right off the main drag by the beach.

Cafe Giai Khat $

Tran Phu.
Peaceful, bamboo laden setting. Small tables are very private. Nice for couples. Romantic in sort of a grungy way.

Hai Au Restaurant $

> *3 Nguyen Chanh;* ☎ *822862.*
> Vietnamese specialties. Superb food at cheap prices.

The Lizard Club and Restaurant $$

> *Le Thanh Ton;* ☎ *821206.*

Nha Trang

46 Cafe $

By the Grand Hotel, Tran Phu.
Standard local fare, nice setting.

Seamen's Club Restaurant $$

72-74 Tran Phu, ☎ *822251.*
I'm not sure about this place, whether it's for seamen only or not.

Dac San Seafood Restaurant $$

Tran Phu, right on the beach south of town.
This is a breezy open air cafe and restaurant under a tent on the beach. Good seafood.

96 Restaurant $

96 Tran Phu.
Tasty Vietnamese seafood.

Kem Cafe $

Tran Phu.
Seafood at cheap prices.

Hanh Green Hat $

Tran Phu.
Vietnamese and Western. Popular.

Directory

Transportation

Nha Trang is 1300 km from Hanoi, 445 km from Saigon, 240 km from Quy Nhon, 215 km from Dalat, 200 km from Buon Ma Thuot, 410 km to Quang Ngai, 105 km from Phan Rang.

By air:

VN has twice daily flights to Nha Trang from HCMC at 6:45 a.m. and at either 8:30 a.m. or 10:00 a.m. A third flight is added on Saturdays (6:45, 8 & 10 a.m.). Flights leave twice daily from Nha Trang to HCMC at 8:15 a.m. and 4:30 p.m., with a third flight added Saturdays at 4 p.m. Connections to Hanoi are four times per week (Mon., Wed., Fri. and Sun. at 1:30 p.m.) and are expensive (about US$130) one way. From Nha Trang, flights to Hanoi leave on the same days at 10 a.m. Flight schedules are subject to change and the prices will go up soon, as mentioned earlier in this edition.

By bus:

The bus station for long-distance travel is located at the intersection of Ngo Gia Tu and Nguyen Huu Huan Streets in the southwest area of town. Express tickets can be purchased at *6A Hoang Hoa Tham Street*, and it's best you buy your tickets in advance. Non-express buses to Saigon cost about 16,000 dong, to Danang 19,000 dong, to Vinh 40,000 dong, Hue 25,000 dong, Quy Nhon 9000 dong, Dalat 8500 dong, and Phan Rang 4000 dong. Express buses to Saigon are about 19,000 dong, Hanoi 55,500 dong, Danang 22,000 dong, Vinh 39,000 dong, Quang Ngai 16,000 dong, Dalat 9400 dong, Vinh 40,000 dong, and Hue 25,000 dong. The local bus station is located across from *115 2 Thang 4 Street*, although there is little reason to travel by local bus.

Bicycles:

Bicycles can be rented from most hotels for about 8000 dong a day (they'll try to get 10,000 from you, but just walk away. They'll call you back). A car and driver can be rented for the day from some of the better hotels, such as the Khatoco Hotel, and popular excursions include an afternoon trip to Dai Lanh Beach up the coast about an hour. Cars and microbuses can also be rented at Tourist Car Enterprise, *1 Nguyen Thi Minh Khai Street*. Prices are different everywhere, either for local excursions or long-distance one-way travel.

Lambrettas

Lambrettas run to Cau Da from the Central Market.

By train:

The train station is located across the street from *26 Thai Nguyen Street*, although you should book in advance at the office at *17 Thai Nguyen Street*. ☎ *822113*.

Cyclos

Cyclos are available all over town. If you want to hire a boat, go to the dock at Cau Da, which is 5–6 km south of Nha Trang. From here, you can visit Mieu Island for about US$8–$10. (The prices keep going up as tourists don't negotiate properly—so the locals can expect more.) Some boats can be hired for the day—the trips include stops for snorkeling—for as little as US$10 per day. Again, see if you can bargain it down a bit. Ferries also run out to Mieu Island for a pittance.

Nha Trang Telecommunications Center

2 Le Loi. Tel: 8458, 821510.; FAX: 84-58-821056. Fax, phone and telex services are here. There's a post office here, too.

Central Post Office

2 Tran Phu Street.

TNT International Express

☎ *821043*.

Hospital

19 Yersin Street. ☎ *822168*.

Banks and Moneychangers

Vietcom Bank. *17 Quang Trung Street*. Will exchange most major currencies and cash travelers' checks. Also will provide cash advances on major U.S. credit cards.

Tourist Offices

Khanh Hoa Tourism. *1 Trang Hung Dao Street*. ☎ *822753*.
Nha Trang Tourism. *3 Tran Hung Dao Street*. ☎ *821231*.

Airline Offices

Vietnam Airlines. *12b Hoang Hoa Tham Street*. ☎ *823797*. *86 Tran Phu Street*. ☎ *821147*. You can also book at *94 Tran Phu Street*.

Nha Trang Environs

Doc Let Beach ★

Doc Let Beach is a magnificent stretch of sand about 30 km north of Nha Trang and another 10 km off Highway 1 just north of Ninh Hoa. The beach is deserted most of the time, and it appears as if someone at some time had plans of developing the area, witnessed by the foundering structures here. Regardless, you can get refreshments and food, and you'll probably be by yourself doing so. It's worth the diversion off Highway 1.

Dai Lanh ★

National Highway 1 passes through the small hamlet of Dai Lanh about 85 km north of Nha Trang. It's a spectacularly scenic location (the lush green mountains descend almost vertically to the beach), the bay's beach being surrounded by casuarina trees that were, unfortunately, virtually ripped from their roots by a devastating typhoon that hit the central Vietnamese coast in December 1993. I mean this area really took a battering. The palms and casuarina trees, the few that remain, look as if they had been totally defoliated during the war—and many tourists will ask their guides if this was indeed what happened to what is normally an amazingly lush mountain-to-sea hamlet. The beach is of clean, white sand and virtually void of beachgoers. Despite the massive typhoon damage to the flora in the area (which is creeping back), Dai Lanh makes for a perfect beach day trip from Nha Trang if you're seeking solitude. The beach touts are few and far between, but they usually offer what you'd want to buy anyway on a hot day—rich local coconut milk and its soft meat to match. There is a restaurant/cafe at the beach (the Dai Lanh Restaurant) as well as an amazingly drab-appearing, unfinished hotel that seems to have been under construction since the Nguyen Dynasty, which will presumably be called the Dai Lanh Hotel. But no one around the area seems to have any idea when or if ever the structure will be completed. It should be, though. Like Ca Na to the south, Dai Lanh has the potential of being one of the more relaxing, remote and unexploited coastal areas in the south. Stop here.

Mieu Island

The principal village on this island off Nha Trang is Tri Nguyen, a small town that's noted for a fish breeding farm, where dozens of species of sea life are raised in separate compartments. There's one "beach" on the island, Bai Soai, which is really nothing more than where the sea meets a bunch of rocks. If you want to lie out in the sun here, bring a bed. If you want to go swimming, bring hiking boots. Means of reaching the island are discussed in the Cau Da section of this chapter.

Bamboo Island ★

You'll have to hire a private craft to reach this island, about 3 km off the coast of Nha Trang Beach and the largest isle in the vicinity of Nha Trang. A decent beach is here (Tru Beach) on the northern end of the island.

Ebony Island

This is just south of Bamboo Island and is noted for its decent snorkeling. Again, you'll have to hire a boat to get out here.

Salangane Island

These are actually two different isles about 17 km offshore (a 3–4 hour boat ride) where salangane nests are gathered for use in bird's nest soup and for their traditional aphrodisiac qualities. The nests themselves are created from the secretions of salangane birds. The red ones are considered the finest and they're harvested about twice a year. It's believed the virile and promiscuous Emperor Minh Mang who ruled Vietnam in the mid-19th century relied on salangane for his legendary sexual longevity.

Ba Ho Falls

About 20 km north of Nha Trang and close to the village of Phu Huu is a beautiful set of three waterfalls set amongst a lush forest. You can get there by bus to Ninh Hoa from Nha Trang's local bus station.

Dien Khanh Citadel

This 17th-century Trinh Dynasty citadel is about 10 km west of Nha Trang and close to the village of Dien Toan. After defeating the Tay Son insurgency, Prince Nguyen Anh, who was later to become Emperor Gia Long, rebuilt the structure in 1793. It's worth only a short visit.

Nha Trang

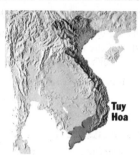

Tuy Hoa

Tuy Hoa

TUY HOA IN A CAPSULE

The capital of Phu Yen Province, but a small town of only a few thousand inhabitants...This is a good place to break the journey north or south along NH1 only if you're tired...There are no real attractions here.

Tuy Hoa is a barely noticeable, small town about 100 km south of Quy Nhon. There's little if anything to do here but stop and eat at a food stall or take a cheap hotel room for the night. You virtually could pass through Tuy Hoa without noticing it. It rests on the coast between Quy Nhon and Dai Lanh Beach. Here NH1 passes over a large river. But the beaches in the area aren't worth noting.

Trang Bridge—the longest bridge in southern Vietnam, built in 1954 by the French, at 1100 meters long—is close by.

Where to Stay in Tuy Hoa

Huong Sen Hotel   **About US$10**
   NH1, center of town.
   This is a peaceful hotel with a surprisingly good restaurant.

Directory

Tourist Office

Phu Yen Tourist
   137 Le Thanh Ton Street. ☎ *823353.*

Quy Nhon

Enchanting islands flank the coast of Nha Trang and Danang.

QUY NHON IN A CAPSULE

The capital of Binh Dinh Province...A dingy city that experienced a good deal of fighting between the Viet Cong, American and South Korean troops during the Vietnam War...Beaches are some of the worst along the central coast...It makes for a decent overnight stop between Nha Trang and Danang.

Quy Nhon, the capital of Binh Dinh Province, is a major seaport supporting a population of about 250,000 people. There's not a lot to see and do here, but it does make for a decent night stop on the road between Nha Trang and Danang. In fact, you've got to leave Highway 1 for about 11 km to get here. There are only two hotels of any note, and they both rest on the palm-shaded Quy Nhon Beach, which I found disappointingly grungy and littered (even near the hotels), and the ocean murky and gray (even on a sunny day). Quy Nhon is definitely not a destination, and you really won't find it worth spending even a full day here. The only "attractions" near town are a couple of small Cham towers on the road off NH1 toward town, about 2-3 km from the central area, or the municipal beach, where the breezes can be quite brisk and even chilly toward the evening hours.

The port here used to be internationally recognized during the 17th–19th centuries. The two Hung Thanh towers near here are worth a visit. The larger of the two towers stands at 23 meters tall and they date back to the 13th century. They were once part of a vast Cham complex here that has been largely destroyed. M. Pigneau de Behaine, French missionary and Bishop of Adran, gave protection to defeated Nguyen survivors while his forces were surrounding the city—which was under the control of the Tay Son—in October 1799. Just two years later, the Tay Son fleet was destroyed from offshore by Nguyen Anh.

Quy Nhon itself is an unremarkable and relatively dirty city and was the site of a great deal of fierce fighting during the war between the Viet Cong and a significant number of South Korean troops, as well as ARVN and American forces.

WHAT WAS THE TAY SON REBELLION?

The Tay Son Rebellion was a peasant revolt in 1771 that was led by the three Tay Son brothers as the country was leaning toward famine. Sensing unease and kinetic revolt and animosity toward the Nguyen Lords and the Trinh amongst the peasants of this region, the brothers were able to unify the peasantry into a ragtag army that soon became a powerful fighting force.

The army soon included others, such as shopkeepers and even intellectuals, who all formed behind the Tay Son brothers. This fighting force soon ruled much of the countryside and cities from as far south as Saigon to Trinh. This is where the Chinese stepped in.

Realizing the country was in turmoil, they sent large forces of troops, as many as 200,000, to annex Vietnam in 1788. Quang Trung, the oldest of the three brothers, proclaimed himself emperor and fought both the Vietnamese and the Chinese viciously and with significant amounts of success. They attacked the Chinese at Thang Long during the Tet new year and decimated the Chinese forces.

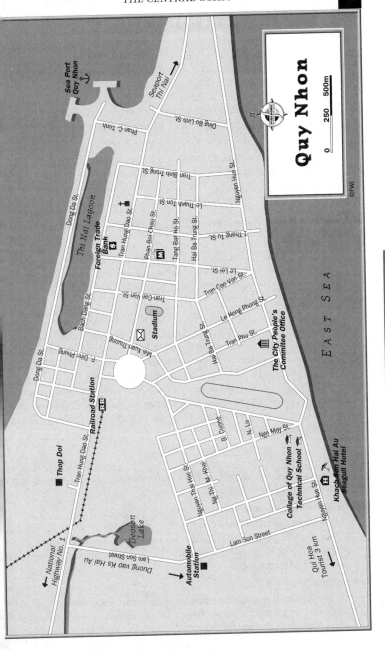

Quy Nhon

EAST SEA

WHAT WAS THE TAY SON REBELLION?

The Tay Son Battle of Dong Da is considered one of the greatest strategically fought battles in the history of Vietnam. The Tay Son brothers then entertained notions of attacking China. Quang Trung initiated a variety of economic reforms, including land reform, education programs and less-demanding tax structures. He attempted to issue to his followers identity cards with the inscription "The Great Trust of the Empire." But Quang Trung died in 1792 and the movement fell apart to such a degree so as not to be in a position to fend off the newly arriving French forces.

Vietnamese Emperor Gia Long then later, in 1802, exhumed the body of the youngest brother and ordered his soldiers to urinate on the corpse while Quang Trung's wife and son watched. Then the corpse was ripped apart by three elephants.

What to See and Do in Quy Nhon and Environs

Thap Doi Cham Towers

Because Quy Nhon was a central Cham area during the Cham Empire, there is a significant amount of the towers scattered about the Quy Nhon area. The two Thap Doi towers, near the edge of town, are perhaps the best examples.

Quy Nhon's Beaches

As I explained above, the beach areas of Quy Nhon are unimpressive stretches of dirty, dark sand and seriously dim the temptation of swimming in the ocean, which is surprisingly cold. The pictures you send back home won't inspire your friends and family to hop on a jetliner to Vietnam. Probably the "best" corridor of beach is by the Quy Nhon Tourist Hotel (which is most likely due to the hotel being run by Saigon Railway Tourism). Along the west side of the beach, you'll find a number of boats and seaside shacks belonging to local fishermen. Another beach is farther west and has fewer people. Its drawback is that part of the beach is flanked by factories and processing plants. Ugh.

Lon Market

Phan Boi Street.

This is the town's central market. It's a relatively new, covered structure where the usual Vietnamese goods and produce can be had.

Binh Dinh/Xiem Reap/Ratanakiri Zoo

As the name implies, this is a "zoo" with creatures imported from Cambodia, namely from the provinces of Siem Reap and Ratanakiri. Here you can see monkeys, bears and crocodiles on a site near the sea. The conditions here aren't as dismal as in other Vietnamese "zoos."

Cu Mong Pass   ★

Cu Mong pass is a spectacularly scenic and steeply graded pass south of Quy Nhon that's great for photos but hell on trannies. On the nearly vertical downgrades engineers have cut out ramps for vehicles that have lost their brakes. Shrines with incense burning, dot the roadway here, marking where motorists have fallen victim to the steep grades and ill-prepared vehicles. The Vietnamese believe that they will avoid the same misfortune if they stop at the shrines and pay their respects for the dead drivers/passengers. The Cu Mong Pass represents the point where the Tonkinese prevailed after the fall of the Vijaya in 1471. From the pass, the Chams were able to prevent invasions from both north and south for nearly 150 years until the early 1600s.

Song Cau

This stretch of NH1, which hugs the coast, offers spectacular views of the surrounding hillsides. NH1 on the outskirts of the small town, particularly to the north, is flanked by rows of "truck stops," (i.e., brothels) where women wait for long distance truck drivers. Here the girls will sit out on the porches and invite you inside for some tea and some sin.

Cha Ban   ★

About 25 km north of Quy Nhon and 5 km from Binh Dinh.
Here are the ruins of what was once an ancient Cham capital. Cha Ban was the capital of Champa from 1000 until about 1470, when it was variously attacked by the Vietnamese, the Chinese and the Khmers. The Vietnamese were defeated by the Chams here in 1377, where the Champa king was killed. The Vietnamese then invaded Cha Ban and captured the Cham king and his royal family. This was considered the last great battle of the Chams. Tens of thousands of Chams were killed and taken prisoner. While Cha Ban was under the control of the Tay Son in 1771, the city was ruled by the three Tay Son brothers. Cha Ban was unsuccessfully attacked again in 1793 by the Vietnamese (Nguyen Anh, who later became Emperor Gia Long). But the city fell to the Vietnamese in 1799. The Tay Son then moved to what is now Quy Nhon, where they conducted their own siege of Cha Ban. The siege of the city continued until 1801, when Vietnamese General Vu Tinh ran out of provisions. Rather than be defeated, Vu Tinh erected a wooden tower, filled it with gun powder and committed suicide inside by blowing the tower into the sky. The Canh Tien Tower, or Tower of Brass, stands in the middle of the compound.

Thap Doi

About 2 km toward NH1 from the Quy Nhon bus station.
Head out on Tran Hung Dao Street and turn right onto Thap Doi Street. These four towers don't possess typical Cham architecture, but instead feature pyramid-type roofs and granite doorways. Some of the brickwork is still in evidence on the granite statuary on the peak of the roofs. Torsos of Garudas are on the roofs of the structures.

Duong Long Cham Towers   ★

About 10 km from Cha Ban.
These are referred to as the Towers of Ivory. There are three towers here with ornamentation depicting elephants and snakes. Huge dragons can be found on the corners of the structures. Bas reliefs over the doorways depict dancers, monsters and animals.

Quy Nhon

Vinh Son Waterfalls

Off Highway 19.

These unspectacular falls are about 19 km off national Highway 19, which run between Binh Dinh and Pleiku.

Quang Trung Museum

The museum is in Tay Son District, nearly 50 km from Quy Nhon. It's about 5 km from the main route. Ask for directions in Quy Nhon at the Binh Dinh Tourist Company (see Directory). But if you don't want to bother (because they'll try to steer you into an expensive tour of the site), take NH19 toward Pleiku. The museum is dedicated to the middle brother of the three brothers that led the Tay Son Rebellion, Nguyen Hue. Later, in 1789, as Emperor Quang Trang, he led a successful defense against an enormous force of about 200,000 Chinese soldiers. The museum features traditional martial art *binh dinh ho* demonstrations performed with bamboo sticks.

Where to Stay in Quy Nhon

> **AUTHOR'S NOTE:**
> **TELEPHONE PREFIXES**
>
> *The following telephone numbers are local exchanges. The country code is 84. The city code id 56.*

Seagull Hotel (Hai Au Hotel)   US$8–$25

48 Nguyen Hue Street. ☎ 821473. FAX: 21926.
45 rooms.

This isn't a bad place save for the suspect staff. It's a beachfront hotel and the rooms on the beach side of the structure offer great views of the ocean and surrounding mountains, which are best at at sunrise and dusk, when the grottiness of the beach isn't so apparent. The higher up, the better. Restaurant, air conditioning, attached bath. But be careful of the staff. Lock your stuff up. The staff has been known to overcharge for faxes and the like, probably pocketing the difference. Ask to see printed rates for hotel services.

Saigon Hotel   US$25   ★

Corner of Dao Duy Tu and Tran Hung Dao Streets.

This is a fairly new and well-appointed hotel that seems designed to entice NH1 travelers to stop by for the night, as the location is convenient at best. Restaurant, air conditioning, attached bath.

Quy Nhon Hotel   US$23–$37   ★

12 Nguyen Hue Street at Quy Nhon Municipal Beach. ☎ 822401.
47 rooms.

On the beach. Air conditioning, restaurant, attached bath. This place has had a bad reputation for cleanliness, and at these prices, that's the first thing you'd expect in a tourist-class hotel.

Thanh Binh Hotel   About US$6–$20

17 Ly Thuong Kiet Street. ☎ 822041.

Overpriced considering the amenities. The cheaper rooms are grimy, while there is air conditioning in the expensive rooms. Private bath. Restaurant.

Hotel Hai Ha   US$20–$30

1A Tran Binh Trong Street, corner of Hai Ba Trung and Tran Binh Trong streets.
☎ *821295.*
Ho-hum. It's a small hotel but relatively clean (it should be at these prices). Air conditioning, attached bath.

Bank Hotel   US$12–$28

257 Le Hong Phong St. ☎ *822779. FAX: 21013.*
Near the bus station, this is a bargain for budget travelers, particularly due to a recent facelift of the rooms.

Dong Phuong Hotel   US$8–$15   ★

39-41 Mai Xuan Thuong Street. ☎ *822915.*
20 Rooms.
Good location near the center of town and the stadium. Recommended by a lot of travelers. Air conditioning, attached bath.

The Peace Hotel   US$30

361 Tran Hung Dao Street. ☎ *822710, 22900.*
64 rooms.
The rates here have soared over the past couple of years, and what I once inferred was a bargain has become much less of one.

Nha Khach Huu Nghi   About US$7–$8

210 Phan Boi Chau Street. ☎ *822152.*
22 rooms.
Popular with backpackers. Doubles with private bath.

Olympic Hotel   About US$10–$20

167 Le Hong Phong Street. ☎ *822375.*
23 rooms.
Next to the stadium and popular. Restaurant, attached bath, air conditioning.

Where to Eat in Quy Nhon

Dong Phuong Restaurant

39-41 Mai Xuan Thuong Street.
Ground floor of the Dong Phuong Hotel. Vietnamese fare.

Tu Hai Restaurant

On the 3rd floor of the Lon Market, Phan Boi Chau Street.
Vietnamese, Asian and Western, but bland.

Ganh Rang Restaurant

Nguyen Hue Street, about 3.5 km out of town on the beach, southwest of Municipal Beach.
This is a great setting, as the restaurant sits on piling above the water. Vietnamese, Asian.

Vu Hung Restaurant

On the roof of the Olympic Hotel, 167 Le Hong Phong Street.
This is a real restaurant. The food's good and relatively cheap for hotel restaurants.

Quy Nhon

Ngoc Lien Restaurant
288 Le Hong Phong Street.
Vietnamese, Asian. Good and cheap.

Directory

Transportation

Quy Nhon is about 680 km from HCMC, 410 km from Hue, 305 km from Danang, 240 km from Nha Trang, 225 km from Buon Ma Thuot, 175 km from Quang Ngai.

By air:

VN has flights to Quy Nhon from HCMC daily except for Thursdays and Sundays at 7:00 a.m. Flights to HCMC leave Quy Nhon Tuesdays and Fridays at 9 a.m., and Wednesdays and Saturdays at 9:50 a.m. Flights to Hanoi leave Wednesdays and Saturdays at 7:30, with a connection in Danang. Flights to Danang leave at the same time. Into Quy Nhon flights leave Danang Wednesdays and Saturdays at 9:10 a.m. The schedule changes often, so check with VN.

By bus:

The Quy Nhon bus station is 1 km northwest of the town center on Tran Hung Dao Street. Express buses leave at 5 a.m. for Hanoi, Hue, Dalat, Danang, Nha Trang and Saigon, as well as other locations. Tickets should be purchased the day before departure. Non-express buses also leave early in the morning for Bong Son, Nha Trang, Am Lao, An Khe, Dalat, Cam Ranh, Danang, Saigon, Hanoi, Phu My, Hoi An, Pleiku, Vinh Than, Tuy Hoa, Van Canh, and Kon Tum, as well as other destinations.

By train:

The train station in Quy Nhon is off the beaten track (express trains do not stop here). The station is 1 km northwest of town on Hoang Hoa Tham Street, which is off Tran Hung Dao Street. To catch an express train, you'll have to go to Dieu Tri, which is about 10 km away.

Post Office

127 Hai Ba Trung Street. International calls and faxes can be made from here.

TNT International Express

☎ *822193* or *22600.*

Banks and Moneychangers

Vietcom Bank, *148 Tran Hung Dao Street*, on the corner of Le Loi Street.

Hospital

102 Nguyen Hue Street.

Tourist Office

Binh Dinh Tourism Company, *4 Nguyen Hue Street.* ☎ *822206, 22524.*

Airline

Vietnam Airlines Booking Office. *2 Ly Thuong Kiet Street.* ☎ *823125.*

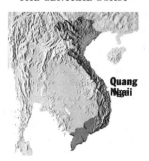

Quang Ngai

QUANG NGAI IN A CAPSULE

Nothing of note in the town itself...gateway to Son My, the site of the My Lai massacre...Great beaches 17 km west of town, although they, also, were the sites of the slaughter of Vietnamese civilians by American troops during the war...Most travelers stop here briefly on their way to Danang.

Most travelers don't spend a lot of time in Quang Ngai, as it's only about 130 km south of Danang, and it's not even on the coast—the beach is nearly 15 km away. It is a small provincial capital of Quang Ngai Province that lies on the banks of the Tra Khuc River (notice the waterwheels as you pass over the bridge). There's a huge market here and a nice cathedral, but the reason why most travelers stop here is to visit Son My (site of the infamous My Lai massacre), which lies about 13 km from Quang Ngai.

Quang Ngai was formerly a center of French resistance during the First Indochina War, inhabited by a number of Viet Minh. During the Vietnam War, the area was part of the South Vietnamese government's Strategic Hamlet Program, which relocated a number of villagers from here into fortified hamlets. This caused a considerable amount of dissent among the townsfolk, and many became Viet Cong sympathizers. The area was considered by the Americans as a VC stronghold, which precipitated the murderous massacre at My Lai in the Son My Subdistrict. Fighting in the district was intense, and you can still see the rusted, ruined bridges that were destroyed by both the Viet Minh and the Viet Cong. The third bridge that NH1 crosses today looks as if had been erected in a day, which it probably was.

The beaches are great—deserted and immaculate—when you get out to them.

What to See and Do in
Quang Ngai and Environs

Son My Subdistrict (My Lai)

Thirteen km from Quang Ngai. Turn right just after crossing the bridge at the monument commemorating the My Lai massacre. This is the site of one of the greatest atrocities during the Vietnam War, and perhaps the most heinous military action ever staged by the U.S. American forces believed the hamlet to be a strategic VC stronghold and thought the villagers were not only VC sympathizers, but fighters and saboteurs as well. On March 16, 1968, units of the 23rd Infantry Division (Task Force Barker) were dropped into the village of Son My. Soldiers were dropped into other hamlets as well, including Tu Cong hamlet and Xom Lang sub-hamlet. Two weeks before the massacre, six U.S. soldiers had been killed after coming upon a mine field. The decision was made to search and destroy Son My subdistrict. Lt. William Calley was responsible for investigating the hamlet of My Lai. Nearly 350 civilians died here under his orders. All were unarmed, and most were women and children. The soldiers of Lt. Calley's 1st Platoon shot and bayonetted fleeing villagers and threw grenades into the hootches and family bomb shelters. As the villagers tried to flee their shelters, they were shot. Women were raped and sodomized. At no time during the massacre did American troops encounter any resistance. As many as 150 villagers were ordered to line up and were mowed down with machine gun fire. The 2nd and 3rd platoons of Charlie Company (under the commands of Lt. Stephen Brooks and Jeffrey La Cross, respectively) were dropped into the zones and "attacked" Tu Cung. Unspeakable crimes were committed here by U.S. troops. Young women were gang-raped—one was reportedly then shot in the vagina. Neil Sheehan reported in his marvelous book, *A Bright Shining Lie*, that, "One soldier missed a baby lying on the ground twice with a .45 pistol as his comrades laughed at his marksmanship. He stood over the child and fired a third time. The soldiers beat women with rifle butts and raped some and sodomized others before shooting them." In all, more than 500 civilians were massacred in Son My, most of them in My Lai. To their credit, some of the soldiers refused to take part in the massacre—one shot himself in the foot. But the vast majority of Capt. Ernest Medina's Charlie Company participated in the worst atrocity committed by any American soldiers during any war involving Americans in U.S. history. In all, more than 500 civilians were killed in the turkey shoot, most in My Lai. The story didn't come out for another eight months as action was taken at every level of the American command to cover up the incident. Finally, soldiers returning home told of the incidents at Son My, and an outraged American public demanded action. This was the "action": A number of American soldiers were disciplined, but only one, Lt. Calley, faced a court-martial—he was found guilty of the murders of 22 (eventually 109) civilians and sentenced to life imprisonment. He was paroled by President Nixon in 1974. Some action. Some president. There is a memorial to the slaughter in Son My in a park where Xom Lang sub-hamlet once existed. There is a museum and graves of the victims. Permits are no longer required to visit the sites, but expect busloads of tourists.

This monument in Quang Ngai directs travelers the way to Son My, the site of the My Lai Massacre.

Bien Khe Ky (Khe Ky Beach)

This is a fine, long beach about 17 km from Quang Ngai, and only about 3 km from Son My. This beach was also the site of another massacre by American troops, Bravo Company this time. Near the bridge across Song Kinh Giang, GIs burned down hootches and blasted automatic weapons fire at the fleeing civilians as they ran on the sand toward the sea. Family bomb shelters were annihilated and torched. Women and children were indiscriminately shot. Others were tortured before being killed. As many as 100 civilians were killed in this mass slaughter. Charges against Lt. Thomas Willingham, Bravo Company's leader, were dismissed. These incidents, although there is little left to remind you of the area's history, will sober your visit to this otherwise beautiful length of beach.

Where to Stay in Quang Ngai

There aren't many places in Quang Ngai where foreigners can stay, but this is changing as tourism to My Lai is booming.

Nha Khach Uy Ban Thi   About US$20–$40

Phan Boi Chau Street. ☎ *82109.*

Absolutely ridiculous price for this place. Restaurant. Used to be a government guest house but foreigners can stay here now. Personally, I'd continue on to Danang or Hoi An.

Song Tra Hotel   About US$30

Next to the Tra Khuc River bridge.

Everyone seems to want to cash in on the tourism boon in My Lai. This place is no exception. The service is lacking, especially for the prices. This used to be the only place foreigners could stay in Quang Ngai.

Where to Eat in Quang Ngai

Food stalls are your best bet in Quang Ngai, but there's a decent restaurant at the Nha Khach Uy Ban Thi hotel, with decent seafood. There are a number of cafes near Khac San So 2, but don't expect much on the menus. Others include:

Nha Hang 155

155 Quang Trung Street.
Average Vietnamese fare. Cheap, but not as cheap as the surrounding food stalls.

Tiem An 72 Restaurant

72 Nguyen Nghiem Street.
Vietnamese, Asian. Cheap.

Directory

Transportation

Quang Ngai is about halfway between HCMC and Hanoi (840 km from HCMC and 890 km from Hanoi). Other distances are 410 kilometers from Nha Trang, 240 km from Hue, 130 km from Danang, 175 km from Quy Nhon.

By bus:

Quang Ngai's bus station is across from *32 Nguyen Nghiem Street*, not far from NH1, which is called Quang Trung Street through Quang Ngai. There is service to Danang, Dalat, Hoi An, Nha Trang, Quy Nhon, Kon Tum and HCMC.

By train:

The railway station is about 3 km west of town. Take Phan Boi Chau Street west from Quang Trung Street. The street name changes to Nguyen Chanh Street, but just keep going. Here you can catch Reunification Express trains either north or south, as the train makes regular stops here.

Post Office

Located at the intersection of Phan Dinh Phung and Phan Boi Chau streets.

Tourist Office

Quang Ngai Tourism, in the Song Tra Hotel. ☎ *82665* or 8*3870.*

Hoi An

Hoi An

he Japanese Covered Bridge in Hoi An was built in 1593.

HOI AN IN A CAPSULE

Perhaps the most unique town in Vietnam...Worth a two-day visit...Ancient seaport that did commerce with dozens of nations, from Europe and even America...Unscathed by the Vietnam War, although there was much damage to the city during the Tay Son Rebellion...Ancient buildings here represent influences from both Asia and the West...Narrow streets flanked by buildings that have remained virtually unchanged for 200 years...Similar in flavor and style to Malaysia's famed port of Malacca...A must-see on the coast.

Hoi An is a beautiful, ancient Vietnamese town, a little more than 30 km to the south of Danang, that will seem to you like a time machine. It sits on the banks of the Thu Bon River near the South China Sea. It was virtually untouched by the fighting during the Vietnam War (although it was heavily damaged during the Tay Son Rebellion), and it retains its centuries-old Vietnamese, Chinese, Japanese and European architecture. It distinctly reminds me of Malaysia's port at Malacca, with its narrow streets and low, tiled roof houses. The influences are from the Japanese, the Portuguese, the Dutch and the Vietnamese. In the 17th–19th centuries, Hoi An was one of the most important ports in Southeast Asia, and wasn't eclipsed by Danang until the end of the 19th century, when Thu Bon River had silted up to such a degree that major commerce by navigation became problematic as the water became too shallow.

Hoi An was probably inhabited as early as 2000 years or more ago, and also has the distinction of being, by most accounts, the first place in Vietnam where Christianity was introduced. The French priest Alexandre de Rhode arrived in the 17th century and later transcribed the Vietnamese language into the Latin-based *quoc ngu* script.

Hoi An was also the site of the first Chinese settlers in southern Vietnam. More than 1500 ethnic Chinese live in Hoi An today. Many Chinese come from all over the southern part of Vietnam to celebrate various Chinese congregational gatherings. Unlike in other parts of Vietnam, there is little friction between ethnic Vietnamese and the Chinese, who have adopted Vietnamese as their first language.

From the 2nd–10th centuries, Hoi An was one of the principal cities in the Champa Kingdom. Archeologists have discovered the bases of numerous Cham towers in the region. Its port was visited by sailors from the Middle East for provisioning. During its heyday, Indian, Dutch, Portuguese, French, Thai, Indonesian, Spanish, American, Japanese, Chinese and Filipino ships came to Hoi An to procure its quality silk, sugar, fabrics, tea, ceramics, pepper, elephant tusks and a slew of other goods.

The Chinese and the Japanese usually stayed in Hoi An for the longest periods of time due to the prevailing winds. In fact, there were "seasons" in which Hoi An experienced the presence of such merchants. Many of the nationalities calling on Hoi An left agents of their respective companies, and this is the reason Hoi An developed its multinational architectural appearance.

Today, parts of Hoi An look precisely as they did two centuries ago. And although Hoi An today remains largely uncommercialized, don't expect that to continue. Foreign tourists were everywhere during my last visit and the city is gearing up for more. Within a year or two, walking the streets of the quaint town won't be dissimilar to strolling through an American theme park. But get there now, before Disney does.

What to See and Do in Hoi An and Environs

There are more than a whopping 840 structures in Hoi An that have been deemed as historical structures. They include houses, shops, pagodas, tombs, etc. We can't possibly describe them all but here are a few worth visiting, especially if you've only got a day to spend in Hoi An. (It's actually worth two or more).

Japanese Covered Bridge   ★★

This is Hoi An's most famous landmark, although there are other structures in town equally if not more compelling. It's located at the west end of Tran Phu Street and connects Tran Phu Street with Nguyen Thi Minh Khai Street. The bridge was reportedly built in the 16th century although there are some experts who think it is much older. It's not a long structure. At the western end of the bridge there are statues of two dogs, and on the east end, two monkeys. Legend has it that the bridge was started in the year of the monkey and finished during the year of the dog. Another tale says that the dogs and monkeys reflect the years that many of Japan's Emperors were born. It was built by the Japanese (although this isn't for certain either) in the same rigid style they built their own bridges—to avoid damage during earthquakes, though there are few in southern Vietnam. It was constructed to link the Japanese quarter of town with the Chinese section. In the 17th century it was the hangout for beggars and the homeless, taking advantage of the hundreds of people who crossed it everyday. During the 20th century the French flattened the bridge's roadway to make it easier to cross by car, but it was restored to its original curvature in 1986. The bridge was once known as the "Faraway People's Bridge," but the name didn't stick. Built on the far side of the bridge is a small pagoda called Chua Cau, where the old Faraway People's Bridge sign hangs.

Phuoc Kien (or Fukien) Pagoda   ★★

46 Tran Phu Street.

This Chinese pagoda was built around 1690 and then restored and enlarged in 1900. It is typical of the Chinese "dialect associations," or "clans" that were established in the Hoi An area. A hall of worship was also added in 1900. This pagoda is a reflection of the Chinese communities to establish within their dialect associations their own schools, hospitals, places of worship, and cemeteries. In Hoi An, there were four associations—the Fukien, Teochiu, Hainan and Kwangthung. This temple, dedicated Thien Hau Thanh Mau (Goddess of the Sea and Protector Sailors and Fishermen), is a large complex in a compound. Thien Hau is the principal figure at the main altar, dressed in an ornate robe. On the right side after entering the pagoda, you'll see a mural of Thien Hau rescuing a sinking ship. Outside there is a model of an old Chinese war junk.

Assemby Hall for Maritime Commerce   ★★

176 Tran Phu Street.

Despite the name, this is also a pagoda that was constructed in the early 18th century and was a refuge for Chinese merchants and sailors of all ethnicities. Tien Hau is the deity worshipped here (who else?). The compound is quite beautiful. For a small donation, the monk will write your name and address on a large piece of red paper and glue it to the inside wall of the pagoda. I noticed that there had been quite a few American visitors in recent months.

Hainan Assembly Hall

Near the corner of Tran Phu and Hoang Dieu Streets.

This was built for the Hainan Chinese congregation in 1833. It is dedicated to the 108 merchants from Hainan Island in southern China who were killed after they were mistaken for pirates by forces of Emperor Tu Duc. There are many plaques commemorating the killings inside the hall.

Ong Hoi Pagoda ★

24 Tran Phu Street, near the intersection of Nguyen Hue Street.

These are actually two temples—Chua Quan Cong and Chua Quan Am behind it. They were probably built sometime early in the 16th century. The pagodas are dedicated to Quan Cong and Quan Am, obviously.

Hoi An Market ★

Right next to the Ong Hoi Pagoda.

This is a huge market that extends along the river and Bach Dang Street. At the market area at Tran Phu street, the products are mostly consumer goods, while farther down, there is a variety of produce and animal meat.

Assembly Hall of the Fujian Chinese Congregation ★★

Opposite 35 Tran Phu Street.

Dedicated to Tien Hau, this assembly hall eventually became a temple. There's a mural near the entrance that shows Tien Hau crossing the sea with a lantern to rescue a faltering ship. A mural depicting the heads of the six Fujian families that escaped China for Hoi An in the 17th century after the overthrow of the Ming Dynasty is on the opposite wall. One chamber contains a statue of Tien Hau. Near the goddess are two figures, one red and the other green. One could see for a thousand miles; the other could hear things from long distances, and it was their responsibility to inform Tien Hau of ships in trouble. There is a central altar in the last chamber that depicts the six families that fled to Hoi An. Behind the altar is depicted the God of Prosperity. There's also a tall glass dome that contains the figure of Le Huu Trac, a great Vietnamese physician. It is said that married couples without children come here to pray for childbirth.

Chaozhou Assembly Hall

Across from 157 Nguyen Duy Hieu Street.

Wood carvings on the altar and beams are the attractions at this temple, constructed in 1776 as an assembly hall. There are also carvings of Chinese girls on the doors in front of the altar.

Chinese All-Community Assembly Hall

31 Phan Chu Trinh Street.

This hall is frequented by all members of the Chinese community in Hoi An. Bamboo blinds and hand-woven carpets are also made here. The hall was built in the early 1770s.

panese Tombs ★

Sugarcane, crushed sea shells, and boi loi leaves were used to build the tomb of Yajirobei, a Japanese Christian merchant who fled his native land and died here in 1647. The Japanese characters inscribed on the tomb are clearly visible to this day. The tomb faces northeast toward Japan. Getting there is a little difficult: Follow Nguyen Truong Street north to its end and then the sand path that curves left until you reach a junction in the path. Here, turn to the right. At the next junction after about 1 km, take a left, and then another left at the next fork. In the open field, you'll cross over an irrigation channel. Take a right on the other side of it and go up the hill. After about 150 meters, turn left for about 100 meters. The tomb is in the middle of rice fields. In the area is also the tomb of Masai, a Japanese who perished in Hoi An in 1629. There are other Japanese tombs in the area. The best bet is to get a guide if you don't already have one.

ao Dai Pagoda

64-70 Huynh Thuc Khang Street.
This is a small Cao Dai pagoda near the bus station. It was built in the early 1950s.

huc Thang Pagoda ★

At the end of Nguyen Trong Street, turn left on the dirt path for about 500 meters. This pagoda, built around 1454 by a Buddhist monk from China named Minh Hai is by far the oldest pagoda in Hoi An. In the main sanctuary, on the roof, Chinese characters depict the pagoda's construction. There are a few big bells here, one made from stone that's at least 200 years old. On the dais is A Di Da Buddha. On each side of the Buddha are Sakyamuni Buddhas. In front of the shrine is the figurine of Thich Ca as a young boy.

huoc Lam Pagoda

On the path past Chuc Thanh Pagoda about 350 meters.
This pagoda was built around the 1750s. Toward the end of the century, the eventual head monk here, An Thiem, who at 18-years-old left monkhood, joined the army in lieu of his brothers and eventually rose to the rank of general. He felt so bad about the number of people he killed, he asked to clean the market in Hoi An for 20 years. He was then asked to enter Phuoc Lam Pagoda as head monk.

loi An Church

Corner of Nguyen Truong To and Le Hong Phong Streets.
This is a new structure where Hoi An's European population was buried.

an Ky House ★★★

101 Nguyen Thai Hoc Street.
This is one of the three central "monuments" of Hoi An. It is a private house built more than 200 years ago for the worship of ancestors. It's one of the oldest and largest private houses in Hoi An. It was recognized by the government's Ministry of Culture as "an ancient building of high value" in 1985. It's basically unchanged in two centuries and reveals evidence of the period when trade with foreigners in this city was booming. During this time, residents used pulleys to raise goods above the floor. There is a combination of priceless ancient Chinese, Japanese and Vietnamese artwork in the house. The builders of the house had also been involved with con-

structing royal sites and palaces in Hue. The carpentry in the house represents both Chinese and Japanese influences. The upper reaches of the house reveal 18th-century Japanese architecture. The timber in the house is joined with wooden pegs. The floor is made mostly of brick and flagstone imported from abroad. Many of the decorative works of art and carvings reveal Vietnamese, Chinese and Western influences. Chinese poems are inscribed in mother-of-pearl. The carved wooden balcony is adorned with grape leaves, another European import. Seven generations of the family have lived here. Members of the family, as well as a couple of young hired guides, give one-hour presentations and they charge you 2000 dong.

77 Tran Phu Street

This private house is nearly 300 years old, and it claims to be the oldest private house in Hoi An. Who to believe? There are magnificent carvings in the house on the walls. Around the courtyard balcony, there are ceramic tiles built into the railings. A small fee is charged to visit this home.

Diep Dong Nguyen House

80 Nguyen Thai Hoc Street.

Built in the late 1800s, this house was constructed for a Chinese merchant, whose family still lives here. The owner has a priceless collection of antiques, including porcelain and furniture, but none are for sale. Some of the items were once on loan to Bao Dai himself. Although there are hours when the house is closed to the public, I just simply knocked on the door and, although I may have spoiled the family's lunch, the owner was more than happy to show me around—without asking for a fee!

Cua Dai Beach

Cua Dai Beach is 5 km from Hoi An, east out on Cua Dai Street, which is what Tran Hung Dao and Phan Dinh Phung Streets become out of town. Although this beautiful stretch of beach has been traditionally deserted, more and more tourists are discovering it. Fortunately Hoi An has so many attractions of its own, still only a handful of tourists make it out to the beach and, once there, don't stay very long. There are souvenir and refreshment kiosks here, but the atmosphere is easy and laid back, and you won't find the hordes of young children hawking chewing gum as you'll find at the nearby Marble Mountains.

Cham Island

About 20 km off Hoi An in the South China Sea. The island is best known for swift's nests, which are exported and eventually find their way into bird's nest soup in other Asian countries. Boats leave Hoi An for Cham Island from the Hoang Van Thu Street dock.

Cam Kim Island

This is a nearby island reachable by boat from the Hoang Van Thu Street dock.

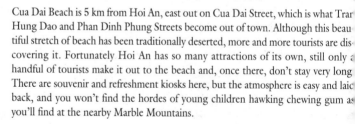

Where to Stay in Hoi An

AUTHOR'S NOTE: TELEPHONE PREFIXES

The following telephone numbers are local exchanges. The country code is 84. The city code is 51.

Hotel Hoi An   US$15–$50   ★

6 Tran Hung Dao Street. ☎ *861445. FAX: 861636*
120 rooms.
Beautiful old colonial building. Fans, air conditioning, restaurant, attached bath. Clean. Friendly staff. Air conditioning isn't so important during the winter, and the rooms are essentially the same, so that's what you're paying for with the top-end rooms. Very popular. Most tourists stay here. Especially busy during the summer and at Christmas. There's a dormitory here which can handle the spillover when it occurs. It usually opens up in the early evening, but only when all the other rooms have been booked. Beds here cost about US$4. Make reservations.

Vinh Hung Mini-Hotel   US$15–$35   ★

143 Tran Phu Street. ☎ *861621.*
14 rooms.
For my money, this is a better choice than the Hotel Hoi An. It's smaller and more comfortable, without the streams of folks found at the Hoi An. Attractive, large rooms with air conditioning, private bath, minibar, hot water. Restaurant; breakfast is included in the price.

Thuy Duong Hotel   US$10–$12

11 Le Loi Street.
9 rooms.
This a comfortable, small place, and a value for the money.

Guesthouse   About US$8

92 Phan Chu Trinh Street.
This place is a dump. Only for those who like cement, cockroaches and the like. Shared bath. Very inexpensive.

Where to Eat in Hoi An

Two specialties in Hoi An are *cao lau*—noodles and croutons with bean sprouts and greens topped with slices of pork. It's mixed with dried rice paper—and Hoi An *loanh thanh*—a delicious wanton soup. There are a number of restaurants offering the same fare up and down Tran Phu Street.

Cafe des Amis   ★

52 Rue Bach Dang.
Superb vegetarian fare at remarkably low prices. No menu and no meat, making it a backpacker's delight. Outspoken owner Nguyen Manh Kim is creating a cult following for the place. A must-do when in Hoi An.

Cao Lau Restaurant

42 Tran Phu Street.

Delicious cao lau.

Floating Restaurant

Bach Dang and Nguyen Thai Hoc Streets.

This is a new, flashy, festive place that sits on the riverfront near the Japanese Covered Bridge. Delicious seafood at reasonable prices. But it's geared for tourists. You can eat more cheaply along Tran Phu Street.

Directory

Transportation

Hoi An is about 30 km south of Danang.

By bus:

The bus station is about 1 km west of the city center at 74 Huynh Thuc Khang Street. Connections to Danang are constant. If you're on only a day trip, the last bus leaves for Danang at 5 p.m. The ride takes an hour. Van buses leave for Danang, Que Son, Dai Loc, Tra My and Tam Ky.

By train:

You'll have to get off the Reunification Express at Danang and find your way south. See the Danang chapter for transport to Hoi An.

By car:

If you're traveling north on NH1, the best way is to get off the highway (a sign is posted) about 27 km from Danang. You'll then travel about 10 km to Nguyen Thi Minh Khai street, which forks as you get into town. Nguyen Thi Minh Khai Street turns into Tran Phu Street on the other side of the Japanese Covered Bridge. From Danang, there are two routes. You can drive south on Trung Nu Street to the Marble Mountains and then continue south along the Korean Highway for about 20 km. Or you can take NH1 south, the sign posted for Hoi An, but this is a longer trip.

By boat:

You can't actually arrive in Hoi An by boat from other destinations, but the docks at Hoang Van Thu Street provide a great way of getting out to see Cam Kim and Cham Islands.

Hoi An

Danang possesses some of the finest ancient Cham relics in the world.

Cham monuments at My Son

Hoan Kiem Lake in the center of Hanoi

ng distance bus in Danang

any historical sights can be reached via boat on Hue's Perfume River.

Danang

Linh Ong Pagoda sits high atop the Marble Mountains, a Viet Cong refuge during the war.

DANANG IN A CAPSULE

Fourth-largest city in Vietnam...The principal port in the central part of the country...A repository of traditional art objects and architecture from the Cham dynasty, which dates from the 2nd century A.D.... It was here that the French originally landed to begin their "excursion" into Vietnam...A century later, the first U.S. combat troops arrived to begin their Vietnam "excursion"...Danang fell to the Viet Cong in March 1975...It signified South Vietnam's defeat in the war...This is an ancient city with a rich cultural history.

The Hai Van Pass, a few kilometers to the north of Danang (or the Pass of the Ocean Clouds), is the thin, snaky stretch of roadway that connects Danang and Lang Co Beach. The weather changes dramatically, truly separating the south from the north. Some of the grades are so steep that the road builders had to construct uphill grades on the downslopes for buses and trucks that lose their brakes, which happens with alarming and deadly frequency.

All along the flanks of the pass, shrines mark where vehicles crashed and their occupants met their demise. It is considered good luck for passing motorists to stop and pay their respects to the dead, as it is believed that the life source of the deceased will be absorbed into the spirit of living motorists and thus prevent them from suffering the same fate.

Laboriously, the pass ascends and then drops to the sugary sands of Lang Co Beach. On top, the pass (also once known as the Mandarin Road because it was reserved only for the use of important ancient mandarin VIPs), snakes through 20 km of spectacular jungle mountains and reaches a height of 500 meters. Here are perhaps the most majestic views in Vietnam. Going by train will not give you these views, as the track cuts a swath through the terrain at the base of the mountains along the sea.

Danang (population about 500,000, and originally known as Cho Han—Market of the Han—and later renamed Tourane by the French) has meant a lot of things for a lot of people—in particular, some of the history wrought by the war, some spectacular scenery, and the friendliness of the locals. But Danang is on the threshold of becoming a major destination of "resort" tourists from Europe, Australia and the U.S. who are accustomed to the amenities found in Bali, Phuket, Pattaya and Tahiti. Hordes of foreign tourists wade in the waters off a US$50 a night hotel beside "China Beach," which actually isn't China Beach at all, but a moniker given to a renamed beach by the government tourism authorities because it's more accessible to tourists than the real China Beach.

Most of the informed locals place the actual China Beach (the popular R&R GI resort of the Vietnam War immortalized by a short-lived, U.S. television show) about three miles up the coast. But, regardless, the bogus China Beach of lore made popular by the American TV series of the same name a few years ago has become the natural destination of those who want to impress their friends at home with T-Shirts. "China Beach" today is Hanoi's exploitation of the adventure tourist trade. And it's paying off.

In October 1993, more than 30 international professional surfers, much to the mixed delight/disdain of the local authorities, descended upon "China Beach" in bourgeois day-glo wetsuits for the first international surfing competition to ever have been held in Vietnam. It was a four-day, US$60,000

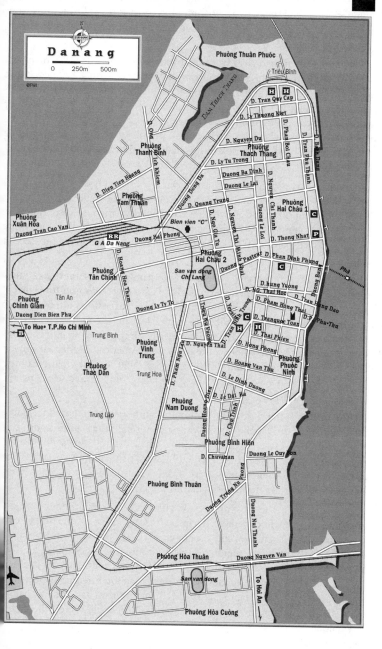

competition called the Saigon Floating Hotel Surf Pro'93, brought to stunning Non Nuoc Beach (the real name for the bogus beach) by Bruce Aitken, director of Sortas Asia.

The entrepreneur had already staged two successful events in Vietnam as a way of promoting surfing and tourism in Vietnam. Surfing has now taken root with the locals, and Vietnam now fields a team of hard-core surfers. Although it's unlikely the perfect wave will ever be found at China Beach, or anywhere else in Vietnam for that matter, the country boasts some 12 "professional" surfers, who took up the sport about nine years ago after some Americans kindly left some boards for the locals; they're all part of the fledgling Danang Surf Club.

Of course, if you're not into surfing, Danang offers a host of other attractions. It serves as an excellent base to make quests to other area sites. There's May Son, about 60 km away, which is considered Vietnam's most impressive Cham site. Some say it's on par with Cambodia's Angkor Wat but, quite frankly, that's usually said by people who haven't had the opportunity to visit Angkor.

When the French took over Danang (Vietnam's fourth-largest city), they renamed it Tourane. It then became Thai Pien before adopting the current name. It's located on a peninsula where the Han River flows into the China Sea. It is the last location in Vietnam that really can be considered southern Vietnam, as the weather changes dramatically on the other side of the pass. Danang is also the site where some of the first American Marines landed in 1965 to control the airfield. Shortly after, by 1966, the city had become a strategic American naval and air base, handling both heavy warships and long-range bombers.

After the fall of the south, the communist authorities attempted to reduce the population of Danang by creating agricultural zones outside the city. The policy had little effect in reducing this bustling port's population. Whereas the port was once frequented by ships of Vietnam's socialist allies, today one sees off its shores ships from Taiwan, Singapore and Hong Kong—and soon, no doubt—ships from the U.S.

Danang is one of the most progressive cities in Vietnam in terms of exploiting Vietnam's new free market principles. It is aggressive in attacting foreign investment, and its cultural and geographical isolation from both Hanoi and Saigon virtually make the region relatively autonomous—not unlike Ha Tien in the Mekong Delta during the 17th and 18th centuries. Danang is one of the leaders in Vietnam in economic reforms (attacting foreign investment at a pace faster than both Hanoi and HCMC), and tourism has certainly helped boost the local economy, as more than 100,000 people visited the city in 1994 alone.

Danang has the stature of perhaps being the most chaotic city in South Vietnam during the war. With both Hue to the north, and Quang Ngai, some 100 km to the south, having fallen to the communists, Danang found itself cut off from the rest of South Vietnam. South Vietnamese troops defected, and on March 29, 1975, truckloads of armed men and women in trucks entered the city and declared it under communist control—without a shot being fired. The only real fighting was between Danang locals and ARVN soldiers battling for space on fleeing aircraft and sea vessels. Two jetliners flew from Saigon to Danang to pick up civilians and soldiers. The scene was utter chaos as soldiers and locals battled one another for space on the planes. Some even attached themselves to the wheelwells of one of the aircraft as the planes took off. They met their deaths as they fell hundreds of feet into the South China Sea, all captured by TV cameras on the second Boeing 727. The only civilians that managed to board the flights were a couple of women and a child.

Danang also contains a beautiful assortment of pagodas, as well as an impressive Cao Dai Temple (which is actually only really impressive if you haven't seen the Cao Dai site at Tay Ninh). The Ho Chi Minh Museum includes a replica of Ho's House. Along Bach Dang Street on the banks of the Han River is the flower market beside the ferry pier.

What to See and Do in Danang and Environs

Cham Museum   ★★★

Located where Tran Phu and Le Dinh Duong Streets meet. This houses probably the best collection of Cham art to be found anywhere in the world. There are more than 300 artifacts in the museum, many dating to the 4th century. There are beautiful sculptures reflecting the 1000-year Cham period. The museum was founded by the École Française d'Extrême Orient, a group of French scholars, in 1915 and was expanded in 1935. Check out the magnificent sandstone carvings. Indonesian and Malay influences are seen in the work before the 10th century, while Khmer influences become more apparent in the work after that date. The museum also features the famous 7th-century altar Tra Kieu, which depicts the wedding of Prince Rama. The building itself is worth the visit. The large rooms are airy and each is devoted to a different period of Cham art. There are displays that range from the 4th through the 14th centuries. Cham art can be basically broken down into two periods: before the 10th century, when the art reflected Cham relations with Indonesia and Mahayana Buddhism, and between the 10th and 14th centuries, when continued conflict with both the Cambodians and the Vietnamese created art with significant Khmer influences. The "Mother of the Country" (Uroja, which, in Cham, means the breast of a woman) is the pervasive image in the museum. You'll see a lot of nipples here. There is also the phallic symbol of Shiva. There are dozens of sandstone sculptures and altars, many of which have required surprisingly little renovation, that span a period of more than a thousand years. You'll definitely need a guide here, as the lingas, reliefs, and garudas are only marginally explained (really only the

Danang

name and date of construction are marked) and only in Vietnamese. Worth a few visits. Open 8–11 a.m. and 1–5 p.m. every day. There is a small admission fee.

Cao Dai Temple ★

35 Hai Phong Street.

It's the second-largest Cao Dai temple in Vietnam, second only to the sect's base in Tay Ninh. There are more than 20,000 Cao Dais in Danang and this is their center-piece. Women enter on the left, marked "Nu Phai," and men enter the temple on the right, marked "Nam Phai." As in all Cao Dai temples, above the main altar is the image of the Giant Eye, which is the symbol of Cao Daism. What I found most interesting about the temple was the sign hanging in front of the altar on the ceiling that says "Van Giao Nhat Ly." It means that all religions have the same purpose. There are also portraits of Jesus Christ, Mohammed, Buddha and Confucius. I didn't see any pictures of Marilyn Monroe or William Shakespeare, though. The temple was erected in 1956. Prayers are held four times a day.

Danang Cathedral

Located on Tran Phu Street.

This church serves Danang's Catholic community. Built in 1923 by the French, it's worth a peek for its single-spire, pink-sandstone architecture.

Ho Chi Minh Museum

Located on Nguyen Van Troi Street.

Also called Bao Tang Ho Chi Minh. Here you can see various weaponry of the Vietnam War from the U.S., China and the former Soviet Union. There's also a replica of Ho's Hanoi house on display. Open 7–11 a.m. and 1–4:30 p.m. Tues.–Sun.

Pho Da Pagoda

Across from 293 Phan Chu Trinh Street.

Not much to see here if you've already seen a lot of pagodas. Built in 1923.

Phap Lam Pagoda

123 Ong Ich Khiem Street.

The main feature here is the tarnished (at least during my visit) brass statue of Dia Tang, the Chief of Hell. The title would make for an interesting business card, I think.

Cho Han Market

At the corner of Tran Phu and Huong Vuong Streets.

This is a new market—clean and worth a visit for essentials.

Cho Con Market

At the corner of Ong Ich Khiem Streets.

A good place for handicrafts and souvenirs.

Beaches

One of the best parts of any Danang visit is the beaches, and there are some good ones in the Danang area. The best time to visit Danang's beaches is from April through July, when the surf isn't as dangerous and there are fewer undertows. **China Beach** was an R&R area during the war and was made popular by the U.S. TV series of the same name, although the real China Beach (**My Khe Beach**) is some three

Danang

miles north. There's a hotel and a number of restaurants in the fake China Beach area. There's also **Nam O Beach**, about 15 km northwest of the city. It's a good place to see the locals' fishing boats. **My Khe Beach** is a little more than 5 km from Danang and one of the better beaches in the area. But watch out for the undertow. **Thanh Binh Beach** in the center of Danang is often packed with locals and can be dirty.

Marble Mountains ★★★

These are the beautiful limestone peaks that rise above Danang. About 10 km from the city of Hoi An and only a stone's throw from Bai Non Nuoc are the five craggy peaks of the Marble Mountains (each represents one of the five elements of the universe), the site of numerous guerrilla attacks on American troops down below from the nearly inaccessible clifflike edifices overlooking the China Beach area. Because of their relative ruggedness and strategic location overlooking Danang, they were a favorite spot of the VC during the war. The VC could snipe at American troops below virtually uncontested.

A trail of steep stairs cuts into the limestone of the most oft-visited peak (Thuy Son), about 900 if I remember correctly. There are a number of natural caves that were once used as Hindu shrines and then of course later by the Viet Cong in their largely successful attempts to harass American troops below, who were picked off like flies on many occasions. The caves were also used as a hospital during the war for wounded Viet Cong soldiers. Getting up the stairs is difficult, and many older people would be foolish making the attempt. Be prepared for hordes of children touts hawking everything from candy to guided tours. I mean there are hundreds of these little kids; all are flawless in their English, as well as fluent in French, German, Italian and a number of other tongues. Each and every single one of them! As many as a dozen at a time won't leave your side from your ascent of the mountain back to the base. If you're lucky you'll only get away with paying one of them for a guided tour. A few thousand dong should do the trick. It's worth it for two reasons. You get a decent tour, and when the other kids see that you already have someone accompanying you as a guide (although he or she may only be 3 or 4 years old) they'll tend to leave you alone.

At the top of the main staircase is the Ong Chon gate, which still reveals bullet holes from the war. Behind that is Linh Ong Pagoda, which has been freshly repainted. Then there are the caverns (Tang Chon Dong) which contain a variety of concrete Buddhas. The passage through the rocks and the caves on the mountain can be very narrow and dark, and it's best to carry a flashlight (the childrens' candles do little to help, especially if you're at the back of a group of visitors. But if you can get up to the top, the scenery is spectacular: miles of crystal clear, unspoiled views of the beaches, Cham Island and the surrounding mountains. You can even see the Hai Van Pass through the Truong Son Mountains to the north. Thuy Son is a village in the mountains that sells local handicrafts. The Tam Thai Pagoda has also been carved into the mountains. The name was given to the limestone mountains by the Nguyen Emperor Minh Mang, who obviously wasn't a geologist. The numerous caves and grottoes on the main Marble mountain were formed by chemical treatments. The main temple up here is the Tam Thai Pagoda, which was built in 1825 by Minh Mang. There's a huge statue of the Buddha Sakyamuni (historic Buddha) which is next to Bodhisattva Quan Am (the Goddess of Mercy). There's also another grotto called Huyen Khong Cave. The roof of the cave has five holes poked into the ceiling to allow dim sunlight to filter through. At about noon–2 p.m., the light shines upon the central statue of Sakyamuni. There's also Linh Nham, a vertical cave with an altar inside. Another cave nearby (Hoa Nghiem) contains a Buddha. There's also the spectacular Huyen Khong Cave, which features an opening to the sky and contains numerous shrines and inscriptions on the walls. This was the cave the VC used as a field hospital during the war. When finished with your visit, you can descend the mountain through the back staircase, which is a lot easier on the heart and lungs. Although you can begin the journey from the back side of the mountain, or rear staircase, it makes more sense to do it from the front, although you'll miss the horde of kids at the base of the front stairs. Cost is 10,000 dong and you should spend at least an hour on Thuy Son. More time does it justice, however.

Bai Non Nuoc (China Beach)   ★★

The hamlet of Non Nuoc is near the fake China Beach. Accommodations are limited at Bai Non Nuoc to the Non Nuoc Beach Hotel. The 60-room Indochina Beach Hotel opened in 1995 after renovations. Managed by Majestic International, based in Hong Kong, the hotel's second phase will include about 300 new villas.

My Son and Dong Duong   ★★★

This is the former site of the Cham's most important cultural, religious and intellectual metropolis back when Tra Kieu was Champa's capital. Although reaching these areas is difficult, they are actually the principal reasons many visitors come to Danang. My Son (which means the Beautiful Mountain) is about 60 km southwest of Danang and it's not an easy journey. To get there, you have to take the road south from Danang about 34 km and cross the Thu Bon River Bridge. About 2 km past the bridge, turn right and follow the tributary of the Thu Bon toward the valley. You'll come across the small village of Tra Kieu after about 7–8 km. Continue to travel upstream for another 28 km to Kim Lam. Turn left for another 6 km. The road here is at times virtually impassable (see INSIDER TIP) during the rainy season. If you're going by car, you'll have to leave it at the end of the "road" and then travel by foot for 8 km on a path that winds through lush hillsides and a lot of brush to reach My Son.

AUTHOR'S NOTE

You should definitely have a guide when traveling to My Son. The area was extensively mined during the war, and many of the mines, still quite lethal, remain beside the roads and paths leading around My Son.

There are more than 70 remarkable Cham monuments in the area, constructed between the 7th and 13th centuries, and it's why many people compare the region with Cambodia's Angkor. (The monuments at My Son are significantly smaller than those found at Angkor in the Cham belief that no grandiose structures should be built.) The small, elegant monuments are surrounded by mountains in a valley with the impressive Cat's Tooth Mountain towering over the basin. There are coffee plantations and clear streams for cooling off.

INSIDER TIP

If you do much traveling into the interior from Danang, remember that roads are often washed out between May and October, which is the wet monsoon season in Vietnam. Medical facilities are next to nonexistent; and doctors will, in many instances, demand cash on the spot or they may not take care of you.

Most of the monuments consist of the classic Cham Tower, which is built high (by Cham standards) to reflect the divinity of the king (Shiva, the founder of the dynasties of Champa). Many of the structures are in incredibly good shape (the bricks were glued together by a vegetable-based cement, according to a number of scientists. Many structures were domed in gold). It's a shame that the remaining buildings aren't in such good shape, the result of incessant B-52 bombing during the war, especially during 1969 (the area was considered a free fire zone at the time). Among those buildings demolished by American sappers was perhaps the most important temple at the site, which was a magnificent tower designated as A1 by French archeologists near the end of the 19th century.

My Son became a major religious area in the 4th century and was bustling until the 13th century. The nearly 1000 years of Cham culture far surpasses religious realms in other Southeast Asia locations. During the early centuries of the dynasties, there was much contact with the Indonesians, as the two empires traded both in commerce and in education. Cham pottery has even been found in Indonesia (Java).

The monuments at My Son were separated into 10 groups (A-K, although, curiously, there are two "A's" and no "I"). The neighboring groups that remain are B, C and D. B and C are two temple enclosures which are about 25 by 25 meters, and lie side by side, although you'll have to use your imagination to distinguish the structures as two separate sanctuaries. Group B is the massive main sanctuary of the southern enclosure. There is a sandstone base and the main building once had eight monolithic columns supporting it.

Temple C is similar to Temple B, more modest in size, measuring 5 by 10 meters but it is a well preserved sanctuary. A small building (C3) is at the southeast corner of the Group C enclosure. Restoration is currently being performed on its interior walls. C7 is in bad shape. C5 and C6 are also being restored.

Temple D is between the Group B and C enclosures and contains six structures. This area is known as the Court of Steles. It's noted for its altars and rows of statues. At the end of the court are two badly demolished buildings. D3 is on the western end where it stands between the gateways to the B and C enclosures.

Dong Duong is about 20 km east of My Son and 60 km south of Danang. In the 9th century, the area emerged as the center of Cham art after King Indravarman II constructed a big Buddhist monastery here. The towers and reliefs at Dong Duong are more intricate and flamboyant than those at My Son. But only a century later, the Cham art and cultural capital returned to My Son. The new towers built at My Son during the 10th century more reflected those at Dong Duong than those that had been previously built at My Son.

Lang Co Beach   ★★

35 km north of Danang over Hai Van Pass.

Lang Co Beach is a kilometers-long stretch of sandy white, palm-lined beach whose only (but significant) misfortune is being located on the north side of Hai Van Pass, where the climate (much of the year) changes dramatically, from hot and sunny to cold and gray. There are incredible views of Lang Co descending Hai Van Pass from Danang when the mountainous region isn't shrouded in fog, which it usually is. But when the sun's out, you'll just be too tempted not to wade in the crystal clear lagoon on the west side of Lang Co, regardless whether you're staying here or simply passing through. Nowhere else in Vietnam have I seen water this azure and clear. You can also walk for kilometers on the beach at Lang Co and neither see a soul nor a sole print for hours. Train travelers like to stop here for the night simply for its pristine peace and quiet. In fact, there's only one place to stay in Lang Co—Nha Khach Cong Doan—situated up a dirt path off Highway 1. You'll have no problem finding it, just ask someone. It's the only digs in town. The small hotel sits on top of a short path right on the beach and is rather run down. Electricity is only available from about 6 to 10 p.m. Rooms have as many as four beds and cost as little as US$4–$5 if you let a Vietnamese do the negotiating for you, perhaps US$10 if you don't. There's a small restaurant here, but it's a lot easier to simply walk down the hill to NH1 and take advantage of one of the many food stalls lining the highway, where the food is cheaper and company cheerier. The area is a popular rest stop for long distance buses heading both north and south, and passengers in hordes pack the roadside food stalls. It's amazing the small restaurant at the hotel is able to remain in business at all. Another important thing to remember about Lang Co: You can show up at the hotel any time during the winter and expect to get a room. But the small hotel is generally packed with foreigners during the summer months when the weather is better. From Danang, you can hire a motorbike driver to take you there and back for about US$3. A good place to find a willing one is at the Marble Mountains Hotel.

Insider Tip

If you hire a motorbike (with or without driver) for a journey over Hai Van Pass to Lang Co, be warned that although it may be sunny and unbearably hot in Danang, the situation changes rapidly as you ascend Hai Van Pass. The fog can be as thick as smoke off the top of a burning Third World textile factory. Bring rain gear or be prepared to get wet.

Ba Na Hill Station ★

50 km west of Danang.

Situated at nearly 150 meters above the sea west of Danang is one of southern Vietnam's best kept secrets—so secret in fact that tourism officials seem to not know about it, which explains why it's so hard to get here and why there's nowhere to stay. This hill station was formerly a French settlement and was often visited by French tourists before 1945. The views here of the mountains to the west and the coastal plain to the east can be magnificent or lousy depending on the cloud cover.

Where to Stay in Danang

AUTHOR'S NOTE: TELEPHONE PREFIXES

The telephone numbers listed here are local exchanges only. The country code is 84. The city code is 51.

Danang Hotel   US$7–$40

3 Dong Da Street. ☎ *821179.*
100 rooms.

This is one of three hotels bunched together on the northern tip of the peninsula and one of the obligatory checkpoints on the backpacker route. The lower end rooms are dreary, but you get air conditioning for $7 so they're a bargain. Shared bath, but check the toilet and shower before accepting the room. Water pressure seems to vary greatly from room to room. For some reason, this hotel seems to be popular with foreign businessmen. One reason may be the hookers. At any given time, you'll run into Cubans, Indians and, of course, the omnipresent French. Downstairs restaurant is okay. At press time, the hotel was being "rebuilt."

Marble Mountains Hotel
(Ngu Hanh Son Hotel)   US$8–$40

5 Dong Da Street. ☎ *823258 or 823122.*
60 rooms.

This is a new hotel next to the Danang Hotel and is far more attractive both inside and out than its neighbor. There are also "flats" available here with a living room, kitchen and two double bed rooms. The hotel offers car rentals and says it can handle visa matters.

Dong Da Hotel   US$8–$15

7 Dong Da Street. ☎ *842216.*
68 rooms.

Next door is this alternative to the Danang Hotel and the Marble Mountains Hotel. This is less run-down than the Danang Hotel, but a little more expensive for budget travelers. The lower-end rooms have a fan, while the others get air conditioning. There is a restaurant.

Ngan Hang Hotel

59 Dong Da. ☎ *821909.*
Inexpensive.

Danang

Orient Hotel (Phuong Dong Hotel)   **US$40–$60**   ★★

   93 Phan Chu Trinh Street. ☎ *821266; FAX: 822854.*
   The lobby is exquisite in this old structure, and many think the Orient is the best
   lodging in Danang. TV; refrigerators; good restaurant upstairs.

Dau Khi Ami Motel

   7 Quang Trung. ☎ *822582 or 824494; FAX: 825532.*
   Inexpensive.

Pacific Hotel   **US$10–$40**

   92 Phan Chu Trinh Street. ☎ *822137.*
   48 rooms.
   Old building. Basic accommodations; TV; refrigerators; restaurant.

Bach Dang Hotel   **US$45–$120**   ★★★

   50 Bach Dang Street. ☎ *823649 or 823034.*
   Situated across Bach Dang Street from the Han River, this may be the nicest place
   to stay in Danang. There is a restaurant and a nightclub.

The Fishery Guest House
(Nha Khach Thuy San)   **US$15–$20**

   12 Bach Dang Street. ☎ *822612; FAX: 821659.*
   15 rooms.
   This seemed a little overpriced, but there's both a restaurant and a nightclub here
   and that may be why. Air conditioning, single and double rooms, hot water.

Phuong Dong Hotel   **US$20–$30**

   93 Phan Chau Trinh Street. ☎ *821266. FAX: 822854.*
   Air conditioning; TV; refrigerators; hot water.

Hai Au Hotel   **US$35–$67**   ★★

   215 Tran Phu Street. ☎ *822722. FAX: 822854.*
   40 rooms.
   Situated across the street from the Danang Cathedral. Good location. Air conditioning; telephones; hot water; restaurant; bar; sauna; massage.

My Khe Guesthouse   **US$30–$35**   ★

   My Khe Beach, Bac My An (6 km from Danang). ☎ *836125.*
   Neat place facing the beach at My Khe. Recommended.

INSIDER TIP

*The American Company DeMatteis Development Corp. plans to construct a
20-hectare seaside resort in Danang. The US$150 million project will include
a hotel, offices, shops, an aquarium, corporate villas and an aquarium.*

Where to Eat in Danang

Ngoc Anh

   30 Tran Phu. ☎ *822778.*
   Vietnamese, Asian.

Trieu Chau

   62 Tran Phu. ☎ *824002.*

Vietnamese.

Nha HangRestaurant
72 Tran Phu.
Vietnamese.

Giai Khat
187 Tran Phu.
Vietnamese.

Tu Do Restaurant ★★
172 Tran Phu. ☎ *821869.*
Chinese, European and Vietnamese food served in a large courtyard. The food is good and many claim this to be Danang's best eatery.

Chin Do
174 Tran Phu. ☎ *821846.*
European and Asian specialties as well as Chinese seafood.

Phuong Nam
205 Tran Phu. ☎ *822806.*
Vietnamese.

Be Thui
207 Tran Phu.
Vietnamese.

Tien Hung Restaurant
190 Tran Phu.
Vietnamese.

Christies Harbourside Bar/Grill Restaurant ★
9 Bach Bang.
Hamburgers, pasta, Vietnamese, fish and chips. Located right on the Han River. There's also a duty free shop here.

Kim Dinh Restaurant
7 Bach Dang Street. ☎ *821541.*
Across the street from the Bach Dang Hotel. Vietnamese and Asian. This sits right out over the Han River. Popular with locals.

Thanh Lich Restaurant ★
48 Bach Dang Street.
Vietnamese, Chinese, and European. Excellent seafood. Right next door to the Bach Dang Hotel.

Que Huong Restaurant
1 Bach Dang Street.
Vietnamese food, karaoke, cafe.

Mien Trung Restaurant ★
1 Bach Dang Street.
Vietnamese, Chinese, and European. Expensive.

Kim Dinh Restaurant
7 Bach Dang Street.

Danang

This stretches out over the Han River. Good food, good views.

Restaurant 72

72 Tran Phu Street.
Great shrimp spring rolls.

Thanh Lich Restaurant

42 Bach Dang Street.
Vietnamese, Asian. Extensive menu.

Directory

Transportation

Danang is 965 km from Saigon, 759 km from Hanoi, 108 km from Hue, 541 km from Nha Trang, 303 km from Quy Nhon, 350 km from the Laos border and 130 km Quang Ngai. Danang has an "international" airport (it has been designated as such to create a better reputation as both a tourist and business destination) located about 3 km from the city. There are regular connections to Saigon and Hanoi (both about US$90) as well as Nha Trang (US$60), Buon Ma Thuot, Haiphong, Vinh and Pleiku (US$30). Flights from HCMC depart from four to seven times daily, starting at 6:45 a.m. and ending at 4:15 p.m. Flights to HCMC from Danang also depart from four to seven times daily, beginning at 8:45 a.m. or 10 a.m. and ending at at 6:15 p.m. or 7 p.m. From Hanoi, planes leave for Danang from three to five times daily, starting at 6:30, 7 or 8 in the morning and ending at 5:10 p.m. (except Friday, when the last flight is at 12:15 p.m.). Planes bound for Hanoi depart four times daily (five times Monday) between 8:30 a.m. and 7 p.m. Schedules change frequently, but you can count on a half-dozen flights a day back and forth from HCMC, and nearly the same number to and from Hanoi.

Like at Saigon's Tan Son Nhat Airport, there are many examples still standing at the airport here of the cement hangars that were built by the Americans during the war, when this was one of the busiest airports in the world. "International" flights (to locations such as Hong Kong, Manila, Paris, Kuala Lumpur, etc.) are always via connections in HCMC or Hanoi; the only difference in the airport being an "international" one is that you can buy a ticket to Bangkok in Danang and not in Nha Trang.

By air:

VN flies to Danang. From HCMC, there are daily flights at 7:20 a.m. and 11:50 a.m. Also on Mon./Wed./Sat. at 9 a.m. and Tues./Thur./Fri./Sun. at 1:50 p.m. Flights from Danang to HCMC are daily at 9 a.m., 1:50 p.m. and 4:20 p.m.

By bus:

The long-distance bus station in Danang is at *8 Dien Bien Phu Street*, about 2 km west of the city. The ticket office is across the street. Here you can get buses to Vinh, Hue, Haiphong, Hanoi and Hong Gai. Next to the Thanh Hotel is a station *(52 Phan Chu Trinh)* where you can get an express bus to Hanoi (about 32,000 dong), Saigon (about 40,000 dong), Nha Trang (about 22,000 dong), Vinh (about 20,000 dong), Dalat (about 32,000 dong), Haiphong (about 34,000 dong), and Buon Ma Thuot (about 27,000 dong). Buses to local destinations such as Hoi An and Marble Mountain leave from opposite *350 Hung Vuong Street*. There is non-express bus service to Trung Phuoc, Hue, Hoi An, Trao Hiep Duc, Tien Phuoc, Ha

Tan, Quy Nhon, Thanh My, Que Son, Dong Ha, Giang Ai Nghia, An Hoa, Giao Thuy, Tam Ky and Kham Duc, among other destinations.

By train:

120 Haiphong Street, at the intersection with Hoang Hoa Tham Street. Optimistically, it takes about 20 hours to get to Saigon and a little less to Hanoi. The views along the coast are spectacular.

Local transportation

Local transportation is by cyclo or rented bicycle. Motorbike riders hang out in front of the Marble Mountains and Danang Hotels and are always available for hire, for either around town or day trips. I paid one to take the 20 km Hai Van Pass over to Lang Co Beach about 40,000 dong. It was too much, as I subsequently learned you can hire a driver for as little as US$5 per day. But you've got to look hard to find one. The Vietnamese know tourist dollars when they see them.

Post Office

46 Bach Dang Street at the corner of Le Duan Street; ☎ *821327*. International telephone and fax services. Faxes can also be transmitted from the Phuong Dong Hotel.

Tourist Offices

Danang Tourist Office. *48 Bach Dang Street*. ☎ *822226. FAX: 822854*.

Vietnamtourism. *158 Phan Chu Trinh*. ☎ *822990 or 822999. FAX: 822854*.

TNT International Express

☎ *821685 or 822582*.

Banks and Moneychangers

Vietcom Bank, *104 Le Loi Street*. ☎ *821024*. Will exchange money and give cash advances on major U.S. credit cards.

Hospital

Hospital C, *35 Hai Phong Street*. ☎ *822480*.

Airline Offices

Vietnam Airlines Domestic Booking Office, *3 Yen Bai Street*. ☎ *822808*.

Danang

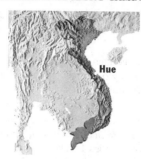

Hue

Hue was the capital of Vietnam during the Nguyen Dynasty 1802–1945.

HUE IN A CAPSULE

Hue served as the capital of Vietnam for more than 140 years...it houses ancient temples...Imperial buildings...and French-style edifices...was established in the 17th century...invaded by the French in 1833 and by the Japanese in 1945...was hammered by U.S. forces during the Tet offensive...many historical monuments were destroyed during this military action...but a great many remain.

The Ancient Capital of Hue (population about 350,000) began to swell with tourists in 1993. Tourism is now the leading generator of hard currency in this historic city that was battered during the Vietnam War. Today, thousands of residents make their salaries from tourism. The five principal provincial tourism businesses reaped in more than 32 million dong in 1994. Simply, the city is going through a tourist boom. Tourism in Hue doubled in a single year (from 1992–93). Foreign currency earnings increased threefold. Responding to the surge in tourism, Thua Thien Hue authorities quickly opened the elegant riverside Hotel Hue, which is the first joint-venture hotel to be opened in the city. Since 1975, when there existed only the dilapidated Huong Giang hotel with 47 gutted guest rooms, tourism authorities have opened at least six "luxury" hotels of international standards with 335 rooms (620 beds). And over the past several years, dozens of hotels have opened up and down the south side of the Perfume River—including the Kinh Do and Dong Ha. The Hoa Hong Hotel on Le Loi Street was the first private hotel to open in the city.

Western visitors in Hue can now find a slew of garden houses and villas as accommodations. Most of the accommodations in the Hue area are enjoying occupancy rates greater than 80 percent, and that's why it's a good bet to book with a particular hotel first rather than simply showing up (although you should always be able to find a room in the city).

By the year 2000 it is predicted that tourism levels will climb to five times higher than their current levels. With the pace of infrastructure developments in the region, this forecast seems reasonable. Officials in the city told me that their predictions will be predicated primarily on the initiation of package tours rather than travel by independent tourists. Hue's Royal Park is being restored, as is the Tinh Tam Lake. Additionally, under construction is the Bach Ma-Lang Co casino. Visits to the "Nine Underground Bunkers," which depict the atrocities of the South Vietnamese Ngo Dinh Diem regime, are in the works. There are reenactments of ancient and royal ceremonies being devised at various locations. Horse-drawn carriages will soon take tourists to the royal tombs, the mountains and the beaches. As well, re-creations of costumes worn by kings, queens, princes and princesses are being sewn as fast as possible for staff at all the new hotels. In short, and regrettably to some extent, this city is gearing up to become a "tour" tourist's destination.

Hue is generally cool, rainy and gray (yearly rainfall can total 152 cm or 60 in.). Although the Citadel and the Forbidden Purple City are well worth visiting, the devastation caused by war to these ancient sites makes them essentially unrecognizable, with patches of weeds and occasional deformed rock formations that were once grand splendors of the Nguyen Dynasty now springing from the earth like outcroppings on a moonscape.

Hue (originally called Phu Xuan and built in 1687), during the Nguyen Dynasty, was the cultural, religious and economic capital of Vietnam. Nguy-

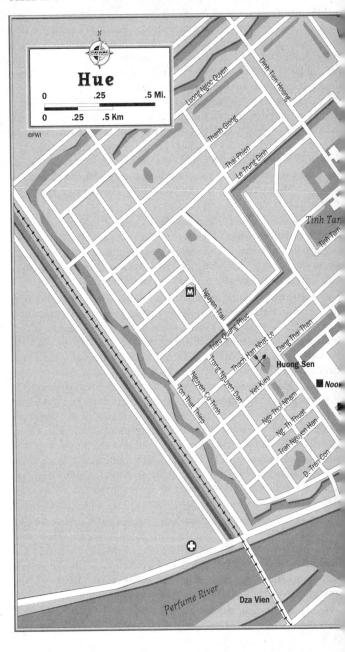

Hue

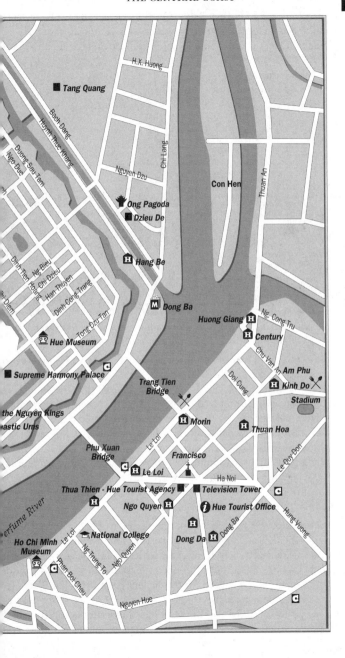

en emperors built the Mandarin Road (Quan Lo) which allowed travelers to remarkably reach Saigon in only two weeks, and Hanoi in under a week. Messengers that were more than two days late were flogged for their tardiness.

Pedestrian crossings don't need to be marked along national highways because most of the pedestrian users wouldn't recognize one if they saw it.

In addition to the Vietnam War, Hue has had an extensive history of conflict. There were no fewer than 100 peasant uprisings in the area between 1802 and 1820. Royalty bickered and fought constantly. The French attacked Hue in 1833 and decimated the population to such an extent that the Emperor Hiep Hoa permitted the city to become a protectorate of France. The French divided the population by their spreading of Christianity. Although the French, and later the Japanese, felt it in their best interests to allow the Nguyen Dynasty to continue, there remained perpetual feuding and power scheming among the Nguyen royalty—and its influence on the population dropped to such a degree that the last Nguyen Emperor, Bao Dai, ceded the throne in August 1945.

Even after World War II, peace would not come to Hue. The Viet Cong took over the Citadel for 25 days during the Tet Offensive in 1968 and their communist flag defiantly flew from the Citadel's flag pole for more than three weeks. U.S. troops ruthlessly counterattacked, and it was this action which caused much of the damage to the ancient royal sites. The Thai Hoa Palace was decimated. More than 10,000 people died in the bitter fighting in Hue during the Tet Offensive. But with the Americans back in control of the area, peace would still not last long. NVA troops, after taking over the city in 1975, reportedly massacred thousands of civilians, beheading many, making the massacre at My Lai look like a mugging.

For shopping, the most unique item in Hue is a hat called *non bai tho*, which is made from palm and bamboo leaves. Inside the hats are proverbs, poems and the lyrics to love songs that can only be seen when facing the hat toward the light. Makes for a great gift.

What to See and Do in and Around Hue

Citadel ★

This is a large, moated and walled area that has a perimeter of some 10 km. It was begun in 1804 by Emperor Gia Long. The Citadel used to enclose the entire city. Its seven-meter-high walls were originally built of earth but it was decided in the 1820s to cover them with bricks. This laborious process took thousands of workers and years to complete. Even today, it is used as a military fortress. The most famous gate is the **Ngo Mon Gate**.

Imperial City ★

This is in the Citadel and was built in the early 19th century and modeled after the Forbidden City in Peking. There are numerous palaces and temples within these walls, as well as towers, a library and a museum. There are also areas for religious ceremonies. The South Gate is the main entrance. The Emperor Gia Long began construction of the city in 1804, and the site eventually encompassed eight villages and covered six square kms. There are 10 gates that surround the four walls of the citadel. It took more than 20,000 laborers to construct the walls alone. Inside two of the gates are sets of large cannons, four through the **Nhon Gate** and five through the **Quang Duc Gate**. These cannons, made of bronze seized from Tay Son rebels, were cast in 1803. They represent the five natural elements and the four seasons. None of the cannons has ever been fired. Each contains a description of how it was constructed as well as firing instructions which, of course, were never followed. The main gate to the Imperial enclosure, the **Ngo Mon Gate** (built during the reign of Emperor Minh Mang in 1834), could only be used by the emperor. On the top of the gate is the Belvedere of the five Phoenixes. The emperor would appear here during important ceremonial occasions. The last Nguyen Dynasty Emperor Bao Dai formally ended his reign here. A Japanese company is completing the process of renovating the gate, albeit a slow one.

Forbidden Purple City ★

The imperial family and its entourage were the only individuals permitted to use this royal palace. There were 60 buildings situated in 20 courtyards. "Feminine" affairs happened in the west area of the complex, while the men did their manly things in the east area. Fighting during the Tet Offensive ruined the complex. The entire area is a depressing pile of rubble and small vegetableless vegetable gardens. Sadly, the only structures that can still be identified here are the two **Mandarin palaces**, the **Dien Canh Can** and the **Reading Book Palace**, but even these are in dismal shape. Work was started in 1983 to renovate the structures, but not much has been done. There are two large urns at the far side of the **Thai Hoa Palace**, cast in bronze and

Hue

decorated with animals, birds and plants. On each side of the urns is a pavilion, the **Huu** and **Ta Pavilions**. One is a souvenir shop. The only really surviving buildings are on the west side of the palace, between the walls of the Forbidden Purple City and the outer walls—and many independent visitors miss them altogether. There is the relatively well preserved **Hien Lam Cac**, where nine large urns made from copper cast in the mid 1830s stand in front of the pavilion. The **Temple of Generations** is next to the urns. This was built in 1821 and features altars of 10 Nguyen Dynasty Emperors. The **Hung Temple** is north of the Temple of Generations. It was built in 1804 in honor of Nguyen Phuc Luan, considered the "Father of the Nguyen Dynasty," and the father of Gia Long. Most blame the American shelling of Hue for the destruction of the Forbidden Purple City, but the complex had been deteriorating over the course of the previous 50 years due to shelling by the French, vandals, natural disasters and termites (not to exonerate the Americans). The only shelling being done here now is the whopping US$4 admission price to get into the Imperial City and Forbidden Purple City.

The Flag Tower

This is the tall, 37-meter-high flagpole between the Nhon and Quang Duc Gates. It was built originally in 1809 and lengthened in 1831. A typhoon knocked it down in 1904; it was rebuilt in 1915 only to be wrecked again in 1947. It was rebuilt in 1949 and that is how it stands today. The VC hung the National Liberation Front flag here for 25 days during the Tet Offensive. A picture of the flag on the pole can be seen in the Ho Chi Minh Museum in Hue.

Bao Quoc Pagoda

Bien Phu Street, near the railway line.

This pagoda was built by the Buddhist monk Giac Phong in the early 18th century. There is a nice stupa behind the pagoda to the left. There are beautiful doors here with Chinese and Sanskrit inscriptions.

Tu Dam Pagoda

At the intersection of Dien Bien Phu and Tu Dam Streets.

This was built in the late 1930s and has the distinction of being the temple where South Vietnamese President Diem sent troops in to silence the residing monks who were reputedly spreading discontent among the populace with the South Vietnamese regime.

Imperial Museum (Museum of Ancient Objects)

3 Le Truc Street.

Built in 1845 and restored in 1923, this is a beautiful museum that houses inscribed poems on the walls. Most of the precious artifacts were pillaged during the Vietnam War, but there are many beautiful items here, including lacquerware, ceramics, royal costumes and furniture. In the front courtyard are giant bells and gongs. Admission 8000 dong. Behind the museum is the **Royal College**, which was moved to this site in 1908 after being built in 1803. This was a school for the sons of princes and high-ranking Mandarins.

AUTHOR'S NOTE

The Vietnamese government has invested more than 1 billion dong (US$1 million) into the primary restoration of the Hue Ancient Museum. The Center for Hue Historical Heritage Restoration has copied the design of the museum in order to restore the whole wooden structure of the museum and retile the roof of Hoang Luu Ly and Than Luy Ly tiles. The fence surrounding the museum has been rebuilt to complement the museum's unique architecture. The restoration is a rapid one and should be completed by the time you read this.

hien Mu Pagoda ★

This is a bizarre sight. Yes, it's a pagoda. But your curiosity is more peaked by something else. It's an old Austin. Yeah, a British car. It was the same car that brought the Buddhist monk Thich Quang Duc to Saigon. There he became the subject of Malcolm Browne's famous photo. It shows the monk immolating himself in 1963. A copy of the photo is pasted on the windshield. Weird.

hu Cam Cathedral

20 Doan Huu Thrinh Street.
The cathedral was built in 1963, but wasn't finished until 1975 (although it isn't entirely finished). There are plans to continue the building, which essentially only requires adding a spire to the cathedral. According to reports, this is the eighth church to be built on this site since 1682.

ang Tau Lake

A royal library was formerly on an island in Tan Tau Lake. There is now a small Hinayana pagoda on the island called Ngoc Huong Pagoda.

inh Tam Lake

This lake is about 500 meters north of the Imperial enclosure and close by to Tang Tau Lake. In the middle of the lake are two islands connected by a bridge. Emperors used to spend lazy afternoons on the lake.

ia Long Tomb ★★

Built between 1814 and 1820, this is a magnificent structure that is unfortunately difficult to visit. There are huge mango trees that surround the tomb. It follows the formula of other royal tombs with a lotus pond surrounding the enclosed compound. Here there is a courtyard with five headless Mandarins. Also there are figurines of horses and elephants. There are steps that lead up to another courtyard where the emperor and his wife are buried. Inscriptions describing the emperor's reign can be found behind the burial area. Gia Long was the first of the Nguyen Dynasty emperors and ruled from 1802–1820, the year he died. He ordered the construction of his tomb in 1814. When the king died, his corpse was washed and clothed in ornate garments. Precious stones and pearls were placed in his mouth. He was then placed in a coffin made of catalpa wood, a type of wood that naturally, through its chemical composition, wards off insects to prevent decomposition.

When a messenger reached the empress a few days later to inform her of Gia Long' death, he found that she, too, was dead—although she could not have known of he husband's death by all accounts. Although Gia Long died on Feb. 3, 1820, he wa not actually buried until around May 20. Next to his tomb is a second grave tha contains items placed that would be useful to the emperor in his next life. A sma donation will be expected at his tomb.

Khai Dinh Tomb

This was the last monument of the Nguyen dynasty and was constructed betwee 1920 and 1931. It sits magnificently on the slopes of Chau E Mountain, about 1 km from Hue in Chau Chu village. It has a long staircase flanked by dragons. Ther are ceiling murals and ceramic frescoes. The emperor reigned over Vietnam fror 1916–1925. The tomb looks entirely unlike the other emperors' tombs aroun Hue. The tomb, combining a gaudy combination of European and Vietnames influences, has become dilapidated over the years. You have to climb 36 steps to g up to the tomb, where you'll reach the first courtyard, surrounded by two pavilion The Honor Courtyard is 26 steps farther up the hillside and features depictions c elephants and horses, as well as Mandarin soldiers. Then climb another three sets c stairs to reach the tomb, which is called Thien Dinh. It's divided into three halls an decorated with various murals. The emperor lies beneath the statue of Khai Dinh.

Minh Mang Tomb

This complex was built in 1840 by King Minh Mang and is known for its magnifi cent architecture, military statuaries and elaborate decorations. It is perhaps th most beautiful of Hue's pagodas and tombs. You can get to this location, about 1. km south of Hue by tour boat on the Perfume River or by car.

Tu Duc Tomb

Seven km from the city, this was once the Royal Palace of Tu Duc, who ruled Hu more than 100 years ago. There are pavilions in a tranquil setting of forested hill and lakes. The tomb was constructed between 1864 and 1867. Tu Duc, who wa the longest reigning Emperor (1848–1883), lived a luxurious life. Fifty chefs and 5 stewards presided over the emperor's meals, enough to feed and serve his 104 wive and numerous mistresses (although he never fathered any sons). The tomb is sur rounded by a wall; there's a lake inside with a small island where the king con structed replicas of various temples. He used to come here to the surroundin pavilions to relax, hunt animals and recite poetry he composed to his many femal companions, and listen to music. To the left of the water is the Xung Khiem Pavil ion; this was one of the emperor's favorite hangouts. Built on pilings over the lake it was restored in 1986. The tomb of his Empress Le Thien Anh and adopted so Kien Phuc is to the left of Tu Duc's tomb. Many of the surrounding pavilions are i dire need of restoration, although you can still feel the serenity Tu Duc must hav found here. With 104 women, it'd be hard not to. It is rumored that Tu Duc wa sterile, and therefore forced to write his own eulogy. The eulogy itself recounts surprisingly sad life (perhaps because of his sterility). Also, the French took contro of Vietnam during his reign, which further saddened the emperor.

ng Khanh Tomb

Seven km from Hue.

Built in 1889, this is the tomb of Emperor Dong Khan, the adopted son of Tu Duc. He assumed the throne as a puppet emperor after the French captured Emperor Ham Nhgi, who had fled Hue after the French stormed the palace in 1885. Ham was exiled to Algeria. Dong ruled the dynasty from 1886–1888. The tomb is the smallest of the royal tombs of Hue.

eu Tri Tomb

About 7 km from Hue.

There are conflicting reports as to when this tomb was built. Some say it was constructed in 1848 and other sources say it was constructed between 1864 and 1867. Trieu Tri ruled Vietnam from 1841 to 1847. The tomb is the only emperor's tomb not to be surrounded by a wall.

ach Ma National Park ★★

55 km southwest of Hue

There has been virtually zero development here and it's not geared up to handle tourists, but it's a gorgeous, mountainous chunk of real estate if you can get access to it. The park is a former French hill station (and a national park since 1991) about 55 km southwest of Hue; it rises majestically 1200 meters from the coast at Canh Duong Beach. The problem is getting in. The 16-km "road" to the hill station is a rutted mudslide, and presently, officials are less than cooperative about letting you use it. One reason may be the numbers of alleged poachers, who are reputed to be armed with AK-47s and quite willing to use them—as there's little chance they'll get caught. These days, the hill station is little more than a few crumbling walls, although the views are magnificent. There are no places to stay nor places to eat. You'll be on your own, save for, of course, the guide who will be assigned to you.

Where to Stay in Hue

AUTHOR'S NOTE: TELEPHONE PREFIXES

The telephone numbers listed in this chapter are local exchanges. The country code prefix is 84. The city code is 54.

en Nghe Guest House US$7–$12

4 Ben Nghe Street. ☎ *823687.*

Attached bath; hot water. Rave reviews from backpackers.

Loi Hue (Hue Guest House) US$25–$70 ★

2-5 Le Loi Street. ☎ *824668, 822161, 822155, 822153 or 822323; FAX: 824527.*

This is an interesting-looking compound of several buildings that looks a little bit like a dormitory quad on a college campus. The cheap rooms are a real bargain. The rooms are small but impeccably clean and comfortable. The more expensive doubles are large and airy. Attached bath in all private rooms and "mini-dorm" rooms, accommodating four or more people. There are a number of outdoor cafes downstairs, as well as souvenir stalls. Bicycle rentals. Very comfortable.

Hue City Tourism Villas   US$25–$35

11, 16, 18 Ly Thuong Kiet Street, and 5 Le Loi Street. ☎ *(11) 823753; (16) 82367*
(18) 823964; (5) 823945.
These four properties get mixed reviews from travelers. Basic accommodation
fans; hot water. Inexpensive.

Century Hotel   US$88–$95   ★★★

49 Le Loi Street. ☎ *823390. FAX: 823399.*
150 rooms.
Largest and the newest hotel in Hue. Air conditioning; tennis courts; two restau
rants; disco; karaoke; swimming pool; post office; gift shop; TV; telephones; refrig
erators; barbers; hairdressers; massage; hot water; all the amenities.

Huong Giang Hotel   US$65–$170   ★★★

51 Le Loi Street. ☎ *822122. FAX: 823424/823102.*
42 rooms.
Built in 1962, but enlarged in 1983. Right on the river. Most rooms offer grea
views (you better get a great view for a hundred bucks). This is one of the mo
expensive hotels in town. Whether it's vastly overpriced will depend on your walle
Friendly staff. Two great restaurants; cafe; large gardens; reception rooms; gift sho
sauna; massage; car and bike rentals; air conditioning; refrigerators; attached bat
rooms; hot water with good pressure. The works, if you've got the cash. Great de
if you can afford a lower-priced room. Often full with the well-heeled. If you're o
a budget, you'll get a kick out of the "modern" architecture as you pass by on th
way to your US$6 guest house.

Kinh Do Hotel   US$30–$35

1 Nguyen Thai Hoc Street. ☎ *823566/824952; FAX: 823858.*
Rooms in three price ranges. Restaurant, bar, sauna, massage, dancing.

Thuan Hoa Hotel   About US$25–$70   ★

7 Nguyen Tri Phuong Street. ☎ *822553/822556; FAX: 823858/823036.*
Basic accommodations if a bit overpriced. Air conditioning, restaurant, attache
bath.

Morin Hotel   About US$20–$40   ★★

2 Hung Vuong Street. ☎ *823866*
Under construction.

Nha Khach Chinh Phu (Gov. Guest House   About US$20–$40   ★★

5 Le Loi Street. ☎ *822161; FAX: 824527.*
This is another recommendation, although it's a bit pricey. Beautiful building o
the Perfume River. Large rooms, private bath, air conditioning. Restauran
Friendly staff and efficient service.

Royal Hotel   US$10–$18

185B Thuan An Street. ☎ *825246/825820.*
11 rooms. Breakfast included. Tell Mr. Ho Dac Dung, director, that Wink
Johnny Tu recommended you to his hotel. We are sure you will get a good rate.

Nam Giao Hotel   US$15

3B Dien Bien Phu Street. ☎ *825736/822140; FAX: 825735.*

14 rooms. Breakfast included.

Von Canh Hotel

25 Hung Vuong Street. ☎ *824130/825672; FAX: 823424/823102.*

Citadel Hotel

9 & 10 Kiem Hue Street. ☎ *826249; FAX: 826252.*
See Ms. Nguyen Thanh Hoa, the hotel manager, and tell her we recommended you, for a good rate.

Via Da Hotel

31 Thuan An Street. ☎ *822352/826145/826146.*
See Mr. Nguyen Viet Tro, the director, for a discount.

A Dong 2 Hotel

7 A Doi Cung Street. ☎ *822765/822766/822767; FAX: 828074.*

Thien Duong (Paradise) Hotel   US$15

33 Nguyen Thai Hoc Street. ☎ *825976/825977; FAX: 828233.*
Breakfast included.

Thanh Loi Hotel   US$15–$20

7 Dinh Tien Hoang Street. ☎ *824803; FAX: 825344.*

Nha Khach 18 Le Loi   US$10–$15

18 Le Loi Street. ☎ *823720.*
Comfortable for the price. Rooms with air conditioning, hot water. Restaurant.

Century Riverside   US$70–$150   ★★★

49 Le Loi Street. ☎ *823391.*
This new hotel is what many are calling the best in Hue—and certainly looks a lot better than the Huong Giang. Rooms with air conditioning, hot water, private bath, TV, minibar and refrigerator, telephone. Restaurant, bar. Nice digs.

Dong Da Hotel   US$40–$80   ★★

15 Ly Thuong Kiet. ☎ *823071.*
Hordes of package guests here. Very comfortable. Rooms with air conditioning, minibar & refrigerator, hot water, TV, telephone. Restaurant, bar, tour services.

Where to Eat in Hue

The food in Hue is generally very good, and there are a number of specialties unique to Hue. One is a dish of shrimp, pork and bean sprouts filled in a deep-fried egg batter *(banh khoai)*. It is served usually with a delicious sesame sauce called *nuoc tuong*. There is also a rice pancake filled with shrimp and herbs called *banh beo*, and a rice pancake with pork called *ram*. The local beer, Huda, is decent but could use some more hops.

Huong Giang Restaurant

51 Le Loi Street.
Vietnamese and European cuisine. Excellent.

Ngu Binh Restaurant

7 Ly Thuong Kiet Street.
Food is average. Great place to meet new friends.

Banh Khoai Thuong Tu   ★

6 Dinh Tien Hoang Street.

Excellent Vietnamese.

Phu Hiep Restaurant ★

19 Ho Xuan Huong Street (opposite 53 Nguyen Chi Thanh Street). ☎ *823560.*
Again, superb Vietnamese fare.

Song Huong Floating Restaurant ★

*North of the Trang Tien Bridge on the bank of the Perfume River, near the intersection
of Le Loi and Hung Vuong.*
Great Vietnamese fare at low prices.

Ong Tao Restaurant

134 Ngo Duc Ke, on the grounds of the Imperial Palace.
Vietnamese, Asian, Western. A little pricey, but this is a good restaurant.

Loc Thien

6 Dinh Tien Hoang Street.
Service is friendly, the Vietnamese and Asian fare good. Cheap.

Pho Restaurant

6 Ha Noi Street.
Vietnamese fare at great prices. The noodle soup *(pho)* is excellent.

Directory

Transportation

Hue is 1070 km from Saigon, 654 km from Hanoi, 370 km from Vinh, 108 km from
Danang, 165 km from Dong Hoi, 94 km from the Ben Hai River, 56 km from Quang
Tri, 72 km from Dong Ha, 152 km from the Laos border, 400 km from the Thai border,
and 60 km from A Luoi, which can only be reached by 4-wheel-drive.

By air:

VN flies to Hue from Ho Chi Minh City Wednesdasy, Fridays and Sundays at 9:50
a.m. Flights to HCMC from Hue leave on the same days at 4:30 p.m. From Hanoi
flights leave for Hue on Wednesdays, Fridays and Sundays at 2:40 p.m. Flights to
Hanoi depart the same days at 12:30 p.m.

By bus:

The An Cuu bus station is at *43 Hung Vuong Street*. This station serves destinations to the south. Buses connect with Lang Co, Quy Nhon, Danang, Buon M
Thuot, Nha Trang, Dalat and Saigon. They usually leave very early in the morning
about 5 a.m. The bus station serving the north (An Hoa Station), at the northwes
corner of the walled city, has connections to Dong Ha, Vinh, Hanoi, Dong Hoi an
Khe Sanh. Again, buses usually leave around 5 a.m. Tickets for all destinations ca
be bought at either station. The local bus station is called Dong Ba (downstrear
from the Trang Tien Bridge on the river side of Tran Hung Dao Street), and fror
here non-express buses depart for Dong Ha, Phu Luong, Cho No, An Lo, Ba
Vinh, Lang Co, Danang, Thuan An and Cau Hai.

By train:

The train station is at the west end of Le Loi Street and serves all points up an
down the coast. It takes about 16 hours to get to Hanoi and 24 hours to Saigor
Book well in advance, especially for sleepers.

Transport around town:

Cars with drivers can be hired at Thua Thien Tourism, Hue Tourist Office and Hue City Tourism.

By bicycle:

Bicycles are easily rented at most hotels for about 8000-10,000 dong per day. It's the best way of getting around town. Unfortunately, it rains so much in Hue, expect to get wet. Bring a rainsuit.

By boat:

There are many ways to rent boats to go up and down the Perfume River. Restaurants can help arrange a boat tour, but they're expensive. Many of the sights in Hue can be reached by boat, including many of the royal tombs, Thuan An Beach, and Thien Mu Pagoda. Also try hiring a boat behind the Dong Ba Market, by the Dap Da Bridge and also the Perfume River Hotel.

Post Office

8 Hoang Hoa Tham Street. You can make international calls and faxes from here.

Hospital

Hue General Hospital. *16 Le Loi Street.* ☎ *822325.*

Banks and Moneychangers

Industrial and Commercial Bank. *2A Le Quy Don Street.* Open from 7 to 11:30 a.m. and from 1:30 to 4:30 p.m. Monday-Saturday.

Tourist Offices

Hue City Tourism. *18 Le Loi Street.* Can arrange for car rentals, guides and traditional Vietnamese musical performances.

Hue Tourist Office. *30 Le Loi Street.* ☎ *822369, 822288.* Can arrange for car rentals and guides.

Hue Tourist Co. (Hue City Tourism). *9 Ly Thuong Kiet.* ☎ *823577.*

Airline Offices

The booking office for Vietnam Airlines is located at *12 Hanoi Street.* ☎ *823249.* There's not much they can do for you here at this primitive, non-computerized office but get you out of Hue. It's staffed by a single employee, so expect to wait a while.

Hue

Hue

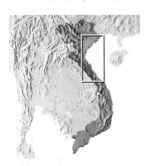

THE NORTH COAST

eep grottoes rise hundreds of meters above Ha Long Bay.

After one sees much of Vietnam's north coast it's easy to imagine why ncle Ho and his buddies wanted to snatch up real estate in the south of the untry. Overall, the south of Vietnam is simply a lot more beautiful than e north. Of course there are some notable exceptions to this: namely Ha ong Bay and the northwest of Vietnam. But the north coast, from the MZ to Haiphong, remains off most visitors' itineraries. Highway 1 is still a eaten track, of course; it's just not that beaten by foreigners.

Above the DMZ (some argue quite well below it, and quite convincingly I ight add), coastal Vietnam becomes rather flat, dreary, drizzly and cold. raveling south to north, peasants in conical hats pushing teams of cows and ting cartloads of rice, or children in funny dresses pedaling rusted bicycles are no longer the fodder for snapshots near Vinh that they were near Phan Thiet. Most of the population centers of the north coast were blasted to oblivion by American warplanes during the Vietnam War, the cities' razed structures being mostly replaced by drab East German concrete blocks. Additionally, the north coast is perhaps the poorest of all of Vietnam's regions. Sure, there are the Phong Na caves and the limestone mountains of Cuc Phuong, but most folks by this point are getting sick of crammed, speeding minibuses (the alternative is to take the train, of course!) and thinking ahead to duty-free shopping at Changi Airport during the layover.

The former DMZ is of most interest to war veterans, and access to places like Khe Sanh, the Rockpile, Dakrong Bridge and other fire bases and battlefields is becoming much easier these days. It's becoming something of "house specialty" of tour agents of the southern north coast to arrange meetings between U.S. veterans and their counterparts in the North Vietnamese and Viet Cong forces. Many a teary "reunion" has occurred in the DMZ in recent years. Looky-Loos won't get much out of a visit to this region.

The Phong Na caves and Ke Bang Desert have mostly been the stomping grounds of geologists and other academics over the years, but have been opened up for tourism over the last few years. The magnificent caves, believed to be the longest and most extensive in the world, are still a relative hassle to get to for most, involving an uncomfortable and lengthy boat journey. Most worth it for the adventurous is the rugged trail to the remote outpost of Son Trach.

Dreary Vinh was bombed back into the Bronze Age during the war, and certainly hasn't been as resilient as Haiphong. It's best for exploring the small villages in the countryside, including Chua, about 14 kilometers northwest of the city, where Ho Chi Minh was born in 1890.

There are a couple of passable beaches on the coast near Thanh Hoa called the Sam Son beaches. Ninh Binh is best for visiting Hoa Lu, an ancient capital of Vietnam. The limestone grottos springing from the rice paddies are reminiscent of Ha Long Bay, but on a rice field.

The coastal industrial city of Haiphong has become pleasant enough again after taking a pounding during the war. But it's best used as a jumping point for Cat Ba Island and the magnificent (when the weather's decent) national park here.

Ha Long Bay is simply a marvel of the world and shouldn't be bypassed a trip to Vietnam. Home to thousands of rugged limestone grottos, the region, regrettably, has become highly commercialized over the last four years.

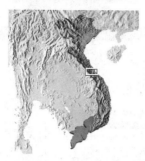

The DMZ

The DMZ was the site of the fiercest fighting of the Vietnam War...Tens of thousands of soldiers died here...The siege of Khe Sanh and battles at Hamburger Hill are considered the bloodiest battles of the war...The former DMZ stretched for 5 km in either direction of the Ben Hai River...Thousands of scavengers have been killed since 1975 unearthing old war materiel to sell as scrap metal and souvenirs...The former DMZ was officially created in 1954...It extends along National Highway 9 from the South China Sea to Laos.

The Demilitarized Zone was the area that extended 5 km both north and south of the Ben Hai river and was the site of some of the bloodiest fighting of the Vietnam War. This was the demarcation line that separated South Vietnam from North Vietnam. The origins of the DMZ were the result of the Potsdam Conference held in Berlin in 1945 (which included representatives of Great Britain, the U.S. and the U.S.S.R.) that partitioned Vietnam into two separate countries. However, the actual DMZ wasn't established until 1954. What was concluded at the Potsdam conference was that Japanese forces south of the 16th parallel would surrender to the British, while occupying Japanese forces in the north would surrender to the Nationalist Chinese Army led by Chiang Kai Shek.

Eventually, in 1954, the governments of France and of Ho Chi Minh agreed in Geneva to an armistice of sorts that would split the south and north—however, not politically. The demarcation line was to be temporary until general elections could be held in 1956. But when these did not occur, the nation was split in half at the Ben Hai River, also referred to as the 17th parallel.

THE DMZ

CON THIEN FIREBASE

American base and scene of intense fighting in Sept. 1967.

BEN HAI RIVER

Demarcation between South Vietnam and North Vietnam and the center of the DMZ.

THE ROCKPILE

U.S. Marine long-range artillery base and lookout station.

NORTH VIETNAM

DAKRONG BRIDGE

Constructed by the North Vietnamese with Cuban assistance after the "official" withdrawal of American troops.

Ben Hai River

Dong Ha

CAMP CARROLL

U.S. artillery base.

Quang Tri River

LAO BAO

North Vietnamese artillery base.

LANG VAY

U.S. Army Special Forces base overrun by North Vietnamese troops in 1968.

KHE SANH

U.S. Marine base besieged by North Vietnamese troops for 77 days in 1968 as a diversion in preparation for the Tet Offensive.

The DMZ

DOC MIEU BASE

American surveillance base used to monitor enemy troop movements along the McNamara Line and in the DMZ.

DONG HA

U.S. Marine command center and South Vietnamese army base.

QUANG TRI

Captured by North Vietnamese army in Eastertide Offensive of 1972 before being recaptured by American troops. During the fighting the city was almost completely destroyed.

GULF OF TONKIN

Quang Tri

Huong Dien

SOUTH VIETNAM

Co Bi

Bo River

A LUOI

U.S. Army Special Forces Base abandoned after North Vietnamese siege in 1966.

A Dang

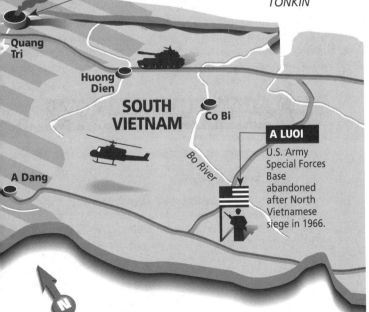

The DMZ

The DMZ extended from the sea to the Laos border. Today National Highway 9 runs along this former border to Laos. As well, the Ho Chi Minh Trail cut across the DMZ, requiring American forces to establish a number of bases and fire bases along the southern side of the demarcation line to prevent the transport of troops and war materiel from moving from the north to the south. Some of the bases along the 17th parallel included Khe Sanh, Camp Carroll, Lang Vay, Cua Viet, Con Thien, Dong Ha, Gio Linh, Cam Lo, Ca Lu and the Rockpile. Khe Sanh, in particular, was the scene of some of the fiercest fighting of the war, with as many as 10,500 soldiers dying during the two-month siege of the base in the beginning of 1968 by North Vietnamese forces—which was only a decoy for the Tet Offensive in February.

Other areas along the DMZ that experienced bitter fighting were Dong Ha, infamous Hamburger Hill, the Rockpile, Camp Carroll, Quang Tri, the Ashau Valley (where Hamburger Hill is located), Con Thien and Lang Vay.

Although the war has been over for many years, the DMZ remains an extremely dangerous area. Thousands of people have been killed by land mines, unexploded bombs, agonizing and deforming white phosphorus shells and other ordnance that is still spread all across the DMZ. Peasants and farmers still comb the area for scrap metal—aluminum, steel and brass—and other items they hope to sell. They earn only a pittance for these efforts and many are killed each year. It is not wise to touch anything on the ground along Highway 9. In fact it would be deadly, because if the Vietnamese have not already scavenged the materiel it is because they are too frightened to move it.

A NOTE ABOUT LAND MINES AND UNEXPLODED ORDNANCE

The Americans recarpeted Vietnam with underground explosives. Even today, scores of Vietnamese and cattle are blown up by land mines and other ordnance. It seems now that it is the Australians who are trying to remove what's still left, especially in port areas.

EXAT is an Australian ordnance disposal firm working with the Vietnamese Army implementing ordnance surveys and clearance services. One contract is with a new cement company on a site near Haiphong heavily bombed by the Americans during the war.

A NOTE ABOUT LAND MINES AND UNEXPLODED ORDNANCE

Another contract is with a mining company in the Central Highlands. Although thousands of bombs near the ground's surface have been defused by the Vietnamese, more sophisticated clearance operations are required for port expansion, sites of new factories, bridge and road building, and open-cast mining operations.

EXAT believes they will achieve a 95 percent success rate in Vietnam, a figure based on their operations in Kuwait, Afghanistan, Cambodia and Pakistan. Much of EXAT's efforts will be training local demining technicians to utilize the sophisticated equipment required for intense, large-scale demining operations.

Travel permits to the DMZ area, once required and extremely costly, have largely been removed. But you should only visit the area with a trained, professional guide. The old bases can be visited by either day trips or through Saigontourist's War Veteran Tours or programs offered by other state- and privately run tour agents.

A Word About Agent Orange

The debate continues even today regarding the effects of Agent Orange on both the Vietnamese and American war veterans exposed to the chemical. Many "experts," particularly in the U.S., insist that the chemical is essentially harmless and that the higher birth defect rates experienced in the south and central parts of Vietnam are due more to malnutrition than anything else. But consider the following: 72 million liters of chemicals, containing 15 types of poisons, were dropped on 1.7 million hectares of forest during the war. That's nearly 20 percent of the total forest area in southern Vietnam. Of these 72 million liters dropped, 47 million of them were Agent Orange, which contained a blend of 170 kg of dioxin. And this estimate of the total amount of Agent Orange (called Operation Ranch Hand, which lasted from 1961–1971) dropped on Vietnam is considered conservative at best. It is believed that 4600 flying sorties sprayed the herbicide mainly in the following areas: Phuoc Long, Binh Dinh, Thua Thien, Tay Ninh, Long Khanh, Binh Duong, Bien Hoa, Quang Nam, Quang Tri and Kon Tum. There were between 300–700 drops in each of these areas. Nearly 50 percent of the Agent Orange dropped fell in these areas.

Despite protests from around the world, the U.S. government asserted that the chemical would have no long-term effects on the Vietnamese people, American soldiers and foliage in the environment. It became indisputedly evident to scientists as early as 1970 (at an international conference in France at Orsay University) that the chemical would have long term harmful effects.

The DMZ

Fielding
WORLDWIDE

1964-1975

BATTLES OF VIETNAM

Area shown

NORTH VIETNAM

CHINA

LAOS

GULF OF TONKIN

DMZ

THAILAND

CAMBODIA

SOUTH VIETNAM

SOUTH CHINA SEA

AN LOC

(Apr. 8–Jul. 11, 1972)
Capital of Binh Long province, which the North Vietnamese laid siege to. The battle ended with the withdrawal of the North Vietnamese from the province.

OPERATION ATTLEBORO

(Sep. 14–Nov. 24, 1966)
The objective was to find and engage Viet Cong forces near the Cambodian border. The first major battle erupted on October 19th and fighting lasted almost a month.

OPERATION JUNCTION CITY

(Feb. 22–May 14, 1967)
Combined U.S. and ARVN forces sought to engage Viet Cong forces in Tay Ninh province. This operation resulted in the movement of Viet Cong forces into Cambodia.

RACH BA

(Sep. 15, 1967)
Amphibious assault that was part of Operation Coronado. The objective was to surround and destroy Viet Cong forces in the Mekong Delta.

Mekong River

Phnon Penh

CAMBODIA

SOUTH VIETNAM

Saigon

MEKONG DELTA

Bac Lieu

OPERATION FREQUENT WIND

(Mar. 11–Apr. 30, 1975) Operation in which the U.S. Navy evacuated remaining Americans and some South Vietnamese before the fall of Saigon.

The DMZ

OPERATION LAM SON

(Feb. 8–Apr. 6, 1971)
Operation in which South
Vietnamese forces with
limited American support
entered Laos in an attempt
to damage the effectiveness
of the Ho Chi Minh Trail.
Like most other attempts,
this attack did little to stop
the vast amounts of troops
and equipment moving up
and down the trail.

Hanoi ✪

**NORTH
VIETNAM**

GULF OF TONKIN

(Aug.. 2, 1964)
Occurred when U.S. destroyer Maddox,
on patrol in the Gulf of Tonkin
allegedly, was attacked by North
Vietnamese torpedo boats. Resulted in
the Aug. 7 Gulf of Tonkin Resolution
that gave Lyndon B. Johnson the
power to "take all necessary measures
to repel an armed attack against the
forces of the United States and to
prevent further aggression."

HAMBURGER HILL

(May. 11–20,1969)
Nickname for Dong Ap
Bia, a hill controlled by the
North Vietnamese. During
the battle for this hill,
heavy casualties were
suffered on both sides.

LAOS

KHE SANH

(Jan. 21–Apr. 7, 1968)
Along with attacks on American
bases at Con Thien, Loc Ninh, Song
Be and Dak To, the North
Vietnamese 77-day siege of Khe Sanh
was a decoy in preparation for the

OPERATION STARLITE

(Aug. 2–18, 1965)
The first major
conflict between
American and Viet
Cong troops. It
consisted of an
amphibious assault
on the Van Tuong
Peninsula backed
by air support and
ground troops
designed to
surround and
destroy the Viet
Cong troops there.

MY LAI

(Mar. 16, 1968)
Incident in which
a company of
American troops
killed about 500
civilians in and
around My Lai in
Son My
subdistrict.

IA DRANG

(Oct. 26–Nov. 27, 1965)
Began when the North
Vietnamese attacked the Special
Forces camp at Plei Mei. American
reinforcements were sent in to
repel the attack and then more
units were sent in to "search and
destroy" North Vietnamese forces
in the Ia Drang valley.

*SOUTH
CHINA SEA*

The DMZ

Regardless, the American military continued to drop the chemical on Vietnam until 1973.

Surveys by scientists have revealed that dioxin is still evident in the blood of the people of Vietnam and in the environment, particularly in the DMZ area and southern Vietnam. In northern Vietnam, blood tests have shown an average of 2.2 picograms (pg) of dioxin in the blood of the people. (In the U.S., the figure is 5.2 pg per person and in Japan 3.2 pg.). However, the levels of dioxin in the blood of southern Vietnamese is staggering. The general figure is between 11.7–14.6 pg per person. Particularly whopping are the amounts of dioxin found in the people of Song Be Province (32 pg per person!), Bien Hoa (28 pg per person) and Danang (18 pg per person).

An analysis of fat tissue taken from 73 people between 1987 and 1992 revealed that of the 25 people living in areas where the chemical was dropped by U.S. warplanes, 84 percent of them contained large traces of dioxin in their blood. Of the 48 people not living in affected areas, 81 percent also showed high levels of dioxin in their blood. This is essentially conclusive evidence that the dioxins of Agent Orange were and still are spread through the consumption of affected food. In fact, people directly exposed to the dioxin absorb about 25 percent of the pesticide, while those exposed to the chemical indirectly through the consumption of food grown in affected areas absorb 98 percent of the dioxin content!

It is conclusive now, most scientists believe, that exposure to Agent Orange causes fetus damage. Newborn babies today usually have about 0.02 pg of the dioxin in their blood. Death rates of children born in sprayed areas is about 30 percent higher than those born in nonsprayed areas. Most believe that the mother's milk containing the dioxin is the principle cause of the higher death rates. Deformities and abnormalities, such as mental retardation are more prevalent in these areas. Instances of stillbirth, cancer and congenital deformity are also higher in these areas.

Only recently has the U.S. government admitted that Agent Orange and dioxin may cause cancer and skin diseases, as well as nervous, lymphatic and respiratory disorders and diseases such as Hodgkin's Disease. There have also been similar long-term effects on the American soldiers who fought in the affected areas. Of the nearly 40,000 lawsuits filed by American soldiers against the government based on their exposure to Agent Orange, to date only about 470 of them have been settled by most recent accounts. It is believed that as many as 200,000 U.S. soldiers were affected by the chemical.

Today, the Vietnamese are still poisoned by Agent Orange through the food they eat and the soil they till. Scientists hope that the spread and effects of Agent Orange will last only another 5–10 years.

What to See and Do Around the DMZ

Ben Hai River

This river, about 20 km north of Dong Ha, marks the former border between South Vietnam and North Vietnam. NH1 passes over the river via a dilapidated bridge. During the war the southern half of the bridge was painted yellow, the northern half red. It was destroyed during a U.S. bombing raid in 1967. After the ceasefire agreements in 1973, the rebuilt bridge had two flag towers built. There are decent stretches of beaches on both the south and north sides of where the river empties into the sea.

Dong Ha

Along National Highway 1 at the intersection of the American-built Highway 9 south of the Ben Hai River, this was the site of a former U.S. Marine command center and later a South Vietnamese Army base. It was fiercely attacked during the spring of 1968 by NVA regulars. Dong Ha is now the capital of Quang Tri Province. Here you can see the **French-built blockhouse** (**Lo Cot Phap**) on Tran Phu Street (about 400 meters of NH1). Captured war equipment, including tanks can be seen on the perimeter. The blockhouse was once used by American and South Vietnamese forces. Near the blockhouse you can stay at the **Dong Ha Hotel** (☎ *8361, 24 rooms*). Other hotels in town include the **Buu Dien Tinh Quang Tri Hotel** (on the south side of town, about US$20), **the Ngoai Thuong Hotel** (also near the French blockhouse and very inexpensive), and the **Dong Truong Son Hotel** (about 3 km out from the blockhouse and rather expensive) on Tran Phu Street. There are a slew of roadside restaurants along NH1 in Dong Ha to choose from. There's a decent restaurant next to the Buu Dien Tinh Quang Tri hotel. There is also a restaurant at the Dong Truong Son Hotel.

Quang Tri

Quang Tri is about 60 km north of Hue and was the site of the Eastertide Offensive in 1972, in which several NVA divisions crossed the DMZ and, using tanks, mortars and heavy artillery, captured both the city and the province. The Americans then carpet-bombed the area with B-52 sorties. South Vietnamese artillery was also employed in the total destruction of the city. In short, the city was leveled in order to retake what was left of it. As a result, there's nothing to see here save for the Quang Tri Memorial and perhaps the ruined citadel, which was formerly an ARVN HQ. There's also another ruined building here that was formerly a Buddhist secondary school, between NH1 and the bus station. If you want, you can visit the bombed-out church where American and VC soldiers fought. It is pockmarked with bullet holes. There are two beaches in the vicinity: Gia Dang Beach and Cua Viet Beach.

Vinh Moc Tunnels ★

Unlike the tunnels at Cu Chi, these elaborate tunnels used by the VC and NVA troops have not been enlarged to accommodate Western tourists (they average 1.2 meters wide and are only 1.7 meters high) and look as they did in the mid-1960s. There are nearly three kilometers of tunnels here, with at least 12 entrances. Seven

Fielding **JAN. 30–FEB., 1968**

THE TET OFFENSIVE

Staged during a ceasefire arranged for the Tet Holiday, which celebrates the beginning of the lunar new year, the offensive consisted of coordinated attacks by Viet Cong and North Vietnamese troops on major population centers of South Vietnam. The offensive was carried out after diversionary attacks on several American strongholds had absorbed troops and attention. While the North Vietnamese and Viet Cong suffered enormous casualties and were tactically unsuccessful, the offensive raised new questions as to the probability of an American victory over such determined enemy forces. While the offensive encompassed all of South Vietnam, the fighting was particularly fierce in Khe Sanh, Hue and Saigon.

SAIGON Jan. 31

The capital of South Vietnam, Saigon was an American stronghold and virtually free of conflict except for isolated Viet Cong terrorist attacks. The second wave of the Tet Offensive brought attacks by disguised Viet Cong troops as well as North Vietnamese troops on strategic locations in Saigon such as the American Embassy, the national radio station and the Presidential Palace. These targets were quickly retaken by American and South Vietnamese troops and the false sense of security that Saigon had enjoyed was shattered.

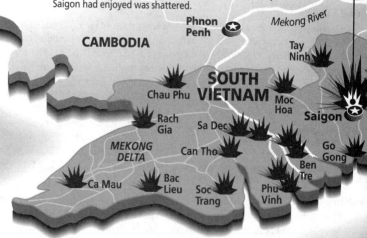

The DMZ

Phnon Penh   Mekong River

CAMBODIA

Tay Ninh

SOUTH VIETNAM

Chau Phu   Moc Hoa

Saigon

Rach Gia   Sa Dec

MEKONG DELTA   Can Tho

Go Gong

Ben Tre

Ca Mau   Bac Lieu   Soc Trang   Phu Vinh

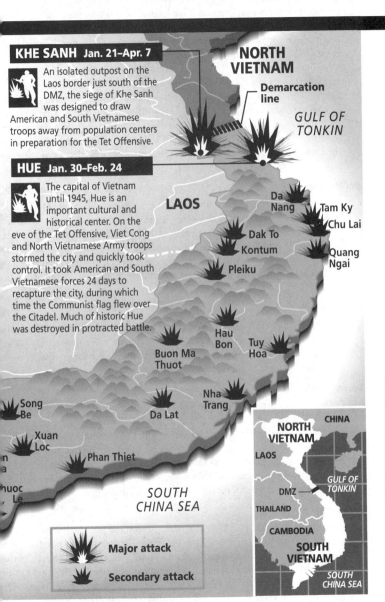

KHE SANH Jan. 21–Apr. 7

An isolated outpost on the Laos border just south of the DMZ, the siege of Khe Sanh was designed to draw American and South Vietnamese troops away from population centers in preparation for the Tet Offensive.

HUE Jan. 30–Feb. 24

The capital of Vietnam until 1945, Hue is an important cultural and historical center. On the eve of the Tet Offensive, Viet Cong and North Vietnamese Army troops stormed the city and quickly took control. It took American and South Vietnamese forces 24 days to recapture the city, during which time the Communist flag flew over the Citadel. Much of historic Hue was destroyed in protracted battle.

NORTH VIETNAM

Demarcation line

GULF OF TONKIN

LAOS

Da Nang

Tam Ky

Chu Lai

Dak To

Kontum

Quang Ngai

Pleiku

Hau Bon

Tuy Hoa

Buon Ma Thuot

Song Be

Nha Trang

Da Lat

Xuan Loc

Phan Thiet

huoc Le

SOUTH CHINA SEA

Major attack

Secondary attack

NORTH VIETNAM

CHINA

LAOS

GULF OF TONKIN

DMZ

THAILAND

CAMBODIA

SOUTH VIETNAM

SOUTH CHINA SEA

The DMZ

of them are at the beach. The entrances have been covered by shrubs and trees. Th
tunnels themselves were built on three levels. Inside the tunnels, there are sma
chambers where families and soldiers lived. There is even a conference hall tha
could fit as many as 150 people who would gather for military meetings and soci
events. (The tunnels themselves usually housed between 2500–3000 people at an
given time.) They can easily be visited by tourists, but only with a guide, because it
easy as hell to get lost in these dark, narrow caverns. If you're on the lam and und
five feet tall, this would be where the bill collectors definitely wouldn't find you
The government uses poisons to keep away snakes tempted to make the tunnel
their home. During the war, the tunnels were bombed, but little damage wa
inflicted. What the inhabitants feared most were the drilling bombs, which burne
their way deep into the earth before exploding. Although electric lighting wa
added to the tunnels in the early 1970s, bring a flashlight.

Doc Mieu Base

Eight km south of the Ben Hai River along NH1. This was the site of "McNamara
Wall," which housed an intricate electronic surveillance site used by the American
to detect VC and NVA troop movements, as the soldiers would cross electrical wire
informing the surveillance station. All around you can see remnants from the war
military uniforms and boots, huge craters leftover from the bombing and shelling
artillery shrapnel and live ammunition rounds. Much has been scavenged by th
locals.

Cua Tung Beach

Bao Dai used to vacation here, which is on the north side of where the Ben Ha
River spills into the South China Sea. Off the coast of Cua Tung Beach is Con C
Island, which can be reached via a three-hour boat ride. Bomb craters of all sizes car
be found in the area around the beach. It's a sobering sight.

Dakrong Bridge

About 12.5 km to the east past the Khe Sanh bus station. This bridge, which spans
over the Dakrong River was built after the "official" withdrawal of American troops.
It was constructed by the North Vietnamese with Cuban assistance. The route that
heads south from the bridge to A Luoi was once part of the Ho Chi Minh Trail.
Although the villagers in the area today are peaceful, they still sling on their backs
automatic weapons and assault rifles leftover from the war. It's a little unnerving,
but there's little danger for tourists.

Camp Carroll

This former U.S. base is 3 km off Highway 9, 24 km east past the Dakrong Bridge
and about 36 km east of the Khe Sanh bus station. There's not much today worth
visiting here but jackfruit trees, shrubs and small weapons shells that litter the
ground, but this is a historical military site that was established in 1966 and named
after a U.S. Marine who was killed during a battle on a nearby ridge. There were
giant artillery pieces at the camp, 175mm cannons that could fire volleys as far away
as Hue. Today the area is utilized to grow pepper. This was also the site where the

South Vietnamese commander of the base, Lt. Col. Ton That Dinh, deserted and joined the North Vietnamese Army.

Con Thien Firebase

This was the scene of intense fighting between U.S. and North Vietnamese troops. When the North Vietnamese attacked the firebase in September 1967 as a diversion leading to the upcoming Tet Offensive, the Americans responded by dropping more than 40,000 tons of bombs on the area via fighter bombers and B-52s. In total, there were more than 4000 sorties flown by American war planes. The normally lush and verdant hills surrounding the base were entirely blown apart, making the area look like a desert of craters and rotting wood. The Americans eventually fought off the siege, but at great expense. Even today, the former firebase is too dangerous to visit due to vast amounts of unexploded ordnance in the area.

The Rockpile

26 km from Dong Ha toward Khe Sanh.

This was exactly as the name implies, a giant pile of rocks, which U.S. Marines used as a lookout and long-range artillery camp. Today, local villagers live in stilt houses and subsist on slash-and-burn agriculture.

Truong Son National Cemetery

This is a cemetery filled with white tombstones of the thousands of North Vietnamese and VC fighters who lost their lives carrying equipment and weaponry down the Ho Chi Minh Trail in the Truong Son Mountains. They were exhumed from where they were originally buried and brought here after the reunification of Vietnam. However, a number of the graves are empty, representing the untold hundreds of thousands of VC and North Vietnamese soldiers missing in action. Above each stone is the inscription *Liet Si*, which translates into "martyr." Disabled veterans maintain this Arlington-type cemetery. The cemetery is divided into five zones, each representing the regions where the soldiers had lived. There is a separate area for decorated heroes and officers.

THE HO CHI MINH TRAIL

The famous and vast networks of roads and paths that connected North Vietnam and South Vietnam were used by VC and North Vietnamese Army troops to transport war supplies, primarily to VC strongholds in the south. Many tributaries of the trail were constructed to avoid any one point from being cut off via the constant U.S. bombing of the intricate path.

As many as 10 secret roadways were constructed, entirely camouflaged in many places. Defoliants and other chemicals the Americans used to reveal the trail were largely ineffective. More than 300,000 full-time workers and another 200,000 part-time North Vietnamese laborers maintained the trail.

THE HO CHI MINH TRAIL

NVA loss rates along the trail are estimated to be only 10 percent, and perhaps only a third of the machinery and vehicles being transported down the trail were ruined by the Americans. At first, supplies were carried on the backs of men and women on bicycles, but trucks from China and Russia later traversed the route(s). By the end of the Vietnam War, the Ho Chi Minh Trail totaled more than 13,350 km of all-weather roadways.

One "trailsman" was reputed to have carried more than 55 tons of supplies down the trail, a distance totalling about 41,000 km—roughly equalling the circumference of the world. Although American bombing did relatively little to ruin the trail and its travelers, the mission of ferrying equipment down the Ho Chi Minh Trail was a damned dangerous one.

A Luoi

60 km west of Hue and about 65 km southeast of the Dakrong Bridge. Here, in 1966, U.S. Army Special Forces units were besieged by the communists and the base here was abandoned. Consequently, it became an important link in the Ho Chi Minh Trail. LZs (landing zones) where bitter fighting took place are located nearby. Included are Hill 1175, Hill 521, Erskine and Razor, and Cunningham LZs. Farther south is Hamburger Hill. This was the site of an incredibly fierce battle in May 1969 and no one seemed to have any reason why it should have taken place, as there was absolutely no strategic advantage of controlling the hill other than "saving face." More than 240 U.S. soldiers died in a week of fighting here that saw possession of the hill change repeatedly. The Americans eventually ceded the area to the North Vietnamese and withdrew.

Lao Bao

On top of a Co Roc Mountain, overlooking the Vietnamese town of Lao Bao from the Lao side of the border was a North Vietnamese artillery position near the Tchepone River.

Lang Vay

This was an American Army Special Forces camp established in 1962 but overrun by north Vietnamese troops in 1968. The base primarily was composed of South Vietnamese, Bru, and U.S.-trained Montagnard soldiers—as well as a handful of U.S. Green Berets. During the attack more than 300 of the ARVN troops died. Ten of the Americans were killed.

Khe Sanh ★

The 77-day siege of Khe Sanh, which started on January 21, 1968, was seen by the American forces as an attempt by the North Vietnamese to create another Dien Bien Phu, when, in actuality, the siege was nothing more than a diversion in preparation for the Tet Offensive. However, as many as 15,000 NVA soldiers lost their lives here, compared with 248 American fatalities (43 of them in a C-123 transport crash). Gen. William Westmoreland, convinced that Khe Sanh was the prime target of NVA forces (reconnaissance revealed that between 20,000-40,000 NVA troops had surrounded the area), had the region carpet-bombed by B-52s and entirely defoliated. More than 100,000 tons of bombs and explosives were dropped by the aircraft. The U.S. Marines at Khe Sanh fired 159,000 shells, including the dreaded white phosphorous type, at NVA positions. Westmoreland would not permit a military humiliation, such as that which occurred to the French at Dien Bien Phu in 1954, to happen to American troops. He even considered the use of tactical nuclear weapons! The area surrounding Khe Sanh was thoroughly leveled. It was a resounding military victory for the Americans (who were able to reopen Highway 9 on April 7, linking the Army with the Marines), but an even greater psychological one for the North Vietnamese—despite their massive losses—as it paved the way to another psychological victory that changed the course of the war: the Tet Offensive, which started a week after the siege of Khe Sanh began. (Westmoreland amazingly continued to believe that Khe Sanh was the primary target, and thought the Tet Offensive was merely a diversion!) After the general's tour of duty was up and he was replaced as Vietnam's military commander-in-chief, American military experts reassessed the significance of Khe Sanh, and forces in the area were silently redeployed after destroying or burying anything of significance. Today villagers inhabit this lush area, many searching for scrap metal and military ordnance, and it's very difficult to believe this was the site of the deadliest battle of the Vietnam War. But all around are shells and remnants of the siege. The area is littered with shell casings. The town of Khe Sanh is set amongst serene hillsides and green fields. Most of the inhabitants here are Bru tribespeople. The thought that comes to mind when visiting here is that the whole affair was an ugly, bloody human travesty. A small (five-room) guest house is at Khe Sanh just south of the Khe Sanh Bus Station.

DMZ Directory

Dong Ha

Transportation

Dong Ha is about 1170 km from Saigon, 617 km from Hanoi, 190 km from Danang, 73 km from Hue, 295 km from Vinh, 40 km from Vinh Moc, 65 km from Khe Sanh, 95 km from Dong Hoi, 22 km from the Ben Hai River, 80 km from the Laos border, and 30 km from the Truong Son National Cemetery. The Dong Ha Bus station is located at the intersection of National Highways 1 and 9. There are connections to surrounding towns, including Quang Tri, Ho Xa, Khe Sanh, Dong Hoi, Lao Bao, Hue and other coastal and interior cities. There is service to Hanoi at least twice a week. The bus leaves at 5 in the morning, stops in Vinh 12 hours later and Hanoi after another 12 hours. Buses south leave for Danang, Con Thien and Ha Tri. The Reunification Express also stops here, with regular connections to the north and south along the Vietnamese coast. The Da Hong Railway station is south of the bus station on NH1 by about a kilometer. Then cross a field to the right of the highway.

Tourist Offices

DMZ Tour Office. *26 Le Loi Street*. ☎ *825242*. Cars, minivans and guides available here, but a better situation is making tour arrangements in Hue through **Thua Thien-Hue Tourism**. *30 Le Loi Street*. ☎ *822369, 822355*.

Quang Tri
Transportation

Buses and Citroën Tractions from the Quang Tri Bus Station (Le Duan Street) connect Quang Tri with Hue, Khe Sanh and Ho Xa.

Vinh Moc Tunnels
Transportation

The best way to get to the tunnels if you're not on a tour is by taking a private car north of the Ben Hai River about 6.5 km to Ho Xa. The tunnels are about 12–13 km from the village.

Doc Mieu Base
Transportation

This is right off NH1 on the right side about 8 km south of the Ben Hai River.

Cua Tung Beach
Transportation

The beach is 8 km on a dirt road to the south of Vinh Moc. If you're headed north, turn right off NH1 exactly 1.2 km north of the Ben Hai River.

Dakrong Bridge
Transportation

Dakrong Bridge is along NH9 13 km east of the Khe Sanh Bus Station.

Camp Carroll
Transportation

To get to Camp Carroll, go about 11–12 km past Cam Lo west on Highway 9 and turn left off NH9 for about 3 km. It's about 25 km east of the Dakrong Bridge and almost 40 km east of the Khe Sanh Bus Station.

Con Thien Firebase
Transportation

Just south of the Ben Hai River, the firebase can be reached from either Cam Lo on Highway 9 or from a turnoff on Highway 1. From Highway 9, Con Thien is about 12 km to the north and 5–6 km from the Truong Son National Cemetery. Con Thien is 7 km east of the Truong Son National Cemetery and 10 km west of NH1. You can reach it by continuing on the road past the cemetery. From the road that connects Cam Lo with the cemetery, you can see the firebase to the east of the road.

The Rockpile
Transportation

To get to The Rockpile, take Highway 9 from Dong Ha for 26 km. The site is off to the right.

Truong Son National Cemetery
Transportation

Thirteen km to the north of Dong Ha, the cemetery is 17 km off of NH1 and 9 km south of the Ben Hai River. A dirt path (only accessible by 4-wheel-drive) connects Cam Lo on Highway 9 with the cemetery. This an 18 km bumpy trip.

The DMZ

A Luoi
Transportation

A Luoi is about 60 km west of Hue and about 65 km southeast of the Dakrong Bridge. If you're already in the DMZ, take Highway 9 and go south at the Dakrong Bridge toward the Ashau Valley and Hamburger Hill.

Lao Bao
Transportation

Lao Bao is about 80 km from Dong Ha, 150 km from Hue, 18 km west of Khe Sanh and 45 km east of the Lao town of Tchepone along Highway 9, near the Tchepone River marking the Lao border.

Lang Vay Special Forces Camp
Transportation

Only 9 km west from the Khe Sanh Bus Station, just off Highway 9 on the southwest side on top of a hill was the Lang Vay Camp. You can also reach it by traveling 7 km toward Khe Sanh from the Lao Bao Market.

Khe Sanh
Transportation

The Khe Sanh Bus Station is along Highway 9 less than 1 km from the junction where the northward road veers off toward the former base of Khe Sanh. There is bus service to Hue, Dong Ha, and Lao Bao. Now that the border with Laos is open, the station has become particularly busy and has added routes in the past year and a half.

The DMZ

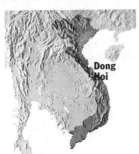

Dong Hoi

DONG HOI IN A CAPSULE

The capital of the Quang Binh Province...Inhabitants regularly struggle with the elements, from constant flooding to typhoons...During the Vietnam War, the area was obliterated by the bombing of U.S. war planes...Millions of unexploded devices are still scattered across the area...Some estimates say that a million unexploded bombs have been unearthed since the war...Dong Hoi makes for a good rest stop along NH1.

Dong Hoi is the capital of the central province of Quang Binh, an area that was obliterated during the Vietnam War due to its proximity to the 17th parallel—the border between South and North Vietnam. Just south of town is the Hien Luong Bridge spanning the Ben Hai River, which split Vietnam in half.

Since the war ended, millions of unexploded bombs and live ordnance have been dug up in the area and, even today, inhabitants of the region are inadvertently killed or dismembered by unexploded materiel. The area was also heavily defoliated during the war, and the effects of Agent Orange are probably more in evidence in this region than in any other area of Vietnam, save for the Mekong Delta. Dong Hoi, of anywhere in Vietnam, is one of the best testimonies to the alleged effects of the chemical.

Today, Dong Hoi is a fishing port where numerous significant archeological finds have been made. In the vicinity of Dong Hoi is the Ke Bang Desert which is the site of perhaps the most extensive and beautiful cave network in the world.

What to See and Do in Dong Hoi and Environs

The Ke Bang Desert & The Phong Nha Cave ★★★★

Ke Bang Desert, which covers more then 10,000 square kilometers from Quang Binh Province in Vietnam to Laos, is the world's largest limestone desert. Geologically evolving over the course of almost 3 million years, the area has been thinly populated due to harsh living conditions. There are also more than 41,000 hectares of primeval forests where biologists and forestry engineers have discovered rare and threatened species of fauna and flora, such as striped leopards, yellow tortoises, black monkeys, violet carp, gayals and 1000-year-old perennial trees.

The people of the region can only reside in the limestone valleys, which are linked with the outside world by tracks clinging on mountains averaging more than 1000 meters in height. Water from rivers and rainstorms is absorbed completely by the limestone, which has created spectacular underground rivers.

The Ke Bang desert really has one community, the remote mountainous village of Son Trach, with a population of about 7000. Although only about 50 km from the city of Dong Hoi, the capital Quang Binh Province, and 35 km from the smaller community of Hoan Lao, getting to Son Trach is like getting from Belize to Panama—but around Cape Horn on the tip of South America.

Son Trach's population, an ethnic enclave of Kinh and Arem people, is spread out through the Son Trach Valleys and in the limestone grottos of the Ke Bang Desert. There is so little water during the dry season there is none available for the rice crops, as canals cannot be dug into limestone.

The weather in the Ke Bang Desert is the most unpredictable in Vietnam. It can be hot and sunny one day and cold and rainy the next, regardless of the season.

But the most spectacular elements of the Ke Bang desert are its caves and grottos, a network called Phong Nha. The Phong Nha cave itself is 7729 meters in length. Discoveries of other caves have also been made, such as the 5258-meter-long Toi Cave, Ruc Mon Cave at 2863 meters, Vom Cave at 13,969 meters, Cha Ang Cave at 667 meters, and Ruc Ca Ron Cave at 2800 meters in length. Eventually, scientists expect to find that this circumference of cave networks is the largest in the world. The natural light in Phong Nha gives the cave a cosmic appearance, with its 10-meter high vault ceilings. There are various compartments, some lacking the beautiful natural light found in Phong Nha's first compartment, where water softly drops from the ceilings like from tree leaves after a spring rain. The fourth compartment contains an array of different stalactites, which look like tree trunks made of diamonds. As you move farther into the cave it becomes narrower. Conversation should be avoided. Just the resonance of a human voice can cause the frail columns of stalactite to fall from the ceiling.

This is a spectacular place that is essentially unknown to the outside world. After the discovery of a 2 km long cave in Malaysia, the Malaysian government poured huge sums of money into making the cave a tourist attraction. They built roads, and soon 11,000 visitors and scientists visited the site annually, pumping millions of dollars into the local economy. But today, the people of Son Trach remain poor, despite

Dong Hoi

their proximity to one of the world's most magnificent geological sites. To date, there have been but a mere 400-500 visitors to Ke Bang Desert's caves, the majority being geologists. The road to Ke Bang is in dismal condition and there are no plans to improve it. To get out there, take NH1 north to the coastal village of Bo Trach; then head west on the dismal road to Son Trach village. Motorcycle taxis are available for the here for the trip to Son Trach, and charge about VND40,000 for the journey. You can either have the driver wait for you at Son Trach or get another when you want to return. From Son Trach, local boats can be hired to go up the Son River to Phong Nha Cave for about US$15 round-trip. The trip to Son Trach takes about three hours, and allow another three or four hours for the round-trip boat ride to the cave.

The closest place to stay is the **Da Nhay Hotel** (☎ *864241*) in Bo Trach, although the hotel is a bit of rip-off, catering almost entirely to package groups. The place new and comfortable, but it's the only game in town and can currently get away with price gauging, both on the rooms and on the car getting out to the caves.

Khe Sanh and the Ho Chi Minh Trail

This is a bit of a trip from Dong Hoi, where you'll really want to stop only to see the caves. Travel about 95 km south to Highway 9 toward Laos. Here, you'll be among the most active areas of the Vietnam War. The Ho Chi Minh Trail crosses Route 9. See the Khe Sanh section and the Ho Chi Minh Trail sidebar in the DMZ chapter for more details.

Beaches

There are a number of sand dunes that line the beaches around Dong Hoi. Kilometers of beach stretch both south and north from the town. The best swimming in the vicinity is **Ly Hoa Beach**. **Nhat Le Beach** lines the mouth of the Nhat Le River.

Deo Ngang Pass   ★

Representing the border between Quang Binh and Ha Tinh Provinces, this is a beautiful pass through the Hoanh Son Mountains which reach from the South China Sea all the way to the Laos border, close to the 18th parallel.

Cam Xuyen and Ha Tinh

Although these small towns are not really at all in the vicinity of Dong Hoi (Cam Xuyen is about 150 km north of Dong Hoi and Ha Tinh a little farther up the coast), they really aren't worthy of chapters of their own, as they're both essentially attractionless—although a surprising amount of foreigners stay at Cam Xuyen's cheap and only guest house.

Where to Stay in Dong Hoi

Phuong Dong Hotel   US$30–$45

20 Quach Xuan Ky Street. ☎ *822276; FAX: 822404.*
35 rooms

This is the best place in town and also the newest. It makes a good base for exploring the Phong Nha caves. Comfortable rooms with hot water, private bath, air conditioning and color TV.

Hoa Binh Hotel   **US$25**

National Highway 1, central Hoa Binh. ☎ *822347.*
18 rooms

This was about the only choice travelers had for a while. Now, gratefully, there are more, as the Hoa Binh is overpriced and turning grotty.

Nhat Le Hotel   **US$10–$25**

16 Quach Xuan Ky Street. ☎ *822180.*
46 rooms

Large riverside hotel that's a bargain, although it's not as nice as the Phuong Dong.

Huu Nghi Hotel   **US$20–$45**

☎ *822567.*
23 rooms

This is another good choice in Dong Hoi. Air-conditioned rooms with private bath and hot water.

Directory

Transportation

Dong Hoi is about 500 km from Hanoi, 200 km from Vinh, 65 km from Hue, 165 km from Hue, and 94 km from Dong Ha. The highway north of Dong Hoi, because it's north of the DMZ, is improving but is not in nearly as good shape as NH1 to the south. There's a ferry crossing 34 km to the north at Cua Gianh. Sometimes it's a long wait.

By bus:

Buses from Dong Hoi serve most major coastal provincial capitals, as most buses traveling along NH1 from Saigon to Hanoi or vice versa stop in Dong Hoi.

By train:

There are regular connections with Hanoi and Saigon.

Tourist Offices

The Dong Hoi Tourist Office is located near the Hoa Binh Hotel in the central part of town.

Dong Hoi

Vinh

Annihilated during the Vietnam War by American and South Vietnamese war planes, Vinh is the capital of Nghe Tinh (or Nghe An, depending on who you talk to) Province (one of Vietnam's most populous and poorest provinces) and a major north central Vietnamese industrial and commercial center. Despite its economic importance, because of the climate, its people are the poorest in Vietnam.

The town had the unfortunate geographical position of being located on a narrow coastal plain, where roads and railways were required to pass through. The city was rebuilt by the East Germans after the war and, consequently, Vinh has the distinction of being perhaps the ugliest city in Vietnam. There's little, if anything, of note in the city to see and do. Its only real attractions are the hotel beds to break up the road journey between Hue and Hanoi.

Its weather could use some improvement—hot as hell in the summer and cold and rainy in the winter. But it's under gray skies much of the year. The area is under the constant threat of flooding and typhoons.

But west of Vinh lie thickly forested mountains inhabited by tribespeople and wild creatures alike. The Muong people live here, as well as the Tai, Meo, Khmer and Tho ethnic groups. The jungles are roamed by elephants, tigers, leopards, deer, rhinoceros, gibbons and other monkeys, giant bats and flying squirrels.

Because Vinh is about halfway between Hanoi and Hue, hotel and eatery owners prosper here, but they're about the only ones in the province who do.

The area is known for its insurgent spirit. The Ho Chi Minh Trail was started in this province and Uncle Ho himself was a native of Nghe An province. There were uprisings against the French led by the population here, and communists in the area (members of the Indochinese Communist Party) in the early 1930s staged uprisings and workers' strikes. These uprisings were generally successfully resisted by the French, utilizing fighter planes to disperse unruly demonstrators.

U.S. bombers and warships off the coast obliterated the area between 1964–1972. It is said that fewer than five buildings remained standing here after the Americans left Vietnam in 1973 (some say only two structures were left intact). But this was also the area where the greatest amount of American warplanes were downed in North Vietnam, and Naval pilots killed or captured.

Vinh (population about 200,000) is located about 15 km from the coast.

What to See and Do in Vinh and Environs

Chua and Sen Villages

The small village of Chua, about 14 km northwest of Vinh, was where Ho Chi Minh was born in 1890. The house is now a sacred shrine, but visitors are welcome. There's a small and unimpressive museum, given the historical significance of this place, close by. Sen village, which is close to Chua, is where Uncle Ho lived starting at the age of 6 with his highly educated father. Ho was actually born to relatively wealthy parents; his neighbors were dismally poor. Although Ho's house itself is nothing more than a crude, thatched shack, it was considered upscale for the area.

Cua Lo Beach

This beach, located about 20 km from Vinh, isn't bad. It's clean and rarely visited, perhaps because the weather here is cold and windy most of the time. There's a modest hotel located here.

Vinh Central Market

At the end of Cao Thang Street.
Despite the amount of people who live here, there is surprisingly little offered, although, like most city markets in Vietnam, it is a bustling, colorful place.

Restoration Project Clinic

Nguyen Phong Sac Street near the Children's Hospital.
A group of California-based war veterans and humanitarians built this structure as a hospital and physical therapy center in 1989. They worked in conjunction with Vietnamese war vets, as well. Nothing of any real interest here. The Nghe Tinh Children's Hospital is also on these grounds.

Anti-Aircraft Guns

Le Hong Phong Street.

Vinh

These giant guns are still active and pointed to the sky to fend off an air attac whom, I couldn't imagine. Perhaps the Belize Air Force.

Worker's Cultural Complex

Le Mao and Dinh Cong Trang Streets.
This is Vinh's "community center," a big structure that features a movie and pe mance theater as well as a dance hall.

Where to Stay in Vinh

Vinh Railway Station Hotel   US$6

Le Ninh Street.
This is right next to the railway station—as you might guess it would be. It's a run-down but it's cheap and popular with backpackers.

Hotel Kim Lien   US$25–$35

Quang Trung Street in the middle of town. ☎ *844751; FAX: 843699.*
76 rooms
This is the biggest hotel in Vinh and the only one you might cautiously refer being up to "international standards." There's hot water, fairly large rooms, air ditioning, restaurant, massage, moneychanging, private bath and a travel ag downstairs. This is the best place in town to rest on the road between Hue Hanoi.

Xi Nghiep Dich Vu Hotel   US$6

Le Loi Street near the corner of Nguyen Si Sach Street, east of the railway station.
The cheapest accommodations in Vinh and popular with backpackers. Don't ex much here but a hard mattress to put your head on.

Hotel Huu Nghi   US$20–$50

Le Loi Street. ☎ *842520; FAX: 8842813.*
78 rooms
This, like the Kim Lien Hotel, is a decent place for Vinh. The price tag will get air conditioning, attached bath, restaurant and hot water. Also recommend you're staying in Vinh.

Chuyen Gia Giao Te Hotel   About US$15–$45

Thanh Ho Street. ☎ *844175.*
Vastly overpriced, rather ugly hotel. Air conditioning, attached bath, hot water, taurant. I'd stay somewhere else in this price range.

Hong Ngoc Hotel   US$30–$40

Le Loi and Nguyen Thai Hoc Streets. ☎ *842165; FAX: 842129.*
18 rooms
If you want to be pampered a little, this is the place to stay. Friendly staff, com able rooms with air conditioning, hot water, private bath, color TV.

Binh Dan Hotel   US$5

☎ *842166.*
20 rooms
Barely worthy of mention, except to say to avoid it at any cost.

Tra Bong Hotel   US$5–$7

Corner Le Mao and Tran Phu Streets. ☎ *842226.*

27 rooms

Another dingy closet but a bargain for the truly cheap charlie. Private bath, but you'll freeze in the winter—the water feels like it was pumped from the deepest depths of a Minnesota lake.

Ben Thuy Hotel   **US$15**

Nguyen Du Street, just a kilometer from the Lam River toward the middle of Vinh. ☎ *855163.*

This is another popular place with backpackers, although expensive and a hike from the train station. No air conditioning, but it does have a small, decent restaurant.

Where to Eat in Vinh

The best place to eat in town is at the restaurant at the **Hotel Kim Lien**, or perhaps the restaurant at the **Hotel Huu Nghi**. But it's less expensive and equally as filling to eat at one of the many restaurants and food stalls at the Vinh Central Market or near the railway station, which has a slew of eateries with dirt-cheap prices. Just point and pay.

Directory

Transportation

Vinh is about 291 km from Hanoi, 365 km from Hue, 197 km from Dong Hoi, 470 m from Danang, 98 km from the Laos border, and 140 km from Thanh Hoa.

By air:

VN flies to Vinh from HCMC Mondays and Fridays at 11:50 a.m. You have to change planes in Danang; the total journey is about 4.5 hours. From Vinh to HCMC, flights depart at 12:10 p.m. on Mondays and Fridays, with a change of planes in Danang. The total journey time is about 5.5 hours.

By bus:

The bus station is on Le Loi Street north of the Central Market by about 1 km. There are express buses that depart for Hanoi, HCMC, Danang and Buon Ma Thuot early in the morning around 5 a.m. There are also express buses that leave for Hanoi at other times of the day as well. Ask at the ticket office (you'd be wise to purchase your tickets in advance). Non-express buses depart for Hanoi, Pleiku, Ba Hai, Ky Anh, Huong Son, Lat, Cau Giat, Hue, Hoa Binh, Yen Thanh, Que Phong, Nghia Dan, Do Luong, Phuc Son and Dung, as well as other destinations.

By train:

The Vinh Railway Station is located about 3 km west of the Central Market about 1 km from the intersection of Le Loi and Phan Boi Chau Streets. The Reunification Express stops here. It's about an 8-hour trip to Hanoi, and 35-40 hours to HCMC.

Post Office

Nguyen Thi Minh Khai Street, about 280 meters northwest of Dinh Cong Trang Street. Hours are from 6:30 a.m. to 9 p.m. International and domestic calls and faxes can made from another office across from the Workers' Cultural Complex (Cong Ty Dien o DienThoai) on Dinh Cong Trang Street close to the intersection of Nguyen Thi inh Khai Street.

Banks and Moneychangers

Vietcom Bank, *at the corner of Le Loi and Nguyen Si Sach Streets*, can provide advances on American-issued credit cards.

Tourist Office

Vinh Tourist Office. *Quang Trung Street*. ☎ *4629*. The travel agency in the Ho Kim Lien can book airline flights.

Hospital

Vinh General Hospital. *Le Mao and Tran Phu Streets*.

North of Vinh

The northern central region of Vietnam contains only one highway, National Highway 1 along the coast. From Vinh to Than Hoa, the road runs many points right along the coast of the South China Sea through tiny, nondescript villages and towns that offer virtually no amenities to travelers save for a sparse number of roadside cafes and restaurants. The northern provinces in this area are the poorest in Vietnam—the soil isn't good for cultivation and the region experiences havoc with the ravages of flooding and seasonal typhoons. The villagers exist on only a marginal subsistence.

The people of this region did not share in the prosperity the Americans brought to the southern half of the country during the Vietnam War. There is little for the independent traveler to do and see between the 140 km that separate Vinh and Thanh Hoa. By the time you've reached this point, you probably have little interest in stopping and exploring these small hamlets.

Some will tell you that the people of north-central Vietnam are not warm to foreigners (especially Americans) as those in the south. While I did not find this to be entirely correct—indeed, smiles were everywhere—there is more reserve on the part of the people of this region, as they rarely see foreigners. But even the North Vietnamese bear little animosity toward Americans and are generally quite friendly. Keep in mind that very little English is spoken in this area, and that you should carry dong rather than dollars stopping in small hamlets and towns along NH1. There are few if any places that will change money for you.

Thanh Hoa

Thanh Hoa is the capital of Thanh Hoa Province (which was the site of the Lam Son Uprising between 1418–1428) and the northernmost point of north-central Vietnam. The 160-meter bridge that spans the Ma River south of Thanh Hoa (Ham Rong Bridge, or "Dragon's Jaw") was an important North Vietnamese military link moving south and was bombed repeatedly by U.S. warplanes during the war. In fact, all around Thanh Hoa are craters left by the bombs of American planes. The North Vietnamese heavily for

·d the bridge and the U.S. lost as many as 70 planes during raids on the idge in the mid-1960s. Finally, in 1972, they were able to take out the idge using laser-guided bombs, but the NVA quickly erected a pontoon idge to replace it. There is a big church on the north side of town, the Cit-lel of Ho, which was built in 1397 when this town was the capital of Viet-im. In Thuan Hoa, you can stay at the **Tourist Hotel**, at *21A Quang Trung reet*; the 25B and 25A Hotels along NH1, or the **Thanh Hoa Hotel** on the est side of NH1 in the middle of town (☎ *852517; FAX: 852104*; US$10-·0). Near the southern edge of town are a slew of cheap restaurants and ca-·s. The Reunification Express train does stop here, linking Thanh Hoa with e rest of the Vietnamese coast. Buses link the provincial capital with a imber of coastal towns, including Vinh (140 km), Hue (500 km), and anoi (153 km). There are two decent beaches in the area called the Sam ·n Beaches, about 15 km southeast of Thanh Hoa. They are mainly fre-·ented by monied Hanoi residents to escape the summer heat. But keep in ind that the weather here is usually cool and damp, and the northerly inds can make a trip to the beaches quite cold. There are some cheap hotels ·d bungalows here. You can also see the remains of fortifications built here · the NVA to protect the Ham Rong Bridge.

Ninh Binh

This is the capital of Ninh Binh province on the Day River, about 60 km ·rth of Thanh Hoa. There is little here for the tourist, and it serves as not ·uch more than an overnight spot. It is linked to other coastal communities · both rail and bus service. Perhaps the best reason to come to this region, ·her than just passing through, is to make the short 10-km trip to the an-·ent capital of Vietnam in the Truong Son Mountains called **Hoa Lu**. Hoa Lu ·as built as the new capital of Vietnam in AD 968 and remained so until AD ·10. This was the time of the Dinh and early Le Dynasties. It was selected ·r its location: in a narrow valley surrounded by limestone mountains with ·ths that were easily defendable against Chinese invaders. Some say it is like ·a Long Bay without the bay. There are still the remnants of ancient tem-·es in Hoa Lu. Elephants and horses were carved into the stonework.

Although today there is little to see here, this was once an area covering ·0 hectares that was dotted with temples and shrines. Hoa Lu was the ·rthplace of Dinh Bo Linh, the founder of the Dinh Dynasty. There are ·ins of the ancient royal citadel here that once covered three square kilome-·s, and the Dinh Tien Hoang royal temple of the Dinh kings. Inscribed on ·e pillar in the central temple are the words *Dai Co Viet*, which the name ·etnam was derived from. Inside this temple are statues of Dinh and his ·ns.

Vinh

The Vault of Dinh is at the base of Mount Yen. During the 960s, Dinh ɪ
Linh was able to pacify the area, and even the warring Ngos accepted ɦ
dominance of the region. But Dinh Bo Linh's kingdom was wracked wi
insubordination. He placed a tiger in the center courtyard and announce
that anyone who violates his rule will be "boiled and gnawed." But rath
than make his oldest blood son, Dinh Lien, the heir to the throne, he cho
instead his younger son, Hang Lang. Trouble then dogged the king. Legeɪ
says that violent climactic events occurred, and, in 979, Lien ordered an a
sassin to kill Hang Lang. Just a few months later, a court official named ᴅ
Thich murdered both Dinh Bo Linh and Dinh Lien as they lay sleeping in
drunken stupor. Do Thich was caught for his crime, and it's said he was e
ecuted and his body fed to the people. Hoa Lu is at the southern edge of tɦ
Red River Delta in Truong Yen village. You'll have to take a car from eitɦ
Hanoi or Ninh Binh to get here.

Near Ninh Binh you can also visit **Bich Dong Pagoda**, a three-hour boat riⅆ
on a tributary of the Hoang Long River. Getting there by car is much quic
er. The boat ride offers magnificent scenery of limestone caves and su
rounding mountains. After getting to the pagoda's landing, there's about

20-minute walk to reach the pagoda. Also visit **Binh Cach**, 20 km to the norɫ
of Ninh Binh. Here are the remains of the citadels of **Bo Co** and **Co Long**. Tɦ
Chinese army was crushed here by General Tran Gian Dinh in 1408. Yⲟ
can also visit the remains of the **Van Phong Citadel** deep in the nearby Ngo ᕁ
Mountains. The small village of Van Lam possesses the **Bich Dong Grottoeϲ**
They can be reached by boat from Hoa Lu or Binh Dinh. The grottoes haˇ
been around since the 10th century, and they were used as hideouts duriⁿ
the First Indochina War by the Viet Minh.

Ke So is 34 km northwest of Binh Dinh on the Song Day River. There iϲ
big cathedral here built between 1879 and 1884 by the French monsign
Puginier. **Nam Trang** (35 km north of Ninh Binh) is where Black Flag reɓ
leader Dinh Kong Trang was born. **Phat Diem** (30 km southeast of Niⁿ
Binh) was a major Catholic center during the French colonial era. The catɦ
dral built here was built of marble, granite and wood. It stands 16 metⲉ
high and is 80 meters long. There is also the nearby **Thuan Dao Church** (buɪ
in 1926) which is a strange looking structure. Monsignor Nguyen Ba Tⲟ
in Phat Diem was pronounced the first Vietnamese Bishop by the Vatican
1930. Places to stay in Ninh Binh include the 100-room **Hoa Lu Hot**
(☎ *871217; FAX: 871200*; US$15–$35) on the west side of NH1 and tɦ
Ninh Binh Hotel, also on the west side of NH1 (about US$10). Ninh Binh iϲ
scheduled stop on the Reunification Express train route. Ninh Binh is abⲟ
115 km south of Hanoi, 200 km north of Vinh and 60 km north of Thaⁿ
Hoa.

Nam Dinh

Nam Dinh (population about 250,000) is a smoky, ugly, gray industrial city about 90 km south of Hanoi. The city is primarily known for its textiles (and lack of tourists). The French built the **Nam Dinh Textile Mill** here in 1899 and it's still up and running. Western missionaries arrived here as early as 1627. Nam Dinh is considered to be the third-largest industrial area in the north. There was a giant square citadel here, built in 1804, that faces southeast toward the sea, that was eventually destroyed by the French in 1891 (only the watchtower is marginally intact) after they seized the city in 1882.

Nam Dinh, which was continually attacked by the Chams during the Champa Empire, was designed as sort of a mini-Hanoi, where quarters were built to house areas of tradesmen and craftsmen. For instance, there was a section for cobblers, another for blacksmiths, one for embroiderers, another for goldsmiths, one for coffin makers, and so on. Some of the "sights" of Nam Dinh are outside the city itself, much of them areas of historical rather than architectural interest, as many of the ancient structures have been ruined. **My Loc**, about 2 km north of the city, is where the Tran Dynasty began and was the birthplace of Tran Bich San. All inhabitants of the city were forced to adopt the name Tran to their own names. **Tuc Mac** is 3 km north of the city. Tu Mac's **Den Thien-Truong** (Royal Temple) was built here. Of its many buildings, one, the **Tran Mieu**, was built in 1239. **Den Co Trach** was constructed in 1895, and was a temple dedicated to Tran Hung Dao. **Pho Minh Thu** was the stupa for King Tran Nhan Ton, who ruled the area in the 13th century. It's a 14-story tower built in the early 14th century that was demolished by the Mings and rebuilt in the 15th century. Subsequent restorations took place in the 17th and 18th centuries.

Fifteen km northwest of Nam Dinh is **Yen Do**, where Nguyen Khuyen was born. **Ky Lan Son (The Mountain of the Unicorn)** was home to Le Hoan, who founded the Early Le Dynasty and was its ruler from 980-1005. He was crowned "The King Who Pacified the South" in 981 after driving back an attacking Chinese force. There were also numerous battles with the Chams during his reign. **Chua Dien Linh**, **Doi Son** and **Doi Dep Pagodas** were built in the 12th century on the hills 46 km northwest of Nam Dinh in Hung Yen valley. **Phu Giay** is a temple dedicated to the immortal Lieu Hanh about 17 km south of Nam Dinh. You might also want to visit the nearby villages of **Dong Dai** (10 km from Nam Dinh), where stands the Phoc Lam Pagoda and stupas of Hung Thien and Hoang Hai; **Van Diem** (20 km north of Nam Dinh) where there is an ancient citadel, and **Doc Bo** (27 km southeast of Nam Dinh), that has a pagoda dedicated to Trieu Viet Vuong, a general who declared himself king of Vietnam in AD 549. In Nam Dinh, you can stay at **Vi Hoang Hotel** (*115 Nguyen Du Street.* ☎ *8439262*). The post office is on Ha Huy Tap Street. Ninh Binh Tourist is at the Vi Hoang Hotel.

Vinh

Haiphong

Haiphong was leveled by American B-52s during the war; some scars still show

HAIPHONG IN A CAPSULE

A once ugly city that is quickly transforming its image...It was heavily bombed by the Americans during the Vietnam War...This is Vietnam's major port...The city itself offers few attractions...But there remains some nice colonial architecture...The First Indochina War started here with the French bombing of the port in 1946...Thousands of civilians died...During the American War, the U.S. lost more than 300 warplanes here...The nicest areas of the region are Cat Ba Island and Do Son Beach.

Haiphong, with a population of more than 1.2 million people, is the second-largest city in the north and Vietnam's major port. For the most part, much of the area surrounding the city is actually an eyesore—a gray urban sprawl pockmarked with factories and bombed-out buildings, despite massive rebuilding in the city.

Now Greater Haiphong, which sits on the mouth of the Cua Cam River, covers an area more than 1520 square meters. In 1872–1874, when the French took possession of the city, it was nothing more than a small port and market town. With the French in control, Haiphong grew at rocket speed. It soon became a major port, in part, because of its proximity to coal supplies. The French didn't leave until 1955, after their defeat at Dien Bien Phu. In fact, the biggest instigation of the First Indochina War was the 1946 French bombardment of Haiphong's civilian residential areas, an action that killed at least hundreds of civilians; perhaps, by some estimates, as many as 5000 people were killed in the raids. All this happened because a French Navy ship had seized a Vietnamese junk. Vietnamese troops fired on the French ship, which so incensed the French commanders, they decided to bomb the hell out of the city. A month later, the war started.

The Americans pounded Haiphong during the Vietnam War and, in 1972, President Nixon ordered the mining of the city's harbor to prevent the shipment of Soviet-made war equipment that was being moved south. As part of the Paris Peace Agreement the same year, the Americans agreed to help dispose of the mines.

The Vietnamese purportedly downed more than 300 U.S. aircraft from the city's antiaircraft batteries during the war. But the Americans achieved many of their objectives in Haiphong. More than 80 percent of the city's above-ground petrol facilities were destroyed in 1966 in the U.S. effort to prevent these precious supplies from reaching the south—although American intelligence was unable to glean that the North Vietnamese suspected such action would be taken and had moved much of their supplies to underground locations.

Today, there's a resort and even Vietnam's first casino in Haiphong. The hotels, though, are generally overpriced. Surprisingly, much of the old French colonial architecture survived the bombardment, mostly in the downtown area around the **theater square**. A couple of kilometers south of the city center is the **Du Hang Pagoda**, said to have been built in the 1600s. Also check out the numerous street markets near Cau Dat and Tam Bac streets, as well as the old colonial architecture on Tam Bac Street.

Despite the "resurgence" of the city, it remains a relatively unattractive metropolis. Tourists don't particularly care for it and, apparently, neither do the Vietnamese. Since 1980, massive amounts of Vietnamese have left the city—

Haiphong

and not merely as boat people in search of a new land and economic opportunities, but to other areas in Vietnam itself.

What to See and Do in Haiphong

Haiphong retains a remarkable amount of its colonial architecture despite being leveled during the Vietnam War.

The Colonial-Style Architecture

If you're going to spend any time in the city at all, at least check out the old French buildings that remained largely undamaged through both Indochina wars. The best area for seeing the old structures is in the center of the city, particularly where Tran Hung Dao and Quang Trung Streets intersect, which is where an old theater can be found.

Du Hang Pagoda

121 Du Hang Street.

This mildly interesting pagoda was built in the 17th century and has been remodeled many times since. Today, it is being renovated again as you read this. The small pagoda was dedicated to Le Chan, who battled the Chinese alongside the Trung Sisters. There's a courtyard and some impressive Vietnamese-style traditional wood carvings.

Nghe Pagoda

51 Ngo Nghe Street.

This pagoda was also built to honor Le Chan, and was constructed during the early part of the 20th century.

Dang Hai Flower Village

About 5 km from the city center. All types of tropical and perennial flowers are grown here and sold to countries all over the world. Worth only a brief stop.

Hang Kenh Tapestry Factory

Wool tapestries are produced at this factory, founded some 66 years ago, and are exported to other nations. Again, worth just a brief stop.

Hang Kenh Communal House

Hang Kenh Street.

This is where you can find an impressive display of about 500 wooden relief sculptures. The area here once belonged to the village of Kenh.

Other Temples

If you're required to spend some time in Haiphong, you might also want to check out the **Thien Phuc Pagoda**, built in 1551, where there is a statue of Queen Mother Tra Huong; the **Le Chan Temple**, which was built in honor of a military commander of the 1st century and **Linh Quang Pagoda**, which was built in 1709 and possesses many fine wood carvings.

Where to Stay in Haiphong and Do Son

> ### AUTHOR'S NOTE:
> ### TELEPHONE PREFIXES
>
> *The following telephone numbers are local exchanges. The country code is 84. The city code is 31.*

Hotel du Commerce US$30–$40 ★ ★

62 Dien Bien Phu Street. ☎ 847206 or 847290.
40 rooms.
This French-era hotel has been renovated and is a very comfortable place to stay. All the rooms have air conditioning, attached bath. Restaurant. Hot water, refrigerators. The lower-priced rooms are especially a bargain.

Duyen Hai Hotel US$22–$40 ★ ★

5 Nguyen Tri Phuong Street. ☎ 847657 or 842157.
This is also an attractive French colonial style hotel not unlike the Hotel du Commerce, in price, ambience and service. Air conditioning, hot water, attached bath. Recently renovated.

Cat Bi Hotel US$25–$35

30 Tran Phu Street. ☎ 846306.
The best thing about this hotel is its proximity to the railroad station. Air conditioning, attached bath. Nothing special.

Hang Hai Hotel US$30–$50 ★ ★

282 Danang Street. ☎ 848576.
38 rooms.
This is one of the nicest hotels in Haiphong, and if you're spending more than a day or two, this would probably be the best place, even though it's located in a grimy area 3 km from the city center. Large, quiet rooms with air conditioning, refrigerators, telephone, attached bath, hot water. Two restaurants and a disco on the top floor.

Haiphong

Bach Dang Hotel   **US$12–$40**

40-42 Dien Bien Phu Street. ☎ 847244.

All classes of rooms in this hotel. But it's a little seedy, especially if you're conside
ing the higher-priced rooms. Air conditioning, restaurant, attached bath, hot wate

Hong Bang Hotel   **US$15–$65**   ★

64 Dien Bien Phu Street. ☎ 842229.
30 rooms.

Recently renovated. Rooms have attached bath, color TV, air conditioning, refrig
erators. Restaurant, massage and sauna. Nice amenities for the price.

Thang Nam Hotel   **US$15–$20**

55 Dien Bien Phu Street. ☎ 842820.

Average. Rooms have air conditioning, attached bath. There's a restaurant an
beauty shop.

Ben Binh Hotel   **US$25–$50**   ★

6 Ben Binh Street, across from the ferry dock. ☎ 842260.

These are large, attractive and spacious villas. Air conditioning, attached bath, ho
water. Friendly service.

Hoa Binh Hotel   **US$8–$19**

104 Luong Khanh Thien Street, opposite the railway station. ☎ 846907.

The lower-priced rooms come with fan; air conditioning in the higher-price
rooms. A convenient and relatively cheap place for backpackers.

Hai Au Hotel   **US$20–$30**

Do Son Beach.
45 rooms.

This hotel is run by Haiphong Tourism and is a reasonably good value. Air condi
tioning, attached bath, hot water, restaurant. There are a slew of hotels strung ou
along the beach, but this may be the best.

Hoa Phuong Hotel

Right near the Hai Au Hotel on Do Son Beach.

Also run by Haiphong Tourism. These are villas that were once used by members o
the Politburo.

Ministry of Energy Guest House
(Nha Khach Bo Nang Luong)   **About US$20–$35**

Do Son Beach.
100 rooms.

This is one of the newest hotels at the beach but it doesn't overlook the beach itsel
Air conditioning, hot water, balconies with the higher-priced rooms, telephone. A
decent deal for foreigners, but the Vietnamese pay half these prices.

Van Hoa Hotel   **About US$8**

Do Son Beach, at the tip of the peninsula.

A favorite among backpackers. Long walk to the beach, however. Bizarre architec
ture. Rooms have a fan.

Where to Eat in Haiphong and Do Son

Haiphong has a great many small and cheap restaurants. The most expensive food can be found at the hotel restaurants, the cheapest on the streets. But the seafood in Haiphong is excellent. At Do Son Beach, try the **Van Hoa Restaurant** at the end of the peninsula in a small park.

Directory

Transportation

Haiphong is 100 km southeast of Hanoi on National Highway 5.

By air:

VN flights leave HCMC nonstop for Haiphong daily at 7 a.m. (Thursday and Sunday at 6:30 a.m. and 12:30 p.m.). From Haiphong, flights depart for HCMC Mon.-Wed. at 10 a.m., Thursday at 9:30 a.m. and 3:30 p.m., Friday and Saturday at 10 a.m., and Sunday at 9:30 a.m. and 3:30 p.m., all nonstop. Flights also serve Haiphong from Danang on Mondays, Wednesdays and Saturdays at 8:45 a.m. Flights to Danang depart Haiphong the same days at 11 a.m.

By bus:

There are regular connections to Hanoi via the minibuses that cruise around the theater area. The trip takes about 2.5 hours and costs about 10,000 dong. Buses also depart from Haiphong's bus station in the Thuy Nguyen District, which is on the north bank of the Cua Cam River, for Bai Chay and Ha Long Bay's Hong Gai (about 3 hours). To reach the station, you have to take a ferry to the north bank of the river. Buses leave Hanoi for Haiphong from the Long Bien Bus Station on the east side of the Red River.

By train:

This is a more popular means of reaching your destination even though the Reunification Express doesn't stop in Haiphong. There is one train that links Hanoi with Haiphong every day early in the morning. From Haiphong, there are two daily trains to Hanoi.

By car:

This is actually a relatively long trip considering the short distance between the two cities. There are a number of bridges that both cars and the train share. If a train is coming, you've got to stop and wait, sometimes for quite a while. This short distance along Highway 5 can take as long as three hours to cover.

By boat:

You can also reach Haiphong from Hanoi by boat. The schedule changes often. If you want, you can even go to Saigon by boat from Haiphong. The trip takes 2.5 days. Ferries also leave from the dock on Ben Binh Street for Hong Gai in Ha Long Bay. The trip takes about four hours and costs about US$1. Ferries from Ha Long Bay usually have the same schedules. As I mentioned, boat schedules in the area change frequently, so find out first. You may end up in Haiphong a day or two longer than you anticipated.

Haiphong

Post Office

5 Nguyen Tri Phuong Street. ☎ *842584.* International calls and faxes can be made from here.

Banks and Moneychangers

Vietcom Bank is located at *11 Hoang Dieu Street*, not far from the Post Office. ☎ *841723.* They give advances on American-issued credit cards.

Tourist Offices

Haiphong Tourist, *15 Le Dai Hanh Street.* ☎ *842957.* This is one of the more useful tourist offices in Vietnam for independent travelers. It offers car rentals and boat charters to Ha Long Bay and Cat Ba National Park.

Hospitals

Vietnam-Czech Friendship Hospital on *Nguyen Duc Canh Street* or the **Traditional Medicine Hospital** on *Ben Vien Dong Y Street* and *Nguyen Duc Canh Street*. The best bet, though, is to get yourself back to Hanoi ASAP if you've gotten sick or badly hurt.

TNT International Express

☎ *847180.*

Airlines

Vietnam Airlines Booking Office. *Cat Bi Airport.* ☎ *848309, 845217.*

Haiphong Environs

Fishing fleet near Yen Hung, Quang Ninh province.

Bach Dang River (Cua Cam)

The mouth of the Bach Dang River (also called the Cua Cam River, Cam iver or the Haiphong Channel) is about 10 km east of Haiphong. This is here the river flows into the sea. It is actually a maze or network of water-ays between Ha Long Bay and Haiphong that has an impressive history. ietnamese forces prevented the Chinese from landing here to do battle ree times: in AD 938, AD 981, and in 1288 by Tran Hung Dao. Antici-ating the Mongol invasion, Tran Hung Dao stopped the Mongols from king over the region by pounding three stone spikes in the harbor during igh tide. The Mongol ships ran into them when they tried to sail away at w tide and sank. The buried remains of the stakes were discovered in 1985 the nearby district of Yen Hung.

Do Son Beach

This beach resort, established in 1888 on what is actually an islet (or a se-es of islets), is 20 km southeast of Haiphong and is popular with the locals. t's not a bad beach but a little dirty due to the hotels that have gone up long the beachfront in recent years. The peninsula is best known for the ine hills called "The Mountain of Nine Dragons," or *Cuu Long*. There's a mall temple on Doc Mountain called **Den Ba De Temple**, which is dedicated o a young woman who leapt to her death after spending the night with a nan she didn't want to be with.

Cat Ba National Park ★★★

30 km to the east of Haiphong and 135 km from Hanoi. Daily ferries leave or Cat Ba from Haiphong's Ben Bach Dang Street Ferry Terminal, usually arly in the morning (however, the schedules are subject to change). Cat Ba sland is the largest island in the Ha Long Bay region. The park represents a mall section of the island of Cat Ba that covers a forested area of 120 square km. The total area of Cat Ba is close to 355 square km. The area was declared national park in 1986 to preserve the island's diverse flora and fauna. The nainly forested park is covered with tropical evergreens, coastal mangrove orests, freshwater swamps and lakes (the biggest being Ech Lake), and sur-ounded by fine beaches with coral reefs offshore. The principal beaches in he park include Hong Xoai Be, Cai Vieng and Hong Xoai Long beaches. There are reportedly three hotels on the island, although I could only locate ne, the Cat Ba Hotel. It's said the other two go by the same name. Don't nake plans to meet anyone at the Cat Ba Hotel. There are also two camping villages near the island's fishing village (Cat Ba Town) that attract a horde of both Vietnamese tourists and foreigners alike.

Cat Ba Island also features small waterfalls and grottoes in limestone rock formations (as many as 350 limestone outcroppings). There are high winds at the top of the grottoes and, frankly, sitting on the beach can get a little nippy at any time of the year, although on the rare summer sunny day, noting beats kicking back on Cat Ba. In fact, there's no real "season" to visit t island, as the winters are cold, drizzly and gray and the summers rattled typhoons.

Of particular interest have been the discoveries of stone tools and hum bones on the island that indicate Cat Ba was inhabited 7000 years ago. Nea ly 20 such sites have been found. Today, the island has at least a dozen sp cies of mammals, including the rare Francois monkey. There are also de and wild boar in addition to birds such as hornbills, hawks and cuckoo Other species stop here on their migration paths. Most of the island's pop lation of 10,000–12,000 people is located in Cat Ba Town. They eke out living mainly through fishing and rice farming and by growing apples, o anges and cassava. Electricity on the island is limited to only a few hours the evening. Some of the best beaches in Vietnam can be found here, that's what Hanoi officials would have you believe. And it may be accurat Cat Ba Island has largely been declared a protected region and, as me tioned, features tropical forests, mangrove swamps, towering dolomite hill waterfalls, lakes, caves and, of course, gorgeous beaches.

Haiphong

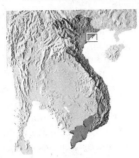

Ha Long Bay

Face Island in Ha Long Bay was aptly named.

HA LONG BAY IN A CAPSULE

165 km from Hanoi to the Bai Chai bus station...Perhaps the most beautiful coastal area of Vietnam...More than 3000 islands in the bay...Spectacular limestone outcroppings and caves...Stalagmite and stalactite formations perhaps the most beautiful in the world...Huge limestone rock formations appear out of the bay like giant deformed monoliths...Bai Chay and Hong Gai are the major "towns" in the region...Reachable by bus, car or boat.

Ha Long Bay

Ha Long Bay, 20 km past Haiphong, is targeted for tourism, and it's quickly taking form. The principal towns tourists get to, Bai Chay and Hong Gai (about 55-60 from Haiphong), have sprouted more new hotels in the last year than tulips in a Dutch flower field in April—particularly Bai Chay, which has become practically unrecognizable in a mere eight months. In fact, the "strip" that runs along the beach from Bai Chay to the ferry to Hong Gai is dangerously starting to resemble the beach strips in Thailand's Pattaya and Phuket (Patong Beach). The resemblance is becoming uncanny. Although the hookers and the bar-beers have yet to arrive, can they be far beyond in what is becoming one of Vietnam's biggest tourist attractions?

A mere two years ago, travelers had only a handful of accommodations to choose from when visiting the area. At last count, I registered 62 hotels in Bai Chay alone—most of them reed-thin five- or six-story structures cemented to one another that stretch up the hill on a dirt road (Vuon Dao-Bai Chay Street—or the "patch") from the new Peach Blossom Hotel at the water's edge—engaged in a classic corner gas station price war. Their owners prowl the street, beckoning wary tourists who have strayed past the Ha Long Hotel by mistake. (And just to make sure they don't wander too far past Bai Chay's milestone Ha Long Hotel, the caravansary now has five hotels! Ha Long 1, Ha Long 2, Ha Long 3...You get the idea.)

Ha Long Bay offers some of Vietnam's most breathtaking scenery, including beautiful limestone formations, sheer edifice cliffs, huge rock arches, peaceful coves and seemingly thousands of limestone islets that rise from the sea like green plaster monsters. If Ha Long Bay was perhaps 1000 km to the south, this would be paradise on Earth. But as it is, the weather here can be horrible—damp, rainy and cold. But catch the area on a good day and you're in for a treat. Boats for hire line the Bai Chay beach area (old day cruisers and overnight boats.) Like the hotels, competition is stiff. Most take groups usually tour groups vanned up from Hanoi. Independent travelers will find better bargains if they can hitch a ride aboard a boat that's relatively full. But I hopped on a day cruiser as a loner for US$10 for a three-hour ride through the islets, grottoes and caves of the islands of Ha Long. (4 hours does the journey more justice.)

INSIDER TIP

It seems like Ha Long Bay is pretty close to the capital—after all, how long could it take to go a hundred miles? A long darn time. It's a trip that can easily take six hours or more—one way. The trip includes both a river and harbor crossing by ferry, starting at Haiphong. So be warned; it's no day trip.

Ha Long Bay (the name means "Where the Dragon Descends Into the Sea") is perhaps the most beautiful area in Vietnam. It's only drawback, and it's a major one at that, is that the area is frequently shrouded in a cold, drizzly fog, particularly during the winter months when, frankly, a stay in the area can be a very uncomfortable one.

Myth says that an enormous beast created the bay and outcroppings as it thrashed its way toward the sea to prevent the forward progress of enemy fleets, even though two major battles were fought here in the 10th and 13th centuries. Legend maybe, but there are sailors who even today report sightings of a giant sea beast called the Tarasque. Locals, in their effort to make a few bucks, offer foreigners a chance to sail out in search of the creature.

Ha Long Bay was also the site where, in 1882, French Captain Henri Rivière was beheaded after sending troops into the area to seize the region's vast coal deposits. His head was put on a stick and paraded from village to village. The incident prompted the French government to launch a full-scale effort to turn the country of Vietnam into a colony of France. The two ports of Hong Gai (called the Pointed Peak, about 120 km from Hanoi in Quang Ninh Province) and Cam Pha (150 km east of Hanoi) are areas of vast coal deposits and are mined by the Cai Bao, Mon Duong and Cham peoples. The territory, in Quang Ninh Province, is Vietnam's largest coal-producing region. Archeological evidence suggests an ancient culture in the area dating back to the Neolithic Era (2000) BC following the Bac Son people.

Ha Long Bay is the north's major tourist center; any trip to Vietnam should include a visit to the area. There are magnificent, fragmented limestone outcroppings in this bay which features, by the best estimate, more than 3000 islands. Beautiful Chinese-type sailing junks dot the waters between the outcroppings—many of the islets ascend to heights of 300 meters or more. Many more reach a height of 100 meters. The area appears like a mountain range in the sea. The mountains, consisting of mainly dolomite and limestone, reach for a distance of more than 100 km and cover 1500 square km. The outcropping formations, caves, grottoes, fjords and tunnels have perhaps the most exotic appearance of any natural wonders in the world. They've been given names founded in wonderment. There is the Isle of Surprise (which is not a surprising name), the Isle of Wonders, and so forth. There are isles named after monkeys, marionettes, toads, turtles and buzzards.

Most foreigners travel to the two principal areas where there is food and accommodations: Bai Chay and Hong Gai on the northern side of the bay. Although some of the more hardy travel to Tra Co next to the Chinese frontier.

What to See and Do in Ha Long Bay

Caves cut through the grottoes of Ha Long Bay.

Limestone Outcroppings and Grottoes   ★★★★

From Bai Chay and Hong Gai, "junks" (actually small, beat-up—but clean—tour boats) can be rented to see the spectacular caves and grottoes in the bay, some of which have names like Fighting Cocks and Customs House Cave. Boats are available all along the beach front in Bai Chay. Expect to pay about US$15–$20 for a three-hour cruise of the bay—although better negotiators will get on board for less. English- and French-speaking guides are available and come with the cost of the boat. Beverages are available on board, but take along food.

Get your guide to bring you to Hang Manh Cave, a giant cave that reaches more than 2 km and offers incredible stalagmite, stalactite and other fantastic rock formations. There is also the Hang Dau Go Grotto, a massive cave of three chambers that can be reached after climbing some slippery steps. In the first hall are scores of stalactites that look like a congregation of small creatures out of a George Lucas film. The cave (translated to the "Cave of Wooden Stakes") derived its name from the famous 13th-century warrior named Tran Hung Dao, who used the third chamber of the cave to store pointed stakes which he later pounded into the bed of the Bach Dang River to sink an invading Mongol fleet. Other boats will stop at Deu Island, where visitors can view a rare species of monkey characterized by its red buttocks. The best time for seeing the monkeys is shortly before dusk. At least this is said by the guides, perhaps to entice you to pay for another hour or two.

You should also see Drum Grotto, which is so called because the wind that blows through the stalagmites and stalactites sounds like the faraway beating of drums. Visitors on longer excursions in the bay can also stop at the Grotto of Bo Nau. Those who want to swim, bring along your bathing suits. Some of the islets offer brief stretches of sandy beaches, although they're becoming increasingly crowded as the dozens of day tour boats tend to bring visitors to the same places. But the numerous secluded coves around many of the grottoes offer superb swimming in glassy-smooth, lime-green waters. When it's raining, forget it. And don't try it during the winter, when the bay is ice-cold. It's generally agreed that the only swimming done in the bay in March is by drunken Siberians on holiday.

Where to Stay in Ha Long Bay

The number of hotels in the area has soared, and more are being built. Most are mini-hotels, tall and thin hospices that reach six stories. Better to get a room on the lower floors. There aren't any elevators in these places.

AUTHOR'S NOTE: TELEPHONE PREFIXES

Phone numbers are listed as local exchanges. From Hanoi, dial 01.33 before the local exchange. The country code is 84. The city code is 33.

Hong Gai

Hong Gai Floating Hotel　　　　　　**About US$8**

Near the ferry dock.
Very inexpensive. No amenities. A place to lay your head.

Hai Au Hotel　　　　　　**About US$10**

About halfway between the Hong Gai and Bai Chay docks.
Hot water, when it works. Basic accommodations.

Bai Chay

Bach Dang Hotel　　　　　　**About US$25**

Near the ferry dock. ☎ *846630.*
Comfortable accommodations. One of the better hospices in town. Hot water, private bath.

Peach Blossom Hotel　　　　　　**About US$40**　　　　★★

Corner of Bai Chay and Vuon Dao streets.
New hotel considered the best in Bai Chay until the next high-rise is finished. Typical of what will become a Ha Long hostelry tradition—famous for a day. Each new high-end roadhouse that goes up in this town will have its 15 minutes in the sun—or not much more than a few moments after that—before something else newer and higher (with more Toyota Land Cruisers parked in front) eclipses both the sun and the real reason to "discover" this corner of Vietnam.

Ha Long Hotel　　　　　　**US$15–$100**　　　　★★★

Bai Chay Road. ☎ *846340 (reservations), 846014 (Ha Long 1).*
This was the place for a good night's rest, decent food and an acceptable if not exceptional degree of comfort that "adventurous, but monied" guests used to rely on when coming to Ha Long. But the management must be getting scared of the "other guys." So now there are no fewer then five Ha Long Hotels, all in a community collegelike campus setting—with collegelike campus service. Ha Long 1 fetches

Ha Long Bay

the big bucks at about US$50–$100 a night. But even Ha Long 5 won't fit a back-packer's budget at US$15. But all in all, it's not a bad place. Service at the restaurant is slow, but you will eat—at least at breakfast. The top end isn't a whole lot different than the "proletariat" dormitory. Rooms with air conditioning, private bath, marginally hot water, satellite TV (and TV that has one station on every channel in the cheap rooms). The "V" channel will get here soon, though, I assure you. This place is either the Harvard or Alcatraz of Ha Long.

Hoang Lan Hotel   About US$15–$20

Vuon Dao Street. ☎ *846318.*
Expensive, but the air conditioning is worth it during the summer. Hot water, private bath. Rooms with color TV, air conditioning, refrigerator.

Bach Long Hotel   About US$25

☎ *846445.*
40 rooms.
This is a good deal, as the rooms are bright, relatively large and clean. Hot water, clean attached bathrooms. Friendly staff. Restaurant.

Navy Guest House (Nha Khach Hai Quan)   About US$30

☎ *84603.*
6 rooms.
These are two colonial mansions overlooking the bay, three rooms in each house. Attached bath, hot water. Moderate.

Peace Hotel   US$15–$20

Vuon Dao Street. ☎ *846009.*
One of the many new Vuon Dao caravansaries. Clean, comfortable and moderately priced. International telephone and a good view of the bay from some of the rooms. Rooms with air conditioning, hot water, color TV, refrigerator. Arranges for boat tours of the bay. Accepts major credit cards.

Hai Trang Hotel   US$12

Vuon Dao Street. ☎ *846094.*
Clean rooms and one of the best deals on Vuon Dao. Rooms with air conditioning, private bath, hot water. Tour boat and car rental service.

Thu Thuy Mini Hotel   US$15

Vuon Dao Street. ☎ *846295.*
Another good value. Mini, sardine-thin "high-rise." Rooms with air conditioning, hot water, color TV, telephone. Restaurant (sort of).

Thuon Loi Hotel & Restaurant   US$15–$20

Vuon Dao Street. ☎ *846209.*
Hotel manager Bui Van Hoa is one of the friendliest on the "patch." Clean, comfortable rooms with color TV, air conditioning, hot water, private bath. Excellent food on my visit (Asian, European, seafood). Karaoke and bay excursions. Taxi service.

Minh Ha Hotel   US$20

Vuon Dao Street. ☎ *846532.*

Reasonable but stretching it a bit as you can find something with the same amenities next door in both directions for a little less. Be nice and Khuat Duy Hai might bring the price down. Rooms with air conditioning, hot water, color TV.

Nhung Hotel   US$10–$15

Vuon Dao Street. ☎ *846121.*
One of the better bargains. Rooms with air conditioning, hot water, private bath. Boat rentals.

Tran Tam Mini Hotel   US$10–$18

Just off Vuon Dao Street, 50 meters from Bai Chay Street (Ha Long Road). ☎ *846469.*
Good rooms, good food, good price. Rooms with air conditioning, hot water, TV. Travel services, bay tours.

Trade Union Guest House   About US$25

Overlooking the beach.
The biggest building in town and relatively new. Make sure the air conditioning is working during the summer before you choose a room.

Post Office Hotel (Khach San Buu Dien)

2 km on the road back to Hanoi.
New and comfortable. Attached bath, air conditioning, hot water. Next door are three relatively new hotels managed by Quang Ninh Tourism: the Bach Long, Ha Long, and Hoang Long Hotels. Each are comfortable and in the US$25–40 price range. For those bucks, you get air conditioning, hot water, attached bath and so on. Restaurant. Each of these four hotels is in the moderate price range.

Van Hai Hotel   About US$10

In the middle of town. ☎ *846403.*
Shared bath. Rooms overlook the sea.

Bac Long Hotel   US$5–$15

Vuon Dao Street. ☎ *846167.*
Perhaps the cheapest rooms on Vuon Dao Street. Rooms with air conditioning, TV, hot water, private bath, refrigerator, telephone.

Other -new mini-hotels are crushed in the Vuon Dao Street area, all offering air-conditioned rooms with private bath, hot water and in-room TVs. All are in the US$12–20 range. They include:

Van Nam Hotel

Vuon Dao Street. ☎ *846593.*

Viet Hoa Hotel

Vuon Dao Street. ☎ *846035.*

Minh Cuong Hotel

Vuon Dao Street. ☎ *846086.*

Minh Minh Hotel

Vuon Dao Street. ☎ *846741.*

Cam Van Hotel

Vuon Dao Street. ☎ *846675.*

Ha Long Bay

Than Lich Hotel

Vuon Dao Street. ☎ *846038.*

Hai Yen Hotel

Vuon Dao Street. ☎ *846126.*

The Olddaling

Vuon Dao Street.

Directory

Transportation

Ha Long Bay is about 165 km from Hanoi, 55 km from Haiphong, and 45 km from Cam Pha.

By air:

Hanoi is the closest airport unless you find a way of hiring a seaplane. Or a chopper.

By helicopter:

Serving the Hanoi-Ha Long route are now two Russian-made Mi-8 and Mi-17 helicopters that have been taken out of service as search-and-rescue choppers to shuttle tourists back and forth from the bay. The route was inaugurated in July 1995 by Northern Flight Service, a branch of the state-run Vietnam Flight Service Corp. The helicopters can hold up to 24 passengers apiece. The flight from Gia Lam Airport (10 km outside of Hanoi) takes 30 minutes and departs from Hanoi on Sundays. The cost? A whopping US$175 round-trip for foreigners—and only US$68 for Vietnamese nationals. Helicopter flights and tours of the bay are also possible either through **Vietnamtourism** or **Vietnam Airlines**. Also try **Helijet-VASCO** *(15 Ngo Quyen, Hanoi.* ☎ *84-4-8266919)* for chopper service out to the bay. And bring your wallet.

By bus:

Buses depart Haiphong for Bai Chay from the bus station on the north bank of the Cua Cam River. The trip takes about two hours. The bus station in Bai Chay is on the waterfront road near the Van Hai Hotel. There are also regular connections with Hanoi until the afternoon. The trip takes five to six hours and there are two ferry crossings (where most of the time is spent).You can also make connections to points south.

By train:

Budget travelers in Hanoi can take the train to Haiphong in the morning, and then the afternoon ferry to Bai Chay. From Bai Chay you can either return to Haiphong by boat or Hanoi by bus.

By car:

This is the best way to get to Ha Long Bay. Go to Bai Chay, spend the night, take a boat tour the next day, and return to Hanoi on the third day. To hire a car and driver from Hanoi will set you back at least US$100 (usually more) for the round trip. The Japanese cars are more expensive to rent than the Russian ones, namely because they're more comfortable. Also expect to pay for the driver's meals and accommodations.

By boat:

Getting around the area isn't much fun unless you've got a boat to tour the islands. You won't need to rent a boat yourself as there will be a slew of foreigners as well as Vietnamese also seeking the same trips. Large boats, carrying up to 100 passengers cost between US$12–$20 an hour. But smaller boats holding up to a dozen people can be had for around US$8 an hour. The smaller boats are privately owned, so you can negotiate.

By ferry:

Ferries depart for Hong Gai about three times a day—in the early morning, mid-morning and late afternoon. But these schedules seem to continually change. The one-way trip takes about 3–4 hours and will set you back at least 10,000 dong, and sometimes much more if you don't let your independent (i.e., non-Vietnamtourism) guide buy your ticket for you. Ferries for Haiphong leave from the dock at Hong Gai at 6 a.m., 11 a.m. and 4 p.m. (Again, these schedules are subject to change). You can also take a ferry from Hong Gai to Bai Chay that leaves constantly during the day and early evening.

Tourist Office

Quang Ninh Tourism. *Bai Chay Street in Bai Chay.* ☎ *846351*.

Quang Ninh Tourism & Ship Chandler. *Bai Chay Street in Bai Chay.* ☎ *846405. FAX: 846226*.

Post Office

Bai Chay opposite the ferry dock. Also at the **Post Office Hotel**.

Banks and Moneychangers

Ha Long Hotel in Bai Chay. ☎ *846014*.

Ha Long Bay

Ha Long Bay

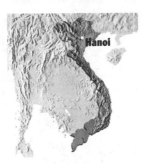

Hanoi

HANOI

Hanoi's One Pillar Pagoda was built in 1049 in the image of a lotus blossom.

HANOI IN A CAPSULE

Hanoi is the capital of the Socialist Republic of Vietnam...it's a city of lakes and parks...about 70 km inland from the Gulf of Tonkin...it sits on the banks of the Red River...the streets are tree-lined...trees are uplifting the pavement...it's been a major settlement since A.D. 1010....it became capital of North Vietnam after the Geneva Agreement of 1954...it's not nearly as kinetic and energetic as Saigon...it is inferior in both tourism and infrastructure...was heavily bombed during the Vietnam War...Like Ho Chi Minh City, Hanoi has had more than a half-dozen names over the years.

Ho Tay
(West Lake)

Tran Quoc
17th Century

Duong Thuy Khue

Duong Hoang Hoa Tham

Duong Buoi

Quan Thanh Temp
11th Centu

Presidential Palace

Ho Chi Minh's House
on stilts

Ho Chi Minh Mausoleum

Pho Doi Can

One Pillar Pagoda 1049

Saigon Pull

Ho Chi Minh Museum

Pho Doi Can

La Thanh Hotel

To Lich River

Duong Buoi

Van Phuc Lake

Ba Dinh District

Pho Kim Ma

Duong Tra

Duong Hung Vuong

Thu Le Zoo

Vol Phuc Temple
11th Cent.

Thu Le Lake

Pho Ngoc Khanh

Popular Opera
Theatre

Pho Nguyen Thai P

Ngoc Khanh

Pho Giang Vo

Transportation College

Giang Vo Lake

Temple of
Literature 1070

Hanoi Hilton

Television Tower

Hotel Dong Do

Pho Giang Vo

Hang Bot Church

Market-National
Showcase

Lang Pagoda
11th Century

Culture

Conservatoire

Foreign
Trade
College

Institute for
International
Relations

Cartographic Mapping
Institute (CMI)

Law College

Industrial Art

Duong La Thanh

Pho Tran Duc Thang

Pho Lang Ha

Thanh Cong
Lake

Pho Lang Trung

Dong Da Lake

Dong Da District

Pho Nguyen Luong Bang

Pho Kha

Duong C2 Thai

Dong Da Hill
1789

Kim Lien

Institute of Acupuncture

Boc
1792

Pho Trung Tu

Duong Chua Boc

Pho Tay Son Nguyen Luong B

Tu Liem District

Water conservancy
College

Duong Lang

Nga Tu So Market

©FWI 1995

Duong Truong Chinh

Water Puppet
Theatre

Air Force Museum

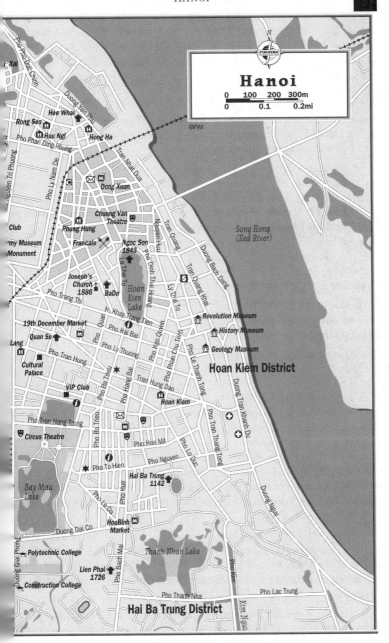

Hanoi

0 100 200 300m
0 0.1 0.2mi

©FWI

t Xai
Pho Phu Doc Chinh
Duong Yen Phu
Hee Whai
Rong Sen
Huu Ngl
Hong Ha
Pho Phan Ding Phung
Nguyen Tri Phuong
Pho Ly Nam De
Tran Nhat Dua
Dong Xuan
Chuong Van Theatre
Phung Hung
Club
my Museum
Monument
Francais
Ngoc Son 1843
La Thai To
Joseph's Church 1886
BaDa
Hoan Kien Lake
Pho Dinh Thai Hoang
Ly Thai To
Song Hong (Red River)
Pho Trang Thi
Ho Khay Trang Tien
Quan
Duong Bach Dang
Tran Quang Khai
Nguyen Huu
Tran Quang
Revolution Museum
19th December Market
Quan Su
Pho Hai Bai
Pho Ly Thuong
History Museum
Geology Museum
Lang
Pho Tran Hung
Cultural Palace
VIP Club
Pho Ba Trieu
Pho Hang Bai
Tran Hung Dao
Pho Phan Chu Trinh
Pho Le Thanh Tong
Hoan Kiem District
Hoan Kiem
Duong Tran Khanh Du
Pho Tran Nang Trung
Circus Theatre
Pho Hoa MA
Pho Ba Trieu
Pho Nguyen
Pho Lo Duc
Duong Tran Thang Tong
Pho To Hien
Bay Mau Lake
Hai Ba Trung 1142
Pho Hue
Duong Ngu
HoaBinh Market
Duong Dai Co
Thanh Nhan Lake
Polytechnic College
Duong Giai Phong
Lien Phal 1726
Pho Bach Mai
Pho Kim
Construction College
Pho Thanh Nha
Pho Lac Trung
Kim Ngu
Hai Ba Trung District

Although not as popular with tourists as Ho Chi Minh City, and certainly lacking the hustle and bustle of its sister to the south, there's still plenty to see and do in the capital. Some of the sights include the Fine Arts Museum, which houses traditional Vietnamese art as well as European-influenced works; the Water Puppet Theater, Vietnam's humorous version of Punch and Judy; Ho Chi Minh's mausoleum (the Vietnamese hero's body reposes in a glass coffin); the Ho Chi Minh Museum, which opened in 1990 in honor of the 100th anniversary of Ho's birth; and the rubble of what used to be the Hanoi Hilton, the prison where U.S. soldiers were kept (it has been torn down to make way for an actual hotel).

Hanoi was founded in A.D. 1010 at the beginning of the Lu Dynasty; it is the oldest capital city in Southeast Asia. The city was racked by constant bombing from U.S. Air Force B-52 bombers from 1966 to 1972. The center of Hanoi itself doesn't reveal a lot of scars, but the outlying areas do. The French colonial buildings of the capital are in desperate need of renovation—at the very least a coat of paint. But like the big city in the south, Hanoi's people are extremely friendly and seem to bear few ill feelings toward Westerners, Americans in particular. In fact, you can almost call this city of more than 3 million charming.

Whereas movement of Westerners in the city was once strictly controlled, tourists today move about Hanoi freely. Bicycles can be hired, and even sights off the beaten track are within easy reach of the traveler.

Perhaps what is most interesting about the city is the enormous changes the war ultimately has brought to the architecture of the capital. Many Hanoi dwelling owners are tearing down their properties and rebuilding in such a way that seriously threatens the character of the capital. These building owners are evidently preparing for what they believe will be a deluge of American customers descending on the capital after the embargo is lifted. Residents are tearing down centuries-old structures as well as ramshackle wooden dwellings and replacing them with multistoried mini-hotels complete with expensive TV satellite dishes. There seems to be little regard for style in these new structures, and they neither conform to any traditional or modern Asian or Western style—nor do they conform to each other. They look odd and out of place.

These new building trends haven't gone unnoticed by Hanoi authorities, who are caught in the dilemma of preserving tradition while faced with the demands of a changing and growing economy so thoroughly dependent on foreign investment—and, yes, buildings that look like six-story inverted railroad cars.

Up to now, Hanoi has been one of the few cities in Asia left entirely void of the western-style boxy business architecture that has completely redefined

ban areas like Bangkok, Manila and Kuala Lumpur. There are two very
nique historical areas: the ancient city of Hanoi near Hoan Kiem Lake that
as settled in the 11th century, and the large French Quarter that was built
y the French during their reign in the region from 1880–1930. The French
uarter is really quite attractive, with its tree-lined streets and small French-
yle houses. Old Hanoi, or the ancient city, is an old network of narrow al-
ys with dilapidated, crumbling houses set on nearly 40 streets named after
e original craftsmen and artisans who settled the area: Gold Street, Baker
reet, etc.

Urban planners in Hanoi, not eager to see either area become infected by
odernization, are seeking to zone areas specifically for the development of
usiness and residential centers that will become necessary as the Vietnamese
onomy expands. But the problem is which areas to earmark.

Although independent travel has become extraordinarily easy throughout
ietnam, the government is still somewhat wary of travelers straying from
e traditional, government-approved sights (many of which are drab and,
uite frankly, boring). This is evident by the fact that Hanoi was, until re-
ently, one of 10 localities in the country where tourist offices administer en-
re tourist establishments and other tourist activities in the area. Now a slew
f private tour agents are operating, and it is easy to move about the city and
s environs quite easily on your own, usually with no hassle from the author-
ies.

Hanoi has a lot of interesting things to see besides the formaldehyde im-
ersed corpse of Ho Chi Minh. The capital has a history of more than 1000
ears. Ho Guam (Restored Sword Lake) features water that has been dyed
ith green ink! There are the golden buffalo in the West Lake (Ho Tay).
here's the bronze-casting village of Ngu Xa, the snake village Le Mat, and
e flower villages of Ngoc Ha and Nhat Tan.

Besides the hundreds of pagodas and temples in the city (if you're not al-
eady entirely "pagodaed"-out) there are more than 35 ancient streets
looming with the same lotus flowers that have existed here for centuries.

But remember that tourism infrastructure in Hanoi is still substandard,
ell below amenities offered in HCMC. There were only a total of about
000 hotel rooms in the city at the end of 1994, and only about a quarter of
hese were considered worthy of "international standards." Roads are in di-
apidated condition, except in central Hanoi. Electricity and the water supply
ontinue to be unpredictable. (Foreign-invested joint projects with Viet-
amese firms, however, are changing these conditions, but at a tortoiselike
ate.)

Hanoi is looking for ways to improve its tourist industry. It's predicted,
ince the inception of the new laws pertaining to foreign investment, that by

Ho Tay
(West Lake)

Tran Quoc
17th Century

Nu Xai

Nam Tran

Ng Khac Hien

Ngu Xa

Lac Chinh

Pho Chau Long

Pho Phu Duc Chinh

Truc Bach Lake

Quan Thanh Temple
11th Century

Dang Tat

P. Nguyen Bieu

P. Dang Dung

Pho Cua Bac

Cua Bac
Church

Pho Phan

Doung Thuy Khue

Duong Hoang Hoa Tham

Presidential Palace

Ng Canh chan

Huong Van Thu

Ho Chi Minh's House
on stilts

Ho Chi Minh Mausoleum

Ngo Ngoc Ha

Duong Hung Vuong

Duong Bac Son

Pho Hoang Dieu

Pho Nguyen Tri Phuong

Pho Cua

One Pillar
Pagoda 1049

Pho Ngac Ha

Ho Chi Minh Museum

Ong Ich Khiem

Poland

Hungary

Slovakia

Albania

Army Club

Flag Tower

Le Hong Phong

Romania

Russia

Czech

Iran

China

Army Museum

Pho Son Tay

Lenin Monument

Popular Opera
Theatre

Pho Nguyen Thai Phu

Duong Tran Phu

Germany

Dien Bien Phu

Belgium

Mongolia

Cao Ba Quat

Tim Hoac Duc

Korea

Pho Cat Linh

Nguyen Khuyen

Ngo Bai

Temple of
Literature 1070

Quoc Tu Giam

Ngo Si Lien

Sao Mai

T An Quy Cap

Hang Bot Church

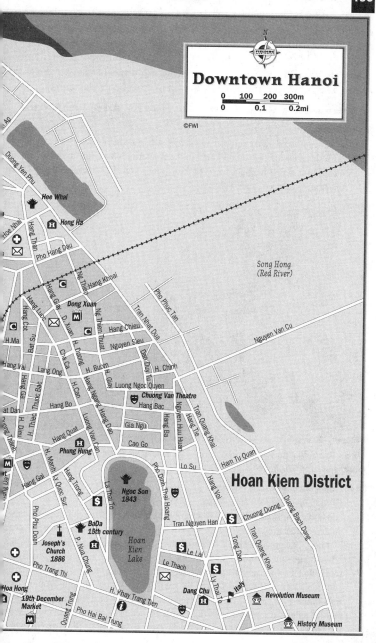

Downtown Hanoi

0   100   200   300m
0   0.1   0.2mi

©FWI

*Song Hong
(Red River)*

Hee Whal

Hong Ha

Duong Yen Phu

Hoe Nha

Hang Than

Pho Hang Dau

Ng. Trinh

Hang Khoai

Pho Phuc Tan

Hang Giay

Dong Xuan

Tran Nhat Dua

Hang Luoc

D. Xuan

Ng Thien Thuat

Hang Chieu

Nguyen Sieu

Dao Duy Tu

H. Chinh

Hang Cot

Hang Ga

Su Bac

H.Ma

H. Duong

Cha Ca

H. Buom

H. Giay

Luong Ngoc Quyen

Hang Vai

Lang Ong

H.Can

Nguyen Van Cu

Thuoc Bac

Hang Ngang

Hang Dao

Chuong Van Theatre

Hang Bac

Hang Bo

Hang Quat

Luong Van Can

Gia Ngu

Hang Ba

Hang Tie

Tran Quang Khai

H. Dieu

H. Thiet

Phung Hung

Cao Go

Nguyen Huu Huan

Lo Su

Ham Tu Quan

Hang Gai

H. Manh

Ly Quoc Su

Hang Trong

La Thai To

**Ngoc Son
1843**

Pho Dinh Tien Hoang

Hang Voi

Hoan Kiem District

Chuong Duong

Duong Bach Dang

Pho Phu Doan

P. Nha Chung

**BaDa
15th century**

**Joseph's
Church
1886**

*Hoan
Kiem
Lake*

Tran Nguyen Han

Le Lai

Chuong Duong

Tong Dan

Tran Quang Khai

Pho Trang Thi

Le Thach

Italy

Hoa Hong

Quang Trung

**19th December
Market**

H. Khay Trang Tien

Dang Chu

Revolution Museum

Pho Hai Bai Trung

History Museum

the year 2000, Hanoi will be attracting US$10 billion in foreign investment capital. Hanoi predicts that in order for the region to become an area of mass tourism that per capita income will need to increase to US$1000 by the year 2000. By then the capital expects to have nearly 20 hotels of international standards. Equally as important, infrastructure projects—largely consisting of decent roadways to the provinces—will have to be implemented.

What to See and Do in Hanoi and Environs

Army Museum

If you want to see tanks and planes and grenades and shells, this is the place. Better to see this museum before checking out the War Crimes Museum in Saigon. It's not as shocking and sobering. However, here you'll find the wreckage of B-52s and American fighter jets, such as F-111s.

Uncle Ho's mausoleum, where Ho rests embalmed, despite his request to b cremated after his death.

Ho Chi Minh Mausoleum and Museum ★★★

Open 7:30–11:30 a.m. Tues.–Thurs. and Sat.–Sun.

Somehow you're not surprised when your guide tells you that this mausoleum wa modeled after the Lenin tomb in Moscow. The structure itself is a huge, imposing building, polygonal in shape. It's no doubt the best-maintained building in all o Hanoi. The inner chamber is where the embalmed body of Ho rests; guards sur round it. The old man's an eerie-looking sight, and his impact on all of our lives thi half of the century, is felt through the glass. From the mausoleum, you can tou **Ho's house** near the Communist Party guest house— which was the former **presi dential palace** and residence of the former French governors of Indochina. Whe the North's quest for independence finally came to fruition in 1954, Ho refused t live in the palace, opting instead for the electrician's meager house on the palace grounds; he claimed the palace belonged to the people.

Hanoi Hilton

Off of Hai Ba Trung Street.

This is the morbidly humorous name given to the grisly, forboding Hanoi prison structure that housed U.S. POWs, namely American flyers, during the Vietnam War. Prisoners were tortured here up until at least 1969. Some were held seven years or longer. This was a dark, eerie sight before it was razed for the construction of a new hotel. If you hurry, you can still peer through portions of the surrounding wall and look at the rubble.

National Arts Museum ★

Open 8–noon and 1–4 p.m. Tues.–Sun.

Vietnamese sculpture is exhibited in this small museum located next to the Van Mieu, Vietnam's first university. The museum also features bronze drums and modern Vietnamese painting.

National History Museum ★

Open 8–noon and 1–4 p.m. Tues.–Sun. There is an admission fee.

This is actually a great place to visit, especially after seeing all the other sights and coming to the conclusion that the Vietnamese must love to yawn. This is Vietnam's leading museum and the center for cultural and historical research. Granted it's tough to know exactly what you're looking at if you don't read Vietnamese or don't have a guide, but the exhibits here are impressive. It's all designed so you can walk though the different periods of Vietnamese history. There are some beautiful bronze Dongson drums and funeral urns, Nguyen Dynasty pieces, models of ancient cities, weapons from the Tay Son revolt, and much more. If you're lucky, you may even get a private tour from one of the museum's curators.

Old Hanoi (The French Quarter) ★★

Check out the old quarter of Hanoi, a maze of narrow back alleys with shops selling antiques, flowers and handicrafts. This area is located in Central Hanoi, and was once located in the southeast part of the city as part of the royal plan for placing foreigners. But the quarter's location was far from the city center (down the Red River, susceptible to pollutants spilled into the river, near cemeteries and a leper colony). When the French took the city in 1882, they moved into the area south of Hoan Kiem, between the former area and the Ambassador Pagoda. This is where they built their new city. In 1884, the first permanent houses were built, replacing the huts that existed in the area at the time. But in order to do so, they had to ruin numerous monuments that stood in the area at the time. The Museum of Mines, which is now called the Museum of the Revolution, is on Tong Dan Street, behind the Opera. So is the History Museum. The style of the two buildings contrast with their surroundings. The Museum of History, especially, is built in a neo-Vietnamese style. St. Joseph's Cathedral is between the French and Vietnamese quarters. It was built in the mid-1880s at the site formerly occupied by Bao Thien Pagoda by Monsignor Puginier. There are two large towers on the cathedral, which was built in the neo-gothic style. According to the local Catholic population, this is the highest seat

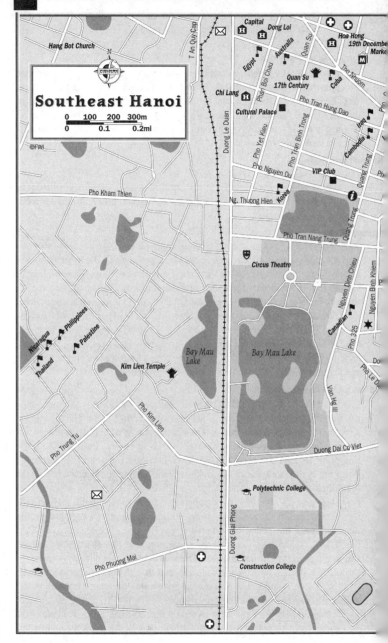

Southeast Hanoi

0   100   200   300m
0   0.1   0.2mi

©FWI

Hang Bot Church

Capital
Dong Loi
Hoa Hong
19th December Market

Egypt
Australia
Quan Su
Quan Su 17th Century
Cuba

Chi Lang

Cultural Palace

Pho Tran Hung Dao

Pho Kham Thien

Pho Yet Kieu
Pho Nguyen Du
VIP Club
Pho Tran Binh Trong

Phan Boi Chau
Iraq
Cambodia
Quang Trung

Ng. Thuong Hien
Korea

Pho Tran Nang Trung

Circus Theatre

Nguyen Dinh Chieu
Nguyen Binh Khiem
Pho 325

Nicaragua
Philippines
Palestine
Thailand
Kim Lien Temple

Bay Mau Lake
Bay Mau Lake

Canadian

Van Hg III

Pho Kim Lien

Pho Trung Tu

Duong Dai Co Viet

Polytechnic College

Duong Giai Phong

Pho Phuong Mai

Construction College

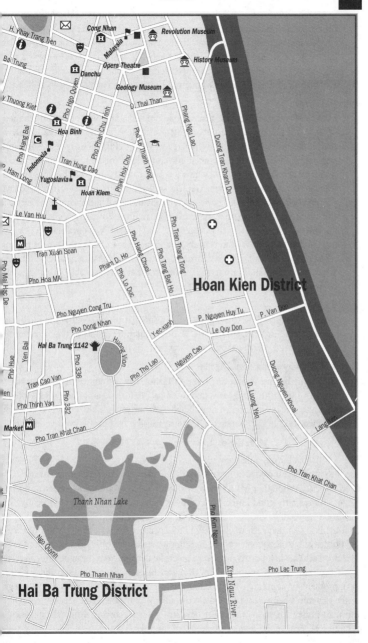

H. Khay Trang Tien

Cong Nhan

Revolution Museum

Malaysia

Bai Trung

Opera Theatre

Danchu

History Museum

Geology Museum

D. Thai Than

y Thuong Kiet

Phang Ngu Lao

Duong Tran Khanh Du

Hoa Binh

Pho Ngo Quyen

Pho Phan Chu Trinh

Pho Le Thanh Tong

Pho Hang Bai

Indonesia

Tran Hung Dao

Phan Huy Chu

o. Ham Long

Yugoslavia

Hoan Kiem

Le Van Huu

Tran Xuan Soan

Pho Mai Hac De

Pho Hoa MA

Pho Hang Chuoi

Pho Tang Bat Ho

Phanh D. Ho

Pho Lo Duc

Pho Tran Thang Tong

Hoan Kien District

Pho Nguyen Cong Tru

Pho Dong Nhan

Y-ec-xanh

P. Nguyen Huy Tu

P. Van Tien

Le Quy Don

Hai Ba Trung 1142

Huong Vien

Pho Tho Lao

Nguyen Cao

D. Luong Yen

Duong Nguyen Khoai

Pho Hue

Yen Bai

Pho 336

Tran Cao Van

Pho 332

Pho Thinh Van

Lang Yen

Market

Pho Tran Khat Chan

Kim Ngau River

Thanh Nhan Lake

Pho Kim Ngau

Ngo Quynh

Pho Lac Trung

Pho Thanh Nhan

Pho Tran Khat Chan

Hai Ba Trung District

of Vietnam's Catholics. When the communists took control of the city, the size of the congregation dwindled, but has now again grown with the relaxing of religious restrictions. Vietnam is second only to the Philippines in Asia in its number of Catholics. The Ambassador Pagoda is at *73 Quan Su Street*. This was formerly a reception house for visiting Buddhist ambassadors. The main temple is in front, while the rear is dedicated to the monk who cured Emperor Ly Thanh Tong of a disease.

Botanical Garden

In the 15th century, King Le Thanh Tong ordered a ring built on an earthen mount so he could better view martial arts demonstrations. After Le died, a temple was built in his honor. For centuries the area was a peaceful sanctuary from the densely populated city. In 1890, the French moved the local residents away and created the Botanical and Zoological Park, which was later named simply the Botanical Garden. The native bamboo and banana trees, as well as the rattan trees were replaced with perennial plants and trees. They created ponds and small hills and, after a short time, the garden became luxuriantly green. Today, many of the trees and plants are imported from Africa, as well as vegetables and flowers from temperate zones. During the first part of the 20th century, the French began bringing in cages for lions, tigers and bears—as well as for leopards, goats, deer, elephants, peacocks and pheasants. Now it's a popular attraction for both tourists and locals alike. It's a great place to spend a hot summer afternoon.

Quan Su Pagoda

Built in the late 1930s this pagoda is on a site that once served as the quarters for visiting Buddhist VIPs. Some of the Buddha sculptures inside the temple are exquisite. This place is usually packed with wayfarers.

Temple of Literature (Van Mieu Pagoda)   ★★★

This is the biggest temple attraction in Hanoi. It was founded in 1070 during the reign of Ly Thanh Tong. It is dedicated to Confucious and purportedly modeled after a temple in Shantung, China. There are courtyards, a big bronze bell, and multistoried roofs in the complex. The courtyards feature beautifully carved stelae.

Where to Stay in Hanoi

It wasn't that long ago that one could stroll down the tree-shaded streets of Hanoi and run into nothing more than a few cyclo drivers clamoring for a fare in this sleepy, slow-paced capital. Although it has a long way to go to catch up with the hustle and bustle of Saigon, some pretty good hotels have been springing out of the concrete recently. Sidewalk cafes, nightclubs and restaurants seem to be opening like barbers at a heavy metal concert. It is said that each week a new hotel opens its doors in Hanoi, most to cater to the hordes of businesspeople converging on the capital in recent years. Even so, the current hotel scheme is still hard-pressed to meet the demand, and it can be difficult to find a hotel room in Hanoi at any time of the year. Building more hotels in the capital has been problematic at best due to the government's increasing involvement in the integrity of the structures being razed to make room for the new hotels (see section on architecture). At present, it seems that most new structures are arising from existing ones, although I've seen a good many exceptions to this "rule."

Construction of the US$30 million Ever Fortune Plaza in Hanoi opposite the United Nations compound and the Australian and Egyptian embassies started during the third quarter of 1994 and were to be completed by press time. The hotel and office plaza will feature a five-story base structure and a 16-floor, 242-room hotel tower. The base area will include offices, restaurants, a bar, meeting rooms and a ballroom. Roof-top swimming facilities will be available as well as a health and beauty center. The new structure will tower high over the opposite seven-story Saigon Hotel on the opposite corner.

Also, an American company (New York-based DeMatteis Development Corp.) will build a 14-story tower on the southern bank of Hanoi's West Lake, an area that will cover 4000 square meters. The building will include office and retail space as well as a restaurant, health club, conference facilities and a movie theatre. DeMatteis hopes to build a number of movie theatres throughout Vietnam. The following establishments are already in operation.

AUTHOR'S NOTE: TELEPHONE PREFIXES

The following telephone numbers are local exchanges. The country code is 84. The city code is 4.

Army Guest House, Army Hotel   US$50–$120   ★★

33C Pham Ngu Lao. ☎ *8252896. FAX: 8259276.*
These two hostelries are run by the defense ministry and are surprisingly clean and well-run considering the ominous sounding monikers. *Just 2 blocks from the municipal theater, and just down the street from the museum of history on Pham Ngu Lao Street,* these two establishments offer 84 rooms with modern facilities, including satellite TV and IDD at moderate prices. Both are popular with expats.

Asean International Hotel   US$145–$375   ★★★★

41 Chua Boc Street. ☎ *8528262. FAX: 8529111.*
International-standard hotel geared for business travelers. Elegant and friendly. All rooms with air conditioning, IDD telephones, safe, minibar, satellite TV and in-house movies. Restaurant with Indian, Malaysian and Western cuisine. Lobby bar, coffeehouse. Full business facilities and health center.

The Dong Loi   US$45–$70

Ly Thuong Kiet Street and Le Duan Street, close to the Hanoi Railway Station. 94 Ly Thuong Kiet Street. ☎ *8255721. FAX: 8267999.*
This hotel is operated by the Hanoi Tourist Services Company (Torseco). It offers old world charm at moderate prices. Built in the 1930s, this 30-room stucco structure features a spiral staircase and wrought iron banisters as well as molded ceilings and art nouveau light fixtures.

Hoa Binh Hotel   US$96–$184   ★★★

Ngo Quyen Street and the corner of Ly Thuong Kiet. 27 Ly Thuong Kiet. ☎ *8253315. FAX: 8269818.*
This place has been around since 1923 and it has an excellent location that ensures a steady stream of both tourists and businesspeople alike. The top-floor bar offers an

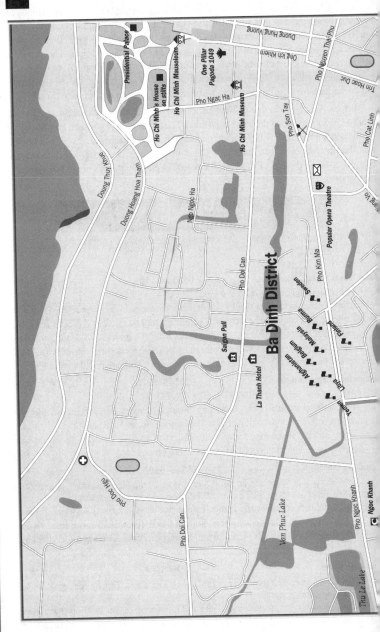

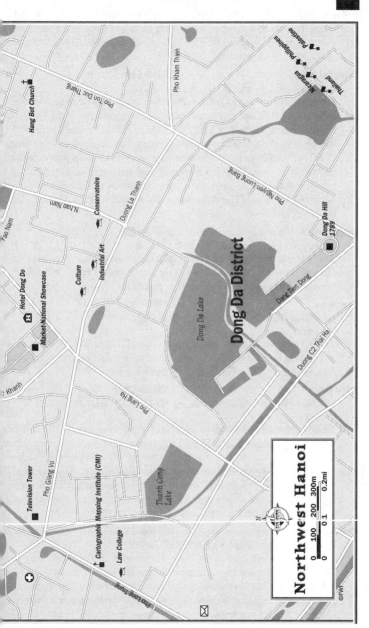

Northwest Hanoi

0 100 200 300m
0   0.1   0.2mi

Hang Bot Church

Pho Ton Duc Thang

Pho Kham Thien

Nicaragua
Philippines
Palestine
Thailand

Pho Nguyen Luong Bang

Conservatoire

Duong La Thanh

N.bao Nam

Tao Nam

Industrial Art

Culture

Hotel Dong Do

Market National Showcase

C Khanh

Dong Da Lake

Dong Da District

Dong Da Hill
1789

Dang Tien Dong

Duong C2 Thai Ha

Pho Lang Ha

Thanh Cong Lake

Television Tower

Pho Giang Vo

Cartographic Mapping Institute (CMI)

Law College

Pho Lang Trung

excellent view of the city and the tree-lined boulevards below of central Hano
Hanoi Tourism runs the place and is in the process of renovating a number of t
rooms; at the last count, there were 112—42 are still open during the renovati
into a three-star caravansary.

Thang Loi Hotel   **US$76–$140**   ★★

Yen Phu, West Lake. ☎ *8268211/5. FAX: 8252800.*

Hanoi Tourism runs seven hotels in the Hanoi area in addition to the Metropole.
is the biggest hotel operator in the region. Many consider the Thang Loi to be t
flagship hotel; it was built as a gift from Cuba in 1975. There are a number of n
lakeside bungalows built from bamboo bringing the existing amount of rooms
175. They're all on beautifully landscaped grounds on a small peninsula jutting o
into the West Lake. There is a swimming pool and a tennis court. Although t
hotel is several kilometers from the city center, you won't mind unless your busin
brings you into central Hanoi frequently. Tourists will relish the rest and relaxati
the Thang Loi affords.

Tay Ho Palace   **US$64–$120**   ★

Quang An, Tu Liem. ☎ *8232381. FAX: 8232390.*

This hotel also borders the lake, and it takes quite a drive to get there. It's a mode
building flanked by lotus paddies, but the service leaves a bit to be desired for
international-standard hotel. I'd avoid it. Expensive.

Boss Hotel   **US$60–$80**

60 Nguyen Du Street. ☎ *8252690. FAX: 8257634.*
15 rooms.

This is a lot closer to the center of Hanoi and faces Thien Quang Lake. It's a sm
and modern hotel, and its VIP lounge is one of the more popular discos in tow
Air conditioning, TV, telephone, refrigerators, hot water.

Hanoi Hotel   **US$169–$390**   ★★★

D8 Giang Vo Street, Ba Binh District. ☎ *8252240/270. FAX: 8259209.*
76 rooms.

Hong Kong built and owned, it is managed by the foreign partner Ever Univer
Company, and is distinctively Hong Kong in taste and styling, and perhaps even
snotty attitude according to a number of visitors. It's a bit cramped, but the 1
year-old structure was recently renovated at a cost of about US$6 million. T
structure is 11 stories high and features a huge Chinese restaurant, a business cent
nightclub and karaoke. Soon there will be a tennis court overlooking the Giang
Lake. Its luxury suites are in the neighborhood of US$300 per night.

Heritage Hotel   **US$105–$120**   ★★

80 Giang Vo. ☎ *8351414. FAX: 8351458, 8343882.*

This is on the same street as the Hanoi Hotel and is under Singaporean manag
ment. This is a favorite among foreign businesspeople, and I'm told this is Hano
only completely new hotel, although I find this hard to believe. The 41-room stru
ture is run by Singapore's Orient Vacation and a Vietnamese local partner C
Company No. 3. There is a nightclub with karaoke booths, and a restaurant offeri
a full range of Southeast Asian cuisine.

Trang An Hotel   US$40   ★

58 Hang Gai Street. ☎ 8268982, 8261135. FAX: 8258511.
Comfortable and cozy, one of Hanoi's skinny high-rises (six stories) with charm and
a guest house feel. Service extremely friendly. Here, you truly feel like a guest. Close
to the lake in the city center. Artwork and antiques cover the lobby. Completely
renovated. Rooms large and cool with modern air conditioning. Hot water, bath
tub, satellite TV, minibar and refrigerator. Great little rooftop restaurant where
breakfast is free. Bar. Car rentals, travel reservations and ticketing, tourist guides.
No elevator, so the rooms on the top floors require a huff and a puff to get to. But
worth it. Recommended.

The Dong Do   About US$50–$75   ★ ★

Giang Vo Street. Close to Giang Vo Lake. ☎ 8343021. FAX: 8334228.
On the top floor is the Sunset Bar, which is run by a Finn and his Vietnamese wife.
It's popular with Expats. They claim to have the longest bar in Hanoi. When you've
imbibed too much, proprietors can usually get away with such claims. The drink list
here includes more than 100 concoctions. Try half of them and you'll be convinced
the Finn's claim to the longest bar in Hanoi is absolutely correct, especially when
you're trying to find the toilet. Rooms with air conditioning, telephone, minibar.

Binh Minh Hotel   US$50

27 Ly Thai To Street. ☎ 8266441. FAX: 8257725.
43 rooms.
Air conditioning, telephones, hot water. Good location.

Bong Sen Hotel   US$50

34 Hang Bun Street. ☎ 8254017.
26 rooms.
Open since 1991 with air-conditioned rooms, TV, refrigerator, attached bathrooms.

Dan Chu Hotel   US$65–$130   ★ ★ ★

29 Trang Tien Street. ☎ 8253323. FAX: 8266786.
A 100-year-old building and it shows. Friendly service. Air conditioning, telephone,
TV, dining room, lounge bar. Excellent location.

Friendship Hotel   US$45–$60

23 Quan Thanh Street. ☎ 8253182.
Singles and doubles. Bar, gift shop.

Hong Ha Hotel   US$40

78 Yen Phu Street. ☎ 8253688.
30 rooms.
North of the railway bridge. Air conditioning, telephones, TV, hot water, refrigerators. Not a bad deal.

Ho Tay Villa   US$35–$80   ★

Quang An, Tu Liem. ☎ 8252393. FAX: 8232126.
On the banks of West Lake. Comfortable and clean. Rooms with air conditioning,
TV, minibar & refrigerator.

Hoa Linh Hotel   US$50

35 Hang Bo Street. ☎ *8250034. FAX: 8243886.*

Air travel booking, car rentals and city tours. Rooms with air conditioning, TV, refrigerator. Good deal.

Kim Lien Hotel   US$50–$75   ★ ?

Kim Lien A, Dong Da District. ☎ *8524930. FAX: 8524919.*

Rooms with air conditioning, satellite color TV, minibar, refrigerator. Conference facilities. Great restaurant if you don't feel like going out.

Lake Side Hotel   US$160–$380   ★★ ?

6A Ngoc Khanh Rd., Ba Dinh District. ☎ *8350111. FAX: 8350121.*
78 rooms.

Set on Giang Vo Lake, this is an impressive—albeit steeply priced—new hotel with all the amenities targeted at the business traveler. All rooms with air conditioning, minibar, IDD phone, color satellite TV. Full business facilities including a conference center. Bar and restaurant.

Melody Hotel   US$40–$60   ★

17 Hang Duong. ☎ *8263029. FAX: 8243746.*

Charming place in a decent location. Rooms with air conditioning, hot water, mini bar and refrigerator.

Hotel Sofitel Metropole   US$180–$400   ★★★★ ?

15 Ngo Quyen Street. ☎ *8266919. FAX: 8266920.*
109 rooms (16 suites).
Reservations: ☎ *(800) 221-4542 in the U.S.*

Totally renovated. This is the grande dame of Hanoi's hotels. It was opened in 1910 and was beginning to show signs of aging before US$9 million was pumped into renovations back in 1989. The original hardwood floors remain, as do the original shuttered windows. Expats and tourists alike congregate here to share news, read the news and take all this luxury in. All the rooms have air conditioning, attached bathrooms, IDD telephones, satellite TV, private safe deposit boxes. Bar, restaurant with French and Asian cuisine with chefs from China and France, live music—traditional Vietnamese, classical, American jazz. Airport shuttle. A new renovation and expansion, costing some US$34 million, has added 135 rooms and 6000 square meters of office space. Architects were careful to preserve the integrity of the structure, including retaining the hardwood floors in the bedrooms and the shuttered French windows. Sooner or later, most visitors to the capital end up here, not necessarily to stay, but at least to sample the fine food created by both French and Vietnamese chefs. This is the only five-star experience in Hanoi. The hotel also features live music, including jazz, traditional Vietnamese music, as well as classical and contemporary. The French, Vietnamese and Chinese chefs make their own pastries, patés and ice cream. The hotel's wine selection is the most extensive in Vietnam. Typically, the hotel runs at 95 percent occupancy and you should book at least a month in advance.

Queen Hotel   US$40–$70   ★

189 Giai Phong. ☎ *8641238. FAX: 8641237.*

Comfortable hotel with the usual amenities in this price range. The drawback is that it's a bit far south of the city center. Restaurant.

⸱se Hotel

20 Phan Boi Chau Street. ☎ *8254438. FAX: 8254437.*

Near the railway station. Singles and doubles. Moderate.

⸱aigon Hotel   US$79–$149   ★★★

80 Ly Thuong Kiet. ☎ *8269499. FAX: 8266631.*

Relaxing rooftop terrace. Sauna, massage. Rooms with air conditioning, color satellite TV, refrigerator, minibar. Restaurant.

⸱pring Song Hotel   US$50–$80   ★★

27 Mai Hoc De. ☎ *8229169. FAX: 8229162.*

27 rooms.

Relaxing atmosphere. Rooms with color satellite TV, IDD telephone. Hey, there's even an elevator here. Unheard of in Hanoi! Good Asian and European fare in the restaurant. Music performances.

⸱huy Tien (Narcissus) Hotel   US$45–$180   ★★★

1C Tong Dan. ☎ *8244775/7. FAX: 8244784.*

60 rooms.

This place has been getting good reviews. All the amenities for the price range. Restaurant, bar. Spacious rooms with air conditioning, TV, minibar & refrigerator.

⸱hang Long Hotel   US$50–$100

Giang Vo. ☎ *8252270.*

Drab 10-story structure near Giang Vo, with service to match. Air conditioning, TV, two restaurant, shop, bar.

⸱rang Tien Hotel   US$10–$20

35 Trang Tien Street.

Basic guest house fare, but popular with the backpacker set. Restaurant downstairs. A good place to trade trail stories.

There are also a ton of mini-hotels in Hanoi (the numbers change daily), the type that the government has discouraged due to the decimating of historic architecture. But not ones to turn down hard currency, the government has allowed these establishments to proliferate as if it were rebuilding the city after a war, which in many ways it still is. According to Vietnamtourism, there are more than 80 such guest houses, although I suspect the number has gone up substantially in the last two years. Among the better mini-hotels are the **Bac Nam Hotel**, just a few blocks from the Metropole on Ngo Nguyen Street. There's also the **Phu Gia Hotel** on Hang Trong Street that overlooks Hoan Kiem Lake in the center of the city. The **Trang An Hotel** on Hang Gai Street has been getting good reviews. The narrow, wedding-cake like building is squeezed between shops in the 36 historic streets section of the city.

HANOI

Where to Eat in Hanoi

INSIDER TIP

Where in Hanoi can you order a plate of bangers and mash and a pint of Bass? Amidst the faded pastel architecture of the capital's Old Quarter, try the Emerald (53 Hang Luoc Street, ☎ 8259258). This is one of the newest eateries and drinking establishments in Hanoi, an authentic Irish pub. There's also Guinness and a variety of Scottish malts. The proprietors—Steven, Patrick and David—go by the acronym SPUD and decided to create their home away from home about a year ago. The interior is graced with Gaelic motifs and glasses hang in brass rail holders over a dark wood counter. The pub offers hamburgers, chili con carne, soups, fries, fish pie, shepherd's pie, and a chicken and mushroom-stuffed pie that some folks complain is too stuffed. The big disappointment is the price of the Bass, which runs US$6 a pint. The owners say it's because the stuff has to go through hell and back, and worse—the Malacca Strait—before it reaches Hanoi.

A Restaurant $

Thang Long Hotel.

One of two of perhaps the most creatively named eateries in Tomorrowland. Basi Vietnamese fare. The place seats hundreds. **B Restaurant** is a lot smaller and has menu in English. Hooray.

Quan Gio Moi $$ ★★★

63 Le Duan Street. ☎ *8229839.*

Located in Lenin Park near the lake, this may very well be the best Chinese eater in the capital. A little expensive but worth every mouthful of succulent hot and sou soup and the roasted chilli prawns.

Khazana $$ ★★★

27 Quoc Tu Giam Street. ☎ *8433468.*

The best North Indian joint in town. The excellent food is prepared in tandoo ovens and served in pewter pots. The surroundings are as authentic as they come The buffet shouldn't be missed.

A Little Italian $$

81 Thu Nhuom. ☎ *8258167.*

Excellent Italian fare. Best for pizza and spaghetti.

The Pear Tree $$$

78 Tho Nhuom. ☎ *8257812.*

Australian-run with an Aussie atmosphere. Expats gather here to soak up the suds and munch on shrimp.

Indochine $$$ ★

16 NamNgu. ☎ *8245097.*

Expensive and fashionable. One of the trendiest eateries in Hanoi. Popular with expat hipsters and yuppies and an increasing number of their Vietnamese counterparts.

HANOI

Restaurant 22 $$$

22 Hang Can. ☎ *8267160.*
Superb Vietnamese and French.

Restaurant 75 $

75 Tran Quoc Toan. ☎ *8265619.*
Vietnamese cuisine. Excellent and inexpensive. Popular with the locals.

Bodega Cafe $$

57 Trang Tien Street.
For good pastries.

Madison's $$$ ★★★

16 Bui Thi Xuan Street. ☎ *8228164.*
Asian and continental cuisine, small portions—but the dishes are superb. If it's available, try the pork medallions with the mango chutney. The menu changes seemingly weekly.

Dan Chu Hotel Restaurant $$

29 Tran Tien St. ☎ *8253323.*
Cheery atmosphere, average food. Menus in three languages.

Darling Cafe $

33 Hang Quat Street.
Decent Western travelers' food, cheap. Popular with backpackers

My Wife's Place $$ ★★★

41 Chua Boc Street. ☎ *8529108.*
Huge buffet offering cuisines from Vietnam, India and Malaysia. At about eight bucks, this is one of the tastiest bargains in Hanoi.

Nam Phuong $$ ★★

19 Phan Chu Trinh Street. ☎ *8240926.*
This may be Hanoi's version of Saigon's Vietnam House. Elegant and traditional Vietnamese cuisine in posh surroundings. Makes for one of the best power lunches in the city.

Hoa Binh Hotel Restaurant $

Hoa Binh Hotel.
This is good, cheap food.

Piano Restaurant $$$

50 Hang Vai Street. ☎ *8232423.*
Features some imported wines and beers; good shrimp and crab; live music.

Restaurant 202 $$

202A Pho Hue Street. ☎ *8259487.*
This used to be the best restaurant in Hanoi before all the trendy joints started opening up in the past couple of years. Still highly recommended. Both Vietnamese and Western food, but specializes in the latter.

Rose Restaurant $$

15 Tran Quoe Tian Street. ☎ *8254400.*
This place is usually quite crowded. Both Asian and Western cuisine.

Sophia Restaurant $$

6 Hang Bai Street. ☎ *8255069.*
There's a cafe downstairs and restaurant upstairs. Average.

Mekki-Lan Anh $$$

9A Da Tuong. ☎ *8267552.*
Known for its Algerian cuisine, of all things. Also Vietnamese and French fare.

Club Opera $$$

59 Ly Thai To. ☎ *8268802.*
Vietnamese and Western food at very French prices. Oo-la-la.

Galleon Steakhouse $$$

50 Tran Quoc Toan. ☎ *8228611.*
Steaks and crepes at outrageous prices, but delicious.

Hot Rock Cafe $$

11A1 Giang Vo. ☎ *8245661.*
It's only a matter of time before the Hard Rock people hire lawyers.

Le Loft $$$

17 Trang Tien. ☎ *8250625.*
Vietnamese and French. Expensive.

The Pastry & Yoghurt Shop $$

252 Hang Bong. ☎ *8250216.*
More a cafe rather than a place for a full sit-down meal. The name says it all.

Mother's Pride $$

53 Ba Trieu. ☎ *8228055.*
Superb Malaysian-style cafe. Satay, the works.

Cherry Blossom Inn $$

18 La Thai Tu. ☎ *8266377.*
If you're into Japanese, this is the place. Packed with Japanese tourists.

Sunset Pub $$

On the roof of the Dong Do Hotel. 10 Giang Vo. ☎ *8351382.*
Great burgers; passable pizza.

Le Coq D'Or $$$

130 Le Duan. ☎ *8524713.*
Packed with the French movers and shakers of Hanoi. If you're anyone else, you'
feel out of place.

Le Bistro $$$

35 Tran Hung Dao Street. ☎ *8266136.*
French and Vietnamese. Expensive.

Marriott's Cook House $$$

65 Ngo Hue. ☎ *8226634.*
Excellent Chinese, Vietnamese and European fare.

The Emerald $$

53 Hang Luoc. ☎ *8259285.*
British-style pub and ale house serving Brit pies, stews and fish & chips.

Gala International $$
33 Nghi Tam. ☎ *8234290.*
Local and European dishes. Karaoke.

Balance Bar $$
25C Phan Dinh Phung. ☎ *8230048.*
European cuisine in a relaxing setting.

Little Dream Snack Bar & Gallery $$$
9 Pham Su Manh. ☎ *8243922.*
Dine to classical music as you're surrounded by original oil paintings. Not popular
with backpackers.

L'Elegant $$$
33 Pho Hue ☎ *8261639.*
Vietnamese the French way.

Cafe de Paris $$$
16A Nguyen Cong Tu. ☎ *8212701.*
Parisian to the max. Expensive.

Five Royal Fish $$
16 Le Thai To. ☎ *8244368.*
Great setting. Vietnamese and Western cuisine.

Viet Hoa $$
119 Hue. ☎ *8266918.*
Great Vietnamese.

La Terrazza $$$
49 Nghi Tam Road (West Lake). ☎ *8238049.*
Homemade pasta and other Italian specialties. Excellent.

Poppy $$
1 Ngoc Khanh. ☎ *8349069.*
A hangout for Swiss expats and tourists. Good Swiss cuisine, including sausages,
racelette and fondue.

The Pear Tree $$$
78 Tho Nhuom. ☎ *8257812.*
Western cuisine, Italian coffee and fresh cakes.

Lucky Restaurant $$
49 Quan Thanh. ☎ *8432888.*
Chinese, specializing in Hainanese chicken rice.

The First Restaurant $$
12 Trang Thi. ☎ *8240060.*
Shanghai specialties. Gathering place for Chinese businessmen. Just opened.

The Green Bamboo $ ★
42 Nha Trung Street. ☎ *8268752.*
Opened in January '94. It was hip while it was undiscovered, but now it's a favorite
among backpackers. Now just another brick in the wall—although still worth it.
Music, outdoor dining, cheap prices in the heart of Hanoi.

The Verandah Cafe & Bar $

9 Nguyen Khac Can Street. ☎ *8257220.*

This place suffers somewhat from an identity crisis: is it a British pub, a bar for expat thirsty suits or an Amsterdam coffee shop? Matters aren't resolved particularly by the cuisine, which seems equally lacking of a genre, and a palatable one at that. But the service is friendly, there's an outdoor dining area and the place is stocked with booze from around the globe. Best bets here are the chili and cheese-stuffed potato skins, the smoked salmon and cream cheese, the grilled tuna (although somewhat bland), and the passable chicken enchiladas. But keep in mind that any culinary experience here will be marred by the the barlike ambience—but in the case of the Verandah, the psychological diversion from the food may work to its advantage.

Tandoor $ ★★

24 Hang Be Street. ☎ *8245359.*

This fine Indian restaurant has a tendency to get quite crowded, much like India itself, and expect to wait around awhile before being served—again, much like India itself. But it's worth it for the chicken samosas, chicken tikka and mutton vindaloo. Only regret besides the slow service is that most of the dishes taste like the bland Indian dishes found in the States.

Hanoi Hotel Chinese Restaurant $$ ★★

D8 Giang Vo Street. ☎ *8452270.*

The dim sum is quite tasty here if you can live with the lackadaisical service. Best for lunch. Characterless but comfortable setting.

Nightlife in Hanoi

Hanoi has always been considered a little more tame than its cousin to the south, Ho Chi Minh City, but the scene is changing rapidly. Although it's still a little tougher to find the constellations and hip clubs in the capital, the underground is beginning to surface. If you don't like to get to bed until the wee hours you might want to consider checking out the following:

Bars

Apocalypse Now ★

☎ *8244302.*

This is exactly like its sister bar in Saigon. Manufactured seediness with decent music. At press time, the bar was relocating, just as the one in Saigon did a short time ago. Expect much of the same when Hanoi's version reopens. Backpackers, rockers and young expats trying to find a job or buy T-shirts.

Sunset Pub ★

Dong Do Hotel. ☎ *8351382.*

Live music on Thursdays and Saturdays. Boasts the longest bar in Hanoi. You can drink yourself from here to Haiphong. Serves pizza that's not half bad.

Green Bamboo

42 Nha Chung. ☎ *8268752.*

Backpackers and young locals hang here. It's above the restaurant. Cheap drinks and a quiet atmosphere. On my visit a loud American was trying to tell a young Vietnamese that shuttlecock isn't a real man's game.

Bar Le Club

Hotel Metropole. 15 Ngo Quyen. ☎ *8266919.*
Forget this place unless you've got a wad of cash and a pressed linen suit handy. Best for businesspeople. Nothing more than a very expensive bar in a very expensive hotel. Do not get drunk here. Well-heeled customers nurse their drinks as they might a glass of gasoline.

The Blue Bar

57 Ly Thai To. ☎ *8249247.*
As the name implies, you walk around in this place feeling like you're under a black light—or that at any moment Willy Dixon and Albert Collins will walk in and sit down with a couple of dobros. But, alas, it's more boring here than that. Karaoke, bad music and warm beer. I always drink mine with ice, so it didn't matter. Mainly expat crowd. Large outdoor area with a pool table.

The White Bar

15 Nguyen Dinh Chieu. ☎ *8228380.*
No relation to the Blue Bar. Stays open all night and attracts Hanoi's expat boozers. Reminds me a little of Bangkok's Thermae Cafe, but without the hookers.

Balance Bar

25C Phan Dinh Phung. ☎ *8230048.*
Decent music and predominantly thirsty Vietnamese customers. The bar says it offers at least 1000 types of drinks.

The Polite Pub

5 Bao Khanh. ☎ *8250959.*
This place is very polite indeed. If you've found a local partner, it's a great place to bring her/him—as neither of you will be offended or distracted by anything. Sterile but cozy.

The Gold Cock

★

5 Bao Khanh. ☎ *8259499.*
Right next door to the Polite Pub. This is one of the most happenin' watering holes in town and anything but polite, although for no particular reason. But on the weekends it's packed with tourists, expats and Vietnamese. It gets loud in here. A good place to imbibe until 3 a.m.

The Pear Tree

78 Tho Nhuom. ☎ *8257812.*
Open until midnight. I kinda liked this place, although at three bucks for a beer, it's a little steep. Satellite TV and a couple of pool tables for amusement between swills. Expats and some locals.

The Pub

52 Ly Thuong Kiet. ☎ *8243054.*

Usually full with expats, this is a quiet bar and good place to bring a friend for a relaxing brew and a game of darts. There's not a lot of action here. Two bar areas with a tree between them that rises up above the roof. Closing time at 2 a.m.

The Billabong Bar ★★

Australian Embassy. 62 Ly Thuong Kiet.

This place is classic Aussie and highly popular with well-heeled expats. All the great Australian beers here. But dress well and don't get too loud unless an Aussie drinking buddy gets loud first. At press time, the club was accepting only members and their guests.

The Verandah Cafe & Bar

9 Nguyen Khac Can St. ☎ 8257220

Take note of the restaurant listing above for this venue of the same name. British pub style and popular with Aussie and Brit expats, mostly journo types.

The Wine Bar ★

82 Hoa Ma Street. ☎ 8263664.

Oh, it's hard to lower myself and call this a bar. But, alas, a place where there is little to do but drink and nibble must be called a bar. But this spade is hardly a spade, more like a sitting room for wine sommeliers, set to jazz music and earthy blues tunes. No beer posters and distillery hostesses—just a simple, elegant environment where fine wine can be enjoyed. The Couly Dutheil Saumur runs US$8 a glass. Also found in the cellar are Chiantis, Chilean sauvignon blancs, Australian chablis and California Beaujolais. And if it's all a little out of your budget, relax with a US$2 glass of the house wine. You'll be tempted to try them all. Just swallow.

Nightclubs/Discos

The Lakeside

West Lake.

Some of the best music and dancing in Hanoi. But be prepared to sweat. There's no air conditioning here and the place gets packed with Hanoi groovsters.

Music City

Near the Bach Mai Hospital.

Large upstairs club at around 2000 square meters. There's a dance floor here but not a lot of people use it. The lighting is a little brash and that may be the reason why. Great sound system, but you'd better be into the squealing of recorded Vietnamese pop.

The Top(Disco) Club

Thuyen Quang Lake. ☎ 8226641.

Nobody ever seems to be in this dark, moody venue, although the music is good and the sound system makes for decent grooving.

My Lan Hotel

Barry Manilow does Guns 'n' Roses here. Small. Pass it by.

Queen Bee ★

42 Lang Ha. ☎ 8352612.

One of the coolest spots in town, or at least it's well on the way. Huge dance floor and Hanoi's version of a grunge-punk crowd. There's live music here, which is its best appeal. Some of the music rocks, by even Western standards. But the heavy stuff comes in spurts, separated by corny pop foot-tappers. The place is usually packed with well-dressed Hanoi hipster youths with earrings, but is attracting a growing number of Westerners. Great dance floor that is always jammed. Get ready to sweat your ass off if you decide to actually dance to this stuff. Tough to get local ladies to dance with you if you're a foreigner.

Chessboard Hotel

This place rocks when there's a decent band on the bill. There used to be a US$15 cover charge here, but it was dropped after customers began dropping off. Although the music can get loud here, not a lot of dancing goes on. Low-key atmosphere. A place where I don't feel out of place not wearing white. It was the first place in Hanoi I felt at home in "naked chick on an Indian motorcycle" T-shirt.

Royal Palace Nightclub

20 Hang Tre. ☎ *8244233.*
Live music, but usually performed by Filipino bands that come across more like another example of Barry Manilow doing Guns 'n' Roses.

The VIP Club ★

62 Nguyen Du. ☎ *8269167.*
Tiny venue. Hot and sweaty. This place was formerly the only joint in town where foreigners could let their hair down.

Shopping in Hanoi

Lacquerware & Souvenirs

The Souvenir Shop

30A Ly Thuong Kiet.
Top-quality handicrafts, including a wide range of lacquerware, stone carvings, woodwork, textiles & fabrics, paintings and ceramics. Definitely worth checking out.

A number of other lacquerware and souvenir shops can be found at **3**, **13**, **17**, **19** and **21**, **Hang Khay**. These shops offer traditional Vietnamese handicrafts as well as watches and clocks from Germany, Russia and France.

Clothing & Fashion

It is pretty difficult to find top-quality Western-made clothing, although it is available. But you didn't come to Vietnam for Levis. Vietnamese silk is among the best in the world. The best places for silk in Hanoi are along Hang Gai Street (Thread Street).

Khai Silk

96 Hang Gai. ☎ *8254237. FAX: 8245150.*
Exquisite raw and refined silk, either in material or apparel form. Tailors on site to create either Vietnamese or Western styles. Recommended.

Kenly Silk

102 Hang Gai. ☎ *8267236. FAX: 8252496.*
Great place for embroidery, lace and silk.

Van Can Street is a good area for purchasing traditional Vietnamese **ao dai** dresses. Fo
Western styles, try the following:

The Leather Boutique

53A Hang Bai.
Western clothes, leather goods and shoes.

Verve Boutique

18 Hang Bai.
This is also a good place for Western fashions, although some of the styles are date

Gourmet Foods

It seems that every potato chip and soda stall in the city are now carrying expensive im
ported foods, wines and liquors. You won't have any problem finding them. Two of th
better centers you might want to check out:

The Food Shop

3 Hom Market, Pho Hue. ☎ *8227557.*
Imported canned and dry foods, as well as French cheeses and expensive importe
wines.

Hanoi Minimart

72 Tran Xuan Soan (2nd floor of Hom Market). ☎ *8229714/5.*
This is one of Hanoi's rare American-style supermarkets, offering a wide variety c
the stuff you're used to getting back at Ralph's, Albertson's or Piggly Wiggly
Expensive, and the place gets jammed aisle-to-aisle with expats and the newly afflu
ent locals.

Lingerie and Cosmetics

Cho Hom (Hon Market)

Pho Hue.
This area contains a number of kiosks offering an array of Western-made and othe
international products. But you'll pay the price.

Musical Instruments

Hanoi Music Center

42 Nha Chung.
Here is offered a large variety of pianos, violins, guitars and other instruments, a
well as modern sound equipment. Really the only place in town if you're looking t
replace that guitar that got smashed up on the flight from HCMC.

Another store at *11 Hang Non* offers a dazzling selection of classical Vietnamese in
struments.

Sports in Hanoi

Health Clubs/Gyms

Catching on to the Western fad of body-beautiful, numerous health clubs and gym
have opened up in Hanoi in recent years and months. There may be as many as 40 gyms/
health centers in the capital, the crux of them frequented by locals only. However, a
growing number cater to expats and tourists, at incredibly low prices. The ladies' centers
offer the most hi-tech equipment, while the men typically go for the traditional free

eights. Most of the men's gyms are stocked with relatively primitive equipment. Keep in
mind that most of these places aren't Gold's Gym. Vietnamese men traditionally work
out barefooted or in sandals—many exercise in their street clothes (some in suit trousers
and wingtips!). In clubs catering to foreigners and locals alike of both sexes, it would be
prudent for Western women to forego thong leotards in favor of baggier gym wear.
However, the Barbie cutie-pie workout fashions made popular by Jane Fonda in the
early '80s are just starting to catch on here, namely leggings, spandex, lipstick and nail
polish in the hue of the spandex, and big hair.) As well, most of the clubs do not offer
medical advice nor guidance on diet to help the body building process. Keeping in shape
in Hanoi is at your own risk, except at the best hotels, which are staffed by qualified trainers.

Army Club

19 Hoang Dieu. ☎ *8233751.*
US$8.40 per month.
Women only. There's a cold shower here. The club accepts locals and foreigners
alike.

Eva Club

3rd floor, Hom Market. ☎ *8226374.*
US$9 per month.
Women only. Multi-gym with saunas and a steam bath. Locals and foreigners are
both welcomed.

Hoan Kiem Fitness Club ★

41 Nha Chung. ☎ *8285530. US$7 for men per month.*
US$12 for women. US$30 for foreigners.
A clip joint. The excuse for the heavy foreigners' tag is that the club is responsible
in the event of an accident. A case of the pre-ASEAN Vietnam blues. Upscale;
there's a swimming pool and even a disco here to flaunt those new flanks. Hot and
cold shower.

Khuc Hao Club

18 Le Hong Phong.
US$4 a month for locals. US$8.20 for foreigners.
Men and women welcome, foreigners and locals alike. Another clip joint. But
you're probably used to price discrimination by now.

October 10th Club

115 Quan Thanh. ☎ *8259559.*
US$4 for men per month. US$5 for women.
Pretty basic. Don't expect any LCDs on your T-cell count here.

Que Lam Fitness Club

Dong Da district cultural house. ☎ *8525278.*
US$3 per month for men. US$5 for women.
This is a bargain for a multi-gym.

Directory

Transportation

Hanoi is 1710 km from Saigon, 765 km from Danang, 660 km from Hue, 420 km from Dien Bien Phu, 165 km from Ha Long Bay, 153 km from Thanh Hoa, 103 km from Haiphong, and 116 km from Ninh Binh.

By air:

Hanoi's Noi Bai Airport is about 50 km from the center of Hanoi and is about an hour's drive by microbus (the new bridge has cut this down to 40 minutes or less), the cheapest and fastest way of reaching the city center, although there are local buses that pick up passengers at the airport's domestic terminal. Expect to pay about US$.60 for the bus ride and at least US$4 for a microbus ride that brings passengers to their destinations in Hanoi and then ends up at the Vietnam Airlines offices at *60 Nguyen Du Street* or *1 Quang Trung Street*. Be duly warned that coming into Hanoi by air is an absolute pain in the ass. The airport itself resembles a warehouse, and the wait for your baggage can take some time indeed. Incoming planes park well away from the terminal, and there is only one baggage conveyor belt in the domestic terminal, sometimes handling luggage from three or four aircraft. Microbuses also depart for the airport many times during the day, but contact the VN office for the exact schedules, as they change and are infrequently adhered to. Microbuses tend to leave when full no matter what time they are scheduled to depart. International passengers can arrange to depart for the airport at the VN office located at *1 Quang Trung Street*. Again, buses leave when they are full. But remember to buy a ticket for the microbus a day in advance. By taxi, the hour trip will set you back at least US$10 and I've talked with people who have paid as much as US$20–$35 for the ride. You can arrange for a taxi to meet you at your hotel or you can hire one at the VN office for the airport. If you're negotiating with a taxi driver, it's better to do it in dong, and be sure the rate agreed upon is for either the car itself or your own personal fare if you're being joined by other passengers. **Touts:** After flying into Noi Bai Airport, you will be greeted by throngs of taxi touts asking US$25 for the one-way trip downtown. These fares can usually be bargained down to US$10–$15.

From five to nine lights leave from HCMC to Hanoi daily between 7 a.m. and 7:50 p.m. Flights from Hanoi to HCMC depart from five to eight times a day, beginning at 7 a.m. and ending at 8 p.m.

Note: Much less English is spoken in the north, and this is particularly frustrating at the airport, where few, if any transportation directors have the ability to say many more than just a few words. They certainly know the meaning of $ signs, however. Conditions are a little more modern at the international terminal, but certainly not up to international standards.

train:

Trains leave daily for Saigon from Hanoi's Ga Hanoi train station, about a 15-minute cyclo ride from the city center. Expect a 50-hour train ride to Saigon from Hanoi.

bus:

Hanoi has four "bus stations." One station *5 Le Thong Street* has two buses a day that depart for Ha Long Bay. The trip takes about five hours. They leave early in the morning, around 7–9 a.m. The Kim Ma station on Nguyen Thai Hoc street services the northwest of Vietnam, including Son Tay, Hat Lot, Phu To, Trung Ha, Moc Chau, Bat Bat, Da Chong, Son La, Yen Bai and Hoa Binh. Kim Lien station is on the southwest edge of Thien Quang Lake and serves destinations in the south, including Vinh, Hue, Danang, Quy Nhon, Ninh Binh, Nam Dinh, Cam Ranh, Nha Trang and Saigon, to mention a few. Again, buses leave early in the morning. The fountain at the northern tip of Hoan Kiem Lake has microbuses that leave regularly for Haiphong.

Transportation around town is usually done by conventional **cyclo**. But their charges to foreigners are usually outrageous. Agree upon a price and put it in writing is the suggestion of many travelers, as the scam in Saigon whereby cyclo drivers claim to be cheated at the end of the ride is an even worse problem in Hanoi. Hiring a bicycle (for about US$1 per day) is the best way of seeing the sights of Hanoi. They can be rented from a number of hotels and bike rental shops across Hanoi.

LAND DISTANCES FROM HANOI

Ba Be Lakes	*240 km*
Bac Giang	*52 km*
Bac Ninh	*30 km*
Bach Thong	*160 km*
Cam Pha	*190 km*
Cao Bang	*272 km*
Da Bac	*105 km*
Danang	*765 km*
Dien Bien Phu	*420 km*
Ha Dong	*10 km*
Ha Giang	*345 km*

LAND DISTANCES FROM HANOI

Hai Duong	56 km
Haiphong	95 km
Hong Gai/Bai Chay	165 km
Ho Chi Minh City	1720 km
Hue	660 km
Lai Chau	490 km
Lang Son	150 km
Nam Dinh	90 km
Ninh Binh	116 km
Phat Diem	120 km
Son La	308 km
Tam Dao	85 km
Thai Binh	110 km
Thai Nguyen	80 km
Thanh Hoa	150 km
Tuyen Quang	165 km
Viet Tri	290 km
Yen Bai	180 km

General Post Office

85 Dinh Tien Hoang Street. The International Post Office is next door at *87 Dinh Tien Hoang Street.*

International Telephone, Fax Services

The necessary international communications services can be found at the International Post Office or at *66-68 Trang Tien Street* and *66 Luong Van Can Street.* All of Hanoi's upscale hotels also offer fax and IDD services. Expect to pay US$7–8 for the first page when faxing to the States and slightly less than that for additional pages. IDD phone calls can be done at a rate of about US$5 for the first minute and slightly less than that for subsequent minutes.

TNT International Express Office

3 Hang Khay Street. ☎ *8257615; FAX: 8255829.*

Immigration Police Station

89 Tran Hung Dao Street.

Hospitals & Emergencies

Bach Mai Hospital
  Giai Phong Road. ☎ *8253731, 8522004.*

K Hospital
  43 Quan Su Street. ☎ *8252143.*

Asia Emergency Assistance
  4 Tran Hung Dao Street, 4th floor. ☎ *8213555*

Dr. Kot Rafi
  Van Phuc A2, Room 101/102. ☎ *8430748. Mobile: 019-041919.*

French Embassy
  57 Tran Hung Dao. ☎ *8252719*

Swedish Clinic
  Van Phuc area. ☎ *8252464.*

Tourist Offices

Vietnamtourism
  54 Nguyen Du Street. ☎ *8255963; FAX: 8252707.*
  30A Ly Thuong Kiet. ☎ *8264154, 8257532.*

Hanoi Tourism Service Co. (TOSERCO)
  1 Trang Tien Street. ☎ *8250876; FAX: 8259209.*
  25 Tran Dung Dao Street. ☎ *8254347*
  94 Ly Thuong Kiet. ☎ *8255721, 8267957.*

Oscan Enterprises
  60 Nguyen Du Street. ☎ *852690; FAX: 857634.*

Vung Tau International Tourist Services
  136 Hang Trong Street. ☎ *8252739.*

Banks and Moneychangers

Bank of Foreign Trade. *49-49 Ly Thai To Street*. This bank, like others in Vietnam, will not change dong back into dollars. On the black market you can change dong back into U.S. dollars. Locations are usually found on Trang Tien Street.

Airline Offices

Vietnam Airlines
  International address: 1 Quang Trung Street. ☎ *8253842, 8250888, 8254440.*
  Domestic address: 60 Nguyen Du Street. ☎ *8255194.*

Singapore Airlines
  15 Ngo Quyen Street at the Hotel Sofitel Metropole.

Air France
  1 Ba Trieu Street. ☎ *8253484; FAX: 8266694.*

Thai Airways
  1c Quang Trung Street. ☎ *8266893; FAX: 8267394.*

  Note: These are also the offices for **Cathay Pacific** and **Malaysian Airlines**.

Useful Taxi Numbers

Hanoi Taxi
  ☎ *8265252, 8535252.*

Metered. US$25-35 one-way to the airport. Local: US$2 for the first 2 km and US$0.67 per km after that.

Thang Long Taxi
☎ *8265241.*

Fujicab
☎ *8255452.*

Unmetered. US$35 one-way to the airport.

Taxi PT
☎ *8533171.*

Metered. US$20-25 one-way to the airport. Local: US$1.5 for the first 2 km and US$0.40 per km after that.

Red Taxi
☎ *8353686.*

A new fleet of metered taxis. Prices comparable with Hanoi taxi.

Embassies in Hanoi

Afganistan
D1 Van Phuc Quarter.
☎ *8253249.*

Australia
66 Ly Thuong Kiet Street.
☎ *8252763.*

Bulgaria
358 Street, Van Phuc Quarter.
☎ *8257923.*

Canada
39 Nguyen Dinh Chieu Street.
☎ *8265840.*

Cuba
65 Ly Thuong Kiet Street.
☎ *8254775.*

Egypt
85 Ly Thuong Kiet Street.
☎ *8252944.*

France
57 Tran Hung Dao Street.
☎ *8252719.*

Hungary
47 Dien Bien Phu Street.
☎ *8252748, 8253353.*

Algeria
15 Phan Chu Trinh Street.
☎ *8253865.*

Belgium
D1 Vann Phuc Quarter, Rooms-105 108.
☎ *8252263.*

Cambodia
71A Tran Hung Dao Street.
☎ *8253789.*

China
46 Hoang Dieu Street.
☎ *8253737.*

Czech and Slovakia
6 Le Hong Phong Street.
☎ *8254335.*

Finland
b3b Giang Vo Street, 2nd Floor.
☎ *8256754.*

Germany
29 Tran Phu Street.
☎ *8252836.*

India
58-60 Tran Hung Dao Street.
☎ *8253406, 8255975.*

Indonesia
> *50 Ngo Quyen Street.*
> ☎ *8253353, 8257969.*

Iraq
> *66 Tran Hung Dao Street.*
> ☎ *8254141.*

Japan
> *E3\Trung Tu Quarter.*
> ☎ *8257902, 8257924.*

Korea (Republic of)
> *60 Nguyen Du Street.*
> ☎ *8269161.*

Libya
> *A3 Van Phuc Quarter.*
> ☎ *8253371.*

Mongolia
> *39 Tran Phu Street.*
> ☎ *8253009.*

Palestine
> *E4b Trung Tu Quarter.*
> ☎ *8254013.*

Poland
> *3 Chua Mot Cot Street.*
> ☎ *8252027.*

The Russia Federation
> *58 Tran Phu Street.*
> ☎ *8254631/2.*

Sweden
> *2-358 Street, Van Phuc Center.*
> ☎ *8254824.*

Thailand
> *63-65 Hoang Dieu Street.*
> ☎ *8253092.*

United States
> *8 Doc Ngu Street.*
> ☎ *8236050*

Iran
> *54 Tran Phu Street.*
> ☎ *8232068.*

Italy
> *9 Le Phing Hieu Street.*
> ☎ *8256246.*

Democratic Peoples' Republic of Korea
> *25 Cao Ba Quat Street.*
> ☎ *8253008.*

Laos
> *40 Quang Trung Street.*
> ☎ *8252588.*
> *22 Tran Binh Trong Street.*
> ☎ *8254576.*

Malaysia
> *A3 Van Phuc Quarter.*
> ☎ *8253371.*

Myanmar
> *A3 Van Phuc Quarter.*
> ☎ *8253369.*

Philippines
> *E1 Trung Tu Center, Rm. 305-308.*
> ☎ *8257948.*

Romania
> *5 Le Hong P`hong Street.*
> ☎ *8252014.*

Singapore
> *B Van Phuc Quarter, Rms. 301-302.*
> ☎ *8233966.*

Switzerland
> *77b Kim Ma Street.*
> ☎ *8232019.*

United Kingdom
> *16 Ly Thuong Kiet Street.*
> ☎ *8252510.*

Yugoslavia
> *47 Tran Phu Street.*
> ☎ *8252343.*

Books, Magazines & Newspapers

The Foreign Language Book Shop
> *61 Trang Tien Street.* ☎ *8257043.*

This place has had a growing number of English language book titles since the demise of the Soviet Union, but is still geared toward culturally correct material, such as politically themed (guess whose politics) art books. Also a good source for maps.

Thong Nhat Bookstore

Hotel Sofitel Metropole, 15 Ngo Quyen Street. ☎ *8266919.*

This provides perhaps the best source of contemporary English-language periodicals and books, although the selection is still pretty poor compared with top-end hotels throughout most of the world, and even to what's available in Ho Chi Minh City.

Xunhasaba (State Enterprise for the Import & Export of Books & Periodicals)

32 Hai Ba Trung Street.

Again, this is a pretty staid shop. These folks aren't the Ministry of Culture, but they may as well be. But there are a number of off-the-wall titles and rare finds.

Hanoi Environs Nearby

Tay Phuong Pagoda ★

Three km from the first left turn at the 34th km marker of Highway 11A from Hanoi. Its initial name was Sung Phuc Pagoda and then it became Hoanh Son Thien Lam Tu before acquiring its current name. It's located in the Thach Xa commune in the Thach That district of Ha Tay Province. On the horizontal board at the pagoda's gate are written four hieroglyphs, *Tay Phuong Co To* (meaning the West Ancient Pagoda). It was built on a 50-meter-tall mountain that locals say looks like a hook. They say that viewing it from a distance, the mountain and the surrounding hills remind them of a buffalo herd. Cau Lau is the herd's leader turning his head back for a drink of water from a lotus pond. After climbing 239 laterite paved steps, you reach the pagoda's gate. There is a main temple and a temple behind it that represent three treasures: Buddha, his law and the bonze (the Buddhist Trinity). Each building features two roof layers. The upper layer is formed by tile with fig leaf reliefs. The bottom layer is paved with square tiles, painted in the five colors of a monk's robe. The surrounding wall of the pagoda is constructed of Bat Trang bricks. The wooden supporting pillars are on bases of blue limestone and decorated with lotus petal ornaments. The roof edges are carved in the form of rolled leaves. On top of the roofs are small figurines. The curved corners of the roofs also feature carved flower, dragon and phoenix reliefs. Its architecture is outstanding, true sculptural art. All over the pagoda are carved mulberry and fig tree leaves, lotus, chrysanthemums, dragons and tiger heads. There's a collection of 76 statues at the pagoda, red lacquered, carved out of jact-tree wood and trimmed with gold. The statues bear only Vietnamese inscriptions, and each has its own facial expression. These sculptures are perhaps unparalleled in Vietnam. Perhaps the most famous is the statue of Tuyet Son. Intricate lines are cut deeply into his face. His thin body and solitary appearance are designed to elicit remorse and loneliness. According to ancient inscriptions on the pagoda, it was restored in 1632. A three-sector upper temple and a back temple with a 20-sector corridor were also added. Four years later a giant bell was cast and the statues carved. The pagoda was again rebuilt during the Tay Son period in 1794. Definitely worth the visit.

Thay Pagoda

This pagoda is in Ha Tay Province about 40 km southwest of Hanoi. This is also known as the Master's Pagoda and is dedicated to the historical Thich Ca Buddha (Sakyamuni) as well as to the 18 monks that achieved Nirvana. The monks are on the central altar. There is also a statue of the 12th century monk the pagoda was named after, Tu Dao Hanh. As well, there is a statue of King Ly Nhan Tong, who was reincarnated from Tu Dao Hanh. There's also a stage here where puppet shows are performed during festivals. There are some magnificent caves in the area. The annual festival here is held for three days during the third lunar month.

Den Hai Ba Trung (Temple)

This temple, well south of Hanoi, was dedicated to the heroines of an aborted revolt against the Chinese in AD 40-43. It was built in 1142 and restored in both the 19th and 20th centuries. Once a year, legend has it, the two sisters return to the temple and walk around it. There's a stone relief depicting the battle, probably carved in the late 15th century.

Chua Lien Phai (Pagoda)

Bach Mai Street, 2 km south of Petic Lac. Built during the Ly Dynasty in the early 1730s, it was restored in 1884. There are many interesting stupas here and a nine-story octagonal tower. There weren't many pagodas built of this style for the tombs of the laity. Interestingly enough, the temple was built over the remains of the wife of an actor from Saigon.

Hanoi Environs to the South

Hung Yen (Formerly Pho Hien)

Next to the Red River 60 km southeast of Hanoi, this historic town with its rich multicultural influences makes for an excellent day or half-day trip. During the 17th century, a number of cities in Vietnam prospered through trade with other Asian nations as well as with the Europeans. Hung Yen was such a place, and brings to mind cities such as Hoi An, south of Danang. Because of its superb geographic location, Pho Hien was developed and thriving as early as the 15th century, and was once considered Vietnam's second-largest com-

mercial center. In the late 16th and early 17th centuries it became a maj
foreign trade center. The Japanese had quite an amount of influence on t
area during the early 17th century. Shortly after, ships from the Philippin
Malaysia, Portugal, England, Holland and France came in to call at Pl
Hien. But the Chinese, who had arrived centuries earlier, still played tl
strongest economic role in the region, especially in the handicraft area. Tl
first Europeans to arrive were the Portuguese in the first part of the 16
century. Long-term business relationships lasted between the Portugue
and businessmen from Pho Hien through the rest of the century. British i
fluence began to be felt in the area around the 1670s. However, by the er
of the 17th century, European traders were forced to abandon Pho Hic
through a magistrate's order, and commerce was performed only with tl
Japanese and Chinese. Many of the goods traded were for royalty and i
cluded gold, bronze, weapons and gunpowder, silver, herbal medicine, te
tiles, jewelry and ceramic products. Exported material from the area includ
silk and painted wood handicrafts. Today, there are still many signs of tl
past on Pho Hien. Its architecture reflects the Tonkin Delta, China's Fukic
Province, and there are other buildings with strong Western influences. Tl
city is packed with ancient antiques and architectural relics. Many of the:
items can be found in the city's pagodas and the Pho Hien Museum. The
are Chinese and Vietnamese ceramic goods, brass bells and laquerwa
items. Even today, ancient relics are still being discovered in Pho Hien.

Ba Vi and Khoang Xanh

Ba Vi National Park is a mountainous oasis some 70 kilometers southwe
of Hanoi that rises from the alluvial plains much like the dragon-spined gro
tos of Ha Long Bay tower over the Gulf of Tonkin. This place, only a coup
of hours from Hanoi, is a world away from the capital and makes for an e:
cellent day trip.

Ba Vi Mountain itself reaches 1272 meters and is covered with lush, pr
mordial vegetation—hundreds of species of tropical plants. Rice fields mear
der between the boulder-strewn, jagged peaks of Khoang Xanh, just to th
southeast of Ba Vi Mountain. The region of Ba Vi is a riverhead forest an
countless streams tumble down the mountainsides. Near the small village o
Van Hoa is located the stream of Suoi Tien (the Ferry Stream), a confluenc
of a number of small brooks and creeks that runs about seven kilometers be
ginning at mid-mountain Ba Vi. The stream is punctuated with magnificer
boulders in myriad, bizarre-looking shapes. During the rainy season, visito:
can be seen cooling off in the currents of the stream.

The summit of Ba Vi Mountain is easily reached by foot, affording fantasti
views of the surrounding countryside (on a nice day, and on a nice day only'

especially of the hills to the southeast. At the base of the mountain is Thien Nga Lake (Swan Lake).

Some cheap guest houses and not-so-cheap restaurants have opened in the vicinity, notably the Khoang Xanh Guesthouse, and the area is becoming popular in a hurry, especially with Hanoi locals on the weekends. A weekday visit generally will afford some solitude.

Cuc Phuong National Park

This is quite a trip, as it's about 150 km south of Hanoi and west of Ninh Binh. Set amidst deeply cut limestone mountains, this national park covers more than 25,000 hectares. It is an important archeological site discovered in 1974 in the Hang Dang (Bat) and Con Mong (Animal) grottoes. There have been numerous discoveries here of prehistoric tools and artifacts. This park is home to thousands of species of endangered and exotic tropical wildlife. A nature preserve was established here in 1962.

Kiep Bac Pagoda

This is 60 km from Hanoi and about 30 km from Bac Ninh. This recently restored pagoda (founded in the early 1300s) was built to honor Tran Quoc Tuan, the famous general who aided Tran Hung Dao in defeating more than a quarter-million Mongol soldiers in the mid 1280s.

Hoa Binh

Hoa Binh is 74 km southwest of Hanoi and the capital of Hoa Binh province. The city, famous for its hill tribes and a large dam on the Song Da River (which created the Song Da Reservoir) can be visited from Hanoi in a day trip. There is a major hydro-electric operation at the dam that generates electricity for much of the north of the country, in fact enough to keep Hanoi from experiencing the constant power failures that put HCMC in the dark. This is also home to members of Muong hill people as well as the Thai. Although there have been problems with foreigners visiting the dam in the past, these obstructions have been largely removed. The tourist office (Hoa Binh Tourism) is located only about 10 km from Hanoi in Ha Dong, at *24 Tran Hung Dao Street.*

Perfume Pagoda ★

Located about 60 km southwest of Hanoi in Hoa Binh Province, this is a complex of pagodas constructed into the sides of the limestone cliffs of Huong Tich Mountain. Here is found **Huong Tich Chu Pagoda** (Pagoda of the Perfumed Vestige), **Giai Oan Chu Pagoda** (Pagoda of Purgatory), and **Thien Thu** (Pagoda Leading to Heaven). This region experiences a great number of pilgrims who come here to fish, hike, explore caves and go boating. There is a festival that begins during the second lunar month and concludes the last week of the third lunar month.

Keo Pagoda

Keo Pagoda is 10 km from the town of Thai Binh in Thai Binh Provin close to Thai Bac. There's a beautiful wood-carved bell at this pagoda, whi was built to honor Buddha and the monk Khong Minh Khong who cur Emperor Ly Than Ton of leprosy. It was constructed in the 12th centu There's a dike nearby that makes for good photo opportunities of the pag da grounds.

Hanoi Environs to the North & East

Buc Thap Pagoda

In Ha Bac Province and nearby Van Phuc Pagoda, about 28 km northea of Hanoi. This pagoda is perhaps best known for its stone four-story stu dedicated to the monk Chuyet Cong. The exact date of its construction is known, however it was built either before or during the 17th century.

Van Phuc Pagoda

About 28 km northeast from Hanoi. This pagoda was built in 1037 and surrounded by lush hills.

Hanoi Environs: North-Central

Ba Be Lake National Park ★★★

Ba Be Lake National Park is one of the better-kept secrets of the north. L cated about 240 km from Hanoi, the park is in Cao Bang province (60 k from Bach Thong and 17 km from Cho Ra) and features magnificent wate falls, caves, sheer rock walls and lakes carved into spectacular jagged mou tains that reach heights of 1800 meters. The largest lake in the park is Ba (Three Bays) Lake, one of three in the area (hence the name). The park is i habited namely by ethnic Dai, whose dwellings are built atop stilts. They be as curious about your presence as you about theirs, although they've se enough tourists these days to start up their own clothing lines.

Puong Cave worms its way 300 meters entirely through one mountain; navigable river sluices its way magnificently through the entire tunnel. Boa are available for the journey. The Dau Dang waterfall is also a draw here, as the Nam Nang River, on which craft can be piloted from the falls to about km above Cho Ra.

Getting to the park has become rather easy during the past year or s Four-wheel-drive vehicles can be hired in Hanoi for the 240-km, eight-ho trip for about US$200. The price usually is for a three-day, two-night jou ney. The road isn't bad until you get to Bach Thong; the last 60 km are a ja

g nightmare. If you go by bus, you'll first have to go to Bach Thong and
en change buses for Cho Ra. The last 17 km will have to be done via the
urtesy of someone's motorbike. If hiring a jeep sounds like a better idea,
t a hold of **Memory Cafe (33 Bis)**, *33 Tran Hung Dao Street, Hanoi
8265854)*. These folks may have started up a service to the area by the
ne you read this.

Hanoi Environs to the North & West

Tam Dao Hill Station ★

About 85 km northwest of Hanoi. In 1907 this hill station (some call it
alat of the north) was founded by the French so that monied colonists
uld make summer retreats to this elevation of 935 meters to escape the
at of the Red River Delta. This is a beautiful, lush mountainous area fearing giant fern trees about two hours by car from Hanoi. Few foreign tour-
s reach this hill station, unlike Dalat, so that Tam Dao has yet to suffer
m duck paddle boats and Vietnamese cowboys dressed like Roy Rogers
at plague Dalat.

Tam Dao Mountain features three summits. Each is about 1200 meters in
ight. The highest is 1265 meters. They're easily seen from Tam Dao. The
lls are teeming with rare animals and plants. The area is also home to a
mber of hilltribe people. Although the buildings in Tam Dao are some-
hat dilapidated, this makes for a beautiful excursion from Hanoi. The sum-
rtime is the best time of the year to come here. It gets quite cold up here
the winter. You can stay at the **Tam Dao Hotel** (virtually all foreigners do).
e tourist office is located in the hotel. ☎ *8306* for both.

Vinh Yen

Vinh Yen is about 60 km northwest of Hanoi. It's a tiny village cut off from
ost everything (even though it's on the main road!) that sees few, if any,
reigners. It lies between the Song River and the Tam Dao Mountains. It
as the site of battles during the First Indochina War. It has the distinction
being the first place in Vietnam where napalm was used (not by the Amer-
ns, but by the French). The attacks killed and wounded thousands of Viet
inh soldiers. The French General who engineered the strategy, Gen. de
attre, was called the Fire General by the locals.

Son Tay

About 40 km northwest of Hanoi. Son Tay is located at the end of the
lta region around Hanoi. There's a small citadel in the middle of the com-
ex that was fortified in 1822, but captured in 1883 by French Admiral
ourbet.

A Hung Hoa

A Hung Hoa is 66 km from Hanoi upriver. There's a famous citadel h (at least for the architecture of its watchtower) that used to stand watch o the Song River. Here the topography descends into the valley where the and Black rivers flow. The local population depends on the river for its li lihood, and the inhabitants here tend to be less friendly to foreigners. L end has it that this was the area where the Hong Bang Dynasty started 2880 BC and ended in 258 BC. It was part of the Van Long Kingdom. capital was Bach Hach (then called Phong Chau), about 80 km from Ha to the northwest in Vinh Phu Province. The site of the Hong Bang kin temple, Den Hung, is close to here in the Nung Hills (80 km west of F noi). The temple, the ruins of which are still precariously standing, da back to the Ly Dynasty. There is the tomb of the mythical leader Hung H Vuong in front of the temple.

Tuyen Quang

Tuyen Quang is located 165 km northwest of Hanoi in Ha Tuyen Pro ince. Tuyen Quang faces Yen Bay from the banks of the Lo River. It wa strategic hamlet for the Nguyen on the path to Yunnan. From 1884-188 the town was occupied by the French and then was occupied by the Chine The Second National Congress of the Vietnamese Communist Party v held here in 1951 in honor of the start-up of the Worker's Party.

Binh Son

Binh Son is 85 km west of Hanoi on the Lo River. There's an 11-st tower here dating from at least the 11th century. When archeologists w working to restore the tower in 1979, they discovered a "blueprint" (scribed on a brick) of the temple that dates back to the 8th century. Betwe Vinh Yen and Tuyen Quang is the village of Thien Khe, which is the site numerous Buddhist rock paintings. Fifteen km before reaching Tuy Quang is the former Binh Ca Fortress. It was built in the early 16th cent by Vu Cong Mat, a famous general. The walls around the fortress are still v ible.

Tan Trao

Tan Trao is situated 150 km from Hanoi, northwest in Ha Tuyen Pro ince. This town has the distinction of once being the capital of revolution Vietnam. Ho Chi Minh organized a mass upheaval here in May 1945. M of the mandates of the Communist Party were drawn up here. Also in T Trao, the Central Committee of the National Liberation was elected. Un Ho was elected president.

Hanoi Environs to the East

The Dong Trieu Ridge and the surrounding area are historically extremely significant in Vietnamese history, particularly to scholars of the country. The ridge averages 500–1000 meters high and borders northern Vietnam with China. During the Cham and Mongol invasions of the 14th century, Tran Dynasty rulers used the area as a hideout and sanctuary. The following areas are extremely remote and rarely, if ever see Western tourists. If you want to visit these areas, as well as the remote areas described earlier in the west, it's extremely important you find a good (a very good) private guide in Hanoi. You should not rely on Vietnamtourism to provide much help in reaching many of these destinations. These communities and sites are well off the beaten track and many are inaccessible by vehicle. Only the hardiest of travelers should attempt visiting these sites. Don't expect any accommodations or decent food and water. Bring your own from Hanoi.

Dong Trieu

Dong Trieu in Quang Ninh Province is 85 km east of Hanoi. This is an important coal mining area. There are vast deposits in the vicinity. The Trans virtually worshipped the surrounding area at the base of Nui Yen Tu. About km away is the village of Ha Loi where there is the Quynh Lam Pagoda, which dates from the Tran Dynasty. There's a giant bell here. Almost 4 km to the north lies the village of Yen Sinh and a temple and tombs of Tran rulers of the 14th century.

Kiep Bac

Kiep Bac is located 60 km northeast of Hanoi. This "quaint" village is north of Hai Duong by about 15 km on the eastern border of the Dong Trieu Ridge, above the Hom Hills. Refuge was taken in the hills here by Prince General Hung Dao, better known as Than Quoc Tuan, in 1285 after being defeated by the Mongolians from Loang Son. The prince then regrouped his forces here and later attacked and beat the Mongols in 1289. After his death in 1300 he was buried in a pagoda that was built here earlier in his honor. Hung Doa is considered a national hero in Vietnam. After his death soldiers used to come to the pagoda when war was pending for luck and signs of the battle's outcome. If a soldier's sword was heard to be removed from its sheath, it meant that the battle would be lost. Pregnant women also came to the temple to pray to the spirits for a safe delivery of the child.

Hai Duong

Hai Duong is in Hai Duong Province, 60 km east of Hanoi. This was a strategic location on the road from Hanoi to Ha Long Bay, as it is located near the summit of the delta in Thai Binh. Today, you can view the remain of a fort that was built here in 1804 by the Nguyen Dynasty.

Nui Yen Tu

Nui Yen Tu is 45 km east of Hanoi. Here there are many pagodas in th surrounding hills that were constructed by Tan rulers, who used Nui Yen T as a retreat. It's damned difficult to get here, but once you reach the area, th views of Ha Long Bay are magnificent.

Mao Khe

About 8 km east of Dong Trieu. This is the most eastern point of the C Bang Hills. The Dong Trieu Ridge begins here.

Con Son

Con Son is 80 km northeast of Hanoi, and 30 km north of Hai Duon The village offers gorgeous views of the surrounding hillsides. Nguyen Tra the trusted advisor and aide to Le Loi, used this location as a retreat.

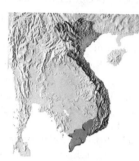

NORTH OF HANOI

...onely fishing vessels idle on the shores of the Gulf of Tonkin.

As the border between northern Vietnam and China becomes increasingly
pen, a burgeoning amount of travel between the two countries has begun.
t has also opened the routes for smugglers. In Lang Son province, which
as opened up in January 1994, one can see swarms of Asian travelers carry-
g on their backs sometimes more than the weight of their bodies. **Dong**
ang has become something of a boom town, and one can see the prosperity
this once shanty town as imported tires, fruit, beer and other consumer
ems are now offered for sale, lining the streets like a gauntlet of entrepre-
urialism. As you head south, you'll notice the rapid construction of multi-
oried brick and tile buildings as this newly found prosperity heads south.
owever, a large degree of this southward-bound caravan of consumer

523

goods has been smuggled into the country or been allowed in through brib-ery. Be cautious in this region. If you're asked by any traveler to help carry goods that appear too burdensome to the carrier, don't be overcome by your sympathies. Carry only your own belongings on both sides of the border.

The beautiful northern Vietnam region of **Son La** province is getting the gears in motion for tourism. To bolster the local economy, the province has been divided into three separate regions. The first, along Highway 6, will be allocated to developing mulberry silk production, coffee and fruit trees. Son La has installed 4000 mini hydroelectric plants to provide power for lighting and agriculture. The telecommunications network is now in synch with the national grid. Tourism is on the rise in the province, mainly because of the magnificent beauty of the surrounding mountains. To date, though, the roads reaching the province from all areas in the north are in dismal shape though the views from the rutted path are spectacular.

Road travelers in Vietnam may soon have an easier selection of routes to take to both urban and rural destinations in the north—a four-lane highway linking Bac Ninh (30 km to the north of Hanoi) and Mong Cai, near the Chinese border. As part of the economic triangle that includes Hanoi, Haiphong and Quang Ninh, the 314-km route is a government infrastruc-ture priority. Additionally, there will also be bridges constructed at Pha La (260 meters) and Bai Chay (800 meters), which will replace the present fer-ries. As well, a new highway has been built from Bac Ninh town to Hanoi's Noi Bai International Airport. The road projects are important as they will connect the Cai Lan port, which is currently under construction in Haiphong with Hanoi and with the Chinese border crossing at Mong Cai.

Road Wearier: Hanoi to Mong Cai the Hard Way— On Two Wheels

Not a lot of Western tourists have heard of Mong Cai, much less been there. The beaten track in Vietnam's northeast ends at Ha Long, where after having endured a "grueling" six-hour ride in an air-conditioned micro-bus, most tourists lather up in the hot showers of the Bai Chay's sprouting caravansaries, wine and dine in relative splendor in the cozy cafes along Bai Chay Street (Ha Long Road) and—the following day—head out in one of the dozens of tourist boats that ply the bay and serpentine through the thou-sands of rugged grottoes that poke from the sea like the scales of an enor-mous dragon, which, of course, is what Ha Long Bay is named after.

Sitting under the shade of Carlsberg umbrellas, sipping banana milk shakes, nibbling on prawns and eel prepared by a Paris-trained chef and watching the camcorder-toting middle-aged tourists strolling along the beachside promenade with their bored children, one feels about as adventurous as an accountant moonlighting as a Little League umpire.

Chinese border crossing (the Friendship Bridge) at Mong Cai.

That is what Ha Long Bay has become in just a very, very short time—a natural wonder that's becoming virtually as accessible as Disneyland is to residents of Anaheim. (Yet it may take a few years before pony rides and those quacky duck-shaped paddleboats make their debut here.)

Three years ago, I would not have looked out of place in Ha Long Bay, my tattered attire and exposed skin having become one with the coal-muddied, rutted roads and paths of Cam Pha, Khe Lang, Ha Tu and Dam Ha—much like the locals look themselves.

Instead, tourists in Levis Dockers shorts and "Saigon Vietnam" T-shirts gazed at me in bewilderment as they passed by my cafe table, as I wolfed down my beef noodle soup and a liter of Tiger Beer. Never mind that it was only 9:30 in the morning—I had been on the "road" (actually a congealing tar and granite path sliced frequently by Mother Nature's and Newton's own "above the law" highways) from Tien Yen since 4 a.m. and it seemed to me to be a perfectly reasonable time to ferment and numb the throbbing of my backside and to forget that my soggy feet more resembled a fisherman's catch than a couple of appendages to bipedal on.

My rip-off Reebok rain suit was in shreds; my French army boots like a sea sponge. Photo prints that I had earlier taken and developed in Mong Cai and the border with China's Dong Hung and had inadvertently stashed in my photog's vest had become a slimy, gloss-dripping brick. The Khmer scarf wrapped around my head had become a checkerboard second skin. My motorcycle seemed sculpted from mud. Earlier, it had broken down during a monsoon between Cam Pha and Khe Lang. Mechanics had squabbled for hours over the ignition problem, none coming up with an answer—but at least trying after I said I was Canadian, not American. (After telling a 10-year-old postcard hawker earlier in Hanoi that I was an American, he spat on me and told me that his father kills Americans. I thought it wise to subsequently don a maple leaf and say "eh" a lot while in the north of Vietnam.)

So the tourists gawked at a road-weary, soiled traveler in a place where only a few short years ago, all those who made it here were road-weary and soiled

Runway 5

The 100 kilometers on Route 5 between Hanoi and Haiphong are some o the most dangerous in Vietnam. The road is in good enough shape—the pavement smooth and wide. And that perhaps explains its dangers. The more convenient something in Vietnam becomes, the more dangerous the Vietnamese make it. Other rutted, pot-holed thoroughfares in Vietnam work under the same principle as speed bumps in the parking lot of the Federal Building in Hartford—they slow people down. But give the Vietnamese an inch and they'll take a mile—rather quickly, too. As the road to Haiphong is like a 100-km-long airport runway, Vietnamese drivers naturally assum that if a Boeing 767 needs to be hurtling along at 170 mph to reach lift-of speed, their own Toyotas need to be traveling at liftoff speed to reac Haiphong. But an aircraft enjoys the luxury of not having to concern itse with oncoming traffic as it makes its way for the sky. Compound this mech anized anarchy with the throngs of bicyclists and pedestrians and it's n wonder to see people lying dead in the road every 40 klicks. Highway 5 is th ultimate game of chicken. On a motorcycle, it's totally nuts.

But I wouldn't have it any other way.

On one stretch of Route 5, the railroad shares the same bridge with aut mobiles, although they both can't use it at the same time. Cars queue to ta turns crossing the 500-meter span. A motorcycle can use the pedestri crossing and avoid the wait.

INSIDER TIP

A new stretch of national Route 5 is being constructed through Hai Duong Town. The road has only a distance of 15 km, but it's still 15 km of less-dilapidated roadways that are the main infrastructure blight of Vietnam. There will be six traffic lanes, and the road will run over three bridges, in Dong Nieu, Phu Luong and Lai Vu.

Accidents along this stretch of roadway invariably lead to fisticuffs between the drivers. In Vietnam, there is no car insurance. In Vietnam, a claims adjuster is the man with a stronger right jab.

At Haiphong, after crossing over the first bridge—the river flanked by old French colonial apartment houses, some still partially razed from the B-52 bombings of Haiphong during the Vietnam War—one makes a left to get to the harbor ferry crossing. A few klicks on the other side of the crossing on the road to Hong Gai, I was flagged down by a team of policemen on the roadside. No words were spoken. One policeman simply wrote on an envelope, "40 USD." He nodded at a tiny dent in my gas tank. No check of my passport, visa, or motorcycle registration. He just wanted 40 bucks because he was quite certain I had it. My only traffic infraction was that my net worth was greater than his own. I told him in English that I was indeed rich, but that my capital was liquid, tied up in Microsoft, Pepsi and Barings stocks. He nearly wept over my plight and settled for 100,000 dong. I was on my way.

After another river ferry crossing 10 or 15 km later, and a relatively stable ride for the next 50 km, I was in Bai Chay.

I did the tourist thing, hired a boat, saw the stalagmite caves. The next day it was off to Mong Cai and the far northeastern tip of Vietnam, about 180 km away. The road becomes rutted and grimy as it passes through the coal towns of Cam Pha and Khe Lang. But the last 90 km from Tien Yen to Mong Cai are a motorcyclist's paradise. The smooth road curves and winds its way through rolling tea plantations. Tiny villages dot the roadside every 15 klicks or so. I stopped frequently to photograph Meo hilltribe people. I came across a couple of young men who had killed a large dog and were pulling the hair from its flesh. It would be dinner—or a few. They invited me to the feast. I couldn't do it, thinking of all the unfetched newspapers that would end up in the guy's driveway in about a week.

Occasionally, groups of soldiers wandered in the desolate, jungle-shrouded roadway, apparently going nowhere, and apparently having come from nowhere. Intermittently, the Gulf of Tonkin could be seen shimmering in the distance to the east.

Near Mong Cai, I was stopped again by the police. But this group was far friendlier than the posse that had bilked me near Haiphong. After a simple inspection of my passport, I was permitted to go on.

The Road Stops Here

Mong Cai is a typical border town and surprisingly large—although it doesn't seem quite as prosperous as Dong Hung, a Free Economic Zone on the Chinese side of the river across from the Vietnamese frontier. The streets of Mong Cai are flanked by an endless gantlet of gutter-side produce and fruit vendors. Some display their wares in the middle of the streets, not satisfied with the relative anonymity of the sidewalk sellers. There are few foreigners in Mong Cai—a scant trickle of travelers bother to make the journey up here. Because there is no real reason to unless you intend to cross the border into China—or truly want to experience the north of Vietnam. I saw one other foreigner—a British woman—an English teacher from Cao Bang who was on "holiday" with her Vietnamese boyfriend, a man half her height and weight. When they held hands, she seemed to be teaching him to walk.

Vietnamese smugglers and traders unload their wares in Dong Hung, China.

The Border

My goal, of course, was to find a way of getting into China without a visa. I headed for the border gate at 8 p.m. Only a short 50-meter bridge separates the two countries. The Chinese military had occupied the area as well as Lang Son to the northwest during a brief border invasion in 1979. I could clearly see the Chinese border guards playing cards—even spotting the grimace on the face of the officer who was winning. If there had once been tension here between the two communist countries, you'd never know it. The trade between the two cities today is bustling.

The crossing had closed at 4:30. At the Vietnamese gate, I was intercepted by the political officer and an English-speaking immigration captain. Without a visa, they would not let me pass. I had been told earlier in Bai Chay by some residents not to initiate a bribe at this particular border crossing. If they were amenable to my passing, they would bring the subject up themselves.

They didn't.

The next day I tried again and was given the same answer: Vietnamese without a passport are permitted to enter Dong Hung for 24 hours to conduct business. They are issued a small booklet which is stamped. But it was absolutely forbidden for a foreigner without a Chinese visa to enter China. They said it was for my safety. Sure, I could get over there, the officers said—but the Chinese might not let me back.

"Then let me take my chances," I said.

"It's not the trouble *you'll* get into we're worried about," the English-speaking officer replied. Point taken.

Later, a Vietnamese woman told me there was another crossing, but that it was an illegal one used by smugglers a kilometer farther up the river. She took me there. Although this was an "illegal" crossing, it was (perhaps unsurprisingly) manned by Vietnamese police. And I could indeed see why it was illegal. Baskets full of endangered pangolins were being hoisted on a flimsy canoe by Vietnamese smugglers, as well as crates of snakes and other goods whose identity I could only imagine. Again, as the covert frontier post was being supervised by police, I was forbidden from crossing. The Vietnamese were paying the police about 20,000 dong for the "ferry" ride. I was told impolitely to go away—and did.

Later that night, at my hotel room, I was paid an unexpected visit by the English woman, her diminutive Vietnamese boyfriend and another Vietnamese man, who explained that he could get me across the river, but that it would take two days to make the preparations—time that I didn't have, and people I didn't have time for.

Lost In Faith

I rode 13 kilometers out of town to the beach at Tra Co and then headed north, to where I thought another less-conspicuous and more-remote crossing could be found. What I found instead was a group of Vietnamese hoeing dirt and digging plant roots from the base of a massive but gutted stone Catholic church in the middle of nowhere, just a few dozen meters from the deserted beach. Young boys and girls as well as old men and women toiled in the searing sun, Christian crosses dangling from their necks. I was told the church had been built by the French in 1914 (others said 1926). A raisin-skinned old man said the North Vietnamese had started tearing the church down during the American War in 1964 to use its stone and wood in the war effort. The Chinese then further ravaged the site during their 1979 invasion and made off with the tower's large iron bell, which they later generously returned at the request of the Bishop of Haiphong.

"We dig and dig and build," the old man said. "No one is paid to do this. We do it for the love of God. But we need money and help. No one knows about us. We are alone. Very alone."

The Tra Co Cathedral was built in 1914 and gutted by generations of war. Th
tower, at 45 meters, is about all that is left of the church.

Indeed, the cathedral is nothing more than a roofless granite shell, it's in
tricately carved bas relief tower rising 45 meters above the flat, alluvial plai
dominating the landscape for miles. From many kilometers afar, the stru
ture looks like Oz at the end of the yellow brick road. The few Catholics wh
live here are indeed alone and very poor, bonded by their outcast faith. Th
work each day reconstructing the church and celebrate Mass without a prie
in a tiny shed alongside the cathedral. A small wooden cross nailed to the to
of the thatched roof lists with the winds from the sea.

The Bishop of Haiphong travels to this remote area "once a month, or maybe once every few months" to celebrate Mass, the old man said. In the meantime, they worship Christ in silence in a dilapidated hootch, waiting for someone to help. I was told these people see foreigners as frequently as they do the Bishop of Haiphong.

(To get here, take the road east out of Mong Cai about 5 km and make a left toward the beach at Tra Co. It's the only left—if you've gone as far as the dirt road, you've gone too far. At Tra Co follow the beach road north another 3-4 km. The church is on the left. You can't miss it. The total journey is about 17 km from Mong Cai.)

A River Runs Over It

The journey back to Hanoi was far more problematic than reaching Mong Cai. Monsoons had swollen the rivers, making the 10 bridges between Mong Cai and Tien Yen impassable. At the first bridge (considered the easiest to pass of the 10 during the monsoons), less than 10 klicks out of town, a mile-long queue of trucks, motorcycles and automobiles waited eight hours for the river to ebb low enough to cross. Young men, charging 20,000 dong a pop to the rider, carried the smaller motorbikes across the torrent using large wooden poles inserted through the wheels (like porters carrying an ancient king), battling the pull of the rushing current like tightrope walkers. My bike was too big and too packed down and gear-laden to be hauled in such a fashion, so I decided to chance a crossing when it was far too dangerous to do so. I had only two options—and neither was particularly attractive: return to Mong Cai and wait out the floods, which might take days, or make a dangerous first-gear crossing in a raging niagara up to my waist, which if I accomplished, might leave me stranded between the first bridge and the even more dangerous crossing 15 km farther—without a town between. I took the precaution of storing up on a couple of day's worth of food and water in anticipation of such a circumstance and barreled through the 90-meter spate. It felt like being terminally caught in the chicane at Willow Springs, but I managed; miraculously the plugs didn't fail. If they had, I would have certainly been washed down river.

It was the same scene at the next crossing. But this was of a much greater distance and the flood waters far higher. Vehicles heading north to Mong Cai stranded on the far side numbered more than 130. The bridge had been closed 12 hours.

I waited two before daring a repeat attempt. Again, success.

Night Crossing

No such luck at Tien Yen. A 300-meter crossing this time, the river raging over the bridge chest-high. Hours passed. I drank beer with the local cops and lamented to them how damn cold Canada gets in the winter. They laughed and we drank more. They said I should move to Los Angeles. We smoked tobacco in giant bamboo bongs. With the scarf wrapped over my head, one of the cops thought I wasn't Canadian at all, but rather Palestinian, and asked if I knew Yasser Arafat. "Sure, I'm his barber," I said. The cop didn't get it.

Dusk now. Again, the same decision. Cross the rage and reach the only hotel in Tien Yen permitted for foreigners—or sleep on the road next to my bike and the curious cops, and say something silly in my slumber like "I wish I was back in L.A."

A night crossing. Perhaps 300 meters. I had just enough of the local suds in my veins to try it. I wasn't the first. I saw a man aboard an old Russian Minsk motorcycle, a giant pig strapped pillion, rip through the roaring current. He was shrouded by the river, engulfed by the rush; the only sight was the white exhaust spewing from the tailpipe into his wake. The squealing of the sow was only a decibel higher than the thunder of the river. Then it, too, became swallowed by the holler of the monster rapids.

I wasn't sure he had made it until I heard cheers from the other side. Hell, if this guy could barge a cheap Russian motorcycle and a 500-lb. hog through Victoria Falls then I could certainly duplicate the feat on an equally cheap Korean motorcycle and a 7-lb. laptop computer.

The bridge, although it couldn't be seen beneath the surging rapids, was straight. If I could just keep the bike upright without steering...

It was like surfing Half Moon Bay under a half moon. My arms struggled to keep the handlebars straight. I actually steered the motorcycle with my feet—not on the ground, but like a tiller on a boat. The water was gushing from right to left. As I was forced left to the abyss, I compensated by dragging my right thigh and calf against the rear wheel, creating more resistance against the tail end of the machine by permitting less water through the rear spokes.

It worked, and I arrived to the other side to even greater applause than the pig received—probably because I was a crazy American...er, Canadian. There's something to be said about being a foreigner in northern Vietnam and getting a bigger hand than a hog.

Somewhere in the World it's Cocktail Hour

I woke up at 4 a.m. My clothes were still wet. Everything was wet. My ignition and electrical systems failed near Cam Pha two hours later. I had to keep the bike running the final 40 km to Hong Gai over muddy, rutted roads—or risk not getting it started again if the engine cut.

Soaked, muddy and exhausted—yeah, I had a beer at 9:30 in the morning when I got to Ha Long. I had three of them. With jet-setting tourists in spiffy new topsiders sipping mineral water at sidewalk cafes while their guides and tour group leaders bargained for tour boats, I may as well have been in Fort Lauderdale.

Or an accountant umping a Little League game.

Doing it:

Unlike in Saigon, it's virtually impossible to rent a bike over 125cc in Hanoi. The authorities are much tighter up here about this, while it is relatively easy to find a larger machine for rent in HCMC. The Vietnamese are not permitted to operate anything larger than 125cc, unless under "special circumstances." Besides, riding a higher-cc machine will only draw more police attention to yourself. I consider myself lucky to have paid only one cop's night out on the town. It easily could have been three or four places where roadside dragnets might have pointed at the nick on my gas tank and demanded BGI money for a month. There are only about 10 places in Hanoi that rent motorcycles to foreigners, and they're hard to find. Machines capable of extended journeys out of Hanoi are even rarer. Best bet is to head on over to the **Memory Cafe (33 Bis)**, *33 Tran Hung Dao Street, Hanoi* (☎ *8265854*) and have a chat with Nguyen Viet Trung and his stepdaughter, Ha Minh Chau, who will take care of the translation. Great folks. Or head over to the **Tourist Service Office** *(18C Ngo Quyen Street; ☎ 8247391, 8517849)*. You'll most likely end up on a Bonus 125cc for between US$9–$12 a day, depending on how long you take it for. If you can get a Honda out of them, you're in better shape, as many mechanics in the boonies (and believe me, you *will* be in the boonies) have never seen Bonus machines before. There's a slight possibility you could land one of those new, fashionable micro-choppers, a Husky 150. It shares the same mechanicals with the Bonus, but is vastly more comfortable. Bring extra spark plugs and a tool kit. Check out the bike carefully. Particularly, check the tires and listen for a valve tap in the cylinder head(s). For a full description of preparing for a motorcycle journey in Vietnam, pick up a copy of *Fielding's Southern Vietnam on 2 Wheels*.

Getting there:

Take Highway 5 to Haiphong, about 95 km east of Hanoi. After the second bridge on the edge of western Haiphong, make an immediate left to the harbor ferry. The boat ride will set you back a couple of thousand dong. After another 16 km or so on the road to Hong Gai, there's another ferry—costing 1000 dong. Between the two ferries, you may run into a police roadblock. Keep some extra cash on hand for bribes. Bai Chay/Hong Gai is about 55–60 km from Haiphong. Allow 5–6 hours of daylight to reach the area by motorcycle from Hanoi. Ha Long Bay makes a great place for an overnight or two. From Bai Chay/Hong Gai, continue north about 90 km to Tien Yen. Stop at any one of the small restaurants near the **Thuy Tien Hotel** for lunch and move on. (If you must stay overnight in Tien Yen, the Thuy Tien is the only hotel in town where foreigners are permitted. About 300 meters from the bridge. A nice place at about US$10–$20 depending on your bargaining skills.)

Nothing to do here. Little to see of any cultural significance. The next 80 km to Mong Cai are the most exhilarating—flat roads, little traffic and few pedestrians. All the kilometers are on a windy mountainous thoroughfare. Let 'er rip here, but keep alert at all times. Remember, the bus drivers also realize there is little traffic on this stretch, and they tend as well to "let 'er rip," using both sides of the road.

Costs:

Motorcycle: US$10–$12 per day. *Fuel*: About US$7–$10 round trip. Check oil at each fuel stop. On a Bonus, it's wise to check every 80–100 km. *Ferries*: 6000 dong round trip. *Bridges*: 2000–4000 dong round trip depending on whether they're manned.

Visas:

If you want to cross the border into China, you will need a visa. No sneaking across. No day trips without one. They can be had at the Chinese consulate in Haiphong or at the Chinese embassy in Hanoi *(46 Hoang Dieu Street.* ☎ *8253736/7)*. It may be possible to arrange for a visa in Mong Cai through "gentlemen" with friends at the immigration office. If you ask at the border bridge, officials will insist you go first to Hanoi or Haiphong and that such "agents" don't exist. These guys don't have offices, but don't worry, they'll find you. So few foreigners visit Mong Cai, they'll spot you quickly. If you're feeling adventurous and have a couple of days to kill to wait for the "preparations," go for it. See if you can save a pangolin or two.

What to See and Do in Mong Cai

The bustling Chinese border town of Dong Hung, as seen from Mong Cai.

The Border

The Chinese border is less than a klick from the center of town. After crossing over the bridge into Mong Cai, hang a left.

• At the first intersection, take another left.

• Where the road Ts after about 100 meters, turn right. This road ends at the bridge that crosses into Dong Hung. Stop and take photos of this bustling Chinese frontier town. If you can find a way to get in, you'll have to change all your money into Chinese yuan, either on the black market or in a bank. Dollars and dong are not accepted. Note that no one, I mean *no one*, in Dong Hung speaks English, including government officials and bank managers. And, as well, virtually no one speaks Vietnamese. Although I was thwarted in my attempts get across into Dong Hung, a Vietnamese friend of mine was a little luckier:

"The legal way for foreigners to cross the border here is to have a prearranged 24-hour visa. But being Vietnamese I showed the Vietnamese border police my identification card and paid them 20,000 dong after telling them the reason I wanted to pass. I had to be escorted by an employee of the Mong Cai hotel where I was staying. After 10 minutes of questioning I was allowed to pass. In Dong Hung I saw a lot of cyclo drivers, many of whom were women. I thought this odd because we do not have any women cyclo drivers in Vietnam. The town looks similar to Mong Cai, but no one can speak any English nor French. I tried to get some information from a few hotels and banks, but managers here weren't able to speak English, as well. I took a 10-minute boat trip along the river for 2 nhan dan te (VND2600), and saw many smugglers. The Chinese police, which also include a number of women, wear white uniforms. Although the town is clean, the hotels are mostly pretty dirty. Many things I see have been smuggled in from Vietnam—silk flowers, frozen fish and different kinds of wild animals, such as pangolins and a variety of snakes, all alive."

Tra Co Beach ★

This is a small beach town about 13 km east of Mong Cai. Take the main road east from Mong Cai, making a left turn after about 10 klicks. The road runs right to the beach. The deserted beach stretches for miles in both directions. The few tourists here are primarily Vietnamese and day-trippers from China who congregate at the beach next to the Tra Co Hotel, about the only place in town. The sand here is less than spectacular, more silt than sand. But it is clean. The sea is generally very rough here. Watch out for dangerous undertows.

Tra Co Cathedral ★★

This is certainly the most engaging sight in the Mong Cai area (see the description above). A large old Catholic church that was gutted by the North Vietnamese Army during the Vietnam War and later by invading Chinese forces in 1979. The small Christian community that lives here toils each day at rebuilding the structure, paid and supported by neither the Bishop in Haiphong nor the Vatican. These believers without a temple toiling under a broiling sun removing weeds and primitively restoring the grand old cathedral are a sight to behold. At their rate of progress, it should only take another century or so to complete. From Tra Co Beach, follow the road north toward the Chinese border along the beach about 3 km to get there.

Where to Stay in and Around Mong Cai

Khach San Huei Nghi   US$15–$25

Center of town. ☎ *(33) 881408. FAX: (33) 881144.*
25 Rooms.

One of the two tourist hotels in town. Comfortable, clean rooms—that appear straight out of a dollhouse—with air conditioning. Photocopier in the lobby for what it's worth. The reception staff seems a little dizzy. Restaurant.

Khach San Thang Loi   US$25

Center of town. ☎ *881002.*

This is the best place to stay in Mong Cai. Large and comfortable rooms, but bland. Downstairs restaurant with a passable American breakfast. The lobby is a good place to hang out and meet other travelers, what few there are here.

Khach San Tra Co   About US$15

Tra Co Beach.

Soviet block-style hotel on the beach in Tra Co. Clean and friendly. Restaurant. But they're getting some competition. Nearly completed is another hotel a few hundred meters up the beach that looks much more attractive.

Where to Eat in Mong Cai

Food stalls abound. There are a couple of good restaurants—one on the left side of the traffic triangle after you cross the bridge into town, and a better one on the southern edge of the town. Go around the traffic triangle 180 degrees. Follow the road all the way back (about 50 meters). It's on the right. Funky atmosphere. Large-screen TV.

Lang Son

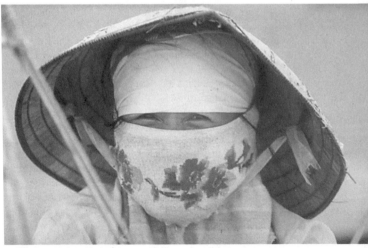

Produce vendor is well protected from the sun near Lang Son.

From Mong Cai, you'll have to double back to Tien Yen before you'll be able to get anywhere else in Vietnam.

Lang Son is about 100 km northwest of Tien Yen (150 km from Hanoi) along what at first appears to be a surprisingly acceptable road. But it deteriorates suddenly, and the final 40 km are pure hell on the rump, on two wheels or four or more.

Lang Son is the capital of Lang Son province and a bustling border town. It is perhaps Vietnam's most important trading outpost with China, and, if you're lucky, you'll be able to cross the border here into China without a Chinese visa for a short stay after taking care of minor details. Since 1992, Vietnam's government has intermittently permitted overland travel for foreigners into China through Lang Son. (In fact, it can also be done from Mong Cai as well, with the proper entry papers.) The number of travelers here has swelled in the past couple of years, namely for this reason—as Lang Son itself isn't particularly an attractive town. (There are some decent caves near Ky Lua district, about 3 km from Lang Son.)

Lang Son, as well as Dong Dang, 20 km to the north, were ravaged during China's 1979 border invasion of northern Vietnam. Today, although there are no longer any signs of tension at the border here, the area is still heavily mined—although it no longer resembles Korea's 38th parallel as it did a few years ago. Chinese and Vietnamese flow across the border to barter and deliver goods, cut business deals, or just get out of their respective countries for an hour or two.

The area is inhabited by a number of ethnic minorities, such as the Dao, Nung, Man and Tho, which makes for another attraction in the area. Nonetheless, most independent travelers come here to cross the border.

In order to cross the border into China, your visa must show Lang Son as an exit point. This can be done at the Foreign Ministry offices in Hanoi and Ho Chi Minh City. If you're without a Chinese visa and just curious how you might be able to get into China for a few hours, the best way is to hook up with a tour packager. Although you won't be traveling independently, Vietnamese guides are usually able to arrange for their flocks to be escorted in and out of China without too much hassle. As in Mong Cai, certain Vietnamese shady-types also have the ability to get you across the border at Dong Dang, but it will cost.

The border itself is at Dong Dang, where there is a 600-m walkway to the Chinese-side "Friendship Gate," that's anything but friendly. Prepare for delays and a number of searches—although these instances are rare when part of a tour.

Doing it:

Go yourself, by bus, by train, by Toyota Land Cruiser—or even by motorcycle. The road between Hanoi and Lang Son is in treacherous condition. If you're traveling by motorcycle, it makes far more sense to visit Ha Long Bay first, and then continue directly on to Lang Son via Trot and Son Dong or by way of Tien Yen. If you want to hook up on a tour, I'd contact **Voiles Vietnam**, *17 Pham Ngoc Thach, Dist. 3, HCMC (☎ 84-8-8296750, 8231589. FAX: 84-8-8231591)*—although they may be dropping the Mong Cai leg of the itinerary during the rainy season (between May and October) due to the constant flooding in the region, washing out bridges for hours, even days, at a time.

Getting there:

It can be done from Hanoi, Ha Long Bay and Tien Yen. By bus, the best bet is from Hanoi. Buses leave from the capital's Long Bien bus station at 6 a.m. It's at least a six-hour ride to hell, as the Hanoi/Lang Son route isn't in nearly as good shape as the roads to the east and northeast. Expect to be jolted, jarred and banged around virtually the entire journey. The cost is about US$6. There are a number of police roadblocks that may or not be functioning, but be prepared to be stopped and perhaps searched by Vietnamese police looking for contraband. If you're doing the trip solo, such as by motorcycle, without a guide, expect to be stopped often and perhaps "fined." By train the journey takes six hours. One leaves Hanoi for Lang Son each morning at 9. If you're going by car, it's necessary that it be of the 4-wheel-drive variety. Nothing else will make it.

INSIDER TIP

If you're traveling through Hai Duong, you have to make a point of trying the town's special cuisine, in particular the green bean cake and Tan Cuong Tea. There is an array of green bean cake dealers (you'll see a sign saying Rong Vuong (Golden Dragon) along the street in the town. Bao Hien Restaurant is where the specialty was originally created, using green beans, white sugar, pig fat, shaddock scent and vanilla. There's a lot of protein in the concoction. These cakes can now be found in other areas of Vietnam, but the real thing comes from Hai Duong. The townsfolk consider the preparation of green bean cake an art form. Green bean cakes are often part of wedding meals and engagement ceremonies, and are offered on the altars of ancestors during the Tet holiday in Hanoi and other northern rural areas. Green bean cakes are also offered to visiting foreign businessmen by government representatives at official functions. The authentic green bean cake comes with the trademark Bao Long. The best restaurants for green bean cake in Hai Duong are the Bao Hien Restaurant (now called the Ngoc Bich) and Nguyen Huong Restaurant. Bao Long green bean cakes are now reaching customers at Hanoi's Noi Bai International airport, upscale eateries in Hanoi, the railway station, Quang Ninh Province and Haiphong, just to mention a few of the areas where the delicacy is available. Green bean cake is now just beginning to be exported to foreign countries. The cakes are perhaps northern Vietnam's best representation of the use of its agricultural products. Try some. Absolutely delicious.

Dien Bien Phu

Meo hilltribe woman.

DIEN BIEN PHU IN A CAPSULE

Famous site of the French defeat to Viet Minh forces in May 1954...The battle marked the end to French colonial rule of northern Vietnam...Extremely remote near the Laos border...Transportation by ground is long, tedious and treacherous...Can now be reached by twice-weekly flights from Hanoi...Spectacular scenery in the Muong Thanh Valley...15 km from the Laos border.

Dien Bien Phu, the site in Northern Vietnam that marked the astounding and tactically brilliant defeat of French forces by Vietnamese patriots on May 6, 1954, has become another hot tourist destination. Not surprisingly, it has become particularly popular with French tourists.

Dien Bien Phu, about 15 km from the Laos border, is a highly inaccessible area 420 km west of Hanoi and has, up to now, been only reached after an exhausting 15- to 17-hour road trip by 4-wheel-drive. If you choose to go by 4-wheel-drive, the trip is perilous, especially along the 40-km pass known as "Where Heaven and Earth Meet," a path that reaches 1000 meters into the sky. It is the only "thoroughfare" that links Lai Chau province in northern Vietnam with the rest of the country.

It was here, across Pha Din, that the Vietnamese cut a path and painfully moved their supplies toward Dien Bien Phu in 1954.

Myth has it that a Meo king once lived in the mountain with a bevy of beautiful women, both Meo and Thai girls. His son fell in love with one of the Thai girls and the woman was mercilessly beaten and punished by the king. After fleeing into the forest to study magic, the prince was finally able to liberate the Thai girl from the clutches of his cruel father. But because there was no path in the mountains to flee, the couple decided to "fly" to heaven. The young prince carried the woman on his back up to Pha Din where they encountered cold weather and were unable to continue farther. As the story goes, they couldn't find the gate to heaven so they embraced each other and turned to stone.

But it was the battle between French and Viet Minh forces that put the location on the map. The day before the Geneva Conference on Indochina was to begin on May 7, 1954, 55,000 Viet Minh forces decisively overran the French unit stationed at Dien Bien Phu. It was a remarkable battle. General Henri Navarre, commander of the French forces in Indochina, deployed 12 battalions during the early months of 1954 to gain and hold control of the Muong Thanh Valley. The French believed the Viet Minh would use the valley as an alley into Laos, where they would seize the Lao capital of Luang Phubang. The high command thought the area to be impregnable.

The French forces were then besieged for 57 days by the Viet Minh, who overcame incredible obstacles to ferry soldiers and supplies to the area (near

200,000 porters were employed to carry the equipment) over impossibly steep mountainsides, and attacked on May 6, 1954. The French soldiers, nearly a third of whom were ethnic Vietnamese, were routed by a Viet Minh force under the leadership of Gen. Vo Nguyen Giap estimated at five or six times stronger than the French. The weaponry was carried by hand through jungles and over mountains and then camouflaged in strategically located sites overlooking the valley.

The first assault on the compound failed. But the Viet Minh then shelled the French encampment continuously for nearly two months and dug a network of trenches and tunnels that were undetected by the French and allowed the Viet Minh to harass the French units unchecked. As the situation became more perilous for the French, the French high command parachuted a half-dozen battalions into Dien Bien Phu to fortify the compound. But a combination of bad weather and the constant bombardment by Viet Minh artillery pieces made attempts at reinforcing Dien Bien Phu largely ineffective.

The French consorted with the Americans. The Americans, of course, wanted to carpet-bomb the valley. (Was it John Foster Dulles' idea to use tactical nuclear weapons in the struggle?) They didn't. On May 6, the Viet Minh attacked the French garrison in force and killed or captured all 13,000 Frenchmen and Vietnamese defending the valley, despite the loss of nearly 25,000 soldiers of their own units. But the battle was decisive and catastrophic, and it signified the beginning of the entire French Vietnam. Interestingly enough, the night before the attack, the Viet Minh played a recording of the song "Song of the Partisans," which was the theme of the French Resistance during WWII. There was a unit of French paratroopers that continued to defend the valley for another 24 hours but, they, too, were overrun.

On July 20, 1954, the French asked for peace and Vietnam was divided into the communist north and the capitalist south at the 17th parallel. Terms set up at the conference included the honorable burial of all forces from both sides killed in the battle. But when South Vietnamese President Ngo Dinh Diem urinated over dead Viet Minh soldiers in the south as a symbolic gesture, Ho Chi Minh decided to let the French lay where they died. During the course of the nine-year war between the French and the Vietnamese, as many as 1 million civilians died, about a quarter-million Viet Minh perished, and nearly 95,000 French troops died.

Today, at the site, rusted French artillery guns and tanks litter the valley. There is a museum dedicated to the battle as well as a hotel to accommodate the increasing number of tourists wishing to visit the area. Also, the headquarters of French Col. Christian de Castries has been recreated. There is a monument to the Viet Minh killed at the former French position called "Elaine."

Today, Route 6 from Hanoi to Pha Din, which passes through the village of Hoa Binh, Moc Chau and Son La, is crowded with vehicles. Highway ends at Tuan Giao. You then have to head southwest for 90 or so kilometers to reach the battlefield at Dien Bien Phu.

Of course, there are easier ways. By air. But it's on-and-off with Vietnam Airlines. The carrier inaugurated flight service to the historic battle site, spurred mostly by French tourist demand to visit the area, in 1994 after years of not serving the desolate location. But as of press time, these flights were no longer. However, they may again resume by the time you read this. You may want to check with Vietnam Airlines once you get in-country. In Hanoi contact ☎ *8250888*; in Danang ☎ *821130*, or in Saigon ☎ *829211, 8230697* or *8299910*.

Dien Bien Phu Environs

Son La

Son La is the capital of Son La Province on the Laos border. Hmong, Black Thai, Muong and White Thai hillpeople live in this heavily mountainous and forested region. Only early in the 20th century was the area annexed by Vietnam; it had been an independent "state" prior to this time, ruled primarily by the Black Thais. This area is within an extremely mountainous area and highly inaccessible. The road from Hanoi is in treacherous condition, and it worsens even still after Ha Dong and Hoa Binh as it turns north. There is a prison here built at the turn of the century, which is the town's only attraction. Other than that, it serves as not much more than a stopping off point for travelers on their way to Dien Bien Phu. Son La is about two thirds of the way between Hanoi and Dien Bien Phu. It was the site of a surprisingly successful uprising against the French by the Thai people, who took control over the town for a brief period. When the French regrouped and recaptured Son La, their revenge on the ethnic minorities of the town was savage. There is a small guesthouse here where most travelers between Hanoi and Dien Phu stay. Bring your own food and water. Buses leave for Son La from Hanoi's Kim Ma Station, near the intersection of Giang Vo and Nguyen Thai Hoc Streets.

Lao Cai

The border into China is now open, and that's the main reason travelers head to Lao Cai. Most are headed for China's city of **Kunming**, capital of Yunnan Province. The scenery around the area is magnificent. Most of the townsfolk have never seen Westerners, although this is changing rapidly. But you will be followed by hordes of villagers wherever you go.

Lao Cai is on the Chinese border, 346 km northwest of Hanoi and 40 km northeast of Sa Pa, at the termination of the rail line. This was a former Black lag capital after the Black Flags drove out the Yellow Flags. The Black Flag :ader, known in Vietnam as Luu Vinh Phuoc, was the former Taipang army :eneral who battled the Manchus. Lao Cai was the last station in Vietnam on he French-built train line to Yunnan in the early 20th century. It cost the 'rench perhaps hundreds of lives to build the train line in this rugged area. n 1979, the Chinese took control of Lao Cai.

If you decide to stay in Lao Cai, there is reportedly a hotel being built for vis- :ing foreigners, but you may end up spending the night in the house of a vil- .ger. A gift to the host would be appropriate, preferably cash. Twenty or 30 housand dong should do it. There is a hotel in Pho Lo near the railway station see Hanoi's "Directory"), but it's run down and dilapidated. You can get to 'ho Lo by train from Hanoi and, although it continues on to Lao Cai, it is .sually reserved for freight. But with the border being open, there have been eports of Westerners reaching Lao Cai by train. Even so, you can change rains at Pho Lo and reach a small village about 10 km from Lao Cai. You can et to Lao Cai by motorbike. Lao Cai is also the gateway to Sa Pa, a magnifi- ent, scenic, small town about 30 km from Lao Cai. (See the Sa Pa chapter.)

Directory

Transportation

Dien Bien Phu is 420 km west of Hanoi, 345 km from Hoa Binh and 110 km from on La.

y air:

VN, up until 1995, flew to Dien Bien Phu from Hanoi on Tuesdays and Fridays. Those flights were subsequently cancelled and DBP went unserviced by air for a year before flights were resumed. Call VN for the latest, as flights seem to be based on seasonal demand.

y bus:

This is an extremely arduous and lengthy trip although the scenery is spectacular. The road is in horrendous condition. When it rains, buses and other vehicles can get stuck in the mud for hours. Buses do leave for Dien Bien Phu from Hanoi but ter- minate in Son La. I don't recommend getting to Dien Bien Phu by bus.

y 4-wheel-drive:

This also is an arduous drive (but far more comfortable than by bus) that takes two full days, but it is a beautiful drive, especially as it nears Dien Bien Phu through hill- tribe villages in the mountains. The best way to do it is by renting a Russian jeep or Toyota Land Cruiser (which is far more comfortable) and sharing the costs with three or four other people. Count on at least 5–6 days for the round-trip journey. There are some incredibly cheap bargain tours out to Dien Bien Phu from Hanoi. I recommend getting in touch with the **Memory Cafe**, *33 Tran Hung Dao Street, Hanoi.* ☎ *(84-4) 8265854.* The reports coming back to me about these folks have thus far been stellar.

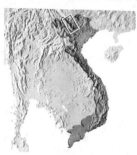

The Chay and Hong Rivers

These are areas where there was a strong colonial presence, and the French influence in the region is evident everywhere. The French called Hoang Lie Mountains the Tonkin (or Tonkinese) Alps. There are two valleys that parallel the Chay and Hong Rivers which form a topographical pass to China Yunnan and the provincial capitals of Kunming and Dali.

The area was a strategic trade route, although access was difficult, betwee Burma and Sichuan. It became a stronghold of Pon Yi refugees who fle Guizhou and now populate the upper valleys. Vietnam's Hoang Lien So Province had the highest mountains in Vietnam. Tourists in the region a few, and only recently have foreigners been allowed basically unrestricted ac cess to the region. Visits to the area will elicit intense curiosity amongst th ethnic hill people, and now that the border to China is open, the inhabitan of this area will be seeing more foreigners, although I dare say that ther won't be many, as the following villages are highly inaccessible from Hano But where there's a will, there's a way. If you haven't drawn up your ow will, you might consider doing so before visiting the far north of Vietnam.

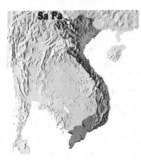

Sa Pa

SA PA IN A CAPSULE

Not easily reached; in fact, it can be treacherous...Sees few tourists but the numbers are growing...Unbelievable mountain scenery...Still retains many French cultural and architectural influences...Has been under the control of at least four countries over the centuries...Unlike other Vietnamese hill towns, different ethnicities cohabitate peacefully here.

Sa Pa is nearly 1600 meters above sea level in the northern province of Lao Cai, 30 km from the border city and provincial capital of Lao Cai. It is known for spectacular scenery (the craggy hills around the area are called the Tonkinese Alps—at least by tourists—and Vietnam's highest mountain, Phan Si Pan, stretching to more than 3100 meters, is in the area) and the amazing hill people called the Hmong. Other ethnic minorities in the region are the White Thai people.

The town has changed hands so many times over the generations, it's difficult to count. It has been under Japanese, French, Chinese and Vietnamese control at various times in its history. It was most recently rebuilt by the Vietnamese, although the French legacy survives in the form of spacious villas. The place was devastated and pillaged by the Chinese in 1979, and all that remains of the Catholic church are crumbling walls and a statue of Notre Dame De France, which has been haphazardly restored. The remaining chunks of the statue are held together by pieces of brick.

More ruins of the Chinese aggression include the remains of a fort that stands on an isolated hill overlooking the Sa Pa Valley. The countryside is broken up by rice terraces surrounded by the clay and thatch houses of ethnic Hmong. These people wear intricately embroidered collars and dark blue outfits fitted with sashes. They also don bizarre-looking black Chinese umbrellas. Many can be seen carrying wicker baskets on their backs containing produce, firewood and clothing for trade at the marketplace, which is becoming a main tourist attraction.

The French influence is still evident among the Hmong, many of whom still wear Christian crosses around their necks. The Hmong people welcome the presence of Western tourists who have increasingly become the villagers best customers of items ranging from hats, handbags, bracelets and sashes to locally produced medicines, produce and liquor—a potent, locally produced libation that'll knock you on your ass.

Unlike a number of other ethnic minorities in Vietnam, the Hmong speak Vietnamese (it's a little more bothersome trying to communicate with the White Thais).

Sa Pa is not easily reached. It's better to do it from Lao Cai by horse than any mechanized means (although horses have been replaced by Hondas in recent years). Some of the roadway is under construction, but the ride is a fitful one—the road is hideously rutted and cratered. Lao Cai itself is accessible by train from Hanoi—an 11-hour ride—and cars or motorbikes can be hired for the final leg to Sa Pa, which even at less than 30 km, can take a couple of hours.

INSIDER TIP

The Hmong are a friendly and warm people, but most will not tolerate having their pictures taken. Instead, use your camera for photos of the verdant countryside. In Sa Pa, if you find yourself surrounded by hordes of curious townsfolk and want to be alone, simply take out your camera. They'll react the way most people react to a skunk—they'll flee. You'll find yourself quite alone rather instantly.

What to See and Do in Sa Pa

Sa Pa Market

The market at Sa Pa is the principal tourist attraction. Here, all kinds of locally made handicrafts, clothes, jewelry and ornaments can be purchased at prices you'll have to bargain for. Despite the Hmong people's friendliness, they are shrewd negotiators. Chances are they'll make out better than you did. But who else on your block back in Indiana will have a genuine Hmong beaded collar?

Where to Stay and Eat in Sa Pa

Currently there are five guest houses in Sa Pa, none of which exceeds minimum accommodation standards—two of them close in the winter time, when temperatures can dip below freezing. But this is expected to change as the number of tourists to the region increases. The best bets in town these days are:

Agriculture & Forestry Guest House   US$10–$25

Western edge of town on the road to Lai Chau.

At 25 bucks, it doesn't get much more expensive in Sa Pa—and it doesn't get you much more than hot water, and only a limited amount..

Trade Union Guest House   **US$5–$7**

Center of town near the church.
This wouldn't be such a bad experience except the place doesn't have any hot water.

Bank Guest House   **US$5–$7**

Center of town.
Another cheapie. The place doubles as a bank, but don't expect to finance your stay. Hot water.

Auberge Hotel   **US$10**

☎ *84-20-871243*

The name's a little redundant, but proprietor Trung is one of the guys in Sa Pa that you'll want to get to know, especially if you want to stay at his popular "auberge" in town. His rooms are the best in Sa Pa, although there are not that many of them. He has a good reputation for finding travelers digs somewhere else in the event the Auberge is booked. He's sought out. You might want to call ahead, although it's no guarantee that you'll get a room.

Eating is at your own risk. There are no real "restaurants" in the town. There are food stalls and such next to the market on the road that leads to Phan Si Pan, but be careful of the cutlery and make sure that any water you consume is either purified or has been boiled. Put simply, Sa Pa is off the beaten track—way off it.

Sa Pa Environs

Of course, there's **Phan Si Pan**, Vietnam's highest peak. It is part of the Hoang Lien Mountains (the Tonkinese Alps), and is accessible by foot from Sa Pa. At present, few foreigners attempt to climb the peak, but the number is growing, as are the number of "guides" in both Sa Pa and Lao Cai who will offer you their services by either car or motorbike (a 4-wheel-drive is the best alternative). Also within walking or driving distance of Sa Pa are the **Thac Bac** (Silver Falls) and **Cau May** (Cloud Bridge) which spans the Muong Hoa River.

Yen Bai

Yen Bai is located about 155 km northwest of Hanoi. This is at the base of the delta. In February 1930, a Vietnamese "army" started an uprising here against the French colonial authorities based on the initiative of the Vietnamese Nationalist Party of Vietnam (Quoc Dan Dang).

Phan Si Pan

Phan Si Pan is 395 km northwest of Hanoi. This area is the site of Vietnam's tallest mountain, at 3143 meters high. The mountain is climbable, but best done in December. There are tremendously steep slopes, and the wind and rain here make the ascent a treacherous affair. For the fittest of the fit (as well as experienced climbers) an ascent of Phan Si Pan is a minimum five-day round-trip trek from Sa Pa. There has been some talk about organized treks up Phan Si Pan, but they have yet to develop. For information about a trek up Phan Si Pan, or to get advice if you're planning on going solo, contact:

Samifana Indochina

21 Phan Dinh Phung, Hanoi. ☎ *(84-4) 8281516.*

This is an adventure travel ground operator that specializes in treks, mountain bike trips and tours for Vietnam veterans. Recommended.

MAJOR ROAD ROUTES OF SOUTHERN VIETNAM

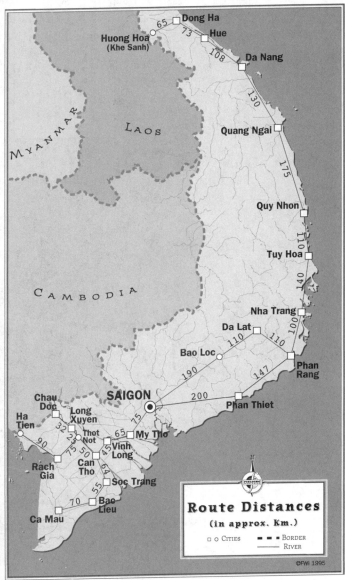

MYANMAR

LAOS

Dong Ha
65
73 Hue
108
Da Nang
130

Huong Hoa
(Khe Sanh)

Quang Ngai
175

Quy Nhon
110

Tuy Hoa
140

CAMBODIA

Nha Trang
100

Da Lat
110   110
Bao Loc
190   Phan
147   Rang

SAIGON
200   Phan Thiet
75

Chau
Doc   Long
Ha   Xuyen
Tien   32   My Tho
22 65
90   Thot
Not   Vinh
75 50 45 Long
Rach   Can
Gia   Tho   64
55   Soc Trang
70   Bac
Lieu
Ca Mau

Route Distances
(in approx. Km.)

□ ○ CITIES   ■ ■ ■ BORDER
              —— RIVER

©RWI 1995

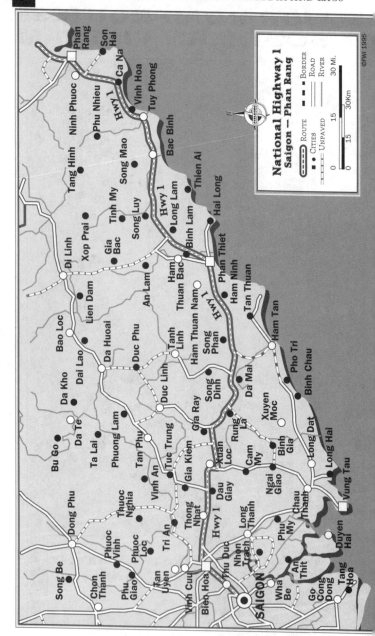

National Highway 1
Saigon — Phan Rang

©FWI 1995

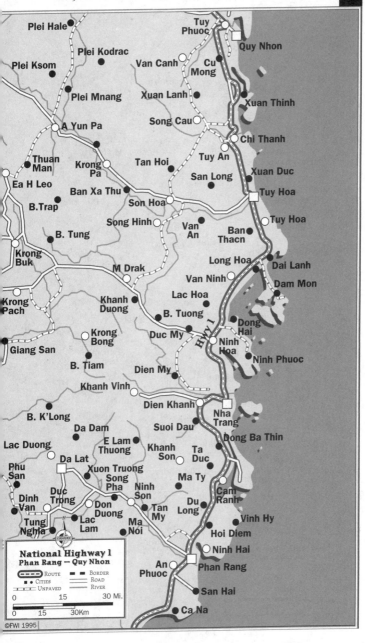

National Highway 1
Phan Rang — Quy Nhon

ROUTE
CITIES
UNPAVED
BORDER
ROAD
RIVER

0   15   30 Mi.
0   15   30Km

©FWI 1995

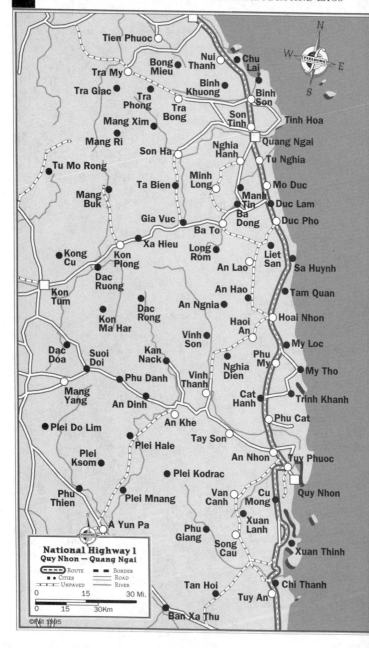

National Highway 1
Quy Nhon – Quang Ngai

⊂⊃	ROUTE
■ ■	CITIES
───	UNPAVED

■ ■	BORDER
───	ROAD
───	RIVER

0   15   30 Mi.

0   15   30 Km

©IWI 1995

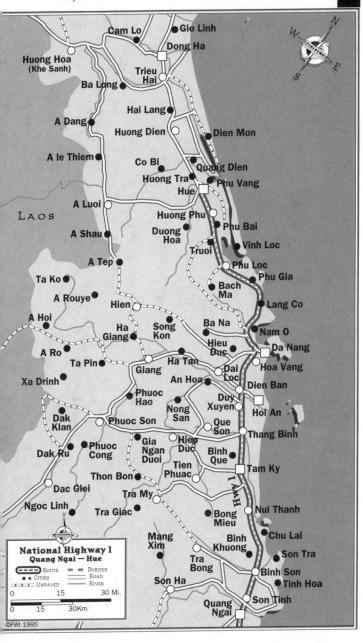

MAJOR ROAD ROUTES
OF SOUTHERN VIETNAM

Cam Lo
Gio Linh
Dong Ha
Huong Hoa
(Khe Sanh)
Trieu Hai
Ba Long
Hai Lang
A Dang
Huong Dien
Dien Mon
A le Thiem
Co Bi
Quang Dien
Huong Tra
Hue
Phu Vang
A Luoi
Huong Phu
LAOS
A Shau
Duong Hoa
Phu Bai
Vinh Loc
Truoi
A Tep
Phu Loc
Phu Gia
Ta Ko
Bach Ma
A Rouye
Hien
Lang Co
A Hoi
Ha Giang
Song Kon
Ba Na
Nam O
A Ro
Hieu Duc
Da Nang
Ta Pin
Ha Tan
Hoa Vang
Giang
Dai Loc
An Hoa
Dien Ban
Xa Drinh
Phuoc Hao
Duy Xuyen
Hoi An
Dak Klan
Nong San
Phuoc Son
Que Son
Thang Binh
Dak Ru
Phuoc Cong
Gia Ngan Duoi
Hiep Duc
Binh Que
Dac Glei
Thon Bon
Tien Phuac
Tam Ky
Ngoc Linh
Tra My
Tra Giac
Bong Mieu
Nui Thanh
Mang Xim
Binh Khuong
Chu Lai
Tra Bong
Son Tra
Son Ha
Binh Son
Tinh Hoa
Quang Ngai
Son Tinh

National Highway 1
Quang Ngai — Hue

ROUTE   BORDER
CITIES   ROAD
UNPAVED   RIVER

0   15   30 Mi.
0   15   30Km

©FWI 1995

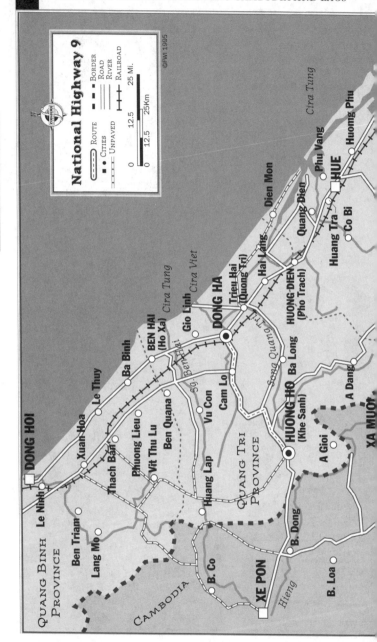

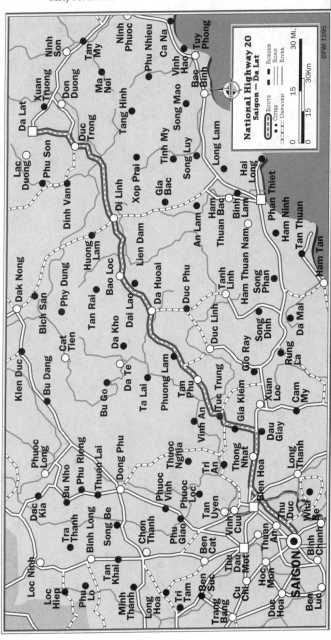

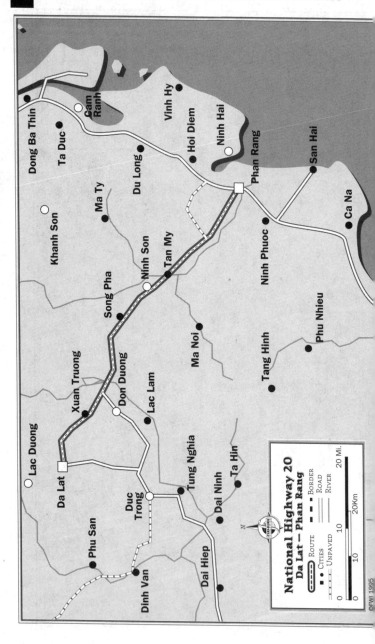

National Highway 20
Da Lat — Phan Rang

©FWI 1995

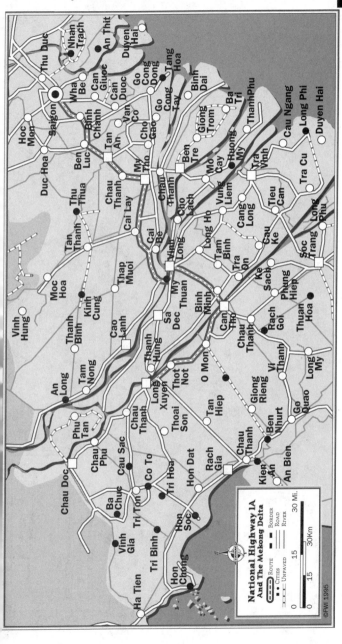

National Highway 1A
And The Mekong Delta

ROUTE — — BORDER
CITIES ═══ ROAD
▬▬ UNPAVED ═══ RIVER

0   15   30 Mi.

0   15   30Km

©RWI 1995

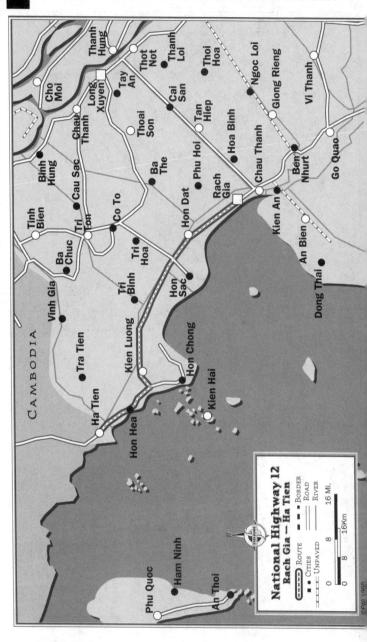

National Highway 12
Rach Gia – Ha Tien

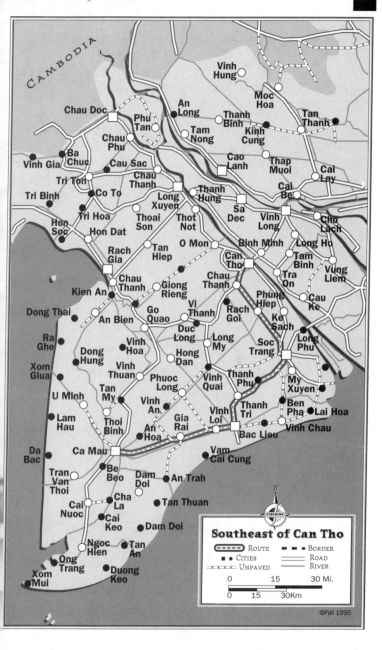

Southeast of Can Tho

⊐⊏ ROUTE ▪ ▪ BORDER
▪ ● CITIES ROAD
⊥⊥⊥⊥ UNPAVED RIVER

0   15   30 Mi.
0   15   30Km

©FWI 1995

CAMBODIA

Cambodia's spectacular Angkor Wat was constructed in the 12th century.

Perhaps no country on earth has so brutally suffered from as many forms of conflict over the past 30 years as has Cambodia. Civil wars, border wars, massive bombardment via a superpower's B-52s, a deforestation rate considered unparalleled anywhere in the world and an autogenicide unprecedented in its savagery—effectively eliminating a full seventh of the country's population—have ravaged this once proud and culturally influential empire.

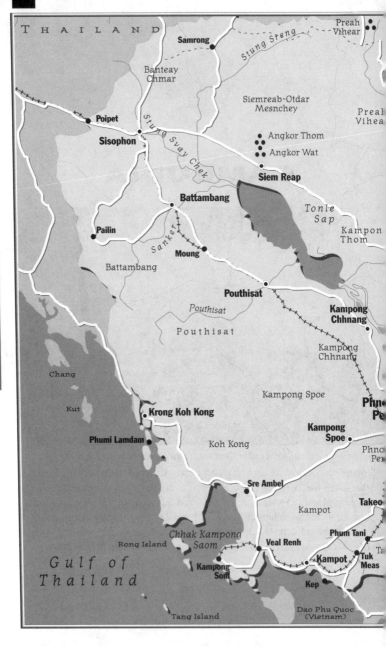

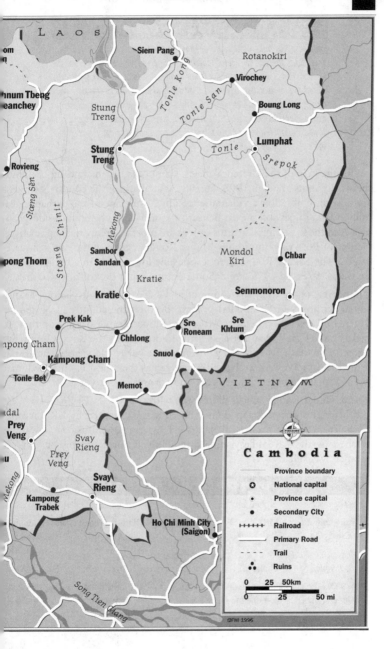

Cambodia

──────	Province boundary
✪	National capital
•	Province capital
●	Secondary City
+++++	Railroad
─────	Primary Road
- - - -	Trail
∴	Ruins

```
0    25   50km
0    25     50 mi
```

©FWI 1996

CAMBODIA

AUTHOR'S NOTE

Cambodia has undergone rapid changes in the last four years which have drastically altered the face of tourism in the country. After the fall of the Khmer Rouge in 1979, Cambodia (then known as Kampuchea) was basically closed to non-Socialist tourists. If they could get in, Western travelers were closely monitored and trundled to and from the attractions in expensive group tours. In 1991, as the UN finalized the Paris Peace Agreements and began organizing its historic peacekeeping mission, the country began to open up for independent travelers.

With the help of the United Nations, Cambodia began crawling back into the world on its knees in 1993, literally, as so many of the country's citizens are missing limbs after accidental encounters with one of the perhaps 6–10 million land mines still buried beneath the surface of the countryside's topsoil. And those not missing arms or legs are most assuredly missing relatives, victims of Pol Pot's murderous Khmer Rouge regime of the mid- and late-1970s. The Khmer Rouge were responsible for more than a million deaths between 1975 and 1979 alone. Some estimates put the toll at twice that.

However, peace didn't last long after UNTAC (United Nations Transitional Authority in Cambodia) peacekeepers left the country in November 1993. In the wake of their departure, the Khmer Rouge stepped up their attacks on the Cambodian People's Armed Forces (now the Royal Cambodian Armed Forces, or RCAF) and gained decisive battlefield victories against an army that one Western analyst characterized as the "most ill-equipped, mal-trained, undisciplined, officer-heavy and corrupt in the world."

And Khmer Rouge attacks didn't stop with the RCAF. In 1994, six Western hostages were kidnapped and subsequently executed by KR guerrillas. Their crime: being tourists. In January 1995, an American couple was ambushed by the KR while visiting a temple site north of Angkor Wat; the woman was killed.

CAMBODIA AT A GLANCE				
The place	*Square km*	*Population*	*Languages*	*Religions*
Kingdom of Cambodia	**181,035**	**10.2 million**	**Khmer, French and English**	**95% Buddhist, also Muslim and animist**
People	*Capital City*	*Pop. growth rate*	*Government*	*Head of State*
90-95% ethnic Khmers, plus ethnic Chinese and Vietnamese	**Phnom Penh (pop one million)**	**2.5%**	**Transitional democracy**	**King Norodom Sihanouk**

CAMBODIA AT A GLANCE				
Per capita income	Gross Domestic Product	GDP per head	World GDP Rank	Inflation
US$180	**US$12 billion**	**US$1266**	**141st**	**3.5%**
Annual Growth	Trading Partners	Major Products/ Industries	Country Code (Telephone)	Currency Exchange
7.5%	**Vietnam, Eastern Europe, Japan, India**	**Rice milling, fishing, wood, textiles, rubber and cement**	**855**	**US$1=2500 riel**

On April 11, 1994, a pair of British citizens and an Australian were abducted from their taxi en route to Sihanoukville along National Route 4 by the Khmer Rouge, brought into the forest, and haven't been heard from since. An American relief worker, Melissa Himes, was released on May 11 after 41 days of captivity by the Khmer Rouge. She was released in exchange for three tons of rice, 100 bags of cement, 100 aluminum roofing sheets, medicines and 1500 cans of fish to be delivered to the KR-occupied village where she was being held. At one point, a KR soldier came to her hut and told her she was going to be killed as Royal Government troops were closing in on the village. When they abandoned their efforts to take the village, the death threat against her was lifted.

Despite the UN-brokered elections in 1993, the Khmer Rouge continued to make life nasty for Cambodians and others up until the end of 1996. Until that time, in many parts of Cambodia, Khmer Rouge 82-mm mortars were felt daily—by Cambodians and the hundreds of thousands of ethnic Vietnamese who have called Cambodia home for generations. It seemed a weekly occurrence for entire villages to be wiped out overnight by Khmer Rouge guerrillas launching rocket-propelled grenades at frightened townspeople from the backs of motorbikes. In one attack, in October 1994, 46 Cambodians were slaughtered by KR marauders in Battambang. Ethnic Vietnamese villages, especially those along the banks of the Tonlé Sap River and the Great Lake of Tonlé Sap, were routinely ransacked, their inhabitants usually marched off into the woods and bludgeoned to death, as the guerrillas chose to save their bullets for the Cambodian army.

Between 1993 and 1996, even the spectacular and highly touristed ruins at Angkor were in occasional danger of attacks by Khmer Rouge guerrillas, who, despite U.N.-supervised elections in May of 1993, continued to control nearly 20 percent of Cambodia's landscape until a pivotal Khmer Rouge leader, Ieng Sary, defected to the government with thousands of KR troops in mid-1996. Shortly before the polls in the spring of 1993, armed guerrillas attacked a U.N. garrison at Siem Reap and injured a Portuguese tourist. A Japanese tourist fled the area on a motorcycle and streaked all the way to the Thai border, nearly 100 miles away. In Siem Reap province itself, not more than 30 km from the temple complex, Khmer Rouge guerrillas were busy "recruiting" soldiers and murdering ethnic Vietnamese.

But all this has changed. Cambodians and tourists alike can be relieved by the fact that the Khmer Rouge has been reduced to essentially a nonplayer these days. The defection of prominent KR leader Ieng Sary, and the subsequent amnesty granted him and his supporters by King Norodom Sihanouk, spawned thousands of other Khmer Rouge rebels to surrender their arms and join the government forces, leaving but perhaps 1000-2000 guerrillas left to do their nasty deeds using as their base Anlong Veng in the northwest of the country.

Regardless of their fall, the mark the Khmer Rouge left on the Cambodian people and the countryside is slow in being erased. In many areas across this lush countryside, bones still spring from the earth like desert cacti, still shrouded with the tattered garments their owners were clothed in on the day they were slaughtered—a testament to Pol Pot's demonic wrath of the mid- and late 1970s. At mass grave sites, human teeth can be found among the rocks and grass like pebbles in an old parking lot.

Red signs depicting skulls and crossbones are tacked to trees, sharing the bark with bullet holes, warning of land mines. Tracers raining back and forth between government forces and the Khmer Rouge in the night sky can sometimes be witnessed by the visitor to this exotic land. To the uninitiated the orange tracers streaking in a large arc across the Asian twilight appear to be a display of grand fireworks that simply aren't functioning properly, some sort of defused celebration—which is, in fact, what Cambodia is.

Cambodia's most significant offering to the world in the 1990s may not be its art, its dancing, its magnificent ancient temples nor its culture; instead, it might be the testament to the country's horrific past. Cambodia's most popular attractions, apart from its ancient *wats*, are museums and fields that depict the mass genocide of its people.

Many of Pol Pot's victims who survived the genocide today roam Phnom Penh's trash-laden boulevards like zombies out of a George Romero film. Some are hideously disfigured; nearly all are penniless, and they follow Western tourists around like gulls behind a shrimper, begging for handouts.

Cambodia just can't seem to shake the shroud of violence that has covered it for more than a generation. No one seems able to shake hands and give peace a chance in this country. If the legacy of Pol Pot isn't enough, today's kinetic environment in Cambodia comes not from the Khmer Rouge but a new factionalism which the guerrilla group's demise has in part contributed to.

*A Cambodian Mine Action Center mine sweeper takes a break from clearing
the estimated 4000 land mines along National Highway 4.*

The elections of 1993 didn't select one leader for Cambodia's future—as most elections do—but two: Prince Norodom Ranariddh's FUNCINPEC party and Hun Sen's CPP, or Cambodian People's Party, the formerly communist government which had been ruling Cambodia until the 1993 UN-brokered polls. Hun Sen simply wouldn't accept the fact that he'd lost the elections to FUNCINPEC, and it was decided, in the interest of peace, to create a copremiership in Cambodia—an uneasy coalition that's providing fodder for new reasons tourists may want to avoid Cambodia.

With new elections coming in 1998, Hun Sen and Ranariddh have been duking it out behind the scenes and in public in consolidating allies in the run-up to the new polls, the first since the country's first free elections in 1993. Of course, bloodshed has been the fruit of their labors. And foreigners have been hurt and killed as each accused the other of murder, kidnapping and mayhem in their efforts to become Cambodia's next sole government. Prominent dissident Sam Rainsy and his Khmer Nation Party (KNP) have invariably been targeted as the fall guys. Four grenades thrown into a KNP rally March 30, 1997 killed at least 15 and injured more than 120 others, including foreigners. A Frenchman who witnessed the attack ended up with a couple of bullets in his head a few days later. Analysts expect stability in Cambodia will worsen in the months preceeding the 1998 elections.

The Khmer Rouge aren't the only Cambodians obsessed with the proper maintenance of their rifles. In fact, the Khmer Rouge may turn out the lesser of two evils for foreigners in Cambodia. At least, even as a formidable force, the KR guerrillas had been cornered into the remote countryside, where few foreigners have reason or means to visit. The current bloodletting is spilling in the streets of the capital. Compound the political problems with an army as divided in its loyalty as the Khmer citizenship and you face a picture which doesn't bode particularly well for tourism.

Cambodia belies itself; it's perhaps the greatest paradox on the planet in its contrast of human warmth and vile indignity. Its people are arguably the gentlest on the globe, sentenced by circumstance to an environment that's utterly raw and entirely untamed. They are struggling to enter the modern world by investing salaries that average as little as US$4 a month on English lessons along Phnom Penh's English Street.

Cambodia is still one of the last frontiers, the Wild West of East Asia, where one can hitchhike from Phnom Penh to Angkor Wat with a relatively good chance of being stopped and detained at rifle point by Maoist guerrillas or highway thugs. It's a place where you can share a ferry ride in a raging storm across the Great Lake of Tonlé Sap on a dilapidated, rusted barge with a dozen sows, cockroaches the size of plums and a few soldiers and joke about the ferry that sank over the same reef last night during a monsoon, killing 50. Or you can sneak across the border from Thailand aboard a speedboat manned by smugglers bound for Kompong Som (Sihanoukville), harboring a cache of Singaporean VCRs, then ride on a train with a reasonable expectation of getting blown up.

Is Cambodia safe?

Fly or take the speedboat to Siem Reap to visit Angkor, and you'll find the experience perfectly safe. Regrettably, though, Cambodia as a tourist destination offers only slim passages of security. Fully 75 percent of the country remains tactically inaccessible to curious foreign travelers.

Rockets and rice—the two staples for survival in the Cambodian countryside.

History of Cambodia

Funan is what much of modern-day Cambodia was called back in the first six centuries A.D. Situated along the Mekong River, the kingdom of Funan was in an ideal location to take advantage of the trade traffic between India and Java and even between India and China, although China's influence on the kingdom, because of its remoteness, was far less than that of India's. It was mainly Indian culture that formed the mores and institutions of early Funan society. It was a society that contained both Hinduism and Mahayana Buddhism in relative harmony.

Ties were established between Funan and the Khmers in the sixth century, and, by the middle of that century, the Kambujans (the term for the predecessors of the Khmers), who lived along the Mekong in what is now Laos, split off from Funan. Chenla, as the new society was called, grew quite powerful and absorbed Funan probably near the end of the sixth century. Quarrels forced the kingdom to be split into Land Chenla and Water Chenla around the eighth century. Land Chenla, in the north, prospered, but Water Chenla, in the south, was constantly plagued with internal strife and power struggles.

The Birth of Angkor

In 802, a Khmer prince named Jayavarman II declared independence from Java and began the Angkor kingdom. Declaring himself a god-king, he began to build temples in his own honor and that of the symbol of Siva around the area of the Tonlé Sap. His successor, Indravarman I, built the vast irrigation systems that permitted the Khmers to live so densely. And it was Indravarman who first started constructing the temples of Angkor.

Yasovarman, next in line, chose Angkor as the site for his new capital, and it was here, sometime in the late ninth century, that the first of the great temples of Angkor were finally built. But it wasn't until 1107, when Suryavarman II took the throne, that Angkor reached its zenith with the construction of Angkor Wat. He also constructed a road network that connected his vast kingdom, which included much of the Malay peninsula, Thailand, southern Vietnam and all of Laos.

Angkor was sacked in 1177, but Jayavarman VII rebuilt and expanded the kingdom, creating hospitals and even more roads, complete with rest houses. Construction on Angkor Thom was started in 1200 by Jayavarman VII, including the Bayon, the last and—next to Angkor Wat—the most imposing structure built at Angkor. The Bayon was supposed to have taken 21 years to complete, draining the labor force, which had kept the vast irrigation system yielding up to four crops per year. Jayavarman VII was also responsible for the shift from Hinduism to Buddhism. This is evident in the construction of the Bayon, where a third level was added to the structure to reflect increasing Buddhist influence on the Khmers. The shift toward Hinayana Buddhism was also responsible for diminishing the godlike reverence Khmers had for the leaders.

Attacks from the West

It was centuries before Angkor was finally abandoned, a process that was aggravated by increasing attacks by the Khmers' neighbors, the Siamese (modern-day Thais). When the irrigation system that the society was so dependent on could no longer be maintained and following an incursion by the Thais that resulted in the takeover of Angkor, the Khmers fled their capital and established a new base near Phnom Penh.

The next few centuries were marked by continual fighting with the Thais, which also included a request by the Cambodian King Satha for the Spaniards to intervene on the Khmers' behalf in 1594. Instead of helping the Cambodians, the arriving Spaniards and accompanying Portuguese found

at Satha had been deposed and replaced by Chung Prei, who had no real
finity for the Europeans. After a number of disputes, the Spaniards raided
e palace and eventually placed one of Satha's sons on the throne.

But Cambodia's real worries continued to rest with the Thais. Between the
7th and 19th centuries, Thailand in effect annexed huge parcels of Khmer
al estate, including the provinces of Siem Reap and Battambang. The only
ason Cambodia continued to exist was due to preoccupations Thailand
d with Burma, while Vietnam continued to battle its own problems on the
ome front.

The French Era

Foreign incursions continued for embattled Cambodia, with the French
king control over the nation in 1863 after King Norodom signed a treaty
aking Cambodia a protectorate of France. This would mark the beginning
f nearly a century of French domination over the Khmers. From the Cam-
odian point of view, this may have been seen as a blessing, as the French
ere able to keep both Thailand and Vietnam away from any designs they
ay have had on further interference with Norodom.

In 1884, Norodom signed another treaty, this time permitting France far
reater powers and essentially making Cambodia a French colony. For two
ears, Cambodians opposed to the treaty harassed and fought with the
rench, to no avail. This would amount to the only real resistance the French
ould meet from the Cambodian people until World War II.

In 1941, the French made Prince Sihanouk king of Cambodia, believing
hey had installed another loyal puppet on the throne who'd do anything the
rench asked for the price of a lavish existence.

Cambodian Independence

Instead, King Sihanouk moved in the direction of Cambodian indepen-
ence. In 1953, he declared martial law and dissolved the parliament. On
November 9, he proclaimed Cambodia an independent state. But internal
ivisions continued to hamper the solidarity among the nation's leaders. In
955, Sihanouk abdicated the throne in favor of politics. His People's So-
ialist Community party was hugely successful and, in fact, captured every
eat in parliament in elections held in 1955. His father, who had gained as-
endancy to the throne after Norodom stepped down five years earlier, died
n 1960. Sihanouk simply assumed both roles, bannered under the title of
hief of state.

Sihanouk's traits as a politician began to become evident. First, he slowly
egan drifting Cambodia toward the clutches of China and North Vietnam
n the early 1960s in the fear that Cambodia's biggest problems would come
rom the United States, Thailand and South Vietnam, even so far as cutting

ties with the United States and permitting North Vietnamese and Viet Cong to use Cambodia for bases of operation during the Vietnam War.

Then, when a conservative and peasant backlash erupted internally, Sihanouk began aligning Cambodia with U.S. efforts to dispose of the communists in Vietnam, an effort that was backed by the army. In 1969, the United States initiated the first of what would become four years of merciless B-52 bombing strikes on eastern Cambodia, thoroughly decimating vast areas of land and killing thousands of people.

In 1970, an apparently U.S.-backed coup deposed Sihanouk and made Prince Sisowath Matak and Army General Lon Nol leaders of Cambodia. Sihanouk himself fled to Beijing, where he still maintains his primary residence today. It was in Beijing where Sihanouk, acting as a leader in exile, nominally held the strings of the newly formed Khmer Rouge.

Lon Nol's troubles, in the meantime, were just beginning. The U.S. invaded Cambodia in 1970, driving North Vietnamese forces further inside Cambodia. Peasants fled en masse to Phnom Penh to escape the fighting. Civil war raged in the countryside. Cambodia's troubles were further compounded by mainly substantiated charges of deep corruption within the government. Hundreds of thousands of people died in the senseless fighting of the early 1970s.

It was this anarchy that played such a formidable role in the ascendancy of the Khmer Rouge. The Maoist guerrillas, amply supplied by the Chinese, were too formidable a force for Lon to suitably suppress, despite heavy U.S aid. The Khmer Rouge rolled into Phnom Penh on April 17, 1975. Two weeks later, Saigon fell to the communists.

On that day in April in Cambodia, everything changed. It was the start of Year Zero.

The Year Zero

Pol Pot evacuated the capital; the entire urban populace was force-marched into the countryside, where individuals were assigned to state-run collective farms. Phnom Penh became a ghost town overnight. It was Pol's objective to reinvent Cambodia, to transform the society into a single vast agrarian collective. Between 1975 and the end of 1978, these efforts had reduced to rubble cities and towns and ancient pagodas. But even more ghastly, more than a million Cambodians had lost their lives at the hands of the Khmer Rouge. Many hundreds of thousands were tortured and executed. Others simply collapsed and died in the fields from exhaustion and malnourishment. All travel was prohibited—currency abolished. Citizens were executed for merely having the ability to speak a foreign language.

The savagery continued for nearly four years. Although Sihanouk returned to Cambodia in 1975 as chief of state, he was kept in Phnom Penh under house arrest until 1978—the year Vietnam invaded Cambodia.

Up to 10 million land mines remain beneath Cambodian soil.

The Vietnamese ousted Pol in just two weeks and took control of the capital on January 7, 1979—installing Hun Sen and Heng Samrin as leaders. The Khmer Rouge fled into the jungles of western Cambodia, to areas near and beyond the Thai border, leaving behind hectares of burning rice fields in their wake. The ensuing famine forced hundreds of thousands of Cambodians to take refuge in camps across the border in Thailand, camps they have only recently returned from.

Meanwhile, Sihanouk, with China's backing, formed a loose opposition coalition dominated by the Khmer Rouge. Although Pol Pot reportedly handed down the reins of his leadership in 1985, he still remains the group's leader, basing his operations over the border in Thailand's Trat Province. Reportedly, he also spends time at the Khmer Rouge's last stronghold in Cambodia, the northwestern town of Anlong Veng.

From 1980 through 1989, government forces engaged in frequent and fierce battles with Khmer Rouge units, which, operating out of their base in Pailin, continued to terrorize the Cambodian countryside, using civilians as human shields and planting millions of land mines across the country. And not to discriminate, Hun Sen's troops were equally guilty of turning the countryside into one big jar of nitroglycerine, by double- and even triple-booby-trapping their own mines.

Although China ceased its quasi-official support of the guerrillas, the Khmer Rouge continued to finance themselves through hardwood logging and gem concessions to Thai businessmen, concessions that have netted the Khmer Rouge more than US$100 million to date. The resultant damage to the environment has been catastrophic; only about 7 million of the country's 16 million hectares of tropical forests remain today. The Thai military, which controls all the checkpoints along the 500-mile border, had—and still has, many charge—a finger in the Khmer Rouge pie. Thailand's historical tacit support of the guerrillas has stemmed mainly from its traditional hatred of the Vietnamese.

The Paris Peace Agreement

Finally, in Paris in October of 1991, after years of intractable negotiations, an agreement was reached to end the civil war in Cambodia, an accord that also called for free elections to be held in May 1993.

More than 22,000 troops and civilian officials descended upon Cambodia, from Japanese policemen and Australian land mine disposal experts, to crack Indonesian and Malaysian combat units. More than US$2.6 billion was spent. Phnom Penh, as it was transformed so suddenly in 1975, was reborn again. But this time with discos and video stores and hamburger joints and international soldiers with US$150-a-day allowances, an amount inconceivable to the vast majority of Cambodians—in a year much less a day.

But, despite the massive presence, the fighting continued. At first, it was still contained between the Khmer Rouge and CPAF troops. But by the beginning of 1993, UNTAC soldiers themselves had become the targets of Khmer Rouge ordnance, including the first Japanese to have been killed on a foreign military mission since World War II. A Bulgarian peacekeeping unit was gunned down by Khmer Rouge guerrillas whom they had invited to lunch. UNTAC helicopters were being shot out of the sky regularly, their passengers being "detained" by Khmer Rouge units. Pol Pot's soldiers attacked Siem Reap, near the site of Angkor Wat. The Khmer Rouge refused to disarm, as the Paris accord required them to do, or to participate in the political process at all.

It seemed that the peace process was doomed, that the elections wouldn't be held at all. The *Los Angeles Times* reported that the "celebratory clinking of champagne glasses in Paris is being mocked by events on the ground."

But, surprisingly, the Khmer Rouge did not follow through on their threats to disrupt the elections, perhaps because of UNTAC's overestimation of their numbers and military capabilities. Polling stations remained relatively violence-free as nearly 90 percent of the Cambodians registered to vote by UNTAC registration teams cast their ballots. The big winner was Norodom Ranariddh, Sihanouk's son and leader of the FUNCINPEC

(Cambodian National Front for an Independent, Neutral, Peaceful and Co-operative Cambodia) party. He overcame what at first were heavy odds in favor of incumbent Cambodian Premier Hun Sen to win the May elections. Hun Sen seemed a shoo-in for many months, but Cambodians became disillusioned as more reports surfaced implicating the government in political violence.

This temple outside Phnom Penh was rocketed and sprayed with machine gun fire during the Khmer Rouge's 1975 orgy of violence.

But the margin of victory was narrow enough (and Hun Sen's threat of a new civil war real enough should he be denied power) that Sihanouk, still considered by most Cambodians as the nation's leader and battling health problems, flew to Phnom Penh from Beijing, where he announced that a coalition between FUNCEINPEC and Hun Sen would rule Cambodia.

In October 1993 the United States, satisfied that the U.N. had accomplished its objective in Cambodia, formally recognized the new Phnom Penh government and established full diplomatic relations.

In January of 1992, Cambodia cautiously opened its doors to tourists. In April 1994, the door was slammed shut—not by the government, but by prospective visitors themselves.

After UNTAC's departure in November 1993, the Khmer Rouge stepped up their attacks on both government troops and foreign tourists alike. In 1994, six Western tourists were abducted and subsequently executed by the Khmer Rouge. A number of unsuccessful peace talks were held between the Khmer Rouge, leaders of the elected Cambodian government and an ailing King Sihanouk in Pyongyang, North Korea.

Because of the Khmer Rouge's continued refusal to disarm under the banner of national reconciliation, the group was outlawed in early 1994. Fierce fighting continued between government troops and Khmer Rouge units in western, northwestern, northern and southern Cambodia. American military advisors were committed to the Phnom Penh government by President Bill Clinton. Although supposedly confined to Phnom Penh, there were reported sightings of U.S. Special Forces soldiers on the front lines.

Tourism dropped as much as 90 percent between 1992 and 1994, according to some officials. There had been 50 flights a week to Phnom Penh from Bangkok in 1992. The number dropped to about 14.

On July 2, 1994, a coup attempt was led by the former regime's Interior Ministry Chief Sin Song and Prince Norodom Chakrapong, King Norodom Sihanouk's son.

Nineteen armored personnel carriers (APCs) with approximately 200 soldiers moved from the eastern Cambodian province of Prey Veng toward Phnom Penh. The vehicles were stopped by government troops 20 km from the capital. There was no fighting, and the soldiers in the vehicles were set free and not charged.

The coup attempt also involved 14 Thai nationals, who were later repatriated after being given suspended sentences. With the aid of his father, Prince Chakrapong fled Cambodia and went into exile in France. Sin Song suspiciously "escaped" from military detention in September 1994, illegally entered Thailand and was subsequently arrested by Thai immigration police in Bangkok and placed in jail, where he remained at press time. France and the United States were among several countries that turned down his request for political asylum. Thai-Cambodian relations were seriously compromised by the Thais' involvement in the abortive coup attempt.

There were questions about the possible involvement of Cambodian Second Prime Minister Hun Sen in the coup attempt. According to statements to his lawyer by senior Cambodian interior ministry official Sin Sen (who received an 18-year sentence for his role in the coup attempt), Hun Sen ordered the APCs to be moved from Prey Veng to the southern province of Kampot to secure the area against the Khmer Rouge. These allegations were also supported by another convicted coup conspirator, Cambodian defense department police chief Tea Choy. However, these claims were not admissible in court.

In October 1994, the government performed a major housecleaning of its cabinet, including the firing of popular Finance Minister Sam Rainsy, a brilliant, French-educated free market reformer, outspoken government critic and ardent anticorruptionist who became a darling of Western diplomats. Rainsy was subsequently stripped of his MP position in parliament and expelled from FUNCINPEC in May 1995. On November 9, 1995, Rainsy launched a new political party in Cambodia called the Khmer Nation Party (KNP). The party was immediately declared illegal by the government, although no direct action was taken immediately to dismantle it or throw its leaders in jail.

Shortly afterwards, on November 18, 1995, Prince Norodom Sirivudh—King Norodom Sihanouk's half-brother, secretary-general of the FUNCINPEC party and a close ally of Rainsy's—was placed under house arrest and full arrest a few days later for the dubious allegation of plotting to assassinate Hun Sen. The move against Sirivudh was seen by many observers as further evidence of the government's intolerance of any form of opposition.

By the end of 1995, the government was routinely using legal (and illegal) processes to harass politicians, close newspapers and arrest their owners. In August 1995, American publisher of the *Phnom Penh Post*, Michael Hayes, was charged with disinformation, incitement, and creating insecurity and instability over an article that appeared in the paper in March detailing security jitters in Cambodia while copremiers Hun Sen and Prince Norodom Ranariddh were both out of the country. At press time, Hayes was faced with imminent conviction and a possible prison sentence, fine and/or deportation.

In August 1995, Thun Bunly, editor of the Khmer-language *Khmer Ideal*, was sentenced to two years in prison or a 10-million riel fine under Articles 62 and 63 of the UNTAC criminal code for accusing the government of being a dictatorship. The judge also ordered the newspaper closed.

In the run-up to the 1988 elections, tensions between the CPP and FUNCINPEC worsened, with both Hun Sen and Ranariddh hurling insults and assassination accusations at each other. The situation was exasperated by the defections of thousands of Khmer Rouge guerrillas to the government, led by prominent KR strongman (and former Pol Pot-era henchman) Ieng Sary, in late 1996, as the two political parties maneuvered both for the credit of the defections and for the rank-and-file KR defectors themselves. Most lined up with Hun Sen's CPP.

Meanwhile, FUNCINPEC took Sam Rainsy's KNP under its wing as it sought to build a coalition of opposition groups that could unite to oust the CPP from power in the 1998 elections. The army remained divided in its loyalty to the two leaders, and by the start of 1997, it could be successfully argued that Cambodia had two different armies, the largest belonging to the CPP. Armed clashes within the army became frequent.

Sam Rainsy, in the meantime, continued to bring his message of anticorruption to the street; some of his followers paid dearfully for it. On March 30, 1997, Easter Sunday, four grenades were thrown into a demonstration being led by Rainsy in Phnom Penh. At least 15 people were killed and 120 more injured, including an American political consultant. Rainsy quickly blamed Hun Sen directly for the attack, in which Rainsy himself narrowly escaped injury. Hun Sen called for Rainsy's arrest. Both Hun Sen and Ranariddh agreed to an investigation of the incident by the Ministry of Interior, although Ranariddh called for an independent inquiry, saying a Ministry of Interior effort could not be trusted.

In April 1997, Norodom Sirivudh attempted to return to Cambodia from exile in France. Hun Sen threatened a blood bath should the prince return to Phnom Penh. Sirivudh attempted to board a Dragon Airways flight from Hong Kong to Phnom Penh, but the airline refused him a boarding pass, fearing the plane would be blown out of the sky should it attempt to land at Pochentong Airport with Sirivudh aboard. Sirivudh returned to Paris and then left for abroad again to muster opposition to the CPP from Cambodians living abroad.

At press time in mid-1997, the coalition government in Cambodia was deteriorating rapidly. Ranariddh expressed his concern—reflecting the view of many diplomats, jounalists and NGO executives in Phnom Penh—that the 1998 elections could not be staged without the help of the UN.

Khmer craftsman strikes a familiar pose.

Cambodia's Land, People and Culture

Ninety percent of Cambodians are ethnic Khmers; the balance are ethnic Chinese and ethnic Vietnamese. Art in Cambodia is largely a monument to the country's glorious past, rather than a progressive attempt to break new ground. This is most typified by the reemergence of the nearly extinct art form of classical Cambodian dance—which was banned and virtually ruined by Pol Pot. Today, dancers who fled the Khmer Rouge to places such as California, Minnesota and Virginia are returning to Phnom Penh and inspiring a new generation of dancers.

Cambodian Classical Dance

Perhaps the one element of ancient Khmer culture the Khmer Rouge were not able to destroy (though they did their best trying) was Cambodian classical dance. Classical dance has been associated with the Royal Court of Cambodia for more than a thousand years. In a mere four, the KR virtually made the art form extinct in its effort to purge all elements associated with the old ways. Dancers and instructors—not to mention the musicians and costume-makers—were executed or maimed, to prevent them from ever practicing their millenium-old craft again. A few fortunate artists made their way to the Thai refugee camps, where they inspired a new generation of dancers. Others found their way to the United States and kept the art form alive there.

Dancers don colorful, intricate costumes and perform highly disciplined movements (kbach) that take years to refine and perfect. Dancers often start their serious training as young as five years old and emerge from all walks of Cambodian life. The poor, the rich and royalty have all produced dancers of the Royal Cambodian Ballet. The ballet was originally only performed for the king of Cambodia, and the only time the dancers ventured away from the Royal Palace (where they's trained since childhood) was when the king himself did.

The dancers were and are seen by the Khmer people as a link to (or a present-day personification of) the ancient apsaras, whose figures are principle images of Angkorian-era architecture.

The repertoire of Khmer dance—many of today's religious dances date from the 12th century—includes myths and epics (such as the Reamker, which is the Cambodian translation of the Hindu Ramayana, the story of Rama and Sita), romances and dramas surrounding Buddha's life.

Cambodian Classical Dance

The Reamker has "evolved" through the centuries, taking on a particularly Khmer flavor. The basic story, composed at least 2000 years ago, involves the story of Prince Rama, an incarnation of the God Vishnu. Rama has been preordained as a great hero before birth but is nonetheless given a test by the gods. However, Rama leaves the throne and is banished along with his brother Lasma and beauitful wife, Sita, to a life of wandering in the forest. Sita gets herself abducted by the bad guys, led by King Ravana. Rama enlists the help of the King of the Monkeys, Hanuman–and together with the God of the Wind's son, justice prevails.

With its 48,000 lines, this epic has had a two-millenium run and, fortunately today, is still playing at a theater near you.

Like their Buddhist neighbors in surrounding countries, Cambodians are very gentle, unassuming people. Never display anger when dealing with them. Respect their religious customs by taking off your shoes before entering a pagoda or a home. Never sit in the lotus, or cross-legged, position while facing a Buddha. Instead, sit with your feet facing behind you. Never point your feet at someone, and don't pat people on the top of the head; it's an insult. And no shorts in religious temples. Women should cover up as much as possible. Cambodia isn't Cancun. Elders are addressed as *ta*, and elder ladies as *yeay*.

OF PONYTAILS AND PROSTITUTES

Compared with Thailand, Vietnam, and other countries in the region, Cambodia is still an "old-fashioned," conservative country which clings to its traditions. Politeness and deference to elders and authority figures is very important. The Khmers are very sensitive to what they may perceive as being "looked down upon." Getting angry and shouting is counterproductive and will "mark" you for exceptionally bad service or treatment in the future.

Women should not be touched in public, the exception being prostitutes in bars; however, be aware that the freewheeling foreigner with his rented "girlfriend" on the back of his motorcycle has done much to sully the reputation of Western men in Cambodia. Be discreet.

Unlike the Thais, however, the Khmer are not as obsessed with personal "neatness." Shorts and T-shirts are generally acceptable, even when visiting temples. Long hair and dreadlocks will be stared at, but will not automatically result in suspicion and hassles. A clean-cut look and decent clothes are, of course, appreciated and will accord the wearer more "status."

Cambodia has an area of about 181,000 square kilometers (70,000 square miles), making it the smallest country in Southeast Asia if one doesn't include the city-states of Brunei and Singapore. Much of the country is forest ed with tropical vegetation dominating the mountains of the southwest and mangrove forest lining the coast. About 75% of the total land area surrounding Tonle Sap is fertile lowland.

Until the 15th century, the Khmer empire reached into eastern Thailand to the Menam River, southern Laos, the Mekong Delta region of Vietnam, the Champa kingdom in central Vietnam and parts of the Malay peninsula.

Tranquil village setting belies the reality here. A child was blown up by a land mine only hours before this photo was taken.

Today, Cambodia shares borders with Thailand, Vietnam and Laos. Although topographically the country is in some parts mountainous, Cambodia is dominated economically and physically by two bodies of water: the Mekong River and the Tonle Sap (Great Lake).

The plains of Cambodia are surrounded by the Cardamon mountain range in the west, the Dangrek mountains to the north, the Eastern Highlands in the northeast and the Elephant mountains to the southwest. The eastern border with Vietnam extends from low-lying Ha Tien, Vietnam on the Gulf of Thailand, up to the rugged and inaccessible Moi mountains.

In the north of the country, the hills that spring from the plains are called *phnom*, and have been traditionally considered holy. Early inhabitants of the area chose to settle at the base of these hills in order to be protected by the gods, who were believed to be seated atop them.

The climate is determined by two monsoon seasons. The relatively cool, dry northeastern monsoon runs from November to April and the humid, rainy southwestern monsoon lasts from May to October. Average annual temperatures vary from 21°C (70°F) to 35°C (95°F). April is the hottest month; the sun reaches its closest distance to Phnom Penh during the latter part of April, rocketing the thermometer to above 40°C (104°F) on some days. The best time to visit Cambodia is from November to April. Although hot, this is the dry season, and getting around the country is far less problematic than during the heavy rains of the southwest monsoon, which make many roads impassable and submerge entire villages.

Cambodia's Food

At its worst, Cambodian food is a good reason to change your airline ticket. At the other end of the spectrum is a cuisine which is perhaps the most exotic in Southeast Asia.

Most Cambodian meals always include local freshwater fish—not surprising considering the Tonle Sap Lake is the largest in Asia—beef, pork or an assortment of other slimy, creepy things that are added to soup and/or rice. Fish is most often eaten, likely to be grilled and wrapped in a leafy vegetable, such as spinach or lettuce. The creation is then dipped into a fermented fish paste *(prahok)* spiced up with peppers and nuts. Other fish dishes are smothered in tasty ginger and peanut sauces. Elephant fish pulled out of the Tonle Sap makes for a particularly tasty and prized dish in Cambodia.

In the countryside, the staple is a broth which consists of every conceivable organ and limb of an animal combined with vegetables such as carrots, onions, fennel, corriander, tamarind, lemongrass and galanga. Accompanying the soup will be a bowl of rice, which is usually consumed separately and un flavored.

Desserts are mostly rice and coconut based puddings and cakes similar to those found in Vietnam, Thailand and Laos—they are absolutely delicious.

Holdovers from the French era include frog legs, turtle meat and baked bread, the latter which is always served with an "American" breakfast. Most attempts at Western food in Cambodia are pretty lame, the exception being found at some of the specialty restaurants in Phnom Penh. The best burrito I've ever had was at The Mex in Phnom Penh—and I'm from Southern California.

As for beverages, Khmers typically wash down a meal with soda water with a dash of lemon. Those without much to do for the rest of the day opt for the local brew—Angkor.

Planning Ahead

Travel Restrictions and Warnings

One can visit Cambodia as part of a group or as an individual. Independent travel opportunities, which were formerly restricted to a few areas, such as Phnom Penh and Siem Reap (Angkor), have improved significantly since the 1993 UN-supervised elections and even more so since the demise of the Khmer Rouge in 1996 and 1997. Provinces and towns such as Sihanoukville, Banlung (Rattanakiri province), Battambang, Krong Koh Kong, Sen Monorom and Stung Treng are now accessible by air from Phnom Penh, and some areas even by road, such as Sihanoukville and Battambang. But it must be said that **any ground travel outside Phnom Penh is at your own risk**. Recently I saw a young child blown up by a land mine by the side of "secure" and newly paved National Highway 4. It could just have easily been me. Although the Khmer Rouge pose a threat in very little of present-day Cambodia, highway banditry is prevalent. There is also a worsening problem of factional fighting between units of the Cambodian army itself due to the strife within Cambodia's coalition government. At the time of this writing, the road to Siem Reap via Kampong Thom was considered unsecure; however, I've been getting reports of foreigners safely making it to Kampong Thom from both Phnom Penh and Siem Reap—but I have yet to hear of a successful land journey the entire distance between Phnom Penh and Siem Reap.

The situation changes daily in this country, and what is written here may no longer apply during your visit. Some officials say that travel is still restricted to Phnom Penh, Angkor, Sihanoukville, Battambang and Banlung. This is not the case. Travel in the northeast of Cambodia is considered "Khmer Rouge-free" (but don't trust this)—the "threats" coming mainly from the region's isolation from the rest of Cambodia; there just aren't a lot of people around should you need assistance.

Officially, travel in Khmer Rouge–controlled areas is restricted. You have absolutely no reason to visit Anlong Veng anyway, the KR's new base of operations, and one of the few remaining pockets of Cambodia still under the guerrillas' control.

Travel Outside Phnom Penh

Despite the huge amount of negative press Cambodia gets in the international media, travel in the country is reasonably safe and secure as long as the traveler avoids certain areas and exercises caution and common sense. As the security situation in the countryside is constantly in flux, when in doubt ask the authorities, the Ministry of Tourism, or at least the management of the Capitol guest house.

Due to the continuing low-intensity civil war between the Khmer Rouge and government forces, travel to western, northwestern, and northern provinces is not recommended. Battambang town may be visited safely, by air from Phnom Penh, but there isn't much to do or see there for the average traveler anyway.

Travel Outside Phnom Penh

Traveling anywhere along the 800-km Thai border is asking for trouble, either with the Khmer Rouge, the Thai border police, or any of the 8 million-plus land mines which are strewn along its length.

Route 4 to Kompong Som is now generally safe due to the reconstruction project, which is being protected by legitimate government troops. Check with other travelers or ask the management of the Capitol guest house for the latest situation updates.

Travel by train is definitely a no-go; *Cambodian trains are notorious for their vulnerability to Khmer Rouge and bandit attacks, even before the tragic abduction and murder of three Western backpackers in July 1994. Trains to Battambang are robbed so regularly that they run a flat car up in front of the engine to absorb explosions in case the tracks are mined. Even locals are reluctant to take the train, preferring to share taxis instead. Take heed of their example, and don't even think of doing it.*

Security along the Mekong River between Kratie and Stung Treng is said to be very shaky, with armed robberies and "checkpoints" set up in many locations. Also, the road between Kompong Thom and Siem Reap is claimed to be infested with bandits, although share taxis ply this route almost daily. Ask the locals in either town to be sure before attempting the trip.

Visas

The cheapest and easiest way to get a visa is on arrival at Phnom Penh's Pochentong Airport. Thirty-day visas on arrival for tourists cost US$20, for business US$25. Bring along a couple of passport photos (and your passport, of course), although they may only require one. Fill out the visa application completely. Most of the air carriers have finally gotten around to passing out visa application forms in-flight, so the paperwork can be done before you arrive. Previously, there was a mad rush at Pochentong's immigration room as visitors raced to speed-write their application forms before queuing on the immigration line.

Your passport and application form will then be processed down a bucket-brigade of passport stampers. The officer on the end of the line (far right) will then hold up your passport for pick-up when the formalities are completed. The whole process usually takes less than 20 minutes (a lot less if you're the first off the plane). And Pochentong can only handle one in-bound at a time presently, typically a half-full Boeing 737.

You can also apply to the **Ministry of Tourism**, Chief of Tour Service Office, *Monivong Street, Phnom Penh;* ☎ *855-23-426107* or *427130*, or FAX *855-23-42630* or *23-426140*.

You will need to send the following: full name, passport number, photocopy of the front section of your passport, date and place of birth, arrival and departure dates and itinerary. They will confirm receipt of application. Visas will then be issued on arrival Pochentong Airport. You will need two passport-sized photos. Visas are good for stays up to 30 days.

You can also try Bangkok, but usually it's a ripoff. Most travel agents there will say you've got to cough up anything from US$80 to US$120 and wait three days for your visa.

Visa extensions can be applied for, but not necessarily granted, in Phnom Penh at the **Foreign Ministry**, *240 Street and Samdech Sothearos Boulevard;* ☎ *724641, 724441, 426122.* Or try the **General Direction of Tourism**, *3 Monivong Street, Phnom Penh;* ☎ *855-23-426107* or *427130;* FAX *855-23-426364* or *23-426140.* Or try the very friendly folks over at **Phnom Penh Tourism**, *313 Samdech Sothearos Boulevard;* ☎ *723949, 725349,* or *724059;* FAX *885-23-426043.* Mr. Yo Sakhan is especially helpful. You can also arrange for visas in Vietnam. Allow three to five days for issue.

Arrival/Departure

If you do it legally, you'll pay about US$280 round-trip from Bangkok and enter by air at Pochentong Airport on a **Royal Air Cambodge** Boeing 737 jet, or on a number of other foreign carriers. **Royal Air Cambodge** flies Boeing 737s internationally and ATRs domestically. Thai Airlines also now flies into the capital, as does Silk Air from Singapore, Dragon Air from Hong Kong and Malaysia Airlines from Kuala Lumpur. You can also enter from Hanoi twice a week on Vietnam Airlines; Vientiane or Pakse twice a week; Saigon four times a week; Bombay, or even from London, on Thai.

Airport Departure Taxes

International flights: US$15

Domestic flights (excluding Siem Reap): US$4

Siem Reap: US$5

The **airport** is a smooth four-mile (7 km) ride from Phnom Penh. You can get to the city by either **taxi** or **motorbike**, whose driver will most likely attempt to convince you to hire him for a day or more as your guide. Private taxis into town shouldn't cost more than US$5 outside (US$4 if you bargain hard). The airport taxi service costs US$7 for a ride into town. There is an astronomical airport departure tax of US$15 for international flights, making the small but recently renovated airport the most expensive one to depart from in Southeast Asia. This was raised from US$10 on November 15, 1995, in a move most observers say is without justification. The tax is almost equal to the cost of a tourist visa (and word is it's going to be hiked yet again to US$20)!

Cambodia's officials do not presently allow visitors to arrive or leave by sea or land from Thailand and Laos, although it's possible (but expensive) to arrive from Saigon via the border crossing at Moc Bai by hired car. Additionally, there is now modern bus service between Saigon and Phnom Penh via Moc Bai. Buses for Saigon leave daily from the corner of 211 Street and 182 Street. At last check, the one-way trip was extraordinarily cheap—about 300 riel. The journey takes about 10–14 hours. Also doable, but risky, is a land or water crossing from Thailand near Trat. But it will be without the correct paperwork. And you'll have to get out the same way. If you are caught, Thai Army units manning the border posts have been known to detain Westerners entering Thailand illegally for up to four days. But even then, you'll still most likely get your passport stamped with a transit visa after you've been "punished."

Entering Cambodia, you are allowed 200 cigarettes and one bottle of liquor.

Money

The **riel (r)** is the currency of Cambodia. The current rate is about 2500 riels to the dollar. The arrival of UNTAC troops in Cambodia in 1992 brought with it a new perception for Cambodians of the concept of currency. With some soldiers luxuriating on US$150-a-day allowances or more, prices throughout Phnom Penh and elsewhere skyrocketed, making the already nearly worthless riel even more so. Exchange dollars into riels, but not a lot of them. Beware: Twenty dollars in riels will fill a backpack. **U.S. dollars** are heartily welcomed and have become Cambodia's real currency. But there still remains some currency control. You must declare all currency on arrival. You can use smaller U.S. bills in-country. Traveler's checks can be cashed at the **Banque du Commerce Extérieur du Cambodge** *(26 Soeung Ngoc Ming Street;* ☎ *724863)* or at the **Bangkok Bank** in Phnom Penh. Visa is accepted at both these banks but with a US$10 use charge. Advances on VISA cards can also be done at the **Cambodia Commercial Bank**, on the corner of Monivong and Pochentong Boulevards. This is probably the most convenient place in town for getting cash advances, but I've had problems there getting any more than US$100 approved off a VISA card, even though the credit limit and availability far exceeded that amount. The bank says it will issue up to US$2000. A case of "This is Cambodia."

Insider Tip: Thai Baht Makes Cents

Thai baht is accepted at a number of stores in Phnom Penh, particularly stores and shops catering to foreigners. If coming from Thailand, it might be worth your while to keep your baht rather than exchange it into U.S. dollars. The dollar is currently so strong against the baht (US$1=27 baht), you'll lose money by exchanging the Thai currency into dollars. However, stores that accept Thai baht in Cambodia give a rate of 25 baht to the dollar. As goods are priced in dollars, using baht instead makes sense.

You can exchange money at the airport. Thai baht and Vietnamese dong can be changed as readily as dollars, although the official line is that Vietnamese dong can't be changed anywhere, even in Vietnam.

There is a slight difference in the rate on the black market. Street changers can be found on sidewalks throughout Phnom Penh and in apothecaries and exchange services in Siem Reap; they offer better rates than the banks.

The exchange rate with U.S. dollars generally hovers around 2500 riel per dollar. New large-denomination riel notes have been introduced by the government to encourage support for the national currency, in 1000, 2000, 5000, 10,000, 20,000, 50,000 and 100,000 notes. The greenback is still preferred in the capital, however, and some unscrupulous restaurants and markets will charge 100–200 riel over the going rate for those paying in riel. Outside Phnom Penh the riel is more acceptable, but be forewarned that large notes in either currency can be difficult to change, especially in remote areas.

A Khmer woman of advanced age with an advanced case of goiter. It's easily cured by an iodine-rich diet.

Medical

Update all your shots and take the usual precautions for **malaria** and other tropical diseases. There are many virulent strains of malaria that are resistant to all phrophylactics. Inoculations are not required, unless you're arriving from an endemic area.

There is no truly modern hospital facility in the country. You will need to buy your own drugs (usually expired). Best to stock up in Bangkok, where many useful preparations can be had over the counter. Carry a first-aid kit and medication. **Dangerous snakes** include vipers, cobras and king cobras, hanumans and banded kraits.

Climate

November to April is the northeastern monsoon season, which brings little rain and temperatures between 25–32°C. (77–90°F.). May through October are the months of the southwestern monsoon. Typically, they're hot, humid and wet—with temperatures above 33°C. (91°F.).

Business Hours

Government offices are open 7:30 a.m.–noon and 2–6 p.m., Monday through Saturday. Banks are open from 7:30–10:30 a.m. and reopen at noon–4 p.m., Saturdays 7:30–10:30 a.m. Some close Saturday and Sunday. Many attractions keep the same hours as banks. Food stalls throughout Phnom Penh open very early in the morning and close at varying times at or after dark. A number of "portable cafes" open around noon every day on the banks of the Tonlé Sap River next to the Phnom Penh Tourism building on Samdech Sothearos Boulevard.

Electricity

It's 220V/50 cycles in Phnom Penh and 220V/50 and sometimes 110V/50 in the outlying areas. Electricity in areas other than Phnom Penh and provincial capitals is mainly provided by portable generators. In Phnom Penh itself, power outages occur daily which explains the ever-present blanket of diesel fumes spewed by portable generators. Electricity in Siem Reap is provided centrally but only available on a limited basis, usually only during the early evening hours.

Communications

Mail from Cambodia is now relatively quick and reliable, but incoming letters sometimes take two weeks to a month from Europe and the U.S. The main post office i Phnom Penh has a telegram, telex, fax and telephone service.

Cambodia has some of the highest international phone rates in the world; at more tha US$5 per minute, calling home can quickly become the most expensive chat with Mo you've ever had. Rates are 20 percent lower on weekends.

The country code for Cambodia is *855*. From the U.S., dial *011*, plus this count code, plus the area code, plus the phone number. If you do wish to call home from Car bodia, dial *1-800-881-001* first. From a private phone, simply dial *00* before the count code. Hand-held cell phones have become required equipment in Cambodia, and ma businesses and residents alike maintain only a cell phone number. The prefixes in Car bodia for cell phones are *015*, *017* and *018*. When calling a cell phone in Cambodia fro abroad, do not dial the *0*.

Faxes average US$7 per page at the post office and at many storefront business cente beware that there is usually a charge even if the fax does not transmit.

Up-to-date information for travelers can be found at the **Ministry of Tourism** (*Monivong Boulevard;* ☎ *426107, 427130).* Also the staff of the Capitol guest house erally knowledgeable, and what you cannot learn from them can be learned from the wd of foreigners in the restaurant, where it seems as if someone has always just re- ned from where you're going.

For the latest news and views about Cambodia, pick up a copy of the biweekly *Phnom ah Post*, the country's premier English-language newspaper. The city map included in ry issue is a must-have for getting around.

Local Transportation

Car rentals are expensive, as high as US$50 a day at the time of this writing. But taxis e become more commonplace, especially in the capital. The easiest way to get around n the back of a motorbike. Phnom Penh traffic is a mish-mash of trishaws (or cyclos), s, trucks, bicycles and motorbikes traversing boulevards without stop lights or traffic as while marginally adhering to Cambodia's right-side-drive hypothesis. Roads outside capital are rutted and cratered by war. It seems every citizen with at least two wheels Cambodia has a de-facto taxi license—and a **motorbike**. Along with its US$5–$10-a- guide/driver, it's the cheapest, easiest and fastest way to get around the country, al- ugh your derrière will pay dearly on longer journeys.

As of this writing, foreigners aren't permitted to travel in Cambodia by **local buses**, this may change if stability is ever achieved. The place to find out is at the bus station, t to the central market in Phnom Penh.

Most of Cambodia's roadways, although easy enough to understand, are marginally sable at best. National Route 4 from Phnom Penh to the coastal port of Sihanoukville National Route 1 to the east—the country's primary link to Vietnam—are in the best pe, namely because the government controls most of these areas.

On the airline scene, Royal Air Cambodge flies Boeing 737s to Siem Reap daily for ut US$55 one-way. As well, there are air connections with Sihanoukville, Battambang Rattanakin via Stung Treng. I suggest going to Siem Reap one way by air and taking speedboat the other. The slower ferry can be a harrowing 24-hour ride across the at Lake and down the Tonlé Sap River when the monsoons hit. It leaves twice a week n both the Psar Cha Municipal Ferry Landing in Phnom Penh and from the lake just th of Siem Reap.

The **cyclo** is the classic way of getting around in the capital. These giant tricyclelike traptions can carry whole families, animals, and almost anything portable. They are ly cheap, averaging 500 to 1000 riel for almost any destination in the city.

Private **motorcycle taxis** are everywhere in Phnom Penh; they can be found outside place where foreigners gather, and merely setting foot on the streets can cause two or ee to rush up and ask, "Moto?" They are fairly quick and cheap—short distances uld be around 800–1000 riel, longer ones 1500 or more.

Small Honda step-through motorcycles, or "**motos**," can be rented from moto-taxi ers around the Capitol guest house for about US$4–$5 per day. These sad scooters usually on their last gasp and should be thoroughly inspected for proper brakes, lights, running before any agreement is made. Any breakdowns are the renter's responsibil-

Larger, "real" **motorcycles** can be rented nearby at **Lucky Motorcycles** (#413 E0 Monivong Boulevard, ☎ 364042) or other such shops in the vicinity. Their selection usually limited to Honda Rebels, a low-slung chopper-clone. The average rate is US per day. These folks fortunately now offer dual-sport and off-road bikes, much more su ed to both Phnom Penh's and the rest of Cambodia's road conditions. These days, y can rent Honda 250cc Degrees and XR-250s. If you're traveling solo and want sor company for out-of-town excursions, check out some of the local bars where the exp hang. **Dis** (Street 178) is a good place to meet folks who like to ride.

Local Time

Local time throughout Cambodia is Greenwich Mean Time plus seven hours, the sar time as in Bangkok, Vientiane, Saigon and Hanoi.

Food

When UNTAC was in town, Western-style restaurants opened in Phnom Penh ar other cities like daffodils after an April shower, featuring cuisines from around the wor Although some shut down after the UN left, others (and more) have taken their pla **Food stalls**, truly a bargain at usually around US$1 a full meal, are located through cities and villages. In Phnom Penh, the big clusters of food stalls can be found at ar around the central market, as well as along the Tonlé Sap river near the ferry landing a the Phnom Penh Tourism building (at last check, however, the "beautification" of riverfront was eliminating many of these).

Local Water and Beverages

Do not drink tap water anywhere in Cambodia. Many physicians suggest even bru ing your teeth with bottled water only, although I both shower and brush my teeth w tap water in Phnom Penh without consequences. **Bottled water** is cheap and available erywhere. Avoid drinking the local fruity-looking "soda pop" that's sold by roadside ve dors. The liquid may come in a Fanta bottle, but, I assure you, this stuff isn't Fanta. You get sick.

There are plenty of **soft drinks**, **beers** and **liquors** both in Phnom Penh and throu out the provinces. Coke is everywhere. The most popular beer swilled in Cambodia is A gkor beer, brewed in Cambodia. Tiger, based in Singapore, is the second choice (the f among the more affluent). It has a refreshing, light taste with a 5% alcohol content. Do confuse the Mekong whisky sold in Cambodia with that of the same moniker found Bangkok. The Cambodia version tastes like lighter fluid. Thai Mekong whisky (as w numerous other pricey imported spirits and wines) can be bought at the Western-st minimarts, such as the Bayon on Monivong Street in the capital.

Shopping

Your best bargains will be the beautifully crafted **gold** and **silver jewelry** fou throughout Cambodia but, in particular, in Phnom Penh's massive, domed Central M ket *(where Charles de Gaulle Boulevard and 118 Street collide, literally)* and a couple smaller outdoor markets on the way to the airport. Most of the other stuff is an asso ment of fake Izods, Levis and Rolexes. And there are mounds and mounds of counter clothing and other products. But if you're looking for fakes, more authentic-look

Cambodian monks make the daily pilgrimage to Angkor Wat via the causeway at the temple's west gate.

Phnom Penh's Royal Palace cannot be visited when King Norodom Sihanouk is in residence.

Battle of Kurukshetra is depicted in the reliefs of Angkor Wat's West Gallery.

Angkor Thom's Bayon reflects both Hindu and Buddhist influences.

forgeries can be found on the streets of Bangkok (although there's been a recent police crackdown there) and Kuala Lumpur in Malaysia.

However, the **gold jewelry** is the real thing, and it can be had for approximately its price on the world market, despite the untold hours of toil Cambodia's artisans have invested in creating its filigree.

Information

The General Directorate of Tourism, *3 Monivong Street, Phnom Penh;* ☎ *855-23-724607* or *723607*; FAX *855-23-426164* or *23-426140.* I've found **Phnom Penh Tourism** more than helpful on frequent occasions. The simple gift of a counterfeit Izod shirt to a staffer will work wonders. Employees here will go well out of their way to help Western tourists, from providing low-cost government hotel rooms, to taxiing them around on the backs of their motorbikes to airline offices, banks, hotels, ferry landings, etc.—at no charge! *Etat du Cambodge, 313 Samdech Sothearos Boulevard;* ☎ *723949, 725349* or *24059*; FAX *855-23-26043.* They can also help with information, car rentals and trips to Angkor.

Tipping

Tipping is traditionally and generally not practiced, although it's become more evident in the past couple of years. Small gifts to Cambodians for special favors are recommended. No need to tip at food stalls; it's not expected (although appreciated nonetheless).

Safety

Phnom Penh is plagued with **petty theft**, so make sure your luggage is locked and/or transported in a canvas cover. Frequent power outages mean you should carry a flashlight when you go out at night. You should not get in the habit of wandering aimlessly at night in the city or the country.

Don't wander off the roads or paths due to **land mines** which, believe me, are everywhere. Warning signs are posted on trees in some areas, including in and around Angkor. You won't see a baseball game played in Cambodia this century. Don't pick up or go near any metallic objects. There is a lot of unexploded materiel lying around all over the country—much of it quite recent—just waiting for the slightest touch to set it off.

Lastly, refuse all offers of **drugs**. I've seen marijuana smoked openly by Americans in Cambodia, even in astonishingly close proximity to soldiers. But if you get your butt dragged in, in this part of the world, forget it. You may as well smoke your airline ticket.

For more information on safety, see the Warnings section at the beginning of "Planning Ahead."

WHEN AND WHERE NOT TO GO OUTSIDE PHNOM PENH: EXCERPTS FROM THE U.S. EMBASSY'S LATEST CAMBODIA CONSULAR INFORMATION SHEET

Areas of Instability: Southeast Cambodia has seen an upsurge in banditry and military activity. On March 31, 1994, an American employee of an international relief organization was abducted in Kampot Province, and on April 11, three non-American expatriates were abducted at a daylight roadblock on National Route 4, the main route to the coast. Lawlessness has also increased along National Route 3 in Kampot Province and on the road that links Kep to the provincial capital of Kampot. The American embassy in Phnom Penh has advised Americans in Cambodia to avoid travel to Sihanoukville and Kampot Province at this time. Several other areas in Cambodia, such as parts of Battambang Province, are also insecure. Americans traveling outside urban areas are urged by the U.S. embassy to exercise caution and restrict travel to daylight hours. [The U.S. embassy official in Phnom Penh told me that "daylight hours" end at 3 p.m.] Travel in vehicle convoys will enhance security. Crime, including armed vehicle robbery, is a serious problem in areas including the capital city of Phnom Penh. Travelers can register and obtain updated security information from the U.S. embassy.

United States Embassy

The U.S. embassy in Phnom Penh is located at *No. 20, Mongkol Iem Street (Street 228), Phnom Penh;* ☎ *855-23-426436, 426438; Cellular: 018-810-465; FAX 855-23-427637, 426437.* The United States established full diplomatic relations with Cambodia in October, 1993. The embassy remains at the site of the former U.S. mission.

Maps

After the May 1993 elections, the newly elected Cambodian government renamed virtually every major street in the capital of Phnom Penh. Maps in other guidebooks as well as those which touts and stores are trying to dump on the street will be useless. Make sure the maps you pick up are current. A tip: If there's a name on it that hints of anything Marxist (i.e., USSR Boulevard, Quai Karl Marx, Lenin Boulevard, etc.), it's an old one. (Although, for some reason, Mao Tse Tung lives!) If you're using an old map, you can substitute the following thoroughfares for the old names:

Achar Mean Boulevard
   Monivong Street
Achar Hemcheay
   Charles de Gaulle
USSR Boulevard
   Pochentong Street
Lenin Boulevard
   Saigon Boulevard
Keo Mony Boulevard
   Issarak Street

Tou Samouth
   Norodom Boulevard
Kampuchea Vietnam
   Kampuchea Krom
Quai Karl Marx
   Samdech Sothearos Boulevard
Sivutha Boulevard
   Preah Sihanouk Boulevard
Pokambor Boulevard
   Monireth Boulevard

FESTIVALS AND HOLIDAYS

Cambodians commemorate a number of days important to their past, in particular, their recent past.

January 7	National Day	*Celebrates the overthrow of Pol Pot and the Khmer Rouge by the Vietnamese in 1979.*
January (late) February (early)	Tet New Year	*Cambodia's ethnic Vietnamese and Chinese celebrate Tet, the Chinese and Vietnamese New Year.*
February 18	Vietnam Friendship Treaty Day	*Celebrates the Cambodia and Vietnam Friendship Treaty signing (1979).*
April 17	Victory Day	*Anniversary of the fall of Lon Nol's government to the Khmer Rouge in 1975.*
April	Chaul Chnam	*The celebration of the Cambodia New Year.*
April	Visak Bauchea	*Celebrates the birth of Buddha.*
May 1	May Day	
May 9	Genocide Day	*Memorial for the victims of the Khmer Rouge genocide of the 1970s.*
May	Chrat Prea Angkal	*The start of the sowing season.*
June 19		*Celebration of the founding of the Revolutionary Armed Forces of Cambodia (1951).*
June 28		*Celebration of the founding of the People's Revolutionary Party of Cambodia (1951).*
September (late)	Prachum Ben	*Offerings are made to the spirits of Cambodians' ancestors.*
October (late)	Water Festival	*Celebrates when the Tonlé Sap River, feeding the Great Lake with the waters of the swollen Mekong since July, reverses its flow back toward the Mekong.*
December 2		*Anniversary of the founding of the Front for National Reconstruction (1978).*

CAMBODIA

Phnom Penh

A new generation reaches for peace.

This is the city you'll most likely use as a base camp to begin your travels, if for no other reason than it's the only city in which you are legally allowed to begin your travels in Cambodia.

Phnom Penh has about a million inhabitants, give or take a million or so depending on who's running the government. During peace (moments of which are few and far between), the population tends to decrease, as Cambodians move back into the countryside to till the soil. But during eruptions of violence and civil war, the population of Phnom Penh swells with refugees from the countryside seeking the relative safety of the big city.

The UN objectives in Cambodia—namely conducting the country's first multiparty, freely held elections, removing all Vietnamese forces from Cambodia and supervising the repatriation of nearly 360,000 Cambodian refugees living in Thai border camps—have been achieved. With the withdrawal of UNTAC troops, however, security across the entire country became compromised, including the capital. Theft and violent crime have increased dramatically. Tourists as well as Phnom Penh residents are targets. Many "citizens" are in possession of assault rifles and will use them to settle arguments—particularly traffic disputes—as well as in the theft of motorbikes and cars—and, of course, the personal belongings of tourists.

Even so, Phnom Penh, which sits on the banks of the Tonlé Sap River where it joins the Mekong in its flow to the South China Sea, retains a great deal of its early colonial charm, despite years of war. The wrought-iron balconies and French architecture give the city the appearance of New Orleans' French Quarter after, say, a hurricane's gone through it. The streets are rutted and garbage-strewn. And they're also home to thousands of Phnom Penhois, who sleep on the crumbled sidewalks by night, cut hair or serve *kuy teav* in food stalls by day. The smell of diesel fuel is incessant, as nearly daily, the portable generators of businesses and hotels are cranked up to inject power back into the veins of a city that just can't seem to keep itself lit at night. Pedestrians, motorists and others swarm across its confusing street system like a massive colony of ants in a maze. Beggars and horribly maimed people are everywhere, frequenting primarily the haunts of the monied Westerners.

INSIDER TIP: CAMBODIA'S FINEST

Cambodia's police are not known for their discipline, helpfulness, or professionalism. Reporting stolen items is almost futile; even if the item is recovered, there is usually a police "fee" for their services. It's best to avoid them if at all possible.

With the arrival of the first U.N. troops at the end of 1991, Phnom Penh underwent a radical physical, economic and cultural transformation. Each day, the capital's skyline seemed to change, towering farther into the sky as yet another hotel was erected. Foreign investment started, and the people of Phnom Penh began tasting material advantages for the first time ever. Young men are now driving cars; the women apply makeup before mirrors in the Central Market. "Essential English" schools line Norodom Boulevard and English Street like Bangkok girlie bars.

Phnom Penh had—and perhaps still has—the potential to become the phoenix of Asia, and now's the time to see it, before either one of two things

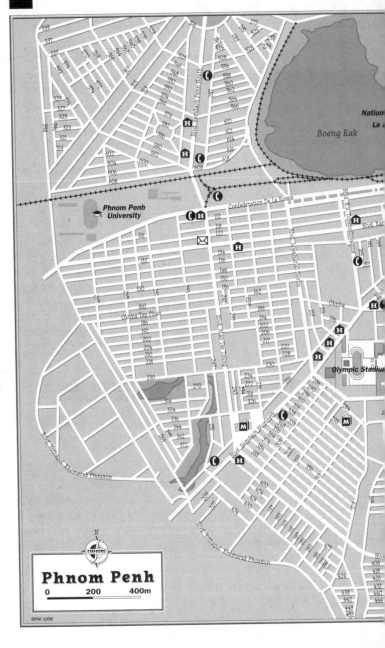

Phnom Penh

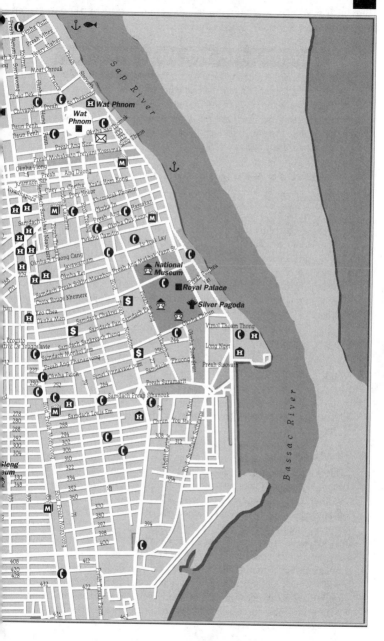

happen: It becomes a war zone, or its wings fully spread en route to becoming just another Kentucky Fried Chicken.

INSIDER TIP: THE MEAN STREETS

Traffic in Phnom Penh and along the interprovincial roads has increased tenfold in the last four years, without a corresponding increase in safety awareness or road improvements. The vast majority of drivers are untrained and ill-disciplined; bloody accidents between motos, cyclos, and larger vehicles can be seen daily in the capital. Thus, the key word is caution if one is to drive and survive in Cambodia.

What to See and Do in Phnom Penh

The Royal Palace   ★★★

Saigon Boulevard.

Built in the mid-19th century by the French, the Royal Palace was the lavish home to King Norodom and was, in effect, France's means of purchasing Cambodia. It is the official residence to Prince Sihanouk. However, the current leader and figurehead is rarely on its grounds, instead making his primary residence in Beijing, due at least in part to medical reasons. Today, sections of the sprawling complex are opened to tourists—but not the residential quarters itself—for a few hours in the morning and a few in the afternoon. When recently checked, the hours were 8 a.m. to 11 a.m. and between 2 p.m. and 5 p.m. There is approximately a US$2 charge to bring in a still camera, US$5 for a video camera.

An area to visit is the Throne Room, with its Bayon-inspired tower that reaches to nearly 200 feet. Here, foreign dignitaries were received. The Khmer Rouge destroyed much of what was displayed here. Opens at 8 a.m., closes for lunch at noon, opens in the afternoon from 2:30 to 5 p.m. Admission fee is US$2 per person, with an extra US$2 added for the use of a still camera and US$5 for a video camera.

The Silver Pagoda   ★★★

This is a beautiful pagoda, also called Wat Preah Kaeo, that truly lives up to its name. The pagoda's floor is constructed from six tons of silver blocks—more than 5000 in all. This is one of the few pagodas that wasn't entirely trashed by the marauding Khmer Rouge, who used the Wat as testament to their supposed efforts at preserving the Khmer glory of Cambodia's cultural past. In the center of the pagoda is a 17th-century Buddha, made entirely of Baccarat crystal. Additionally, another 198-lb. gold Buddha is encrusted with 9584 diamonds! Permits once issued only by the tourist office for gaining entry are no longer required, at least as of this writing. And remember to leave your shoes outside. Opens at 8 a.m., closes for lunch at noon, opens in the afternoon from 2:30 to 5 p.m. Admission fee is US$2 per person, with an extra US$2 added for the use of a still camera and US$5 for a video camera.

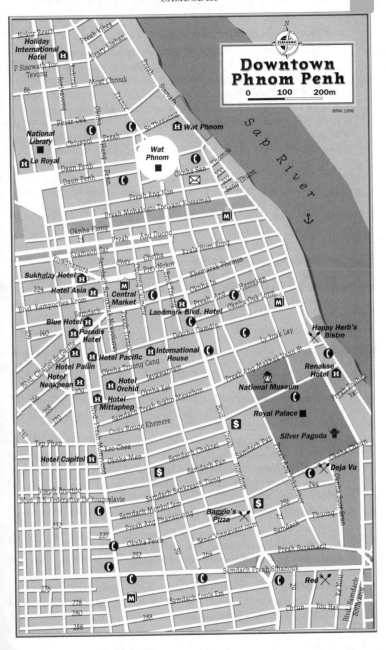

The National Museum   ★★

On 184th Street and 13th Street, across from the Royal Palace.

The National Museum was built in 1920. Colored a deep brick-red, the museum houses Cambodia's largest collection of ancient Khmer art, dating all the way back to the Funan period (first–sixth centuries). Additionally, many exhibits date from the Angkor period. More than 5000 of Cambodia's most important works of art from the pre-Angkor and Angkor eras are housed here, just north of the Royal Palace. The distinctive red building, constructed in classic Khmer style, was inaugurated in 1920 during the French colonial period. In 1994 an extensive restoration was completed, funded by the Australian government, which repaired the leaking roof and isolated the artworks from the droppings of some 20 million bats which live under the eaves. The droppings, or *guano*, are now collected and sold as an excellent fertilizer. The interior of the museum is a peaceful, palm-shaded courtyard surrounding lotus ponds. Visitors can relax in this idyllic environment and contemplate the timeless wonders of the ancient Khmer empires. This is a must-stop if your only destination in Cambodia is Phnom Penh. Although a highly worthwhile stop if you've got plans to visit Angkor, the museum is only a pale substitute for the trip west. If you're doing both, do the museum first. It'll be a letdown if you've seen the temples first. There is a shop that sells reproductions of Cambodian art from Angkor, so keep your receipt in case you get hassled by an obstinate customs officer on your return. The National Museum opens from 8:30–11:30 a.m., and in the afternoons from 2 until 5 p.m. Admission is US$2 per person. No photos or videos permitted at last check.

Tuol Sleng Museum   ★★★

Here we leave the vibrant, mystical history of the Khmers for the bloody, terrifying realities of their present. Located in a suburban neighborhood of the capital, Tuol Sleng is where the horrors of the Khmer Rouge years hit you in the face—hard. This place, the former Tuol Svay Prey High School, is nothing short of shocking. Pol Pot converted these sprawling (by Phnom Penh standards) two-story buildings into a blood-spattered, horrific campus of terror called Security Prison 21. The large classrooms were transformed into crude brick 2-by-4-foot cells which reach to the ceiling. Here, tens of thousands of innocent Cambodians were forced to live out their final days in unimaginable circumstances while preparing for their deaths in the interrogation rooms on the first floor. More than 17,000 people were incarcerated, tortured, and executed in the prison over a three-year period; less than 10 survived.

After the Khmer Rouge fled during the first days of 1979, the newly installed regime of Hun Sen did absolutely nothing to the premises to lead any subsequent visitors to the school to believe the place was anything short of the slaughterhouse it was. Inside each of these rooms of torture is a single rusted steel cot. An enlarged black-and-white photograph above each gruesomely depicts the bodies the liberating Vietnamese soldiers discovered on the cots the day they entered the compound. Blood still covers the walls and tile floors of the rooms. The walls of another room are covered with head shot photos of Pol's victims at Security Prison 21. Chillingly, some prisoners smile shyly for the executioner's lens, despite being bloodied and obviously in or near varying states of torture.

Tuol Sleng is not an attraction for the squeamish.

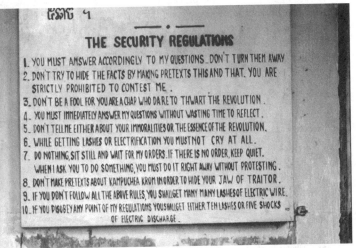

THE SECURITY REGULATIONS

1. YOU MUST ANSWER ACCORDINGLY TO MY QUESTIONS—DON'T TURN THEM AWAY
2. DON'T TRY TO HIDE THE FACTS BY MAKING PRETEXTS THIS AND THAT, YOU ARE STRICTLY PROHIBITED TO CONTEST ME.
3. DON'T BE A FOOL FOR YOU ARE A CHAP WHO DARE TO THWART THE REVOLUTION.
4. YOU MUST IMMEDIATELY ANSWER MY QUESTIONS WITHOUT WASTING TIME TO REFLECT.
5. DON'T TELL ME EITHER ABOUT YOUR IMMORALITIES OR THE ESSENCE OF THE REVOLUTION.
6. WHILE GETTING LASHES OR ELECTRIFICATION YOU MUST NOT CRY AT ALL.
7. DO NOTHING, SIT STILL AND WAIT FOR MY ORDERS. IF THERE IS NO ORDER, KEEP QUIET. WHEN I ASK YOU TO DO SOMETHING, YOU MUST DO IT RIGHT AWAY WITHOUT PROTESTING.
8. DON'T MAKE PRETEXTS ABOUT KAMPUCHEA KROM IN ORDER TO HIDE YOUR JAW OF TRAITOR.
9. IF YOU DON'T FOLLOW ALL THE ABOVE RULES, YOU SHALL GET MANY MANY LASHES OF ELECTRIC WIRE.
10. IF YOU DISOBEY ANY POINT OF MY REGULATIONS YOU SHALL GET EITHER TEN LASHES OR FIVE SHOCKS OF ELECTRIC DISCHARGE.

The rules at Phnom Penh's Khmer Rouge horror house, Security Prison 21.

Grisly paintings show the various methods of torture used by the KR cadre whose task was to extract "confessions" from the prisoners, thus justifying their imprisonment and execution. One classroom contains a bare metal bed frame and leg shackles. Dried blood still stains the floor. Entrance to Tuol Sleng is ostensibly free, but you may be requested to make a small donation.

Chrouy Changvar Bridge

Just off Monivong Street, north of the city center.

One of the dominant features of Phnom Penh's physical layout is the newly repaired Chrouy Changvar bridge that spans the Tonlé Sap river. The bridge was blown up by the Khmer Rouge in 1975. Before being rebuilt in 1993–94, it made for an eerie but compelling sight. You could walk along the bridge about a quarter of the way across before it dropped off about a hundred feet to the murky brown waters of the Tonlé Sap below. From its summit, you have a good view of the city, the dilapidated foreign-registered freighters at anchor below, the imposing Oz-like Hotel Cambodiana on the bank of the snaking Tonlé Sap looking south and the Mekong River in the distance. Food stalls used to open in the late morning along its span, some precariously close to the bridge's unfenced abyss. Today, however, the reconstructed bridge is like any other modern bridge. If there hasn't been national reconciliation yet achieved in Cambodia, at least the two sides of the Tonlé Sap River have been reconciled.

Wat Phnom

Next to the former UNTAC headquarters.

Phnom Penh

Wat Phnom, which is where the city gets its name, is situated on the small, man-made hill in Phnom Penh, next to the former UNTAC headquarters, which was also formerly the French colonial Wat Phnom Hotel. The pagoda itself, built in 1373, is reached by a long staircase on the east side of the structure. Stone stairs flanked by *naga* serpents and Angkor-style lions lead up to an old *chedi* and Preah Wihea (chapel) at the summit. A fenced-off area on the north side of the hill contains the half-finished Sakyamuni Chedi monument, construction of which has now been abandoned as unfeasable. Older *chedis* containing the remains of royalty dot the hillside. Ascending the stairs, you'll see smaller pavilions and offerings to Buddha of chickens and other fowl.

On Sundays, the area around the pagoda, a serene wooded park, can become quite crowded. I'd suggest another day to bring a camera, which I successfully used in the pagoda, without flash and without being banished from the country.

Wat Phnom Hotel

The massive Wat Phnom Hotel was a guest house for visiting heads of state before the U.N. made the compound headquarters for its military, political and transitional operations in Cambodia. The building was a beehive of military and civilian traffic while UNTAC was in town. The white Toyota Land Cruisers of the UNTAC forces filled the streets in the vicinity of the structure like a car dealership. It was difficult to enter the compound without official business—Pakistani and Bangladeshi soldiers guarded the gates with automatic rifles—but there were not a lot of foreigners in Phnom Penh who weren't there on official business. I found entry into the headquarters relatively easy. Inside, with soldiers and civilians from dozens of nations scurrying about, you really had the thrilling feeling of being part of the destiny of Cambodia. Today, the Raffles company of Singapore is transforming the building into a magnificent new hotel, the Hotel Le Royal.

Wat Lang Ka

274th Street and Norodom Boulevard.

This *wat* used to be one of the most beautiful in Phnom Penh before it was ruined by the Khmer Rouge in the mid 1970s. Today, it has been mostly rebuilt and houses some beautiful depictions of Buddha's life on its walls.

Central Market

At the intersection of Charles de Gaulle Boulevard, 118th Street and about a dozen other streets.

Some of the finest gold and silver jewelry in all of Indochina can be found here at incredibly cheap prices, which explains why it was so thickly frequented by UNTAC personnel when they were in the city in force. Almost everything conceivable can be had at this perpetually crowded market center, from Thai silk to bogus Rolexes. Food stalls abound. One dark wing, covered by a sagging cloth canopy, has so many eateries they appear to be one. The aisles couldn't be any tighter, nearly filled with the overflow of colorful garments and rattan, making passage through them an adventure in itself. The New Market (also called the Central Market; in Khmer: Psar Thmei) is the biggest in Phnom Penh. Housed in a huge Art Deco–ish structure built by the French in 1937, the market is truly vast, and, as the saying goes, if you can't find it here, you don't need it.

Tol Tom Pong Market

Also called the Russian Market (during the Communist years all the Russian advisors shopped here), this is the city's best spot for souvenir-hunting. Apsaras, Bayon heads, statues of Hindu gods, and hundreds of other trinkets are available, made of wood, stone or iron. Bargain hard. Also on sale are samples of the various currencies of Cambodia's former governments: the People's Republic, Lon Nol-era, Sihanouk's Popular Socialist Party of the '60s (the most colorful), and even some notes from the Khmer Rouge period depicting black-pajama-clad cadre manning machine guns and building dams, which were never put into circulation.

English Street

Near the corner of Norodom Boulevard and 184th Street.

Take a stroll down English Street after sunset and hear classroom after classroom filled with young Cambodians learning "Essential English." The small one-story bungalows are crammed next to each other, lit softly inside by kerosene or candles, as the choruses of children in differing stages of syntax make for a cacophony floating across the humid Phnom Penh night. It's a scene unimaginable 15 years ago.

The Former French Embassy Building

On Monivong Street.

People like to say this building was made famous by the film, *The Killing Fields*. It wasn't; rather it was made infamous by the 800 or so foreigners and 600 Cambodians who sweated out their fates within its gates, while the Khmer Rouge figured out what to do with them after the capital fell to Pol Pot's merry henchmen in April 1975. The foreigners were trucked out and the Cambodians were taken away and killed.

The Former United States Embassy Building

Near the corner of Norodom Boulevard and Samdech Sothearos Boulevard.

Although it isn't much to behold now, the former U.S. Embassy was the scene of utter chaos as the Khmer Rouge entered Phnom Penh in April 1975. On April 12, five days before the Phnom Penh government would capitulate to Pol Pot, U.S. helicopters—in a frantic rush to get Americans, their dependents and selected Cambodians to safety—dropped hundreds of Marines to secure the embassy zone while the mass evacuation took place. Hundreds of other Cambodians, seeking to be evacuated with the Americans, congregated in panic outside the embassy's gate, only to be turned away to meet their fates at the hands of Pol Pot's approaching soldiers.

Where to Stay in Phnom Penh

Phnom Penh used to be crawling with journalists, technicians and aid workers, as well as thousands of UNTAC soldiers. However, with the withdrawl of UNTAC, stepped-up Khmer Rouge activities (mainly victories against government troops and the executions of Western tourists), and a plunge in tourism, hotel prices plummeted and many projects half-completed were abandoned. Today, however, there's been a resurgence in foreig investment in the hotel sector.

Because of the rapidly changing conditions in Cambodia, prices may be different tha stated below. Keep in mind that many lodgings raise and lower their prices with the de mand. However, at press time, with a return to greater numbers of tourists coming t Cambodia, prices have become more stable.

Phnom Penh has a growing number of luxury hotels aimed mainly at package touris and businesspeople. The capital also has an abundance of mid-range ($25–55) hotel which are usually converted villas or shop houses and offer more amenities (television, a conditioning, hot water) than guest houses, at reasonable rates. Ant-trail backpacker need look no further than the Capitol Hotel. Some hotels in PP are little more tha brothels in disguise, however; only the more reputable are listed below.

Hotel Sofitel Cambodiana   US$140–$275   ★★★★

313 Sisovath Quay. ☎ 426288; FAX 426392.

This is one of the few places where you might forget you're in Cambodia. Air-con ditioned chalet-style rooms with views of the Tonlé Sap and Mekong rivers. It's th best hotel in Cambodia and is always full, though it's been a little easier to stay her since UNTAC withdrew. Run by the French hotel group, Accor. Single rooms star at US$140 per night; doubles at US$170, and suites go up to US$275. The Cam bodiana boasts French and Chinese restaurants, several bars and cafes, a swimming pool, tennis courts, business center, travel center, health center, shops, and othe amenities one would expect from a "four-star" hotel. The atmosphere, however, i rather stuffy and artificial, and totally removed from the realities of the surrounding environment.

Motel Cambodiana (Cambodiana Inn)   US$44–$48

313 Samdech Sothearos (Sisovath) Boulevard. ☎ 725059; FAX 426139.

Don't get this confused with the Hotel Cambodiana, although it's nearly as com fortable. Located along the Bassac River, it offers individual bungalows, starting at US$44 for singles and US$48 for doubles. A large disco and restaurant are located on the premises. You can also eat next door at the Hotel Cambodiana.

Inter-Continental   US$120+   ★★★★★

296 Mao Tse Toung Blvd. (just south of the city center on the road to the Killing Fields ☎ 424888; FAX: 424885; e-mail: phnompenh@interconti.com.

At press time, this place was just opening—they've already gotten it up to 15 floors, making it the tallest building in Cambodia. This will be the only real alternative to the Sofital Cambodiana when fully complete. Expect all the amenities, and expect the intro rate of US$120 to climb big-time.

Hotel Monorom   US$30

89 Monivong Street. ☎ 426149, 724799; FAX 426149.

You're back in Cambodia. Air-conditioned rooms without the style or elegance of the above two hotels. If you book your lodgings stateside, chances are you'll prob ably end up in one of these three hotels. Run by Phnom Penh Tourism.

Phnom Penh

Juliana   **US$120–$140**   ★★★

16 152nd Street. ☎ 366070.
Singles at US$120, doubles US$140. Thai restaurant, disco, excellent "legitimate" Thai massage parlor.

Allson Phnom Penh   **US$90–$115**   ★★★

128 Monivong Boulevard. ☎ 362018.
Singles at US$90, doubles US$115. Asian and Western restaurant.

Sharaton [sic]   **US$100–$110**   ★★★

47th Street, near Wat Phnom. ☎ 360393.
Singles at US$100, doubles US$110. Asian restaurant, swimming pool. The hotel also has a disco which stays open till the wee hours, and can be quite rowdy.

Landmark Boulevard Hotel   **US$50–$120**   ★★★

63 Norodom Boulevard. ☎ 428461/4, 426943; FAX: 428506.
Offers "budget" rooms at US$50, standard singles at US$60, doubles US$66, and suites from US$90 to US$120. Rooftop garden restaurant and bar, 24-hour cafe. IDD, meeting and banquet rooms.

Rama Inn 1   **US$35–$42**

17 9th Street. ☎ 362161.
Singles at US$35, doubles US$42. Both Rama Inn 1 and 2 are comfortable, tastefully appointed houses with gardens.

Rama Inn 2   **US$35–$42**

10 282nd Street. ☎ 725667.

Phnom Penh Garden   **US$60–$80**

66 Pasteur Street. ☎ 427264.
Singles at US$60, doubles US$80.

Regent Park   **US$80**

58 Sothearos Boulevard. ☎ 427131.
Across from the Cambodia-Vietnam Friendship Park and near the Royal Palace, has singles and doubles for US$80.

Diamond   **US$40–$60**

172–182 Monivong Boulevard. ☎ 426535.
Centrally located on the city's main street; singles US$40, doubles US$60. Borders on classy. Friendly staff, passable, comfortable rooms with air conditioning, private bath, hot water, TV. Restaurant. Travel services. Good value.

Asie   **US$25–$35**

73 136th Street. ☎ 427826.
Centrally located; singles US$25, doubles US$35. The Miramar, a good Asian/French restaurant, is on the ground floor.

Green Hotel   **US$25–$30**

145 Norodom Boulevard. ☎ 426055.
Good location near Independence Monument. Single are US$25, doubles US$30. A rather pricey Japanese restaurant (with sushi!) is on the ground floor; sauna, weight room and massage parlor are on the top.

Phnom Penh

La Paillote   US$20–$25

234 53rd Street. ☎ *426513.*

Central location directly across from the New Market (Psar Thmei), with singles at US$20, doubles US$25. An excellent French restaurant is on the ground floor.

Holiday International Hotel   US$50   ★★

84th Street. ☎ *427400/4, 427502; FAX: 427401.*

Expensive during civil wars and between them. New hotel; rooms with air conditioning and all that you'd expect for the price. IDD phone, 10-channel satellite TV, minibar, etc. Fitness center, three restaurants, swimming pool. This plush hotel is best known for its casino, but offers both single and double rooms for US$50.

International House   US$20

178th Street. ☎ *426246; FAX 426246.*

Not as good a bargain as the Orchide, but certainly acceptable. Air conditioning.

Lotus Guesthouse   US$5

121st Samdech Sothearos Boulevard.
Cheap and clean. Restaurant.

Orchide Hotel   US$20

262nd Monivong Street. ☎ *22659.*

Rooms with air conditioning. Restaurant. Nice, relatively new hotel that's a bargain for the Khmer Rouge–lowered room rate specials.

Paradis Hotel   Rates on Request

Monivong Street, south of Charles de Gaulle Boulevard. ☎ *22951.*

Good location. Amid the hustle and bustle of Monivong Street. Relatively new establishment. But aren't they all.

Phnom Penh Floating Hotel   US$100+

On the Tonlé Sap River downtown. ☎ *725231, 6585; FAX 26567.*

Another of the new hotels that were added to the lineup prepared to scoop in all that foreign hard cash that stopped comin' in. This place was of marginal international standards with air conditioning, a good restaurant, and swimming pool. At press time, it had been dragged from dockside and now sits grotesquely mothballed out in the middle of the Tonlé Sap River, looking strangely like a battered Carnival cruiseliner after having gone through a time warp.

Renakse   US$20

40 Sothearos Street. Off Saigon Boulevard, across from the Royal Palace. ☎ *426036, 22457; FAX 426036.*

This is a charming old French colonial hotel that had previously been an office until 1991. Inexpensive for the amenities. Fax, air conditioned, restaurant. Excellent location on the Bassac riverfront across from the Royal Palace, this is the last of the "old-fashioned" colonial-era hotels of Phnom Penh. A bit grungy and frayed at the edges, it offers both singles and doubles for US$20.

Royal (formerly Hotel Le Phnom)   Rates on Request

92nd Street and Monivong Street. ☎ *723051.*

French colonial hotel popular with journalists during the war(s). Can be booked with or without a tour. Cool place if you like 'em seedy and nostalgic.

oyal Phnom Penh Hotel US$150 ★★★

Samdech Sothearos Blvd. ☎ *360026, 360697, 360698; FAX: 360036.*
Well manicured, country club-style hotel with comfortable air-conditioned rooms.
Restaurant, business center, swimming pool.

ukhalay Hotel US$20

126th Street at Monivong Street. ☎ *426140; FAX 426140.*
Another Vietnam War–era journalists' hangout. Basic amenities, including air conditioning and a restaurant.

apitol Hotel US$5–$6

14 AEo Tep Phan Street (Road 182). ☎ *64104.*
The basic essentials. Rooms with bath. No hot water. This is the city's most popular
guest house and hangout A good place to find out the latest regional travel data,
rent motos, and meet fellow travelers. This alone is the reason to stay here. Highly
popular with the backpacker set. This place used to run as high as 20 bucks U.S.
when UNTAC was in town. Open-air cafe downstairs serves good Cambodian fare
and is a great place to meet other travelers and plot Angkor strategy. Cycle and
motorbike drivers wait on the street four or five deep, vying for work and generally
taking in the oddities called Western tourists. Good place to get a guide to "the Killing Fields." Unfortunately, the Capitol is a lousy place to stay; the surrounding area
is filthy, and the traffic noise begins at 4:30 in the morning. Don't even think of eating in the restaurant (though all of its guests do). Shoddy, closet-like singles are
US$5, doubles US$6.

umber Nine US$2–$6

Off Monivong, behind Ministry of Information. ☎ *68289.*
Located on the Boeng Kak lake, this guest house is a cluster of traditional Khmer
wooden shanties run by Mr. Sri from Malaysia. In the evenings, backpackers from
around the world gather on the lakeside pavilion to take in the cool breezes blowing
across the lake and listen to Sri's excellent tape selection. A variety of food is available and singles go for US$5–6, dorm beds US$2.

Bert's Guesthouse and Bookstore US$3–$6

79 Sisowath Boulevard. ☎ *015-916-411.*
Run by a former UN employee, Bert's has a great view of the Tonlé Sap River from
the upper patio and a good location near the post office and Wat Phnom. Hundreds
of used books are for sale on the ground floor. Singles and doubles with private
baths are US$6, and there are several "backpacker" rooms on the roof for US$3.

Lucky Inn US$10–$20

11 254th Street. ☎ *427044.*
Clean and quiet location, singles for US$10, doubles US$20. Small restaurant.

City Lotus US$10

72 172nd Street. ☎ *62409.*
Singles and doubles US$10, including breakfast.

Tai Seng US$10–$20

56 Monivong Boulevard. ☎ *427220.*

Singles US$15, doubles US$20. All rooms with private bath. Asian restaurant o
ground floor.

Indochina   **US$10**

251 Sisowath Street. ☎ *427492.*
Riverside location, singles US$10, doubles US$10.

Where to Eat In Phnom Penh

Like hotels, restaurants started to proliferate in Phnom Penh over the last few years
Most are quite inexpensive. Others, though, wouldn't look a gift horse in the mouth
when they saw it. The gift horse being, of course, those outrageous allowances UNTAC
soldiers could spend on gold, Viet hookers and French food.

Food stalls are a great way to eat well and shamefully inexpensively. Food stalls are lo
cated throughout the city, but in concentration in and around the Central Market, the
Psar Cha Municipal Ferry Landing and across Samdech Sotheros Boulevard from the
Phnom Penh Tourism building on the banks of the Tonlé Sap River.

The best food in town is invariably found at the pricier hotels, such as the **Cambodi**
ana, the **Monorom**, and the **International House**. But a number of very good trendy in
ternational "designer" eateries have opened up in the last two years, serving everything
from bulls' testicles to tacos.... Remember, though, some of the following establishment
may come and go with the simple pull of a grenade pin.

Key
$ = most dishes under US$4
$$ = US$5–8
$$$ = US$8–10+

Thai

Eid's   **$**

118 E0 Sotheros Boulevard.
Tasty Thai food prepared before your eyes by the gregarious Miss Eid (rhymes with
"eat"). She also does Western dishes, breakfasts, and scrumptious spaghetti on Sundays.

Ban Thai   **$$**

1 306th Street, off Norodom Boulevard.
Thai and Khmer food in a traditional Thai wooden house with gardens.

Boeng Thong   **$$$**

Near Boeng Kak Lake. ☎ *368030.*
Outdoor dining on the water. Pleasant atmosphere, large à la carte menu plus
nightly buffet.

Chao Praya   **$$$**

67 Norodom Boulevard. ☎ *22752.*
Indoor and patio dining with nightly buffet, featuring all-you-can-eat seafood.

Hua Nam **$$$**

   753 Monivong Boulevard. ☎ *364005.*

Thai and Chinese food in a fancy Western setting.

Western

Deja Vu **$$$**

   22 240th Street. ☎ *018-813-103.*

Light Mediterranean-style cuisine in a picturesque old villa. Full bar.

Red **$$$**

   56 E1 Sihanouk Boulevard, near the Independence Monument.

Constantly changing menu of delicious European cuisine. Posh setting, good service.

Starlight Cafe **$$$**

   In the Landmark Boulevard Hotel, 63 Norodom Boulevard. ☎ *428461–4.*

Possibly the only 24-hour restaurant in Cambodia, the Starlight has decent Western and Asian food, albeit slightly pricey. For curing the munchies at 3 a.m., however, it's a bargain.

California Restaurant 1 **$**

   55 Sihanouk Street.

Both California 1 and 2 serve hamburgers, sandwiches, and other Western dishes. Great pancakes!

California 2 **$**

   317 Sisowath Boulevard. ☎ *725645.*

Happy Herb's Bistro **$$**

   345 Sisowath Boulevard. ☎ *362349.*

Great pizza and calzones along the riverside. Also try the feta cheese salad and the prawns sautéed in whiskey sauce. Happy Herb's also delivers, a lifesaver on rainy nights.

Ettamoogah Pub **$** ★

   154B Sihanouk Boulevard.

Named after the famous Ettamoogah Pub in Australia, this storefront restaurant offers lambchops, pies and mash, and other down-home Aussie treats. The hamburgers are arguably the best in the country.

La Paillote **$$$**

   234 53rd Street. ☎ *426513.*

Delicious French and European cuisine. A longtime favorite in Phnom Penh, La Paillote looks classy but is actually quite reasonably priced considering the quality of their food. The service is also snappy.

Baggio's Pizza **$$**

   14 51st Street. ☎ *362758.*

Pizza, pasta and calzones. Killer garlic bread! Free delivery.

The Mex **$** ★

   111 Norodom Boulevard, just south of the Independence Monument. ☎ *360535.*

Phnom Penh

Mexican food in Phnom Penh??! The Mex has it: tacos, nachos, chili, and great fajita burritos, as well as submarine sandwiches and hamburgers. Outstanding value. Puts most places in East L.A. to shame. Recommended.

Wagon Wheel Steak House $$$
353 Sisowath Boulevard.
Steaks, salads, and other traditional American favorites.

Cafe No Problem $$
Next to the National Museum on 178th Street.
Memorable continental restaurant in a restored colonial mansion. This is where a number of Western expats hang out.

Khmer

Special Rice Crust Restaurant $$$ ★
506 National Route 2, Chak Angre Kraom.
Located about three kilometers past the Monivong Bridge roundabout in Chak Angre district, this large Sino-Khmer restaurant is worth the drive for its delicious Special Rice Crust *(Bai G'dang Piseh)*, which is crispy fried rice served with a spicy sauce containing shrimp, squid, pork and beef. Most other popular Chinese and Cambodian dishes are available.

Ponlok Restaurant $$$
319–323 Sisowath Boulevard. ☎ *426051.*
This gaudy Khmer-Chinese place is a mecca for the Phnom Penh cell phone set. Wide selection of dishes; the English menu alone is cause for a visit ("Boiled Stomach with Cambodian Cheese," "Foods Made of Pigeon's, Frogs and Ducks." Try the fried bread—like a Cambodian pizza.

Phnom Khieu $
138 Sihanouk Street, corner of 63rd Street.
Run by a Khmer who resided in France for many years, this little cafe is popular with the local Francophone set, but is a nice place nonetheless. The outside patio is a pleasant place to observe the chaotic intersection traffic. Wide selection of Khmer, Chinese, and a few Western dishes, at bargain prices. Try the Special Fried Shrimp.

Indian

Royal India Restaurant $
310 Monivong, corner of 240th Street.
Offers good basic Indian dishes. Exceptionally tasty are the *raita* (yogurt with cucumbers and spices) and the Kashmire-style naan.

Indian Restaurant $$
81 Monivong Boulevard, in front of the railway station.
Like the name, Indian Restaurant is simple and to the point. A must-try is the Special Vegetarian Thali (US$5), a selection of nine—count 'em, nine—different curries served in little glasses, with rice, chapatti and a crispy *papadam.*

Korean

Lucky Restaurant $$
217–213 Sisowath Boulevard. ☎ *360414.*

Featuring tasty Korean treats. Especially recommended is *Bul Gogi*, listed on the menu as "Beef from the back of the ribs," tender lean beef you cook yourself on a tabletop brazier, served with different varieties of *kim chi* (pickled vegetables).

Travelers' Food

apitol   **$**

At the Capitol Hotel.

Street level foreigners cafe. Ho-hum Cambodian fare and travelers' food (i.e., Kal Kan). The most popular in town with budget travelers. The food's pretty bad—even by Phnom Penh standards—but cheap. More a social center.

Miscelleneous

rackers   **$$$**

13 90th Street.

French and expensive.

ecko Club   **$$**

114 61st Street.

Noted for its Sunday brunch.

a Mousson   **$$$**

55 178th Street.

Superb French cuisine. Also expensive.

idori   **$$$**

145 Norodom Boulevard.

Excellent Japanese.

ereipheap   **$$**

76 Monivong Boulevard, near the Monorom Hotel.

French, Vietnamese and Cambodian cuisine.

estaurant Tonlé Sap   **$$**

Samdech Sothearos Boulevard and 106th Street.

They actually have dancing here when they're open, and not the Cambodian variety either.

Nightlife in Phnom Penh

Do I dare say it? Phnom Penh has actually become a pretty cool place to hang out hese days after dark if you can dodge the bullets of nervous soldiers guarding even more ervous government co-ministers on your way home.

When the sun goes down in Phnom Penh, government officials find somewhere to ide while the expats hit Martini's, Dis or the grungy Heart of Darkness for cheap brews-is, cheaper babes or to slam head-of-state wannabes between tokes on puissant, head-ammering ganja spliffs. Even a glistening Harley or two can be spotted as if they were orses tied to a post outside these expat watering troughs. For a more staid, colonial-type tmosphere, the Foreign Correspondents Club offers a more expensive taste of home.

As a rule of thumb—one which is broken constantly by imbibed expats—stay off the treets of Phnom Penh after 10 p.m., unless you want to see your Harley hitched up to omeone else's post. Swill at your own risk.

Phnom Penh

Bars/Discos

Martini Pub

402 Mao Tse Tung Boulevard.

Regarded by many as the city's hot spot, this place is a combination disco, restaurant and beer garden, populated by a large variety of expat men and glassy-eyed ladies of the night. The small dance floor is often packed to capacity; after working up a sweat, one can take in a movie on the big screen TV in the courtyard, or simply sit and people-watch. Decent Western and Asian food is available. Definitely a late bloomer, the Martini is best after 11 p.m. Beware the moto-parking mafia, who will damage your bike if not parked in their "designated areas."

Dis

178 Street.

This new edge-type hole-in-the-wall is run by an American longhair, and it's gaining popularity quickly, especially with the American journos. "Hip" tourists won't be far behind. Not as popular as the broodish Heart, but a lot more amiable. Owner Alex blasts the best and latest alternative rock from the States. Awesome libations. The place is small, friendly and has a pool table. Recommended for seasoned Third World bar crawlers accustomed to staggering out into war zones and gang turf at 4 in the morning—and highly at that. Starts cookin' around 11. The best place in town for milkshakes, but not the kind Dairy Queen sells.

The Heart of Darkness

26 51st Street.

A dimly lit grunge bar with black and red walls and a single pool table, the Heart is a favorite among resident expats and travelers alike. A formerly great tape selection has begun sounding like a scratched record, though. The type of joint for those who've been away from home for a long time, are looking for something to remind them of home, but forgot a long time ago what home is like. The Heart starts happening around 10 p.m.-plus.

The Foreign Correspondents' Club of Cambodia

363 Sisowath Boulevard. ☎ *015-911-383* .

Don't let the name put you off; the FCCC is open to all. A classy bar and lounge on the top floor of a colonial-era building on the riverside, the FCCC is a well-known gathering point for expats. Features include a full bar, restaurant, pool table, and business center. Movies on laser disc are screened every Tues. and Sun. evenings for US$2.

Tabou

7 84th Street.

A Francophone bar featuring light snacks, pool, and occasionally dancing.

Cathouse

4, corner of 51st and 118th streets.

A bar done up in "tropical motif" (like the entrails of a grass hut), the Cathouse has a pool table and satellite TV. Tenanted mostly by working-class Aussies.

Cinema

The Foreign Correspondents' Club of Cambodia

363 Sisowath Boulevard. ☎ *015-911-383.*

Recent-release Hollywood flicks on laser disc are screened here every Tues. and Sun. evenings for US$2.

Casinos

The Cambodian government has recently allowed several international companies to open casinos in the capital, ostensibly for the income that such businesses would generate for the national coffers, and as a draw for tourism. Cambodian nationals are supposedly forbidden to enter and play in the casinos, but it seems the pols have been turning a blind eye and indeed some of the highest rollers have been Khmer officials and the military, who, when they lose a few riel at the tables, have a propensity for kidnapping the tables' owners.

The biggest is the **Naga Resorts Floating Casino**, a converted cruise ship anchored behind the Cambodiana Hotel on the Bassac River. This ultra-glitzy operation is open from 2 p.m. to 6 a.m., and features all the usual games and diversions. The Naga is owned by Ariston International, an obscure Malaysian company with extensive business interests in Cambodia. Ariston has planned to invest some US$1.3 billion dollars in casinos and resorts in Kompong Som in the next few years, but so far little has materialized. Stay tuned.

Phnom Penh's second casino is located in the **Holiday International Hotel**, and is open 24 hours.

Directory (Area Code 23)

Note on Phone Number Changes

Phnom Penh recently went through overhauling its phone number sytem, changing the five-digit exchanges to six-digit numbers. It's been a pain in the ass for locals and visitors alike. If you need to telephone someone but only have a five-digit number, let the following serve as a basic key to make the call:

1) Five-digit numbers starting with 23 through 25, add a 7 in front.

2) Five-digit numbers starting with 26 through 28, add a 4 in front.

3) Five-digit numbers starting with a 6, add a 3 in front.

4) Cell phones: With 017 numbers, substitute 81 for 20 and 21.

For now, if you dial a five-digit number, a recorded voice will give you the correct number. I dunno how long that will last, however.

Transportation

The **cyclo** is the classic way of getting around in the capital. They are fairly cheap, averaging 500 to 1000 riel for almost any destination in the city.

Royal Air Cambodge **flies** ATR-72s four times daily to Siem Reap for about US$55 one-way. There are air connections with Sihanoukville, Battambang, Krong Koh Chong, en Monorom, Stung Treng and Rattanakiri. RAC flies to Banlung (the capital of Rattanakiri) five times a week (Monday, Wednesday, Thursday, Friday and Saturday. The Monday and Thursday flights are via Stung Treng). Flights to Krong Koh Kong leave Phnom Penh on Tuesday, Friday and Sunday. RAC flies to Battambang daily. On Tuesday and Saturday the flights are via Siem Reap. Flights to Sen Monorom leave PP on Monday and Thursday. Flights to Stung Treng leave five times a week—Mon.-Thurs. and Saturday; On Wednesday and Saturday the flights are via Banlung. I suggest going to Siem Reap one way by air and taking the speedboat the other. The slower ferry can be a harrowing 24-hour ride across the Great Lake and down the Tonlé Sap River when the monsoons hit. It leaves twice a week from both the Psar Cha Municipal Ferry Landing in Phnom Penh and from the lake just south of Siem Reap.

Airport tax is a whopping US$15 on international flights and US$4 on domestic flights (except Siem Reap, which costs US$5). Expect this to jump to US$20 and US$10 respectively in the near future. Outrageous!

Car rentals are expensive, as high as US$50 a day. But **taxis** have become more commonplace, especially in the capital. There is a new "official" taxi service which serves downtown from Pochentong Airport. The fare is US$7 and the badge-donning touts are quite persistent for your business, if not downright annoying. Skip the sanctioned taxi and head for outside arrivals where private taxis will bring you into town for US$4-5. If the driver seems like a reasonable and friendly enough chap (and his car's in good shape) it would pay to get his mobile phone number. For in town, taxis are difficult to get except outside the major hotels. There aren't any numbers to call. If you need a ride by car, simply call the guy who brought you into town from the airport and strike a deal. The going rate is about US$20 a day, or US$10 per half day—if you bargain hard. If not, expect to shell out about US$5 per hour to be ferried around town.

The easiest way to get around is on the back of a **motorbike**. Private **motorcycle taxis** are everywhere in Phnom Penh; they can be found outside any place where foreigners gather. Or you can simply stand out in the street and undoubtedly within a minute or so some industrious soul with a motorbike will stop and ask if you need a ride. Around town prices are negotiable. But on the average, every kilometer will cost about 500-1000 riel for the moto taxis—sometimes more at night.

Of course you can rent your own moto, as well. Old Honda 250cc Rebels starting arriving in Phnom Penh by the container-load a few years ago. Not too hard to spot: most still sport their California license plates—with tags which expired in 1983. They can be had for a daily rental rate of about US$7 at a few shops along Monivong Blvd., next to the Hong Kong Hotel around the corner from the Capitol Hotel. These shops in recent months have started getting more practical bikes for Cambodia: Honda 250cc Degree trail bikes, as well as some XR250s. The chopper crowd and guys who just bought their first cell-phone go for the Rebels, while those who want to have fun in the countryside (and a less ass-grinding ride within Phnom Penh) go for the dual-sports. I recommend the dual-sports for experienced riders and the Rebels for those whose last bike was Schwinn.

Insider Tip

You bust up a rental bike and you've bought it—that's if you want to see your passport back. Bend up a US400 Honda Rebel and expect to shell out what it would normally cost for a Harley Heritage Softail—after it's been tricked out for a show at Sturgis.

It isn't permitted for foreigners to travel in Cambodia by **local buses**.

Hospitals

SOS International Medical Center
> *83 Issarak Boulevard;* ☎ *015-912-765, 364127.*
> Emergency medical care, up to limited Western standards.

Calmette Hospital
> *Monivong Boulevard.* ☎ *723173.*
> This is the place those go who can afford to get sick.

Access Medical Services
> *203 63rd Street;* ☎ *015-913-358.*
> Australian nurse, vaccinations.

European Dental Clinic
> *195A Norodom Boulevard;* ☎ *62656, 018-812-055.*

Clinique Borei Keila
> *172 Tehcoslavaquie.* ☎ *360207.*

Kantha Bopha-II
> *Paediatrics Hospital, Vithei Oknha Chun.*

Maternite Somphop Panya
> *282 St. Kampuchea Krom.* ☎ *366046.*

Polyclinic and Maternity Angkor
> *75 St. Oknha Pich.* ☎ *018-811237.*

Poyclinic & Maternity Psar Chas
> *38-40 110 Street.* ☎ *426948, 360436.*

Polyclinique Aurore
> *58-60 113 Street.* ☎ *018-810339.*

Raffles Medical Center
> *Sofitel Cambodiana, 313 Sisovath Boulevard Office 3, Ground Floor.* ☎ *017-204088, 426299 (ext. 631/7).*

Tropical & Travelers Medical Clinic
> *No. 88 Street 108.* ☎ *366802.*
> Dr. Gavin Scott is the capital's senior Western private doctor, and the only native English speaker.

Psalok Polyclinic
> *80 Monireth Boulevard.* ☎ *427069, 365160.*

Post Office/Overseas Calls

Directorate of Posts and Telecommunications (DPT)

Corner of 102nd and 13th streets.

Banks

Banque Indosuez

70 Norodom Boulevard; ☎ *427233; FAX 427235.*

Tourist Offices

The General Directorate of Tourism

3 Monivong Street, Phnom Penh. ☎ *855-23-24607 or 23607; FAX 855-23-26164 or 23-26140.*

Travel Agents and Tour Operators

Diethelm Travel

8 Samdech Sothearos Boulevard. ☎ *426648; FAX 426676.*

East-West Group

84 Samdech Sothearos Boulevard. ☎ *427118, 426189; FAX 426189.*

Transpeed Travel

19 106th Street; ☎ *427633.*

Airline Offices

Dragon Air

19 106th Street; ☎ *427665.*

Royal Air Cambodge

Head Office: 24 Kramuon Sar Avenue. ☎ *428830/1, 428901/3, 428891/4; FAX (855) 17-812-757, 428806.*

Reservations Office: 206A Preah Norodom Boulevard, ☎ *428891/4, 428055, 017- 812300, 018-811143; FAX: (855-23) 427910.*

Pochentong Airport: ☎ *017-816183.*

Malaysia Airlines

Hotel Diamond, Monivong Boulevard, ☎ *426688, 426665.*

Couriers

DHL Worldwide Express

28 Monivong Boulevard. ☎ *427726, 427656; mobile: 018-810916; FAX 018-810-83*

United Parcel Service

8 134th Street. ☎ *366323; FAX 366323.*

Federal Express

(Rep company: Transpeed) 19 109 Street. ☎ *426931; FAX: 427633.*

Overseas Courier Service

Sofitel Cambodiana, 313 Sisowath Boulevard, Office No. 1B. ☎ *810227; FAX: 42635*

TNT

139 Monireth Boulevard ☎ *360602; FAX: 366604.*

Malaysia Airlines

Hotel Diamond, Monivong Boulevard, ☎ *426688, 426665.*

Western-Style Markets

Phnom Penh now has several Western-style markets which sell all manner of goodies from back home. **The Lucky Market** (*160 Sihanouk Boulevard*, open 9 a.m.–8 p.m. daily) is the largest and most popular. **Bayon Market** *(133–5 Monivong Boulevard)* and **Seven Seven Supermarket** (*13 90th Street*, behind the Royal Hotel, open 7 a.m. to 10 p.m. daily) offer similar goods.

Embassies

Australia
No. 11 Street 254.
☎ 426000/1; FAX: 426003.

Canada
No. 11 Street 254.
☎ 426001/1; FAX: 426003.

Cuba
No. 98 Street 214.
☎ 427428, 724181; FAX: 427428.

Germany
No. 76-78 Street 214.
☎ 426381, 426193; FAX: 427746.

India
777 Monivong Boulevard.
☎ 725981; FAX: 427566.

Korea, North (DPRK)
No. 39 Street 268.
☎ 912567; FAX: 426230.

Malaysia
No. 161 Street 51.
☎ 426176; FAX: 426004.

Poland
767 Monivong Boulevard.
☎ 426250, 723582; FAX: 426516.

Singapore
92 Norodom Boulevard.
☎ 360855/6; FAX: 810840.

United Kingdom
No. 27-29 Street 75.
☎ 427124; FAX: 427125.

Vietnam
436 Monivong Boulevard.
☎ 725481; FAX: 427385.

Bulgaria
No. 177/227 Norodom Boulevard.
☎ 723181; FAX: 426491.

China (People's Republic)
No. 256 Mao Tse Tung Boulevard.
☎ 427428, 724181; FAX: 426271.

France
No. 1 Monivong Boulevard.
☎ 430020; FAX: 430037.

Hungary
463 Monivong Boulevard.
☎ 722781; FAX: 426216.

Japan
75 Norodom Boulevard.
☎ 427161/4; FAX: 426162

Laos
No. 15-17 Mao Tse Tung Boulevard.
☎ 426441; FAX: 427454.

Philippines
No. 33 Street 294.
☎/FAX: 280048.

Russia (CIS)
213 Sotheros Boulevard.
☎ 722081; FAX: 426776.

Taiwan
Taipei Economic and Cultural Representative Office, 15bis, Sokun Meanbon Street.
☎ 725055, 725908; FAX: 724855.

United States of America
No. 27 Street 240.
☎ 426436; FAX: 426437.

Phnom Penh Environs

One great aspect of Phnom Penh is that if you tire of its chaotic hustle, escape is only a few kilometers outside the city. Urban streets quickly change to rural villages, fields and jungle, where friendly residents welcome foreigners.

More than 17,000 Cambodians were slaughtered at Choeung Ek.

Choeung Ek

"The Killing Fields." There are no words to quite describe the horror that awaits visitors here, about eight miles south of the capital. On approach, it's hard to imagine the human butchery that occurred in these sunny, peaceful fields in the late 1970s. More than 17,000 Cambodians—men, women and children—were killed here by the Khmer Rouge and buried in shallow mass graves.

Most killed here had been tortured at Security Prison 21 in downtown Phnom Penh first, then brought to these fields to be bludgeoned to death. **The Memorial Stupa**, a 20-foot-tall glass monolith, stands near the shallow bone craters. It houses hundreds, perhaps thousands, of human skulls that have been exhumed in recent years—although only a fraction of the remains buried here have been recovered. The skulls grotesquely line the shelves of the memorial. Most have been tagged: "Asian, Male, 15–20 years old," "Asian, Female, 5–10 years old." They all bear gaping holes in their sides marking where they had been struck by axes. Many have two chasms.

Clothes have been recovered and are stuffed into a separate shelf. Human teeth are everywhere. You'll be asked by the guide to sign a guestbook and leave a message for the future of Cambodia. Quite understandably, you'll be too numb to devise anything appropriate.

Koki Beach

On Sundays, it seems as if half of Phnom Penh is here, vying for tiny parcels of real estate near the river in which to relax, eat, socialize and sleep. You can get here by motorbike or taxi by taking National Route 1 eight miles past the Monivong bridge; hang a left.

Oudong

Oudong was the capital of Cambodia between 1601 and 1850; its last remaining structures are a few *chedis* and temples situated on a hilltop about 40km north of Phnom Penh along Route 5. Climb up the steep stairway to the top and enjoy a magnificent view of the Cambodian countryside. Best in the cool season when the weather is pleasant and the paddies are electric green.

Phnom Basit

Phnom Basit is two extinct volcanoes jutting up approximately 300 meters high off the flood plains north of Phnom Penh. The southern hill has a popular Chinese temple, often crowded with worshippers on weekends. The remains of an Angkor-era temple stand on the northern hill, along with a reclining Buddha and a modern *wat* at its crest. Both hills offer excellent views and can be scaled by vehicles along dirt roads.

Located about 10 km south of Oudong, Phnom Basit is reached by a 15-km dirt road leading west from Route 5. The turnoff is approximately 12 kilometers north of Phnom Penh, just past a large lumber yard and near a market. Turn left at the small police pedestal on the left side of Route 5.

Tonle Bati

About 30 km south of the capital on Route 2, Tonle Bati is a small village in the midst of rice fields. The main attraction is the 12th-century temple of Ta Prohm, which boasts some fairly well preserved bas reliefs of *apsaras.* On weekends the area is crowded with locals from Phnom Penh, and traditional Khmer music is played in the temple courtyard. *Kru teay* (fortune tellers) lurk in the doorways. Nearby is a lake with food stalls and small huts along the water for rent. On a darker note, one of the largest "security prisons" of the Khmer Rouge was located just across the lake in a former teachers training college. The bones of some of its thousands of victims are stored in a roofless classroom.

Beware of the high prices charged by the lakeside vendors for food; always ask and bargain before buying. Also, if you arrive on moto or in a car, there is a "parking fee" of 2000 riel per motorbike, more for four-wheelers.

Kien Svay

This is another popular weekend getaway for Phnom Penhoise. Kien Svay is actually the name of an entire district located about 15 km southeast of the city along Route 1, but the entertainment area runs along the Mekong River approximately 500 meters from the highway. The main attraction is hundreds of wood-and-thatch houses built on stilts on the river. Families come out to picnic; there are also many brothels in the area, which will surely be pointed out should any single men venture into the area.

Kien Svay has little to recommend to it. The food available from the local vendors is of questionable hygiene and is grossly overpriced. The area itself is rather dirty; garbage and food are swept directly into the river, so swimming is unsavory. Also, the crowd tends to be rowdy and drunk, and foreigners may attract unwanted attention.

Phnom Chiso

Phnom Chiso is located in Takeo province approximately 45 km down Route 2 to Takeo. An Angkorian temple sits at the top of a 155-meter hill which also boasts a fine view of the surrounding countryside. The peak is accessible by two long staircases, one new, one original; if you choose the latter, located on the east side of the mountain, be prepared for a very steep exhausting climb. What's neat is that it provides an insight into the ways of the pilgrims and priests of yore; as you huff and puff your way up the mountain, think of the faithful who came here almost 1000 years ago, carrying bowls of fruit and offerings to the Hindu gods high above. Unfortunately there were no cold soft drinks waiting for them at the top as there are today.

At the foot of the mountain, you'll notice large piles of rocks, slowly being broken into gravel by hundreds of workers using only hammers. The "tap tap" sound is like rain on sheet metal.

If you're going there yourself, the turnoff is on the left about three kilometers after you pass the hill.

Angkor

An arched gateway to Cambodia's ancient city of Angkor Thom.

The temples at the lost civilization of Angkor may very well be the most spectacular architectural ruins found on earth. What French naturalist Henri Mouhot "discovered" in 1860, an endless complex of hundreds of overgrown carved stone temples and structures, was a lost city that reflected the zenith of Khmer history.

In its prime, Angkor stretched 15 miles east to west and six miles north to south. Constructed between the 9th and the 13th centuries, the temples were built around the Khmer interpretation of Indian religious and political beliefs that ultimately evolved from Hinduism to Buddhism. The complex architectural grandeur of Angkor Wat itself, with its remarkable bas reliefs, towers and pools, and absolute immensity is arguably unmatched among an-

Fielding **CAMBODIA**

ANGKOR WAT (A.D. 1113–1150)

Constructed sometime between 1112 and 1152, Angkor Wat was erected to honor the god-king Vishnu. Its walls tell dozens of Khmer legends and depict ancient invasions. The temple features the largest bas relief carving in the world. An enormous network of canals and moats served to irrigate the once thriving capital city.

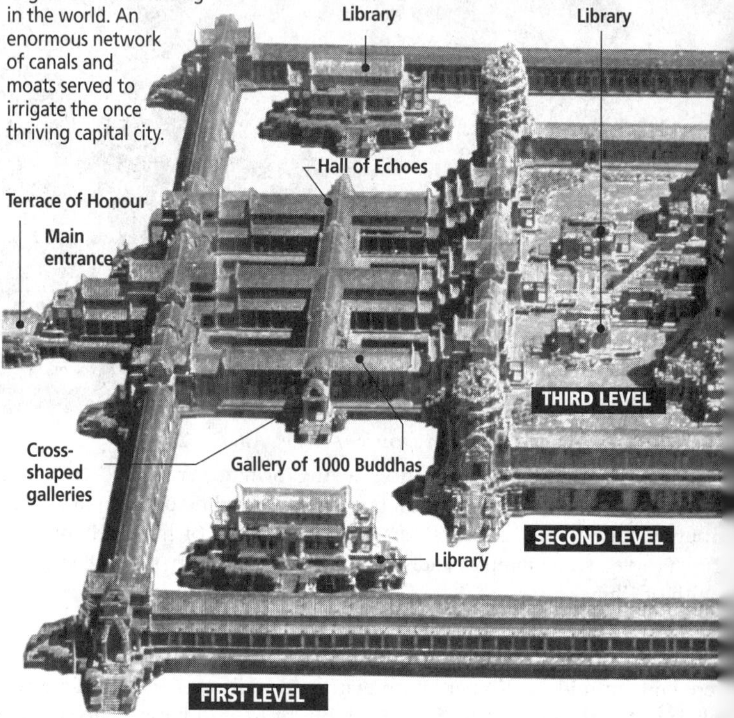

Map labels:
N
ANGKOR THOM
Prah Kahn
Ta Som
Bayon
EAST BARAY
East Mebon
West Mebon
WEST BARAY
Ta Prohm
Siem Reap
Srah Srang
Banteay Kdei
ANGKOR WAT
0 1 2 miles

Photo labels:
Library
Library
Hall of Echoes
Terrace of Honour
Main entrance
THIRD LEVEL
Cross-shaped galleries
Gallery of 1000 Buddhas
SECOND LEVEL
Library
FIRST LEVEL

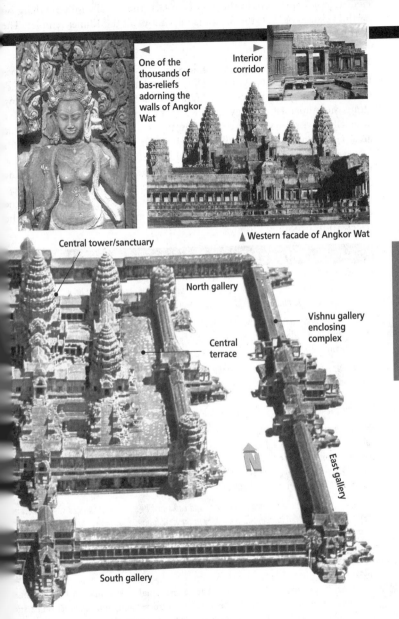

One of the thousands of bas-reliefs adorning the walls of Angkor Wat

Interior corridor

▲ Western facade of Angkor Wat

Central tower/sanctuary

North gallery

Vishnu gallery enclosing complex

Central terrace

East gallery

South gallery

Angkor

cient temples anywhere in the world. In fact, there really isn't anything on earth like Angkor Wat, the most magnificent of all the Khmer temples. The Acropolis in Athens and the Colosseum in Rome come to mind, but can't compare in sheer vastness.

You should put aside at least two days for viewing the temples. Three does the visit more justice. Neighboring Siem Reap has comfortable and cheap accommodations. Even if you've brought along a map and a guidebook, bring along the human kind with you, as well—if for no other reason than to give yourself a favorable chance of avoiding the many land mines buried in the area. Guides are easily available throughout Siem Riep. The going rate for Angkor guides is between US$10 and US$20 a day (depending on the means of transport). The fees for entrance to the temples are US$20 for one day, US$40 for three days, and US$60 for one week, with unlimited access to all temple sites. Tickets can be purchased at the checkpoint gate on the road leading to the temples, or at the tourist information office across the street from the Grand Hotel.

Unearthing More than Mines

Land mines have killed thousands of Khmers over the last 30 years and injured many more. Since relative stability came to Cambodia in 1993, teams of international experts have been tasked with the removal of perhaps 10 million land mines buried beneath the Cambodian countryside.

Demining engineers have concentrated particularly on Siem Reap province, home to the famed Angkor temples, but also the venue for some of the heaviest fighting between government troops and the Khmer Rouge between 1979 and 1996.

But the mine removal experts are unearthing more than booby traps these days. If there can be anything positive gleaned from laying land mines, that is removing them and discovering relics which shed new light on ancient Khmer civilization. The discoveries of ancient kilns in the Angkor area by demining personnel are intriguing the scientific world.

Three different ceramic production sites have been discovered to the northeast of Angkor Archaeological Park. In the rice fields and villages themselves experts are finding vases, pots, urns and roof tiles deep in the soil—some are fragmented, some completely intact. These discoveries will no doubt aid researchers in answering questions such as: How did the ancient Khmers eat? How did they store water and grain? How did they bury their dead?

After these sites are more thoroughly explored and explained by such organizations as UNESCO and APSARA, undoubtedly a museum will open here in the near future, allowing visitors a more complete glimpse into ancient Khmer civilization.

What to See and Do in Angkor

Angkor Wat

With its phenomenally preserved **bas reliefs**, Angkor Wat may well be the most spectacular ancient temple in the world. Constructed sometime between 1112 and 1152 on a low flat alluvial delta surrounded by the most elaborate irrigation system of any ancient city in the world, Angkor Wat was erected to honor the god-king Vishnu. When the Khmers relocated their capital to Phnom Penh during the 15th century, Buddhist monks occupied the structure and protected it from both invaders and the natural elements. Its walls tell of dozens of Khmer legends and depict ancient invasions by monkeys and men alike. In fact, the temple features the largest bas relief carving found in the world.

Angkor Wat is surrounded by an enormous network of **canals** and **moats** once teeming with crocodiles that served to irrigate the then-thriving capital city. Most of the crocs, as well as the gibbons in the trees, are gone now from this jungle. Many of the finer statues in the complex were removed and taken to France by archeologist Louis Delaporte in 1873. Restoration on the temple began in earnest in 1898 and the resulting two-volume book, *Les Monuments du Combodge*, is still acknowledged as the most comprehensive depiction of the site. The book also served to intrigue a variety of visitors, treasure hunters, robbers and vandals (mostly European) who began the tradition of looting and defacing the sculpted city.

The wholesale destruction of Angkor Wat didn't start until 1971 when the Khmer Rouge used the temple complex as a headquarters. To generate income and to simply kill time, the guerrillas began methodically dismantling statues and carvings and removing Buddha statue heads—which were then sold to art dealers in Bangkok. They also heavily mined the jungle and fields surrounding the temples. These mines and others buried by government troops are numerous and widespread and very, very operable. Stay only on marked paths.

After a disastrous period of clumsy restoration, with workers using acid, cement and abrasive tools on the temple, UNESCO has implemented a plan to begin a comprehensive and enduring restoration of Angkor Wat. The temple, though, remains one of the best preserved structures at Angkor. The most plausible explanation is that the sandstone used to construct Angkor Wat was imported from many miles away, as opposed to the predominant use of local stone in the construction of other temples at the complex.

Angkor Wat is one of the few temples facing west and, consequently, the best time for viewing it is during the late afternoon.

Ta Prohm ★★★

If Angkor Wat is spectacular for how well it is preserved, then Ta Prohm is known for how well it isn't. The jungle has literally grown up right through this Buddhist temple constructed during the 12th century. Massive trees are attached to dismembered parts of the structure like molasses, roots oozing through the stone of the courtyards to the jungle floor. Bas reliefs are choked by moss and thick, spiraling vines in this unique osmosis between jungle and stone.

Angkor Thom (The Great City)

The southern gate is 1.5 km from Angkor Wat.
This is the 10-sq-km ancient city which features the Bayon as its highlight. An estimated 100,000 to 1 million inhabited this magnificent ancient metropolis, built originally by Udayadityavarman II (1050–1066) and renovated and largely

Fielding **CAMBODIA**

ANGKOR THOM

This Spread	Next Spread
Preah Palilay Tep Pranam	North Kleang Thommanon
Royal Palace	Ave. of Victory
Baphuon	South Kleang Chau Say Tevoda
Bayon	

ANGKOR THOM (central)

Angkor Thom is the 10 sq. km. ancient city built originally by Udayadityavarman II (1050–1066), then renovated and largely expanded during the reign of Jayavarman VII between 1181 and 1201. The city was surrounded by walls and a 100-meter-wide crocodile-infested moat. Five imposing 20-meter high gates lead into the town after crossing a causeway over the moats flanked by demons and gods. A fifth gate, the Victory Gate, is 500 meters north of the east gate. The gateways are each decorated with three -headed stone elephants. At the center of Angkor Thom, is Bayon, Jayavarman VII's temple mountain. More than 200 faces carved on its 54 towers are an awesome sight and a favorite with visitors.

ROYAL PALACE

PHIMEANAKAS

Gate

BAPHUON

South Gate of Angkor Thom

BAPHUON

This temple (the name means copper tower) 200 meters northwest of the Bayon features excellent lintels and columns as well as a second-story wall shaped in the image of a reclining Buddha. The temple was built as the center of Angkor Thom and was constructed during the reign of Udayadityavarman II between 1050 and 1066. The pyramidal temple was built to depict Mt. Meru.

PREAH PALILAY

A reclining Buddha is on the east side of the entry tower and a finely carved seated Buddha is on the south side. The pediments of the entry towers depict Buddhist scenes. A standing Buddha on the north pediment rests his hand on an elephant. The remains of two headless guardians and two lions stand between the terrace and central sanctuary.

TEP PRANUM

Tep Pranum is one of the most serene areas of Angkor. A large Buddha assembled from various stones is seated on a lotus pedestal. The entrance is bordered by double boundary stones at the corners and features a cross-shaped terrace.

PREAH PALILAY

Gate

TEP PRANUM

Gate

TERRACE OF THE LEPER KING

ROYAL ENCLOSURE

This important, but now rundown and jungle-infested complex of temples, wooden buildings and sandstone pools was built during Jayavarman VII's reign. The official palace was in front with domestic quarters behind. The gardens were surrounded by a wall and a moat.

Gate

Ave. of Victory
CENTRAL SQUARE

Northern Ave.

Angkor

BAYON

To South Gate

TERRACE OF ELEPHANTS

To East Gate →

Built by Jayavarman VII at the end of his reign in the early 13th century, this was the grand reviewing stand for the kings of the Angkor era. From the 350-meter long terrace, the royals would observe ceremonies, parades, sporting events and pageants. Walls depict elephants, lions, gladiators and the five-headed horse Balacha.

ANGKOR THOM (continued)

TERRACE OF THE LEPER KING

This terrace was built in the early 13th century by Jayavarman VII and named after the founder of Angkor, Yasovarman, who died of leprosy. It is believed to have been a cremation platform for Angkor aristocrats. The lower tiers of the six tiered terrace feature carved nagas and fish. The upper tiers contain bas reliefs of sword-bearing kings.

TEP PRANUM

Northern Ave.

TERRACE OF THE LEPER KING

CENTRAL SQUARE

NORTH KLEANG

TERRACE OF THE ELEPHANTS

SOUTH KLEANG

PRASATS SUOR PRAT

According to Cambodian legend, these 12 towers were used as anchors for ropes used by performing acrobats at festivals. Others say the towers served as a depository for the crown jewels. The towers are connected by galleries and entrance porches. The interior of each tower has two levels.

NORTH AND SOUTH KLEANGS

These stately structures on the east side of the central square are believed to have been used as accommodations for foreign envoys. The North Kleang was the idea of Javavarman V. Javavarman VII added the 12 victory towers called Prasat Suor Prat. (See left)

Fielding

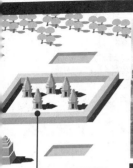

PREAH PITHU

Located across from
Tep Pranam, Preah
Pithu is a cluster of five
12th century Hindu and
Buddhist temples
enclosed by a wall.

THOMMANON

This shrine to Vishnu was constructed
by Suryavarman II (1113–1150). There
is a huge tower shrine and three
false doors. The east and west
gates are still standing.

ANGKOR THOM

**VICTORY
GATE**

Ave. of Victory

Angkor

Previous Spread	This Spread

Preah Palilay — Tep Pranam

North Kleang — Thommanon

Royal Palace — Ave. of Victory

Baphuon — South Kleang — Chau Say Tevoda

Bayon

CHAU SAY TEVODA

This temple dating from the same period as
Thommanon differs only slightly from its
neighbor. The difference is that Chau Say, the
temple tower (which looks much like the towers
of Angkor Wat) is linked to the rest of the
structure. The false windows give the impression
the building has more stories than it actually does

**GATE OF THE
DEAD**

Fielding CAMBODIA

TEMPLES OF ANGKOR

The temples of the lost civilization of Angkor may very well be the most spectacular architectural ruins on earth. Conceived as a stone likeness of the Hindu Universe, Angkor flourished as the center of the Khmer Empire from the 9th century A.D. The complex was based on a wax model and built over 37 years by artisans, workers and slaves. The Hindu temple city dedicated to the god Vishnu became a Buddhist shrine with the fall of the empire in the 15th century. In its prime, Angkor stretched 15 miles east to west and six miles north to south. The intricate architectural grandeur of Angkor Wat itself, with its remarkable bas reliefs, towers, canals and moats, is the most compelling reason to visit Cambodia.

PHIMEANAKAS (A.D. 910–1000)

This is a three-terraced pyramidal temple started by Jayavarman V (968-1001) and completed by Udayadityavarman II (1050-1066). It is not in superb condition, but it's still an engaging sight. The three tiers are of unequal height. Lions and elephants decorate the terrace corners.

PHNOM BAKHENG (A.D. 900)

Constructed on a hill, Bakheng was the first temple of Angkor. It is a pyramid formed by five terraces. The vista from the summit is best seen at sunset for a panoramic view of Angkor Wat and other temples. Seated lions are on each side of the slope near the summit and at each end of the five tiers.

PRASAT RULUH

PRASAT KAS HO

WEST BARAY

WEST MEBON (A.D. 1010–80)

Situated at the center of an artificial lake on a circular island, West Mebon was at one time surrounded by a square enclosure with three entry towers and a sanctuary crowned by a lotus. Animals in small squares are carved on the sides of the towers.

PRASAT TA NOREAY

PRASAT TRAPEANG ROPOU

Angkor

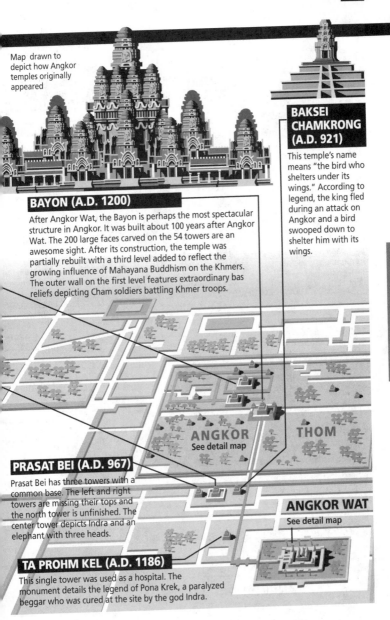

Map drawn to depict how Angkor temples originally appeared

BAKSEI CHAMKRONG (A.D. 921)

This temple's name means "the bird who shelters under its wings." According to legend, the king fled during an attack on Angkor and a bird swooped down to shelter him with its wings.

BAYON (A.D. 1200)

After Angkor Wat, the Bayon is perhaps the most spectacular structure in Angkor. It was built about 100 years after Angkor Wat. The 200 large faces carved on the 54 towers are an awesome sight. After its construction, the temple was partially rebuilt with a third level added to reflect the growing influence of Mahayana Buddhism on the Khmers. The outer wall on the first level features extraordinary bas reliefs depicting Cham soldiers battling Khmer troops.

ANGKOR
See detail map

THOM

PRASAT BEI (A.D. 967)

Prasat Bei has three towers with a common base. The left and right towers are missing their tops and the north tower is unfinished. The center tower depicts Indra and an elephant with three heads.

ANGKOR WAT
See detail map

TA PROHM KEL (A.D. 1186)

This single tower was used as a hospital. The monument details the legend of Pona Krek, a paralyzed beggar who was cured at the site by the god Indra.

Angkor

TEMPLES OF ANGKOR (continued)

PREAH KAHN

PREAH KAHN (A.D.1191)

Covering a vast 140 acres with four enclosing walls, Preah Kahn is surrounded by a moat. Inside are a maze of pavilions, chapels and halls. Giant serpents and garudas are found on many reliefs and some walls feature tapestry patterns with bases of scrolls, lotus petals and rosettes. The surrounding jungle can be seen on the path to the Central Sanctuary.

TA PROHM (as it looks today)

TA PROHM (A.D.

The jungle has literally grown up right through this Buddhist temple constructed during the 12th century. Massive trees are attached to dismembered parts of the structure. Bas reliefs are choked by moss and thick, spiraling vines, while roots ooze through the stone of the courtyards.

NEAK PEAN

PHIMEANAKAS

SIEM REAP RIVER

THOM MANON

ANGKOR **THOM**

BAYON

PHNOM BAKHENG

BANTEAY SREI (A.D. 967)

This temple has suffered the collapse of many galleries and porches. It is notable for its many distinctive carvings.

ANGKOR WAT

Angkor

TA KEO

TA KEO (A.D. 1000)

Ta Keo is one of the few temples at Angkor lacking bas relief decorations and sculptures. Its five towers are laid out in a cruciform pattern. Ta Keo was the first temple built entirely of sandstone and it was never completed. It scales 22 m. (72 ft.) giving an impression of power by its sheer simplicity.

TA SOM (A.D. 1200)

A single tower surrounded by three enclosing walls, Ta Som has entry towers east and west carved with four faces. The first entry tower is bordered with serpents and large garudas. The main tower, in the shape of a cross, has four porches.

EAST BARAY

EAST MEBON

PRE RUP (A.D. 961)

Pre Rup was constructed with a square plan on an artificial mountain. The name of the temple is derived from a cremation ritual. Long galleries surround the courtyard and there are two groups of three towers. Carvings include plant motifs and divinity depictions.

Angkor

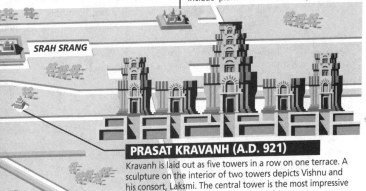

SRAH SRANG

PRASAT KRAVANH (A.D. 921)

Kravanh is laid out as five towers in a row on one terrace. A sculpture on the interior of two towers depicts Vishnu and his consort, Laksmi. The central tower is the most impressive with brick carvings unique in Khmer architecture.

expanded during the reign of Jayavarman VII between 1181 and 1201. The city was huge even by European standards, and was surrounded by walls and a 100-meter-wide crocodile-infested moat to make any incursions by hostile powers such as the Chams rather problematic. Five imposing 20-meter-high gates built by Jayavarman VII (featuring the giant faces typical of the Jayavarman VII style) lead into the town along its four walls (the fifth, the Victory Gate, is 500 meters north of the east gate) after crossing a causeway over the moats flanked by demons and gods. Outside the gates, with their backs to the city, sit the 54 gods and demons (the gods to the left of the causeway and the demons to the right). The gods hold a giant serpent across their knees.

The Royal Enclosure

In the center of Angkor Thom.

This important but now run-down complex of temples, wooden buildings and sandstone pools was built during Jayavarman V's period.

The Baphuon (Copper Tower)   ★

About 200 meters northwest of the Bayon.

This temple features some excellent lintels and columns, as well as a second-story wall shaped in the image of a reclining Buddha. The temple was built as the center of Angkor Thom and was constructed during the reign of Udayadityavarman II between 1050 and 1066. The west-side wall was reshaped into a reclining Buddha in the 15th century. The pyramidal temple itself was built to depict Mt. Meru, and appears as such today. However, it was one of the more shabbily constructed temples of the time (using a lot of wood to support the masonry), and the elements over the centuries have not been good to it. Guesses are that the cone of the hill-temple once reached 50 meters high.

Terrace of Elephants

On the Great Square, west of the north-south street.

Built by Jayavarman VII at the end of his reign in the early 13th century, this was the grand reviewing stand for the kings of the Angkor era. From this 350-meter-long terrace, the royals would observe magnificent ceremonies, army parades, sporting events and religious pageants. The terrace features three platforms standing at three different heights, reached by five flights of stairs. Walls depict elephants, lions, gladiators and the five-headed horse Balacha (north frontage).

Terrace of the Leper King   ★★

North of the Terrace of Elephants on the Great Square.

This terrace was built by Jayavarman VII in the early 13th century and named after the founder of Angkor, Yasovarman, who died of leprosy in 910. The lower tiers of the six-tiered terrace feature carved *nagas* and fish. The upper tiers contain bas reliefs depicting sword-bearing kings. Although many historians have argued the terrace was a place of cremation for royalty, modern thought says that such activities would not have occurred in such a notable location.

The Bayon   ★★★★

In the center of Angkor Thom.

After Angkor Wat, the Bayon is perhaps the next most spectacular structure in Angkor. A few kilometers north of Angkor Wat, this spooky, ambiguous temple was built directly in the center of the ancient city of Angkor Thom. After its construction, the temple was partially rebuilt, with a third level added to reflect the growing influence of Mahayana Buddhism on the Khmers. The outer wall on the first level features extraordinary bas reliefs depicting Cham soldiers battling Khmer troops.

The Bayon was built during the Khmer transition from Hinduism to Buddhism; its spooky architecture reflects the influences of both faiths.

Phimeanakas

Royal Palace, center of the second courtyard.
This is a three-terraced pyramidal temple started by Jayavarman V (968–1001) and completed by Udayadityavarman II (1050–1066). Not in superb condition, but still an engaging sight. The three tiers are of unequal height. Lions and elephants decorate the corners of each terrace.

Thommanon

About 2 km from the Triumph Gate of Angkor Thom, on the Little Circuit.
This shrine to Vishnu was constructed by Suriyavarman II (1113–1150). There is a huge tower shrine and three false doors. The east and west gateways are still standing.

Chau Say

Opposite Thommanon.
This temple dates from about the same time as Thommanon and varies only slightly in design from its neighbor. The difference is that in Chau Say, the temple tower (whick looks much like the towers of Angkor Wat) is linked to the rest of the structure. The false windows (balusters) give the impression that the building has more stories than it actually does.

Ta Keo

About 1 km beyond the Thommanon on the Little Circuit.

This is one of the few temples at Angkor lacking bas relief decorations and sculptures. If Albert Speer had been Jayavarman's architect, this would have been the result. It's rather geometrical and plain-looking, but quite large, even though it was never completed. It was to have reached a height of about 50 meters, but, perhaps because of the labor needed to work with the massive sandstone blocks, work was never completed by Suriyavarman. The temple appears as if it had been stripped of its onamentation, but none ever existed. Some believe the temple was used as a place of human sacrifice, although this hasn't been proven either.

INSIDER TIP: BANTEAY SREI

The Banteay Srei complex, located some 30 km outside of Siem Reap, was off-limits after the ambush and murder of an American tourist near the temples in early 1995. The road has recently been repaired, however, and travelers may be permitted to visit the site with a police escort. Check at the tourist information office for the latest update.

Siem Reap

This quaint little village will be your base while you visit the temples at Angkor. It was also a provincial base for UNTAC, which made the town an occasional target for Khmer Rouge rocket attacks during 1993. So don't let its apparent cheerfulness fool you—Siem Reap is the definition of sanguinity. There have been numerous other Khmer Rouge assaults, campaigns and slaughters in the region since then, and Siem Reap province itself is a Khmer Rouge stronghold. But not to fear; the KR is largely gone (entirely from the region surrounding the temples) an no longer a threat to visitors to Angkor.

For the most part, the village—the provincial capital of Siem Reap province—is pretty quiet, its inhabitants working in the surrounding jungle collecting resin from the gum trees. The town center itself is a little dilapidated, but there are a few minor attractions here other than the temples at Angkor.

Because everyone knows each other here, festivals are fun. A number of bands get together in a large field behind the Grand Hotel d'Angkor and play Cambodian and Thai popular dance tunes during the celebration that marks the end of the rainy season (Festival of the Reversing Current) in October. In days not long past, during the night around Siem Reap, it wasn't unusual to see the tracers of artillery rounds being exchanged by warring factions in the countryside.

Getting There

The two primary ways of getting to Siem Reap and Angkor are via daily flights from Phnom Penh aboard a Royal Air Cambodge ATR-72, or by daily early-morning speedboats that leave from Phnom Penh and take about 4-5 hours to get up to Siem Reap (get tickets and make transportation arrangements at the Capitol Hotel). The real adventurers' alternative is the twice-weekly ferry out of Psar Cha Ferry Landing. If you take the ferry, stock up on provisions for this interesting and occasionally bizarre 24-hour journey across the Tonlé Sap Lake and down the Tonlé Sap River. And get a hammock. They can be bought at the Central Markets both in Phnom Penh and Siem Reap for about US$3. It'll be your only means to get some sleep.

The flight is about 45 minutes and goes for US$55 one way; the speedboat ride is US$25 one-way. The ferry's only a couple of bucks. Hope you don't mind a few cockroaches—giant ones.

Adventure tourists used to regularly hitchhike National Route 6 between Phnom Penh and Siem Reap. However, the practice today is nothing short of suicide. It's most assured you'll be headed for trouble. Big time.

Cambodia's Tonle Sap: Saving the Great Lake

What a small, remote savana watering hole is to elephants, zebra, gazelle and other wildlife, Cambodia's Tonle Sap Lake is to most of the Khmer population, who depend upon its bounties for their very survival. However, the Great Lake is hardly small; it is the largest inland body of water in Southeast Asia, even during the dry season, when it covers some 2700 square kilometers. Nearly 3 million people live around the lake, more than a quarter of Cambodia's population. But the Tonle Sap may be the most remarkable lake in the world. During the rainy season-from May to November-the lake's girth swells to a rotund 16,000 square kilometers, a six-fold expansion. This is due to the swollen waters of the Mekong River-which in their massive surge to the South China Sea-force the Tonle Sap River, a Mekong tributary, to reverse its current toward the lake. This river running in the wrong direction makes the lake some of the most fertile fishing grounds in the world. The rising water covers the nutrient-rich inundated forest, making a perfect spawning area for the fish brought in by the surge. When the waters finally recede some seven months later, the lake has yielded about 100,000 tons of fish, providing nearly three-quarters of Cambodians' intake of protein. The lake is so vital to Cambodians' subsistence that each November, in a ceremony centuries old, the king slashes a leather vine which has been spanned across the river, symbolically setting the waters of Tonle Sap Lake free and allowing them to flow back toward the sea. But things haven't been going the Tonle Sap's way, so to speak, in recent years. The population around the northwestern edge of the lake has surged some 15-20 percent since 1992; this is home to the ecologically-fragile inundated forest so key to this environment's life cycle. Fishermen and recent arrivals have turned to cutting down the forest's trees for firewood-there's been a nearly 20-percent decrease in forest in the area since 1992. This, of course, makes the terrain less desirable as a spawning area for fish. Fewer fish and more fishermen have inspired new tactics to pull from the lake what remains. Traditional fishing practices have given way to the use of dynamite, electric shocks and huge fishing nets. Also, there's talk of damming the Mekong-which runs its entire length from the Himalayas to the South China Sea without any man-made obstructions-which would mark nothing short of an environmental catastrophe for the Tonle Sap. The potential for environmental disaster is serious enough that at least nine foreign NGOs have committed US$6 million to saving the Tonle Sap. The number of agencies involved is expected to grow, upping the aid figure to US$12 million by the end of 1997. If this is enough to keep things going in the wrong direction remains to be seen.

What to See and Do in Siem Reap

Central Market

The busy Central Market in Siem Reap (about a mile east of the Siem Reap River) is a muddy, bustling marketplace best for stocking up on fresh fruit and local delicacies. Both the pineapple and the durian are the sweetest I've ever tasted. Here, you can also watch artisans creating magnificently filigreed gold jewelry. But wear boots during the southwestern monsoon season. Although marginally covered, this place never dries out.

Siem Reap Zoo

The zoo, located on the road to Phnom Krom, is really not much more than what's outside the zoo, but with a fence around it. However, there's a bunch of large crocs lounging about that make the stop worth it. Also, don't screw around with the monkeys, who roam the grounds freely. If you get between a mama gibbon and her kid, she may end up on your back. It hurts. Across from the zoo is where a number of townspeople bathe in the sometimes raging Siem Reap River.

Where to Stay in Siem Reap

New hotels, mostly the high-end variety, are springing up around Siem Reap town like mushrooms, in preparation for an anticipated tourist boom. There are also quite a few moderate- and low-priced accommodations available for the budget traveler. Note that many hotels have minimal addresses and some guest houses are known only by numbers. This should be no problem as the local taxi drivers will know where they are.

Hotels in the higher-end price range usually have air conditioning, hot water, satellite TV, and other amenities.

Diamond Hotel US$45–$55

Vithei Achasva Street. ☎ *015-913-130.*
Rooms have air conditioning, TV, hot water and refrigerator. Singles are US$45, doubles US$55. A restaurant is on the premises. Opened up in the spirit of the free elections in 1993 in anticipation of a tourist barrage. During 1994, it was nearly deserted, but business was picking up at press time.

Grand Hotel d'Angkor N/A—but a bundle

Located on the road to Angkor, about a hundred yards north of National Route 6. ☎ *015-911-292.*
Once considered the finest hotel in town if not all of Cambodia, the Grand fell into such disrepair it differed little from the nearby temples it was built to serve—but 600 years later. It was recently purchased by the Raffles Group of Singapore and is currently undergoing a massive renovation. At this writing, the hotel was closed while undergoing a complete transformation. At least 131 rooms will open after the first phase of the restoration is complete, and an additional 172 will open later. There will be six restaurants and bars as well as meeting and business facilities. After a searing day of temple-hopping, guests can kick back in the 25-meter swimming pool. The gardens will feature more than 20,540 trees and the 60,000 sqm frontage will make for a grand entrance indeed.

Siem Reap

Baray Hotel   Rates on Request

On the road to the temples, on the right, just a short distance after the Grand Hotel.
This was a hangout for Aussies building prefab buildings for UNTAC in the jungle
in '92. Definitely a frontier, last-chance-type place. Last check: bar, restaurant, TV
in the outdoor bar.

International House (Vimean Thmei)   US$15–$20

No. 021 Street Sivatha, Mondol 1, Quarter 2 (opposite Monorom Restaurant). ☎ 063-
963494, 015-630-070; FAX: 063-380102.
Unremarkable hotel with unusually friendly service, clean rooms and a strong
shower. Fifteen bucks for a room during most of the year, but they jack it up to 20
during holidays. Friendly and tasty Singapore Restaurant adjoins the hotel..

Ta Prohm   US$55–$100

Psar Chas Street, on the Siem Reap River. ☎ *015-911-983.*
Modern for the surroundings. Rooms with air conditioning, satellite TV. Nice digs.
Singles US$55, doubles US$65, suites US$100.

Dr. Ith Kim Phan's Guesthouse   US$10

0129 Achar Hem Chiev.
Dr. Ith and his wife are the warmest people this side of tomorrowland. They're popular with the villagers, so staying here is a great way to get to know your new neighbors. The rooms are cozy, clean and comfortable. The stilt home has an airy,
woodsy feel. And it's cheap, about US$10 a night. There's a cafe out back that was
popular with the UNTAC crowd.

Kok Thlok   US$80–$90   ★★★

National Route 6. ☎ *015-912-608.*
Built like a miniature replica of the Cambodiana in Phnom Penh. Until the Grand
Hotel's facelift is finished, this is about the best place to stay around Siem Reap. At
this writing, it was also the only hotel in town to accept major credit cards. Despite
its awkward and poorly planned location on the highway to the airport (and, thus,
close to nothing), that's something to keep in mind. Singles are US$80, doubles
US$90.

Banteay Srei   US$55

National Route 6.
Singles and doubles both US$55. The restaurant on the ground floor serves Chi-
nese, Khmer and Western food.

Bayon   US$30–$35

Achar Swa Street. ☎ *015-911-769.*
Pleasant location on the riverside. Restaurant on the ground floor. Singles are
US$30, doubles US$35.

Stung Siem Reap   US$25–$30

☎ *015-912-379.*
Singles at US$25, doubles at US$30.

Hotel de la Paix   US$25–$30

Sivutha Street.
Singles at US$25, doubles at US$30.

Bopha Angkor US$30–$35

26 Eo Street 310. ☎ *015-917-176.*
All rooms with air conditioning, hot water, TV and refrigerator. A restaurant and
gift shop are on the premises. Singles are US$30, doubles US$35.

Angkor Village US$35–$50

Wat Bo Road. ☎ *015-916-048.*
This hotel features individual bungalow-type rooms, with singles at US$35 and
doubles US$50.

Mr. Ouk Soeum's Guesthouse US$5–$10

Behind Angkor Conservation Complex.
Located on a forested road along the Siem Reap River, this large concrete house is
one of the most tranquil and idyllic guest houses in town. It's also conveniently
located only 3 kilometers from the temples. Mr. Soeum and his family are friendly
and can arrange motos, taxis and other transportation. At present, there are only a
few rooms for rent, at US$5 for a single, US$10 double, but a new 10-room building is being finalized behind the house which will offer private bathrooms.

Sunrise Guesthouse US$5–$6

0592 Wat Bo Road.
Run by two jovial Khmer women, offers basic singles for US$5, US$6 doubles.

Mom's Guesthouse US$5–$8

99 Wat Bo Road.
Singles US$5, doubles US$6, doubles with private bath US$8.

Mahogany Guesthouse US$5–$6

0593 Wat Bo Road.
Singles US$5, doubles US$6.

Pailin Guesthouse US$5

0594 Wat Bo Road.
Singles US$5.

Garden House US$5–$6

0129 Wat Bo Road.
Singles US$5, doubles US$6 and US$8.

Guesthouse #0027 US$5–$12

Along the Siem Reap River, east of the Stone Bridge.
Singles US$5, doubles US$6, air-conditioned rooms US$12.

Freedom Guesthouse US$15

On Route 6 near Psar Leu Market.
Singles and doubles US$15; all rooms with air conditioning and TV.

Where to Eat in Siem Reap

Food stalls and restaurants can be found throughout Siem Reap. The road running
north along the east side of the Siem Reap River has a number of the largest ones. Like
Phnom Penh, full meals can usually be had for under US$1 at the stalls and twice that at
basic restaurants. Additionally, food stalls and refreshment stands can be found in and
around the temple sites.

Sampheap $

Next to the bridge near the Grand Hotel d'Angkor.

This place used to be packed with UNTACers, but is now usually empty. Semi-open cafe with good food while the troops were in town. Cambodian, Chinese and continental fare. Recommended.

The Mine Field Beer Bar $

Sangkat I, near the Baray.

American fare in this seedy joint. It's like: "Hey, man, you're in Cambodia."

Bayon Restaurant $

0098 Wat Bo Road.

Serving a wide selection of well-prepared Khmer, Thai, Chinese, and some Western dishes, this is probably the best restaurant in the town. The backyard garden area is a pleasant place to have a beer and relax at any time of the day. Don't be alarmed by the machine-gun toting diners.

Green House $

58 on the road leading to the airport.

Features mediocre Thai and Khmer food in an open-air pavilion.

Singapore Restaurant $$

Next to Vimean Thmei Hotel, 21 Sivatha Street.

New spot owned by guess who—a Singaporean. Some outdoor seating. Western-style dishes (breakfast is particularly expensive) seem to be airline leftovers, but the Cambodian and Chinese fare is excellent. Laid-back, but attentive, friendly service.

Directory

Transportation

By **air**, Royal Air Cambodge flies both Boeing jets and ATR turboprops to Siem Reap several times daily. Fare is US$110 round-trip.

By **boat**: There are now several companies running a **speedboat** service via the Tonlé Sap River. The trip takes about five hours from Phnom Penh; foreigners pay US$25, Khmers 50,000 riel one-way. Scenes of rural life along the waterways as well as on the vast Tonlé Sap Lake are added benefits of taking the boat.

Two types of boats make the run: long, enclosed boats bought second-hand from Malaysia, and comparatively new, smaller speedboats with twin outboard engines run by a Chinese company. The long boats are the more comfortable, with aircraftlike interiors, air conditioning, and real (if tiny) toilets. Be sure to bring toilet paper as none is provided. Earplugs are also a good idea, as the drone of the engine competes with Chinese video dubbed in Khmer and played at top volume. The smaller speedboats are supposedly a bit faster, but the double-row bench seats get uncomfortable after an hour, and the "toilet" is a roofless box at the stern.

Both boats depart every morning at 7 from the Psar Toit area north of the Japanese Bridge. A free shuttle to the pier leaves at about 6:30 a.m. from the Capitol Hotel.

Travel to Siem Reap is also possible on the slow **cargo boats**, which depart Phnom Penh regularly and take a full 24 hours. The boat anchors in the middle of the river for the night; travelers must bring their own sleeping gear. Price is about 35,000 riel one way.

Note that storms in the rainy season (June–October) can cause high waves on the Tonlé Sap Lake, making travel in the boats very uncomfortable.

By **road**, Siem Reap can be reached via share taxis, which take National Route 5 to Battambang and then swing east around the Tonlé Sap Lake. The trip is long and arduous, however, and security on the Battambang-Siem Reap leg is chancy. National Route 6, the most direct road from Phnom Penh, is still insecure between Kompong Thom and Siem Reap due to many bandits with big guns which can fire many bullets with one squeeze.

Siem Reap Environs

Phnom Kraom

Peaceful scenes of rural Khmer life can be observed along Route 29, which follows the meandering Siem Reap River to Phnom Kraom about 15 km from downtown. The area is redolent with the powerful smell of fermented fish paste *(prahok)*, a popular condiment, which is stored in big wooden barrels with lids weighted by rocks. Hike to the top of Phnom Kraom for a magnificent view of the Tonlé Sap Lake and the surrounding countryside. There are several ancient monuments and a modern *wat* at the summit of Phnom Kraom, as well.

The Outer Limits

Young monks take a break restoring a temple near Pray Veng.

Along the Coast

Cambodia isn't known for its beaches, and that's what perhaps makes them such a treat when you reach them. The country has more than 200 miles of coastline, most of it totally unspoiled. What's kept people away from these areas has been the Khmer Rouge, who ruined entire towns and villages in the late 1970s in their maniacal upheaval, including the once popular resort of Kep. In fact, by the time Pol Pot fled Phnom Penh, not a single structure was left standing in this town. The Khmer Rouge also still control some areas at night that you'll need to pass through to reach the coast. As of this writing, reaching ports such as Sihanoukville by car or motorcycle is quite doable, but only during daylight hours. The train is absolutely out of the question.

Kampot also suffered at the hands of the Khmer Rouge. But if the FUNC-INPEC/Hun Sen government starts tapping the coasts for resort develop-ment, Kampot is one area expected to be targeted.

Kompong Som, Cambodia's only seaport, is another area that may experi-ence relatively significant growth over the next few years.

Koh Kong is a small island in the Gulf of Thailand, only about 20 miles from the Thai border. It's surrounded by calm, azure waters—a diver's par-adise in the winter months. This area, too, has been targeted for tourism.

Sihanoukville (Kompong Som)

Talcum-powder-soft white sand and palm-lined beaches with limpid blue waters are the ingredients that make Sihanoukville (also known as Kompong Som) a favorite getaway spot for locals and travelers alike.

The town itself—hardly the eyesore you'd expect of a Cambodian port town (although I wouldn't quite call it charming)—consists of only a few streets and a market and is built on the sides of windswept, grassy hills. On the west side of town is the country's biggest port. Great views of the coast can be enjoyed at the top of the town's highest hill, easily discerned by the *vat* which rests near its summit.

INSIDER TIP

The best time for visiting Sihanoukville is during the dry months between November and May; from June to October is the rainy season and showers occur almost daily.

Cambodian soldiers strike a pose beside their armored personnel carrier south Kompong Spieu.

Still seedy, the number of brothels will make your head spin. It's not unual to find sex tourists here as well as procurers looking for gals to smuggle Bangkok. At present, though, Sihanoukville still has the sleepy atmohere of a provincial town. The Cambodian government has big plans for it, wever, with an international airport, a billion-dollar casino on one of the nearby islands, and scores of high-end hotels to be built in the next few years. Enjoy Sihanoukville now before it's taken over by tourists.

What to See and Do in Sihanoukville

The Beaches

Sihanoukville has three main beaches, the first near the now defunct seven-story **Hilton Hotel**; **Sokha Beach**, the second and most popular; and **Ochateal Beach**, a vast stretch of sand marked by the white prefab buildings of the old UNTAC provincial headquarters. The Hilton and Sokha beaches draw the most crowds, mainly locals, on the weekends, as they have shade trees and restaurants, while Ochateal Beach is usually deserted. Other than hanging out at the beach, there ain't a helluvalot to do here. Keep in mind that the rainy season, from May though October, brings gusty, chilly winds, high seas and slate-gray skies on most days. To me, this place seems a long ride just to drink beer.

Where to Stay in Sihanoukville

Sihanoukville presently offers mostly mid-range hotels; budget accommodations are available, but must be sought out through moto-taxi drivers.

Seaside   US$20–40

Ochateal Beach.

Good location facing the ocean. Singles are US$20, doubles US$40.

Eagle's Nest   US$12–20

Ochateal Beach. ☎ *015-914-657.*

Run by gregarious Aussie Colin Jerram, the Eagle's Nest faces the ocean and has small restaurant with Western food. Singles with satellite TV, hot water, and air conditioning are US$12, doubles US$20.

Sam's Place   US$5–10

100 meters from the Vietnamese Monument.

There's about a half-dozen basic but clean rooms (with private bath) at this guest house/restaurant overlooking the sea. Very backpacker friendly, superb food; owners couldn't be any friendlier. Best for drinking beer and trading travelers' tales in the open air cafe.

Sokha Motel   US$40

Sokha Beach.

One of the town's first hotels, the Sokha is a series of bungalows in a coconut grove along Sokha Beach, with a great tropical atmosphere. The bungalows are in a sad state of repair, however, and overpriced at US$40 per night. Nevertheless they always seem full.

Cobra Hotel   US$10

Ochateal Beach.

Offers small bungalows for US$10. A thinly disguised brothel, the Cobra becomes a karaoke joint in the evenings and attracts a boisterous, sleazy crowd.

Hawaii   US$10–12

Ekreach Street, in town.

A good value with singles at US$10, doubles US$12. All rooms have air conditioning, satellite TV, and hot water. A Chinese-Khmer restaurant is on the ground floor.

Sorya   **US$15–25**

Ekreach Street, in town.

This large hotel offers singles for US$15, doubles for US$25. All rooms have air conditioning. The top floor is a "dancing restaurant"-style disco, and can get a bit rowdy into the wee hours.

New Hong Kong Motel   **US$20–30**

On road to Sokha Beach.

Individual bungalows with air conditioning, hot water, satellite TV, and other amenities for US$20 single, US$30 double.

Ekreach   **US$5**

Mondal 1, district 2, Mittapheap.

A government-run guest house with all rooms for US$5.

Where to Eat in Sihanoukville

For all its good points, Sihanoukville has a poor selection of restaurants serving fair to miserable cuisine. Most eateries are located in hotels, such as the Hawaii and the Phnom Pinh, which serve only Khmer and Chinese dishes. Western food is almost nonexistent.

Sokha Beach Restaurant   **$$**

Sokha Beach.

A large, open-air pavilion on the beach which makes up for its overpriced, mediocre food and abysmal service with a great atmosphere. Often crowded on weekends.

Crocodile Restaurant   **$$**

Hilton Beach.

Similar to the Sokha, with the same menu and high prices. Dubious hygiene.

Directory

Transportation

By **road**, Sihanoukville is a pleasant and sometimes eventful three-hour drive from the capital along the freshly reconstructed National Route 4, which can be made by share taxi for US$25 each way, or by rented motorcycle. Share taxis depart Phnom Penh in the early morning from Psar Depot, north of the water tower near the Olympic Stadium. From Sihanoukville, taxis congregate near the central market.

By **air**, Royal Air Cambodge flies to Sihanoukville three—sometimes four—days per week; flights on Tuesday and Sunday stop in Koh Kong province first. Round-trip fare is US$70 from Phnom Penh.

The Road to Sihanoukville

On April 11, 1994, two Britons and an Australian were abducted at a daylight Khmer Rouge roadblock on Highway 4, the main route to Sihanoukville and the coast, and later executed. On July 26, 1994, three other Westerners were abducted after a Khmer Rouge rocket attack on a train traveling from Phnom Penh to Sihanoukville. They were executed two months later near Vine Mountain. On January 14, 1995, an American woman was killed by bandits—and her husband seriously wounded—in Siem Reap province.

Not good press for a country whose lifelines are illegal timber concessions, gambling and tourism.

Is travel in Cambodia safe for foreigners in 1997? The government seems to think so and invited Fielding to see for itself.

I received a fax from Veng Sereyvuth, Cambodia's Minister of Tourism and a member of the Royal Family, inviting me to dinner.

"Mr. Dulles, in response to your willing to revisit Cambodia to reassess the country's safety," the fax read, "I have the honor to cordially invite you for a dinner...I believe that this meeting is evidently the best way to have the correct and better overview on tourism in Cambodia."

Two days later, a Royal Air Cambodge 737 dumped me on the tarmac at Phnom Penh's Pochentong Airport beneath a searing sun, rare for the monsoons of August. They'd done plastic surgery on the small cozy terminal since my last visit.

Halfway into town, my taxi driver stopped. A police motorcycle carrying two of Phnom Penh's finest had pulled out onto Pochentong Boulevard from a side street directly in front of a small Toyota, which slammed into the rear of the bike, splattering the cops on the pavement. The bike was eaten by the sedan's grille and lay crumpled beneath the undercarriage. One of the cops staggered away in shock. The small Toyota was packed with perhaps eight Khmer passengers. The other cop bolted to his feet and raced to the right front door of the car.

He opened it, dragged out a young Cambodian man and began kicking the daylights out of the poor lad, pummeling his rib cage with his military boots. It seemed to make no difference that the steering wheel of the Toyota was on the left-hand side, the actual driver of the car grimacing in either the realization of imminent pain and arrest or in the delight that his car had been smuggled into Cambodia from Vietnam and not Thailand.

I checked into the Capitol Hotel, the seedy mecca of Cambodia's long-nose ganja trade. Tattered, weathered cyclo and motorbike drivers looking for customers meandered around the perimeter like gulls on a shrimp trawler. Hippies loafed about, swilling from tall bottles of Angkor beer, feigning boredom—like all way-cool people do in the Third World.

Policemen strapped to AK-47 assault rifles lounged on stools on the street corners, smoking in tedium. I ordered some rice and bought that day's edition of the Cambodia Daily from a kid street hawk. That day's banner announced that four foreigners on motorcycles had been cut down by machine gun fire in the capital the previous night in two separate incidents. They were mistaken as potential terrorists who earlier sprayed some weapons fire at Second Prime Minister Hun Sen's house in a drive-by.

The Road to Sihanoukville

There was a report of troop movements a hundred klicks to the south, suggesting a possible coup attempt against Hun Sen. Hun had ordered his personal troops to set up roadblocks in the street. The foreigners had been accused of disobeying orders to stop–as well as warning shots–and had consequently been shot. An hour later, the second duo, aboard a Honda Rebel, were mowed down in a hail of tracers. Lying on the asphalt wounded, the military cops robbed them of a cell phone and cash.

The "coup attempt" and the "troop movements" to the south turned out to be no more than Co-Premier Norodom Ranariddh's bodyguards on their monthly jog to the airport. The foreigners had been returning home from a bar. No one fires warning shots in Cambodia, one of them later said.

I called Veng Sereyvuth to schedule dinner. He was busy dedicating something somewhere, but his assistant told me to meet him the following night at 7:30 at the Cambodiana, Cambodia's queen of hotels and a good place to convince someone that land mines don't maim a few hundred Cambodians a month or that Khmers' per-capita annual income isn't below 170 bucks a year.

I rented a Honda Rebel, the Tonka Toy of choppers, and headed back to the Capitol to find a guide to go to Sihanoukville. My Khmer is as fluent as my Swahili, and I didn't want to get stuck in the sticks trading my wallet and underwear for smiles with the locals.

I was swarmed with applicants on the street and chose the guy who seemed most capable of talking his way out of a hole. He went by the name of Tall Man. Appropriate, as he was over six-three, making him the King Kong of Khmers. I gave in to his insistence that we bike out past the airport to a military firing range to do some target practice with their AKs and M-16s. We bought ammo at a black market dump on the edge of town and hooked up with a unit of the military police at the range 5 kilometers on the other side of the airport. At 50 meters, I hit the target twice in 30 attempts. Outstanding.

I met with Sereyvuth the next night at the posh Cambodiana. The tourism minister was tall and a lot younger than I expected, and dressed in an Italian double-breasted suit sans tie. His dark face was strong but boyish. His broad smile deserved a spot on a box of toothpaste. He brought with him a strapping, husky Australian named Trevor, whose own smile couldn't be seen beneath mustache whiskers spilling over his mouth like stalagmite from the roof of a cave. He was introduced to me as an attorney. He looked more like a retired boxer.

Forty-dollar dishes appeared at our table and sat as props. Veng teased some pasta with his fork. The Aussie made no such pretensions of hunger. His crab and shrimp cured beneath the lamps of the overhead chandelier, as he spent the next hour running down the delicate intricacies of composing a Casino Democracy. I had upset their grandiose plans to lure offshore currency with the publication of accounts which suggested that Cambodia wasn't particularly safe for tourists, and both men were hardly pleased with my announcement that I would be retracing the routes to Sihanoukville of the six Westerners who had been abducted and executed by the Khmer Rouge a year earlier. In no uncertain terms, I was warned not to travel to Sihanoukville by train.

"There's a way of doing things in this country," Trevor warned, "and there's a way of not doing them. Do not go to Sihanoukville."

The Road to Sihanoukville

"Tomorrow," Veng cut in, "go to Angkor Wat and have a good time. You'll see that Cambodia is certainly safe." He was smiling. I decided not to bring up the four foreigners who were splattered by the troops.

* * *

Foreigners are still not permitted to purchase the discounted tickets for the first three cars of the train, which can only be had by Cambodians. At last check, clerks at Phnom Penh's train station refused to sell any tickets at all to foreigners on any of Cambodia's train routes.

"That's how those guys were hit," Martin Flitman, a long-time Phnom Penh-based photojournalist told me. "They were seen buying tickets at the station. Word goes down the line into KR territory. The KR knew those tourists were on the train before it got there. You might be able to make it today, but not if you buy your ticket at the station. Get aboard after Pochentong and you may make it."

Flitman was the type of guy who might try it. Rail thin, with an electric shock of hair, crazy eyes and a vestful of lenses, he was like Dennis Hopper in Apocalypse Now. Or Timothy Leary telling the world he was looking forward to his imminent death, as it would be the ultimate trip. Guys like this made up your mind for you.

The train was out of the question. The risks weren't worth it simply to make a point. I'd take the bike down to the coast—via National Highway 4, the route the April '94 trio had taken, where they were seized at a Khmer Rouge roadblock in broad daylight.

The dawn brought a steady rain. I went to the U.S. embassy and registered my itinerary. I was told the Khmer Rouge had blown up a portion of Highway 4 near the boonies 120 kilometers from the capital with a couple of crude diesel and fertilizer bombs the previous morning. I was warned only to travel between 10 a.m. and 3 p.m.—and do it in a convoy. Great. I went over to the Capitol to pick up Tall Man.

Kompong Som—or Sihanoukville, the quaintly renamed port of the south—is 230 kilometers south of Phnom Penh at the other end of a marvelously well-paved ribbon of asphalt which cuts a swath through the flat rice fields around the Mekong River and winds its way through the Elephant Mountains before descending into the sleepy seaside port town. Route 4 is Cambodia's lifeline—and its deathline.

Highway 4 is generally considered to be safe for 50 klicks out of Phnom Penh. The villages flanking its shoulders are large, and psychologically comforting, modern Western-style petrol stations spring from the rice fields every 5 kilometers or so. As the road cuts into the hills, the villages become fewer and farther between. The Shell stations cease. Rice fields cede the topography to rolling parcels of dense brush, much of the scrub blanketing many of the country's millions of land mines.

This is Khmer Rouge territory. During daylight on most days, the guerrillas hide in the hills between 5 and 10 klicks off the highway. At night they creep to the roadside and lay fresh mines and—along with other groups of thugs, bullies and bandits—stop vehicles and rob motorists.

The Road to Sihanoukville

As the route winds though KR turf, every half-klick a small group of soldiers can be seen lounging by the roadside beneath makeshift lean-tos. The small bridges along Highway 4 are manned by troops 24 hours a day. The soldiers sleep beneath tarps strung in the trees just off the road. They have the special responsibility of preventing the KR from blowing up the bridges. A number will step into the road, attempting to halt cars for bribes. Few motorists pay them any heed, speeding past. They know they won't have such an escape opportunity at the larger, more fortified checkpoints. At these points, the line of cars and trucks waiting to pay the road "toll" can reach a kilometer long. Until recently, foreigners traveling in taxis were routinely hit up for kickbacks at the military roadblocks. Gratefully, such instances are rare these days.

We were halfway to Sihanoukville, and I was surprised we hadn't been stopped by the soldiers. "It is good we are on a motorcycle," Tall Man said. "The army won't stop us because they think we are poor. They stop cars because anyone with a car is rich. Only poor people would ride a motorcycle to Sihanoukville."

About 50 klicks from Sihanoukville, Tall Man tapped my shoulder. He had to pee. I saw a bright red "DANGER! LAND MINES" sign off the road and parked the bike on the pavement next to it. Not on the soft road shoulder. There was a way to do things in Cambodia, and a way not to do them.

Three soldiers approached the bike, their automatic rifles slung like purses. They seemed friendly enough. I gave them cigarettes and Mr. DP stickers. Tall Man chirped with the lazy soldiers in Khmer and then turned to me to translate.

"A child stepped on a land mine," he said. "About an hour ago. Right there." He pointed.

It started to rain again. I rolled the bike about 50 meters up the asphalt. A small compound of brightly painted hootches on stilts were off to the right, just off the road. Tinny, reverbed Khmer mourning music blared from a small loudspeaker. Beneath an overhang stood a circle of people.

I was struck by the blood-soaked blanket covering the corpse, as the circle opened up to let me through. An old man, on seeing my camera, removed the shroud and stripped the dead 12-year-old. The child had caught the blast in the groin. His eyes were milky, his tiny hands folded on his chest. He looked as if he had taken awhile to die.

The old man was the child's grandfather. He said his grandson had been walking the family cow. The cow had stepped on the mine, then ran off into the forest on three legs. It explained why the boy's legs were fine. He said the mine had been planted by drunken government soldiers about a month ago.

We made it to Sihanoukville, escaping detainment, arrest, theft, abduction and execution. I got drunk on Thai whisky. The next morning we headed back for Phnom Penh. I stopped to photograph the village where the child had died. The grandfather had sent a messenger to a faraway province to summon the child's parents.

The Road to Sihanoukville

After another 60 kilometers, we came upon a unit of the Cambodian Mine Action Committee (CMAC), tiptoeing on Highway 4's shoulder with metal detectors. The team was led by a young Canadian army captain and supported by Royal Cambodian tanks and armored personnel carriers. A Khmer was slumped asleep behind the wheel of a Nissan pickup. In its bed, a huge Browning machine gun mounted on a turret was aimed toward the eastern mountains. It looked like the "technicals" used by the thugs and warlords in Somalia. Another soldier stooped by the side of the highway wiping a pair of B-40 rockets. Steamrollers were pressing new asphalt. We had come upon the spot where the KR's diesel and fertilizer bombs had detonated a couple of days earlier. I reported our discovery to the Canadian. Tall Man gave his Khmer assistant the details and location.

"Thanks for the report," the Canadian said. "I didn't know there was any action down there. We'll report it to Phnom Penh, and they'll send a team down there to clean up the area soon."

"The old man said government troops buried it about a month ago," I said.

"Unlikely. Probably old. But even we can't tell how long they've been under."

The Canadian had been in-country six months, charged with clearing Highway 4 from Phnom Penh to Sihanoukville. He'd made it about halfway, saying his team had removed 1800 mines. The kid's mine had made it 1801.

Krong Koh Kong

Koh Kong is on Cambodia's far southwestern coastline not far from the Thai border and is making for a remote alternative to Sihanoukville these days. With regular flights and the Khmer Rouge all but a has-been in the region, Koh Krong is just beginning to be inked onto the Cambodian tourist map.

The town itself is a pleasant if not terribly distinct fishing community, but some of the best coastal scenery in Cambodia can be found here. Mountains ring the area and a number of pristine islands, accessible by private craft, can be found just off the coast. The beaches here are the most extensive along the Cambodian coastline. The waters are generally clear and make for great snorkeling during the dry season months. During the rainy season, from May through October, the waters can become rough and unpredictable.

There are extensive mangrove swamps in the region which are home to rare and exotic wildlife. It's worth chartering a small boat to get to them for half-day of kickback leisure.

Koh Kong is reached by Royal Air Cambodge three times a week from Phnom Penh: Tuesdays, Fridays and Sundays.

Central and Western Cambodia

Other than Siem Reap, these areas of Cambodia remain largely inaccessible, for political, military and infrastructural reasons. In other words, much of Cambodia is either a war zone or remains essentially lawless and inaccessible. The U.S. State Department, as of this writing, is still urging Americans to avoid any form of travel in central and western Cambodia. The Khmer Rouge formerly controlled approximately 20 percent of the country, with most of the area located in the west. Pailin, near the Thai border, for instance, was entirely under Khmer Rouge control until the end of 1996. The guerrillas made Pailin their principal base. A government assault on the KR provisional capital in April 1994 failed. But the defection of Khmer Rouge leader Ieng Sary and most of his soldiers to the government side in mid-1996 put Pailin ostensibly under government control. See "Pailin" below.

AUTHOR'S NOTE

Ironically enough, according to the International Union for the Conservation of Nature, despite decades of war, rather than being decimated of its wildlife, Cambodia has emerged as a haven for endangered animal species and plants that have been all but eliminated in neighboring Thailand and Vietnam. According to IUCN, Cambodia has abundant wildlife, including elephants, bears and tigers that are an eco-tourist's dream. The conservation agency says that Cambodia could become a major Southeast Asian destination for environmental tourists within a few years if stability comes to a majority of the country.

Although little scientific work has been conducted in the northwest of Cambodia due to the Khmer Rouge's continued domination of that region, surveys in the northeastern part of the country have revealed a number of species that are extinct—or close to it—in other countries, including tigers, elephants, kouprey and wild cow. The kouprey is Cambodia's National Animal, although none has been sighted since 1963. But evidence suggests that as many as 20 of the creatures exist in remote areas today. Three varieties of stork, which are on the verge of global extinction, are known to breed freely in Cambodia. Rare birds are frequently sighted in the northeast. New species of flora and fauna are expected to be discovered in coming years.

The Outer Limits

AUTHOR'S NOTE

King Norodom Sihanouk signed a bill in 1993 which called for the "creation and designation of protected areas." Consequently, there are plans for environmental protection laws and the creation of at least seven national parks and 10 wildlife sanctuaries. But quite frankly, any terrain the Khmer Rouge control can be considered a "wildlife sanctuary." There's certainly more than 10 of 'em—and I'm not talking about those for endangered microscopic worms and minnows. (Human beings are endangered enough.) Storks aren't abducted by the guerrillas and only released after their genus agrees to a 5000-egg ransom for purchasing "shells." Cambodian plans for the preservation (or extinction) of the not-so-endangered Cambodian "guerrilla" species aren't so ambitious at present.

Battambang

Battambang, with a population estimated at 90,000, is the country's second-largest city. It's also along Cambodia's main rail route. But the city continued to be shelled regularly, although rarely accurately, by Khmer Rouge units until the start of 1997. It is certainly not a place most tourists would consider a destination. But some hardy souls manage to get there, if only to say they've been there.

Battambang is 292 kilometers from Phnom Penh and sits on the banks of the Stung Sangker River. It was founded in the 11th century and you might expect the city to be the site of some spectacular ancient temples. Well, i once was. What remains today is hardly recognizable as such. Wat Ek wa constructed during the 11th century by Suryavarman I and is about 8-9 ki lometers from town. Wat Toul Baset, which is in relatively decent shape afte having endured 1400 years, features bas reliefs depicting scenes from the In dian epic Mahabaratha.

Wat Sengkar, Wat Po Khnong, Wat Bopharam and Wat Kandal are worth visit on the east side of the river. Wat Po Veal Museum has a selection of an cient Khmer art. However, the most important pieces from the region are i the National Museum in Phnom Penh.

Royal Air Cambodge has flights to Battambang daily from Phnom Penh. I is also possible to take a taxi from the capital with a reasonable degree of pe sonal security these days.

Pailin

For the last 20 years Pailin has been perhaps the most forbidden city in th world. After the fall of the Khmer Rouge to the Vietnamese in Phnom Per in 1979, the rebels retreated west toward the Thai border—and Pailin b came their base for the next 18 years. The only foreigners to see the town a quarter-century were UN peacekeeping troops during UNTAC's supervision of the 1993 elections. Even these folks shivered in their boots.

In mid-1996, one of the KR's top leaders, Ieng Sary, defected—along with an estimated 10,000 of his troops—to the government side. In return for his defection, which essentially eliminated the Khmer Rouge as a threat to national security and ended 30 years of civil war, Ieng Sary was given control of Pailin and permitted to run the city as an autonomous region. Although his soldiers now wear government uniforms with Angkor Wat patches on the sleeves, little has changed in this community, which knows nothing else but Khmer Rouge occupation—and supports nothing but KR control.

Today, loudspeakers still blare public messages to the town's 12,000 residents at 6 a.m.—"No crime; no prostitution or gambling; no monopoly business." Signs still posted around town display the Big Brother messages of the Khmer Rouge: "Corruption and robbery bring social instability."

Indeed, there is little crime in Pailin. It is said that thieves and other criminals are simply executed without a trial, as they were during the Khmer Rouge years. There are no jails in town. The official line is that social offenders are sent off to re-education camps in the forest. Of course that was Phnom Penh's line in 1978, during the genocide of perhaps a quarter of Cambodia's population.

The royally pardoned Ieng Sary—a ruthless executioner for Pol Pot during the Khmer Rouge regime of the mid- and late-1970s—still runs Pailin, this in exchange for his defection to the government. He and his cronies are fabulously wealthy from the gem and hardwood trades, which is how the Khmer Rouge financed its civil war in the 1980s and 1990s. The central government in Phnom Penh sees none of the wealth which is still being accrued by Ieng Sary and his autonomous municipal hierarchy.

Consequently, Pailin has been booming. In 1997, buildings were going up by the dozens. Pailin gem and hardwood traders were signing lucrative contracts with Thai companies.

The town still remains essentially closed off to outsiders. The lucky journo can get in.

Northeastern and Eastern Cambodia

Rattanakiri

Cambodia's northeastern region is sparsely populated and extremely inaccessible. Population centers in the east are found primarily along or near National Route 1, the route to Saigon. But one area in the northeast accessible by plane is Rattanakiri.

A vast, forested province, Rattanakiri has been virtually cut off from the rest of the country for years. Even today there are no overland links to Phnom Penh; Highway 9, a lone dirt road, connects the provincial capital, Ban Lung, with Pleiku in central Vietnam.

Rattanakiri's isolation has played an important role in recent Southeast Asian history. In 1963, the Khmer Rouge, led by the infamous Pol Pot, established one of their first strongholds in the area, as it was safe from incursions by the Phnom Penh army forces. Later the province was used by the North Vietnamese Army for smuggling weapons and cadres south along the Ho Chi Minh Trail; as a result, the area was carpet-bombed by US B-52s.

With 70,000 inhabitants, dense jungle, volcanic lakes, picturesque waterfalls, and roughly 30 different ethnic groups, Rattanakiri is a natural paradise, completely different from the rest of Cambodia. The province is very secure; there is virtually no crime, land mines, nor problems with the Khmer Rouge. Twenty-four-hour electricity is provided by a local hydroelectric power plant.

The sleepy village of **Ban Lung** consists of several dirt roads linking a few official buildings, a small market, and several basic guest houses. The best is the **Mountain Guesthouse**, a deal at US$4 per night including breakfast. The Mountain also has a bakery which churns out the town's supply of French baguettes. Motorbikes are available for rent at around US$5–6 per day. There is absolutely nothing to do or see in Ban Lung, but it's a pleasant, mellow place nonetheless.

Around Ban Lung, attractions include **Boeng Yeak Laom** ("Lake Surrounded by Giants"), formed from an ancient volcanic crater. Locals claim that giants live on the bottom, 250 meters down; however, a recent study by an American scientist measured the depth at only 45 meters. Nevertheless, the lake has a surreal, dreamy air about it; the crystal clear waters invite swimming and the shores have plenty of idyllic picnic spots. Locals come out in force on weekends, mostly converging on the pavilion built by UNTAC troops.

Along the roads leading to the lake, you'll see members of the Tampuon or Jarai tribes, who live nearby in simple wood-and-thatch huts. The women often smoke long pipes and go about topless.

A tall, mossy waterfall (*teuk chu* in Khmer), located some 5 km outside Ban Lung just past the rubber tree plantations, is also a great picnic spot. Check out the water before diving in, however, as the waterfall lies downstream from a small village and may contain unpleasant effluvium.

Outside Ban Lung are uncounted kilometers of dirt roads leading to more rubber plantations or villages. Going north you'll encounter ethnic Lao villagers. One can wander for hours down these tree-lined paths without seeing a soul.

Royal Air Cambodge flies directly to Rattanakiri on Mondays, Thursdays and Fridays. On Tuesdays and Sundays, there are flights leaving Phnom Penh which stop in Stung Treng province. Fare is US$100 round-trip.

Stung Treng

Only about 30 kilometers from the Laos border on the eastern bank of the Mekong River, the Lao influences are evident in Stung Treng. The population is a mish-mash of ethnic Khmer, Lao and Thai.

Stung Treng is home to working elephant camps and it's possible to arrange for elephant rides here, although the best thing to do is just take in the river life and check out the few waterfalls. Not spectacular, but peaceful. At the time of this writing Stung Treng was secure and offers basic accommodations for foreign visitors.

Royal Air Cambodge flies here from Phnom Penh five times a week.

Sen Monorom (Mondulkiri)

This is about as remote as any place you can get to by air in Cambodia, and that's saying a lot. Other than by air, the town is entirely cut off from the rest of Cambodia. Densely forested and mountainous, the area is home to thousands of Phnong hill people. These folks make up the majority of the 30,000 or so people who live in Mondulkiri province. This colorful hilltribe is getting more accustomed to seeing foreigners, but still few get out here—you'll have no company when enjoying the region's many waterfalls, the best being the Sen Monorom Waterfall.

Royal Air Cambodge flies here from Phnom Penh twice a week, on Monday and Thursday.

The Outer Limits

Khmer Glossary

A CRASH COURSE IN KHMER

GREETINGS AND FORMALITIES

Hello	*Joom reab/Suor sdei*
Good morning	
Good afternoon	
Good night	*Rear trei suor sdei*
Good-bye	*Lear heouy*
Please	*Suom*
How are you?	*Tau neak sok sapbaiy jea te?*
I am doing well, thank you	*Sok touk jea thom-ada te*
Thank you	*Ar kun*
No, thank you	*Te ar kun*
Yes (men)	*Bat*
Yes (women)	*Jas*
No	*Te*
Excuse me	*Suom tous*

PRONOUNS

I	*Khjoom*

NUMBERS

1	*Mouy*
2	*Pee*
3	*Bei*
4	*Boun*
5	*Bram*
6	*Bram-mouy*
7	*Bram-pee*
8	*Bram-bei*
9	*Bram-boun*
10	*Duop*
11	*Duop-mouy*
12	*Duop-pee*
13	*Duop-bei*
14	*Duop-boun*
15	*Duop-bram*

A CRASH COURSE IN KHMER

16	*Duop-bram-mouy*
17	*Duop-bram-pee*
18	*Duop-bram-bei*
19	*Duop-bram-boun*
20	*Maphei*
21	*Maphei-mouy*
22	*Maphei-pee*
30	*Samseb*
40	*Sairseb*
50	*Haseb*
60	*hokseb*
70	*jetseb*
80	*Peitseb*
90	*Kavseb*
100	*Mouy-rouy*
500	*Bram-rouy*
1000	*Mouy-paun*
10,000	*Mouy-meoun*
100,000	*Mouy-sen*
1 million	*Mouy-rouy-lean*

DAYS OF THE WEEK

Sunday	*Tha-ngai attit*
Monday	*Tha-ngai chan*
Tuesday	*Tha-ngai angkea*
Wednesday	*Tha-ngai puot*
Thursday	*Tha-ngai preuo-haou*
Friday	*Tha-ngai sok*
Saturday	*Tha-ngai sav*
Yesterday	*Masel menh*
Tomorrow	*Sa-ek*
Morning	*Preouk*
Afternoon	*Reuseal*
Evening	*La-ngeech*

Khmer Glossary

A CRASH COURSE IN KHMER

Right now	*Eilov nees*
In the morning	*Neouv pel preouk*
In the afternoon	*Neouv pel reuseal*
In the evening	*Neouv pel la-ngeech*
At night	*Neouv pel yuop*
This week/month	*Atit/khe nees*
Last week/month	*Atit/khe muon*
What time is it?	*Eilov nees moung ponmaan?*
When?	*Pel na?*
Night	*Yuop*
What day is today?	*Tha-ngai nees jea that-ngai ei?*
What is today's date?	*Tha-ngai nees trouv jea tha-ngai khe ei?*
At what time?	*Muong ponmaan*

MONTHS OF THE YEAR

January	*Makara*
February	*Kumphak*
March	*Meenear*
April	*Mesa*
May	*Ou-saphea*
June	*Me-thuna*
July	*Kakkada*
August	*Seiha*
September	*Kanh-nha*
October	*Tola*
November	*Vichika*
December	*Tha-nou*

USEFUL WORDS AND PHRASES

Where is the...?	*Tau...nouv eir na?*
Bus station	*Ben lan*
Railway station	*Sathani rout phleoung*
Airport	*Veal youn huos*
Tourist office	*Kariyaleiy samrap puok tesajor*
Bus	*Lan thom deouk monuos*

A CRASH COURSE IN KHMER

Train	*Rout phleoung*
Boat	*Tuok*
Ticket office	*Kanleng luok suombuot*
I want a ticket to…	*Khjoom junh ban suombuot teou…*
When does it leave here?	*Tau ke jeng domneur moung ponmaan?*
When does it arrive here/there?	*Tau ke teou/mouk doul moung ponmaan?*
How many hours does it take?	*Tau domneur nees sie pel ponmaan muong?*

ACCOMMODATIONS

I want a…	*Khjoom joung ban…*
Room	*Bantuop*
Bed	*Kre mouy*
Single room	*Bantuop kre samrap mouy neak*
Double room	*Bantuop kre samrap pee neak*
Triple room	*Bantuop kre samrap khnea pei neak*
Room with private bath	*Bantuop deil meen thlang gnout teouk*
Room with a shower	*Bantuop deil meen teouk phka chouk*
Do you have a cheaper room?	*Tau neak meen eiy deil thuok jeang nees deir te?*
Could I see the room?	*Tau khjoom suom meul bantuop sen ban te?*
How much does the room cost?	*Chnoul mouy bantuop tleiy ponmaan?*

FOOD AND DRINK

Soda water with lemon	*Soda kroch chhmar*
Ice	*Tuk tak*
Beer	*Bia*
Whisky	*Wi-sa-kee*
Coffee	*Ka-fae*
Meat	*Saach*
Chicken	*maan*
Fish	*Trei*
Soup	*Suop/somlor*
Noodles	*Kuy teav/Mee/Moum banjuok*
Eggs	*Poung sat*
I can eat…	*Khjoom hope toul tean saach…*

Khmer Glossary

A CRASH COURSE IN KHMER

I cannot eat...	*Khjoom toam...*
Market	*Psar*

TRAVEL/TOPOGRAPHY/ARCHITECTURE

Town on the water	*Kompong*
Lake	*Boeng*
River	*Tonle*
Mountain (hill)	*Phnom*
Pagoda	*Wat*

EMERGENCIES

This is an emergency	*Nees jea pheap ason*
I want a...	*Khjoom joung ban...*
Please call...	*Suom jouy hao...*
Doctor	*Krou peit*
Dentist	*Peit thamenh*
Ambulance	*Lan peit*
Police	*Police*

MEDICAL

I have...	*Khjoom...*
Diarrhea	*Reak*
I have a fever.	*Khjoom krun.*
I have a cold.	*Khjoom padasay.*
I have constipation.	*Khjoom toul leamouk.*
I have a headache.	*Khjoom chheu kbal.*
I have diabetes.	*Khjoom meen rouk teouk nuom pa-em.*
I'm allergic to penicillin.	*Khjoom min trouv theat neoung thanam pe-neecilleen.*
I have cramps.	*Khjoom romuol krapeu.*

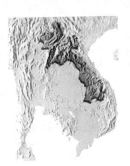

LAOS

Plain of Jars in Xieng Khouang province of Laos covers 1000 square meters.

Travelers are either awed with Laos or lullabied to sleep by it, depending on where this technically communist country fits into their Southeast Asia itineraries. First-timers to Indochina will marvel at sights like Vientiane's That Luang, the Plain of Jars, Luang Prabang's Pak Ou caves and the Khone Prapheng waterfalls in Champassak; while others, who've already experienced Angkor Wat, climbed Vietnam's Phan Si Pan Mountain, elephant trekked Karen rebel territory on the Thai-Burma border, broken bread with ethnic Gia Rai in jungle longhouses in Buon Ma Thuot and weathered ferry rides up the Tonle Sap may ask what all the fuss is about.

Suffice it to say that Laos is the least explored country in Indochina. It may lack the spectacular ancient temples of Cambodia, the Hawaii-like coastline of Vietnam and the racy nightlife of Bangkok, but travel in Laos offers the intrepid adventurer the chance to see and experience a people and land few foreigners before him have. There are no real transportation and communication networks here. You'll be tossed back into the Stone Age in many places in Laos, and the only tourist map you'll have is your own ingenuity. You may as well have been pushed from a plane over the Amazon with a compass and a change of underwear. Laos, in other words, is a good place to get lost.

Laos, these days, is being touted in the Sunday travel sections as the last great frontier. Travelers with a memory longer than Ronald Reagan's will recall these same editors making similar pontifications about Vietnam and Cambodia just a few short months ago. Laos certainly may not be the "last" frontier, but the country does make Third World Vietnam and Cambodia look like shopping centers in Singapore.

With the exception of being able to get into Vientiane across the Mekong River from Nong Khai in Thailand for a limited stay in the capital, landlocked Laos has been mostly closed to tourism since 1975 and has only recently opened the door for travel elsewhere in the country. As a result of the 15-year ban on tourism to the country, there have been few infrastructure improvements and you will be among the first Westerners to explore this heavily damaged but fascinating country. Laos is much like Europe after 1945, as many of its ancient monuments are damaged and many areas of the country are moonscapes; the consequences of the United States' secret war against Laos are apparent.

As with Myanmar, the Laotian government is gradually opening up areas of the country for unrestricted travel—Laos no longer directly controls where travelers can go and what they can see and do except in a few very isolated regions. Even in these areas, however, enforcement capabilities (and motivation, it seems) are lacking. You can get a short visa to gain entry and then try creating your own trip once in Vientiane. The fact of the matter is that the situation in Laos changes regularly regarding how you can enter the country and get around once inside. The "authorities" are hard-pressed to keep track of you and, as it turns out, rarely do. If you're considering visiting this beautiful country, the best thing to do is question other travelers in places such as Bangkok, Saigon and Phnom Penh who have recently been to Laos themselves.

The best time to visit is November to March, when it's cooler and drier. The higher elevations such as Plain of Jars and Bolovens plateau can drop below freezing, and the rest of the year it's hot—real hot.

Few governments envy Laos, a landlocked, rugged land, populated by diverse ethnic groups and bordered on all sides by pugnacious neighbors. With an annual per-capita income of $180, most (75 percent) of the four million

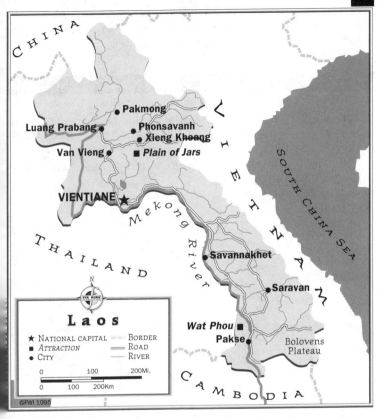

residents of Laos are agrarian subsistence farmers. Only 10 percent of the country lies anywhere near a road.

We don't want to ponder too long on the savagery of the undeclared war the United States wrought on Laos, but suffice it to say that Laos has the dubious distinction of being the most thoroughly bombed country in history. U.S. warplanes dropped more than 2 million tons of bombs on this primitive country for nearly nine years in the '60s and early '70s. That's more than the total tonnage dropped on Europe in WWII.

Little wonder why Laos had been living entirely on Russian aid until the collapse of the Soviet Union and its aftermath. Now with that source of income gone, Laos has looked begrudgingly to tourism to generate badly needed dollars. Laotians do not wish to throw open their doors to unbridled commercialism and, like Myanmar, are taking it one step at a time. Still, a trip to Laos in 1997 or 1998 will make you one of the vanguard who will see this country without makeup and in the cold light of its transition from communism to capitalism. Rather than take you through the tongue-twisting list of rulers and dates, we will try to put some order to the various eras of Laos by providing a brief overview of its history.

LAOS AT A GLANCE				
The place	*Square km*	*Population*	*Languages*	*Religions*
Lao People's Democratic Republic	**236,000**	**4.75 million**	**Lao, various dialects of Lao, French**	**85 % Theravada Buddhist. 15% animist**
People	*Capital City*	*Pop. growth rate*	*Per capita income*	*Government*
50% Lao Loum (Lowland Lao), 30% Lao Theu (Lower Mountain), 10-20% Lao Sung (high mountains, mostly Hmong)	**Vientiane (pop. 300,000)**	**2.9%**	**US$180**	**Socialist republic**
Gross Domestic Product	*World GDP Rank*	*Inflation*	*Annual Growth*	*Chief Exports*
US$9.6 billion	**151st**	**6.7%**	**8%**	**Rice, coffee, tobacco, timber, opium**
Trading Partners	*Timber Exports*	*Country Code (Telephone)*	*Currency Exchange*	*Average Annual Rainfall (Vientiane)*
Thailand, Vietnam, Japan, Malaysia	**450,000 square meters**	**856**	**US$1=925 kip**	**1720 mm**

History of Laos

The mountains of Laos acted as a wall against the Mongols of Kublai Khan. The Tai tribes fled to Laos, gradually absorbing culture and influence from India rather than from China.

The Khmer empire was under the control of Lannathai in the 11th century and under the Sukhothai. It was not until 1349, with the fall of the Ayutthaya Dynasty, that the kingdom of Laos was created.

Called **Lane Xang**, the land of a million elephants, it claimed as an empire an area similar to present-day Laos and was ruled from Luang Prabang by Fa Ngoum, a prince from Angkor Wat in what is present-day Cambodia.

Theravada Buddhism was the official religion, and the Golden Buddha, from which Luang Prabang gets its name, was a gift from Fa Ngoum's Khmer father-in-law.

In 1369, his son Samsenethai took over and set up the system of *muangs* (districts) that was in effect until 1975. When he died, Wat Manoram was built to house his ashes.

Chaiyachakkapat-Phaenphaeo ruled from 1441 until 1478, years that marked the beginning of Vietnam's incursions into Laos. His son, King Suvarna Banlang, drove the Vietnamese out of Luang Prabang. King Visunarat, who ruled from 1500 to 1520, is remembered for building Wat Visoun in Luang Prabang. It was then Vientiane's turn to be Indochina's prominent center under King Phothisareth from 1520 to 1548. His union with a Chaing Mai princess created Setthathirat, one of Laos' best known and loved monarchs. He ruled from the new capital Vientiane and was responsible for building Wat Phra Kareo and bringing the Emerald Buddha (the same one that is now in Bangkok) inside. When he expired in 1574, the kingdom of Laos split into factions, with Vientiane (called Vieng Chan) ending up under Burmese rule and Luang Prabang in the north splitting away.

Seven years later, the two kingdoms were unified under Nokeo Koumane, who ruled for five years. His successor, Thammikarath, lasted from 1596 until 1622. The next ruler, King Souligna Vongsa, lasted until 1694 and it was about this time that Europeans caught their first glimpses of this strange and wonderful land. Jesuit missionaries and the Dutch trader Gerrit van Wuysthoff were some of the first to see it. Laos was considered too remote and too poor; Europe's expansionist attention turned to the more lucrative lands of America and Indonesia. After the benign reign of Souligna Vongsa, Laos never regained its peaceful state again. The kingdom of Laos became a succession of small kingdoms, foreign-run vassal states and colonial empires.

In 1778, Vientiane (Vieng Chan) was sacked, and both the Emerald Buddha and Phra Bang were taken to Bangkok. Run by the puppet King Anou, the Thais ruled Laos from afar. It wasn't until the French assumed control of Laos in 1887 that the country began to enjoy a 50-year period of *laisse faire* colonialism, with the Chinese and Vietnamese given control of most of the country's trade.

The Japanese never technically invaded Laos but ousted the French administration in a coup in March of 1945. When the Japanese surrendered, the seeds of independence were planted in Lao minds, as they were in the minds of most of Asia. Faced with returning to their colonial landlords or fighting

LAOS

for independence, the Lao chose freedom. The governor of Vientiane, Prince Phaya Khammao, formed a national government and declared independence on September 1, 1945.

In typical fashion, the French fought to regain their colony, and it wasn't until 1953 that the French granted Laos its freedom, being careful to make Laos a French protectorate.

The Pathet Lao (the Lao Nation) faction, which ruled the north, had different ideas, and when the Viet Minh under Ho Chi Minh beat the French in Vietnam, the United States became concerned that Laos could fall to Communist influences from the north, which would begin destabilizing Southeast Asian countries one by one. The Domino Theory, as it was called, assumed that China, or all "Commies" for that matter, were bent on world domination. Laos plunged into a three-way civil war in the late '50s between left wing, right wing and neutral factions. America chose to draw the line not in Vietnam, but in Laos in the early '60s.

The United States was determined to stop the flow of arms and supplies along the Ho Chi Minh Trail that ran through Laos into Vietnam. The concept was simple, but the execution was the stuff of pulp novels. The CIA, Army Special Forces (nicknamed the Green Berets), Thai mercenaries, Laotian soldiers and an amazing army of 30,000 Hmong tribesmen, all supported by a CIA-owned-and-run airline called Air America, began a war that would ultimately escalate into the Vietnam War.

At the time, the idea of remote wooden forts inhabited by A-Teams, mercenary pilots in cowboy hats and jeans who flew soldiers and supplies in and opium out, sounded like the Wild West, or a bad Stuart Woods novel. To some extent, this was the reality. In this isolated, backwater whore-hootchdom there were no rules, just guns and dope, and a lot of both. Excess was the order of the day. The bombing of the area around the Ho Chi Minh Trail easily exceeded the ordnance dropped in WWII. Little is known or recorded about this covert war that essentially punched Laos back into the Stone Age.

In August of 1975, what some called "peace" came to Laos and the People's Republic of Laos was born. The monarchy was abolished and a period of even greater darkness, if that could be imagined, descended upon the Laotion people—a time not unlike the dreaded Khmer Rouge years in Cambodia during the mid 1970s. The Pathet Lao communist government began to "reeducate" the population. Intellectuals were sent to concentration camps; village autonomy was ended. The king and his family were arrested; they died in squalor at a reeducation camp. In all, more than 10 percent of the population fled Laos between 1973 and 1975. Three hundred thousand people, mostly educated property owners and shopkeepers, fled to the West or to refugee camps in Thailand.

Laos Today

The Economy

The government of Laos—one of the five remaining official Communist states, along with Vietnam, China, North Korea and Cuba—has been decentralizing control and encouraging private enterprise since 1986. But unlike Vietnam, which essentially transformed its centralized economy into a free market in a mere seven years—Laos has been much more deliberate in its reforms. The results, however, starting from an extremely low base, have been startling—growth has averaged 7.5% annually since 1988.

Regardless of the push forward, Laos is still a landlocked country with a primitive infrastructure. It has no railroads, a basal road system that can be called a "road system" on maps only (if you can even find one of those!), and only embryonic external and internal telecommunications. Electricity is available in only a few urban areas—and even in many of these places, only for a few hours a day. Subsistence agriculture accounts for half of GDP and provides 80% of total employment. The predominant crop is rice. In non-drought years, Laos is self-sufficient overall in food, but each year flood, pests, and localized drought cause shortages in various parts of the country.

For the foreseeable future the economy will continue to depend on aid from the IMF and other international sources; aid from the former USSR and Eastern Europe has been cut sharply. As in many developing countries, deforestation and soil erosion will hamper efforts to maintain the high rate of GDP growth.

Today Laos is still run by an autocratic, Marxist regime, but communism is definitely out of fashion. Same group, different song. You can decide if your tourist dollars are better spent in other countries. For now, we recommend Laos only to the most experienced independent travelers.

Illicit Drugs

Laos is an illicit producer of cannabis and opium poppies for the international drug trade. The country is the fourth largest opium producer in the world (85 metric tons were harvested in 1994 alone). With the heroin labs of Thailand being forced to run for the hills after that country got tough on drugs in the 1980s, many of them ended up on the other side of the border in Laos, turning the country into a major heroin producer. Laos is also increasingly used as transshipment point for heroin produced in Myanmar.

Geography and Environment

Laos is bordered by Myanmar (Burma) to the west, Vietnam to the east, Cambodia to the southeast, China to the north and Thailand to the south. The majority of Laos' terrain (75 percent) is rugged mountains and high plateaus, with the Mekong River (Nam Khong) being the only major commercial byway. It is the largest river in Laos and runs the entire length of the country, demarcating Laos' border with Thailand most of the way. As well, the Mekong is the largest transportation route in the country. It's estimated that only 10 percent of Laos' terrain can support agriculture, much of this area being in the fertle plains found near the Mekong.

Laos is heavily forested with high plateaus and has the lowest population density in Asia (18 people per square kilometer). The population is 4.75 million, who reside within 236,800 sq. km. (Eighty-five percent of the population lives in rural areas.) The high plateaus are grassy savannah, the northern area has pine forests and the lower elevations are hardwood forests. About 50 percent of Laos is primary forest, and 30-35 percent secondary forest. Although Laos is the most densely forested country in Indochina (and the most pristine, say most observers) the country loses 450,000 square meters a year to commercial logging, and perhaps another 100,000 square meters to agricultural pursuits.

Phu Bia, at 2819 meters, is the tallest mountain in Laos. It's found in the northern part of the country. The largest mountain chain in Laos is the Annamite Chain, whose peaks average between 1600–2900 meters in height. The chain runs generally parallel with the Mekong River in the eastern half of the country and also borders Vietnam. At the base of the chain in southern Laos is found the temperate crop-yielding Bolaven Plateau, which reaches across 10,000 square kilometers. Here is where the country's coffee and tea are produced.

Flora and Fauna

The wildlife of Laos is still very impressive, with elephants, rhinoceroses and Asian elk still quite evident—despite carpet bombing and defoliants the U.S. pummeled Laos with back in the 1960s and 1970s. And Laos is taking its wildlife preservation seriously (if not its forests). In Laos, there are 17 Biodiversity Conservation Areas located in different areas of the country. There are many unique bird species; reptiles are in abundance—and predators such as leopards, tigers and bears liven up a jungle hike. Indigenous to Laos or found in the wild today are the snub-nosed langur, concolor gibbon, Siamese hare, Javan rhino, Irrawaddy dolphin, raccoon dog, Javan mongoose, leopard , Asian tiger and lesser panda.

In mid- and low-lying areas, vegetation is generally tropical, featuring coconut, bamboo and banyan trees, as well as hardwood trees typical of monsoon forests. At the higher elevations in the mountains are vast pine forests and trees associated with temperate climates.

Climate

The climate of Laos is technically tropical, but it can get quite cold in mountainous northern Laos, with temperatures dropping below the freezing mark in the winter. Precipitation increases with altitude. The average rainfall in Vientiane is 1720 mm per year. The lowlands receive an average of 1250 mm per year. And the highlands receive twice that. The rainy season is between May and October. In the highlands, it can drop below freezing in December and January. It is quite pleasant during the cool dry season, with temperatures between 10 and 20 degrees Celsius from November to February. March to June is the hot dry season, when temperatures climb daily to 35 degrees Celsius plus. The best time to visit, in terms of weather, is between December and February.

The People and Culture of Laos

INSIDER TIPS

Use the wai when greeting: Put your hands together as if in prayer and bow your head. Remove shoes in temples and private homes. Do not point. Ask permission before taking pictures. You should wear long-sleeve shirts and long pants when visiting a religious site. Address people by their first name. Tipping is not widespread, except for your guide.

The people of Laos are gentle and generally accommodating to foreigners, although some are fearful that contact with outsiders will somehow be construed as an act of treason by the secret police. There are many different tribes in Laos, principally the Thai-Lao of the lower valleys, the Indochinese of the highlands and the Tibeto-Burman peoples of the higher mountains.

Laos has been heavily influenced, of course, by its common ancestry with the Thais. This is particularly evident in the lowlands, where the two cultures seem virtually indistinguishable, save for the modern technological and pop influences seen in many Thais. However, traditional Lao art, dance and music might be called Thai by all but the most learned Lao scolars. The traditional festivals are the same, as is the religion from which their inspiration is drawn from: Theravada Buddhism.

Theravada Buddhism is predominant in Laos, practiced by perhaps 85 percent of the population. (The remaining inhabitants subscribe to a hodge-podge of animist beliefs, as well as a religion called *phii*, a form of spirit worship which is prohibited by the government). The largest ethnic minority in Laos, the Hmong, practice animism. Unlike Vietnam, which was also colonized for many years by the French, there is virtually no Christian population in Laos. After French colonial rule, Vietnam emerged with the second largest Christian population in Southeast Asia (behind the Philippines), but Laos remained virtually unscathed by the missionaries from the West. The only Lao you'll find as Christians probably don't live in Laos—much of the French-educated, elite Lao Christian population fled Laos in 1975. There is a small element (statistically insignificant) of the Lao population which believes Jesus Christ will come again and pull up in a jeep dressed like Rambo.

Buddhist teachings reached the land that is modern Laos and Thailand within a few hundred years of the death of Gautama, the historical Buddha, in 543 B.C. As this was well before the formation of anything that resembles the modern day nation, you could say the religion predates the state. Buddhism arrived via two routes, the north and the south. The two approaches were Mahayana and Theravada, and they diverged increasingly in the way the teachings were interpreted.

Theravada is the more traditional, relying directly on the teachings of Gautama; this was the sect that took ground in Laos and Thailand. The Mahayana sect dominated in the south and east of Indochina, including Vietnam, some parts which were part of the Khmer empire.

Theravada Buddhism now claims nearly nine-tenths of the modern Lao population. Traditionally, the *wat*, or Buddhist temple, has been the center of the people's social, cultural and spiritual lives. Every male enters the monkhood for a period (usually before marriage), and most report that this time away from school, job, and more worldly cares has a significant positive effect on their lives. Although the practice is still widespread, many young men today (especially in and around Vientiane) become monks for shorter periods of time, and go through the exercise more to please their parents than for their own spiritual development.

The clergy and other Buddhist institutions traditionally receive a lot of respect, and the value of merit making in the form of providing monks food and supporting the local *wat*, are deeply entrenched in the Lao psyche. Indeed, it has been noted that Buddhist beliefs about impermanence, suffering, karma, detachment, and so forth are so interwoven into Lao cultural values that you can't spot where the religion begins and the culture ends.

At the same time, indigenous animistic beliefs have been incorporated into the local Buddhism. The spirit houses do not have a Buddhist source. Each house or office building must lure intrinsically mischievous spirits out of the human abode by offering them their own digs. Food and incense are provided daily. In the country, one sometimes comes across temporary spirit houses constructed of beautifully folded grasses. A peasant taking a nap or camping out for the night will often feel moved to provide a little shelter for nearby spirits so that they will leave him and his dreams in peace.

In cities and towns, if expansion or redevelopment requires moving the spirit house, the only thing that will convince the spirits not to cause bad luck to the property owners is building them a bigger, finer spirit house along with the improved or enlarged human construction. The old spirit house is set to the side (never thrown away or resold) and left to be dismantled by the elements of time and weather. It is the monks from the local temple who determine the correct placement of the spirit house, and bless it. They act as sort of middlemen to the spirits, and can even convince them, when expediency demands, that the optimum placement of their home is atop a sewage treatment plant. The administrators of one large office building in Bangkok were advised this would be okay as long as the new spirit house was elevated an extra nine (not eight or 10) steps.

In the same way, the ficus trees which are adorned with incense and garlands are not Buddhist shrines in the strictest sense. These trees are believed by many to harbor spirits and memories of tragedies befalling the people who have occupied the property. While the practice is inherently dangerous because it may incur the wrath of these spirits, sometimes the only way to get rid of the sadness or bad luck is to chop down the trees. A house surrounded by what is considered "too many" large trees shading the dwelling is found to be very scary by many Thais. All these are examples of animistic, or folk, beliefs which coexist happily with Buddhism.

While on the subject, a word about ghosts *(phii)*. Many Lao believe in these, and have a wealth of fascinating personal anecdotes to prove their existence. For this reason, they don't much care for old houses or hospitals. Both of these are known to harbor ghosts, because so many people have died there. The logic is airtight. Similarly, not just spirits, but also ghosts, can inhabit large old trees or wooden buildings. In the case of wooden structures, beyond an occasional sighting, the ghost will often hint of his/her presence by oozing sap down a column or beam. Fortunately, once such a dead giveaway is provided, most Lao will know exactly what to do to keep the ghost from escaping or causing harm. There are special nails available (often provided or blessed by a monk), and one of these need only be driven into the offending ooze to trap the inhabitant in the wood. The same remedy is applied to trees which house ghosts.

The folk beliefs held by most, but not all, Lao people probably developed over centuries in small villages during long rainy seasons when there wasn't much else to do but watch the rice grow. Telling ghost stories is still a favorite pastime among the people. So, when visiting the country and looking for a way to make contact with the locals, a good ghost story provides an excellent icebreaker or conversation starter.

Fielding **NORTHERN LAOS**

SCENIC WONDERS OF LAOS

WAT XIENG THONG
Founded in 1550 and one of the city's more prominent temples

Laos is a scenic country of remote hilltribes and ancient kingdoms. The most primitive of all Southeast Asian countries, it contains incredible sights that make it a great destination for adventurers and history buffs.

CHINA
This Spread
VIETNAM
LAOS
THAILAND
Next Spread
CAMBODIA

PHONGSALI
Phongsali

Muang Khua

Luang Nam Tha
LUANG NAM THA

BOKEO
Vieng Phukha **3**

2 **4**

Muang Xai **Nambak** **1**

Huey

UDOMXAI
Muang Houn

LUANG PHABAN

2

13

Muang Pakbeng

Pac Ou Cave

Luang Phabang

SAINYABULI
Sainyabuli

13

Ben Jiang

Nam Ngum Res.

VIENTIANE
Suvannaphun
Phon Hong

Pak Lai *Mekong River*

13

Vier

PAK OU CAVES
Located 25 km. upriver from Luang Prabang and across the river from Pak Ou village, the Tham Thing and Tham Phum sacred caves are a spectacle with their thousands of gold and wood statues of Buddha. The caves are located in the mouth of the Ou River. Steps lead up to Tham Thing. Tham Phum is higher and cuts deeper into the mountain.

LAOS

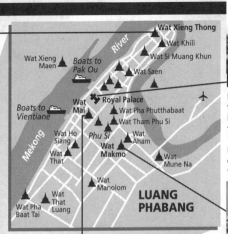

ROYAL PALACE

Built in 1904, the palace has been the repository of some of the most important and revered Buddha figures in Laos. Be sure to see the 15th–17th century statues and the Khmer bronze drums. Much of the decor is modern and there are gifts from many countries on display.

WAT MAKMO

Built in 1514, it forms part of Wat Vixun, the stupa was named because it resembles a watermelon, or makmo.

WAT MAI

This wat took more than 70 years to complete and was begun in 1821 during the reign of King Manthatourath. The five tiered roof of the wooden sim is the traditional Luang Prabang style. Three stupas have survived and a number of festivals are held here.

PLAIN OF JARS

This remarkable field of giant urns is a 1000 sq. meter plateau covered with more than 300 jars ranging in size from one to 3.5 meters high. The mysterious jars have never been accurately explained. From the tops of the hills, the jars cover the barren landscape in all directions. Some say they are ancient burial urns; others say they were used to store wine. While war damage has ravaged the area, the jars remain an impressive sight.

LAOS

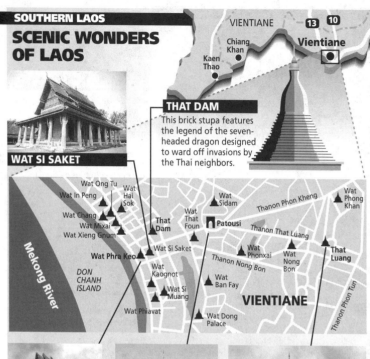

SOUTHERN LAOS

SCENIC WONDERS OF LAOS

WAT SI SAKET

THAT DAM

This brick stupa features the legend of the seven-headed dragon designed to ward off invasions by the Thai neighbors.

VIENTIANE

Chiang Khan

Vientiane

Kaen Thao

Wat Ong Tu
Wat In Peng
Wat Hai Sok
Wat Sidam
Wat Phong Khan

Thanon Phon Kheng

Wat Chang
Wat Mixai
Wat Xieng Gnum

That Dam
Wat That Foun
Patousi

Thanon That Luang

Wat Si Saket

Wat Phra Keo

Wat Phonxai
Wat Nong Bon

That Luang

Mekong River

DON CHANH ISLAND

Wat Kaognot

Thanon Nong Bon

Wat Ban Fay

Wat Si Muang

VIENTIANE

Wat Phiavat

Wat Dong Palace

Thanon Phon Tun

LAOS

WAT PHRA KAEO

Built in 1565 by King Xayasethathirath, this wat was restored in the 1950s. It was the original home of the Emerald Buddha now found in Bangkok. It is now a museum worth visiting for its collection of Burmese, Khmer and Lao art.

PATOUSI

Formerly known as Anousavary, this monument on Lan Zang Avenue is now called the Arch of Triumph and was built in 1958, taking its inspiration from the Arc de Triomphe of Paris, yet instilling typical Lao motifs.

THAT LUANG

That Luang is the national symbol and commands the top of a hill 3 km. northeast of the city. Built in 1566 by King Say Settathirat in the typical Lao style, it has been plundered and restored at various times since then.

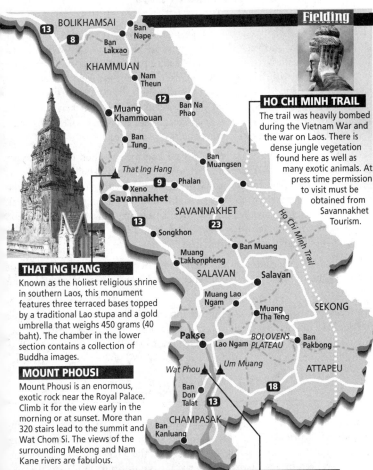

Fielding

HO CHI MINH TRAIL

The trail was heavily bombed during the Vietnam War and the war on Laos. There is dense jungle vegetation found here as well as many exotic animals. At press time permission to visit must be obtained from Savannakhet Tourism.

THAT ING HANG

Known as the holiest religious shrine in southern Laos, this monument features three terraced bases topped by a traditional Lao stupa and a gold umbrella that weighs 450 grams (40 baht). The chamber in the lower section contains a collection of Buddha images.

MOUNT PHOUSI

Mount Phousi is an enormous, exotic rock near the Royal Palace. Climb it for the view early in the morning or at sunset. More than 320 stairs lead to the summit and Wat Chom Si. The views of the surrounding Mekong and Nam Kane rivers are fabulous.

WAT PHOU

Wat Phou is 200 years older than Angkor Wat and was discovered in 1866 by a French explorer. The lost city features brilliant carvings, impressive scales and a fantastic setting with the majestic mountain Linga Parvata in the background. A number of reliefs depicting Hindu gods and goddesses on the main temple are the best preserved features of the complex.

◀ **Wat Phou sculpture**

LAOS

The Food of Laos

Like the food of Thailand, Lao food is hot and spicy. It's served in communal dishes of meat and vegetables. The upscale hotels add a little less fire to their culinary creations to appease the Western palate. Lao specialties include soups, rice soup with fish, noodles, chicken, fried eggs, fried noodles with soy sauce, crisp-fried fish, steamed and grilled fish, fried rice, stir-fried vegetables, fresh spring rolls, roasted duck, grilled chicken, chicken fried with chiles, spicy green papaya salad, spicy beef salad, spicy fish salad, egg, custard, banana in coconut milk and sticky rice in coconut.

Of course, rice is the staple for nearly all Lao meals (when noodles aren't used). Garnishes are as important in Laos as they are in Thailand in providing food with its characteristic spicy flavor. In fact, without them, you'd be hard-pressed to enjoy any meal in Laos. Lemongrass, lime juice, sweet basil, green and red chiles, garlic, mint, ground peanuts, ginger, coconut milk, tamarind juice, fermented fish sauce, vinegar and fresh coriander are added to Lao dishes to give them a little "heat."

Soups are also common, using noodles from rice or wheat; chicken, beef or pork; vegetables such as lettuce, and garnishes of sweet basil and bean sprouts.

In recent years, a number of upscale international and specialty/boutique eateries have opened, catering to the growing number of expats in Vientiane. The small sois off Samsenthai Rd. is where to start your search, as well as Nam Phu Square and Setthathirath Rd. near Wat Ong Teu and Wat Inpeng

The Language of Laos

Lao, the official language of Laos (the dialect and written form in Vientiane) has five principal dialects and dozens if not hundreds of subdialects but at its most fundamental, it is a member of the Thai-Kadai family of languages, and resembles Thai very closely. (It is also quite similar to the languages spoken in China's Yunnan province and northern Burma). But most foreigners will quickly compare the language with Thai. Thais living in the northeastern region of Thailand speak a variation of Thai that more closely resembles Lao than Thai, and many Thais even in Bangkok can understand much of Lao when it is spoken. As well, the Lao easily understand most dialects of Thai, not only because of the similarities between the two languages but also because of their exposure to Thai TV and radio programs.

The scripts of the two languages differ but not enough so that even uneducated Bankokians can readily understand about half of what they read i

Lao. Northeastern Thai is virtually interchangeable with Lao (in fact, most say what the northeasterners speak is indeed Lao).

Lao is monosyllabic and tonal with six different tones, as opposed to Thai's four. The script consists of 32 consonants and 28 vowels and dipthongs. See the "Glossary" at the end of this chapter.

Pronunciation

th as in "tea"	*t* as in "thirty"	*Vowels should be pronounced as they are in the "Glossary" for Thailand. For instance, ii as in "tee," o as in "low," aw as in "saw," and iu as in "you."*
ph as in "pot"	*p* as in "dipper"	
kh as in "kite"	*ng* as in "ring"	
k as in "god"	*ny* as in "pinion"	

Monks wait for dawn alms during That Luang festival in Vientiane.

Planning Ahead

Travel Restrictions

The limits to where you can and cannot go in Laos have largely been removed. Where-s in recent years, you could go no more than 15 km outside Vientiane (so they said), it now possible (and legal) to roam most of the country freely. You do not have to travel a group. Tourists, traditionally required to have a local guide approved or provided by ao National Tourism, can now travel to all areas except a few—those namely being here there is a particularly large amount of unexploded war ordnance and regions con-dered sensitive due to insurgent activity and the growing of opium. Guides can be hired n arrival for a daily fee (US$12), expenses and tip. Permits are still required in some areas. However, these areas change, and the government doesn't openly explain which regions require permits. You no longer need permits to visit the following areas: Attapeu, Champassak, Luang Prabang, Saravane, Savannakhet and Xieng Khouang.

Laos is no longer hung up on keeping people together in groups, nor are officials particularly concerned any longer with unescorted travel in Laos. If you are traveling in remote regions, first make sure you are allowed to be there. If you're in the wrong place at the wrong time without the proper paperwork or without a guide, they do not fool around or look the other way. You will be detained, bounced out of the country and not have much luck in getting any prepaid portions of your trip refunded.

Visas

It's all a little confusing, but as we go to press Laos issues three types of tourist visas: a 15-day tourist visa, which can be had through a Lao embassy in a third country; a 30-day tourist visa, which can be obtained at the Lao embassy in your home country; and a 15-day checkpoint visa, which is issued at authorized land border checkpoints. Most travelers pick up their Lao visas from a third country such as Thailand, but are left with only a couple of weeks to tour the country. Heading to a Lao border checkpoint through a third country without a Lao visa is always chancy. But more on that in a moment.

Insider Tip: Visas on Arrival

With Laos expected to join the Association of Southeast Asian Nations (ASEAN) as a full member in 1997, tourism officials say the country will soon adopt visa policies similiar to those found in neighboring ASEAN nations such as Thailand and Malaysia, where most Western tourists are permitted a free stay of up to 90 days without an embassy-issued visa; their passports are simply stamped on arrival. Cambodia, also expected to join the regional body, already provides visas on arrival–but for a US$20 price tag. What the new Lao on-arrival visas will cost–if there is indeed a cost–has yet to be determined.

Lao embassies abroad will usually issue independent tourist visas, but not necessarily at all embassies. And even the same embassy may or may not issue you a tourist visa. Instead you may be told to get a visa through a travel agency, which is a better way, anyhow. Still the best way to get into Laos is on a 15-day tourist visa issued through a travel agency approved by the Lao Tourism Authority. Fifteen-day tourist visas vary vastly in cost: from US$15–100. You'll be hard pressed to find the US$15 price, though. In Bangkok, you best bet is to stop by **MK Ways** *(57/11 Wittayu (Wireless) Road, Patumwan, Bangkok (right down the street from the Vietnamese Embassy);* ☎ *254-4765 or 254-7770, FAX (662) 254-5583).* The cost will run you about 1600 Thai baht (US$64). Bring two passport photos. You are no longer required, in order to obtain a visa, to book a two-day tour. (At press time, tours were not required, and independent travel for the entirety of your visit was permitted. Check first.)

For the businessperson, you need sponsorship from somebody in Laos—a Lao citizen, travel company or another company—who will issue an invitation combined with a fax is sued by the Ministry of the Interior. These documents must be sent to the closest Lao embassy or consulate. There are offices in Canberra, Australia; Paris, France; Washington, D.C., U.S.A., or Stockholm, Sweden. If you are in Asia, there are consulates or embassies in Bangkok, Hanoi, Phnom Penh and Yangon.

At press time, 15-day tourist visas were available for 2300 Thai baht (about US$92) at the Thai border checkpoint of Nong Khai. At the bus terminal on the Thai side of the Friendship Bridge is located **B.S. Tour & Shipping** (☎/*FAX: 042-465119*). Get to these folks before 10 a.m. Monday–Friday, and they'll have your Lao visa ready to be picked up by 4 p.m. The cost is B2300. This service is not available on the weekends. Same-day 15-day visas can also be had in Nong Khai at the **International Meeting Place**, a budget travelers' guesthouse and restaurant *(1117 Soi Chuanjit)*, for about B2700. Americans have reported 15-day Lao visas can be had in only one working day for B300–400 at travel agents and tour operators in the Isan city of Khon Kaen along National Highway 2 linking Bangkok and Nong Khai. If you're traveling by land to Nong Khai with a Lao visa, it would be well worth your while to check this out. A new Lao Consulate-General opened in Khon Kaen not long ago, and travelers report obtaining 30-day tourist visas through this office for between 100–1000 baht (US$4–40) depending on your nationality. The new consulate is on Potisan Road.

Thai nationals were permitted to obtain permission to enter Laos at the Nong Khai border, and then only for three days. For foreigners, five-day transit visas could also be obtained if you presented evidence of your onward movement (i.e., Hanoi or Bangkok). Although these visas could be had for only US$10, they did not permit you to travel outside Vientiane. Check with a travel agent on the latest visa policies; they change.

Insider Tip: Just Maybe...

If you are traveling up to Vientiane by land from Bangkok without a Lao visa, or just plain have to, it may be possible to pick up a visa guarantee from a travel agent in Bangkok and then pick up the actual visa at the border in Nong Khai, Thailand. The visa will set you back about 2750 Thai baht (US$110) depending on the travel agent used (shop around). You pay 2000 baht (US$80) at the travel agency, where you will pick up a faxed "guarantee." Bring this document to the border where you'll pay the additional 750 baht (US$30) for the actual visa. I haven't tried this myself, but I know some folks whom it's worked for. Because of the expense, it's really only worth it for those traveling by land to Laos who don't want to hang around Bangkok for the week it takes to get a visa processed.

Visas other than transit visas are extendable once inside Laos. You can apply for (although you may not be granted) an extension through a Vientiane tour agency or directly through the Ministry of the Interior on Thanon Lane Xang in Vientiane across from the Morning Market. Fifteen-day extended visas can be had for US$4 per day, or US$60 for the 15-day extension. It's best to do it through a tour company. I suggest heading for the **Lao National Tourism Company** which houses **Lana Tours** *(08/2 Lane Xang Ave., Vientiane;* ☎ *216671, 212013; FAX: 212013)*. If you go through these folks, they can extend your visa twice (an additional 30 days) beyond your original visa. Keep in mind the implication that a two-week tourist visa is indcative of how overjoyed the Lao authorities are at having you as a guest in their country in the first place.

If you overstay your visa, don't be alarmed. You won't be tried as a spy. But you will be fined US$5 a day for your overstay, perhaps more if you try to leave the country at a checkpoint which happens to be "closed."

Insider Tip: Dog Days of Nong Khai

To play it safe, it's best to obtain a Lao visa in advance from abroad. I've known quite a few travelers who ventured to Nong Khai, Thailand, by land from Bangkok only to be turned back at the border. They've either had to return to the Lao embassy in Bangkok or hole up in Nong Khai for a week or more while their passports were sent by a local travel agent to Bangkok for a stamp. Waiting it out in Nong Khai is about as appealing as a summer vacation in your backyard–if you've got a really small back yard. But at the time of this writing, same-day visas were available at the border.

If you have it in your mind to pick up a Thailand tourist visa (not to be con fused with the 30-day transit visa) while in Laos consider the following: On January 2, 1997 the rules changed, and now it's a bit of a pain in the ass, at least according to some folks . And the process requires your presence at the Thai embassy in Vientiane for three consecutive days. On the first day, you show up at the Consular Section of the Thai embassy after 2:30 p.m. (if you want to waste some time, get there earlier). Bring your passport. You'll receive an application form and a number. That's it. The next morning show up again and wait for your number to be called. (Make sure the application form is completed and that you have glued a passport-sized photo to the upper right-hand corner.) Then you pay what you owe: transit visa—200 baht (US$8), tourist visa—300 baht (US$12),and non-immigrant visa—500 baht (US$20). On the third day show up at the "Official and Diplomatic Passports" office at the embassy during regular working hours and pick up your visa. Whatever you do, don't start the process on a Thursday or Friday. If Day 2 happens to be on a Friday, Day 3 is on Tuesday! Ugggh!

Others report that Thai visas can still only be had in one day at the embassy. For sure, a 30-day transit visa to Thailand can be had on the Thai side of the Friendship Bridge on arrival, and at no charge.

Entry By Air and Land

For the less adventurous, we recommend entry by air from Bangkok to Vientiane's Wattay Airport (the only legal arrival and departure point for foreign airline passengers) via THAI Airways ($184 round-trip). THAI flies to Vientiane once daily, except Wednesday. Much improved Lao Aviation operates flights daily, except Saturday. You can also enter from Hanoi via Lao Aviation or Vietnam Airlines ($160 round-trip, twice a week). There are two flights a week from Phnom Penh ($244 round-trip Wednesdays and Thursdays). There are also flights to and from Ho Chi Minh City (Saigon), Singapore, Yangon (Rangoon) and Guangzhou and Kunming in China.

Up until just very recently, internal flights relied on Lao Aviation's relatively ramshackle collection of Russian and Chinese turboprops. You would long for the hot crowded buses after one circuitous up-and-down flight. Not recommended, except for travelers with a lot of flight insurance and very few reasons to live. However, I must say that Lao Aviation is doing its best to upgrade both its equipment and safety standards. Hey, you can actually fly on a Lao Aviation ATR-72 these days (most domestic flights employ these aircraft now). Good thing it's the tropics. Wattay International airport is 3 km from Vientiane, and there is a US$5 departure tax.

There is **land** entry from Nong Khai to Tha Dua, about 25 km from Vientiane and across the Mittaphab Bridge (Friendship Bridge) linking Nong Khai with Vientiane (bring some 10 baht coins for the bus across the bridge; pedestrians aren't allowed). You can cross from Chomeck to Pakse as well, but it requires special permission if you leave this way. Once inside Laos, conditions go from primitive to nonexistent. You can enter Laos by land from Thailand and Vietnam, and there are many companies who will supply package tours in Bangkok, Ho Chi Minh City or Hanoi. In particular, I'd like to recommend Bangkok's **MK Ways**, *57/11 Wittayu (Wireless) Road, Patumwan, Bangkok (right down the street from the Vietnamese Embassy);* ☎ *66-2-254-4765 or 66-2-254-7770, FAX (662) 254-5583.* (See "Tour Operators" below.) From Saigon, in Vietnam, I recommend **Ben Thanh Tourist**, *121 Nguyen Hue Street, District 1, Ho Chi Minh City;* ☎ *84-8-8295597, 8222506; FAX: 84-8-8296269 or 8295060.*

Lao-Thai Borders Open to Foreigners

From (Thailand)	To (Laos)
Nong Khai	Tha Deua
Nakhon Phanom	Tha Khaek
Chiang Khong	Huay Xai
Mukdahan	Savannakhet
Chong Mek/Ubon Ratchatani*	Pakse*

* A visa valid for entry at Chong Mek from Pakse must be obtained in advance.

Land entry points are the following (although the rules regarding foreigners crossing these points fluctuate): Boten at the border checkpoint with China's Yunan province Luang Namtha province (Laos-China border); at the Houixay border checkpoint in okeo province (Laos-Thailand border); at the Mittaphab Bridge, Tha Deua or Thaaleng border checkpoints at Vientiane city (Laos-Thailand border); at Savannakhet Laos-Thailand border), and at the Savanh checkpoint in Savannakhet province (Laos-ietnam border).

Borders between Thailand and Laos are opening quickly. In Thailand's Nan province, ere is now a permanent border crossing at Baan Huay Kone, Thung Chang district. wo smaller checkpoints have opened in Huay Sa Taeng and Baan Mai Chai Daen in hung Chang district and Song Kwai subdistrict, respectively. Huay Kone is expected to be promoted to an international checkpoint in the future. From Baan Huay Kone, it is now possible to travel to Laos, Vietnam and China. It's only 152 km to Luang Prabang and 100 km to Chaiyaburi in Laos. From the border to Muang La in Sipsongpanna, China is 284 km and 408 km to Dien Bien Phu in Vietnam. Two more checkpoints may have already opened by the time you read this: at Baan Nam Pi in Wiang Sa district—3 km from Paklai—and at Baan Sob Mang in Bo Klua subdistrict to connect with Phieng in Laos. From Phieng, it will be possible to proceed to Pak Rai and return to Thailand via Uttaradit province. The Thai Interior Ministry relaxed the regulations at Baan Huay Sa-taeng in 1993, shortening the journey to Pak Baeng in Laos to 54 km. The road continues from there to the Sipsongpanna region in China about 180 km away. The Baan Huay Sataeng checkpoint is being heavily promoted as a permanent checkpoint to give tourists the option of getting off the oft-trodded Vientiane-Luang Prabang route.

Insider Tip: Beware Lazy, Lousy Lao Gatekeepers

I've heard a couple of stories from travelers who report getting shaken down for money by Lao immigration officials when trying to exit Laos via the Mittaphab (Friendship) Bridge to Nong Khai, Thailand. It seems that if you attempt to cross when the immigration post isn't "open," officials there will charge you a "special processing fee" to slap an exit stamp into your visa. This might not sound unusual or unjustified until you consider that these guys seem to be arbitrarily, conveniently "closed" at such hours as 10 a.m. or 2:15 p.m.—hours, of course, when the checkpoint is supposed to be open. The bridge is open to foreign travelers between 8 a.m. and 6 p.m. Don't say you weren't warned.

By overland, most travelers enter Laos from Thailand. By **bus**, the best way to Laos from Bangkok is via buses departing from Bangkok's Northern Bus Terminal (Mor Chit bus terminal). Both air conditioned and nonair-conditioned buses leave about every hour for Nong Khai. Once in Nong Khai, you can easily find the motorcycle version of a tuk tuk, also called a tuk tuk, at the bus station for the short B20 ride to the Friendship Bridge.

By **car**, Thai motorists can drive across the Friendship Bridge from Nong Khai to the Lao side, but aren't permitted to go any further with their cars, as driving in Laos is on the right hand side of the road. Those with vehicles must park them—after paying customs fees on both sides of the border—and take a taxi. The taxis aren't a bad value. A day tour inside Laos by taxi runs only about 300 baht (US$12). Don't expect to be permitted to bring a rental vehicle across the bridge from Thailand into Laos. If you're renting a car in Thailand, take the bus across the Friendship Bridge and leave your car in storage at the bus terminal facing the Immigration house on the Nong Khai side. The cost for this secured parking is about B100 (US$4) per day. A motorcycle garaged here will set you back B50 per day (US$2).

Buses run when full across the Friendship Bridge from the small bus terminal at the bridge. The cost is B10 one-way. On slow days you may wait awhile, even an hour or more. If you can't wait, a car or minibus can be hired at the terminal to make the crossing for a hefty B200 (for the vehicle, not per-person).

Once on the other side, you'll have to go through the basically painless process of going through Lao immigration. But it doesn't come cheap. First, at Customs, you'll be asked to fork over B20. Why? God knows. The uniformed guys here, when asked, will tell you it's for inspecting your bags, but then will not explain a moment later why they didn't inspect your bags. (I don't know any travelers who ever once asked a Customs officer why he *didn't* inspect their belongings. And probably neither do Lao Customs officers.) Then you'll be asked for another B60 by the passport stamper at Immigration. Why? God knows.

From the Lao side of the bridge, you can take either an old, slow taxi the 20 km to Vientiane or an even slower motorcycle *songthaew* (called a tuk tuk). If you pay more than B100 for the taxi to Vientiane, you didn't bargain very well. (Note: Remember, Thai baht is accepted once inside Laos.)

By **train**, State Railways of Thailand has put together weekend tours to Nong Khai and Vientiane from Bangkok for groups of 10 or more. The trips start late Friday night from Hualamphong station in Bangkok and get back early Monday. The tour costs 2890 baht (US$116), not including the train fare. Call ☎ *(66-2) 225-0300 (ext. 5217) or 225-964* to mak reservations, which should be done two to four weeks in advance. Otherwise, there is daily train service to Nong Khai from Bangkok.

From Vietnam, it is possible to enter Laos via Highway 9 from Dong Ha to Lao Bao cross Vietnam's former demilitarized zone. This seems to be an on-again, off-again deal for foreigners. According to the Lao consulate in Ho Chi Minh City, travel by bus across the border at Lao Bao was possible, and visas for travel through this border checkpoint could be had at the consulate in HCMC. Refer to the Lao embassy in HCMC: *181 Hai Ba Trung Street, District 1;* ☎ *(84-8) 8299262, 8297667.*

From Myanmar, forget the idea of traveling by land into Laos—at least legally. Ditto with Cambodia. China's a different story, though. From Baan Huay Kone in northern Thailand, it is now possible to travel to China via Laos. From this Thai/Lao border checkpoint, Muang La in Sipsongpanna, China, is only 284 km (hard kilometers!) away. From Baan Huay Sataeng, Thailand, another open Lao/Thai border post, the journey to Bok Baeng in Laos is 54 km. The road continues from there to the Sipsongpanna region of China about 180 km away.

From Vietnam, land entry is also possible into Laos. It has to be at the Lao Bao checkpoint at the Vietnamese termination of Highway 9, which runs across Vietnam from Dong Ha through the former DMZ to Lao Boa. The only problem here is that your Vietnamese visa must specify Lao Bao as your exit point. If yours specifies another (most are either Hanoi or Ho Chi Minh City), you can have it changed to Lao Bao through travel agents in Vietnam's major cities, This generally costs about US$15 in Hanoi, about US$10 in Ho Chi Minh City and about US$20 in Danang. From Lao Bao, the last bus to Savvanakhet leaves around 3 p.m., getting into Savannakhet around midnight.

If you plan to fly in, the best places to get a Lao visa are in Bangkok or Ho Chi Minh City. They're also the cheapest places. But shop around. As it is with trying to get a visa for Cambodia, you'll run into as many procedures and prices as there are travel agents. And it seems that anyone who has a phone in Bangkok does some moonlighting as a travel agent. Tourist visas typically take between two and seven days to get. A transit visa takes less time and only about 10–20 U.S. bucks, depending where you get it and if you can get it. But remember, a tourist visa will give you more freedom of movement in the country.

Tour Operators

Although a formal tour of Laos is no longer required, a lack of a decent transportation and accommodations infrastructure makes touring Laos independently attractive only to adventurers and experienced backpackers. For a little more comfort (and for a lot more money), you might consider a tour of Laos. The following is a partial listing of the U.S., Laos, and Thailand-based tour operators offering packages to Laos. Call around. Check out the prices and the itineraries that suit your budget and level of intrepidity. Some will merely bus your buns around the beaten track. Others will put you on a motorcycle odyssey where you've got a decent chance of doing some pretty outrageous things.

(Note: Local numbers are for information; toll-free numbers are for reservations). In the U.S., you can contact:

Absolute Asia
155 W. 68 Street, Suite 525
New York, NY 10023
☎ *(212) 595-5782; (800) 736-8187*

All Adventure Travel
5589 Rapahoe, Ste. 208
Boulder, CO 80303
☎ *(800) 537-4025*
FAX: (303) 4404160

Archaeological Tours
271 Madison Avenue, Ste. 904
New York, NY 10016
☎ *(212) 986-3054*

Bolder Adventures ★
P.O. Box 1279
Boulder, CO 80306
☎ *(303) 443-6789; (800) 642-2742*
FAX: (303) 443-7078

Creative Adventures Club
3007 Royce Lane
Costa Mesa, CA 92626
☎ *(714) 545-5888; (800) 544-5088*
FAX: (714) 545-5898

Adventure Center
1311 63rd Street, Ste. 200
Emeryville, CA 94608
☎ *(510) 654-1879; (800) 227-8747*
FAX: (510) 654-4200

Apex World Travel
4620 West Commercial Way, Ste. 3
Pamarac, FL 33319
☎ *(305) 733-4144; (800) 666-0025*
FAX: (305) 733-4456

Asian Pacific Adventures
826 South Sierra Bonita Avenue
Los Angeles, CA 90036
☎ *(213) 935-3156*
FAX: (213) 935-2691

Chinasmith
330 West 42nd Street
New York, NY 10036
☎ *(212) 239-2410; (800) US-CHIN*
FAX: (212) 643-1598

Diva Worldwide
☎ *415-777-5351*
FAX: (415) 334-6365

Thousands of gold and wood Buddha figures in Pak Ou Caves, 25 km from Luang Prabang, Laos

Mekong River, between Laos and Thailand

EastQuest

1 Beekman Street, #607
New York, NY 10038
☎ (212) 406-2224; (800) 638-3449

Far East Destinations

1001 4th Avenue Plaza, Ste. 2401
Seattle, WA 98154
☎ (206) 224-0117; (800) 879-2976
FAX: (206) 467-9186

Himalayan Travel

112 Prospect Street
Stamford, CT 06901
☎ (203) 359-3711; (800) 225-2380
FAX: (203) 359-3669

IPI/InterPacific Tours International

111 E. 15th Street
New York, NY 10003
☎ (212) 953-6010; (800) 221-3594

Intrepid Tours

315 Post Road West
Westport, CT 06880
☎ (203) 221-0332; (800) 558-2522
FAX: (203) 221-0816

Mountain Travel Sobek

6420 Fairmount Avenue
El Cerrito, CA 94530
☎ (510) 527-8100; (800) 227-2384
FAX: (510) 525-7710

Natrabu Indo-American Travel

433 California Street
San Francisco, CA 94104
☎ (800) 628-7228
FAX: (415) 362-0531

Pacific Holidays

2 West 45th Street, Ste. 1102
New York, NY 10036
☎ (212) 764-1977; (800) 355-8025
FAX: (212) 764-2396

TBI Tours

787 Seventh Avenue, Ste. 1101
New York, NY 10019
☎ (212) 489-1919; (800) 223-0266
FAX: (212) 307-0612

Express Travel

1050 S. Jackson Street
Seattle, WA 98104
☎ (206) 324-6530
FAX: (206) 328-6334

Gannon Tours

11495 Sunset Hills Road
Reston, VA 22090
☎ (703) 471-9700; (800) GAN-TRVL
FAX: (703) 742-0063

InterNation

620 Kearny Street
San Francisco, CA 94108
☎ (415) 392-0244; (800) 553-3533
FAX: (415) 392-3369

Here Today, There Tomorrow

1901 Pennsylvania Avenue, N.W., #204
Washington, D.C. 20006
☎ (202) 296-6373; (800) 368-5965

Lotus Tours

2 Mott Street
New York, NY 10013
☎ (212) 267-5414
FAX: (212) 608-6007

Myths and Mountains

976 Tee Court
Incline Village, NV 89451
☎ (800) 670-6984
FAX: (702) 832-4454

Overseas Adventure Travel

349 Broadway
Cambridge, MA 02139
☎ (800) 221-0814
FAX: (617) 876-0455

Sino-American Tours

37 Bowery
New York, N.Y. 10002
☎ (212) 966-5866; (800) 221-7982

The Global Spectrum

1901 Pennsylvania Avenue NW
Washington, DC 20006
☎ (202) 293-2065; (800) 419-4446
FAX: (202) 296-0815

Top Guides

> 1825 San Lorenzo Avenue
> Berkeley, CA 94707
> ☎ (510) 527-9884; (800) 867-6777
> FAX: (510) 527-9885

Travcoa

> 2350 SE Bristol Street
> Newport Beach, CA 92660
> ☎ (714) 476-2800; (800) 992-2003
> FAX: (714) 476-2538

Trade Services Co.

> 565 5th Avenue
> New York, NY 10017
> ☎ (212) 697-1558; (800) 872-3386
> FAX: (212) 697-2609

Abercrombie & Kent International

> 1520 Kensington Road
> Oak Brook, IL 60521-2106
> ☎ (708) 954-2944; (800) 323-7308

Or in Bangkok, Thailand, you can contact (country code, 66—city code, 2):

MK Ways ★

> 57/11 Wireless Road
> Patumwan, Bangkok 10330
> ☎ 254-4765, 254-7770, 255-2892,
> 255-3390
> FAX: 254-5583

Lam Son International Ltd.

> 23/1 Sukhumvit Soi 4,
> Bangkok 10110
> ☎ 255-6692/3/4/5
> FAX: 255-8859

Vikamla Tours

> Room 401 Nana Condo, 23/11
> Sukhumvit Soi 4
> Bangkok 10110
> ☎ 252-2340, 255-8859

Exotissimo Travel

> 21/17 Sukhumvit Soi 4
> Bangkok 10110
> ☎ 253-5240/1, 255-2747
> FAX: 254-7683.

Red Carpet Service & Tour

> 459 New Rama 6 Road
> Phayathai, Bangkok 10400
> ☎ 215-9951, 215-3331
> FAX: 662-215-3331

In Chiang Mai (country code: 66, city code: 53), for a motorcycle adventure in Laos and southern China, contact:

Chiang Mai Motorcycle Touring Club

> 21/1 Ratchamankha Soi 2, Chiang Mai 50301
> ☎ 278518
> FAX: 278518

In Udon Thani (country code: 66, city code: 42), I recommend:

Arunya Tours

> Udon Thani
> ☎ 240881, 247320
> FAX: 247320

After a brief open-door policy in 1989, Laos decided to filter out the backpacker tourist and focus on big-dollar group tours. In 1991 the government began to privatize tour packaging and encourage the influx of tourism dollars. Since then, there has been a proliferation of Vientiane tour "specialists." Like in Vietnam, the tour business is a fledgling one in Laos and, at many operators, the level of service simply isn't acceptable to a num ber of foreign customers, while others walk away perfectly satisfied. The following is a listing of operators in Vientiane and elsewhere in Laos. I cannot personally vouch for any one of them. They appear here for directory purposes only. It can be safely assumed that operators such as Diethelm Travel—with years of experience in Southeast Asia markets— can be counted on.

Bokeo Travel Co.

> *144/1 Saikang Road, Houaisa, Bokeo province.*

Chackavane Travel & Tour

> *92 Thongkhankham Road, P.O. Box 590, Vientiane. ☎ 216444; FAX 214743.*

DAFI Travel/Tours Co.

> *Head Office: 146–148 Ban Thaluang, Pakse district, Champassack province.*
> *Branch Office: 093/4 Samsenthai Road, Vientiane. ☎ 216721; FAX 217335.*

Diethelm Travel Laos

> *Namphu Square, Sethathirath Road, P.O. Box 2657, Vientiane. ☎ 215920; FAX 217151.*

Hoongthip Tour

> *Phetsalath Road, P.O. Box 682, Savannakhet; ☎ 212262.*

Inter Lao Tourism

> *50 Setthathirath Rd., Vientiane. ☎ 214232; FAX: 216306.*

Lao National Tourism Co.

> *08/02 Lane Xang Avenue, Vientiane. ☎ 216671; FAX 212013.*

Luang Prabang Tourism

> *Sisavangvong Road, P.O. Box 356, Luang Prabang. ☎ 212198.*

Lane Xang Travel & Tour

> *Pangkham Road, Vientiane. ☎ 212469, 213198; FAX 215804.*

Sode Tour

> *114 Quai Fa Ngum, Vientiane. ☎ 216314; FAX: 216313.*

Language

Lao is the language of the people. French is widely spoken by the older and more educated. And Russian is popular but waning; there aren't too many Russians around to practice with anymore. Many people will try to speak English, as Laos is slowly climbing on the English bandwagon, so do your best to help local folks practice. Government officials, some shopkeepers catering to tourists and guides will have a basic understanding of English.

Money

Kip is the currency. There are about 925 kip to one U.S. dollar. There are no coins. You'll feel like a rich dude because the largest bill is 1000 kip—a little more than one U.S. dollar. Carry U.S. dollars or Thai baht; traveler's checks are hard to cash; there is no black market and U.S. currency and Thai baht are the most accepted currencies in large cities— baht for smaller purchases and dollars for the larger ones. Out in the country spend your kip. Don't change too much unless you like to collect worthless Third World currency. It cannot be exchanged outside the country. Your credit cards are novelties and are only accepted at the largest hotels.

Electricity

It's 220 volts/50 cycles in cities, 110 volts some places in the countryside. Bring a two-pin socket and a multivoltage converter. Don't plan on having electricity 24 hours a day outside the main cities.

Weights and Measures

Metric. Drive on the right side of the road.

Postal

Mail service is not reliable anywhere except for Vientiane—and even there incoming mail from abroad may not reach its recipient. But try it for postcards. They might even arrive by the time you get back. Don't attempt any important mailings from up-country. The post office in Vientiane is located on the corner of Lane Xang Avenue and Khou Viang Road, across from the Morning Market.

Communications

If you want to call home, use the major hotels or the international telephone office in Vientiane. The chances of being able to get a line in the countryside are slim to none. You must place the call through an international operator (☎ *19*), who will let you know when your call is ready. At this time, there is only one line to Western countries, so don't talk too long if you do get through!

Within the country there is better service, including faxes in major offices and hotels.

The country dialing code for Laos is *856*. Dial *011*, plus this country code, plus the area code, plus the phone number. Inside Laos, when dialing a number in another province, dial '0' before the area code. Do not do this when dialing into Laos from outside the country.

Newspaper, TV, Radio

VCRs and Thai TV stations are the most popular media. There is a national station. If you're dying for news, bring a shortwave radio. Government-controlled newspapers are of the old-school socialist type, good for souvenirs but not for news. *Khao San Pathet Lao News Bulletin* is published daily in English and French. You can also find Western publications in Vientiane, if you ask around. The English-language weekly in Vientiane is called the *Vientiane Times*. Most periodicals are limited to Thai teeny-bopper rags.

Health

Technically, you will only need shots if you come from an infected area. But since you are coming into a Third World country with limited health or medical facilities, take all precautions. Make sure you are current on cholera, hepatitis, polio, tetanus and typhoid. Carry any medication and first aid. Take a prophylaxis for malaria, a small mosquito net and bug juice, and wear long-sleeve shirts and long pants. Domestic animals may have rabies, so don't go petting scabby boonie dogs with a fluffernutter froth at the mouth.

WARNING:
BEWARE CHOLERA

In 1992, the World Health Organization released a warning about the wide-spread cholera epidemics of Asia. Among the countries it specified were Laos, Cambodia,Vietnam and China. Cholera outbreaks have officially only been reported in Laos since 1993. In that year, the National Institute of Hygiene and Epidemiology recorded outbreaks in two provinces in southern Laos, involving 6600 cases and 340 deaths. In 1994, the disease was found in nine provinces and resulted in 616 deaths. Only 37 percent of the rural population of Laos has access to year-round supplies of clean drinking water.

Don't drink the water; bilharzia can be contracted from stagnant or slow-moving water. And don't swim in the Mekong or eat fish from it that haven't been properly cooked. Liver flukes, small worms found in the Mekong and freshwater fish, can make life a pain in the ass, literally. Symptoms include fatigue, fever and/or a swollen, tender liver. These little rascals are a bitch. You can snuff 'em with 750 mg of Biltricide three times a day for about a week.

There is a ratio of one doctor to every 1362 people. Take a number if you get sick. There are two hospitals in Vientiane—Mahasot and Settathirath—or you can visit the Australian or Swedish embassies. If you can wait, go to Bangkok. For a complete description of medical problems in Southeast Asia, refer to "Medical Problems" in the Vietnam section of this book.

Of course, myriad health complications can result from stepping on a land mine or some other unexploded device. Much of the unexploded materiel that has littered Laos for the last 30 years has yet to be surgically removed from the ground, making wandering off marked roads and paths potentially fatal. According to government sources I talked with, most of the country these days is quite safe in regard to buried bombs and other nasty things underfoot. But I was frankly told Houaphan province in the northeast remains a virtual bed of nails, and that wandering anywhere in the province should be avoided entirely. The same goes for northeastern Xieng Khouang province, which borders Houaphan province. Advice you may want to heed.

Local and Long Distance Transportation

There is not even a **bus** system for the locals—if you do find a bus, don't count on it getting where you want to go. There is bus service inside the prefectures. All roads are bad and there is erratic to nonexistent service between the states; some are subject to travel restrictions.

Taxis are rolling antiques and have no meters. Negotiate a day rate in the main towns or a flat rate for each trip. Count on spending a buck a mile or 10-12 dollars for the day.

Trishaws are relatively plentiful. Agree on a price before you get in.

There is **car rental** in Laos. You can rent Toyota Land Cruisers, Volvos or nondescript passenger cars for anywhere from $25–$40 a day. With or without a driver.

Bicycles are popular for getting around town. They can be rented in Vientiane and Luang Prabang, and nowhere else that I know of. And there are **boats** for river trips on the Mekong.

Small **motorbikes** (under 100 cc) can be rented in Vientiane and some of the larger provincial capitals, such as Savannakhet and Luang Prabang, for about US$15 per day. (Don't count on them being available anywhere else.)

Laos' **river network** is dominated by the Mekong River. It flows through 2030 km of Laos and provides a natural means of transportation. However, its navigability is limited to 1330 km, primarily due to the severe rapids between Savannakhet and Pakse, as well as the Khong Falls and generally low water levels during the dry season. In addition to the Mekong, other navigable rivers include the Nam Ou, Nam Khan, Nam Tha, Nam Hgum and Se Don.

In April 1994, the 1.2 km Friendship Bridge linking Nong Khai in Thailand with Vientiane was opened, making overland entry into Laos possible from Thailand's northeast. The bridge was financed by US$30 million in aid from Australia. The bridge is open from 8 a.m.–6 p.m. Travelers can obtain visas to Laos either from travel agencies Bangkok, Khon Kaen and Nong Khai itself in order to cross the bridge. Visas to Laos from Nong Khai can be processed the same day. For a complete description of all land entry oints into Laos, see the "Visas" and "Entry by Land" sections.

The **road system** in Laos can be considered dismal, however, the road to Luang Prabang from Vientiane has been improved considerably, allowing some of the cowboy tour van drivers to make the 410 km trip in under seven hours, even six hours. The intraprovincial bus system can also be called lousy—and expensive. A lot of travelers, especially in the northern part of the country arrange rides with locals, truck drivers, or cargo trucks converted to haul passengers.

Laos possesses 13,100 km of roadways, excluding forest and mining roads, which consist of national, provincial and local roadways. The national routes linking provincial capitals, major towns and international borders total 3390 km, 1620 km of which are paved. The balance of the roadways are often dilapidated earth trails linking villages within provinces. National Highway 13 is the country's major artery. It totals 1370 km, connecting Pak Mong in the north with Khong in the south, passing through the larger urban areas of Luang Prabang, Vientiane, Savannakhet and Champasack. National Highway 9, an other important international artery, links Laos with Vietnam. Much of the road is im passable during the rainy season by motorcycle and even by car.

Local transportation is either on foot, by bicycle or by motorcycle tuk tuk. In place such as Vientiane, simply wave down a passing tuk tuk and bargain a price for your desti nation. You shouldn't pay any more than 500 kip per kilometer. Laos' prehistoric taxi generally can't be hailed from the street for trips around town. Instead, they're use mainly to shuttle visitors back and forth from Vientiane Wattay Airport and from th Friendship Bridge connecting Laos with Thailand, 20 kilometers from Vientiane. Th bridge trip should be 100 Thai baht, or 3700 kip. If you should need a taxi, it's best t find one on your own, as hotels have a propensity for tacking on outrageous servic charges for a simple phone call. There is no intracity bus service to speak of. However in tercity buses connect Vientiane with all of Laos' provinces. The main bus station in Vientiane is behind the Morning Market on Mahosot Street. Here, buses leave for Luang Prabang, 420 kilometers to the north, and elsewhere in Laos when full. The trip to Luang Prabang takes 7-10 hours depending on the driver (public buses take the longest) over a much improved roadway.

Duty Free

Customs allows 500 cigarettes, two bottles of wine and one bottle of hard liquor. You may bring in or take out as much currency as you wish. There is a limit on the amount of Thai baht (100,000 baht) that can be brought in. Do not attempt to export antiquities or any images of the Buddha.

Accommodations

Hotels are basic, dull and uninspiring, save for a couple in Vientiane. If you are visiting the south, try to get into one of the colonial houses or chalets. Keep in mind that lodgings in Laos are surprisingly expensive, most hotels costing at least 50% more than similar hotels in Vietnam and Cambodia—even Thailand.

Food and Beverages

Lao food is similar to Thai food—by way of China and without the variety. What you will eat in Laos either clucked, oinked, swam or was just yanked out of the ground. You may find yourself enjoying certain dishes more than others, as marijuana is a common addition to dishes. Some meals include pounded raw meat marinated in lemon juice *(laap sin)*. If it's made with fish, it's called *laap pa*. You'll also find glutinous rice *(khaaw niaw)*, fermented fish *(paddek of nam pa)* and soups such as bamboo shoot soup *(keng no may)*, veggie broth and buffalo skin soup *(keng khi lek)*. The soups are for the end or the middle of your meal. Don't go out of your way to find "typical" Lao home cooking because French cuisine is so popular. You also might want to patronize the Vietnamese or Chinese establishments in town.

If you develop a thirst, there is a good but expensive selection of imported beer and alcohol. The local beer is called Laobeer, and is the cheapest bottled brew you'll find in Laos. It's available everywhere. The local rock-gut is rice wine, which is a tempting mixture of local river water and fermented rice *(lau-lao)*. Try it but be prepared to suffer the consequences. You may want to bring home a bottle of Sticky Rice to impress your friends. At least they will have a doctor nearby.

As in the rest of Indochina, stay away from the tap water and stick to bottled water only everywhere in Laos. For more on the cuisine of Laos, see "The Food of Laos" section.

Shopping

Laos is famous for textiles and weaving. Try to bring home some of the more ornate embroidered sarongs *(pha sin)* or shawls *(pha baeng)*. Also look for silverware, tribal jewelry, wood carvings and antiques. Wood, gold, silver and precious stones are sold in a number of shops. But it is prohibited to take antique items such as Buddha images and other cultural artifacts out of the country. Any silver or copper items bought in Laos will require a customs duty according to the weight upon departure at the airport.

Safety

One of the positive effects of totalitarian governments seems to be a lack of petty crime. Before you get too complacent, though, you could end up being shot or injured if you are caught in a rebel attack while traveling in the Nam Ngum or Luang Prabang regions. As you are probably getting tired of hearing, the Golden Triangle area is not a good place to wander because of the tight and rather brutal control by opium smugglers.

INSIDER TIP

The Xieng Khouang province, The Ho Chi Minh Trail and the Bolovens Plateau will never be safe due to the thousands of unexploded cluster bombs delivered free of charge during the Vietnam War by the USAF. There are anti-personnel mines, unexploded cluster bombs and other unexploded ordnance in many areas of Laos.

FESTIVALS AND HOLIDAYS

January 1	New Year's Day	
January 6	Pathet Lao Day	*Parades.*
January 20	Army Day	*Public holiday.*
January	Boun Pha Vet	*Celebrates King Vessanthara's reincarnation.*
February	Magha Puja	*End of Buddha's monastic term and prediction of his death.*
February	Chinese and Vietnamese holiday	*Jan./Feb. New Year. Businesses shut down for three days.*
March 8	Women's Day	*Public holiday.*
March 22	People's Party Day	*Public holiday.*
March	Boun Khoun Khao	*Harvest Festival.*
April	Lao New Year	*Three-day holiday calling for rain and celebrating the Lao New Year.*
May 1	Labor Day	*Parades in Vientiane.*
May	Visakha Puja	*Celebrates the birth, enlightenment and death of Buddha.*
May	Boun Bang Fai	*Two-day Buddhist rain-making festival using bamboo rockets.*
June 1	Children's Day	*Public holiday.*
June	Khao Phansa	*Start of Buddhist fasting.*

LAOS

FESTIVALS AND HOLIDAYS

August 13	Lao Issara	*Public holiday.*
August 23	Liberation Day	*Public holiday.*
August	Ho Khao Padap Dinh	*Celebration of the Dead.*
September	Bouk Phansa	*End of Buddhist fasting.*
October 12	Freedom from the French Day	*Public holiday.*
November	That Luang	*Weeklong festival.*
December	Hmong New Year	
December 2	Independence Day	*Public holiday.*

Vientiane

Vientiane

Simuoag temple in Vientiane houses an undated Khmer boundary stone.

With a population of 464,000, the capital city is made up of smaller villages *(ban)*, built around their respective *wats*, which are then grouped into districts *(muang)*. Most travelers will start their visit in the quiet river city of Vientiane. Not particularly distinctive nor historic compared with some other Southeast Asia capitals, it has a selection of religious monuments and a mix of old, drab colonial buildings.

Vientiane began life some 1200 years ago and became an important religious, cultural and economic link with India and China, as well other nations in Southeast Asia. During those times, the name of the city was Ban Nong Khanthach village. As the story goes, there lived in the village a man named

Chanthabury Oay Luay, a simple farmer who had little save for a firm belief in Buddhism. His beliefs were noticed by King Sumittatham of the Marukhanakhorn Empire. For his good deeds, Sumittatham made Chanthabury the King of Vientiane. Chanthabury was renamed Phraya Chanthabury Prasithisak, and the village of Ban Nong Khanthach was rechristened Vientiane, after its new king. Chanthabury's kingdom extended to the Kading River in the south.

In 1375, Vientiane was the site of a great celebration by King Fangum after he unified the Lane Xang kingdom. In 1560, Vientiane became capital of the kingdom after it was moved from Luang Prabang. Since then, the city has been plundered, looted and pillaged countless times—abandoned, rebuilt, deserted and rebuilt again. Its latest reconstruction was at the start of the 20th century.

Today Vientiane sits lazily on the east bank of the Mekong River, and is more like a backwater provincial town than a national capital. Save for such sites as the Victory Monument, you'd think you just happened along another northern Isan town whose folks drive on the wrong side of the road. Most experts think that the name Vientiane is a Romanized derivation of Wieng Chan, which means Moon City, or Sandalwood depending on who you talk to. But the place isn't called Moon City because of its reputation as a party town. Quite the contrary, one could fall asleep just walking around Vientiane's quaint streets. During the weekdays, the old French colonial streets are about as bustling with traffic as they are with anti-government protesters. At nighttime and on Sundays, they're just plain dead. Most of the folks here still use bicycles to get around. Although motorbikes and cars have made their debut here and are on the rise, there is hardly the massive, anarchic ant nest of motos that plague such cities as Saigon. The centers of social activity, as in Thailand, are the city's temples. And on Sundays locals and tourists alike can be found at the most impressive: Pha That Luang, Wat Pha Keo and Wat Si Muang. These temples, of course, form the crux of tourist attractions in Vientiane. Regrettably, the government cannot afford to restore other temples in both the capital and elsewhere in the country, many of which house sacred objects.

Have fun getting around Vientiane, as the streets are referred to by both their pre- and post-revolutionary names. This probably does not matter, as there are no street signs to add to the confusion. The best way to get around Vientiane is by foot, because the city is compact enough—with its attractions in close proximity to each other—to be fully explored in a single day. *Samlors* and *tuk-tuks* are also in abundance and can be had quite cheaply. Keep in mind that bargaining is expected. Drivers will accept Thai baht as well as Lao kip. A ride out to That Luang (the tourist attraction furthest from the city

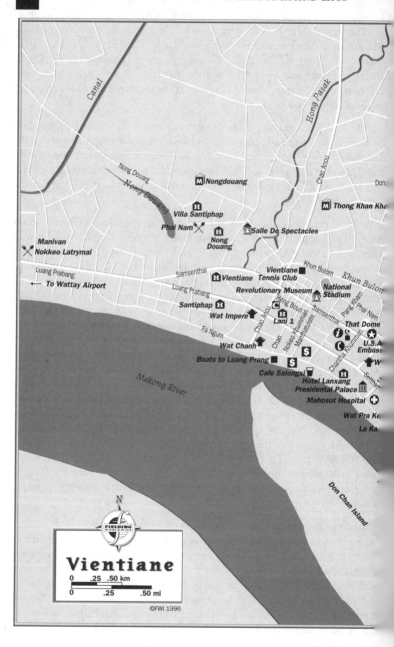

Canal

Hong Pasak

Chao Anou

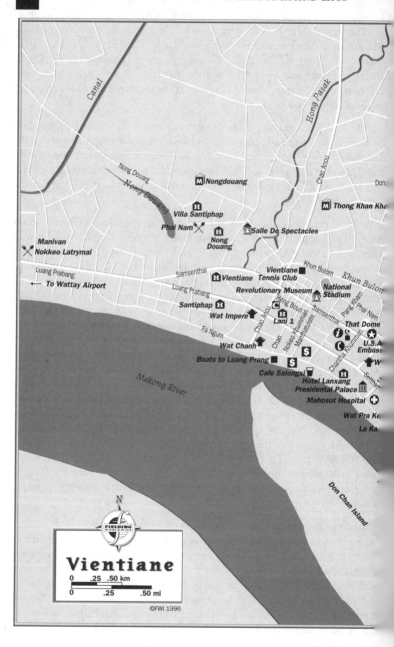 M Nongdouang

Nong Douang

Nong Douang

Don

M Thong Khan Kha

H Villa Santiphap

Phai Nam ✕🍴

H Nong Douang

🎭 Salle De Spectacles

✕ Manivan
Nokkeo Latrymai

Khun Bulom

Khun Bulor

Luang Prabang
← To Wattay Airport

Samsenthai

H Vientiane Tennis Club

Vientiane ■

National Stadium

Luang Prabang

Revolutionary Museum

Samsenthai

Pang Kham / Phai Nam

Santiphap H

Heng Boun

Chao Anou

C

That Dome

Wat Impere 🌳

H Lani 1

Nokeo Khummane

Manthatulat

i

C

U.S.A
Embass

Fa Ngum

Chan

Chantha Khummane

Wat Chanh 🌳

$

🌳 W

Boats to Luang Prang ■

$

Sethath

Cafe Salongxi 🍷

Hotel Lanxang H

Mekong River

Presidential Palace 🏛

Mahosot Hospital ➕

Wat Pra Ke

La Ka

Don Chan Island

N

FIELDING
WORLDWIDE

Vientiane

0   .25   .50 km

0   .25   .50 mi

©FWI 1996

Vientiane

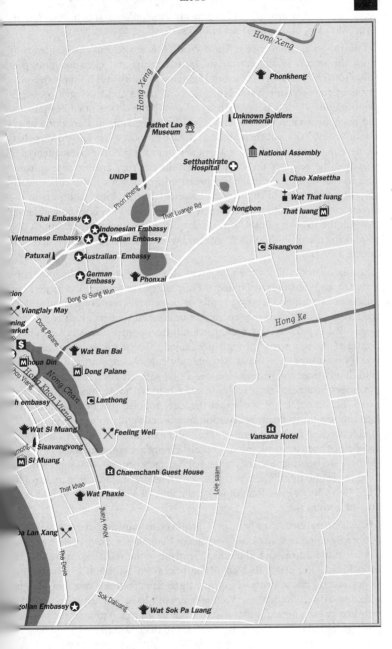

Hong Xeng

Hong Xeng

Phonkheng

Unknown Soldiers memorial

Pathet Lao Museum

Setthathirate Hospital

National Assembly

Chao Xaisettha

Wat That luang

That luang

UNDP

Phon Kheng

That Luange Rd

Nongbon

Thai Embassy

Indonesian Embassy

Vietnamese Embassy

Indian Embassy

Patuxai

Australian Embassy

Sisangvon

German Embassy

Phonxai

Dong Si Sung Wun

Hong Ke

...tion

Vianglaly May

...ning ...arket

Dong Palane

Wat Ban Bai

Nhoua Din

Dong Palane

Hong Khon Vieng

...hou Vieng

Lanthong

...h embassy

Wat Si Muang

Feeling Well

Vansana Hotel

Sisavangvong

Nong Chan

Si Muang

Chaemchanh Guest House

That khao

Wat Phaxie

Loie saam

...a Lan Xang

Khou Vieng

The Deua

...golian Embassy

Sok Daluang

Wat Sok Pa Luang

center) from downtown and back again shouldn't set you back any more than 3000 kip, or about 80 baht (US$3.20).

Two things in abundance at Third World tourist sites but curiously missing from the streets of the capital are both beggars and chewing gum/post card/souvenir hawkers. At each of Vientiane's tourist sites is simply one government-run souvenir stand. No clusters of kiosks and food stalls nor children tugging at your sleeve with boxes of Wrigleys. Deformed beggars and old haggard women toting seemingly half-dead infants in search of a handout are conspicuous in their absence. I have no doubt the Lao powers-that-be have made the nice folks of Vientiane quite clear of the consequences of smearing the best face they've mandated the citizenry don for foreign tourists. In this regard, Vientiane is a breath of fresh air for those either heart-torn or simply tired of the poverty-in-your-face the visitor confronts in the streets of Laos' neighbors. Yet, when attired in $120 Reeboks and sweating beneath the strap of a $600 Sony camcorder, it still remains quite impossible to remain entirely without guilt in a land where the average annual income is a mere US$180.

Equally as noticable by their apparent absence are the both the local constabulary and the military. Unlike in Phnom Penh or Saigon, Vientiane's finest cannot be found directing traffic or posted at street corners surveilling the scene. Neither does one encounter uniformed soldiers glued to AK-47s positioned in pill boxes or loafing around street corner cafes smoking cheap cigarettes. Take a stroll through the capital, particularly on a Sunday, and you'll be astounded by what is seemingly either a content, self-governing community from the pages of Walden Pond without any need for a law-enforcement structure, or a self-contained halfway house for lobotomy patients. I cannot determine whether the local populace has been skull-beaten into submission and stoic resignation by a brutal xenophobic regime and no longer needs to be monitored, or if half of the strollers on the city's sidewalks and half of the city's tuk tuk drivers are simply government agents in plain clothes—accounting for the other half's adherence to conformity. But I imagine, in the tightly knit but relatively transparent (say, compared to Ho Chi Minh City or even Rangoon) social fabric of Vientiane, there may be a little of both in there.

If you've traveled elsewhere in Third World Southeast Asia, it will undoubtedly come as a shock how expensive Vientiane is. For its crude amenities (or I should say lack thereof), Vientiane is the most expensive city in Indochina. Sure, classy digs at orbital prices can be found in Hanoi and Saigon, even Phnom Penh—but these three cities feature a vast mid-budget accommodations foundation. Vientiane doesn't have that luxury (nor even truly luxury-class hotel for that matter), but seems to flip tourists the bird regardless. Hotel rooms that don't fetch more than US$20 a night in Saigon cost twice that in Vientiane. And, generally, you don't get a lot of bang for the buck. Aloof service and lifeless rooms in sterile, Soviet-style buildings are the norm. There are a growing number of exceptions to this rule, but still a rule nonetheless. For some discerning visitors, especially those considering only a day or two in Vientiane, it makes more sense to simply go back to one of Nong Khai's comfortable hotels for the evening rather than spend the night in Vientiane.

Budget travelers will find food stall fare more expensive than in Cambodia and Vietnam (even Thailand), about 20 percent. City maps cost an outrageous US$6. And your jaw will drop when you take a trip to the Morning Market in Vientiane, especially if you've done some souvenir shopping previously in Thailand. The same items—from embroidery and fabric to electronic goods—found in the markets of Thailand generally cost 25 percent lower. A visit to the market in Vientiane is something of a disappointment, simply because there is so little there which is Lao.

Although Vientiane is arriving in the late 1990s as a world hot spot for the "been there, done that" set, the city is still searching for its identity (if it is even searching at all). Other than for the few French-worded building signs, the city has been snipped of its former colonial identity—yet has emerged as more Thai than Lao. Thai game shows pop from color TVs in Vientiane's cafes and hotel lobbies. Thai pop hits blare from the sound systems of neon-accented Isuzu pickups—Bangkok style. Lao girls get their toenails painted and hair done like Thai soap stars. When asked, Thai tourists in the capital will tell you Vientiane reminds them far more of an upcountry Thai town than the capital city of a foreign country.

I hesitate to call Vientiane the Gateway to Laos, as I think of Bangkok in Thailand. But for entirely different reasons. If Vientiane is indicative of Laos, it is only in its patience. Like the rest of Laos, it seems in little hurry to get anywhere. Which makes Vientiane unique among all Southeast Asia metropolises, and worth seeing for this reason alone.

What to See and Do in Vientiane

That Luang ★★

At the top of That Luang Rd.
Open daily from 8:30–11:30 a.m. and 2–4:30 p.m. except for Mondays and holidays.
Admission: 200 kip.
Built in 1566 by King Say Setthathirat during the heyday of the Lane Xang kingdom, That Luang was constructed in the typical Lao style and plundered and restored at various times since then. The current restoration is from the 1930s. It is believed to contain a relic of Buddha. The highlight of the temple is the 45-meter-high, gold-colored lotus bud stupa, which is an impressive sight as you near the complex coming up the road from the Victory Monument. The stupa was formerly surrounded by four monasteries. Two of those can be found today. An important

monument, That Luang impressively commands the top of a hill 3 km northeast of the city. That Luang is the Lao national symbol. The best time to see it is in the late afternoon when the sun turns the stupa an electric shade of gold. Photos are best at this time, and from in front of the stupa. There's a temple north of the monastery where Laos' Supreme Patriarch lives. A statue of Setthathirat can be found at the entrance to the stupa.

Morning Market (Talat Sao)   ★

Lane Xang Avenue, across from the Joint Development Bank
Open 7 a.m.–6:30 p.m.

Get here early and bring your camera and your kip. A good place to find souvenirs and local handicrafts if Vientiane is your only stop in Laos. A good selection of traditional Lao textiles can be found here (ground floor, left side of the building), as well as a bunch of imported electronic goods. Gold, silver and antiques can be found on the first floor of the far right pavilion. The central pavilion houses a "department store." But be warned, far more of the stuff here is from Thailand than Laos. Rest assured that you will pay more than you should, even if your guide does the bartering for you. Goods and crafts in Vientiane are more expensive than the same items found in markets south of the border. What you might assume to be a Lao handicraft may simply be a tablemat or satchel woven in Udon, with the import price tag to boot. Save the souvenir hunting for upcountry, as this market's best for locals and expats.

Revolutionary Museum

Samsenthai Rd., next to the National Stadium.
Monday–Friday 8–11:30 a.m. and 2–4 p.m.; Saturday between 8 a.m.–11:30 p.m. Admission is 200 kip.

The Revolutionary Museum is housed in an old, dilapidated colonial-era buiding and is said to display "memorabilia from the period of struggle for freedom and independence" and "achievements recorded by the Lao PDR since 1975." Don't expect a laser show here, folks. The museum was formerly not open to the public, but now we can all sneak peaks at these glorious Pathet Lao achievements.

Patu Xai (Victory Monument)   ★

At the head of Lane Xang Avenue
Open daily 8 a.m.–5 p.m. Admission: 200 kip

Formerly known only as Anousavary (monument), this monument on Lane Xang Avenue is now called the Arch of Triumph (or Victory Monument) and was built in 1962, taking its colonial inspiration from the Arc de Triomphe of Paris, yet instilling typical Lao motifs, namely *Kinnari* figures—half-woman, half-bird creatures. Although decidedly French inspired, the monument is rich in elaborate Lao bas relief ornamentation. Photographers wait outside for those who want an expensive photo taken of themselves by the arch. You can climb the stairs inside to the top for an impressive view of the city, the Mekong River, and Thailand beyond. The stairs are open until 5:00 p.m. Beneath the arch are a couple of souvenir kiosks and a few tables for picnicking.

Wat Si Saket ★

Setthathirath Rd., near the corner of Lane Xang.
Admission is 200 kip. Open daily 8:30 a.m.-4:30 p.m. except for Mondays and holidays,
closed midday from 11:30 a.m.–2 p.m.

Wat Si Saket is a traditional Lao monastery and the only temple in Vientiane to have survived the destruction of the city by the Siamese in 1828. Built in 1818 by King Anouvong, it is said to be the oldest existing *wat* complex in Vientiane. Inside the main hall *(sim)* and the courtyards surrounding it are hundreds of small niches and shelves containing a total of 6840 Buddha images dating from the 16th–19th centuries, as well as murals and typical Lao-style architecture. There's also a library here housing palm leaf manuscripts.

Wat Pha Keo ★

Setthathirath Rd., next to the Presidential Palace and across the street from Wat Si Saket.
Admission is 200 kip. Open daily 8:30 a.m.-4:30 p.m. except for Mondays and holidays,
closed midday from 11:30 a.m.–2 p.m.

Across the street from Wat Si Saket, Wat Pha Keo was built in 1565 by King Setthathirat—when he moved the capital of Lane Xang to Vientiane—and restored in the 1950s. This is the original home of the Emerald Buddha now found in Bangkok. King Setthathirat brought the Buddha from Chaing Mai. The king used the wat as his own personal place of worship and, as no monks were ever in residence here, the temple can't technically be called a wat. The Emerald Buddha was stolen by the Thais in 1778 and the temple destroyed in 1827. This small temple was formerly the royal residence but was rebuilt into a museum in 1936 to house Buddha images. It became a religious arts museum in 1968 and a monument museum in 1988. Both Wat Pha Keo and Wat Si Saket are museums worth visiting for their collections of Burmese, Khmer and Lao art from other *wats* in Vientiane.

That Dam (Black Stupa)

30 meters from both Lane Xang Avenue and Samsenthai Road.

This brick stupa, just down the street from the Metropole Hotel and about 20 meters high, features the legend of the seven-headed dragon, or naga, designed to ward off invasions by the Thai neighbors. The stupa today seems oddly placed, but most likely there was a reason for it in its day.

Wat Ong Teu and Wat Chan ★

Setthathirath Rd., near the intersection of Chao Anou Street.

The best place to experience the **That Luang Festival**, Wat Ong Teu is also home to a very large Buddha. In fact, *ong teu* means big, real big. The *wat* is called the Monastery of the Heavy Buddha, the name deriving from this huge 16th-century bronze Buddha enshrined in the main hall. Worth a peek for its carved wooden doors and interesting architecture. Here is also found the Institute of Buddhism. Monks from all over the country come here to study Buddhism under Laos' most revered and senior abbots. The day after the That Luang Festival, a wax pavilions procession (Phasat Pheung) is held here. Wat Ong Teu is surrounded by four other temples: Wat Impeng to the north, Wat Mixay to the south, Wat Haysok to the east and Wat Chan to the west. **Wat Chan** is the site of a bronze Buddha, although not much remains after the Thais wrecked the surrounding temple in 1827.

Vientiane

Wat Si Muang ★

Wat Si Muang, perhaps the most visited temple in Laos (attracting hundreds if not thousands of visitors a day), houses an undated Khmer boundary stone called a *lak muang*, or town pillar. There is also a larger-than-life monument to King Si Sawangwong, the last Lao monarch, in front of the temple. The temple was built by King Setthathirat in the mid-16th century (1566) when he moved Laos' captial from Luang Prabang to Vientiane. As legend has it, during the construction of the temple, a young pregnant woman named Nang Si decided to sacrifice herself—and her unborn child—jumped into the hole where the temple was being built and was crushed by *lak*. Today, she's considered the protector of Vientiane by those who revere her.

Nam Phu Square

This was a former roofed market which is home today to a number of decent restaurants. There is little left of its former appearance: arched buildings surrounding an attractive fountain, which was constructed in the late 1960s. Today, the area is best known for international cuisine.

Try to see the Mekong River in Vientiane at sunset.

Where to Stay in Vientiane

Anou Hotel   **US$18–$25**

01-03 Heng Boun Rd. ☎ *213360.*

A little disheveled, but the rooms are decent and the place has a good restaurant, serving even "international cuisine." Rooms with air conditioning, color TV, private bath, hot water.

Ambassador   **US$50**

Pang Kham Rd.

Also disheveled, but the rooms (with air conditioning, color TV, private bath, hot water) are large. Good restaurant here.

Settha Guesthouse   US$16

80/4 Samsenthai Rd. *213241, 216062; FAX: 215995.*
Very basic but clean guesthouse near the Revolutionary Museum. Rooms with air conditioning, private bath, hot water. Downstairs is the attached, air conditoned Hong Kong Restaurant with good Chinese food and friendly service.

Pornthip Guesthouse   US$10–$15

Across from No. 5 Rue Impeng, 20 meters from the intersection of Rue Inpeng and Fa Ngoum Quay. *217239.*
Very quiet relaxing setting on a small soi just a few meters from the banks of the Mekong. Small courtyard for relaxing and writing postcards. A favorite of backpackers. Clean rooms.

Asian Pavilion   US$24–$50

379 Samsenthai Road. *213430/1; FAX: 213432.*
Run-of-the-mill rooms (many without windows) with air conditioning. Large airy lobby with connected cozy restaurant. Rooms with satellite color TV, hot water and private bath. Five floors but no elevator, so it's a hoof to the top if that's where they tell you to go. If you're staying only a night, management will try to steer you to the least attractive room in your price range. Friendly and comfortable, but overpriced. Be warned: don't get the hotel to call a taxi for you. They mark up the rate at least 100 percent. A total ripoff, and they should be ashamed.

Lane Xang Hotel   US$90–$150   ★★

Fa Ngum Road. *214100/2, 214106; FAX 214108, 213432. 109 rooms.*
This is the most interesting hotel in town and still one of the capital's better hotels. Large Soviet-era concrete block with an interior design that archaeologists might discover a few centuries from now and determine to be an old "Miami Vice" set that was somehow displaced from South Florida via Moscow to Southeast Asia by a flood or two. Rooms with air conditioning, satellite color TV, telephone, minibar, hot water. Good continental restaurant; swimming pool, snooker club, tennis court, sauna, "minigolf courts." But still vastly overpriced. But given that everything is inflated in Vientiane, it's not a bad deal. And don't be surprised if a 50% off special is being offered—as it often is here. Price includes breakfast. An outrageously expensive restaurant under the same management is located across the street on the river.

New Apollo Hotel   US$69–$79   ★

Luang Prabang Road, Chanthabuly district. *213244/6; FAX 213343. 75 rooms.*
Totally renovated. Rooms with air conditioning, hot water, telephone, color TV, minibar. Restaurant with Thai, Chinese and Western fare. Night club, laundry service, gift shop. Worth the price, although it's gone up 10 bucks in the last year.

Novotel Vientiane   US$90–$140   ★★★

Unit 9, Ban Koun Ta Thong, Km 2, Samsenthai Road., Muang Sikhotabong. *213570, 213574, 214338; FAX 213572/3. 233 rooms.*

One of the two best hotels in Vientiane. Surprising amenities and comfort. Rooms with air conditioning, satellite color TV, IDD telephone, minibar. Also featuring fitness center, massage, sauna, swimming pool, tennis and gambling. Two restaurants with local and international cuisine. Karaoke, disco, business facilities, conference hall, banquet facilities for up to 250 people. One of the few professional, properly-trained staffs in Laos.

River View Hotel   US$42–$80

Khaemkhong Road, Sikhotabong district, Quai Fa Ngoum. ☎ *216224, 216231/2; FAX 216232. 32 rooms.*

A bit off the beaten track. The only thing this place has going for it, for the steep price, is that some of the rooms have a view of the Mekong River. Rooms with air conditioning, minibar, telephone, color TV. Restaurant. Only double rooms.

Metropole (Ekalath)   US$22–$33

Thanon Samsenthai and Chantha Khumman. ☎ *213420; FAX 213421. 34 rooms.*

Not one of the Metropoles you might be used to in Saigon or Hanoi, but accommodating enough despite the fact the place needs a facelift. Good location. The "upscale" rooms are doubles (some with air conditioning when it works), most with fans. No hot water. Rooms with satellite color TV; some rooms with shared toilets. Attached guest house has the cheapest rooms. Vietnamese restaurant. Some of the lowest hotel—as opposed to guesthouse—prices in Vientiane, but still overpriced. Beware that this place doesn't take credit cards, and that on my last visit, management would not allow two people in a single, unless they paid double the price. One couple had to take a double, although they were married. Bogus.

Santisouk   US$8–$20

Thanon Nokeo Khumman. ☎ *215567; FAX: 217449.*

Private bath in some of the rooms. Decent restaurant downstairs. Popular with backpackers.

Lao-Paris Hotel   US$25–$35

100 Samsenthai Rd. ☎ *222229, 213440; FAX: 216382.*

Cozy and in a good location; good deal for the price. Rooms with air conditioning, color satellite TV, telephone, refrigerator, private with hot water. Empty restaurant serves passable Euro dishes but better local and Thai fare at stiff rates.

Auberge du Temple   US$10–$20

Wat Khounta, Sikhotabong. ☎ *214844.*

Small and quiet. Clean rooms with air conditioning. Private bath.

Mekong   US$22–$25

Thanon Tha Deua, between 3–4 km from town toward the Tha Deua ferry. ☎ *212938; FAX: 216119.*

A great bargain, although far from town. But it's often full.

Tai-Pan Hotel   US$54–$68   ★

2–12 Francois Nginn Street, Chanthabouly district. ☎ *216906/7; FAX 216223. 3C rooms.*

Decent relatively upscale caravansary. Rooms with air conditioning, minibar, color TV, telephone. Laundry service. Restaurant, nightclub.

Royal Dokmaideng **US$88–$150** ★★★

Lane Xang Avenue, Chanthabouly district, central Vientiane. ☎ *213090, 214455, 214477; FAX 214454. 83 rooms.*

Perhaps Vientiane's nicest. Air-conditioned rooms and suites with private bath, minibar, satellite TV. Plus restaurant, karaoke, swimming pool, gift shop arcade, business services, conference facilities.

Where to Eat in Vientiane

The Taj **$$$** ★★

75/4 Pangkham Road, Nam Phu Square. ☎ *212890; FAX: 216214.*

Exquisite Indian fare in a casual but trendy setting. If you want to forget you're in Laos, start here.

Le Souriya **$$$** ★

Pangkham Road, Nam Phu Square area. ☎ *215887.*

The next night go here. French and Asian; upscale ambience.

Royal Dokmaideng **$$$** ★★

Royal Dokmaideng Hotel, Lane Xang Ave. ☎ *214455; FAX: 214454.*

If you want to avoid the way locals eat altogether, dine here the third night for expensive continental and gourmet Lao cuisine.

Le Vendome **$$$** ★

Wat Impeng. ☎ *216402.*

French at some its best in the capital.

Ban Haysok **$$** ★

Opposite the Anou Hotel. ☎ *215417; FAX: 215639.*

Basic Lao and Thai, but clean and well prepared for Western tastes.

Belle Ile **$$$** ★

24/1 Lane Xang Ave. ☎ *214942.*

Expensive Euro and Asian fare with a good bar. Gets a lot of expats.

Lao-Thai Restaurant **$$**

Lao-Paris Hotel. 100 Samsenthai Rd. ☎ *222229.*

Relatively sedate but tasty Lao and Thai concoctions for the farang palate.

Koualao **$$** ★★

111 Samsenthai Road. ☎ *214813; FAX: 215777.*

Great Lao dishes near the Lao-Paris Hotel. Perhaps the best Lao restaurant in the country. Live traditional Lao music accompanies the experience, in an antique setting—antique furniture with Lao textile covering the walls. Recommended.

Dao Vieng **$**

Heng Boun.

Popular place with a great local menu.

Dong Palan Night Market **$**

Near the Lang Thon Cinema off Ban Fai.

Check out any of the food stalls here. Not to be missed.

Vientiane

Chez Mo $$

352 Samsenthai.
Vietnamese cuisine.

Vientiane Department Store $–$$

Morning Market.
Sort of the Robinson's for Lao food. But cheap beer.

Arawan $$

472–480 Samsenthai.
Decent French fare.

Santisouk $$

Thanon Nokeo Khumman. ☎ *215567. Under the hotel.*
Maybe the best food in Vientiane for the price. Continental, decent French.

Le Santal $$

Thanon Setthathirat, across from Wat Ong Teu.
French and pizza. You figure it out. Great for the price.

Thai Food Garden $$

Samsenthai near the Russian Cultural Center.
Great Thai fare.

May 1 Restaurant $$

The corner of Pang Kham and Fa Ngum.
On the river. Good Lao fare. Formerly popular with the Soviets and Cuba's best.

Nightlife in Vientiane

There ain't much. The Asian scourge of karaoke is spreading epidemically in this sleepy capital, and finding a Western-style roadhouse here is more for a team of archaeologists than thirsty travelers. The Russians are pretty much gone. But in their wake, the Russian Bar (Mixai) still remains, and is popular because brewskis can still be bought with rubles—or the equivilant, which isn't much.

The Fountain Bar seems to be the most popular hangout for expats and yupsters, as well as the few hookers hanging out at the perimeter tables. Try a disco here and you'll do one of two things: throw up at the live music or dance to it, a cantankerous cacophony of hybridized, sour Thai bubble gum and fractious, nasal renditions of "Yumpin' Lack Frash." But go ahead, take a chance. Feel lucky? Well, do you, punk?

Oh yeah, the beer around here is called Beerlao. It's a punchless brew that reminds me a little of the old Rheingold beer brewed in the States—i.e., you won't guess it in any taste tests. And it won't win any medals in Munich for a couple of centuries. It has 5% alcohol and is a lot cheaper than Tiger and the other imports.

Malibu

Samsenthai Road.
The latest in a string of expat bars to open in the capital. California motif. Imported beers, pool, etc. This might become Vientiane's version of Phnom Penh's Martinis.

Anou Cabaret

Anou Hotel. Thanon Chao Anou at Thanon Heng Boun.

Mirrors line the walls of this loud, sweaty, this-side-of-hell dance hall. Live music (can't anyone play the drums in Asia anymore?) and outrageous *lam wong* spinoffs to poppy-pop.

Checker Pub

Opposite the Novotel, 7/073 Luang Prabang Rd. ☎ *222799.*
Part bar, part coffee shop. Killing time is the best thing to do here.

Feeling Well

Thanon Ban Fai (Thanon Dong Pulan).
About 200 meters past the Dong Pulan Night Market. Few *farangs* venture into this place, extremely popular with the local kids. Anything else said would be superfluous.

Foster's Modern House

Thanon Touran at the Thanon Heng Boun end.
Where Nine-Inch Nails might stop in for an amber ale in a "my-loft-is-cooler-than-yours" setting.

Fountain Bar

Thanon Phang Kham, Namphu Garden.
Croat manager of this setting for NGOers and cub reporters. Folks catch a buzz here.

Haan Kin Deum Mixai

Across from the Mixai Guesthouse, 30/1 Thanon Fa Ngum.
This is what the infamous Russian Bar is now called, but not by anyone who's had more than a couple of beers.

Vienglaty Mai

North of the Morning Market on Thanon Lane Xang.
Live music at this disco with the best-looking Lao lasses this side of Luang Prabang.

Sports in Vientiene

Tennis

Unless you're a guest at one of the few well-heeled hotels in Vientiane that do have tennis courts, you won't have many options. If you're not a guest, try asking anyhow. I'm sure, for a large fee, the following will let you use their courts. If that doesn't work, try heading to the Tennis Club, near the National Stadium.

Novotel Vientiane

Unit 9, Ban Koun Ta Thong, Km 2, Samsenthai Road., Muang Sikhotabong. ☎ *213570, 213574, 214338; FAX 213572/3.*

Lane Xang Hotel

Fa Ngum Road. ☎ *214100/2, 214106; FAX 214108, 213432.*
The Lane Xang has one court.

Swimming

Municipal Swimming Pool

Corner of Phai Nam Road and Ky Huong Road (at the National Stadium).
A large, clean pool can be found here with enough chlorine to raise the eyebrows of UN chemical weapons inspectors. And beware of the puddle-jumpers on Sundays,

who, no doubt, were never told by their parents not to pee in water they happen to be immersed in. You can also count on being an oddity here as the only farang. And save the G-strings for Club Med.

Sokpaluang Swimming Pool

Sokpaluang Road, about 3 km southeast of downtown.

Fitness Centers

L'Eden

Wat Phaya Wat. ☎ *213528.*
Weight room and aerobic center.

Gym-Tonic Body Building & Aerobics

Dong Palan Road, next to the Lane Xang Nightclub.
Free weights and aerobic exercise machines.

Novotel Vientiane

Unit 9, Ban Koun Ta Thong, Km 2, Samsenthai Road., Muang Sikhotabong.
☎ *213570, 213574, 214338; FAX 213572/3.*
The Novotel has a weight room with free weights and aerobic exercise machines.

Jet Skiing

Vientiane itself offers no jetskiing on the Mekong River I'm aware of, but the Thailand side of the river does. The best bet is to check out the Holiday Inn in Nong Khai.

Holiday Inn

222 Jamanee Beach, Nong Khai, Thailand 43000. ☎ *66-42-420024; FAX: 66-42-421280.*

Shopping in Vientiane

As I mentioned earlier, things are a bit pricy on this side of the river, and it's probably best to do your souvenir shopping upcountry in Luang Prabang or Phonsavan. But there are certainly a number of places in the capital where textiles, jewelry and electronic goods can be found. The best source, of course, is the **Morning Market** on Lane Xang Avenue. The following are some other suggestions.

Textiles

Carol Cassidy

82/5 Ban Mixay. ☎ *212123; FAX: 216205.*
This is where the Diethelm tour buses stop for their customers to load up on expensive traditional Lao textiles.

Handicrafts/Antiques

Yani

Khoun Boulom Road. ☎ *(020) 513190.*
Lao handicrafts and interior decorations. One of the classiest stores in the capital.

Tang's Antiques

103 Street. 14/02 Bane Thongkhang village, Sisattanak district; ☎ *313223.*
Specializes in old Lao textiles, artifacts, paintings and silver.

Kanchana Boutique

That Dam, 102 Samsenthai Road (opposite Ekalath Hotel), Chanthabuly district
☎ *213467.*

Lao handicrafts and antiques.

Directory (Area Code 021)

Transportation

On arrival at Wattay International Airport, **taxis** are available for transport into town for about US$5. The airport is about 10 minutes outside of the city center, and taxi prices are posted in the airport lounge. There are some metered taxis, but it doesn't make any difference what taxi you decide upon.

When departing from Wattay airport, there is a US$5 departure tax. Allow an hour for check-in and immigration procedures for international flights. And confirm your international reservations at least two days before departure at the Lao Aviation office. It's better to make the confirmation in person.

Lao Aviation connects Vientiane with the following provincial capitals: Luang Prabang, Savannakhet, Luang Namtha, Xieng Khouang, Pakse, Oudomxay, Xayaboury, Houixay, Tha Khek, Samneua and Laksao. See the Lao Aviation Time Table below.

Laos' **river network** is dominated by the Mekong River. It flows through 2030 km of Laos and provides a natural means of transportation. However, its navigability is limited to 1330 km, primarily due to the severe rapids between Savannakhet and Pakse, as well as the Khong Falls and generally low water levels during the dry season. In addition to the Mekong, other navigable rivers include the Nam Ou, Nam Khan, Nam Tha, Nam Hgum and Se Don.

In April 1994, the 1.2 km Friendship Bridge linking Nong Khai in Thailand with Vientiane was opened, making overland entry into Laos possible from Thailand's northeast. The bridge was financed by US$30 million in aid from Australia. The bridge is open from 8 a.m.–6 p.m. Travelers can obtain visas to Laos either from travel agencies in Bangkok, Khon Kaen and Nong Khai itself in order to cross the bridge. Visas to Laos from Nong Khai can be processed the same day. For a complete description of all land entry points into Laos, see the "Visas" and "Entry by Land" sections.

Laos has 13,100 km of **roadways**, excluding forest and mining roads, which consist of national, provincial and local roadways. The national routes linking provincial capitals, major towns and international borders total 3390 km, 1620 km of which are paved. The balance of the roadways are often dilapidated earth trails linking villages within provinces. National Highway 13 is the country's major artery. It totals 1370 km, connecting Pak Mong in the north with Khong in the south, passing through the larger urban areas of Luang Prabang, Vientiane, Savannakhet and Champasack. National Highway 9, another important international artery, links Laos with Vietnam. Much of the road is impassable during the rainy season by motorcycle and even by car.

Local transportation is either on foot, by bicycle or by motorcycle tuk tuk. In places such as Vientiane, simply wave down a passing tuk tuk and bargain a price for your destination. You shouldn't pay any more than 500 kip per kilometer. Laos' prehistoric taxis generally can't be hailed from the street for trips around town. Instead, they're used mainly to shuttle visitors back and forth from Vientiane Wattay Airport and from the Friendship Bridge connecting Laos with Thailand, 20 kilometers from Vientiane. The bridge trip should be 100 Thai baht, or 3700 kip. If you should need a taxi, it's best to find one on your own, as hotels have a propensity for tacking on outrageous service charges for a simple phone call. There is no intracity bus service to speak of. However intercity buses connect Vientiane with all of Laos' provinces. The main bus station in Vientiane is behind the Morning Market on Mahosot Street. Here, buses leave for Luang Prabang, 420 kilometers to the north, and elsewhere in Laos when full. The trip to Luang Prabang takes 7-10 hours depending on the driver (public buses take the longest) over a much improved roadway. Foreigners are are permitted to travel independently by bus in Lao. The cost for foreigners is 12,000 kip one way to Luang Prabang.

Insider Tip: Beware of Bandits

Traveling by public bus is certainly the most dangerous way to see Laos, and not only because of the decrepit condition of the vehicles. Banditry is a big problem on the Vientiane-Luang Prabang route, particularly where the road heading north forks to Luang Prabang and Phonsavan from just inside Vientiane province. Some foreigners were held at gunpoint at this juncture in October 1996, after the bus they were riding in was stopped and raided by armed banditos. From time to time, the army moves in and cleans things up a bit for a short time, but the highwaymen move right back in when the soldiers are gone—which is most of the time. Bus drivers and tour groups time their trips to Luang Prabang and Phonsavan very carefully, making certain they reach the fork in daylight. The National Tourism Authority flat out warns foreigners against taking the public buses north due to the possibility of encountering gun-toting rebels-turned-robbers.

Emergencies

Police

> Emergency: ☎ 412536.
> Chanthabouri District: ☎ 213907/8.
> Xayasettha District: ☎ 412455, 412457
> Sikhottabong District: ☎ 212712.
> Sisatanak District: ☎ 212711.

Hospitals

International Medical Clinic (Mahosot Hospital)

> Fa Ngum Road; ☎ 214018, 214022, 214025. Open daily 24 hours.

Australian Embassy Clinic

> Next to the Australian Embassy, Nehru, Stret Phonexay. ☎ 413603, 413610, 312343.
> Open Mon., Tues., Thur., Fri. 8:30 a.m.–noon and 2–5 p.m. Open Wed. 8:30 a.m.–noon.

Swedish Clinic

> Close to the Swedish Embassy, Sok Paluang. ☎ 315015 (clinic); ☎ 217010, 3150.
> (embassy).
> Open Mon.–Wed. and Fri. 8 a.m.–noon and 2–4 p.m. Open Thurs. 8 a.m.–noon.

Setthathirath Hospital

> Phonesaad Street. ☎ 412783.

Friendship Hospital
Phontong Street. ☎ *413306.*

AMFA
Phontong Street. ☎ *412663*

Post Offices/ Express Couriers/Freight Forwarders

Vientiane Post Office
On the corner of Lane Xang Aveenue and Khou Viang Street (across from the Morning Market). ☎ *215480.*

This is the only place you should post mail in Vientiane. Even from here it's chancy. It's best for post cards. If it's important, send it DHL.

DHL Worldwide Express
Ban Wattay Noy Thong. ☎ *214868, 216830; FAX: 214869.*

Express letters and packages. Minimum charge about US$50. Packages take 3-4 working days to reach addressees in the U.S.

Calberson (Freight Forwarding)
089 Ban Phonesavan Tay, Sisattank. ☎ *& FAX: 313210.*

International Phones

Central Telephone Office
Setthathirath Road (at Chanta Khoumane Rd.), near Nam Phu Square (Nam Phu Fountain). Open 8 a.m.–10 p.m. daily.

International calls and faxes can be made from here. IDD is available in Laos. The country code for Laos is 856; the Vientaine city code is 21.

Airline Offices

Lao Aviation
2 Pangkham Road
☎ *212051/3; FAX 212056.*

Silk Air
Lane Xang Avenue
☎ *217492; FAX: 217491.*

Malaysia Airlines
Unit 9, Samsenthai Road
☎ *213570; FAX: 213572.*

Singapore Airlines
Lane Xang Avenue
☎ *217492; FAX: 217491.*

Embassies

Australia
Nehru Street, Wat Phonsay area;
☎ *413610, 413805, 413602.*

China
Vat Nak Street, Sisattanak area;
☎ *315103, 315100, 315101.*

France
Setthathirath Road.
☎ *215258.*

India
That Luang Road.
☎ *413802.*

Cambodia
Saphathong Nua area.
☎ *314952; FAX 312584.*

Cuba
Ban Saphanthong Neua.
☎ *314902*

Germany
26 Sokpaluang Road.
☎ *312111*

Indonesia
Phon Kheng Road;
☎ *413910, 413909, 413907, 413914.*

Japan
> Sisangvone Road.
> ☎ 212623, 414400; FAX 414403.

Malaysia
> That Luang Street, Wat Phonsay area;
> ☎ 414205.

Poland
> Tha Deua Road, Km 3.
> ☎ 313940.

Sweden
> Vat Nak Street, Sokpaluang.
> ☎ 315018.

United States of America
> That Dam.
> ☎ 212580/2, 312609; FAX 212584.

North Korea (DPRK)
> Vat Nak Street, Sisattanak;
> ☎ 315261, 315260.

Myanmar
> Sokpaluang Street, Sisattanak;
> ☎ 312439, 314910.

Russia
> Thaphalanxay.
> ☎ 312219

Thailand
> Phonkheng Road;
> ☎ 214582/3, 214585.

Vietnam
> That Luang Road;
> ☎ 413400, 413409, 413403.

Government Offices

Presidential Palace
> ☎ 214210

Customs and Taxes Department
> ☎ 213810.

National Geographic Department
> ☎ 214914.

Ministry of Information & Culture
> ☎ 212406.

Ministry of Foreign Affairs
> ☎ 414015.

Ministry of Trade
> ☎ 412003.

Ministry of Defense
> ☎ 412801.

Prime Minister's Office
> ☎ 213653.

Immigration Department
> ☎ 212520.

Police Headquarters
> ☎ 412530.

Ministry of Interior
> ☎ 414107.

Ministry of Finance
> ☎ 412401.

Ministry of Justice
> ☎ 414103.

Ministry of Public Health
> ☎ 214000.

Banks

Joint Development Bank
> 31–33 Lane Xang Road. ☎ 213532/6, 215595; FAX 213530.

Bank of Ayudhya
> 79/6 Lane Xang Avenue. ☎ 213521, 214575/6; FAX 213520.

Car Rentals

Yes, you can indeed rent a car in Laos, with or without a driver. The options aren't many, but you may find yourself behind the wheel of a Land Cruiser or late model Volvo

Asia Vehicle Rental
> 08/3 Lane Xang Ave. ☎ 217493; FAX: 217493.

Vientiane

Rents late model 4-wheel-drive vehixles and passenger cars for about US$50 a day.

Computer Equipment and Supplies

Micro Info
> *Sidamdouan Street.* ☎ *215515; FAX: 212117.*

Microtec
> *168 Luang Prabang Rd.* ☎ *213836; FAX: 212933.*

Minimarts

With the increasing number of expats and NGO workers arriving in the capital, a few small, Western style minimarts have opened up offering imported Western foods and beverages. Two of the most popular are found on the corner Samsenthai Road and Chanta Khoumane Road, near That Dam. One is located beneath the Metropole Ekalat Hotel.

Newspapers and Magazines

Vientiane has an English-language newspaper, the *Vientiane Times*. But it's a weekly and best for wire reports and overviews of what's going on in Laos and the rest of the world. Vientiane isn't a good place for getting foreign periodicals yet.

Vientiane Times
> *Phangkham Street.* ☎ *216364; FAX: 216365.*

Art Galleries

Carol Cassidy
> *82/5 Ban Mixay.* ☎ *212123; FAX: 216205.*

Performing Arts

Lao Opera (L'Opera Lao)
> *Khoun Boulom Street (at Thongkhankham Street).*
> Traditional Lao music, song and dance performances.

Circus

Vientiane Circus
> *Savang Road and Dong Palep Road.*
> For Laos, this is the big tent. An assortment of acts, mostly with clowns and animals, can be found here. Not worth going out of your way for unless you claimed small children at Customs.

Zoo

Vientiane Zoo (Vientiane Zoological Gardens)
> *Ban Kuen (Km 59, northeast), Muang Toulakhom, Vientiane Province. Office: 193 Set-thathirath Rd., Ban Kaonhoth, Muang Sisattanak, Vientiane.* ☎ *216341/3; FAX: 212360.*
> A shake from town, and worth a stop (if Third World zoos don't bother you) if you're headed out of town in that direction. The zoo seems surprisingly well maintained, with clean, apparently well-treated inhabitants..

Tour Operators

ane Xang Travel & Tour
> *Pangkham Road, Vientiane.* ☎ *212469, 213198; FAX 215804.*

Lao National Tourism Co.

08/02 Lane Xang Avenue, Vientiane. ☎ 216671; FAX 212013.

Chackavane Travel & Tour

92 Thongkhankham Road, P.O. Box 590, Vientiane. ☎ 216444; FAX 214743.

DAFI Travel/Tours Co.

Head Office: 146–148 Ban Thaluang, Pakse district, Champassack province.
Branch Office: 093/4 Samsenthai Road, Vientiane. ☎ 216721; FAX 217335.

Diethelm Travel Laos

Nam Phu Square, Setthathirath Road, P.O. Box 2657, Vientiane. ☎ 215920; FAX 217151.

Vientiane Environs

Vientiane province, with a total population of 305,000, borders Vientiane municipality and the provinces of Luang Prabang, Xieng Khouang and Bolikhamsay. Within the province, Phonhong is the largest town. The eight other districts of the province include Thourakhom, Keo Oudom, Feuang, Vang Vieng, Kasy, Saysomboom, Hom and Sanakham.

INSIDER TIP

If you decide to wander off toward the Hmong and Yao areas near Luang Prabang, you may find the countryside is both scenic and dangerous. Hmong rebels will attack some convoys. For this reason, foreigners have been quickly deported if found. But as the region has stabilzied, these areas have become more accessible.

KM-6 (Silver City)

Six kilometers south of Vientiane is an interesting area for those who have a military bent. This was the headquarters of the CIA staff and spotter pilots who ran the secret war in Laos up until 1975. After the Americans left, the communists made Silver City their headquarters and their operatives earned the nickname "Silvers." Ask your guide if he is a Silver—don't be surprised if he proudly confirms your suspicions.

Suan Vatthanatham Banda Phas (Ethnic Cultural Park)

Open daily 8 a.m.-4:30 p.m. Admission: 500 kip.

This is an attractive little park along the grotty road linking the Friendship Bridge with Vientiane. It's located not even a kilometer from the bridge. Here there are mock-ups of ethnic hilltribe dwellings and a small, pointless zoo. It's a good place to come for local musical performances along the banks of the Mekong. There are also some small shops and cafes. Foreigners don't usually bother to stop here; few people do between the bridge and the capital.

Suan Xieng Khuan Park (Buddha Park)

Open daily 8 a.m.-4:30 p.m. Admission: 200 kip.

Located a few kilometers closer to Vientiane than the Ethnic Cultural Park is this concrete statue garden built in the late 1960s, which appears like a miniature Wat Kaek across the river in Nong Khai. The statues represent both Buddhist and Hindi mythology. The most unusual sight here is the three-story-tall pumpkin with its three levels depicting heaven, purgatory and hell. It'll remind you more of a Charlie Brown special.

Vang Vieng

This is perhaps the most scenic district of Vientiane province, which offers some of the best weather in the country as well spectacular vistas of of rock and limestone mountains not dissimilar to those found in the northeast of Vietnam. Pha Tang and Pha Tho Nokham are perhaps the most magnificent. They offer numerous caves and outcrops over the Xong River. Tham Phra, Tham Baat and Tham Leusi are considered holy caves in the Chang Mountains and are situated only about 3 km from Vang Vieng. The surrounding countryside is fertile for both rice and temperate vegetables, including watermelon and cabbage. Namoug and Nagnao are hand-woven-silk production centers—locally known as Khun Lou and Nang Oua's Hill.

Xieng Khonane (Garden of the Buddhas)

Avoid this ticky, tacky Asian theme park built in the 1950s by a priest.

Saam Haa Yai (555 Park)

These gardens are about 14 km outside town. They're more inclined to serve the local need for recreation than to inspire wonder and amazement. Skip it.

Prabat Phonsanh

An impressively situated *wat* on a volcanic plug that contains a footprint of the Lord Buddha and a reclining Buddha. It's 80 km east of Vientiane toward Paksane.

Ane Soung

Thirty km north of Vientiane on the Luang Prabang road, you will come across a partial cave with a sculpture of the Buddha inside. There is supposed to be a footprint of the Lord Buddha at the entrance.

Ban Thalet and Nam Ngum Dam

Ninety km from Vientiane on Route 13, this large man-made lake boasts a hydro-electric dam, most of the electricity being routed into Thailand. The lake has perhaps thousands of small islands (actually submerged hilltops). The Nam Ngum River offers beautiful scenery, and travelers are allowed to stay at the **Nam Ngum Hotel**. There is a growing number of bungalows, and boats can be hired for excursions on the lake. Fishing villages ring the shoreline. On the way to the lake, a short detour will lead to Vangsang, an 11th-century Buddhist archaeological site where early Buddha images are carved into the rockside. A traditional salt factory can also be seen in the vicinity at Ban Keun. Nam Ngum is also a jumping-off point for adventurers heading north to Luang Prabang.

The Outer Limits

The lure of northern Laos depends on whether your travels are for business or pleasure. If you are interested in traditional Hmong and Lao villages, then this is the place. You will need a guide (not an official one) and plenty of kip (it costs a lot to get around and to get out). The area between here and China is home to some of the least-visited tribes in the world. These tribes are tough, independent and very wealthy—wealthy because 60 percent of the world's heroin supply comes from this area. Myanmar and Afghanistan are the only two bigger producers of opium. Much of this wealth is used to pay for weapons and manpower to fight the current regime. How can you tell when you're in an opium smuggling area? Look for ponies. They are used for one purpose: transporting heroin over the mountainous terrain to Chaing Mai, Thailand.

If you are here on business, you know that the poppy fields are not for flower arranging. Raw material is transported overland to the Chaing Mai area of Thailand. There is also significant mining of sapphires. Timber poaching by the Thais is rampant. The Plain of Jars in Xieng Kouang province is not to be missed.

Someday it would be fun to do the Ho Chi Minh Trail, but cluster bombs litter the trail like thistles.

Southern Laos offers tranquil Lao Theung villages on the banks of the Mekong River, spectacular waterfalls such as the Khon Prapheng falls and mysterious Wat Phou near Champasak. Elephant rides deep into the jungle to explore remote hilltribe villages can be had at the Tat Lo Lodge near Pak song.

Luang Prabang

Not much left of this historic and scenic but oft-razed city. Worth a trip for its more than 60 temples, perhaps 30 of which are still in good enough shape to visit. Many of the *wats* are locked, so make sure you contract with a local guide.

Luang Prabang, situated at Mount Phousi, was the capital of different kingdoms for more than six centuries and was established in the 14th century by Fa Ngum, the first monarch of Lane Xang. The city sits at 300 meters above sea level and is an easygoing municipality of 16,000 or so inhabitants. The population of Luang Prabang province is about 365,000.

After the French made Laos a "protectorate" in the early part of the 20 century, they permitted the Laotians to retain the Luang Prabang monarch although on paper only. The monarchy was quickly dismantled after the Pathet Lao took over the area in 1975.

Today, Luang Prabang is little changed from the last 100 years. Of course, there is a smattering of cars and motorbikes, but most folks still ride bicycles. The streets are quiet and lazy. There seems little need for electricity, for what little of it exists seems never to work.

The city is worth about a two- or three-day visit, as many of the remaining *wats* and other sights are all within walking distance of each other.

Thousands of gold-and-wood Buddhas are in Pak Ou Caves, near Luang Prabang.

What to See and Do in and Around Luang Prabang

Royal Palace (National Museum) ★★

Built in 1904, the palace has been the repository of some of the most important and revered Buddha figures in Laos. Make sure you see the 15th- through 17th-century statues and the Khmer bronze drums. The Golden Buddha inside is a copy; the original is 90 percent solid gold, 83 cm high and weighs over 90 kg. It was created in Ceylon in the first century, brought to Cambodia and then to Vientiane in 1563 by King Setthathirat. It was taken to Thailand in 1779 and then returned in 1839. It was "rediscovered" in 1975 in the palace chapel. Much of the decor is modern (1960–1970), as befitting for the last king, Sissavong Vattana. There are a variety of state gifts from other countries on display (there's even a moon rock from the Apollo missions). You will need to arrange for special entry with the LNT office if it is not part of your tour.

Wat Mai

This *wat* took more than 70 years to complete and was begun in 1821 during the reign of King Manthatourath. It was once the residence of Phra Sangkharaj, the patriarch of the Buddhist clergy in Laos, until he moved to Vientiane in 1975. The five-tiered roof of the wooden *sim* is in the traditional Luang Prabang style. The *wat* features beautiful architecture. Three stupas have survived from the period. The *wat* has a number of boats which are used during festivals in the local boat races. The New Year festival, *Pimai*, also takes place here.

Mount Phousi   ★

An enormous, exotic rock. Climb it for the view early in the morning for sunrise or at dusk for sunset. Enjoy the very Asian, very spiritual feeling that this rock has inspired for centuries. The hill rises up from the middle of town—the Royal Palace is at its base. **Wat Chom Si** sits on the summit and was built in 1774–1804 during the reign of King Anurut. It was restored in 1962 and completely renovated in 1994. More than 320 stairs lead to it and the climb rivals the huffing and puffing it takes to reach the temple at the summit of Chiang Mai's Doi Suthep in Thailand. But the views of the surrounding Mekong and Nam Kane rivers are fabulous. The best time of the day is at sunset during the dry season. The anti-aircraft guns dampen the mystical feeling somewhat. The giant drum here is beaten 33 times (the number of the Buddha's commandments) four times a day. Or at least it used to be until the drummer died. No word on his understudy. Along the main road, there are a number of important religious sites, monks living in many of them. **Wat Phra Bath Nua** features a three-meter-long footprint of the Lord Buddha and was renovated in 1965. **Wat Sene** was built in 1718 and is a Thai-style temple. **Wat Xieng Thong**, built in 1559 by King Xiengthong on the banks of the Mekong River, is a well-cared-for royal *wat* with a reclining Buddha, which was shown at the 1931 Paris Exhibition on a 12-meter-high, gilded funeral chariot used to transport the burial urn of King Sisavang Vong. **Wat Pak Khan** has a pretty location but not much else. **Wat That** is known for its ornamental doors and pillars. **Wat Phra Bath** features a large Buddha footprint in a scenic setting. **Wat That Luang**, built in 1818, is the burial place of King Sisavang Vong, the last king. **Wat Manorom** is the site of a two-ton Buddha from 1372; it's one of the oldest Laotian Buddha images.

Wat Visoun

Wat Visoun was built in 1513 during the reign of King Visounnarat and rebuilt in 1898. It's an ancient-looking *wat* with a good collection of religious art and the largest Buddha in town. The Phrabang, a fine gold Buddha image, was the religious symbol of the kingdom. It was enshrined here from 1504–1715, and from 1866–1874. In 1942, it was turned into the Museum of Religious Arts and housed collections of Buddha images and religious artifacts dating from the 14th century. Within its confines is the huge That Makmo (Watermelon Stupa). Originally known as That Patum, or Lotus Stupa, it was constructed in 1503. Its neighbor, **Wat Aham**, was built in 1823 and has two Bodhi trees.

Wat Phra Phone Phoa

Just out of town and modeled after the Shwedagon in Yangon, Myanmar. Check out the rather absurd depiction of the fates that await a variety of sinners.

Wat Chom Phet

Wat Chom Phet is a popular scenic viewpoint on the other side of the river from Luang Prabang. Nothing notable about this 20th-century temple other than its location.

Wat Long Khoun

On the far side of the river, Wat Long Khoun dates from the 18th century but was destroyed twice. There is a carved door which dates from 1937.

Wat Tham

Far side of the river.
This *wat* is a dark, dank cave with steps and carved-out stone. Bring a flashlight to see the dilapidated Buddhas inside.

Ban Chan

This is downriver from Luang Prabang and is a good place to buy large water jars and other pottery. Ban Hat Hien (near the airport) is known for its knives made from scrap.

Ban Phanom

Old village 3 km out of town (on the far side of the Nam Kane River) known for weaving. Three hundred years of weaving and selling to visitors makes this a tough place to cut a deal on the beautiful fabrics that were originally made for the royal family. The Lu people here originally came from Sip Son Panna in the southern Chinese province of Yunnan. They were used as servants of the royal court. The women began weaving again in earnest after 1947.

Wat Sangkhalok

About 6 km from the village of Ban Phanom.
This *wat* was built to protect the city in 1527. It was razed by a storm in 1883 and rebuilt in 1904.

Kuang Si Waterfall (Tad Kuang Si)

About 25 km from Luang Prabang toward Vientiane on Highway 13.
The Lao Lum village of Ban Xom and a Lao Theung village called Ban Thapene lie along the road to the waterfalls.

Long Lanh

This is a highly inaccessible Hmong village about 30 km off the main route.
The journey can only be done during the dry season, and then just by off-road motorcycle or four-wheel-drive. The trip is especially worth it for the stunning mountain views and a chance to see a traditional Meo village without other busloads of gawkers. The trip takes about two hours, and the last few hundred meters have to be done by foot.

Henri Mouhout's Tomb

If you'd like to pay your respects to fellow explorers, here's your chance. The discoverer of Angkor Wat was buried here in 1860—he died of malaria—but his grave was just discovered in 1990.

Pak Ou Caves ★★★

About 25 km upriver from Luang Prabang.

We recommend the boat trip and the sacred caves, **Tham Thing** and **Tham Phum**, for their thousands of gold-and-wood statues of the Buddha. You'll need to bring a flashlight. In April, hundreds of townspeople journey upriver to celebrate Pimai. The caves used to be the home of monks. The journey itself takes a couple of hours, depending on the season and boat employed. A relatively high powered boat usually takes two hours to get upriver and an hour to get back downstream. You can actually try your hand at some gold panning here during the dry season, when the water level is low enough for it. Villagers supplement their meager incomes with occasional flakes and small nuggets that can be sifted from the silt. You'll pass the village of Ban Xang Hai. Stop and sample the local fire water, *lao lao*. Wow. In the mouth of the Ou River is where the caves are located. Steps lead up to Tham Thing. Tam Phum is the higher of the two caves, which also cuts deeper into the mountain. Here can be found numerous Buddha images which have been "donated" by the faithful. On the opposite bank of the river is the small stilt-house village of Pak Ou.

Royal Cemetery

Not all people can be cremated, so the remains of the royal family who died as infants or from contagious diseases are buried here. Do you believe in ghosts? You will after you see the look on the face of your guide when you ask to visit here.

Xang Hai

If you develop a terrible thirst or a death wish, head upriver about 20 km to the home of *lao lao*. The distilled wine is potent and definitely an acquired taste. If you visit the wine makers, they take great pleasure in watching you grimace as you sample their wares.

Xayabouri (Xayyabuli)

It's a one-day trip to this area of ethnic minorities and provincial capital from Luang Prabang. By boat, the town can be reached in about four hours, depending on the river conditions. Take the boat. Along the way, the Mekong is flanked by numerous minority villages, where working elephants can be seen hauling teak trunks to the river and other tourists can't be seen at all. The province has several peaks higher than 1000 meters. Temples in the town itself include Wat Ban Thin, Wat Ba Phapoon and Wat Natomoy.

Houayxay (Houixay)

This town lies in the westernmost point of Laos in the Golden Triangle. The region is highly mountainous and inaccessible, although there are plane connections. Depending on who has the guns in the area, you may be able to cross into Thailand's Chiang Khong. Wat Chom Khao overlooks the town from a hill. In the hills around Houayxay can be found Lantene and Nong Thane minority villages, as well as the Lu village of Ban Poung. These villages are known for their goldsmiths, as the area is rich in gold, sapphires and rubies. There is a very basic guest house in Houayxay.

Luang Namtha

This is the northernmost province, bordering China to the north and Myanmar to the northwest—and surrounded by towering mountains reaching 2000 meters. Luang Namtha lies along Route 3 as well as the Nam Tha River. France, China, Siam (Thailand) and the kingdom of Luang Prabang all bickered about sovereignty of the area, and the city was once plagued by Chinese ruffians. Although the security picture has improved here, this is a major opium production region. There are flights here from Vientiane, but minimal accommodations. Treks can be arranged into the surrounding hilltribe communities, many who have seen few if any foreigners. Thirty-nine different ethnic groups make up the population of 125,000 here. The place to stay in Luang Namtha is the Luang Namtha Hotel, clean and relatively new with 15 rooms.

Where to Stay in Luang Prabang

Mouang Luang Hotel   **US$35–$80**   ★★

Bounkhong Road, Luang Prabang. ☎ *212790/1. FAX: 212790.*
35 rooms, 2 suites.

This is definitely my choice when in town. Clean, modern and attractive using traditional Lao motifs. Large air conditioned rooms tastefully furnished with excellent bathrooms. The rooms have minibar, refrigerator, telephone. TV hasn't gotten here yet. Conference room with fax service, dry cleaning, swimming pool. Restaurant serves tasty Lao and Euro dishes. Only drawback: this is where they toss all the tour groups.

Phousi, Kitsarath Settharhirath   **US$30–$35**

At the intersection of Kitsarath Settarhirat and Prothisarat, Luang Prabang Province. ☎ *212192.*
Air conditioning; restaurant; bar.

Phou Vao Hotel   **US$72**

Luang Prabang. ☎ *212194.*

Villa de la Princesse   **US$45**

Rue Sakkdrine, Luang Prabang.
10 rooms.
Formerly the private house of Princess Khampha. Now a quaint and highly popular guest house. Restaurant.

Manolak   **US$35**

Luang Prabang. ☎ *212250.*
The price gets you hot water, private bath and air conditioning.

Santy   **US$45**

Luang Prabang. ☎ *212267.*
Air conditioned rooms with hot water, private bath.

Rama Hotel   **US$10–15**

Wat Visoun, Luang Prabang. ☎ *212247*
Basic. No hot water. Restaurant.

Where to Eat in Luang Prabang

The **Nam Khan Restaurant** on the banks of the Nam Khan River gets the best reviews.
Kudos also goes to the restaurant at **Villa de la Princesse**.

Directory (Area Code 071)

Transportation

Luang Prabang is 420 kilomters north of Vientiane on Route 13. **Buses** depart when
full for Luang Prabang from the bus station in Vientiane on Mahosot Road behind the
Morning Market. The trip takes between 8-10 hours. The one-way fare for foreigners is
12,000 kip (US$13).

By **air**, Lao Aviation flies to Luang Prabang three times daily (twice daily on Thursday
and Sunday). The flight takes 40 minutes.

Tour Operators

Luang Prabang Tourism

Sisavangvong Road, P.O. Box 356, Luang Prabang. ☎ *212198.*

Xieng Khouang

Travel outside Vientiane used to require a special permit and a tour (with
guide). However, areas such as Xieng Khouang province are now accessible
to independent travelers.

Best known for the region "Plain of Jars," the province was the site of severe bombardment during the Vietnam War. By air, coming into the province, you'll notice massive craters left by B-52s and T-28 warplanes. The B-
52s used to jettison their loads over the Plain of Jars on their way back to
Thai airbases after unloading on Hanoi.

The province was also the recipient of tens of thousands of cluster bombs,
many of which are still unexploded and haven't been unearthed. Scrap metal
from the war materiel is in abundance and can be found all over the province. Xieng Khouang itself was leveled during the war, and the principal city
today is Phonsavanh (Paradise Hill), with a population of around 6000.

Xieng Khouang lies on a high plateau some 3000 meters higher than Vientiane. From the air, you'll notice the vast devastation caused by the bombers—the craters so close together that only small plots of rice can be grown
between them.

Most of the population of the region fled during the Vietnam War, or second Indochinese War. Most haven't returned. The entire province today
only numbers about 190,000 inhabitants. Of these, many are hilltribes people: Lao Lum, Lao Theung, Lao Soung (Hmong Khao and Hmong Lay

and Black Thai. There is some rebuilding going on in the area, but scars of war are everywhere. Bombed-out houses, temples and other buildings remain abandoned.

Muang Phouane was the principal town of the province and offered a number of historical sites, such as Siphom temple, Phia Wat temple and That Chom Phet, each of which were reputedly built 250 years before the establishment of the Lane Xang Kingdom.

What to See and Do in Xieng Khouang

Phonsavanh (Phone Savanh)

This is the new capital of Xieng Khouang. The major town has a daily market and a Revolutionary Museum with some unimpressive, but authentic mementos of the war. From Phonsavanh there were formerly only two side trips allowed—the first 10 km southeast to the Plain of Jars and the other to Xieng Khouang itself. But this has changed.

Plain of Jars (Thong Hai Hin)   ★★

Maybe one of the better-known areas in Laos to Westerners. This remarkable field of giant urns begins 7 km east of Phonsavnh on the road to Muong Khouane and stretches as far as Lat Sene, 30 km to the south. There is a second site in Muong Sui district at the 27-km marker near the road to Luang Prabang and still a third near San Tio, a Meo village between Muong Phan and Muong The. The land itself is rather featureless, hilly, brown and treeless. From the tops of the hills, the jars cover the landscape in all directions. The Plain of Jars is exactly that: a 1000-sq.-meter plateau which is covered with 300 or so 1- to 3.5-meter-high jars that have yet to be accurately explained. Some say that they are 2000-year-old burial urns with the size of the jar being relative to the deceased's station in life. No one is sure how they came to be here and exactly what their purpose was. The ancient jars, according to Lao history at any rate, were made during Khun Chuang's time to store wine for the celebration of his conquest of Xieng Khouang (called Pakanh at the time). The former theory seems to be more accurate as evidenced by the human bones found in the vicinity as well as other artifacts. Modern researchers believe the urns were constructed by a megalithic Austronesian people sometime between 2500 and 3000 years ago. The same culture can be traced to many other regions in Southeast Asia, including Myanmar, Malaysia and Indonesia—even the area south of the Red River Delta in Vietnam.

The jars vary in size and shape, and even in the materials from which they were constructed. Some resemble footballs with the ends cut off. Others are straight-sided with rounded edges. Most of the urns appear to have been carved from limestone or granite, while others seem molded from a number of different materials.

In February 1970, the United States began bombing this area. B-52s on their way back to Thailand from Hanoi used the area to jettison their bombs—putting the total tonnage dropped here well above the official estimate of half-a-million tons of explosives. Even though the bombing ruined many of the jars, the sight is still impressive enough. On the far southern edge of the plain, about a kilometer north of Lat Sene off the road to Luang Prabang, are a couple of caves standing atop one another. Tam Kap and Tam Mat formerly contained some important Buddha images until they were stolen in 1911.

This area was also the site of fierce fighting between the Hanoi-backed Pathet Lao and U.S.-backed Hmong mercenary forces.

Xieng Khouang

It's 36 km south of Phonsavanh over a dilapidated road. Another town that was demolished during the war, this is the site of many temples that are now totally destroyed or defaced by shrapnel. **Wat Phia Wat**, **That Chomsi** and **Wat Si Phoum** are the only sights worth seeing here. Tha Joh and Ban Na Sala are typical Hmong villages. The latter is the more traditional of the two. The town lies about 1200 meters above sea level and was formerly the capital of the province with the same name. It has since been changed to Muong Khoun. The temples were heavily damaged during the war but are in the process of being rebuilt.

INSIDER TIP

You will see plenty of war surplus in this area, including unexploded bombs. Keep to the paths and touch nothing. Dozens are killed every month in Laos from unexploded bombs.

Muong Kham

It's 51 km away from Phonsavanh along a decent road. Muang Kham is the location of Tam Phiu Cave, the scene of a 1968 air attack that killed eleven families. Used as an air raid shelter, it is now a war memorial. The remains of the dead still poke through the dirt next to the cave mouth. For those with a more hedonist bent, there is a hot springs near the Nam Mat River. The springs are 52 km north of Phonsavanh in Muang Kham district, Bao Nam Haon village. The hot springs here can reach temperatures of 60 degrees celsius. On the way to Muong Kham, you'll pass Ban Tha Chock, a Meo village tucked away up in the mountains where a number of caves can be found that were used as shelters by resistance fighters and bomb shelters by frightened villagers when the B-52s dumped their payloads. Tam Phiu is the most famous of the caves. In 1969, an American bomb killed more than 650 villagers here. The village outside the cave, Ban Nam Eun, was also leveled.

Nong Het

This is a small border town along Highway 6 going southeast from Xieng Khouang. The border here with Vietnam was closed, then opened a couple of years ago. Check to see the current status if planning to travel into Vietnam.

Where to Stay in Xieng Khouang

Auberge (Hotel) Plaine de Jarres   US$10

Just outside Phonsavanh on the road to Muang Khoune.

Two-story house with four bedrooms, little water, and even less food. The electricity here is on only from 6-10 p.m. Popular with backpackers.

Phou Phieng Xieng Khouang

About 1 km east of Phonsavanh.
This is a relatively new hotel with a good view.

Phou Pha Deng   **US$40–$45**

Xieng Khouang. ☎ *212613.*
15 rooms.
Clearly the best hotel here, it can get away with its prices because this is where the tour groups stay. As such, it offers hot water, air conditioning, private bath and a restaurant.

Dokkhai   **US$15**

Xieng Khouang.
15 rooms (5 singles, 10 doubles).

Phonsavanh   **US$20**

Phonsavanh.
15 rooms (5 singles, 10 doubles)

Mitaphab Hotel   **US$15–$25**

Xieng Khouang Province. No telephone nor fax.
Shared bath, cold water. A good place to find a guide.

Saravan and Savannakhet

These provinces were decimated during the war—in particular, the town of Saravan. Perhaps the biggest attraction here is the heap of war materiel that was cleared away when the airport was reconstructed. The area is also home to vast numbers of bombed-out temples, as U.S. warplanes followed no rules of avoiding striking pagodas during their metallic carpeting of Laos. The market in the town of Saravan is stocked with the riches of the jungle surrounding the Ho Chi Minh Trail, including wildlife that would (and does) give U.S. Fish and Game Department officers conniptions.

The capital of the province, Saravan city has a population of about 42,000, many returning after having fled the region during the massive bombing of the Vietnam War. The town was obliterated during the war and was rebuilt without any architectural inspiration.

Savannakhet province is home to about 692,000 people, according to the government, about half that according to independent sources. The real importance of the province is its strategic location on Highway 9, commercially linking Thailand with Laos and Vietnam. Khanthabouly is sometimes the name used for the capital city of the province, although most folks (and maps) refer to the city as Savannakhet. Its population is about 45,000, and the town lies at an altitude of about 300 meters. Despite its drabness, the province is considered one of the most prosperous in Laos.

There is a Thai/Laos border crossing here, linking Savannakhet with Mukhadan in Thailand, which is open-again, closed-again to foreign tourists. Traditionally, tourists have been required to have a special permit. But that hasn't been the case lately. Speak with the Laos embassy in Bangkok if you want to get into Laos this way. At press time, the border checkpoint was open to foreign tourists with the proper visas.

What to See and Do in and Around Saravan and Savannakhet

Savannakhet

This is a bustling and highly entrepreneurial town with a population of maybe 25,000 (or 45,000, depending who you talk to), that serves as a gateway to the south for travelers. Although it isn't of much interest to travelers in itself, there are some nice surrounding areas. Kengkok is an especially nice village to visit. **That Inheng** is about 11–12 km north of Savannakhet and is worth a stop.

Ho Chi Minh Trail

This is a surprisingly undisturbed part of the country, which may have more to do with the amount of unexploded bombs found here than its inaccessibility. The trail itself was heavily bombed during the Vietnam War and the undeclared war on Laos. There is dense jungle vegetation found here, as well as a lot of exotic animals, if you can spot any. At press time, permission was needed to visit the trail from Savanna-khet Tourism.

Wat Chom Keoh

This was formerly one of the most spendid temples in Laos, until it was obliterated in a 1968 U.S. air raid. Nothing to see here anymore, save for a couple of posts still standing.

Where to Stay in and Around Saravan and Savannakhet

Sensabay Hotel   US$3–$8

Thanon Tha Dan, two blocks east of the ferry, Savannakhet.
Some rooms with air conditioning and private bath.

Hoongthip Hotel   US$24–$36

Phetsarat Road, Savannakhet. ☎ *(856-41) 212262; FAX 212860.*
One of the two nicest digs in town. Rooms with air conditioning, TV, hot water, balcony, telephone, private bath. Restaurant.

Nanhai Hotel Guangdon China   US$24–$75

Ratsavong Seuk Road, Khanthabouly district. ☎ *(856-41) 212370/1.*
Huge sterile block, but relatively modern. Rooms with most conveniences, including satellite TV, minibar. Probably the best choice in town.

Santiphap   US$4–$8

Across the street from the Sensabay.
Currently shabby and in need of renovations. Some rooms with air conditioning. Restaurant.

Savanbanheou   US$8–$10

Savannakhet. ☎ *212202.*
Basic, but a good choice for shoestringers.

Directory (Area Code 041)

Transportation

Lao Aviation serves Savannakhet from Vientiane with a single flight daily. The flight takes 65 minutes. Flights to Vientiane from Savannakhet also depart daily. Flights are also available to Savannakhet from Pakse on Monday, Wednesday, Friday and Saturday. Flights to Pakse depart on the same days. Flying time is 45 minutes.

Tour Operators

Hoongthip Tour

Phetsalath Road, P.O. Box 682, Savannakhet; ☎ *212262.*

Savannakhet Tour

Senna Road, Savannakhet; ☎ *212202.*

Nongsoda Travel

Khemkhong Road, Savannakhet; ☎ *212522.*

Phonepaseut Tour

Santisouk Road, Savannakhet; ☎ *212158.*

Champasak

This is an agricultural province on Boloven Plateau (coffee and tea center), interesting for its diverse ethnic mix and the impressive lost city of **Wat Phou**. Many villages were destroyed during the Vietnam conflict, but there are very colorful and unusual ethnic centers.

Pakse (meaning the mouth of the River Se), the capital of the province at 300 meters above sea level and with a population of about 60,000, has had a tumultuous past. It was formerly the northernmost province of the Khmer empire of Angkor from the 10th through the 13th centuries. In the 15th century, after the fall of the Khmers, the Lane Xang empire extended its reaches into the province, and in 1800 the Champasak empire was established at Pakse.

During the Vietnam War, the prince of Champasak, Boun Oum, allied the region with efforts against the Vietnamese Communists by the Americans and Thais.

There is little of interest in Pakse itself—the town is not much more than a few buildings and a lot of stilt houses. The only temples here date from this century. However, the surrounding countryside along the Mekong River is quite scenic, the largest mountain being the volcano-shaped Ma Long.

The main attraction of the province is undeniably Wat Phou, an ancient stone palace on the eastern slope of Kao Mountain about 45 km from Pakse.

The Outer Limits

What to See and Do in Champasak

Boloven Plateau

This is a fertile highlands area covering some 10,000 square km at an altitude of 1200 meters. The highest peak in the region is the 1716-meter-tall Mount Phia-may. The eastern area of the plateau contained an arm of the Ho Chi Minh Trail and was heavily bombed by the United States during the war. The climate on the plateau is perfectly suited for the cultivation of tea, coffee and temperate vegetables.

Pakse

There is little to do or see here in the town itself. **Boun Oum Palace** is the six-story home of Prince Boun Oum of Champassak. This is an unfinished monument to waste, bad taste and excess. **Wat Luang** is the oldest *wat* in Pakse, built in 1830 and restored in 1990. It's near the site of the largest monastic school in southern Laos.

Hona Se Waterfall

On the Nam Se River, off Highway 13 to Cambodia, 10 km from Pakse. These are nice falls close to Pakse and easy to reach. About 14 km farther, the road branches off toward Paksong.

Paksong (Pak Son)

At 13 km past Pakse on Highway 13, a small road winds its way over the plateau to Paksong. Predecessors of the Khmers, the Chen La settled here at this small town until the end of the fifth century. Paksong is known for its proximity to the **Tat Phan** (or Sexet) waterfall, which is 130 meters high. We recommend staying at the **Tat Lo Resort** built at the top of the falls. This is a very scenic location, and the resort is a relaxing chalet-type facility. It's located on the the northern edge of the plateau right beside the falls. The bungalows here are quite exotic, and the place offers elephant journeys to surrounding Alak minority villages and Kalum.

Champasak

The journey to Champasak meanders through minority villages and teak forests. Along the way from Pakse, you'll come to the Lao Theung village of Tha Muong, beautifully set on the Mekong and dominated by outstanding vistas of Kao Mountain, home to Wat Phou. Here, a ferry operates across the Mekong, which is nearly a mile wide at this point. Champasak itself , with a population of about 25,000, was once a royal capital, and the only real attraction in town is the Great House. This was the home of Prince Boun Oum and has some magnificent artifacts from Wat Phou, including golden Buddhas.

Wat Phou   ★ ★

Eastern slope of Kao Mountain, 45 km from Pakse. If you come to Laos for one reason, this is it. Two hundred years older than Angkor Wat and discovered in 1866 by French explorer Francis Garnier, the lost city of Wat Phou features brilliant carvings, impressive scales and a fantastic setting with the majestic mountain **Linga Parvata** in the background. Wat Phou was constructed in the 10th century as a shrine to Shiva by King Jayavarman IV in the Koh Ker style (921–944). It was connected to Angkor by a road about 100 km long and marked with stones, according to many historians. Ninety *naga*-lined steps lead to the temple on top of the hill, although the *nagas* are barely recognizable. Unfortunately, the whole complex is in a rather shabby state. It is surrounded by an outer wall. The hill temple is also surrounded by walls. On the main temple can be observed a number of reliefs depicting Hindu gods and goddesses, probably the best-preserved features of the complex. The vistas from the top of the hill are superb. Today, the temple is inhabited by a few monks. In the third lunar month on the day of the full moon, there is a three-day Buddhist festival here called Boun Wat Phou. On the full moon of the seventh lunar month, a water buffalo is sacrificed near the Wat to Chao Tengkam, the local earth spirit. There is ongoing restoration and archaeological work and a small charge for entry and photography.

Note: Most tourists get out to Wat Phou either through a tour group or by hiring a guide and/or private transportation. Some travelers have reported getting to the wat via public local bus, and then getting back to Champasak by asking someone for a ride. If you're on your own, this might be the way to go. The bus stops within 100 meters of the temple.

Hindu sculpture at Wat Phou. Most of the temples at Linga Parvata date from the fifth and sixth centuries.

Tha Teng

Village known for its export of wild honey collected from the surrounding hills.

Ban Khian and Tad Soung

Unusual Alak villages with grass-thatched huts. The Alak family head builds the coffins for his family out of hollowed logs and then stores them under the rice huts.

Ban Paleng

Tay-Oy Village, which is the site of a three-day sacrificial festival in February or March. A water buffalo is donated by each family and then sacrificed.

Ban Saphay

Village known for its silk weaving and a *wat* featuring a statue of Ganesh, Indra and Parvati.

Oup Moung

This is a romantic ruin about a half-hour walk from the river. It was built around the same period as Wat Phou, but there is little left of this sixth-century temple. The full extent of this site has yet to be explored.

Where to Stay Around Champasak

Tat Lo Resort   US$32

Tat Lo, right on the waterfalls.

Beautiful location for this modest but charming complex of bungalows set on the Tat Lo waterfalls. The water is clean and great for swimming. Bungalows have balconies and rocking chairs. Great restaurant. The "resort" also runs elephant treks. Relaxing place. Don't miss it.

Hotel Residence Du Champa   US$26–$31

No. 13 Road, Pakse district, P.O. Box 504. ☎ *(856-31) 212120, 212765; FAX 212765. 25 rooms.*

Near the museum and small stadium. For Pakse, this is the best place for mid-budget travelers. Rooms with air conditioning, hot water, private bath. Also restaurant, car rentals, gift shop.

Champasak Palace   US$36–$54   ★

Pakse District. ☎ *212263.*

Clearly the best hotel in Pakse, and this is where Lanatours brings the tour groups. Air conditioned, comfortable rooms with hot water. Good restaurant.

Directory (Area Code 031)

Transportation

Lao Aviation serves Pakse from Vientiane with daily flights (once a day). The flight takes about 80 minutes. Flghts return to Vientiane daily, as well, with one flight a day. Lao Aviation also connects Pakse with Savannakhet. Flights to Pakse from Savannakhet leave Monday, Wednesday, Friday and Saturday. Flights to Savannakhet leave on the same days. The flight time both directions is 45 minutes. By bus, there are several which connect Pakse with Champasak every day. Most leave quite early in the morning, and when full, not at a particular time. Buses also connect Pakse with Savannakhet, also leaving on the early morning.

At the current time, it is possible to cross the border from Pakse into Thailand at Chong Mek without a permit being obtained in Pakse. From Pakse, take a ferry over the river, and then a taxi to the border. The trip takes about 40-60 minutes and costs 200 baht (7400 kip). An exit stamp can be had at the border for 300 kip. Travelers crossing on Sundays have complained of being overcharged (up to 2000), but it seems the Lao passport stampers are on overtime (technically, they are) and charge more for crossing when they are "working" those long hours. From Chong Mek, you can take a bus into Ubon Ratchathani, about 60 km away, for about 20 baht, or hire a taxi (500-600 baht for the car) for the trip.

Tour Operators

DAFI Travel/Tours Co.

  Head Office: 146–148 Ban Thaluang, Pakse district, Champasak province.
  Branch Office: 093/4 Samsenthai Road, Vientiane. ☎ *216721; FAX 217335.*

Sode Tour

  Pakse Office: Thabak, Wat Luang, Pakse. ☎ *8056.*
  Vientiane Office: 114 Quai Fa Ngum, Vientiane. ☎ *215489, 213478, 216314; FAX 215123, 216313.*

Mekong Islands

There are around 4000 islands in the wide Mekong in southern Laos on the Cambodia border. They're covered with lush tropical foliage. Worth visiting for the impressive **Li Phi** and **Khon Phapheng Falls**, the largest waterfalls in Southeast Asia and the working elephants at **Pha Pho**. There's even an amethyst mine where you can try your luck.

Don Khong is the largest island in the river, and there's even a town here, called **Muang Khoune**. You can visit **Li Phi Falls** by taking a boat from **Ban Na-kasong**. On Ban Khone Thai (**Don Khone**), there's a short railway line that was built by the French during the colonial era. It was the only railway built by the French in Laos.

Just to the east of Don Khone are the **Khon Phapheng Falls**, which offer great views. The falls are about 130 km from Pakse and are inarguably the most beautiful in all of Southeast Asia. The unique but nearly extinct **Pa Kha iver dolphins** inhabit the waters here.

An amethyst mine is located a few kilometers off the main road linking Ban 'hang Beng and Attapeu. The stones are primarily bought by the Thais who else?).

Where to Stay on the Mekong Islands

overnment Resthouse   **US$5**

  Khong Island (Donekhong).

ala Sithandone   **US$25**

  Khong Island (Donekhong), to the left of the jetty.
  Airy, comfortable accommodations. Air conditioning; restaurant.

ala Donekhong   **US$40**   ★

  Donekhong Island.
  They've got you by the short hairs here. But the setting is indeed beautiful. The best place to stay on the island.

Directory

Transportation

From Pakse, several buses each morning make the trip to Donekhong (Kong Island).

Lao Glossary

A CRASH COURSE IN LAO

GREETINGS AND FORMALITIES

Hello	*Sa-bai-dii*
Good morning	*Sa-bai-dii*
Good afternoon	*Sa-bai-dii*
Good night	*Sa-bai-dii*
Good-bye	*Sa-bai-dii*
How are you?	*Sa-bai-dii baw?*
I am doing well, thank you.	*Khawy sa-bai-dii.*
Thank you	*Khap jai*
Thank you very much	*Khap jai lai lai*
You're welcome (or "never mind")	*Baw pen nyang*
Yes	*Men*
No	*Baw*

PRONOUNS

I	*Khawy*
You	*Jao*
She	*Lao or Kao*
We	*Hao or Phuak khawy*
They	*Phual lao*

NUMBERS

1	*Neung*
2	*Sawng*
3	*Saam*
4	*Sii*
5	*Ha*
6	*Hok*
7	*Jet*
8	*Paet*
9	*Kao*
10	*Sip*
11	*Sip-et*
12	*Sip -sawng*
13	*Sip-sam*
14	*Sip-see*
15	*Sip-ha*

A CRASH COURSE IN LAO

16	*Sip-hok*
17	*Sip-jet*
18	*Sip-paet*
19	*Sip-khao*
20	*Sao*
21	*Sao et*
22	*Sao sawng*
30	*Sam-sip*
90	*Kao-sip*
100	*Neung hawy*
110	*Neung hawy sip*
200	*Sawng hawy*
1000	*Neung phan*
10,000	*Neung meun*
100,000	*Neung saen*
1 million	*Laan*

DAYS OF THE WEEK

Sunday	*Wan a-thit*
Monday	*Wan jan*
Tuesday	*Wan ang-khan*
Wednesday	*Wan phoot*
Thursday	*Thu nam*
Friday	*Thu sau*
Saturday	*Thu bay*
Today	*Meu nii*
Yesterday	*Meu wan nii*
Tomorrow	*Meu eun*
Right now	*Dio nii*

USEFUL WORDS AND PHRASES

My name is...	*Khawy seu...*
What is your name?	*Jao seu nyang?*
Can you speak Lao?	*Jao paak phaa-saa lao dai baw?*
I can speak a little Lao.	*Khawy paak phaa-saa lao dai nawy neung.*
I can't	*Khawy baw dai*
I would like...(plus verb)	*Yaak...*
I would like...(plus noun)	*Yaak dai...*

A CRASH COURSE IN LAO

I would not like…(plus verb)	*Baw yaak…*
Do you understand?	*Khao jai baw?*
I understand	*Khao jai*
I do not understand	*Baw khao jai*
I want to go…	*Yaak Pai…*
I need…	*Tawng-kaan…*
Where do you come from?	*Jao maa tae sai?*
I come from…	*Khawy maa tae…*
How much for this?	*Thao dai?*
Expensive	*Phaeng*
Very expensive	*Phaeng thae*
Cheap	*Theuk*
A little	*Nawy neung*
Small	*Nawy*
Big	*Nyai*
Buy	*Seu*
Sell	*Khai*
Give	*Ao hai*
Market	*Talaat*
Cafe	*Haan kin deum*
Post office	*Pai-sa-nii*
Station	*Sa-thaa-nii*
Bus	*Lot pa-jam thaang*
Fast	*Wai wai*
Slow	*Saa saa*
Samlor	*Saam-law*

ACCOMMODATIONS

Hotel	*Hohng haem*
Restaurant	*Haan aahaan*
Room	*Hawng*
Bathroom	*Hawng suam*
Toilet	*Hawng nam*
Hot water	*Nam hawn*
Cold water	*Nam yen*
Bath/Shower	*Aap nam*
Towel	*Phaa set tho*

A CRASH COURSE IN LAO
FOOD AND DRINK

Drinking water	*Nam deum*
Boiled water	*Nam tom*
Ice	*Nam -khawn*
Beer	*Bia*
Rice whisky	*Lao lao*
Coffee	*Ka-fae*
Chinese tea	*Nam sa*
Lao tea	*Saa*
Hot Lao tea with sugar	*Saa dam hawn*
Hot Lao tea with milk and sugar	*Saa hawn*
Iced Lao tea with sugar	*Saa dam yen*
Iced Lao tea with milk and sugar	*Saa yen*
Hot Lao coffee with milk and sugar	*Kaa-fae nom hawn*
Hot Lao coffee with sugar	*Kaa-fae dam*
Ovaltine	*Oh-waan-tin*
Milk	*Nom jeut*
Orange soda	*Nam mak kang*
Soda water	*Nam soh-daa*
Yogurt	*Nom som*
Beef	*Sin wua*
Sour hot beef	*Yam wua*
Chicken	*Kai*
Pork	*Muu*
Prawns	*Kung*
Fried rice	*Khao phat*
Thai curry	*Kaeng phet*
Indian curry	*Kaeng kari*
Curried chicken	*Kaeng Kai*
Fried eggs	*Khai dao*
Scrambled eggs	*Khai kuan*
Hard-boiled egg	*Khai tom*
Rice	*Khao*
Omelette	*Khai jii oh*
Grilled fish	*Paa jii*
Fish	*Paa*

A CRASH COURSE IN LAO

Shrimp	*Kung*
Fried prawns	*Kung jeun*
Chicken fried with chiles	*Kai phat maak phet*
Stir-fried vegetables	*Phat phak*
Roasted chicken	*Kai piing*
Lemon soup	*Tom yam*
Chicken fried with ginger	*Kai phat khing*
Chicken in coconut soup	*Tham kaa kai*
Fried chicken	*Kai jeun*
Roasted duck	*Pet ping*
Spicy chicken salad	*Laap kai*
Spicy beef salad	*Laap sin*
Spicy green papaya salad	*Tam som maak hung*
Grilled prawns	*Kung ping*
Fried fish	*Paa jeun*
Steamed fish	*Paa Neung*
Grilled fish	*Paa jii*
Catfish	*Paa duk*
Giant Mekong catfish	*Paa beuk*
Carp	*Paa waa*
Serpent	*Paa Khaw*
Rice soup with chicken/fish	*Khao tom kai/paa*
Lemon grass soup with fish	*Tom yam paa*
Soup with pork and vegetables	*Kaeng Jeut*
Sticky rice cakes	*Khao nom*
Sticky rice in coconut milk	*Khao laam*
Sticky rice in coconut cream	*Khao nio daeng*
Banana in coconut milk	*Na waan maak kuay*
Banana	*Maak kuay*
Guava	*Maak sii-daa*
Betel nut	*Maak*
Mango	*Maak muang*
Durian	*Maak thu-rian*
Jackfruit	*Maak mii*
Papaya	*Maak hung*
Rambutan	*Maak ngaw*

A CRASH COURSE IN LAO

Pineapple	*Maak nat*
Watermelon	*Maak moh*
Rose apple	*Maak kiang*
Orange	*Maak Som*
Mangosteen	*Maak mang-khut*

EMERGENCIES

Doctor	*Maw*
I want to see a doctor.	*Tawng-kaan maw.*
I am sick.	*Boh sa-bai.*
Hospital	*Rong pha-ya-ban*
Diarrhea	*Kii lai*
Dysentery	*Bit*
Stomachache	*Jep thawng*
Malaria	*Khai baa*
I have a fever.	*Mii khai.*
I have no appetite.	*Baw hieu.*
I have a toothache.	*Jep kheo.*
I have a headache.	*Jep Hua.*
I have a backache.	*Jep lang or Jep aeo.*

Lao Glossary

HOTEL INDEX

RESTAURANT INDEX

INDEX

X

Y

Z

Order Your Guide to Travel and Adventure

Title	Price	Title	Price
Fielding's Alaska Cruises and the Inside Passage	$18.95	Fielding's Indiana Jones Adventure and Survival Guide™	$15.95
Fielding's America West	$19.95	Fielding's Italy	$18.95
Fielding's Asia's Top Dive Sites	$19.95	Fielding's Kenya	$19.95
Fielding's Australia	$18.95	Fielding's Las Vegas Agenda	$16.95
Fielding's Bahamas	$16.95	Fielding's London Agenda	$14.95
Fielding's Baja California	$18.95	Fielding's Los Angeles	$16.95
Fielding's Bermuda	$16.95	Fielding's Mexico	$18.95
Fielding's Best and Worst	$19.95	Fielding's New Orleans Agenda	$16.95
Fielding's Birding Indonesia	$19.95	Fielding's New York Agenda	$16.95
Fielding's Borneo	$18.95	Fielding's New Zealand	$17.95
Fielding's Budget Europe	$18.95	Fielding's Paradors, Pousadas and Charming Villages of Spain and Portugal	$18.95
Fielding's Caribbean	$19.95	Fielding's Paris Agenda	$14.95
Fielding's Caribbean Cruises	$18.95	Fielding's Portugal	$16.95
Fielding's Caribbean on a Budget	$18.95	Fielding's Rome Agenda	$16.95
Fielding's Diving Australia	$19.95	Fielding's San Diego Agenda	$14.95
Fielding's Diving Indonesia	$19.95	Fielding's Southeast Asia	$18.95
Fielding's Eastern Caribbean	$17.95	Fielding's Southern California Theme Parks	$18.95
Fielding's England including Ireland, Scotland and Wales	$18.95	Fielding's Southern Vietnam on Two Wheels	$15.95
Fielding's Europe	$19.95	Fielding's Spain	$18.95
Fielding's Europe 50th Anniversary	$24.95	Fielding's Surfing Australia	$19.95
Fielding's European Cruises	$18.95	Fielding's Surfing Indonesia	$19.95
Fielding's Far East	$18.95	Fielding's Sydney Agenda	$16.95
Fielding's France	$18.95	Fielding's Thailand, Cambodia, Laos and Myanmar	$18.95
Fielding's France: Loire Valley, Burgundy and the Best of French Culture	$16.95	Fielding's Travel Tools™	$15.95
Fielding's France: Normandy & Brittany	$16.95	Fielding's Vietnam including Cambodia and Laos	$19.95
Fielding's France: Provence and the Mediterranean	$16.95	Fielding's Walt Disney World and Orlando Area Theme Parks	$18.95
Fielding's Freewheelin' USA	$18.95	Fielding's Western Caribbean	$18.95
Fielding's Hawaii	$18.95	Fielding's The World's Most Dangerous Places™	$21.95
Fielding's Hot Spots: Travel in Harm's Way	$15.95	Fielding's Worldwide Cruises	$21.95

To place an order: call toll-free 1-800-FW-2-GUIDE
(VISA, MasterCard and American Express accepted)
or send your check or money order to:
Fielding Worldwide, Inc., 308 S. Catalina Avenue, Redondo Beach, CA 90277
http://www.fieldingtravel.com
d $2.00 per book for shipping & handling (sorry, no COD's), allow 2–6 weeks for delivery

International Conversions

TEMPERATURE

To convert °F to °C, subtract 32 and divide by 1.8. To convert °C to °F, multiply by 1.8 and add 32.

Fahrenheit	Centigrade	
230°	110°	
220°	100°	Water Boils
210°		
200°	90°	
190°		
180°	80°	
170°		
160°	70°	
150°		
140°	60°	
130°		
120°	50°	
110°		
100°	40°	
90°	30°	
80°		
70°	20°	
60°		
50°	10°	
40°	0°	Water Freezes
30°		
20°	-10°	
10°		
0°	-20°	
-10°		
-20°	-30°	
-30°		
-40°	-40°	

WEIGHTS & MEASURES

LENGTH

1 km	=	0.62 miles
1 mile	=	1.609 km
1 meter	=	1.0936 yards
1 meter	=	3.28 feet
1 yard	=	0.9144 meters
1 yard	=	3 feet
1 foot	=	30.48 centimeters
1 centimeter	=	0.39 inch
1 inch	=	2.54 centimeters

AREA

1 square km	=	0.3861 square miles
1 square mile	=	2.590 square km
1 hectare	=	2.47 acres
1 acre	=	0.405 hectare

VOLUME

1 cubic meter	=	1.307 cubic yards
1 cubic yard	=	0.765 cubic meter
1 cubic yard	=	27 cubic feet
1 cubic foot	=	0.028 cubic meter
1 cubic centimeter	=	0.061 cubic inch
1 cubic inch	=	16.387 cubic centimeters

CAPACITY

1 gallon	=	3.785 liters
1 quart	=	0.94635 liters
1 liter	=	1.057 quarts
1 pint	=	473 milliliters
1 fluid ounce	=	29.573 milliliters

MASS and WEIGHT

1 metric ton	=	1.102 short tons
1 metric ton	=	1000 kilograms
1 short ton	=	.90718 metric ton
1 long ton	=	1.016 metric tons
1 long ton	=	2240 pounds
1 pound	=	0.4536 kilograms
1 kilogram	=	2.2046 pounds
1 ounce	=	28.35 grams
1 gram	=	0.035 ounce
1 milligram	=	0.015 grain

cm 0 1 2 3 4 5 6 7 8 9

Inch 0 1 2 3